THE NOTRE DAME
FOOTBALL
ENCYCLOPEDIA

Fourth Edition

BY
MICHAEL R. STEELE

Introduction by Ara Parseghian
Forewords by Ed Krause and Rocky Bleier

SPORTS
PUBLISHING

Sports Publishing books may be purchased in bulk at
special discounts for sales promotion, corporate gifts,
fund-raising, or educational purposes. Special editions
can also be created to specifications. For details, contact
the Special Sales Department, Sports Publishing, 307
West 36th Street, 11th Floor, New York, NY 10018 or
sportspubbooks@skyhorsepublishing.com.

Sports Publishing® is a registered trademark of
Skyhorse Publishing, Inc.®, a Delaware corporation.

Visit our website at www.sportspubbooks.com

10 9 8 7 6 5 4 3 2 1

Library of Congress Cataloging-in-Publication Data is
available on file.

ISBN: 978-1-61321-076-5

Printed in Canada

For my family

and

for all those who have ever wanted to play football for Notre Dame.

————————————————————————

CONTENTS

ACKNOWLEDGMENTS

The gestation period for this book was more than eight years in duration. It would have been impossible without the generous, selfless help of people such as John Heisler, Susan McGonigal, Herb Juliano, and Jethrow Kyles of Notre Dame, especially in the early stages; and Alex Toth, who labored in the Pacific University Library throughout the process. The entire staff of the Notre Dame Sports Information Department must be mentioned, with special thanks to Pam Carnes. My deepest gratitude goes to former Irish head coach, the late Dan Devine, and his family, for their friendship and guidance in all matters related to coach Devine's years at Notre Dame. I also have a special place in my heart for three of Coach Devine's players—Vagas Ferguson, Jerome Heavens, and Dave Duerson, who have kindly helped me with various matters over the years. Others at Pacific University helped considerably with the statistics and viewpoints, particularly Chris Carley and Jon Stine. Numerous student assistants at Pacific have had a hand in this as well. A thank you to all of them. I am indebted to my dean at Pacific, Tom Beck, for his unwavering support…and to my former student and good friend, our assistant athletic director, Jeff Grundon, who has always offered kind words of encouragement. My wife, Geri, has always been understanding and kind about my passion for Notre Dame…and my children—Erica, Jared, Matt, and Sean—know well how to put up with a dad who occasionally tries to recover televised fumbles in his living room.

Within the Notre Dame football family special thanks go to John Heisler, who has helped with my various Irish projects since 1979, former head coaches Gerry Faust and Bob Davie, and their secretary, Jan Blazi, as well as former AD Gene Corrigan, Assistant AD Brian Boulac, and Special Assistant Joe Yonto. Carol Copley and Paul Anthony worked quickly and efficiently to update photographs from the archives for this fourth edition. Drew Mahalic, who played for Ara and has been a friend for twenty-five years, has always offered quick answers and insights when called upon. Very special regards go to the memory of Moose Krause, who was always available to help. I am particularly obliged to Skyhorse Publishing Inc. of New York, a company who resurrected the book from oblivion. Thanks to their former editor Meg Distinti, who got the project started. Niels Aaboe has worked diligently with me as the editor who at last brought the book into print. Julie Ganz worked overtime with a short deadline to handle the many small details that go into the final product. Karissa Hearn has been a pleasure to work with as the Skyhorse publicist assigned to this project.

Those are the people personally known to be involved. There are many others. On a December night in 1979, I worked late at the Notre Dame Library—with the personal help of Chet Grant, George Gipp's quarterback on the 1920 team. Grant had me going through the paces of the famous Notre Dame shift—I was the fullback, and two library chairs represented the halfbacks. In retrospect, Gipp must have been there watching the proceedings as the spry, nimble-witted Grant brought to life a style of football not seen for half a century. So, thanks also to the memory of George Gipp, who represents all of Notre Dame's players since 1887 (though few bear much resemblance to Gipp).

Finally, very special thanks go to Jim Peterson, whose act of faith in this book brought it back from the afterlife more than a decade ago.

—*Mike Steele*

INTRODUCTION

When I became head football coach at Notre Dame, I quickly realized that it was more than just a midwestern university. I had coached in the Big 10 for eight years, and I assumed that the transition would be a simple one. I realized after sitting in the head coach's chair a very short period, that interest in Notre Dame was not just regional or even national; it commanded international interest and attention.

Much of this respect came from the university's ability to blend the academic and athletic programs without compromising either. The principal reason for enrollment was an education and a goal of developing the whole person. Within these objectives were opportunities in other activities. In spite of its great athletic success, the academic programs were never overshadowed by athletics, and both continued to prosper.

The *Notre Dame Football Encyclopedia* is a beautiful reconstruction of Notre Dame history. It originally took nine years to complete and is a wonderful source of information on the 1,083 games, with more than 300 player profiles. In addition, one can digest statistics and photos to relive many historical moments. This allows all ages to reminisce and relive every Notre Dame game from the beginning. I do not know of any other book that covers the entire history of Notre Dame football with the completeness and accuracy you'll find here.

I'm sure you will enjoy this encyclopedia as much as I have.

—Ara Parseghian

A SPECIAL FOREWORD
FROM THE FIRST EDITION

In my 62 years of involvement with the University of Notre Dame, I have been privileged to know and work with some of the greatest men in the pantheon of collegiate football—from Rockne to Layden, Leahy, Parseghian, Devine, and Holtz, as well as their tremendously gifted players. I have also come to know and appreciate the young men who are not football heroes on a Saturday afternoon in the fall, but who worked diligently to play the game to the best of their abilities while also succeeding in the difficult world of academics.

From Knute Rockne I learned important lessons about teamwork, cooperation, accepting adversity, winning properly, practicing self-discipline, and loyalty. These lessons are still emphasized at the University of Notre Dame today along with the same emphasis dedicated to academic success that Rockne preached. These have been constants at Notre Dame ever since I began my association with the University.

The brilliant story of Notre Dame football encompasses all of these lessons, the coaches, and the players. It also represents the struggles and successes of all the coaches and the young men who have played college football. There are so many valuable, important stories to be told regarding collegiate football, tales that help us better understand ourselves and the unfolding drama of athletics and sports in America.

Many, many books have been written about Notre Dame football. This encyclopedia is a compendium of all of those games, the people, and the events that have gone on in more than 100 seasons of football under the Golden Dome. Notre Dame has been blessed to have its many worthy opponents on football fields across America; this book will thrill not only the fans of Irish football but also the many millions who cheer Notre Dame's opponents. We would not have had the opportunity for these wonderful athletic contests without our honored opponents.

Follow Notre Dame football game by game and season by season in this encyclopedia. Watch the development of individual stars through their years…and feel the drama of those careers became great struggles with adversity. Feel the uplifting triumphs and grieve the sad losses. But all the time recognize the blessings we all share as they are detailed in Michael Steele's *Fighting Irish Football Encyclopedia*.

—Ed "Moose" Krause
Emeritus Athletic Director
University of Notre Dame

FOREWORD

When Mike Steele contacted me to write the foreword for his second edition of *The Notre Dame Football Encyclopedia* I was quite honored, especially following in the footsteps of Moose Krause and Ara Parseghian.

I felt some apprehension and a whole lot of inadequacies to undertake this task, primarily because my official contact with Notre Dame football was the four years I spent on campus from 1964 to 1968. You won't find my name in the record books or as an administrative official or as a coach. But like thousands of other young people, you will find my name on the scrolls of those who have graduated from that great institution.

I don't consider myself a *football fanatic* and I wasn't raised in a *Notre Dame* family. Having grown up in Appleton, Wisconsin, living above my father's bar, the only thing I knew about Notre Dame and its football tradition was when I was required to read *Knute Rockne, All American* in the fifth grade. My awareness and knowledge increased about the Fighting Irish during junior and senior high school when I would watch Notre Dame reruns, every now and then, on Sunday mornings. This sparse education was augmented by the patrons sitting around the bar arguing about the game. The reason I say "every now and then" and "sparse education" is because if you look up in this encyclopedia the years 1956 to 1963, Notre Dame wasn't necessarily setting the world on fire...but you probably knew that already.

Two factors changed my perspective on Notre Dame. The first was when I attended the University. I learned about *Fair Catch Corby, Number One Moses!* and *Touchdown Jesus*. I learned about pep rallies, the fight song and the stadium. Then there were the Grotto, the Rockne Memorial and the Heisman Trophy winners. I learned about the lore and tradition, the impact of the alumni and what it all meant.

The second factor that changed my perspective was meeting a fireman in Pittsburgh, Pennsylvania, by the name of Charlie Jones. He taught me the universal love a group of people called *Subway Alumni* have for this university. Charlie, a.k.a. "the Lumper," continued my education by impersonating the voice of Joe Boland, the great Notre Dame announcer. He would do the radio broadcast from kickoff to the final gun. I have to tell you it was quite entertaining and very informative. But after listening to the same games over the last 25 plus years, I have to say that it is a little more than any good Notre Dame grad can take.

So if you're like me, or even if you're not, you're going to love *The Notre Dame Football Encyclopedia*. For, you see, now I don't have to listen to "the Lumper" anymore or the guys that hung out at my dad's place or feel inadequate about some Notre Dame lore I should know. Now I can get that information at my fingertips and especially relive those exciting Notre Dame games I played in, and truly feel, at least in my own mind, that I am a legendary athlete.

—*Rocky Bleier*
March, 1996

PREFACE

All Fighting Irish fans have their favorite memories—those moments suspended in time when an athlete in his youthful prime performs a miraculous feat. Such memories have been fostered by 114 seasons of heroics, painful losses, great comebacks, and excellence in pursuit of a good life as the football playing sons of Notre Dame.

Notre Dame students rub shoulders with these young men for four years. They see them in their normal dimensions—in the dorms, the cafeteria, around campus, and in classes. And they seem not much larger than life, except they are gone in the fall in the late afternoons and much of the weekends.

Yet something happens when these student-athletes are near the stadium. They *do* seem larger, as if the monolithic stadium imparts ruggedness to their frames, their shoulders, their chests. Some pause near the blue door of the team's locker room to sign a shy child's game program, to speak to hometown friends, or to meet someone's aunt who has made her first trip to the football shrine.

They enter the locker room and perform their rituals away from the public eye. They go on the field and do some stretching in a nearly empty stadium. They return to the locker room for full pads. Specialty teams warm up and then the whole team, by units. Back to the locker room for final words, thoughts and prayers. They go down the narrow steps to the tunnel under the north stands, their cleats clacking on the pavement, and touch the sign about champions above the steps for good luck.

The brilliant light of an Indiana autumn reflects off their newly painted gold helmets. They mass near the edge of the concrete and the field, then jog forward into full view of 59,075 people, and bear to their right—to the west, the Fighting Irish side of the field. And most of the 59,075 go slightly crazy. Some variation of this ritual has taken place hundreds of times since the dedication of the stadium in 1930, and similar rites met the needs of the players and fans before that.

After all this, for some three hours, a game is played—a football game—on the field that Rockne built.

And it is here that we properly find the subject of this encyclopedia—in the game.

But how can all those glorious moments become mere fodder for statistics in a book? Let us not fool ourselves. This book is not Fighting Irish football; it is about Irish football. Yet this book can still serve to fix in words and pictures some of the memories Fighting Irish fans love to ponder.

So, let's try to see Red Salmon slam into a turn-of-the-century pile up—and emerge angrily to go dashing toward his football destiny…

There is Gipp, a shy Huck Finn grown-up, drop-kicking a 62-yard field goal even though he was told to punt—he grins, he has a toothpick…

The Horsemen, four magicians, synchronized to absolute perfection—the Notre Dame shift, the other team jumps, and the ball is snapped to a Horseman who has just the slightest advantage; he breaks it outside and is down the sideline…

The 1929-30 team of Carideo, Brill, Schwartz, and Metzger, tough but smooth. Fancy football on splendid fall afternoons—double laterals and a forward pass or old "51" (Rock's favorite)…

Leahy's powerhouses, big, mobile worldly-wise war vets. The passing of Bertelli, the confidence of Lujak, or gigantic Leon Hart madly loose on an end-around, careening through, and caroming off frightened defenders, running into…

Hornung—a golden moment in a dim era—a throwback to the old triple threats that Walter Camp so admired. He has a bit of the Gipp insouciance. There, see the little smile…

Ara, intense, brooding, impatient and demanding. "I don't know how many games they will win, but they will be in condition in the fourth quarter, I promise that." They were, too. See Ara, in agony at USC in 1964? And overjoyed at Alabama in 1973 and 1975? Ara…

Eric Penick, first play of the second half, 1973 USC game, takes the ball and swings wide left, cuts it up and turns it on, nobody touches him for 85 yards—so much speed…

Over there—not Huck Finn this time, but Tom Sawyer—call him Joe Montana. Smooth, quick release, a la Namath. Surrounded by such great players—Vagas and Big Mac. Joe's got his arms raised, imitating the umpire's touchdown call…

Or Bob Crable introducing himself to Charles White, "You might beat this team, but not *me*." White gingerly picks himself up, but takes a count or two on the ground longer than usual. Crable looms over him, then jogs back…

Rocket Ismail—who changes forever the way teams handle the kicking game. Holtz said he was the only person he ever saw play tennis with himself…

Or Jerome Bettis—slamming through defenses for 23 touchdowns in his sophomore campaign. With so much promise for the future.

Kory Minor totally stuffing a surprised USC runner on a goal-line stand, firing up the Irish in a great 38-10 home win over the Trojans in 1995.

Ivory Covington's goal-line tackle on an Army tight end to preserve a one-point win over the Cadets in a 1995 game played at Giants stadium.

Julius Jones's 100-yard TD run with a Nebraska kickoff, blasting past the Cornhuskers up the left sideline in the classic 2000 contest.

Or the explosive, graceful Arnaz Battle, reaching his full potential after seasons of injuries, with long TD catches for wins over MSU and FSU in 2002.

The memories continue with such remarkable figures as Michael Floyd or Jeff Samardzija, defeating smaller defenders with sheer speed, guile, and strength. Or Manti Te'O roaming intensely just behind his D line, angling to the ball carrier with incredible ferocity.

It's magic. We all know these moments, these faces. They are etched into our lives. Let this book complete the process—and keep them forever young.

—*Mike Steele*

CHAPTER ONE

THE PLACE

Many generations of young people have made the trek to north-central Indiana to begin their college studies. If they were lucky, they caught a glimpse of the Golden Dome soaring majestically above the flat, fertile Indiana landscape. After seeing the Dome from afar, their cars are slowly drawn to that central location. You cannot help but stare the first time in wonderment at the Dome as it moves in and out of view.

There are certain places in this country where the visitor feels a special relationship to a locale—the Lincoln Memorial, the Statue of Liberty, Mt. Rushmore, and Arlington National Cemetery come to mind as such places where the individual meets the past, and feels a tangible quality that permeates the air.

Notre Dame is also such a place. It is calm there. In a world of senseless violence, confused values, seemingly irreparable breaks with the past, and with little hope for the future, you can find a measure of peace at Notre Dame, a sense of values not frustrated by contemporary confusions, a sense of the past and its traditions. You feel there. It is indisputable. Many writers and commentators have attempted to articulate this special sense, but you must visit to fully comprehend it. Go to the place.

But there is more. On five or six Saturdays each fall, in the midst of the serenity, the classical quietude of the academy, and its tree-lined cloisters, there is another activity—the noisiest, most raucous, most volatile student-body support for intercollegiate football that can be found in this land. They are not the "Fighting Irish" for nothing.

Paradoxically, Americans like both underdogs and winners. Notre Dame's history embraces both, which perhaps is part of the secret of its enduring success. Founded in 1842 by a visionary French priest, Father Edward Sorin, the school attracted upwardly mobile young Catholics. And they took up the game of football with an abandon and flair that caught the fancy of fans. The school imparted discipline and demanded excellence—both in the classroom and on the playing field. Early on, the institution decided that the whole individual would be molded—body and mind, spirit and flesh. The active life of the mind would not be estranged from the active life of the body. Add to this a crusading spirit, and the framework for the unfolding history of Notre Dame football is complete. To understand completely what makes Fighting Irish football what it is, we must speak in the abstractions above, before going on to the concrete necessities of excellence in recruiting, rigorous training, perfection in teamwork, dedicated and brilliant coaching, and the sheer athleticism so often displayed in Notre Dame games.

The place, like the dancer and the dance, cannot be separated from what goes on there or from the intangible Notre Dame spirit. Countless commentators have remarked about the spirit of the place. Thousands of visiting players have felt it. The saying is that you can cut it with a knife as you walk around the campus.

Spirit is many things. As a noun, spirit is an animating or vital principle, a supernatural being, disposition of mind, a special attitude or frame of mind, a brisk quality, a firm disposition. And as a verb, it means to infuse or animate. All of these are involved in the unique spirit that is Notre Dame. It is a sense that this place throbs and pulses quietly, confidently, with concern for the higher things of human life. It is also composed of memories—so many young men and women have dreamed great dreams, have lived intense lives, have burned with the deepest thoughts, and have rejoiced in the beauties of youth and vigor in their games. Those tens of thousands of lives, many already finished, have left tangible vestiges of their intensity amid the tree-lined walks of the campus, to reside in the halls of learning, and to remain by the playing fields.

Ultimately, spirit (delivered from the Latin *spirare*, to breathe) is just that—a breath of life, hope, and determination to excel. Here we have it: Notre Dame, dedicated to Our Lady, has its purpose firmly dedicated to the best to which mankind can aspire. And this is the finest aspect of the spirit that characterizes Notre Dame football. In the game, we find humanity's dualities—flesh and spirit—united in an effort to do one's best.

2

WHY FOOTBALL?

There is really no telling why certain sports appeal to certain people, or why different cultures appreciate a particular sport, even to the exclusion of other widely accepted sports.

Our nation is barely more than 200 years old, and football has been with us for more than half of that period. It has been the dominant sport for many decades, not so much because of spectators or the numbers who play the game, but really for what it says about who and what we are.

There is an aesthetics of football. Well-edited film clips, played in slow motion, reveal a ballet-like quality to the motions of the players. The acrobatic catches of a well-executed pass route, or the gliding power of a halfback cutting through a crack in the defense is a wonder of human mechanics. Irish fans still marvel over the synchronized, hypnotic, musical quality of Rockne's carefully planned and executed shift plays. Even the ponderous agility of the defensive and offensive linemen have an artistic quality. All these movements are choreographed in precise ways just as in a dance—or like a stage production. The players follow a "script," also known as a game plan, often like a Greek drama with agonistic conflict. But once performed, the movements and delivery of lines cannot be exactly recreated. Yet people like to remember those vivid moments when

something truly heroic happened—the pass that won one for the Gipper, Shakespeare's heroics in overcoming Ohio State, the "perfect plays" from Leahy's tenure, Hunter's run that helped beat Alabama, Clements's pass to Weber that saved the game, Penick's long run to beat USC, the defensive gallantry against Campbell's Texas team in the Cotton Bowl, or the intensity of the rivalry with Miami. These become etched in the collective consciousness of Fighting Irish fans and are passed on from one generation to the next.

Then there is the sheer physical courage that football, properly played, requires—the courage required to match one's physical gifts against those of another similarly gifted athlete before millions of witnesses. Humans like to test themselves in this fashion, a confrontation of egos and intellects. And there is a vicarious sense of identification on the part of the spectator.

People like to be associated with excellence. And from any viewpoint, Notre Dame football is the finest example of excellence in college football—and has been for most of this century. Many seek it out, wish to become close to it, or become a part of it. The emotional identification between the Fighting Irish fan and the team should not be underestimated. When the team triumphs, it is shared with its legions of fans. The fan can taste victory and empathize with defeat, wishing for those moments that might have turned the game around. The fan can enjoy the sense that he or she knows how it should have been. Thus, even after the game has been played, there is another "game" played alone with the raw data of the game, re-arranging facts, and creating a mythical re-enactment. The game lives on in the minds of the beholders.

And Notre Dame's Fighting Irish have probably provided more such memories than any other college team in the country.

CHAPTER THREE

VARIOUS ALL-TIME FIGHTING IRISH TEAMS

There is a certain unfairness about any all-star team. In a team sport, the other players have as much to say about an individual's performance as does the individual. Many players have had weaknesses buttressed by the strength of the men next to them. And memories fog when we try to recreate performances of stars from the past. Much of the brilliance of the great stars from the past is not recorded on film; we have only written accounts that must serve as the record until well into the mid-1930s when film became a standard coaching tool. Still, there is a desire to want to define the best.

There are many variables in selecting an all-star team. Size is one of the most important. Modern training methods guarantee that today's players are stronger, faster, and bigger. Tackles from the first quarter of this century might be big enough today to play as defensive backs. For example, it would be hard imagining 149-pound Bert Metzger doing very well against Mike McCoy, almost twice his weight, or Metzger stopping the pass rush or punt blocking charge of a player like Chris Zorich.

To do away with part of the bias that creeps into the selection of all-time teams, herewith is a sample of the best of the smallest and the largest players in the annals of the Fighting Irish.

The Best "Small" Offensive Players (under six feet):

LE	Knute Rockne	5'8", 165	1910-13
LT	Joe Bach	5'11", 181	1923-24
LG	Clipper Smith	5'9", 164	1925-27
C	Al Feeney	5'11", 180	1910-13
RG	Bert Metzger	5'9", 149	1928-30
RT	Sam Dolan	5'11", 210	1906-09
RE	Eddie Anderson	5'10", 163	1918-21
QB	Harry Stuhldreher	5'7", 151	1922-24
HB	Allan Pinkett	5'9", 184	1982-85
FB	Jerome Bettis	5'11", 247	1990-91
FL	Rocket Ismail	5'9", 175	1988-90

*Note: the entire backfield could have come from the Four Horsemen.

Most of these men either played with or for Rockne, except for Dolan, Pinkett, Bettis, and Ismail. Rock liked the "small" players, since he was one himself, and he preferred speed, quickness, and agility over what he called "the bovine."

The Best "Big" Offensive Players (six feet and taller)

LE	Ken MacAfee	6'4", 249	1974-77
LT	Larry Williams	6'6", 284	1981-83
LG	Tim Grunhard	6'3", 292	1986-89
C	Dave Huffman	6'5", 245	1975-78
RG	Ernie Hughes	6'3", 253	1974-77
RT	George Kunz	6'5", 240	1966-68
RE	Leon Hart	6'4", 245	1946-49
QB	Joe Montana	6'2", 191	1975-78
LH	George Gipp	6'0", 180	1917-20
RH	Vagas Ferguson	6'1", 194	1976-79
FB	Wayne Bullock	6'1", 221	1972-74
K	George Gipp		

This mammoth group averages 6'3" and almost 236 pounds. They are five inches taller than the best of the small men and outweigh them by 60 pounds. The two offensive lines look like this: the small men average 5'10", 173 pounds while the big men average 6'4", 248 pounds, for a six-inch height differential and 75 pounds in weight. The backfield is closer in size, probably because sheer speed has an outside limit as far as size goes. The small backfield averages 5'9 1/4" and 187 pounds whereas the larger backfield is 6'1", 196 1/2 pounds.

The Best "Small" Defensive Players

LE	Knute Rockne	5'8", 165	1910-13
LT	Hunk Anderson	5'11", 170	1918-21
RT	Dick Arrington	5'11", 227	1963-65
RE	Eddie Anderson	5'10", 163	1918-21
LLB	Jack Alessandrini	5'11", 197	1950-52
MLB	Nick Buoniconti	5'11", 210	1959-61
RLB	Al Ecuyer	5'10", 190	1956-58
LCB	Reggie Barnett	5'11", 180	1972-74
RCB	George Sefcik	5'8", 170	1959-61
SS	Mike Crotty	5'9", 180	1969-71
FS	Tom Schoen	5'11", 178	1965-67

This is a most interesting group, cutting across several of the eras; good, small defensive players can expect to play some football. A very interesting game would be played between this group and the small offensive team. This defensive group is about the same height as their offensive counterparts, but weighs a bit more. As much as we would want to see a good game between this group and the large offensive team, it would probably be a mismatch.

The Best "Big" Defensive Players

LE	Ross Browner	6'3", 248	1973-77
LT	Chris Zorich	6'1", 266	1988-90
RT	Kevin Hardy	6'5", 270	1964-67
RE	Alan Page	6'5", 238	1964-66
LLB	Jim Lynch	6'1", 225	1964-66
MLB	Bob Golic	6'3", 244	1975-78
RLB	Bob Crable	6'3", 225	1978-81
LCB	Luther Bradley	6'3", 202	1973-77
RCB	Stacy Toran	6'4", 195	1980-83
SS	Jim Browner	6'3", 214	1975-78
FS	Mike Townsend	6'3", 183	1971-73

Like the big offensive team, this group is not representative of the sweep of Fighting Irish football. It is composed exclusively of men who played for or after Ara Parseghian, not because he set the trend to larger men, but responded to it. The linemen average 6'3 1/2" and 254 pounds; the linebackers are 6'2 1/2" and 231 1/3 pounds; the backs average 6'3", 198 1/2. Make no mistake, there is speed in this group. Browner caught Tony Dorsett from behind on a long run once and Page outran a Purdue halfback for a touchdown with a blocked punt, not to mention Bradley's record-setting return of a Purdue pass. The interior linemen, Hardy and Zorich, had it all—but especially lateral mobility and quickness to go with their great strength. The linebackers are a superb group, with plenty of speed on the flanks behind the quick ends, and even more speed behind them among the backs. Sad to say, this group would crunch the small offensive team, but what a game could be played between this team and the large offense! The lines match up well, with the offense coming in at 6'4", 258 pounds and the defense slightly smaller.

All-time Notre Dame Players by Era

The following players have been selected from among their Notre Dame peers as the best of their respective eras.

1887-1910:

LE	John Farley	5'9", 160
LT	Pat Beacom	6'2", 220
LG	George Philbrook	6'3", 225
C	John Eggeman	6'4", 256
RG	Rosy Dolan	5'11", 210
RT	Ralph Dimmick	6'0", 225
RE	Frank Lonergan	5'10", 168
QB	Nate Silver	5'8", 150
LHB	Red Miller	6'0", 175
RHB	Dom Callicrate	5'11", 160
FB	Red Salmon	5'10", 175
K	Red Salmon	

1911-1930:

LE	Knute Rockne	5'8", 165
LT	Frank Coughlin	6'3", 215
LG	Hunk Anderson	5'11", 170
C	Adam Walsh	6'0", 187
RG	Clipper Smith	5'10", 160
RT	Buck Shaw	6'0", 185

RE	Eddie Anderson	5'10", 163
QB	Harry Stuhldreher	5'7", 151
LHB	George Gipp	6'0", 180
RHB	Don Miller	5'11", 160
FB	Ray Eichenlaub	6'0", 210
K	George Gipp	

1931-1940:

LE	Wayne Millner	6'0", 184
LT	Moose Krause	6'3", 217
LG	John Lautar	6'1", 184
C	Jack Robinson	6'3", 200
RG	Joe Kuharich	6'0", 193
RT	Joe Kurth	6'2", 204
RE	Johnny Kelly	6'2", 190
QB	Wally Fromhart	5'11", 180
LHB	Marchy Schwartz	5'11", 167
RHB	Ray Brancheau	5'11", 190
FB	George Melinkovich	6'0", 180
K	Marchy Schwartz	

1941-1950:

LE	Jim Martin	6'2", 205
LT	George Connor	6'3", 225
LG	Bill Fischer	6'2", 230
C	Bill Walsh	6'3", 205
RG	Marty Wendell	5'11", 198
RT	Ziggy Czarobski	6'0", 213
RE	Leon Hart	6'4", 245
QB	Johnny Lujack	6'0", 180
LHB	Terry Brennan	6'0", 175
RHB	Creighton Miller	6'0", 185
FB	Emil Sitko	5'8", 180
K	Johnny Lujack	

1951-1960:

LE	Monty Stickles	6'4", 225
LT	Frank Varrichione	6'1", 205
LG	Ray Lemek	6'1", 207
C	Art Hunter	6'3", 226
RG	Al Ecuyer	5'10", 205
RT	Bob Toneff	6'1", 230
RE	Bob Wetoska	6'3", 225
QB	Paul Hornung	6'2", 205
LHB	Joe Heap	5'11", 180
RHB	Johnny Lattner	6'1", 190
FB	Neil Worden	5'11", 185
K	Paul Hornung	

1961-1970:
Offense:

LE	Jim Seymour	6'4", 205
LT	Jim Reilly	6'2", 230
LG	Larry DiNardo	6'1", 235
C	George Goeddeke	6'3", 228
RG	Dick Arrington	5'11", 232
RT	George Kunz	6'5", 240
TE	Jim Winegardner	6'4", 225
QB	Joe Theismann	6'0", 170
LHB	Nick Eddy	6'0", 195
RHB	Rocky Bleier	5'11", 195
FB	Bill Barz	6'2", 216
K	Scott Hempel	6'0", 235
P	Kevin Hardy	6'5", 270

Defense:

LE	Walt Patulski	6'6", 260
LT	Mike McCoy	6'5", 274
RT	Kevin Hardy	6'5", 270
RE	Alan Page	6'5", 238
OLB	Jim Lynch	6'1", 225
ILB	Nick Buoniconti	5'11", 210
ILB	Jim Carroll	6'1", 225
OLB	Mike McGill	6'2", 225
LCB	Clarence Ellis	6'0", 178
RCB	Tony Carey	6'0", 190
S	Nick Rassas	6'0", 185

1971-1980:
Offense:

SE	Kris Haines	6'0", 181
LT	Rob Martinovich	6'5", 260
LG	Frank Pomarico	6'1", 250
C	Dave Huffman	6'5", 245
RG	Ernie Hughes	6'3", 253
RT	Tim Foley	6'5", 265
TE	Ken MacAfee	6'4", 249
QB	Joe Montana	6'2", 191
HB	Vagas Ferguson	6'1", 194
FB	Jerome Heavens	6'0", 204
FL	Pete Holohan	6'5", 228
K	Dave Reeve	6'3", 198
P	Joe Restic	6'2", 192

Defense:

LE	Ross Browner	6'3", 248
LT	Steve Niehaus	6'5", 260
RT	Mike Fanning	6'6", 250
RE	Willie Fry	6'3", 237

OLB	Bob Crable	6'3", 225
ILB	Bob Golic	6'3", 240
ILB	Steve Heimkreiter	6'2", 224
LCB	Luther Bradley	6'2", 202
RCB	Dave Waymer	6'3", 182
SS	Jim Browner	6'3", 204
FS	Joe Restic	6'2", 192

1981-1990:
Offense:

SE	Tim Brown	6'0", 195
LT	Mike Perrino	6'5", 278
LG	Tim Grunhard	6'3", 292
C	Mike Heldt	6'4", 267
RG	Tom Thayer	6'5", 268
RT	Larry Williams	6'6", 284
TE	Derek Brown	6'6", 252
QB	Steve Beuerlein	6'3", 201
HB	Allen Pinkett	5'9", 183
FB	Jerome Bettis	5'11", 247
FL	Raghib Ismail	5'10", 175
K	John Carney	5'10", 170
P	Craig Hentrich	6'1", 197

Defense:

LE	Jeff Alm	6'7", 248
NT	Chris Zorich	6'1", 266
RT	Mike Gann	6'5", 256
OLB	Frank Stams	6'4", 237
ILB	Michael Stonebreaker	6'1", 228
ILB	Demetrius DuBose	6'2", 234
OLB	Cedric Figaro	6'3", 232
LCB	Stacy Toran	6'4", 206
RCB	Todd Lyght	6'1", 181
SS	George Streeter	6'2", 212
FS	Dave Duerson	6'3", 202

1991-2000:
Offense:

SE	Derrick Mayes	6'1", 204
LT	Aaron Taylor	6'4", 299
LG	Jeremy Akers	6'5", 286
C	Tim Ruddy	6'3", 286
RG	Mike Rosenthal	6'7", 302
RT	Mike Doughty	6'7", 304
TE	Jabari Holloway	6'3", 260
QB	Ron Powlus	6'3", 220
FB	Marc Edwards	6'0", 237
TB	Autry Denson	5'10", 202

FL	Lake Dawson	6'1", 202
K/P	Craig Hentrich	6'1", 197

Defense:

LE	Bryant Young	6'3", 277
LT	Jim Flanigan	6'2", 276
RT	Cedric Hilliard	6'2", 290
RE	Grant Irons	6'5", 275
MLB	Courtney Watson	6'1", 232
OLB	Rocky Boiman	6'4", 240
CB	Shane Walton	5'11", 186
FS	Tony Driver	6'2", 220
SS	Glenn Earl	6'1", 210
CB	Bobby Taylor	6'3", 191
KR	Allen Rossum	5'8", 174

2001-2010:
Offense:

LT:	Ryan Harris	6'5" 290
LG:	Chris Stewart	6'5" 318
C:	Jeff Faine	6'3" 291
RG:	Trevor Robinson	6'5" 311
RT:	Sam Young	6'8" 310
QB:	Brady Quinn	6'3" 230
RB:	Julius Jones	5'10" 211
WR:	Michael Floyd	6'3" 230
WR:	Jeff Samardzija	6'5" 225
TE:	John Carlson	6'6" 251
P/K:	D. J. Fitzpatrick	6'2" 206

Defense:

DE:	Justin Tuck	6'5" 270
DT:	Trevor Laws	6'1" 304
DT:	Derek Landri	6'2" 290
DE:	Victor Abiamiri	6'4" 270
OLB:	Darius Fleming	6'2" 255
MLB:	Manti Te'O	6'2" 255
OLB:	Courtney Watson	6'1" 246
CB:	Shane Walton	5'11" 195
CB:	Vontez Duff	5'10" 193
FS:	Tom Zbikowski	5'11" 200
SS:	Harrison Smith	6'2" 214

All-time Notre Dame Players by Position

Pre-1942: The following players were selected as the best at their positions. Their careers were over before Leahy introduced the T-formation in 1942. Invariably, they were one-platoon players.

LE	John Farley	
LT	Moose Krause	
LG	Hunk Anderson	
C	John Eggeman	
RG	Clipper Smith	
RT	Ralph Dimmick	
RE	Eddie Anderson	
QB	Harry Stuhldreher	
LHB	George Gipp	
RHB	Don Miller	
FB	Ray Eichenlaub	
K	George Gipp	

Post-1942: The following players have been selected from among those whose careers took place after 1942, the year that modern football began at Notre Dame.

LE	Jim Seymour
LT	George Connor
LG	Tim Grunhard
C	Dave Huffman
RG	Tom Thayer
RT	George Kunz
RE	Ken MacAfee
QB	Joe Montana
HB	Allen Pinkett
FB	Jerome Bettis
FL	Raghib Ismail
K	John Carney
P	Craig Hentrich

Best All-time Teams

The following players represent the best two offensive and defensive units from the history of Notre Dame football. These players would have excelled in any era, under any coach, under any conditions, against all opponents. There are probably some surprises here—the center and fullback, for instance. Two players make both offense and defense—George Gipp and Leon Hart.

	All-time offense:	*Second team:*
WR	Michael Floyd	Jim Seymour
LT	George Connor	Moose Krause
LG	Tim Grunhard	Larry DiNardo
C	John Eggeman	Dave Huffman
RG	Tom Thayer	Dick Arrington
RT	George Kunz	Aaron Taylor
TE	Ken MacAfee	Leon Hart
QB	Joe Montana	Johnny Lujack
HB	George Gipp	Allen Pinkett
FB	Jerome Bettis	Ray Eichenlaub
FL	Raghib Ismail	Tim Brown
K	George Gipp	Craig Hentrich

	All-time defense:	*Second team:*
LE	Ross Browner	Walt Patulski
LT	Chris Zorich	Kevin Hardy
RT	Steve Niehaus	Mike Fanning
RE	Alan Page	Leon Hart
OLB	Bob Crable	Frank Stams
MLB	Bob Golic	Jim Carroll
OLB	Jim Lynch	Steve Heimkreiter
LCB	Todd Lyght	Luther Bradley
RCB	Bobby Taylor	Stacey Toran
SS	Jim Browner	Nick Rassas
FS	George Gipp	Dave Duerson

CHAPTER FOUR

SEASON REVIEWS

THE EARLY YEARS: 1887 TO 1899

1887

Notre Dame football had an inauspicious beginning. The young men who wanted to start up a team found that the university did not own a football. They also had no playing field, no uniforms, and no opponents.

In March, Henry Luhn, a student, called a meeting in Brownson Hall and 15 students showed up. Brother Joachim was charged in that meeting with buying a football; in two weeks a football arrived in South Bend from Chicago. The campus literary society took over fundraising and acquired clean, white cotton uniforms—but only eleven of them.

A field of sorts came into being near Sorin Hall, about 100 yards south of the Golden Dome; the sidelines marked by two rocks, the goals by two trees. Soon two old poles were put up for goal kicks. Practices were organized for the original 15 enthusiasts, and bystanders were cajoled into the fray as well. Experience was not a high priority, but eventually 11 players were selected—because that was the number of uniforms they had.

The Founding Fathers of Notre Dame football. Standing: Hepburn, Houck, Sawkins, Fehr, Nelson, Melady, Springer. Sitting: Jewett, Cusack, Luhn, and Prudhomme.

An inauspicious beginning: the 1887 Fighting Irish.

The first trial "game" was with the South Bend Shamrock Athletic Club in April. The Club team threatened to make this a memorable affair, and Notre Dame students responded in kind. Intimidated officials hired for the game failed to show up, so a "cheerleader" for the A.C. team became the referee, and John Burke, a janitor from Brownson Hall, served as umpire. Notre Dame won 8-4, with touchdowns being scored by Joe Cusack and Luhn for the home team. In this period, touchdowns were valued at four points, field goals at five points, and point after kicks at two points. Several players were knocked senseless during the melee; Notre Dame finished the game with only nine players.

Emboldened by their modest success, Luhn's team arranged for a regular game with representatives from the University of Michigan. On November 23, the Michigan team took the train to South Bend and were warmly greeted with a sight-seeing tour. Then they played a demonstration match of rugby, with mixed teams. The groups reorganized into their original teams and the football game commenced.

The playing conditions were horrible—the field a quagmire—and the game ended early after a partial—"inning" (what is now called a quarter). Michigan shut out Notre Dame 8-0. It would be six more years before Notre Dame's record indicates more wins than losses, but the enterprise was begun. The student newspaper commented on the enthusiasm displayed and stated its hope that "...coming years will witness a series of these contests."

Record to date: 0-1-0 (.000)

1888

Undaunted, Notre Dame invited the University of Michigan back to help celebrate their first anniversary of football. Michigan players stayed at the Sheridan House in South Bend and were met by a group from Notre Dame on April 20. The game was played off campus at Green Stocking Ball Park. Festivities began with a 100-yard race, with Michigan's James Duffy nipping Notre Dame's Harry Jewett in the elapsed time of 11 seconds. The game began at 3 p.m. but the first half was marred by arguments with the referee, who was from Ann Arbor and would play against Notre Dame the next day. Michigan's experience earned them a 24-0 lead before Notre Dame's Frank Springer wrestled the ball away for an apparent touchdown; the referee disallowed the score. Jewett thus gained football immortality when his subsequent score became the first official Notre Dame touchdown. Ed Prudhomme made the conversion and the Fighting Irish lost 24-6. But they were on the right path.

The boys were learning fast and almost upset Michigan the next day. Sprague, the referee of the day before, switched with Babcock. The game was played on campus and Notre Dame jumped out to a quick 4-0 lead based on two safeties—Michigan's center, W.W. Harless, was tackled with the ball behind his goal, as was Duffy. Yet another rules argument started and Michigan's Sprague took off with the ball and scored an unmolested, but not uncontested, touchdown. The ball was not in play, the Fighting Irish claimed, and besides he had stepped out of bounds. Babcock ignored them. Michigan scored again. Jewett responded with a touchdown, but Babcock disallowed it. Notre Dame lost 10-4. It would be 21 years before a Michigan team would lose to Notre Dame.

The young team practiced hard. There were some new faces for the Irish, and Jewett and Cusack switched positions. Their next game was in early December with Harvard School of Illinois, who deemed themselves champions of that state. Notre Dame won 20-0, and declared themselves champs of both states.

1888 record: 1-2-0 (.333)
Record to date: 1-3-0 (.250)

1889

Perhaps sensing something good, the team scheduled an away game with Northwestern University. They prepared diligently with early morning runs around the campus lake. The Fighting Irish turned in a successful 9-0 shutout in their first road game. Play was still ragged—one opponent's dash to the goal was stopped when a Notre Dame player simply sat on the runner. Notre Dame's first field goal was drop-kicked by Dezera Cartier, who distinguished himself later in the game, according to the accounts of the time, when he "dribbled" the ball for a 25-yard gain, the best on record to that point. The Fighting Irish showed ingenuity in scoring when quarterback Ed Coady hid the ball, making it appear that end Steve Fleming had it. As Northwestern chased Fleming, Coady ambled into the end zone with a touchdown and the first recorded Fighting Irish fake.

The win wrapped up Notre Dame's first undefeated season—and also marked the end of playing the game at Notre Dame for more than two years. Football ended because it was only a club sport, and the students were unable to maintain its momentum.

1889 record: 1-0-0 (1.000)
Record to date: 2-3-0 (.400)

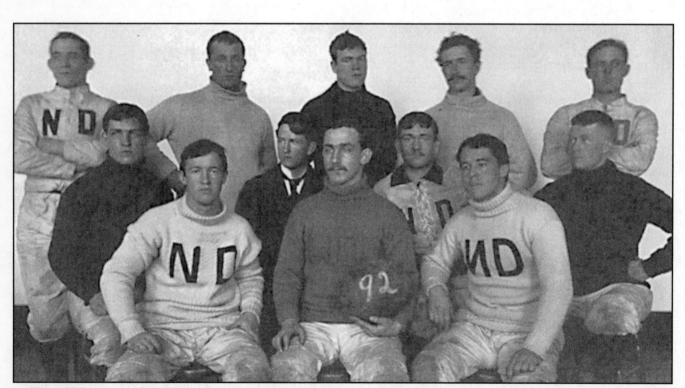

The 1892 team revived the game after a lapse of two years. Captain Pat Coady with the ball.

1892

The team had to start over by recruiting personnel. Only Pat Coady, the new captain, had any connection with the previous teams, since his brothers had been quarterbacks in 1888 and 1889. Fred Schillo at left tackle would be a fixture until 1897, and several other players were in for the duration. This continuity appears to have been a crucial factor in reviving the program.

The schedule was not very ambitious. In playing South Bend High School, Notre Dame established a trend of playing some rag-tag outfits well into the new century. The ambitious high schoolers suffered a 56-0 loss as Notre Dame's Ed Brown became the school's first game-breaker with five touchdowns. The next game with Hillsdale College was a well-played, hard-hitting affair ending in a 10-10 tie. It was the first time Notre Dame rallied from a halftime deficit (6-4) to avert a loss.

Football was back.

1892 record: 1-0-1 (.750)
Record to date: 3-3-1 (.500)

1893

In 1893, there was an attempt to schedule serious major opponents. (Earlier encounters with Michigan had been the result of mutual friendships, with Michigan helping out the new kid). The most important addition to the season was scheduling the University of Chicago for the final game, a school that was challenging the smug eastern football powers for recognition.

Kalamazoo folded easily 34-0 in the opener. Albion lost 8-6, thanks to a safety made by Ernest DuBrul. Schillo impressed people with his running from the dreaded "tackles back" formation. DeLasalle collapsed 28-0 in a blinding snowstorm; Fighting Irish tackle Charles Roby scored with a "turtle crawl"—on all fours with three DeLasalle players smothering his body. Roby capped his day's work by carrying Schillo, who carried the ball, for a five-yard gain. Such was football in 1893. Another snowstorm hit a week later, but the game with Hillsdale went on. Notre Dame's 22-10 win that featured a 50-yard run by John Barrett. For New Year's, the team went to Chicago, but the University of Chicago won 8-0. In spite of that loss, the 1893 season showed that Notre Dame could play with the established teams and pummel lesser ones.

1893 record: 4-1-0 (.800)
Record to date: 7-4-1 (.625)

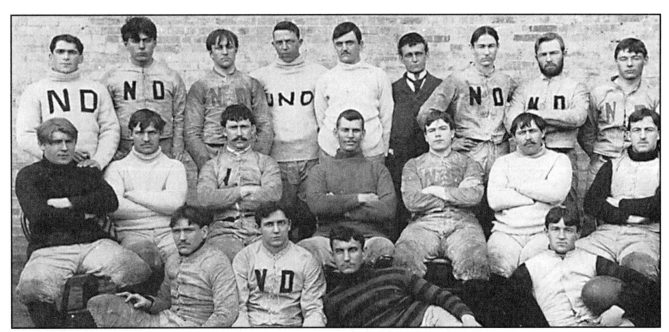

The 1893 Fighting Irish, with almost double the number of players from 1892.

The 1894 Notre Dame football team.

1894

Notre Dame took a significant step toward respectability, prominence, and stability when they hired a part-time coach, bearded James L. Morison. Morison had once played tackle for the University of Michigan. He stressed conditioning, speed, and an abundance of end runs. Such tactics led to an opening 14-0 win over Hillsdale. Next came Albion, fresh from a 26-12 loss to Michigan, who proved to be tough. The game ended in a 6-6 tie when substitute fullback John Studebaker fell on a fumble for the only Fighting Irish touchdown. Next, Wabash was dispatched easily, 30-0; the score might have been higher, but Wabash left the field with 18 minutes to go in the game. Notre Dame then whipped Rush Medical 18-6 in a workmanlike game, serenaded by a band led by a Professor Prescott. The season finale was a 19-12 loss to Albion in a return match, although Notre Dame felt the game was stolen from them when it was called due to darkness.

1894 record: 3-1-1 (.700)
Record to date: 10-5-2 (.647)

1895

The new season brought a new coach, H.G. Hadden, who emphasized creating depth behind the starters. In fact, he was the substitute for portly Rosy Rosenthal at center, a fairly common practice in those days.

The Fighting Irish won their opener 20-0 over Northwestern. Next, Notre Dame tallied an 18-2 win over the Illinois Cycling Club due to better tackling. The win streak ended against Indianapolis Artillery, however, a team that boasted a former All-American player named Osgood. Somerville, the referee, apparently did not detect an offsides penalty when it took place, maybe because his brother played for the Artillery squad. The Fighting Irish also lost two costly fumbles on a slick field. Coach Hadden, however, did his best to help his team win: game accounts tell of him playing left tackle, returning kick offs, recovering a fumble, running the ball four times, and making tackles, although he was unable to stop the referee's brother from dashing 90 yards for a touchdown. A Renaissance figure on the field, Hadden next served as a referee as his scrubs, an early version of junior varsity, romped 46-0 over LaPorte High School. Less than a week after that, more medical students from Chicago came to the campus, only to lose 32-0. Notre Dame's backfield duo of Bob Brown and Lucian Wheeler

The 1895 team: Jack Mullen, far left second row, became the only three-time captain for Notre Dame.

combined to rush for more than 150 and 116 yards, respectively, the first time Notre Dame had two players break the century mark in one game.

1895 record: 3-1-0 (.750)
Record to date: 13-6-2 (.666)

1896

This was a pivotal season. Notre Dame was led by its first full-time coach, Frank Hering from Bucknell—a football nomad (he played for the University of Chicago in 1893 and 1894, and was the Maroon quarterback in Notre Dame's 8-0 loss in 1893), a bit of a dreamer (he

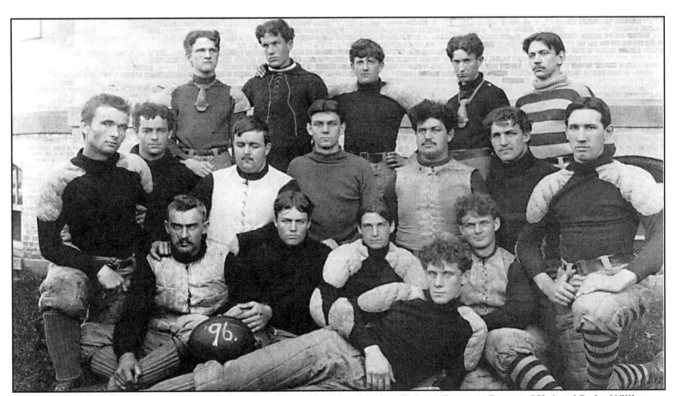

The 1896 squad. Front: Frank Hering; second row: Charles Moritz, Robert Emmett Brown, Michael Daly, William Kegler; third row: John Mullen, Frank Hanly, Thomas Cavanaugh, Frank Lyons, Jake Rosenthal, Fred Schillo, John Murphy; top row: Joseph Corby, Angus McDonald, Houser (trainer), Thomas O'Hara, William Fagan.

was responsible for campaigning to put Mother's Day on the national calendar), a heady tactician, and a believer in positive reinforcement. He came to Notre Dame in the triple capacity of coach, quarterback, and captain.

He coached an advanced form of the game imported from the east, especially involving line play, and he arranged an expanded schedule of seven home games. His team lost its first game 4-0 to Physicians and Surgeons, partially because they left the field to protest a bad possession call. Then Hering's former Chicago teammates shut out Notre Dame 18-0, based on strong line play and weak Irish tackling. Two weeks later, Hering's coaching paid off in a 46-0 rout of South Bend Commercial Athletic Club. Notre Dame's Bob Brown had another big day with 50- and 65-yard touchdown runs and Jack Mullen scampered 90 yards for another. Hering, who had earlier berated the student body for heckling the players at practice, had the playing field enclosed with a fence. Next Albion fell 24-0 as the Fighting Irish tuned up for the state championship game with Purdue. In that game, the Irish offense clicked, but the defense faltered in a 28-22 loss. Three muffed conversion kicks sealed the team's fate.

That loss spurred the team on to an 82-0 win over Highland Views. Only three starters for the Fighting Irish did *not* score in the blitz of 15 touchdowns. Mike Daly booted 11 conversion kicks and Brown ran for three touchdowns, each more than 60 yards. A highly touted

Beloit team arrived next, fresh from tying undefeated Wisconsin and Northwestern. Notre Dame slogged to an 8-0 win on a wretched field. Hering had put together a very solid team in his first campaign.

1896 record: 4-3-0 (.571)
Record to date: 17-9-2 (.642)

1897

Hering returned for his second year as coach and the Western Conference was created (now the Big Ten). Notre Dame applied for membership but was told, more or less, to grow up some more. Two new players must be mentioned—John Farley at left end (he would later become a priest and spend his life under the Dome) and massive John Eggeman (6-4, 256 pounds) became an instant fixture at center for Hering's sophisticated brand of football. Farley would be the best player for the Fighting Irish until Red Salmon matriculated a few years later. He personally demolished Chicago Dental Surgeons in his third game by rushing for 464 yards.

The season started with another shutout—a 0-0 tie with Rush Medical. Farley and Eggeman played well, and the big center used his bulk to push fullback Bill Kegler "into the line like a battering ram." Similar tactics helped the Fighting Irish win 4-0 over DePauw (TDs

The 1897 team: first row: Bauwens, Kearney, Kegler, Captain Mullen, Daly, Fennessey, Monohan, McNaughton; middle row: Healey, Schillo, Swonk, Eggemen, Lins, Niezer, Farley; top row: Powers, Dr. Berteling, Coach Hering, O'Malley (manager), McDonald, Murray, Waters, Bouza, Williams.

were worth four points in 1897), with Kegler registering the lone score. The next game was Farley's big day of 464 yards against the dentists—more than twice the yardage of any Fighting Irish back of any era. He scored four touchdowns, one on a short run and others on runs of 25, 50, and 45 yards. The last time anyone saw him he was scooting 85 yards with a backwards pass on the last play of the game.

The euphoria of this 62-0 win lasted two weeks until Chicago dumped Notre Dame with a bruising 34-5 win. The scoring machine found new life a week later, however, when St. Viator was demolished 60-0. The season ended on a 34-5 victory over Michigan Agricultural College. Kegler and George Lins led the way with two touchdowns each. This was probably the best of Hering's three teams as head coach.

1897 record: 4-1-1 (.750)
Record to date: 21-10-3 (.661)

1898

Facing a rugged schedule, Hering had the team go to a resort hotel at Hudson Lake for preseason training. Seventeen hopefuls made the trip and the week-long stay seems to have helped them avoid the slow starts of the previous seasons. Hering also noted that touchdowns were now valued at five points, the same as a field goal, and conversion kicks were worth only one point. They were bold enough to open on the road, at the University of Illinois in Champaign, winning 5-0, thanks to a late field goal by Charles Fleming and Eggeman's block of an Illini field goal try. A desperate Fighting Irish defense stopped the Illini on the last play of the game with the ball on the six-yard line.

The Aggies of Michigan Agricultural College were next, fresh from being whipped 39-0 by the University of Michigan. Notre Dame was still trying to measure itself by the Michigan standard and piled up an impressive 53-0 rout. Farley, now oddly known as "Tiger Lily," made 11 runs for 225 yards and three touchdowns, including scoring bursts of 38 and 45 yards.

The Irish traveled to Ann Arbor to try their luck, but Michigan prevailed 23-0. The field was a mud bath, and Michigan players had long cleats, which the Irish lacked. Michigan triple-teamed Eggeman and nullified the rest for the win.

Six days later, Notre Dame rebounded for a 32-0 rout of DePauw. Then downstate rival Indiana pinned them with an 11-5 loss. Farley tallied the only Fighting Irish touchdown on a 14-yard sweep around left end. Unable to claim the state championship, they vented their frustrations on Albion, winning 60-0 to close the season. Angus McDonald streaked 95 yards for a touchdown on the opening kickoff, and scored twice more. Eggeman also racked up a touchdown on a 15-yard run.

It was a frustrating season, perhaps blighted by overconfidence after the good start. The Fighting Irish were still not ready to defeat a major power.

1898 record: 4-2-0 (.666)
Record to date: 25-12-3 (.662)

1899

Frank Hering would coach the team through only five games before turning it over to rough, abrasive James McWeeney, who would prove to be a problem in later years as an assistant coach under Pat O'Dea. Hering launched the team on a 10-game schedule, a first for Notre Dame, although most of the opponents were nearby.

The first game was with Englewood High School, who put up a good fight before losing 29-5. Then Michigan Agricultural College was defeated 40-0. The opportunistic Irish blocked two late field goal attempts to save the shutout.

Riding this modest crest, the Fighting Irish met up with the great Amos Alonzo Stagg's Chicago team, but were disappointed in a 23-6 loss. Farley scored the only Fighting Irish touchdown, dashing 15 yards with a recovered fumble. But his effort was eclipsed by Chicago's Hamill who ran 105 and 100 yards for touchdowns, the latter coming on a blocked field goal try.

Ten days later, only 325 spectators watched Notre Dame blank Lake Forest 38-0, with Angus McDonald using the new-fangled "Princeton kick" (using a holder rather than the dropkick) for a field goal. Then Michigan again and another loss, 12-0. For some unrecorded reason, Eggeman kept the time for the game. The Michigan team kept Farley in check, although he dropped a Wolverine runner who seemed destined for a long touchdown run.

The Fighting Irish rebounded by beating Indiana 17-0 to make a partial claim on the state championship. The student body helped out with a cheering contest and asked the referee—former coach and player Hadden—to give a speech. Farley racked up two punt returns of 45 yards each, other runs of 40 and 35 yards, and a stop on an opposing player who threatened the shutout. Four days later, Notre Dame blanked Northwestern 12-0, again blocking field goals to save the shutout. Eggeman and others missed that game and the 17-0 whitewash of Rush.

Injuries mounted, and new players were thrust into unfamiliar positions as Notre Dame went to Purdue to claim the rest of the state crown; the game ended in a 10-10 tie, with McDonald salvaging that with a field goal from the 40-yard line.

A crowd of some 2,000 showed up for the finale with Chicago Physicians and Surgeons, a mature, experienced bunch good enough to use a former All-Western player only as a substitute. Eggeman had quit, and his replacement had only three days to prepare. The overmatched Fighting Irish played a good game, bowing 5-0, and used McDonald's punts of 68 and 82 yards to keep the other team bottled up.

Notre Dame's student paper pointed out that Indiana and Purdue had each lost an in-state game, whereas they had not, so a modest claim for the state title was made.

1899 record: 6-3-1 (.650)
Record to date: 31-15-4 (.660)

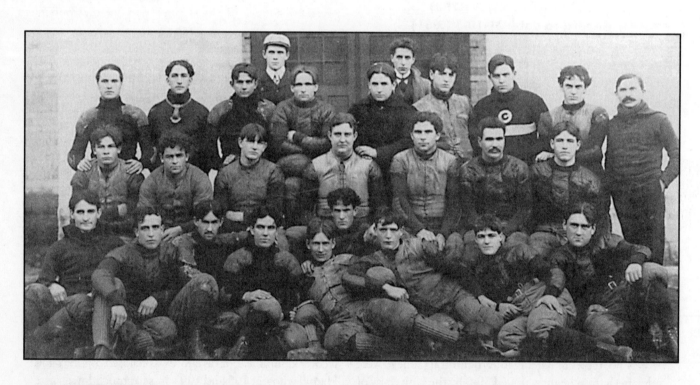

The 1899 Fighting Irish: front row: Monohan, Kuppler, Fleming, Daly, Duncan, McDonald, Hayes, Glynn, Winters; second row: Schneider, Hanley, McNulty, Eggeman, O'Malley, Wagner, Fortin; third row: Pym, Smith, Coleman, Captain Mullen, Lennon, Hayes, McWeeney, Farley, Engledrum (trainer); top: Coach Hering, Crumley (manager).

1900-1909

1900

Pat O'Dea and McWeeney were the coaches for the year. O'Dea had been an All-America fullback and kicker for Wisconsin, and McWeeney established rapport with those who liked a rough game. Chet Grant recalled McWeeney's advice to runners: "double your fist when you run into the line and they'll get the message." This probably missed the point, since their line needed good replacements. Farley moved from left end to fullback, an interesting change since his backup was named Red Salmon. Other moves were made to shore up the depleted squad.

The changes looked pretty good when Notre Dame demolished Goshen College 55-0. Farley and Fortin had four touchdowns between them; five others were spread around. Englewood High School, who had just held Stagg's Chicago team to 27 points, lost to the Fighting Irish 68-0. Farley's score on a 75-yard run was the play of the game. The South Bend Howard Park lost 64-0, with George Kuppler and Jim Faragher scoring three touchdowns each and Farley and Fortin two each. The momentum continued through a 58-0 demolition of Cincinnati, with Kuppler scoring three times and Farley

twice. One of Farley's scores came on a "fake kick," which he converted for a score on a 90-yard run.

Having scored 245 points to 0 in four games, there was a reason to expect the Fighting Irish to be a power in the state, but Indiana shocked them 6-0. Then Beloit College added to the skid with a 6-6 tie, although Fighting Irish honor was upheld with a valiant four-play stand at their one-foot line. The downward slide was completed a week later when Notre Dame lost to the University of Wisconsin 54-0, the worst defeat on record to that point. Farley was injured early in the game to make it worse.

With ample reasons to be depressed, the Fighting Irish faced a tough Michigan team. But the team pulled together, played solid defense, matched Michigan punt for punt, and even drove to the Michigan three-yard line, but could not score. A recovered fumble led to a touchdown for Michigan and Salmon was caught for a safety, resulting in a 7-0 win for the Wolverines. For Notre Dame, it was their best game against a powerhouse team and showed promise for the future.

Rush Medical then came to Notre Dame where a drenching rain turned the field into a lake. Farley blocked a kick and ran 35 and 70 yards to help Notre Dame win 5-0. Salmon scored the only touchdown

The 1900 edition of Notre Dame Varsity Football.

in his first game starting at fullback. The season ended with another 5-0 win over Physicians and Surgeons, with Frank Winters kicking a 40-yard field goal into a stiff wind.

1900 record: 6-3-1 (.650)
Record to date: 37-18-5 (.658)

1901

The 1901 season did not start well. A replacement team had to be found for the scheduled opener; South Bend Commercial Athletic Club gladly filled in for Milwaukee Medical, too gladly as it turned out. They held the Fighting Irish to a scoreless tie. Captain Al Fortin, only 19 years old but in his fourth season with Notre Dame, saved the day when he blocked a field goal try. Then the Fighting Irish took a long road trip to Columbus, to play Ohio Medical University. There they were glad to escape with a 6-0 win, with Fortin scoring the only touchdown. Irish fumbles made the game tighter than it should have been. Traveling in the opposite direction the next week, the Irish visited Northwestern, only to find the mud there four inches deep. Salmon could not operate in the wet conditions, and a bad snap on a punt from his end zone resulted in a safety and a 2-0 Northwestern win. Notre Dame

then played Chicago Medical College at home and won handily, 32-0. With the defense playing well, a tough Beloit squad fell 5-0; their offense was stymied by Salmon's booming 70-yard punts. Yet another shutout, the fifth in six games, took Lake Forest to defeat, 16-0. Salmon scored a touchdown and booted a field goal.

Coach O'Dea planned on a first-half schedule of easier opponents to prepare his team for the perceived challenges in the state, an early version of Fighting Irish scheduling that was practiced for many years. His plan worked as Purdue came to Notre Dame, only to run into an aroused student body that had even written special songs for the occasion. O'Dea's offense was designed around Salmon's vicious line bucks followed by ponderous tackle back plays, a crunching combination that earned a 12-6 win. A week later, the in-state sweep became a reality as Notre Dame whipped Indiana 18-5. Salmon scored twice on short runs and also had a 55-yard kickoff return. Physicians and Surgeons were dispatched 34-0; running backs switched positions with linemen to allow them scoring chances. Both guards and the center scored, and another center who took over at fullback also scored a touchdown.

The finale was against the South Bend Commercial Athletic Club (with O'Dea as its kicker). The Fighting Irish won 22-6 as Salmon outkicked his coach, although O'Dea scored the club team's only touchdown.

Notre Dame thus concluded its most successful season yet. They claimed a state championship, six

The 1901 Notre Dame University Football Team.

shutouts in 10 games and only three touchdowns scored against them. The Fighting Irish were on the verge of reaching the prominence they had been seeking for a decade.

**1901 record: 8-1-1 (.850)
Record to date: 45-19-6 (.685)**

1902

O'Dea moved on to coach at Missouri, the Cornell coach who was supposed to replace him did not show up, so Salmon took on the job. His first chore was to find a new interior line before playing Michigan Agricultural College. His backs looked good, scoring two touchdowns in the first moments, and Notre Dame kept the pressure on for a 33-0 blitz. Lake Forest fell next, 28-0, led by Salmon's two touchdowns.

The Fighting Irish had played Michigan both at home and in Ann Arbor, so they tried them in Toledo for a change. Michigan won 23-0, although Salmon's spirited play and leadership caught their attention, especially in the first half when Notre Dame was behind only 5-0. Before it was over, Salmon was knocked out four times—and showed it.

Although disappointed once again in that big test, Notre Dame bested Indiana 11-5. A recovered Salmon broke loose for two touchdown runs (40 yards and a short plunge). His line smashes set up a nice 55-yard ramble by Jim Doar on a fake when the Hoosiers went after Salmon. After this win, Notre Dame went to Columbus, Ohio, winning 6-5. A booming Salmon punt of 65 yards was misplayed into Notre Dame's only score. The team moved on to Rock Island, Illinois, for a game with Knox College, losing 12-5, although Salmon left the 3,000 spectators agog with an 85-yard punt. He also plunged for Notre Dame's only touchdown near the end of the game.

The road trip behind them, the Fighting Irish met American Medical, winning 92-0. The longest touchdown run, by Frank Lonergan, was 106 yards. Fighting Irish ball carriers racked up no less than 940 yards on 12 long-distance scores and seven players joined the century mark for the day! The 92 points were scored in just 32 minutes of play, with American Medical leaving the field early. The season's fourth shutout was handed to DePauw, 22-0. Salmon did his

usual thing—one touchdown on a fierce run, a 75-yard punt, and a field goal.

The instate rivalry ended sourly in Lafayette with a 6-6 tie with Purdue. Salmon was Notre Dame's only scorer. He played on a badly sprained ankle, which spoiled his last-minute drop-kick effort to win the game. Purdue used 35 players in the second half to wear out the 12 Fighting Irish who suited up. The tie left the state championship to be shared.

**1902 record: 6-2-1 (.766)
Record to date: 51-21-7 (.689)**

1903

This was the year for which the Fighting Irish had long waited. Salmon, as head coach and a senior in college, led the team to an undefeated, unscored-upon season. Michigan Agricultural College fell first, 12-0. Newcomer lineman Pat Beacom, 220 pounds of mean on the line, hit the Aggies all day. Salmon tinkered with his line assignments before the next game, and an improved squad downed Lake Forest 28-0, with Salmon scoring three times in the second half.

It rained for the DePauw game, both precipitation and points, as Notre Dame prevailed 56-0. American Medical showed some improvement from the previous year, but lost 52-0. Frank Lonergan scored three touchdowns. The Missouri Osteopaths were the next losers, 28-0. Salmon led the way, and Nate Silver saved the shutout when he tackled a Missouri player on the four-yard line after an 80-yard run.

The Fighting Irish played Northwestern in the American League baseball park of the day, a sign of the game's growing popularity; the game ended in a 0-0 tie. Lonergan scored a touchdown on a 45-yard burst, but Salmon was called for illegal use of the hands on the block. The Fighting Irish stunned the spectators with their defense when consecutive punts from their end zone went awry, at their two- and five-yard lines, but the Wildcats could not score in six tries. The team traveled to Toledo again to play Ohio Medical, winning 35-0. Four Notre Dame players scored two touchdowns each, including Salmon. He closed the scoring with a 20-yard burst with three opponents dangling from his shoulders. Notre Dame finished its season with a 35-0 romp over Wabash (who had whipped Indiana) and made some noises about the state crown.

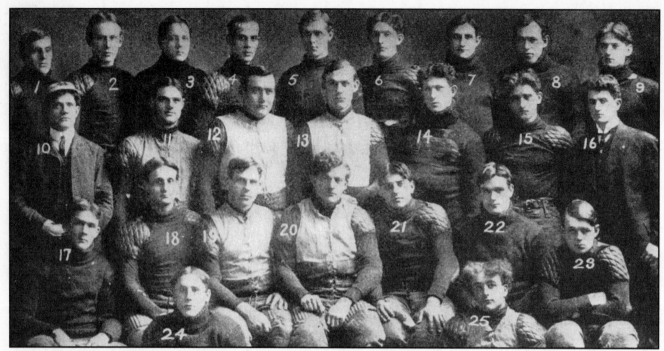

The 1903 squad, the best to date, undefeated and unscored upon.

For his illustrious efforts, Salmon made Walter Camp's All-America third team.

1903 record: 8-0-1 (.944)
Record to date: 59-21-8 (.715)

1904

Salmon coached a third season since he had to finish his engineering studies; his team was strong in desire but weak in talent and experience. Injuries would make matters worse. Salmon purchased a "charging machine," similar to the one used at Northwestern, to train the linemen "to charge fast and low and together." The rulesmakers had tinkered with the scoring values again: touchdowns were still five points, but field goals were reduced to four points.

Armed with the latest technology, the Fighting Irish charged against Wabash in an unimpressive 12-4 win. Frank Shaughnessey looked good on some long runs and a 30-yard sprint with a fumble he recovered in mid-air. Pat Beacom thrilled the fans when he charged through the Little Giants on a punt play and forced the punter into surrendering the ball. American Medical was next, losing 44-0. Newcomer Bob Bracken ran for three touchdowns and Shaughnessey followed up a blocked kick with a 101-yard touchdown dash.

After that, the deluge. The Fighting Irish took 25 men to Wisconsin (with 60 on its squad). Notre Dame played stoutly for 14 scoreless minutes, then a series of injuries decimated its players. Wisconsin won 58-0. Beacom was the only ray of light in an otherwise gloomy picture.

With injured players at many positions, quarterback Silver tried to compensate against Ohio Medical by exchanging backs with linemen. Left guard Beacom scored twice as Notre Dame struggled to a 17-5 win. Shaughnessey dislocated his collar bone to keep the bad luck going. Similar emergency plans allowed for a 6-0 win over Toledo, but disaster struck in practice the next week when fullback Bill Draper sprained an ankle. Shaughnessey at least had his shoulder sling removed.

Taking plenty of lineaments and plasters, the Fighting Irish made their longest road trip, to the University of Kansas in Lawrence. They played as well as they could with four starters out, but fell 24-6. Captain Shaughnessey could not bear to just watch and inserted himself over the roaring protests of Salmon; he promptly ran 100 yards for the only Irish touchdown. Bad luck went on the trip too—even the substitutes were hurting when Keefe and O'Neil saw action for two plays and were kicked unconscious. It would be 30 years before Notre Dame played Kansas again.

The 1904 Irish: first row: Sudheimer, Silver, Coad; second row: Holland, McInerney, Shaughnessey, Guthery, Daley, Coach Salmon; third row: Funk, Donovan, Beacom, Fansler, Sheehan, Murphy, Bracken; top row: O'Neill, O'Keefe, Draper, Church, Healy, Waldorf.

A two-week breather helped the Irish prepare for DePauw and Purdue. They needed it. DePauw played tough but lost 10-0; Draper broke his collarbone after booming a 75-yard punt. Notre Dame limped on to Lafayette to meet Purdue but it was no contest with Purdue winning 36-0. The team played like madmen though; Salmon had to take Shaughnessey out of the game when he was so weak no one could hear his signals. Beacom was a pillar of strength, but it was not enough.

1904 record: 5-3-0 (.625)
Record to date: 64-24-8 (.708)

1905

Salmon moved back east to pursue his career in civil engineering, and former quarterback Henry McGlew advanced to become head coach. Having helped Salmon late in the 1904 season, he knew the players well, and there were some good ones. But the season started on a sour note when unfounded charges in the press of favoritism regarding starting positions and personnel eroded team morale following the opener with North Division High School. Nate Silver, a North Division grad, played well, but three North Division recruits on the Notre Dame bench abruptly quit the team following

the expected 44-0 rout; they were apparently lured to Wisconsin. In the game, Beacom scored twice and Bill Downs scored three times. The brouhaha welled up a few days after the game; it was the last time Notre Dame played a high school team.

Michigan Agricultural College tried again, but lost 28-0; six players scored touchdowns, all on short runs. The Fighting Irish could not sweep MAC's ends, so they went up the middle. On to Wisconsin, a tough assignment in view of the controversy regarding the preseason charges, plus the defection of players from Notre Dame to Wisconsin. Notre Dame lost 21-0, but not before serving notice that they could play with the Badgers. Some clear scoring chances were lost while Beacom unceremoniously stuffed the tentative plays sent in his direction. The Fighting Irish were good enough to earn accolades from Alonzo Stagg: they "looked every bit as good as Chicago, and in several particulars seem to have the better of the argument." The Notre Dame student paper called it a "glorious defeat."

Glorious it might have been, but the students ran out of words in the 5-0 loss to Wabash. Although statistically they had twice the yardage of Wabash, they could not score from the one-foot line, they fumbled on the Wabash 10, *etc.* Two consecutive shutout losses, one to tiny Wabash.

It was too bad for American Medical that Wabash beat Notre Dame. The student paper told the story:

The 1905 Notre Dame team.

"NOTRE DAME 142; AMERICAN COLLEGE OF MEDICINE AND SURGERY, 0."

"That looks good anyway. Rather relieves the feeling after the Wabash game."

Every starter scored, 142 points in 33 minutes. There were 27 touchdowns (with 21 mercifully missed conversion kicks—a pattern for many Fighting Irish blowouts in later years); interior linemen scored 11 of them. The longest drive was five plays; most were only two. (Remember, in those days the team that scored received the following kickoff.) Ten scores came in eight minutes. Four players scored three times each, six scored twice, and newcomer Dom Callicrate wandered into the end zone once.

DePauw lost by a 71-0 score. Bill Draper scored six touchdowns. Indiana, however, was not impressed and beat Notre Dame 22-5. The lackluster loss was followed by a modest 22-0 win over Bennett Medical College. Then Purdue finished the season in rude fashion with a 32-0 win over the Fighting Irish. Henry McGlew had seen enough of coaching.

1905 record: 5-4-0 (.555)
Record to date: 69-28-8 (.695)

1906

With McGlew gone, Notre Dame looked eastward again and came up with Thomas Barry, one of Camp's All-American choices for 1902. Barry had coached at Brown and Bowdoin and played minor league baseball in Buffalo and Montreal between stints at Harvard Law School. He inherited a good talent pool and newcomers who would soon make their marks. One of these was Harry "Red" Miller, the first of the great Miller clan to attend Notre Dame (they would keep coming right into World War II). John Eggeman's "little" brother showed up, all 220 pounds of him, to line up next to Beacom for a powerful left side.

The rules had changed, too, but Notre Dame would not take advantage of them for awhile. There would be less "mass play" and the forward pass could be thrown—cautiously, carefully, and conservatively.

Barry did not favor ridiculous scoring and told his players to take it easy on Franklin College. The opening kickoff turned into a Fighting Irish touchdown. Beacom strode in for a touchdown four plays later, then again moments later. Barry in the second half unloaded the bench. The game was marred by more than 100 yards of penalties because of the exuberant Irish who could not break their habit, now illegal, of hurdling the line. Notre Dame won 26-0. Hillsdale was next, losing 17-0. The first half was a restrained 0-0 tie—too much for Beacom to take. He scored twice soon after the half.

The 1906 Notre Dame varsity.

Physicians and Surgeons fell 28-0. Barry was scouting Purdue's game with Chicago and let Captain Bracken handle the game. Beacom scored three touchdowns.

Barry's professionalism emerged after his scouting trip when he ordered lights for the field house for three night practices before the Purdue game. But first, Michigan Agricultural College, aware of the new rules, came to Cartier Field ready to play flashy football. They had improved, but lost their sixth straight shutout to Notre Dame 5-0; the lone score came on a blocked kick.

Next up was Purdue. Two straight shutouts at their hands rankled, so the Fighting Irish returned the favor, 2-0, thanks to a bad snap on a punt that earned a safety. The game was marred by fumbles and penalties.

Next was Indiana for the state crown. But it was not to be. The Hoosier punter kept the Fighting Irish bottled up with 18 punts, the big Notre Dame linemen tired, and Indiana prevailed 12-0. Notre Dame ended the season on a high note with a 29-0 victory over Beloit, the sixth shutout of the year.

1906 record: 6-1-0 (.857)
Record to date: 75-29-8 (.705)

1907

Barry wanted to practice law, but stayed for one more year. Hopes were high that the elusive state crown would be won. The schedule was not very demanding, except for Purdue and Indiana. Barry was a master of defense—six shutouts in 1906 and four more would be added in 1907.

Physicians and Surgeons opened the season and the Irish held them to one first down in a 32-0 wipeout. There were many long runs for touchdowns, although some were called back for infractions. Franklin tried again but lost 23-0. For some reason, Red Miller was at center, although he still scored two touchdowns. Tiny Olivet was next; they had beaten Michigan Agricultural College in 1906 and also earned respect in a 22-4 Fighting Irish win. They had good team speed and used it in a variety of trick plays, onside kicks, and forward passes. Callicrate broke it open, with a touchdown plunge from the five-yard line, followed by a touchdown run of 100 yards. Olivet at one point used a play with five forward passes.

Indiana was a different story. They were tough. The game ended up in a 0-0 tie, which was marred by fumbles, lost possessions on incomplete passes (a rule then), and stalled drives. Miller seemed to be everywhere to stymie Hoosier plans.

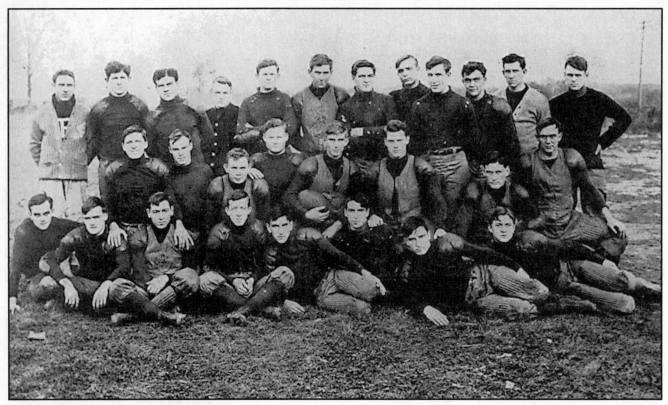

The 1907 Notre Dame football team.

Knox lost 17-0 even though Barry rested his starting backfield for Purdue. The Knox quarterback weighed only 117 pounds and spent most of his day trying to avoid the Notre Dame linemen. The Fighting Irish met Purdue without Red Miller, who was suffering from an abscess on his leg, and won 17-0. Callicrate successfully made up for the absent Miller. The season ended with a poorly played 21-12 win over St. Vincent's. Oddly enough, for a reward, Miller made the All-State team as a center.

1907 record: 6-0-1 (.928)
Record to date: 81-29-9 (.718)

1908

Barry left to coach at Wisconsin. Notre Dame continued its practice of hiring easterners when Victor Place, an All-America from Dartmouth, was hired. He specialized in power football, a throwback to the pre-1906 rules. Place came to be known for grueling practices and constant scrimmaging. Red Miller spoke of his two-a-days running for two and a half hours in

the morning with three and a half to four hours in the afternoon. Scrimmages would last up to two hours. All this tended to make the players overtrained.

In the opener against Hillsdale, the Fighting Irish scored within the first three minutes, got 23 points before the half, and held Hillsdale to one first down. Paul McDonald had the play of the day, a 65-yard touchdown sprint. Pete Vaughan scored twice, once on a 35-yard line buck intended for short yardage. His methods seemingly vindicated by the 39-0 score, Place continued to work his charges hard. Mismatched Franklin was pounded 64-0 and never earned a first down. The Irish were conducting a sprinter's clinic with several long touchdown runs when history was made as quarterback Don Hamilton tossed a forward pass to second-string left end Fay Wood, who turned the play into a score—Notre Dame's first recorded touchdown through the air. There were more passes after that, but McDonald racked up three touchdowns on the ground in the second half to attract most of the attention.

Miller had been rested in that game to be ready for Michigan. UM's coach and athletic director Fielding Yost's team was a bit past its "point a minute" express featuring Willie Heston, but they were a national power nevertheless. Michigan won again, 12-6, but the Fighting Irish scored the only touchdown when

Pete Vaughan dashed 50 yards on a double pass play. Michigan's Allerdice scored three field goals. Perhaps the game was lost on a mistaken out of bounds call that nullified McDonald's 85-yard TD run. In the loss, however, Notre Dame sacked the Wolverines six times and stopped their ground game all day.

Physicians and Surgeons watched an amazing performance by a bevy of Fighting Irish runners, losing 88-0 in 40 minutes of play. Notre Dame accumulated 1,316 yards rushing (to minus 15 yards for the opponents). Miller scored three times while Ulric Ruell and McDonald tallied twice each. Eight other players scored touchdowns. They also kicked a field goal and scored a safety just to make sure.

Ohio Northern University fell next 58-4. Ruell had a touchdown and a run of 85 yards within the first 40 seconds of the game. Miller and McDonald scored three times each and four others scored once. ONU managed a 40-yard field goal to keep the Fighting Irish record intact of not having an opposing player cross the goal with the ball.

Having established that they could play stifling defense, Notre Dame went to Indianapolis to meet Indiana. The Hoosiers managed to reach Notre Dame's 20-yard line, but that was all as the Fighting Irish won 11-0. Left tackles Kelly and Edwards scored twice and Miller piled up 175 yards rushing, with 150 yards of that in five end runs.

Wabash was outmanned but tough because of their coach Jesse Harper. It was a defensive game with all the scoring coming on field goals in an 8-4 Irish win. Vaughan intercepted two passes to ice the game. St. Viator was defeated in a 46-0 rout and a tough Marquette squad lost 6-0. (Marquette had tied Illinois and lost a close 9-6 game with Wisconsin.) The first half was scoreless, and Place opted to put in his speedsters, McDonald and Schmitt. Their outside speed resulted in the lone touchdown by McDonald, after his long passes to Rosey Dolan and Joe Collins. Marquette had a chance when it pinned Notre Dame on its one-yard line, but Vaughan sidestepped a charging tackler and broke a 35-yard gainer. The Milwaukee paper praised Irish tackling as "brief and to the point" so that "the play stopped right there." This was the key to the season in which no opposing team scored a touchdown, as the Fighting Irish racked up 326 points to 20. In the last 24 games, only two touchdowns had been scored against them while they registered sixteen shutouts.

The Fighting Irish had reached an important threshold—they were ready to beat a major power.

1908 record: 8-1-0 (.888)
Record to date: 89-30-9 (.730)

1909

Place was replaced by Frank "Shorty" Longman, a former fullback for Yost at Michigan from 1903 to 1905. He had coached at Arkansas and Wooster; at Wooster he had beaten Ohio State, the first time in 18 tries for the small school. In picking Longman, Notre Dame signaled the end of the domination of eastern personnel and methods.

The Fighting Irish had some good players— especially Miller and Vaughan in the backfield and the linemen Ralph Dimmick and George Philbrook. The school also now had its own song, the "Notre Dame Victory March." The scene was set for a good year of football. It should be noted that this was the first season in which the field goal scored the three points known in modern football.

Olivet opened the season, losing 58-0. The Fighting Irish had a big lead at the half but still used an onside kick. Longman also showed a preference for "smash-mouth" football, as his big linemen scored five touchdowns.

Rose Poly befell a similar fate, 60-11. Longman showed that he could combine power with passing by turning loose the towering Philbrook as a receiver. He promptly scored on a 50-yard touchdown pass. Dimmick also scored, but on the ground. Miller scored four times and Vaughan three. Rose Poly did score a touchdown when a Fighting Irish onside kick went astray and a Rose Poly player snatched it just in time to see Philbrook steaming after him. Notre Dame blocked a field goal try that ended up in a touchdown for Rose Poly.

A still-improving Michigan Agricultural College lost 17-0 in a well-played game. Dimmick ran in a touchdown from the 20-yard line, and Vaughan scored twice. Then Notre Dame went east to begin a series with Pitt and escaped with a 6-0 win; the issue was settled with the first game-winning touchdown pass in Fighting Irish history, a 35-yarder from Don Hamilton to Lee Mathews. The referees were so objectionable that

Pete Dwyer, substitute QB (second team) protested too much, was ejected, then tried to hit a referee. They invented a 45-yard penalty to end the argument.

After that, Ann Arbor must have seemed peaceful. But the 5,000 Michigan fans were stunned by a thrilling 11-3 Fighting Irish win. Walter Camp was there, too. Longman had been showcasing a long passing attack, but changed to a patient, short game. He still liked the onside kick, but it backfired when Allerdice recovered the first one and scored a field goal. Vaughan replied with the first Irish touchdown, shocking the fans when the end of his run he also ran into and demolished the goal posts. Michigan fought back, but a blocked field goal try was recovered by Notre Dame on the Michigan 35-yard line, setting up Billy Ryan's touchdown. A dejected Yost said afterwards, "Those are the worst kind of games to lose. They leave a worm in a man's heart to gnaw and gnaw." Longman introduced Miller to Yost the next day, and Yost promptly complained that Miller had called for fair catches too late three times, earning cheap penalties. A week later, Yost changed his tune completely: "… we went into the game caring little whether we won or lost." He would eventually define it as a "practice game"—even though 5,000 fans came to the proceedings on November 6, and Camp just happened to drop by.

The Fighting Irish high lasted through a 46-0 win over Ohio Northern. Longman turned his tackles loose on tackle-around plays and Philbrook and Dolan garnered two touchdowns each. Wabash was dispatched 38-0. Harper liked what he saw and chose seven Fighting Irish players for his 11-man All-State squad.

Mounting injuries contributed to a scoreless tie with Marquette to end the season. Vaughan was out; Dolan broke his collarbone early in the game, although he continued to play. The field was a sticky mess and the referees called a tight game. Still, the team thought Marquette was the best team they'd seen all year. Dimmick, Dolan, and Vaughan made All-Western; Dimmick earned honorable mention All-America. Walter Camp praised Miller.

1909. Let it stand with the other great years and other great teams. After waiting 22 years, Notre Dame had finally reached the point that it considered commensurate with its destiny. Although there would be genuine national championships ahead, but this was a year to cherish for its special accomplishments.

1909 record: 7-0-1 (.937)
Record to date: 96-30-10 (.742)

The 1909 squad—names are incorrect in three places: "Schmitt" should be Vaughan, "Maloney" should be Schmitt, and "Vaughan" is Maloney.

1910-1919

1910

The team lost a number of excellent players. Gone were Miller, Dolan, Vaughan, Ryan, Hamilton and other stalwarts. The 1910 team would be hard-pressed to do as well.

Dimmick and Philbrook were back, and a little guy named Dorais was an early lock at quarterback. Olivet was scheduled for the opener, and Longman used it to check out his new players. College football was beginning the process of sorting out the large schools from the small schools; Olivet had been able to compete earlier, but not anymore. Notre Dame won 48-0. Longman used every player, including a small, balding fellow with a broken nose and a funny name as third-string fullback. "Rochne," the papers reported—Knute Rockne, new to college after several years with the Post Office. Longman thought maybe he could eventually contribute something.

The coach of Buchtel (Akron) erred in judgment when he said that ND's colors contained a shade of yellow. His team was highly ranked in Ohio circles. Fifty-one Fighting Irish points later, he probably regretted the remark. Philbrook started the touchdowns and captain Dimmick took the honors with three scores. Philbrook made the play of the day when he started around end, fumbled, recovered, blasted through three converging would-be tacklers, and ran 75 yards for his second touchdown.

But Michigan Agricultural College turned the tables, winning 17-0. Notre Dame suffered a mental breakdown—fumbles, miscues, muffed punts, weak running, and poor blocking. The night before the Michigan game, University of Michigan Coach Yost cancelled the scheduled game between Notre Dame and Michigan, claiming that Philbrook and Dimmick had exhausted their eligibility in the Pacific Northwest before coming to Notre Dame. Yost's point probably had a point worth considering, but his tactics were not. There was the lingering suspicion that he did not want to run the risk of consecutive losses to the upstart Fighting Irish. Wabash coach Jesse Harper also had to cancel their game because of the death of a player. Rose

The 1910 Notre Dame team—Knute Rockne, far left, second row.

Poly substituted for them, only to lose in a 41-3 rout. Dimmick scored three touchdowns; Dorais hit three conversions and a field goal.

Ohio Northern became the 100th victim of the Fighting Irish football program. Ryan sprinted 95 yards for a score, Mathews ran 75 for another, and Dorais went cross country for a third to go with seven conversion kicks.

Marquette spoiled the finale with a 5-5 tie. Joe Brennan, Notre Dame's backup center in 1909 (and father of Terry Brennan, a later star under Leahy, and head coach, 1954-58), scored for Marquette on a one-yard plunge. Bill Martin recovered a fumble for Notre Dame's score. Although this had not been a particularly good year, there were some impressive players working their way to the starting lineup—men who would launch Notre Dame from a regional powerhouse into the national spotlight.

1910 record: 4-1-1 (.750)
Record to date: 100-31-11 (.742)

1911

Jack Marks from Dartmouth replaced Longman; he was assisted by Philbrook for the line and Hamilton for the backs. Losing Dimmick and Philbrook left yawning holes in the line, but speed was the order of the day. There was not a 200-pounder on the 1911 line. Only fullback Ray Eichenlaub, a rock-hard, 205-pounder, had any size.

Ohio Northern started the second 100 wins for Notre Dame with a 32-6 loss to a team with only four monogram winners in starting positions. A new brand of football was unveiled for Notre Dame—speed turned loose on end runs and long passes, but also a shift formation, the predecessor of the famous Notre Dame shift used later by Harper and Rockne. Scoring was distributed among the players, and the starters even rested for a quarter before they went back in to score three touchdowns in the last six minutes. Eichenlaub set up one of those scores with a 20-yard pass to Dorais. The ONU score came on an official's error when a blocked pass hit the ground but was not called incomplete; a surprised halfback named Stump scooped up the ball and scored what was to become the only touchdown against the Fighting Irish for the year.

The Irish dismantled St. Viator 43-0 in the next game. Dorais kicked an early field goal and paced a second-quarter, five-touchdown scoring burst with a touchdown pass to Dutch Bergman and a quarterback sneak for another.

A reputedly strong Butler team looked good through much of the game, down only 6-0 at halftime. The Fighting Irish were killing themselves with fumbles, so Marks sent his second team in for the third quarter, then blitzed a tiring Butler with his starters to end the game. The final score was 27-0. Eichenlaub scored twice, the second with most of the Butler team along for the ride. Bergman returned a 65-yard punt for a score that was the play of the day.

In the next game, Loyola of Chicago was immolated 80-0 in only 54 minutes of play. Dutch Bergman returned a kick-off for 105 yards, but missed a touchdown by five, due to the longer field in use back then—a record that may never be broken. Marks used his substitutes liberally against Loyola; back-up halfback Art Smith racked up seven touchdowns, the last one a 75-yard effort. Bergman pitched in with three.

The Fighting Irish headed for the University of Pittsburgh with 20 good players and Marks's caution was accurate; the Panthers fought to a tough 0-0 tie. Notre Dame stopped Pitt twice near the goal, once from the two-yard line, and Rockne lost a 40-yard touchdown dash on a recovered kick (the referee said the whistle never blew). Pitt lost a touchdown on an offside call and Dorais narrowly missed a late field goal. It was a game of lost opportunities for both teams.

Marks rested his starters against St. Bonaventure, and the reserves won 34-0. Joe Pliska scored three touchdowns, Heine Berger added two more, and Bill Kelleher one. Wabash was next and Wabash coach Harper had his team ready, duelling the Fighting Irish to a stirring 6-3 Notre Dame win. Wabash took the early lead with a dropkick and then made it last until the fourth quarter. Facing defeat, the Fighting Irish marched the length of the field, and Berger scored from the Wabash two for the win. Modern rules would have declared Wabash the winner, since their touchdown pass was disallowed for going more than 20 yards.

Marquette tied Notre Dame for the third straight year, in yet another scoreless affair. Notre Dame did manage a drive to the Marquette two, but a holding penalty killed the chance for a score. Dorais flubbed two field goal tries. Eichenlaub played well, and Charlie Crowley intercepted a pass to end a Marquette scoring threat.

The 1911 season marked a gradual shift into a brand of football similar to the modern game. All the early signs were there to indicate what would eventually happen at West Point in 1913.

1911 record: 6-0-2 (.875)
Record to date: 106-31-13 (.750)

1912

Marks continued his quiet ways, emphasizing team speed. After he filled holes and tinkered with personnel, he had what he wanted—a very fast squad, mostly of small men, with Eichenlaub for the hammer. Rockne and Crowley were great ends and Gus Dorais was a gutsy quarterback. This was the first season for college ball in which the scoring values were virtually the same as today, except for the two-point conversion, instituted in 1958.

St. Viator had the misfortune to field a team that was *both* smaller and slower, losing 116-7. Sheer speed accounted for 19 Fighting Irish touchdowns, with Berger

garnering five, sub Curly Nowers four, and Eichenlaub and Eddie Duggan three each; the rest were sprinkled among the masses. The tradition of botching conversion kicks in routs continued; Notre Dame made only seven of 19.

Marks opted to try to slug it out with Adrian College, a much larger, more physical team, in a display of old-fashioned straight football. The Irish enjoyed the anachronism, winning 74-7. Berger and Pliska got four touchdowns each; Dorais booted eight conversions and consistently put the Fighting Irish in excellent field position with brilliant punt returns.

Morris Harvey, from West Virginia, put up a good fight before bowing 39-0. Eichenlaub stunned them with a 50-yard touchdown sprint in the first minute, but they played well for a long time after that. All the Notre Dame backs scored, but not in bunches.

Wabash was next; and they had pulverized a good DePauw team where Indiana and Purdue had not, so Fighting Irish fans were buzzing about the implications. It ended in a 41-6 Notre Dame win and indicated the end of mythical intrastate championships. Still, Wabash played well until the third quarter. Notre Dame's Freeman Fitzgerald broke it open when he grabbed a

The 1912 football team. First row: Harvat, Finegan, Gushurst; second row: Jones, Pliska, Rockne, Dorais (Capt.), Crowley, Lathrop, Feeney; top row: Fitzgerald, Yund, Banbar (manager), Cotter (manager), Coach Marks, Berger, Eichenlaub.

risky Wabash pass and scored. Eichenlaub scored twice to lead the Irish, and a long pass earned the final Irish touchdown.

If Notre Dame was to be a national force, it needed to beat Pitt on the road. They did, but only on Dorais's fourth-quarter field goal for a 3-0 final score. A similar Pitt kick just missed. Rockne helped the cause with a 33-yard pass play from Dorais.

St. Louis fell easily 47-7. (Ironically, St. Louis, under coach Eddie Cochems, had showcased the passing game for easy wins in 1906.) They couldn't stop Eichenlaub's runs and Berger executed a perfect stiff arm on a defensive back on his way to an 85-yard score. Pliska chipped in three touchdowns and Dorais hit five conversions and two field goals.

Tired of ties with Marquette, the Fighting Irish exploded for 69 unanswered points to end the season. Dorais set the tone early when he smashed his 145 pounds into, through, and over seven potential tacklers during an 80-yard touchdown run. Eichenlaub dragged four opponents for the better part of 70 yards before the mud slid him to a stop. But he scored four touchdowns for the day anyway.

The rout completed Notre Dame's first unblemished season since the one-game 1889 season and showed that the Fighting Irish could play good teams outside the Midwest and beat them.

Marks compiled an impressive two-year record of 13 wins and two ties as the Fighting Irish piled up 611

points to 36. The average score under Marks was almost 41 to 2. He can be credited with initiating the trademark Notre Dame blend of speed, quickness, and passing that would come to full fruition under Harper and Rockne.

1912 record: 7-0-0 (1.000)
Record to date: 113-31-13 (.761)

1913

Any Fighting Irish fan knows about this year—it is the stuff of legends. Jesse Harper, formerly the Wabash coach, was a son of the Midwest, from Pawpaw, Illinois. He played for Stagg at Chicago in 1902 and 1905, subbing at quarterback for Rockne's boyhood hero, Walter Eckersall. He also played for Stagg's baseball team. He first coached at Alma, losing only three football games in four years. His 1907 baseball team won the state championship, beating Michigan to do it. His best year at Wabash was 1910, when he was undefeated with four shutouts before a player died in the St. Louis game. He beat Purdue three times in four tries. Notre Dame wanted him for his obvious coaching skills but also for his keen business acumen since the Irish were launching themselves on the national scene with Penn State and Texas. Army was substituted for a cancelled opponent.

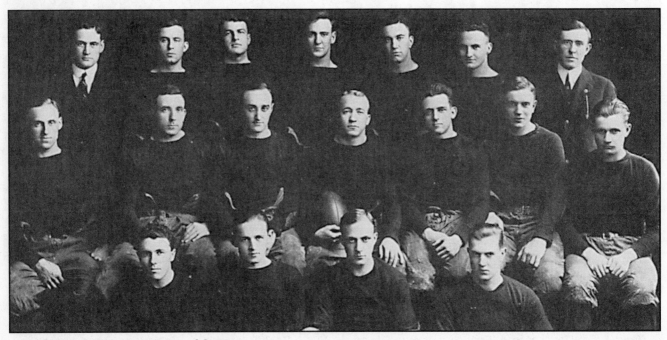

The 1913 team: conquerors of Army.

The completion of one of the startling "Dorais to Rockne" passes which beat the Army in 1913 and modified the entire game of football. Here's Knute making a touchdown.

Rockne loose in Army's secondary with a pass from Dorais in the epic 1913 game.

This was the beginning of the national scheduling that Rockne would insist on a decade later.

Ohio Northern came up short again, 87-0. Eichenlaub scored four touchdowns and Pliska three more. Rockne tore rib cartilage and was out early. Then a scrappy South Dakota team showed up, bold enough to score within the first minute. They played a tight, containing defense and were vulnerable to Dorais's passing, which made them spread out a little, which then made them easy prey for Eichenlaub's smashes—in other words, modern football. The later win over Army got all the credit for ushering in "modern football," but Notre Dame beat South Dakota 20-7 with an integrated passing and running attack that befuddled the defense. Eichenlaub responded to the South Dakota score, then Dorais hit two field goals before throwing a pass to Curly Nowers for a 40-yard touchdown to end the scoring.

Alma fell next, 62-0, on good, fundamental, patient drives, killing time as much as gaining ground. Rockne, who had missed the previous game, was back to make a nuisance of himself—good defense, solid blocking, an occasional run, and his patented pass receptions caught on a dead run. Al Feeney somehow intercepted three passes from the center (nose guard) position. Pliska scored three times; Eichenlaub twice, and Dorais returned a punt 65 yards to score.

On Thursday, October 30, the team left on a train for its first trip to the eastern seaboard, to West Point. The Cadets were spurned by other eastern teams because some of their players had already graduated elsewhere. While the Army was willing to play the Fighting Irish, they were not overwhelmed by the prospect. No top-notch sports writers were assigned to the game. One New York paper had Notre Dame coming from South Bend, Illinois.

But cadet Omar Bradley saw something strange the evening before the game—the Notre Dame players doing some sort of running with and juggling the football; it was hard to tell. He failed to report the intelligence, however, unless he mentioned it privately to injured Army punter Dwight Eisenhower. What he had seen was the Fighting Irish practicing their passing game.

Army went into the game undefeated, having beaten Stevens 34-0, Colgate 7-6, and Tufts 2-0. Myth has it that Army simply thought it had the game won by showing up, but respect was closer to what they felt; they still did not know a great deal about Notre Dame.

The first Fighting Irish score came on an 85-yard drive, keyed by passes from Dorais to Pliska for 30 yards, Dorais to Rockne for 35 yards, to Rockne for 10 yards, and capped by Pliska's five-yard touchdown run. Army scored twice in the second quarter using "straight" football tactics. Dorais fired a 25-yarder to

Rockne for a score. The last play of the first half found Dorais and his center on one side of the field with all the others on the opposite side. Dorais threw long to Rockne, but it was intercepted. Notre Dame led 14-13 at halftime. In the third quarter, Dorais missed a 45-yard field goal try, and the Cadets threatened with a drive to the Notre Dame two. Rockne got under the runner, flipped him to a stop, then assisted with a sack on the next play to set up a Dorais interception of an Army pass for a touchback. The Irish steamed back into a drive ended by an Eichenlaub touchdown burst. Army stalled. Then it was Pliska's turn—a 30-yard run to their five-yard line, and a pass from Dorais for the score. Thoroughly baffled, the Cadet defense surrendered an insurance touchdown to Eichenlaub to end the game: ND 35, Army 13. Midwest football had arrived in the east with a vengeance; the same day Michigan blasted Syracuse 43-7. And Colgate beat Yale 16-6 (remember, Army had already dumped Colgate). Dorais hit 14 of 17 throws for 243 yards and two touchdowns, one to Rockne and one to Pliska.

The Irish then faced a Penn State team that had not lost at home since 1894. Notre Dame pulled off another "upset" by a 14-7 margin. Penn State threatened first with a field goal after recovering a fumble, but it was blocked. Dorais set to work: a 40-yard strike to Pliska, a quarterback keeper for 35 yards, and a short touchdown pass to Rockne to conclude the three-play drive. Harper killed the third quarter using Eichenlaub for three-fourths of the ground game before his touchdown put the game out of reach.

The Irish headed towards Texas but stopped for a courtesy game with Christian Brothers in St. Louis. Harper used his substitutes. The field was wet; the Brothers took a 7-0 lead. Send in the regulars, Harper said, but they weren't in synch either. Finally, Eichenlaub scored; Dorais dashed 65 yards to score on a punt return and again on a 40-yard end run for a 20-7 win.

More rain awaited the Fighting Irish in Texas, but they won 30-7. Dorais called a beautiful game, directing the runners to 248 yards gained on 77 time-consuming carries, while booting three field goals. He connected on 10 of 21 passes for 200 yards (Texas hit two of six). The first score confused the Texans when Dorais faked a pass and ran 15 yards for a touchdown. Eichenlaub shrugged off some Texans from their two-yard line for a touchdown, and Rupe Mills intercepted a terrible Texas pass and dashed to the end zone.

Surely, this season surpassed Harper's fondest hopes. Eichenlaub and Dorais made All-America teams, and Rockne got Camp's attention as a third-team All-American.

1913 record: 7-0-0 (1.000)
Record to date: 120-31-13 (.771)

1914

The 1913 season was a hard act to follow. Notre Dame had not tasted defeat since 1910. The class that played with Rockne and Dorais had a marvelous career: 24 wins, one loss, and three ties (a .910 winning percentage.) The Fighting Irish had grown from a state and regional power to a position of modest national prominence. Notre Dame consciously tried to schedule eastern teams—Army, Syracuse, and Yale—for 1914.

The season started with the expected rout of Alma, 56-0. Harper kept out Eichenlaub and play straight football, using only two passes, one for a touchdown. Pliska racked up three touchdowns: 50 yards up the middle, another 50 around end, and a punt return for 65 yards. Kelleher snagged the touchdown pass and Cofall added two more.

More conservative football smashed Rose Poly 103-0. It was a blocking clinic; Irish ball carriers literally had nobody to run over, by, or around. The starters played briefly, and the second unit gave the Fighting Irish a second-half cushion of 75 points. Cofall scored four touchdowns, Kelleher three, and Bergman, Finegan, Duggan, and John Miller two each.

Harper worked the team hard the week of the Yale game; Tuesday's practice ran six hours. He took 23 players to New Haven, but the game did not live up to its advance notices. Too much may have been expected of the Fighting Irish, and Yale was splendidly prepared. The Elis used a new weapon—lateral passes—and Notre Dame had not expected that twist. They started well with five first-quarter first downs to none for Yale, but both teams muffed the ball too much. Then Yale opened up with a triple pass for a 13-yard gain. Yale's first score came on a backward pass and a circle route around Notre Dame's left end. Eichenlaub started to punish the Elis, but Notre Dame had not scored when the half ended, although they reached the Yale 3. The field was getting soggy; Yale scored on a 32-yard run with Fighting Irish tacklers slipping and missing. Harper

Stan Cofall, the first of a long series of All-American left halfbacks for the Fighting Irish.

opened up the passing game but Yale intercepted. In the fourth quarter, Bergman drove the Irish to the Yale two, but an illegal substitution killed the drive. Yale won 28-0. The Irish had 16 first downs to Yale's 15, completed six passes (Dorais was missed), and struck deep into Yale territory often enough to have kept the pressure on Yale. Eichenlaub had two 40-yard runs and Bergman was a one-man drive with 55 yards on two carries. The glum Irish returned to the campus to be met by their mates—classes had been cancelled to welcome them back, thus starting the tradition of cheering the team after a tough loss.

Feisty South Dakota was next, holding the Fighting Irish scoreless for the first half. The team finally pulled out of the doldrums, scoring 33 unanswered points. Cofall scored the first touchdown on a run and passed to Harry Baujan for another. Bergman scored twice and Pliska one.

A tough Haskell squad from Nebraska fought hard before losing 20-7. Their star halfback, Richards, carried 11 consecutive times for 75 yards on a desperate second half drive. Although they did not score, they earned a great measure of respect. Bergman used a double pass for Notre Dame's first touchdown, then he sped 85 and 80 yards with punts in the second half to end the scoring.

Although Notre Dame won, observers thought that the line play had slipped since the Alma game, and Army was up next.

Against Army, the Irish developed fumble-itis—on Army's first punt. Bergman booted it and Army recovered on the Notre Dame 15-yard line to lead to an easy touchdown. In the third quarter, Cofall and Pliska teamed on a drive that ended with Cofall's one-yard plunge for their only score. Army won 20-7 and was bidding for another score at the end when the Fighting Irish stopped them at the one.

Eichenlaub came back after missing a month of play, probably due to injury, against Carlisle, played in Chicago's Comiskey Park, and Notre Dame rolled 48-6. There were some stunning plays: Bergman sprinted 50 yards after a fumbled punt; Cofall punted for 90 yards; a triple pass set up a 30-yard touchdown run by Bunny Larkin. Pliska scored twice on long hauls.

The Fighting Irish downed the Syracuse Orangemen 20-0. Syracuse had beaten Michigan; it was a huge team by 1914 standards—210 pounds across the line—but they wilted rapidly under Eichenlaub's insistent hammering. Cofall, Bergman, and Finegan were the scorers.

The year's two losses in the east rankled but they weren't blowouts. Perhaps too much was expected too soon.

1914 record: 6-2-0 (.750)
Record to date: 126-33-13 (.770)

1915

Harper had a good core to work with for the new campaign. The line would be the largest since Dimmick and Philbrook were there. Younger brothers Bergman and Miller (Arthur and Walter) arrived. Bergman took over the important left halfback position (which would be the key position for the Irish offense for the next quarter century). Cartier Field, in use until about 1930, was improved by adding practice fields for the frosh and varsity, saving the main field from overuse.

Alma was the opener and made their best showing in South Bend in a 32-0 loss. The halftime score was a surprising 13-0 and the third quarter yielded only one Fighting Irish touchdown on a tough drive. Harper sent in his reserves in the fourth quarter; they scored two quick touchdowns.

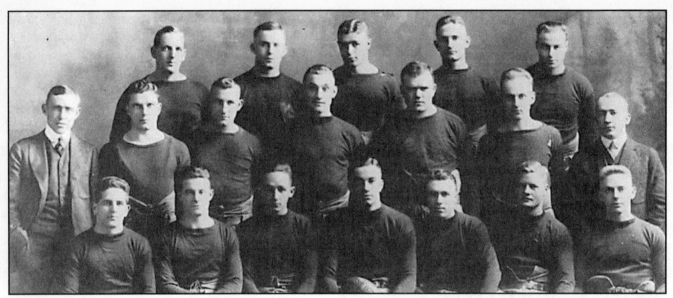

The 1915 Notre Dame monogram winners.

Everyone remembered Haskell from the year before. Harper moved Jim Phelan to starting quarterback and Rockne worked the line hard after a mediocre showing against Alma. On the first drive, Phelan ran the kickoff to the 40, Cofall zipped around right end for 20, Bergman went left for 10, Bachman punched through the middle for 10, and then Cofall turned right end for the score. Haskell soon had to punt, and Bachman sped 60 yards with the kick for another quick touchdown, breaking six tackles. Cofall added another touchdown later and Bergman roared for a 50-yard touchdown on a punt. Reserves held on for a 34-0 shutout.

The Irish went to Nebraska to meet the powerful Cornhuskers, undefeated for three seasons. Notre Dame lost 20-19 in a great game with a big Nebraska team using a modest passing game (five completions in eight attempts) as an instrumental part of three touchdown drives. Notre Dame had several good drives finished off by penalties. Baujan scored what would have been the winning touchdown after chasing a loose ball on a punt, but one official "did not see" the play, and another claimed the whistle stopped the play when the receiver touched the ball. A missed conversion after Notre Dame's first score also hurt badly. Cofall scored the first two touchdowns and Bergman the third, but that conversion was missed as well.

The loss lingered as a factor in the next game, a 6-0 Fighting Irish win over perennially tough South Dakota. The Coyotes played dead even with Notre Dame in the first half. In the second half, Bergman scored the only touchdown on a criss-cross play.

Army was next and they were not having a good year. Notre Dame barely sneaked out of town with a Hudson River cliffhanger, 7-0. The score came on a 50-yard pass from Cofall to Bergman in the final moments. Army almost scored with a field goal try, but it hit the crossbar and fell back on the field. The Irish missed three field goals and had just two completed passes in seven attempts for 73 yards and the touchdown. The running game was strong with 261 yards to Army's 75.

Red Miller was now coaching at Creighton, but his team was no match for Notre Dame, losing 41-0. Cofall scored twice, once with a lateral pass from Bachman. Phelan also scored twice, and Bergman and Bachman each scored. Notre Dame racked up 25 first downs to eight, and nine backs tromped 468 yards to 174 for Creighton.

After seeing the Illinois-Chicago game on their off day, the Irish went to Texas for two games. The Longhorns lost four fumbles on the way to a 36-7 loss. Their lone score came when someone fell on a loose ball in the end zone. Bergman took scoring honors for Notre Dame with two touchdowns, one from 75 yards out. Cofall, Bachman, and Malone each scored. The Fighting Irish hammered the middle of the line on 14 plunges for 147 yards. But the real story was in 42 trips around the ends for 315 yards.

Two days later, Notre Dame dismantled the Rice Owls 55-2. The deluge came in the second half after Rice played respectably for a 14-2 halftime disadvantage. But in the second half, Cofall returned a kickoff 90 yards for a touchdown; on the next series he capped it with a 30-yard scoring jaunt. Bergman scored on his favorite play, a double pass from 20 yards out. Cofall got his third score of the quarter scooting around end for seven yards. Bachman and Keefe also scored, the latter when he started a Fighting Irish drive with a recovered fumble and finished when he recovered a fumble for a touchdown.

Only two missed conversions and a disputed touchdown kept Notre Dame from enjoying its third undefeated season in four years. Nebraska joined Army as a major rival.

1915 record: 7-1-0 (.875)
Record to date: 133-34-13 (.775)

1916

A Notre Dame baseball player, Dolly Gray, enters the picture now. During the summer of 1916 in upstate Michigan, he gave a good sales talk about the university to a friend by the name of George Gipp from Laurium. Gipp borrowed the money for the train ride to South Bend, but he seemed to be having some trouble coming to terms with his new environment. He would start up something and quit—interhall football, basketball, baseball (Notre Dame had a full team for each of its dorms). He was 20 years old but still liked to play games, perhaps to break up the monotony of the classes he had never excelled in as a teenager. He'd grab an acquaintance (few were close enough to be his friend) and go out to one of the open spaces to kick the ball around.

Like 1913, this is the stuff of legends. As the story goes, Rockne was on his way to practice when he saw a guy drop kick a ball for 70 or 80 yards at a time. Rockne introduced himself, and a diffident Gipp was not impressed. Yet Gipp took up Rockne's challenge and played a little ball for Notre Dame. In so doing, Gipp's short life, little more than a thousand days under the Dome, would enter American culture and sports immortality. In his freshman year, he would stun his coaches and fellow players. In a freshman game against Western Normal (now Western Michigan), on his own 45 and with instructions to punt, he drop-kicked a 62-yard field goal instead. This was typical of the man—a player who loved the challenges found on the gridiron, willing to take almost any legal route to victory, but who was also utterly uncaring about the whole deal. More about Gipp later.

Harper had a team with several legitimate All-American candidates. Even his substitutes were talented and would fill starting positions soon. In Gipp's class was another older fellow, Chet Grant, a speedster at quarterback who would be involved with Notre Dame for nearly three quarters of a century. The schedule was not very demanding, especially since Western Conference teams (now Big 10) were not scheduling games with the Irish. Not one of them had met Notre Dame since 1909—the year Yost's Michigan team lost.

Case Tech was pummeled 48-0. Grant, nervous in his first game, made the mistake of fielding a punt on his five-yard line and then having to look for help—a zig here, a zig there—find some blockers, up this sideline, one guy to beat (Baujan got him), and a 95-yard touchdown for the record books. Western Reserve met an identical fate, 48-0. But these blowouts were costly in terms of injuries: Miller, Grover Malone, Bergman, and Cofall.

Haskell was next. The Native Americans playing for their college fought brilliantly, but sheer talent overwhelmed them 26-0. Then, Wabash, who a few seasons earlier had been in the picture with the bigger schools of the state, was obliterated by Notre Dame. Rockne's pregame pep talk, as it was recalled, urged the team to "go out there and kill 'em, crucify 'em." Fortunately for Wabash, they stopped short of that, 60-0. Nine touchdowns came on end runs and tackle smashes. Cofall got a touchdown from his 40-yard line on the first play. Harper pulled his starters in the second quarter but put them back in when it looked like Wabash would hold on for a 39-0 loss. At the half, three former Irish greats (Dorais, Art Bergman, and Pliska) toured the field in a car driven by the senior class president, Royal Bosshard. Three more touchdowns ended the affair. The ref for the game was Guernsey Van Riper, who would later write *Knute Rockne; Young Athlete*.

Notre Dame now faced Army. The Cadets featured Elmer Oliphant, the former Purdue star, who was big, fast, daring, and a fine passer. The Irish played well in the first half, down only 6-3, but then the sky fell. Oliphant passed for three touchdowns and kicked two field goals for a 30-10 triumph. Bergman got Notre Dame's lone touchdown. Reporters thought the Fighting Irish the better team in all phases, except passing.

Notre Dame blanked South Dakota 21-0. Then they went to East Lansing to meet Michigan Agricultural College, who had not been on their schedule for six years. The Fighting Irish won 14-0, with Cofall scoring twice to avenge the 1910 loss. (MAC was not in the Western

Conference then.) Alma lost 46-0; the Fighting Irish were tuning up for the grudge match with Nebraska.

In Lincoln, Notre Dame got the 20 points it so badly wanted in 1915, and left the Huskers scoreless. Bergman got the first score on a 55-yard run that saw him break into the secondary with no less than four blockers still with him. In the second quarter, Baujan emerged from a pileup on a busted punt to score from the 22. John Miller wrapped it up with a 55-yard touchdown strike to Bergman. The Fighting Irish defense broke up nine of Nebraska's 10 passes, the other fell incomplete. Notre Dame garnered 11 first downs to Nebraska's four. The Huskers ran for 89 yards to Notre Dame's 324. The Fighting Irish held the Huskers to only seven yards running in the second quarter, and to only six in the fourth. This was the eighth Irish shutout in nine games this year.

Cofall, Bachman, and Slip Madigan, a reserve, made All-American honors. Arnold McInerney and Frank Rydzewski achieved All-Western accolades. And the best player on the team had never even played for the varsity. He would, though, in 1917…George Gipp.

1916 record: 8-1-0 (.888)
Record to date: 141-35-13 (.780)

1917

This would be Harper's last season at Notre Dame. The war was beginning to make inroads into the team's personnel and Harper would be hard pressed to match the stunning 1916 results. Talented sophomores would have some impact: the gangly, indifferent Gipp and Pete Bahan would replace departed starters in the backfield. Dave Philbin filled the spot vacated by Arnold McInerney, who had joined the Army (and would later be killed in France). A brace of smallish guards, Madigan and Clyde Zoia, averaging 159 pounds, showed Rockne's emerging influence on line play.

Kalamazoo was first on the Notre Dame schedule, losing 55-0, Notre Dame's fifth straight shutout. Bahan ran 75 yards for a touchdown on the season's first play from scrimmage. When the dust settled, Phelan and Bahan led the rout with three touchdowns each.

After defeating Kalamazoo, the Irish traveled to Wisconsin. (The Irish were now both wanted and unwanted by the Western Conference—wanted as opponents, unwanted as a member due to philosophical

differences, i.e., Notre Dame was not academically oriented, too interested in sports.) The game ended in a 0-0 tie, the sixth straight shutout for Notre Dame. The Badgers missed four field goals. Phelan's try hit the left upright and fell the wrong way. It was a tight game.

Then a rematch with Nebraska, who enjoyed a 15-pound advantage per man on the line, and had eight returning starters to Notre Dame's two. They won 7-0 although the Irish almost scored on a drive to their 10-yard line. Quarterback Phelan played the whole game knowing he belonged to the Army one hour after the game, yet observers said it was his best game ever directing the attack, and he played demonic defense. Gipp made his first appearance for the Fighting Irish, carrying 15 times for 31 yards but returning five punts for 69 yards.

Harper rested his starting interior linemen in a 40-0 blitz of South Dakota. Gipp flew 40 yards on the first play to set up the first score, then Walter Miller dashed 40 for the tally. Tom Spalding received a double pass—quarterback Tex Allison to Gipp to Spalding—for a touchdown. Three more touchdowns ended the show. Gipp's second game for Notre Dame was his first over the 100-yard mark—24 carries for 110 yards.

Notre Dame and Army had split four games previously; this one would be for bragging rights. Army practiced diligently to stop the expected aerial game. Harper gave them off-tackle plays instead, mixed with short passes to keep them off balance. Joe Brandy scored the game's only touchdown on a seven-yard run to end a drive he had started on his 23 with an interception. Gipp set up his score with a 13-yard run from the 20. Army was held to eight first downs, five in a furious fourth quarter. Brandy and Philbin recovered late fumbles to save the win. The 11 Irish starters never saw a substitute the entire game. Gipp punted 11 times, a sign of the game's defensive intensity.

Gipp broke his left leg against Morningside the next week after a 35-yard gain; a tired, crippled Notre Dame squad escaped with a 13-0 win. Rydzewski speared an interception and ran 40 yards for a touchdown to go with one earned later via passing. But the Fighting Irish were hurting.

Against Michigan Agricultural College, Notre Dame suffered more injuries—right guard Basil Stanley broke a leg and quarterback Allison strained his back. Irish numbers were thinning quickly. When Allison went down, the passing game stopped too. Clipper Smith moved from right half to fullback and scored a touchdown on a 10-yard bolt up the middle; Bahan and Barry both scored 50-yard touchdowns to lead Notre Dame to a 23-0 win. Rydzewski, upon returning to South Bend, received a silver loving cup from proud Polish fathers.

An exhausted squad went east to play Washington and Jefferson. Brandy's 45-yard field goal ended the scoring for a 3-0 win.

Massive injuries and military call ups made this season a difficult one to coach. But Harper got his men to produce four more shutouts (17 in his last 25 games). They were only a handful of points from another undefeated season.

1917 record: 6-1-1 (.8125)
Record to date: 147-36-14 (.781)

1918

The death of a relative forced Harper to take over a family ranch near Sitka, Kansas. He made sure that his choice for the vacated position would get the job—Knute Rockne. He had taken a team poised for success beyond its wildest dreams and he left it in extremely capable hands.

Harper's fate was inextricably bound up with Rockne's, both as the man he coached to modest stardom in his senior year, as his coaching mentor for four years, and as the man who would be asked to fill the athletic director's job following Rockne's death on March 31, 1931. It was perhaps fitting that his 30,000-acre ranch was less than 100 miles from the isolated hilltop near Bazaar, Kansas, where Rockne died in an airplane crash. Of Fighting Irish coaches with more than five seasons on the job, Harper's .863 winning percentage places him second only to Rockne, ahead of Leahy's .855 and Parseghian's .836. In 40 games, he won 34, and shutout the opponents 25 times.

Knute Rockne—there is no greater name in Fighting Irish football. The man's background is as unbelievable as his coaching record was impressive; a Norwegian immigrant...grew up in a tough Chicago neighborhood...learned his new culture mostly through street and sandlot games...never graduated from high school because he was caught skipping school to practice track...worked for the U.S. Post Office for five years to save money for college...passed an entrance exam for Notre Dame and threw himself into the strange life of an over-age undergraduate...sports (football, track)...campus theatre, music...life of a hustler (pool, boxing) to make ends meet...brilliant student in chemistry and pharmacology...All-American football player...learned lots about good and bad coaching...*magna cum laude* graduate 1914...matriculated in medical school in St. Louis in 1914 but they would not let him work to cover expenses...returned to Notre Dame, now married, and a flip of the coin sent Dorais to Iowa and kept Rockne under the Dome...taught chemistry, coached football and track...learned how to temper himself under the calming influence of Harper. Horatio Alger could not have created a more interesting fictional life. He loved Notre Dame. He never left the place...to this day.

The Fighting Irish of 1918 had almost nothing to fight with or against. The war had taken scores of the best athletes. The schedule was curtailed to six games. But there were some impressive players on hand: Gipp, freshman guard Heartley "Hunk" Anderson (Grantland Rice later called him "the toughest man, pound for pound, I have ever known"); Clipper Smith, Eddie Anderson, Bahan, Lambeau from Green Bay, and Norm Barry.

The Fighting Irish opened away from home for the first time in 20 years, at Case Tech. Notre Dame was down 6-0 in the early going so Rockne sent in Bahan and Gipp to spark matters. They did and Curly Lambeau scored the first touchdown of the Rockne era at Notre Dame. Rockne probably gave them an earful at the half, because in the second half, Gipp shifted into high gear to score two touchdowns, gained 88 yards on the ground, and hit five of 12 passes for another 101 yards for a 26-6 win.

October went by without a game. Rock tried to schedule a game with Municipal Pier, but it had to be cancelled by medical authorities because of the influenza epidemic that was killing tens of thousands of people across the country. Practices were cancelled. Then a game with Camp Custer was cancelled. Rockne scrimmaged the varsity against the freshmen, loaning the freshman team Gipp, Bahan, and himself, and they tied it 7-7 with a Gipp fumble.

The Fighting Irish mangled Wabash 67-7. It was a spur of the moment game; no one knew until Friday night that there would be a Saturday game. The team left at 4:00 a.m. Saturday. Bahan, Lambeau, and Gipp each scored two touchdowns and the subs did the rest. Gipp racked up his second game with century-mark running, 119 yards on 16 rushes. With government permission, the team stayed overnight in Crawfordsville.

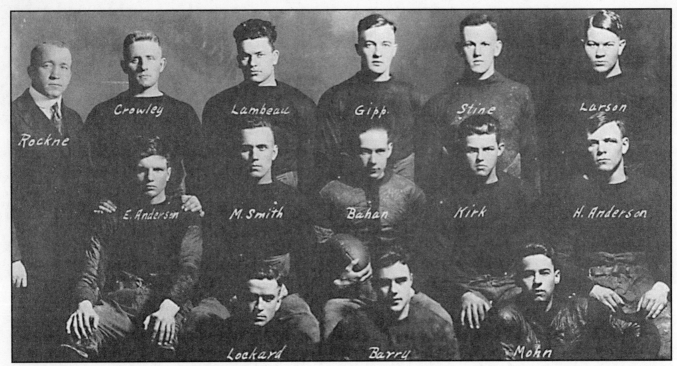

The 1918 Notre Dame war-depleted team.

Refamiliarized with winning, they faced a formidable Great Lakes Naval squad loaded with good players—Paddy O'Driscoll, George Halas, and Notre Dame's erstwhile Bachman. The papers made it out to be a hopeless case for the college boys, but Rockne willed a 7-7 tie. The touchdown was scored by Bill Mohn after some great running by the other backs. Gipp missed a 40-yard field goal, carried 15 times for 69 yards, hit two of seven passes, and punted eight times.

A truly sloppy field and injuries to Bahan and Gipp took away whatever advantages Notre Dame might have had over Michigan Agricultural College; the Aggies won 13-7. This was followed by another road trip (only one home game all year) to Purdue. The Irish were banged up, tired, sick, and coming off an upset defeat. The broken blood vessel from the MAC game in Gipp's face had healed enough for him to play; he led the Irish with 137 yards on 19 carries good for two touchdowns, and he kicked a point after with his bad leg. He sped up a drive at the end with two runs covering 37 yards for his first score, then later passed for 22 yards twice, the second for a score to Bernie Kirk, and capped his day with racking up almost all of the yardage from the Notre Dame 20 for a score. Mohn returned a 73-yard punt return for a touchdown. Gipp led the way though, and he played the game hurt.

The season was wrapped up at Nebraska also on a sloppy field. Notre Dame garnered 12 first downs to 0. Nebraska also scored no points. Unfortunately, neither did the Irish. The Fighting Irish had a score disallowed by a referee who claimed Lambeau helped Barry with his belt, then a whistle stopped a pass play at the Husker 8. Gipp played heroically with 15 carries for 76 yards, four completions in nine throws for 65 yards, a kick off return of 40 yards, and 12 punts.

Rockne's first season was not overtly the stuff of legends, but it was an incredible coaching job in the face of nearly insurmountable problems—the war, the flu epidemic, injuries, horrible weather, and all-star teams.

1918 record: 3-1-2 (.571)
Record to date: 150-37-16 (.778)

1919

After the trials of 1918, Rockne must have been pleased to see the return of his war vets: Walter Miller, Dutch Bergman, Grover Malone, Slip Madigan, Frank Coughlin, and Cy DeGree. Their return duplicated what the great postwar Leahy teams enjoyed—a sudden infusion of mature talent from previous squads. The end result would be two consecutive undefeated teams. In essence, Rockne had the heart of the great 1916 team again. Add them to the 1918 starters—Gipp, Hunk Anderson, Eddie Anderson, and Pete Bahan—and there was the making of an awesome football team that would lose only one game in the next 28.

Half of the 1919 schedule was composed of major or emerging powers (Nebraska, Army, Purdue, Indiana, and Michigan Agricultural College) and the rest were pretty good teams. Kalamazoo fell first, 14-0. Gipp lost touchdown runs of 80 and 68 yards because of tight calls by the referees. (After his second futile run, he told the referees to give him two whistles as a sign to keep running, one whistle to stop.) He still managed to rush for 148 yards. Bergman scored on a 55-yarder.

The defending champs of Ohio, Mt. Union, played the Irish to a 7-7 first-quarter tie. Then Gipp ran for two touchdowns on identical runs of 30 yards, threw two passes for 49 yards, added another 63 yards in incidental rushing, and raced 56 yards on two kickoff returns. All ambulatory backs scored: Bergman, Fritz Slackford, Phelan, Malone, John Mohardt, Cy Kasper, and Earl Walsh, as Notre Dame won 60-7.

Nebraska knew all about Gipp's running, and prepared for it, but they had not counted on his other talents. Bergman had the play of the day in the first Fighting Irish series with a 90-yard touchdown run on a lateral pass. Guess who tossed the lateral? Gipp also completed five of eight passes, good for 124 yards, all on a wet field. The Huskers tied it, so Gipp took charge with his passing in the third quarter: he hit Bergman with a 33-yard gain, then Kirk for 20 more to the 16-yard line, then he ran for five, passed to Kirk for 10 more, but the drive stopped there. Nebraska punted out of trouble, and Gipp started again. He passed to Bergman who ran 45 yards, Miller ran for four on a criss-cross, and Gipp passed for five yards to Bergman to set up Bahan's one-yard dive for the winning touchdown. Near the end of the game, a Husker dropkicked a field goal for a 14-9 Irish win.

The Irish then beat Western Normal, recent winners over Michigan Agricultural College, 53-0. Malone scored first and Gipp twice in the first quarter, then Brandy and Barry shook loose in the second quarter.

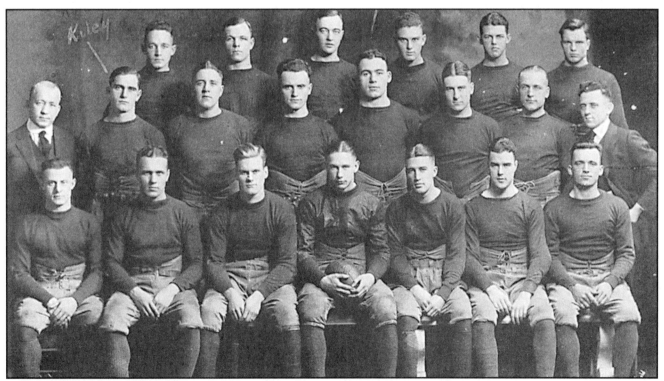

The undefeated 1919 team.

It was all subs after that, although Rockne put the starters in for a while and Bergman went long distance for the final touchdown.

Indiana and Notre Dame met in Indianapolis in rain and mud. Rockne wanted to save the starters for Army, so most of them didn't play. Gipp played some—82 yards on 18 carries, 57 yards on three of seven passes, and a drop-kicked field goal. Bergman scored the touchdowns for a 16-3 win, but he hurt his knee and didn't go east to Army.

Gipp had to pick up the slack; he rushed for 70 yards and hit seven passes for 115 yards as Notre Dame beat Army 12-9. The Fighting Irish stopped Army several times inside their 5.

Michigan Agricultural College was next—physically a much bigger team—and they even brought a 50-piece marching band with them. The Fighting Irish sent them home with a 13-0 loss, but it was probably too close to Rock's liking. Gipp passed well, ran at will around their ends, and had two interceptions; but Rockne had to come up with a tackle eligible play for Notre Dame's clinching score.

The following week, the Fighting Irish played even with Purdue, in that they beat Purdue by the 20-point margin of 1918, this time 33-13. Purdue scored first, but it was all Notre Dame after that. Gipp completed 11 of 15 passes for 217 yards and two touchdowns to go with those scored on interceptions by Anderson and Trafton.

Gipp had been hurt in the 1918 Morningside game and it looked bad when they trapped him on the Notre Dame 11 on a busted punt play. Morningside scored, and with Miller and Bahan out it appeared gloomy. Gipp took over in the second quarter, orchestrating a long drive that he capped with a three-yard touchdown burst. In the third quarter, a bad punt gave Notre Dame the ball at Morningside's 10. Gipp probed left end for a yard, then went back for the rest on the next play. Later he added a 25-yard run and iced the game with an interception. With the win, Notre Dame commanded the west and only Harvard, at 9-0-1, made noises about the national crown being theirs.

1919 record: 9-0-0 (1.000)
Record to date: 159-37-16 (.787)

1920-1929

1920

The 1919 effort showed what a Rockne team could do with a full complement of players; many of those stars returned in 1920. The schedule had a mix of easy marks with traditional tough challenges. Kalamazoo opened and hoped to give the Fighting Irish a second rough go, but Notre Dame was ready. Chet Wynne earned the first score, then Gipp got in the saddle on the third possession, scampering for 30 to set up two short runs for a touchdown. In the third quarter he rambled for 30 again, then hit Kiley with a 28-yard pass to set up Norm Barry's touchdown. Paul Castner intercepted a pass to set up a Joe Brandy for a touchdown. Reserve Cy Kasper grabbed a fumble and ran 35 yards to set up his own touchdown a little later. The other reserves punched over another score for the 39-0 win. It was Gipp's best game as a runner—183 yards on 16 carries.

Another Michigan team, Western Normal, met a similar fate, 42-0, even though three touchdowns were called back. Gipp mangled their defense for 123 yards, two touchdowns, and three point-after kicks. Mohardt rambled for two touchdowns; Phelan had the best touchdown run, a 55-yarder; Castner powered in from 35 yards out; and Brandy returned a punt for a touchdown.

Chet Wynne, two-time starter at fullback in 1920 and 1921.

The Fighting Irish moved west for the game with Nebraska. Husker coach Schulte had rested his starters in the Colorado game the week before, barely winning 7-0. At first, the game was a punting duel, until Notre

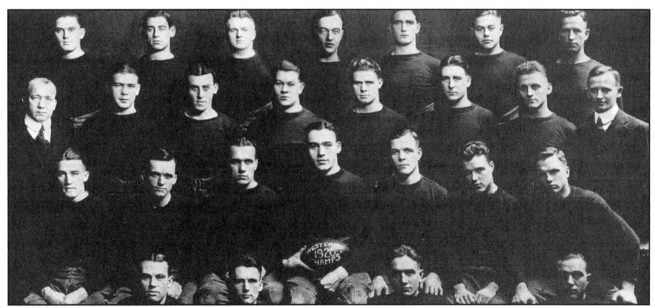

The undefeated 1920 national champs.

Dame put together a drive to the Husker two, where it stalled. Following common practice for those days, the Huskers immediately went into a punt formation to kick out of trouble. Buck Shaw blocked the kick out of the end zone for a safety. In the next quarter, two more Fighting Irish drives fizzled. Gipp took command after that, hitting Eddie Anderson with two passes for 60 yards to set up Brandy's one-yard plunge for the touchdown. Late in the game, Gipp hit Anderson again with a 28-yard pass to set up his own seven-yard touchdown run. Notre Dame won 16-7, but statistically the Huskers dominated: 13 first downs to 6; 550 total yards to 174; 425 yards rushing to 135; 10 of 28 passes good for 125 yards to four of 18 for 39 yards. Gipp owned 218 yards of Notre Dame's total offense for the day.

Against instate foe Valparaiso, Rockne unveiled another pet project: starting the second unit as "shock troops." This let his starters build motivation while assessing the other team's strengths and weaknesses. Rockne liked the inherent suspense. His only requirement was that the subs have a good punter to keep them out of the hole. He'd send in his starters after the first quarter to save the day. Valparaiso took advantage of the move and drove for a field goal and the lead. Castner took his cue and started booming towering punts to avoid trouble. The subs tired and Rockne sent in the cavalry. Gipp hit Kiley with a 38-yard pass but his next one was intercepted. In the third quarter, a quick drive ended with a Wynne touchdown, and Gipp scored shortly thereafter. Rock tried a tackle eligible play on which Gipp

hit Coughlin for 32 yards, but the drive failed. Mohardt and Gipp led a two-play drive, with Gipp going in from 25 yards out. Mohardt ended the scoring with a crashing run from the five-yard line for the 28-3 final score.

Army waited, undefeated. It would be Gipp's finest hour, even though trained observers might have noticed the early stages of the debilitating illnesses that would claim his life in a matter of weeks. (He'd ignored his physician's advice that summer to have his infected tonsils removed; he just wanted to play ball.)

Army recovered an early fumble by Wynne to register the first touchdown, but their two first downs on the drive would be half their total for the game. Notre Dame drove to midfield but a penalty threatened their momentum. Gipp fired a pass to Kiley, Gipp slanted off tackle, and then he swept end, and Mohardt tied the game. Army punted and the Fighting Irish struck with a 35-yard touchdown pass to Kiley. But Army ran back a Gipp punt 60 yards for a touchdown and used a bad kick for an easy field goal to lead at halftime 17-14. Notre Dame's center, Ojay Larson, had been playing with a dislocated hip and had to leave the game. In the second half Rockne tried everything, but they still could not buy another score. Finally, in the fourth quarter, Gipp set up a Mohardt touchdown; then he dashed for 50 yards and threw short passes to set up Wynne's 20-yard sideline sprint for a touchdown and a final score of 27-17. Gipp rushed for 150 yards, returned kicks for 207 yards, and passed for 123 more, for a total of 480 yards. Cadets who saw him in the showers after the game

Action from the 1920 game against Nebraska. Quarterback Brandy has just spun and pitched the ball to Gipp; Castner is getting ready to block in front of Gipp.

Cover of the program and menu for the dinner honoring the 1920 team.

recalled later that he looked a bit emaciated.

On November 6, Notre Dame enjoyed its first Homecoming against Purdue. Red Salmon was there as an honored guest and he saw Notre Dame win 28-0. Shock troops (the subs used to start a game until Rock sent in his starters) started and scored when Grant ran 50 yards with a pass. Rock tried to rest a tired Gipp and let him play only briefly, but that was all he needed: he careened through Purdue's team for a 35-yard touchdown, fired passes good for 128 yards to Anderson and Kiley, rushed for 129 yards, and kicked three conversions. Buck Shaw recovered a Barry fumble for a touchdown; and Mohardt stopped a drive late with an interception to preserve the 28-0 shutout. With this win, the Fighting Irish had defeated all intrastate rivals since 1906.

With Notre Dame behind 10-0, the Indiana Hoosiers almost broke that streak. Gipp piled into the Hoosier line for the first Notre Dame score—even though he had a separated shoulder. Later, the Hoosiers stacked their defense at the end of an Irish drive to stop Gipp, only to see Joe Brandy run in the winning

touchdown in a 13-10 nail-biter. The wear and tear was showing; Hunk Anderson played the whole game with cracked ribs.

Notre Dame traveled to Chicago for a game with Northwestern, billed by alumni as "George Gipp Day." The day was bitterly cold and Rockne did not want to play his sick star, but the fans chanted for their man. As it turned out, all Notre Dame scoring resulted from the passing game, perhaps a first. Coughlin recovered a fumble deep in Northwestern territory to set up a five-yard touchdown pass from Brandy to Eddie Anderson. Mohardt, in for Gipp, grabbed a Wildcat pass to set up a Barry touchdown. Danny Coughlin grabbed a fumble, and later intercepted a pass which set up a pass from Mohardt to Anderson for the third score. The crowd got its hero in the fourth quarter. In two plays, he threw a long pass to Kiley for a touchdown, and another to Barry for a 25-yard touchdown. In addition to completing five of six passes for 157 yards, Gipp also tried to run back a punt, but his strength was failing him. The papers noted that the respectful Wildcat tacklers brought him down as gently as possible. With that poignant moment, Gipp had played his last game. The Irish won 33-7 before 20,000 people. George Gipp stayed in a frigid Chicago an extra day to help an old friend with a punting clinic.

In mid-week, at the team banquet, Gipp left early and checked into a South Bend hospital, where he died three weeks later. There was much mourning following Gipp's passing, including a lights-out memorial on the campus. The team later went on to East Lansing for the finale with Michigan Agricultural College. The subs got things rolling as the Fighting Irish won easily 25-0. Danny Coughlin flashed 95 yards with the opening kickoff to score and served notice that Notre Dame meant to finish undefeated. In the third quarter, Paul Castner racked up two touchdowns. And Anderson strolled 25 yards to pay dirt with a blocked punt.

The win assured Notre Dame of its first undisputed national championship, its first consensus All-America player in Gipp, and the nation its first truly great college football immortal when Gipp died December 14 at the age of 25. Kiley also earned All-America accolades. Rockne, at 32, was on the verge of becoming a national phenomenon.

1920 record: 9-0-0 (1.000)
Record to date: 168-37-16 (.796)

1921

Rockne enjoyed another strong year. His seniors had suffered only one loss in their careers. This was the first attempt at what came to be known as a "suicide schedule"—two easy games followed by nine strong challenges.

Kalamazoo capitulated 56-0. Chet Wynne won the game on the opening kick with an 80-yard touchdown run. Frank Thomas scored two touchdowns, Wynne another one on a dive play, Mohardt ran for touchdowns on plays covering 39 and 40 yards, Frank Desch—the fastest man for the Irish—tallied a 15-yard touchdown run, and fifth-string quarterback Frank Reese scored twice but one was negated by a penalty. Kalamazoo completed its first pass in the third quarter—for a loss. Fighting Irish defenders caught more of their passes than they did.

DePauw was obliterated 57-10 to complete the tune-up portion of the year. Wynne and Mohardt shared four touchdowns and solos went in the books for Desch, Thomas, Kiley, and Frank Seyfrit.

But Iowa beat them in the next game, 10-7. Statistics are for losers, it's said, and this case appears to prove it: 456 total yards for Notre Dame to Iowa's 216; 239 yards on the ground against 206 for Iowa; 227 yards passing to Iowa's 10; and 22 first downs to Iowa's 14. Fighting Irish penalties aided Iowa's touchdown scoring drive in the first quarter and they ended their scoring with a field goal on their second drive. Notre Dame never caught up, though Mohardt hit Kiley for

a 50-yard touchdown in the second quarter. Castner was a force, blasting a punt 70 yards and just missing a 50-yard field goal.

The Fighting Irish were not accustomed to coming off a loss. As in 1918, they faced Purdue after a loss, winning this time, 33-0. Notre Dame was invincible in the first half—scoring 30 points and holding Purdue to no first downs. Hunk Anderson scored two touchdowns within three minutes, incredible for a guard in modern football. Anderson's feat came when Eddie Anderson blocked a punt his way, and moments later when Castner's punt was mishandled just as Hunk arrived in the vicinity, and took it 25 yards for the score. Mohardt garnered two more on short runs. Castner hit a late field goal as Rockne used the second half to improve the kicking game, and Seyfrit saved the shutout with his nose while blocking a Purdue field goal try.

Nebraska wanted this game; they had not beaten Notre Dame since 1917. They were frustrated again, 7-0. A poor Husker kick gave the Irish good field position, and Mohardt took it in. In the fourth quarter, Nebraska used an impressive air attack, but the Fighting Irish backs played great defense.

Indiana went down 28-7. After the subs mixed it up early, Rockne sent in the starters and Coughlin quickly scored from the three-yard line. An Irish fumble led to a short drive for the Hoosiers and their only score. Mohardt clicked on a series of medium-length passes and Wynne scored. Coughlin tallied his second touchdown on a 10-yard end run in the fourth quarter. Castner grabbed a Mohardt pass for an 11-yard touchdown. Castner stopped an aroused Hoosier team in the final

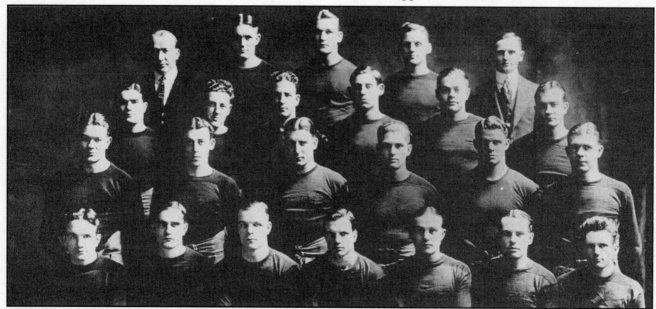

The 1921 team—only a field goal away from being Rock's third consecutive undefeated team.

Eddie Anderson, three-year starter at RE from 1919-1921, on two national championship squads, All-American in 1921.

moments with three interceptions. Such defense had allowed the last three opponents a total of 10 first downs.

Rockne scheduled four games in 14 days, starting with Army. The Fighting Irish passing game was too much for the Cadets in a 28-0 rout. Mohardt fired to Kiley who ran it in from 47 yards out. Then Mohardt threw a 40-yarder to Wynne. The Cadets backed off a bit to accommodate Notre Dame's speed. So Mohardt threw under them and Kiley scored again. In the last quarter, Mohardt used his own 45-yard kick return to start a drive he finished with a 15-yard sprint to the end zone. The Cadets lost an interception to Castner, and the Andersons grabbed fumbles. Notre Dame had 16 first downs to two for Army. So went Saturday, November 5.

Tuesday it was Rutgers. Castner appeared well rested since he took the opening handoff and sped 55 yards for a touchdown. Rutgers punted; Notre Dame probed twice, then Wynne struck for a 35-yard score. Castner drop kicked two field goals to end the first half. Mohardt passed to Kiley for an eight-yard score in the third quarter and Castner added a touchdown from the Rutgers' one-yard line. Frank Thomas swiped a pass and Desch slipped around end for a six-yard touchdown. The final score was 48-0. Notre Dame scored 76 points in two games played within three days.

On Saturday, November 12, Notre Dame obliterated Haskell 42-7. Castner ran for three scores, one from 50 yards out. Earl Walsh, third-string left halfback, added two more, and Desch one. The starters played a total of four minutes. Rockne didn't bother to attend the game; he scouted Marquette.

Marquette did not fold easily. They scored first after they stuffed a Castner punt. Mohardt scored a 48-yard touchdown on the next possession, with Wynne blocking. Then he fired a pass to Eddie Anderson for a 45-yard score and the lead. His 35-yard jaunt later in the game set up Wynne's closing score for a 21-7 victory.

Thursday, November 24, Notre Dame bested Michigan Agricultural College 48-0 in a home game. MAC gained no first downs. Harry Mehre, Notre Dame's center, intercepted a pass and lumbered for the first touchdown. Mohardt, who was playing with a broken nose, passed for more than 100 yards and scored a touchdown to go with those he set up for others. Desch's speed got a touchdown and Joe Bergman closed the scoring for the season.

Six players received All-America honors: Kiley, Eddie and Hunk Anderson, Mohardt, Castner, and Shaw. The Fighting Irish were tantalizingly close to a third consecutive undefeated season. They were also now wanted for post-season bowl play. The Rose Bowl showed some interest, but some players got caught playing semipro ball, and Rockne did not push the matter.

1921 record: 10-1-0 (.909)
Record to date: 178-38-16 (.801)

1922

The new season appeared problematic. Some excellent players were gone, especially Hunk Anderson. The seniors had played with Gipp and would serve as transitional figures to the Four Horsemen, who were sophomores in 1922. The basic problem was to mold a backfield unit out of the young raw material. Rockne had seen leadership quality in a 1921 freshman, Harry Stuhldreher. There was fine speed in sophomores Elmer Layden and Don Miller. Castner would start at fullback.

Kalamazoo lost to Notre Dame, 46-0. Rockne used three different backfields. He liked what he saw as they ran all over, but something was missing that he couldn't quite define. St. Louis was next. They played well but

The 1922 team, with the Four Horsemen as sophomores.

succumbed 26-0; fewer backfield combinations were tried. The defense was solid enough to allow the young backs to learn the intricacies of the Notre Dame shift.

The Irish next met Purdue, coached by Notre Dame alumnus Jimmy Phelan. The Boilermakers tried hard but couldn't score. The Fighting Irish scored three touchdowns for a 20-0 win, but lost tackle Tom Lieb with a broken leg. (Note that converting on extra points was more difficult back then, because the ball was shaped differently, and special teams were not in use. Great kicking games did not occur until the late 1960s.) DePauw broke the shutout string the following week, but lost 34-7. Rockne could see that the kids were learning.

Just in time, too, for Georgia Tech. Rockne had the team work out with terrible noise around so that the infamous Rebel Yell wouldn't fluster the youngsters. Tech outplayed the shocked troops for a 3-0 lead when Rockne, who had seen enough, sent in his starters. This added pressure caused Tech's Red Barron to muff a punt at the Tech 42, which Notre Dame recovered. They took their time on a careful drive; Stuhldreher fired a short pass to Castner off a line fake for the touchdown. The game settled into a defensive stalemate in the middle quarters, with Castner's booming punts keeping Tech at bay. Good Irish defense caused fumbles to kill Tech drives, but the Irish couldn't capitalize. In the fourth quarter, however, two Tech lapses in the secondary allowed Stuhldreher to complete some medium range passes, followed by a run to their one-yard line. He sneaked it in to clinch a 13-3 win.

Homecoming against Indiana belonged to Castner. He did virtually all the scoring and played great defense

in a 27-0 win. Castner drop-kicked two field goals of 45 and 35 yards, scored touchdowns from the 20 and 22, intercepted a Hoosier pass on their 35 to zip in for a touchdown, and kicked three conversions in a performance to rival Gipp's 1920 Army marvel. A crushing Fighting Irish ground game reduced their need to pass; only four were attempted. Indiana tried five, and the Fighting Irish snagged three.

Castner should have saved some for the Army game, which ended in a 0-0 tie after both teams did what they could to lose it. The Cadets drove to the Notre Dame 12 but could not score. Layden stopped another deep threat with a pass interception, but nothing eventuated.

Paul Castner, a 1922 All-American, played with both Gipp and the eventual Four Horsemen.

In the fourth quarter, the Fighting Irish put together a drive, mixing delayed passes and off-tackle slants, to reach the Army four-yard line. But Castner fumbled on a line plunge. On Notre Dame's next possession, with a broken nose and a sprained ankle, Castner tried a 55-yard dropkick that missed.

Rockne nursed his big fullback all week hoping he would recover for Butler. He did but was lost for the season in an early pileup. At first they thought he had a dislocated hip and manipulated it back into place, but it was really broken. The Fighting Irish won the game handily, 31-3, but Rockne had to replace his All-America fullback within a week. He asked Layden to try moving from left halfback, the glamour spot then, to fullback, and Crowley moved up to fill the halfback position. It worked—and Rockne had four sophomores for his backfield. He had also just created the Four Horsemen. Rockne recognized that this backfield unit now had what had been missing—perfect timing for the shift, a blend of speed, power, rhythm and headiness for this deceptive offensive tactic.

In the next game, Carnegie Tech opened the game with old-fashioned mass plays, vintage 1905, to rumble for two quick first downs. The Notre Dame defense clamped down, stopped them, got the ball back, and showed Carnegie modern football—Bergman zipped for 27 yards; then from the 10, Layden did the shake and bake, but lost the ball; however, Stuhldreher recovered it for the score. Don Miller scored on a 10-yard burst. In the fourth quarter, good passing finished off the Scots as Crowley scooted for 25 yards to set up a 10-yard touchdown pass from Stuhldreher to Layden. The 19-0 win was the sixth shutout of the season.

They all knew that Nebraska wouldn't be as easy. Another week of intense practice gave the young backfield a better grasp of the offense, but it wasn't enough to beat a loaded Husker squad in a game attended by WWI hero General Pershing. The Huskers ran for two quick touchdowns in the second quarter, on a two-yard plunge and a 38-yarder. The Fighting Irish passing game was not clicking, although Layden hit Miller in the flat for a score. It wasn't enough and Notre Dame lost 14-6.

Those few (Castner, Thomas, and Carberry) who would graduate after 1922 could say they had played with the immortal Gipp—and with the Four Horsemen. It had been a transitional year from 1921, when the Irish should have won it all, to the great 1923-1924 years. The 1922 team played with distinction. And Rockne

Glen Carberry, left end and captain of the 1922 team.

knew he had a good thing in his backfield, but perhaps even he did not fully know just how good they would prove to be.

1922 record: 8-1-1 (.850)
Record to date: 186-39-17 (.803)

1923

Starting his sixth year, Rockne had the longest tenure of any Fighting Irish head football coach. The backfield was set, but no opponent knew how good they'd be. The new center, Adam Walsh, was talented enough to be called the best Irish center long after he was gone. Joe Bach and Noble Kizer would become excellent linemen. The whole team had great speed, and the line had the quickness this backfield needed.

Kalamazoo was demolished 74-0. Red Maher took the kickoff 90 yards on a touchdown run that saw all 11 opponents flattened. His next carry was for 53 yards; then he scored from the seven (and this was a sub—shock troops started the game). Miller tallied from 59 yards;

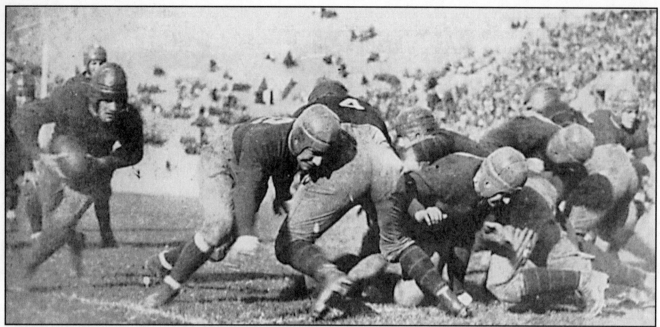

The beginning of a perfect play in the 1923 Princeton game.

Rex Enright from the 25; Crowley from the 68; Bernie Livergood, Bergman, and Max Houser all scored, before the substitutes got three final touchdowns. Kalamazoo never earned a first down. The two teams never met again.

Lombard tried next. Rockne played it very tight in a 14-0 win with basic football—Army was scouting. Rockne usually prepared no more than 12 plays for a whole season, so when he hid the offense, the scouts learned very little.

The Army-Notre Dame game was now being played at Ebbets Field in New York City. The Cadets, with their usual supply of fifth- and sixth-year college students, were much bigger players than Notre Dame, but lacked speed. The Cadets came out wearing bright yellow jerseys rather than the usual blue. The Fighting Irish shock troops sparred with Army for the opening quarter, then the regulars came in: Stuhldreher hit Miller for a 35-yard gain to the Cadet 21; Layden ran to the 6-yard line, and a pass resulted in a touchdown. Notre Dame's defense throttled the slow Army attack; Crowley intercepted a pass and ran it 37 yards to their 24. He went around end for 15; Miller started in the same direction, then he reversed field and scored untouched. Army was beaten 13-0. Army's size was humiliated: two first downs to Notre Dame's 13, 0 completions in 11 tries (and three interceptions), and 49 yards rushing to Notre Dame's 165.

A week later, Notre Dame completed its conquest of eastern football with a 25-2 blitz of Princeton, who had been undefeated since 1921. Notre Dame's superior talent showed: 27 first downs to five; 465 yards of total offense to 101; 241 yards rushing to 54. Miller scored first with a burst around end in the first quarter; Stuhldreher sneaked in from the one-yard line in the next quarter; and a Layden-to-Stuhldreher pass set up Red Maher's 21-yard run for the third tally. Late in the game, Layden picked off a Princeton pass and sped 40 yards to score. The east had fallen.

The south was next. Georgia Tech found Irish speed too much, losing 35-7. Miller ran 59 and 23 yards for touchdowns, and lost an 88-yarder on a penalty. Tech relaxed when Maher replaced Miller near the end, but Red dashed 46 yards for a touchdown on a cut back. Joe Bach blocked two punts, the second going to Gene Mayl for a score.

Purdue was again the Homecoming opponent. Miller starred, with at least four runs over 25 yards each, to go with 50 yards receiving and two touchdowns; Enright and Maher both scored. Notre Dame had 22 first downs to Purdue's five. The final score was Notre Dame over Purdue, 34-7.

Next, Nebraska defeated Notre Dame on the strength of two Dave Noble scores, 14-7. The Huskers mounted a fine pass defense that stymied the Fighting Irish most of the day. Rockne tried to energize matters in the third quarter with substitutes, and Bill Cerney scored on a 20-yard toss from Stuhldreher, but the rally fell short.

Butler was easy, losing 34-7. As in 1922, however, Butler knocked out a star. It had been Castner the year before; this time it was Don Miller, with a broken rib. He had scored early in the game, and was seemingly on his way again with a 38-yard dash when the play ended in injury. Layden scored twice, both on short runs. Stuhldreher ran 65 yards for a score on a punt return. Ward Connell registered the final score as the subs took over. Butler scored on a blocked punt; otherwise, they had five first downs to Notre Dame's 22.

The Irish played Carnegie Tech at Forbes Field in Pittsburgh. The Fighting Irish scored in each quarter for a 26-0 victory. Layden scored first with a short dive to end an 86-yard march. Connell looked like he should be a starter when he ran 41 yards around end to score in the second quarter. He also scored in the third quarter on a short run to end a meticulous, time-killing drive. More subs came in and Red Maher, who probably would have been a three-year starter anywhere else, got the final score.

The season finale was with St. Louis at Sportsman's Park, with three inches of mud on the field. Notre Dame won 13-0 and survived a scare when a big lineman, Kalkman, blocked a Layden punt and recovered it on the 18, but he was apparently unused to carrying the ball, especially in a mudbath. A mud puddle felled him, ending the threat. Most of the day was spent slithering, sliding, and mucking in the mud. It was a good play when someone actually managed to maintain balance.

The year could be summed up in one distasteful word—Nebraska. The Irish wanted Nebraska.

1923 record: 9-1-0 (.900)
Record to date: 195-40-17 (.807)

1924

This season should be displayed as a monument to excellence. Notre Dame football was at the pinnacle of the collegiate game, replacing the fading eastern triumvirate. Rockne had it all: a devastating backfield and a powerful, quick line. His shift was operated by men with an appreciation for its subtleties. A late-season trip to the Rose Bowl would give Rockne the expertise needed to begin the series with the University of Southern California in 1926, creating the first coast-to-coast agenda in college football.

Kalamazoo, outscored 284-0 in six games against the Irish, was dropped from the schedule. Lombard took their place, losing 40-0. Miller scored the first touchdown of the year, then the subs scored on runs of 50 and 57 yards. Crowley, Bill Cerney, and Miller again scored. Cerney literally somersaulted into the end zone for his touchdown after being hit. Quarterback Stuhldreher did not play due to a minor injury.

Wabash closed its series with the Fighting Irish with a well-played 34-0 loss. Rockne played mostly substitutes, watching them carefully, and kept the regulars ready for Army. Crowley scored on one of his classic end runs, and Ward Connell had a long gainer with five Wabash players in tow. Still, the Irish seemed preoccupied with thoughts of Army.

This game with Army completed the transition of Notre Dame from a state power to a regional power to a national power. Rockne personified all that was deemed admirable in college football. His backfield would be immortalized as media heroes in ways unknown before Grantland Rice wrote his famous story of the game. For the rest of his career, Rockne and the Fighting Irish would play the game as if on a plateau removed from mortal teams.

Both teams were undefeated and star-laden. The crowd at the old Polo Grounds reached 55,000, almost twice the live gate of any previous Notre Dame game. And Rice would write the most famous sports story ever written. Heroic feats would happen: Irish captain and center Adam Walsh would play most of the game with two broken hands and still manage to intercept an Army pass and return it 20 yards.

The first quarter was spent reconnoitering and punting. Notre Dame opened up in the second, from their 15. Crowley burst for 20 around end, then Miller for 11 yards. Stuhldreher fired a pass to Crowley for 12 more, and Miller went outside for 20 more. After two thrusts, Layden took it in. In the third quarter, Layden intercepted a Cadet pass to start another march, capped by Crowley's 20-yard flanking end run for the touchdown. Army tried; Wood ran for 45 yards once, but the drive died. Poor punting led to an Army score, but Notre Dame prevailed 13-7. The game was played nearly 80 years ago, so words cannot relay the speed, power, and grace of the shift, nor fully capture a swarming defense that stifled a fine Army team. The team was welcomed back to South Bend the next day with a huge crowd, speeches, and an impromptu parade.

When the excitement subsided, there was a week to prepare for Princeton, one of the old lions of the east. The Fighting Irish dominated them, although the 12-0 final score did not reflect that. Crowley scored both touchdowns and ran 250 yards, virtually uncontested. Notre Dame racked up 20 first downs to Princeton's four and never let them get beyond the Notre Dame 30-yard line. Rockne let the shock troops have the whole first quarter; they held Princeton to one and a half yards on 20 runs. When the regulars came in, a five-play drive of 50 yards ended in a Crowley touchdown. In the fourth quarter Crowley scored on a run in which he was hit four times and spun away from each. When Princeton kicked off in the second half, Rock intentionally used a flying wedge formation to return the kick. Don Miller almost topped this with a 35-yard run, dodging three tacklers while running backwards, after being spun around on the play.

The next week, Notre Dame spotted Georgia Tech a field goal, then roared back for a 34-3 win. Stuhldreher was hurt; Red Edwards started and the Fighting Irish didn't skip a beat. The first score came on a fourth-down play when Crowley hit Miller for an 11-yard touchdown; the drive started with Miller's 35-yard run. Layden soon ran for another; John Roach sparked a drive with a 45-yard scamper, capped by his three-yard touchdown plunge. The same pass play that worked for Crowley and Miller also worked for Eddie Scharer and Roach in the fourth quarter. Bernie Livergood, who owned the right side of the line with his dashes, scored the final touchdown. The fans enjoyed seeing the surviving members of the 1887 team honored at the game. It was, appropriately enough, the 200th career win for Notre Dame.

Wisconsin held the subs to a 3-3 standoff before Rockne sent in the starters, who rocked the Badgers for four touchdowns before the subs went back in. Miller and Layden scored once each, and Crowley twice, one on a pass from Stuhldreher. Roach scored after Joe Harmon intercepted a Badger pass. Notre Dame won 38-3.

The close losses to Nebraska in 1922 and 1923 rankled. Rockne, determined to break the streak, did so, 34-6. The Huskers scored first following an Irish fumble, then the sky fell. Stuhldreher and Miller scored quickly in the second quarter. Miller scored again in the third quarter, and Crowley steamed 65 yards with a pass from Layden, who had thrown it from a prone position, which was then allowed. After that, Notre Dame just pounded the middle, and Layden scored the last touchdown. Notre Dame had 24 first downs to Nebraska's three; 566 yards total offense to 76; eight of 11 passes for 101 yards to one of seven for 20; and 465 yards rushing to 56.

Northwestern turned tough at Soldier Field in Chicago. Two early Wildcat field goals made Rockne send in the regulars. The passing game turned the tide. Stuhldreher threw a long one to Crowley, who ran it to the Northwestern nine; two plays later, a quarterback keeper tied the game. And in two more plays, Stuhldreher snagged a pass and ran it back 40 yards for the winning touchdown in a 13-6 cliffhanger.

Carnegie Tech ended the season, losing 40-19, although the game was closer than the score shows. At the half, the Scots had fought to a 13-13 stalemate. When it was over, their three touchdowns were the most scored by anyone since 1916. It took a great Fighting Irish passing game to earn the win; at one point Notre

The 1924 national champions, line: Hunsinger, Rip Miller, Kizer, captain Walsh, Weibel, Bach, Collins; and backs: Stuhldreher, Miller, Layden, Crowley.

The Four Horsemen, somewhat baffled by their newfound identity. From the left, Miller, Layden, Crowley, and Stuhldreher.

Dame completed 12 consecutive passes. Miller scored first with a 40-yarder from Crowley and Cerney bolted in from the three to tie the game. Stuhldreher fired two touchdown strikes in the third quarter, one to Livergood and one to Crowley. Livergood and Stuhldreher wrapped it up with short runs for scores. It was a fierce game. Adam Walsh was knocked out six times before leaving the field.

Three weeks later, 33 Irish players took a train to the Rose Bowl. After many stops, practices, and festivities, they arrived in Pasadena, each man about eight pounds lighter. The game against Stanford highlighted two different approaches, the Rockne System vs. the Warner System. Stanford used a wingback offense designed to move the ball in long, time-consuming drives, led by an all-time great, fullback Ernie Nevers. Rockne's system was designed for the lightning-quick strike (the "perfect play") executed from anywhere on the field; theoretically, if all 11 players executed as designed, the play should score. Opposing defenses faced this possibility on each play. Under Warner, a defense was nibbled to death while Rock went for the jugular.

Stanford opened the scoring with a 27-yard field goal, and the Fighting Irish shock troops stalled. With the starters in, Layden capped a 46-yard drive with a three-yard plunge. As the Notre Dame defense set up, Rockne made a subtle shift in Layden's alignment, a few inches from his regular spot so he could read Stanford's passing game better. (Years later, Bert Metzger would

say that Rockne coached "in inches.") Five minutes into a meticulous Stanford drive, Layden saw what he wanted—a handoff to Nevers, who floated a bit wider than usual, opening up an area just behind the linebackers. Nevers fired the ball in the direction of an end, but Layden intercepted it for a 78-yard touchdown, helped by right end Ed Hunsinger's blocking. Both men were involved in the next score when Stanford's Solomon couldn't handle one of Layden's punts; Hunsinger recovered and ran 20 yards for the score. Four minutes later, Stanford scored on a seven-yard pass. But they kept misfiring—three missed field goals, Solomon in the open field with a long pass dragged down by a speedy Horseman, and so on. Then Layden saw it again—the handoff to Nevers, who swings a bit wide, the soft spot just behind the linebackers, and the pass. And just as before, he had it all the way, tipped it to himself, and ran 70 yards for the touchdown.

It wasn't easy. Stuhldreher played most of the game with a broken ankle, and Bach went against much bigger Stanford linemen with two cracked ribs. Stanford won the statistics, but Notre Dame won the game, 27-10. Warner's offense could move the ball; Rockne's could score at any moment. The game also showed that football is not a game of territory, but of opportunity. Stanford amassed 316 yards to Notre Dame's 186, 17 first downs to seven, and 138 yards passing to 56. But Rockne's scouting and coaching led to eight turnovers as the opportunistic Irish intercepted five passes and recovered three fumbles. Stanford simply made too many mistakes and the Fighting Irish capitalized on them. Notre Dame was crowned the national champion.

Four players won first team All-American awards: Layden, Stuhldreher, Crowley, and Walsh. Rockne was 58-4-3 (.915) after seven seasons, with three undefeated teams and the others only with one loss.

1924 record: 10-0-0 (1.000)
Record to date: 205-40-17 (.814)

1925

The basic challenge for the 1925 season was to replace the entire starting unit. All 11 men had graduated. Rockne's shock troop theory fortunately provided a large number of players with game experience. There were some dependable, if not particularly flashy, players available: Red Edwards for quarterback, Clem Crowe and Joe Boland on the left flank, and Rex Enright at fullback. A lanky Texan, Christy Flanagan, showed promise.

Baylor, defending two-time Southwest Conference champion, was first. Rockne tried eight different backs in the game. The passing game worked well enough, eight completions in 11 tries (while Baylor showed how not to pass—0 for 15). Tom Hearden scored first from the 11 after Edwards got them there passing. More passing, especially from Eddie Scharer to Joe Prelli, followed by persistent smashes by guard/fullback Dick Hanousek, led to Flanagan's first touchdown, an end run from the six-yard line. Prelli scored the third touchdown by sweeping Baylor's left end. In the third quarter, Fighting Irish speed kept Baylor in trouble; Harry O'Boyle broke six poor tackles to score from the 18. Baylor's right side allowed Hearden to score the next one, and Bucky Dahman made a leaping catch of a pass from Charlie Riley to conclude a 41-0 rout.

Lombard was blitzed by the Irish, 69-0. Lombard used a huddle, something that had not been seen before at Cartier Field. It looked like they were trying to kill time (players in those days got up, aligned themselves, and waited for the signals). The Irish rampaged for 10 touchdowns. O'Boyle and Prelli capped good drives in the first quarter; in the second, John Roach had a long-distance score on his first run; then Lew Cody was a one-man drive on three runs. Before it was over, Hanousek scored three, and O'Boyle, Dahman, and

Flanagan were the other scorers. The winning streak was 15, half of them shutouts.

The next week, the Fighting Irish had a rude awakening when Beloit scored first with a field goal and then used something new—a screen pass. The defensive subs took a while to adjust to this. But in the second quarter with the veterans in, O'Boyle scored on a short run. Later, Prelli slashed off tackle for a 67-yard scoring burst. Lew Cody intercepted a Viking pass and ran 47 yards to the end zone for the 19-3 Irish win.

Army, with only one tie in the previous seven encounters with Notre Dame, ruined the season with a 27-0 win, exposing all of Notre Dame's weaknesses in the process. The line play was deficient in blocking and on defense. Army rolled at will. They scored twice in the second quarter and twice in the fourth. The Irish played fairly well in the third quarter; they blocked an Army punt, but the threat ended when a Cadet blocked the ensuing Irish punt and scored a touchdown in the melee.

More than 5,500 students and fans went to Minnesota. Notre Dame did not play well through the third quarter, when the score was tied 7-7. Poor Minnesota punting let the Fighting Irish take the lead when Flanagan went 40 yards on two runs on a 28-yard

Bucky Dahman, Christy Flanagan's running mate from 1925 to 1927, from his right halfback position.

Joe Boland, a tackle on the 1924 and 1925 squads, later a coach at Notre Dame, and still later the voice of the Irish on the national radio hookup.

touchdown drive (a penalty took place between the runs). On the next series, Red Smith grabbed a Gopher fumble at the 28. Flanagan ran for 24, and Enright took it in from the four-yard line. Joe Boland recovered two fumbles and Art Parisien recovered a fumble at the Notre Dame two and ran it back 80 yards.

Notre Dame went to the deep south to play Georgia Tech. Edwards intercepted a Tech pass and the Fighting Irish were in business at the Tech 25. Flanagan ran for 11 of that before he scored from in close. In the second quarter, Flanagan marched 51 yards with a 20-yard burst past left end and a 10-yard scoring run to the opposite side. A Ramblin' Wreck drive ended as Hearden intercepted a pass at the Fighting Irish 25 to seal the win, 13-0.

From there, the Fighting Irish traveled to Penn State. The Nittany Lions allowed the Irish backs to run around the field almost at will, but when they neared the end zone, Penn State shut them down. The field was so bad from heavy rain that Enright's field goal try from the 13 failed miserably. Captain Clem Crowe tore a back muscle and was lost for the year. The 0-0 tie pleased no one.

Back on campus for Homecoming, Notre Dame whipped Carnegie Tech 26-0. The Irish got off to a

slow start with the subs being used through nearly two quarters; and then it took two drives after that before the regulars hit stride. From the Tech 35, Enright slammed into the middle, and Flanagan went wide for 24. Enright pounded the middle twice; Flanagan finished it off for the touchdown. Enright scored in the third quarter to end a drive, then scored again on a fumble recovery. The subs finished; Riley faked a pass and rolled in for a 20-yard score.

Northwestern visited Cartier Field and shocked everyone with a 10-0 halftime lead. The Wildcats had also held the Irish to no first downs. Rockne reminded the team at halftime that memory could not recall the last team to do what Northwestern was doing. The team got the point. Flanagan carried for 25 yards. A quick march, led by Flanagan and Enright, finished with an Enright touchdown from the four-yard line. On the next drive, Flanagan ran for 29 yards to the Northwestern 17, then for 12 more; Enright ran for no-gain, and Flanagan raced in for the touchdown and a final score of 13-10.

Flanagan was injured and Nebraska was next. The Huskers had not played the weekend before. Rockne started the subs again, but it backfired. A strong Nebraska team shredded them for two touchdowns in the first quarter to sink Fighting Irish hopes. They added a field goal in the third quarter. Notre Dame's passing game disappeared; they hit one of 12, with Nebraska intercepting three. The season ended on this sour 17-0 note, but Rockne had overcome the loss of his entire 1924 starting team to keep this young team in contention much of the season.

1925 record: 7-2-1 (.750)
Record to date: 212-42-18 (.812)

1926

Rockne had to deal with two key points: the schedule for 1926 was the most demanding ever, and a full second stop was now mandatory after the shift (in 1924, the Horsemen could all be in motion, as a unit, at the snap). He was not overly concerned on either score.

Beloit was the only breather in the nation's first coast-to-coast schedule, from Yankee Stadium to the Los Angeles Coliseum. Rockne had hired Tommy Mills, the Beloit coach who scared the Irish in 1925, so Beloit was hurting even before the Fighting Irish obliterated them 77-0. Of Notre Dame's 11 touchdowns (10 rushing),

Flanagan's 95-yard kickoff return in the third quarter was the best. Vince McNally scored two touchdowns and Hearden, Dahman, John Niemiec, Jack Chevigny, Red Edwards, Fred Collins, and Joe Maxwell each scored.

Minnesota was much tougher, so much so that Joe Boland and Collins were lost for the year. Dahman opened up Notre Dame's scoring with a 65-yarder designed to be a short gainer. For two quarters, it was a defensive struggle, then Flanagan broke the log jam with another 65-yard touchdown run. Hearden wrapped up the 20-7 win on a late drive with a 20-yard run and a 15-yard scoring burst.

Hugo Bedzek's Penn State team wanted to avenge the 0-0 tie, but Notre Dame was ready. Parisien, working with the subs, fired a 35-yard strike to Harry O'Boyle who ran 15 yards for a touchdown. Penn State stalled and punted. Parisien threw to O'Boyle, who was open again and turned it into a 53-yard touchdown. Penn State stiffened, stopping four Irish drives. Edwards finally shook loose for a 48-yard touchdown run in the second quarter. Jack Chevigny ended it in the fourth quarter when he crashed through seven Penn State tacklers for a 17-yard touchdown and a 28-0 win. Notre Dame gained 506 total yards to Penn State's 85. Northwestern christened its new stadium against Notre Dame and played well for nearly four quarters. With only five minutes left, Rockne sent in Parisien. He promptly hit Chile Walsh with a pass play for 66 yards to the Northwestern 14. Then he hit Niemiec with a touchdown pass, but the point after was missed. Superb punting kept the Wildcats at bay, and Hearden later intercepted a threatening pass for a 6-0 win.

Georgia Tech came north and ran into John Roach: from the Tech 40, he gained 20 yards, and slammed in for a short yardage touchdown. After several punts, O'Boyle ran to the Tech 40 but left hurt. Niemiec passing set up a short run for Dahman and a 12-0 final score.

Indiana swooned 26-0. Parisien was hurt early. But Flanagan started to roll in the second quarter: a 20-yard gain and a short touchdown sprint; and later, a sideline-to-sideline touchdown ramble. Dahman took over the second half with two touchdowns for a 26-0 win. This was Notre Dame's fifth shutout in six games.

Army would be difficult with many players back from the 1925 win over Notre Dame. But Rockne had used the train ride home a year ago to challenge the team to make this game their top priority. The team won a thrilling 7-0 game; the score came on the old "51" play—the left halfback, Flanagan, off tackle with plenty of blocking to escort him for the 68-yard touchdown run.

Drake made their first visit to the Dome. The Bulldogs played even with the shock troops; in the second quarter, Drake drove to the three-inch line before being stopped. Notre Dame took over on a 95-yard drive that ended when Edwards took it in from the two-yard line on a quarterback sneak. Drake came back but John Wallace intercepted a pass, turning it into a 30-yard touchdown. As the snow fell, Riley pitched a 21-yard touchdown strike to O'Boyle for a 21-0 win.

Six shutouts for the year so far. Only Minnesota had scored. The next game against Carnegie Tech would be a shutout, too. Confident of an Irish victory, Rockne went on to Chicago to scout a 1927 opponent, Navy, and saw a 21-21 tie game. The team went to Pittsburgh under

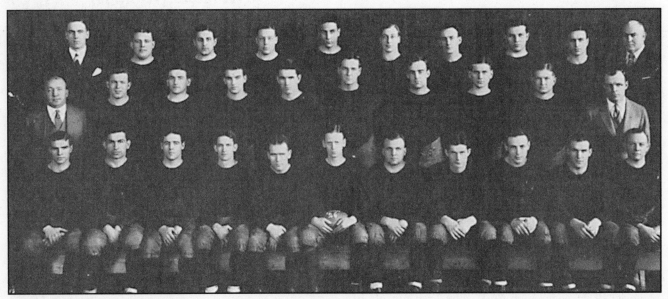

The 1926 Fighting Irish team.

Hunk Anderson to meet Carnegie Tech. In Chicago, Rockne got the news of the stunning upset—Tech had destroyed a championship year with a 19-0 win over Notre Dame. Two touchdowns on the ground and two field goals were scored against the Fighting Irish defense, who had trouble with the running game all day.

On to University of Southern California. This game set the tone for the series, including the surprise ending that would be duplicated more times than either team would care to remember. Notre Dame scored first as Riley led a drive to USC's 20, then faked a plunge and broke outside for the touchdown. Notre Dame missed the point after kick. USC earned a touchdown following an interception, but also missed the conversion. In the fourth quarter, USC's Wheeler ran 44 yards on five carries for the go-ahead touchdown. USC missed another conversion, but led 12-6. The Fighting Irish struggled to get back into it but did little until Rockne sent in Parisien with 90 seconds left. He immediately fired passes to Niemiec, good for 50 yards and the winning touchdown; the final score was 13-12.

It had to be painful for Rockne to contemplate seven shutouts and sustained success in college football's first truly national schedule, almost gone for naught due to Carnegie Tech.

1926 record: 9-1-0 (.900)
Record to date. 221-43-18 (.815)

1927

Fighting Irish fans could expect only three games with genuinely good teams this year—Minnesota, Army, and USC. The team, though not great, was certainly good, led by Flanagan (second team All-American in 1926) and underrated Bucky Dahman who had exceptional speed and good hands. The left side of the line was intact and the right side was filled capably as good men moved up.

Rockne, as usual, played his hand close to his vest early in the season so that Navy's scouts (the third game scheduled) would learn little. Notre Dame toppled a scrappy Coe team, 28-7, and then Detroit, 20-7. The starting unit was quite capable, but the quality dropped off quickly after that.

The Irish took a train to Baltimore to meet Navy. Niemiec bobbled a punt early in the game to give Navy good field position and Navy's Spring ran for a six-yard

touchdown. Rockne pulled the subs out and tried to stay close. In the third quarter, Notre Dame twice blocked Navy punts; a penalty killed the first one; but John Frederick's block of the second punt was recovered by Chile Walsh for a touchdown. On the next drive, Flanagan ran 35 yards off tackle and 25 yards past right end, and Riley attacked the other side for a 12-yard touchdown run. Niemiec redeemed himself with sharp passing on a 44-yard drive, capped by his touchdown. The Fighting Irish escaped with a 19-6 win, but their passing game was not sharp throughout.

On to Bloomington—different town, different team, same score (19-6). It had the same start, too, when Indiana's Reinhardt streaked through the subs for a 45-yard touchdown. Niemiec tallied in the second quarter with a plunge from the one. A quarter later, Dahman completed a five-play drive with a touchdown bolt. Flanagan completed the scoring.

Undefeated Georgia Tech came to South Bend. The shock troops did better, playing even for their quarter. The starters relieved them and began moving—Fred Collins started it with a 20-yard run and finished it with a 17-yard touchdown jaunt. In the third quarter, Tech fumbled and Collins dashed 25 yards for a score from scrimmage. In the fourth quarter, Chevigny sparked a score with a 25-yard run, capped by Billy Dew's four-yard touchdown on a fullback dive. Tech lost 26-7.

Minnesota, with stars Bronko Nagurski at guard and Herb Joesting at fullback, came next. Early in

Clipper Smith, one of Rock's great "watch-charm guards" at 5'9", 164 pounds. Started at left guard in 1926 and 1927, and was an All-American in 1927.

1927 Notre Dame starting team, in the line (l-r): Charlie Walsh, John Polisky, George Leppig, Tim Moynihan, John Smith, Fred Miller, and John Voedisch. In the backfield: Bucky Dahman, Charlie Riley (QB), Elmer Wynne, and Christy Flanagan.

the game, Clipper Smith grabbed a fumbled punt at Minnesota's 18, and Niemiec scored on the next play for a 7-0 lead. For almost three quarters after that the defenses dominated; neither Joesting nor Flanagan was able to shake loose. In the fourth quarter with 15 seconds remaining (or so they were told), Niemiec went into punt formation but Riley called for a plunge to kill the time. Somebody missed the call because the ball was snapped into the middle of the backfield and Nagurski

fell on it at the Notre Dame 15. After three Joesting runs, Minnesota scored with a pass and tied the game as time expired. It was a superb defensive game, but Minnesota showed that the Fighting Irish could not run up the middle with impunity.

On to Yankee Stadium and Army, another star-laden team, led by Christian Keener Cagle at halfback. Army was a good, big team and handled Notre Dame with some ease, 18-0. Cagle scored twice on a run of

The 1927 football squad.

48 yards and with a pass of 32 yards; quarterback Billy Nave intercepted an Irish pass and sped 60 yards for the final score.

Notre Dame took out its accumulated frustrations on Drake, 32-0. Rockne had the offense practice its off-tackle smashes and its passing game against the Bulldogs, and he rested the starters as much as possible, saving them for USC. Jack Elder, Rockne's fastest player, took an interception 86 yards for a score and also threw a short pass to John Colrick for another. Niemiec had opened the scoring, and Dahman and Prelli closed it, on a 14-yard touchdown catch and a 15-yard run, respectively. Flanagan was held in check, with 23 yards being his longest gain.

USC came to Soldier Field in Chicago. The records show 120,000 fans attended, but 135,000 is probably more accurate. Fans stood on top of the colonnade circling the upper deck; others were on ladders between the columns. It was, and still is, the largest crowd ever to see a college football game. The Fighting Irish thrilled these packed masses with a 7-6 win. Bucky Dahman was the most valuable player of the game: he caught a 25-yard touchdown pass from Riley after four Flanagan runs netted 28 yards; he kicked the winning point after; in the fourth quarter he kicked a 65-yard punt to the USC two; and then he intercepted a Trojan pass on their 20 to ice the game. Notre Dame killed the clock, won the game, and concluded the season.

There were three All-Americans: Flanagan, Clipper Smith, and John Polisky at tackle, a second-team choice. In retrospect, the 1927 team lacked a knockout punch. They had also been lucky in escaping injuries. They would not be so lucky in 1928.

1927 record: 7-1-1 (.833)
Record to date: 228-44-18 (.817)

1928

There are cycles in football. The 1928 Fighting Irish team was a transitional team, akin to the 1921 team sandwiched between the passing of Gipp and the arrival of the Horsemen. With Flanagan and key supporters gone, Rockne had to look for help from sophomores, and hope that the team could sustain the effort through a tough schedule. This team, like last year's, also lacked a knockout punch. Rockne moved some veterans so that the left side of the line was solid; other spots were filled

with former reserves. The running backs were good: Chevigny, Niemiec, and Elder as halfbacks and Collins and Moon Mullins at fullback. There were some bad knees here and there. Rock knew he'd have a difficult season.

The Wolf Pack of New Orleans's Loyola University provided the first test. Notre Dame's 12-6 victory was won in the final moments against a determined Loyola team. The Wolf Pack had a 6-0 lead through the first half, then Elder brought Notre Dame back with 48-yard touchdown sprint. The teams traded punts and miscues until late in the game, when Rockne inserted new ends, Johnny O'Brien and Tom Murphy. Niemiec lofted a long pass to O'Brien, who took it to the Loyola eight. Niemiec hit him again at the two, then took it in himself, going off left tackle—all in less than a minute.

Playing Wisconsin in Madison, the Fighting Irish simply did not look good. They lost key fumbles, seven in all, and scored only once (Chevigny from the three). Elder was trapped for a safety, so they Irish clung to a 6-2 lead until the third quarter. They fumbled at their 20, recovered it but lost eight yards, then promptly fumbled again; Wisconsin recovered it on the Notre Dame three-yard line. The Badgers took the lead for good on the next play, a touchdown sweep. In the fourth quarter, Wisconsin pitched a 65-yard pass and run to close it out 22-6. Notre Dame, although they moved the ball,

Jack Chevigny scored the first TD of the great 1928 win over Army, shouting, "That's one for the Gipper!" as he crossed the goal.

The 1928 team, the group that "Won one for the Gipper."

could not sustain a drive.

Against Navy in Soldier Field, Rockne had to do something—so he suited them up in Kelly Green. The Fighting Irish moved the ball well, but scoring was another matter. Rockne played the regulars from the start. Notre Dame won the game in the fourth quarter with a slant-in pass from Niemiec to Colrick for the game's only touchdown. Other long drives fizzled. The 120,000-plus spectators were treated to a stifling defense that allowed Navy only 93 total yards. The final score was Notre Dame 7, Navy 0.

The passing game failed against Georgia Tech, who held onto an early lead and waited. Father Lumpkin from Tech intercepted two Notre Dame passes, running the second one to the Irish three-yard line to set up the clincher. Georgia Tech won 130. Guard John Law was injured, and a glaring deficiency at fullback was exposed when insistent line smashes close to the Tech goal were stopped fairly easily.

Drake provided a breather. Notre Dame won handily, 32-6, and Rockne saw that moving Moon Mullins to the fullback spot improved things. Niemiec hit Colrick with a touchdown pass, then Chevigny scored. Carideo was next, crawling under a pile of Bulldogs. Sub Dinny Shay scored and Joe Nash, a center,

Action from the first quarter of the 1928 Army game, John Niemiec has the ball setting up for a pass, which was incomplete. This is what the play looked like that went to Johnny O'Brien for the winning TD.

Babe Ruth showing them how a southpaw does it, circa 1928.

grabbed an errant pass and ran 50 yards to complete the scoring. Mullins did not score, but showed great doggedness in resisting tackles. Drake's score came on an 80-yard pass and run.

Notre Dame beat Penn State 9-0, but the score could easily have been higher. Carideo crawled in, literally, for a score. Colrick's speed netted a safety in the fourth quarter. Eddie Collins sacked a Penn State back for minus 20 yards, then recovered a fumble on the next play.

After six games, the Fighting Irish were 4-2, but Rockne knew that matters ahead looked grim. The team *had* to beat Army to prevent a losing season. He had a thought. He told Grantland Rice the night before the game that he might have to use the ghost of George Gipp to help the Irish play beyond capacity. The rest is, as they say, history.

Army was a loaded ream built around Cagle. The Irish defense showed that it could play with the larger Cadets and neutralize Cagle. The first half ended in a 0-0 deadlock. At the half, Rockne played his ace—the now famous "Win One for the Gipper" ploy. They'd have to keep Cagle in check, an assignment they almost blew when play resumed. Cagle shook loose for a 20-yard gain, then fired a 41-yard pass to spark a Cadet touchdown and a 6-0 lead. He also stopped Irish backs that his mates let loose. Then Chevigny matched the touchdown, on a fourth-down plunge, highlighted by his cry, "That's one for the Gipper!" A little later he was hurt recovering a fumble. Rock substituted; he sent in Johnny

"One Play" O'Brien to march his height against the diminutive Nave, the hero of the 1927 game. Niemiec got the hall and saw Cadets breaking through his front wall. He heaved a prayer in O'Brien's direction—who caught it and stumbled for the score, just out of Nave's desperate reach.

Cagle inspired a long drive deep into Notre Dame territory, but had to be removed, totally exhausted. With mere seconds left in the game, Army reached the one-

Johnny "One Play" O'Brien won the 1928 Army game with a TD reception from John Niemiec.

foot line, but lost possession on downs. The Irish line held, each man driven by the ghost of Gipp perhaps, and the game ended. Rockne had succeeded in pumping up a mediocre team to beat a superior foe. It is doubtful that Gipp said "Win one for the Gipper," as Rockne claimed, (both Castner and Grant have said that Gipp never called himself that) but it is the best example in Notre Dame's history of the use of motivational psychology.

The rest of the season was anticlimactic, although the Fighting Irish had to face even better teams— Carnegie Tech and USC. The Scots were led by a 230-pound fullback named Karcis, who was too much for the smallish linemen to handle. Tech won 27-7. Mullins earned the only Irish score on a 10-yard fumble recovery. It was the first defeat at Cartier Field in 23 years, and also the first time a Rockne team had lost three games.

Notre Dame moved on to the west coast for USC, the 300th game for the Fighting Irish. They lost 27-14, but played gamely. Chevigny scored on a 51-yard run, and Albert Gebert, a sub quarterback, tallied the other. The defense drilled USC four times while dug in at the Notre Dame four-yard line.

Rockne's most painful season was at last behind him. Things could only get better.

Fred Collins, starting fullback for the star-crossed 1928 team.

1928 record: 5-4-0 (.555)
Record to date: 233-48-19 (.808)

1929

R ockne felt good about prospects for 1929. The line was solid and Carideo had matured. Elder's blazing speed was perfect for left halfback, and his backup was excellent—Marchmont Schwartz. Marty Brill, a transfer from Penn, was big, strong, and fast. Mullins was at fullback, with Joe Savoldi behind him.

This was a transitional backfield since the days of the shift were severely numbered. Rockne knew he would need bigger players, especially as backs. The metamorphosis was complete by 1930, when the backfield would average 20 pounds more per man than the Horsemen.

It was a suicide schedule, with all games on the road. Cartier Field was a memory, dug up for a new stadium under Rockne's watchful eye. He was already aware of something called television, and intuitively knew the entertainment appeal of college football. He designed his teams with this in mind—the uniforms, play selection, shock troops, tiring road trips, and manipulation of the media. It was all there. Now he was constructing the perfect stadium.

Off to Indiana. The shock troops started and played even. Savoldi and Schwartz showed flashes of brilliance. Elder scored on a 20-yard streak, having set it up with a pass to Mullins. He ended the scoring with a 60-yard sprint that left the defense in the dust (he held the world sprint record for 75 yards). The Hoosiers did not threaten, and the Fighting Irish lost scoring chances with fumbles and other slips for a final score of 14-0.

The real news of the game happened on the sidelines; a pileup smashed into Rockne and bounced him around. It was almost fatal since phlebitis set in; he was confined to bed much of the season. Although he went to extraordinary lengths to stay active in coaching, it probably cost the team a little bit of edge. He would never again be the active, vigorous man of before.

The team that week went to Rockne's house to prepare for Navy; quarterbacks spent 14 hours there that week, enjoying Mrs. Rockne's cooking. Before the game, Rockne spoke to each starter on the phone and fidgeted upon hearing that Navy scored first. Carideo brought Notre Dame back, hitting Elder with a touchdown pass thrown kneeling on one knee after absorbing a hit.

The 1929 national champions.

Carideo broke Navy with an interception, running it back to their 32. The ensuing drive included runs of seven and 17 by Brill, setting up Mullins's one-yard TD plunge and ND's 14-7 win.

Rockne started attending practices in a specially arranged hearse from the McGann funeral home. The squad worked out well. At Soldier Field, Wisconsin threatened early, but Savoldi hit pay dirt twice, from 40 and 71 yards out, runs before and after Elder's 43-yard touchdown run. The Fighting Irish won 19-0.

Carnegie Tech's victory over the Irish in 1928 had smashed the home winning streak that started before most of the current players were born. Tech fielded a huge team, and Notre Dame knew it would be a rough game. As expected, it was a scoreless game in the third quarter; finally, Carideo returned a punt to mid-field, and Elder ran to the 17. Brill crashed to the eight. Savoldi came in against Tech's 230-pound Karcis. Savoldi ran up the middle three straight times, with grudging inches gained on each. On the fourth down, Savoldi went in for the winning touchdown. And in the midst of all this was Jack "Boom Boom" Cannon, the last lineman for Notre Dame to play sans helmet. The final score was 7-0.

The 1928 national champions, Georgia Tech, hosted the Fighting Irish next. Tech grabbed a Mullins fumble on the Notre Dame 19 and took a 6-0 lead. The Irish came right back: Brill returned the kickoff to the 40, and Elder ran 53 untouched yards to finish the drive with the go-ahead touchdown. Cannon used his bare head to block a punt, allowing Mullins to score

for a 13-6 halftime lead. After intermission, Carideo danced 75 yards with a punt return for a touchdown. In the fourth quarter, Schwartz gave Tech a glimpse of the Fighting Irish future with an eight-yard touchdown run for the 26-6 final score.

Fresh off the victory over Georgia Tech, the Irish were quickly brought back to earth as Drake grabbed

John Law, starter at TG in 1928 and 1929, captain in 1929.

a 7-0 lead. Rockne let the subs extricate themselves; Al Howard dashed 35 yards before going another three for a touchdown. Late in the third quarter, Elder zipped 17 yards to score and Mullins crunched the tiring Bulldogs for a 23-yard touchdown late in the game. Notre Dame won 19-7.

Against his doctor's order, Rockne went to Soldier Field for the USC game. It was a close game, almost decided by Bucky O'Connor's swollen black eye. With the eye freshly shut, he never saw the Trojan touchdown pass play coming his way that put USC ahead. Elder could throw, too, and he hit Tom Conley for a 54-yarder to tie it 66. Savoldi led a ground attack and scored the next Irish touchdown. USC ran the kickoff back 92 yards, but missed the conversion. Notre Dame escaped with a 13-12 victory.

Rockne stayed home for the Northwestern game and told the team to win for him—it would be his 100th. He was wrong (and knew it), but the Fighting Irish got his wish for him, 26-6. Three touchdowns were scored against Northwestern in the second quarter: it started with a Schwartz run of 40 yards to the Northwestern 40, and Savoldi ran it in. Next Schwartz passed to Brill for 25 yards, reaching the Wildcat 10; Schwartz slanted in standing up. Northwestern started passing and Carideo intercepted for an 85-yard touchdown. Late in the game, Savoldi careened for 32 yards and then plunged in to end the scoring.

The finale matched Army, and its star halfback Cagle in his last game against Notre Dame. Yankee Stadium, and a frozen field, was the locale for their 16th

meeting. They sparred at first, until a Cadet rushing a punt knocked Elder into Carideo, the Notre Dame kicker, and Army was set up on the Notre Dame 13. Two runs and two yards later, Cagle threw a pass in the left corner to Carlmark and the massed Cadets cheered—but a blur cut in front of Carlmark and snatched the ball. Elder running, dodging three tacklers, sidestepping more Cadets, was gone—100 yards for the game's only touchdown. Carideo kicked the point after and the national championship turned on this one play. Notre Dame intercepted three more of Cagle's passes to ice the game.

The Irish won the Rissman Trophy—the equivalent of the national championship—based on comparative schedules. They never played a home game and did not have their coach for six games. Their statistical dominance was complete in all categories. No Fighting Irish team to date had faced more adversity and performed better.

1929 record: 9-0-0 (1.000)
Record to date: 242-48-19 (.813)

The conclusion of Jack Elder's 100-yard interception and TD runback to beat Army in 1929.

1930-1939

1930

If anyone was capable of performing an exciting encore, it was Rockne. The 1929 team had been great, but the 1930 edition was stupendous. The line produced three All-Americans (149-pound guard Bert Metzger, Al Culver, and Tom Conley), while the backfield could be favorably compared to any under the Dome. Carideo, Brill, Schwartz, and Savoldi posed a fearsome set of problems for defenses to solve. Rockne added "spinners" to the shift—the quarterback took the ball and spun around to lateral or handoff, or rolled out to pass—a concept close to the veer offense used by Parseghian 40 years later.

The stage was set for the defending national champions as they opened in South Bend at the new stadium against pass-happy Southern Methodist University, three-time defending Southwest Conference champs. Four plays into the game, SMU scored on a 48-yard catch and run play. Savoldi bobbled the ensuing kickoff slightly, then raced up the middle for a 98-yard touchdown. It was 7-7 after five plays. In the second quarter, Carideo returned a punt to the SMU 11, and Schwartz took it in two plays later off tackle. Three long SMU passes made the halftime score 14-14. It was a

stand-off into the fourth quarter until a Schwartz pass to Ed Kosky, good for 48 yards, landed the ball at the SMU 27. Schwartz tried Conley but he was decked at the four—pass interference. Schwartz ran a cut back past left end for the touchdown. Tommy Yarr's three interceptions iced the game, 20-14.

The stadium was formally dedicated before the Navy game. Three previous games with Navy had been close, but the Fighting Irish won easily this time, 26-2. Mullins was hurt and Savoldi filled in, scoring three touchdowns while rushing 11 times for 123 yards. A third-string back, Clarence Kaplan, had 96 yards on six carries, enough to make Navy marvel at Notre Dame's depth. Navy played a modified wingback offense, like Warner's, but didn't have a Nevers to ram it home. Savoldi's first score came on a 23-yard lateral from Brill, repeated moments later for a 55-yard scoring play. In the third quarter, Savoldi muscled in from the 8, then retired to the bench exhausted. Kaplan owned the fourth quarter, setting up Fritz Stuab's touchdown for the final score.

Carnegie Tech was next. Notre Dame won this one, 21-6. Carnegie Tech's score capped the only time they were in Notre Dame territory. Kurth and Culver dominated Tech's linemen. After a placid first quarter,

The 1930 national champions, Rockne's last team; Line (l to r): Conley, Kurth, Metzger, Yarr, Kassis, Culver, Kosky; backs (l to r): Carideo, Brill, Mullins, Schwartz.

Marchy Schwartz scores the winning TD against SMU in 1930.

Rockne unleashed a series of spinners, reverses, and laterals that dizzied defenders. Schwartz ended a scintillating drive with a 13-yard touchdown pass to Kosky. The teams exchanged interceptions; Notre Dame reached the Tech two-yard line, and Schwartz piled in for the touchdown. A 72-yard run for a score by Tech's Eyth brought them close in the third quarter but Schwartz threw a 44-yard strike to Conley for the closer.

Notre Dame moved on to the University of Pittsburgh, also undefeated in 1929. Pitt's Jock Sutherland worked his charges hard to stop the expected aerial show, but Rockne told Carideo to keep it on the ground. The result was Notre Dame 35, Pitt 19. Pitt's plans evaporated on the first play from scrimmage when

Schwartz had a 60-yard touchdown run. Notre Dame scored four more times before the half ended: Mullins in from the one; Savoldi recovered a fumble to lead to his blast from the one; Savoldi picked off a Pitt pass and ran 42 yards for a score; and Bucky O'Connor ran 32 and 45 yards before Mike Koken rallied from the five-yard line. Pitt got two consolation touchdowns on drives and a third on a fumble recovery.

Against Indiana, Savoldi started things with a 33-yard scoring run, and Schwartz raced around right end 26 yards for a touchdown. Later, Schwartz set Brill up with a 79-yard kickoff return and Brill scored on a nine-yard run; he scored again on a 23-yard jolt. Notre Dame's racehorses compiled 432 yards of offense to

Marchy Schwartz throwing a pass in the 60-20 rout of Penn in 1930. Penn's Paul Riblett (5) applies the pressure a bit late.

Indiana's 76 for the 27-0 win.

The Fighting Irish sent Penn back east, 60-20. Brill had been told that he was not good enough for Quaker football, so he had given the Fighting Irish a try. Running with the starters, Brill saw his work rout Penn 43-0 before the subs went in. On his first carry, Brill scored a 65-yard touchdown. He added two more on similar runs. Carideo, Schwartz, Savoldi, Mullins, and O'Connor also scored. Penn never moved the sticks against the starting unit.

Against Drake, Rockne unveiled yet another threat, Dan Hanley. As a sub, he scored on a 32-yard canter. (Savoldi, secretly married but already divorcing, had been expelled, so the fullback position needed the help Hanley provided.) Drake scored, but Schwartz ran the kickoff back to Drake's 13. The running game got them to the three-yard line; Carideo faked a pass and handed off to Brill for the touchdown. Schwartz's passing paved the way for a Mullins touchdown in the third quarter, and Schwartz wrapped it up with a 43-yard score. Notre Dame won 28-7.

Northwestern had played to a 0-0 tie with only 10 minutes left. They even reached the Fighting Irish five-yard line twice in the first half, but came up empty. Finally, Schwartz scored from the Northwestern 18. Hanley secured the 14-0 win with a one-yard touchdown plunge a bit later.

Then came the annual game with Army, also undefeated, but with one tie. Conditions were wretched at Soldier Field, but the Fighting Irish worked another perfect play, and Schwartz scored on a 54-yarder. Army scored on a blocked kick moments later, but Notre Dame blocked their conversion try. It was a bruising affair, won by the Irish 7-6.

Too bruising, in fact, since Mullins went down, leaving Hanley to face a monstrous USC team. USC was undefeated. They had beaten assorted opponents 389 points to 39. On the long trip west, Rockne orchestrated an elaborate ruse, as Bucky O'Connor practiced in the guise of Hanley, purposely running slowly, fumbling a lot, and showing sophomore jitters. The ruse was designed to prepare USC for a slow fullback; in fact, O'Connor was almost as fast as Elder, two steps faster from scrimmage than the Trojans expected. Only Notre Dame alumnus and writer Francis Wallace knew of the trick. All the other reporters took it in hook, line, and fullback.

The Trojans literally never knew what hit them. Entering the game as nine-point favorites, they left defeated, 27-0. O'Connor ran for an 80-yard touchdown in the second quarter, and later zipped in from the seven-yard line with a lateral (he also lost a 60-yard touchdown run due to a penalty). He averaged 11 yards per carry. Following a USC fumble, Schwartz fired a 19-yard pass to Carideo. USC back Marshall Duffield tried to avert a big loss on a fumble by kicking the ball out of the end zone—his end zone—for a safety. Hanley intercepted a USC pass and Nick Lukats scored from the 11. The Trojan offense gained only 140 total yards while the Fighting Irish punched out 433.

Action in the 1930 ND-USC game. Marchy Schwartz makes a short gain.

Joe Kurth, two-time consensus All-American at right tackle, won his starting spot in the spring of 1930 and held it for three years.

With its perfect 10-0 record, Notre Dame thus officially became the first school to win consecutive national titles in football.

The Depression was in full force. Rockne coached charity All-Star games against the New York Giants and a Northwestern team, with the proceeds going to the needy. He visited the Mayo clinic for his bad leg and spent the week in bed next to a Fighting Irish player who had missed his senior year with a back injury. He was from Winner, South Dakota. His name was Frank Leahy.

Rockne headed south for some Florida sun. He left his family in Miami while he went back to South Bend to organize spring practice and to tidy up some Studebaker business. Then he went to Chicago to celebrate his mother's birthday early. From there he moved on to Kansas City to see an old friend, Dr. D.M. Nigro. He was on his way to Los Angeles to sign a contract for a Lew Ayres movie about *The Spirit of Notre Dame*. He waited an extra 20 minutes in Kansas City to see his two sons who attended boarding school there, but the flight couldn't wait any longer and he missed them by minutes.

The weather was miserable but the plane took off anyway. They never reached their next stop in Wichita. Over Bazaar, Kansas, the plane went into a violent spin, flinging Rockne from the cabin 650 feet above ground before crashing.

A terrible earthquake hit Managua, Nicaragua, that same day, March 31, 1931. Thousands it were killed, but their deaths received about a quarter of the U.S. newspaper space that Rockne's did. At the funeral, his players served as pallbearers. He was knighted posthumously by King Olaf of Norway. They knew well what kind of man Knute Kenneth Rockne, 43 years old, had been.

1930 record: 10-0-0 (1.000)
Record to date: 252-48-19 (.819)

1931

An era had come to a terrible, abrupt end. But the pieces had to be picked up. Notre Dame's authorities, led by President Charles O'Donnell, appealed to Jesse Harper to assume the athletic director's position. Harper did so. Hunk Anderson became the head coach. Anderson had been a fine assistant coach, but he did not have the flair for the head coaching job. He would coach for three seasons, the last a total dud. It would be a decade before the team's fortunes would be placed in the hands of someone with Rockne's flair, intensity, and drive—Frank Leahy.

Anderson inherited a solid team. The line was good, only Schwartz returned in the backfield (Hanley would miss two seasons because of injuries). How the players would conduct themselves in the absence of Rockne was anyone's guess.

Rockne seemed to be with them for the opener, a 25-0 shutout of Indiana. Three units played and all scored. Joe Sheeketski scored on a 70-yard effort capped by a fake. Reserve center Kitty Gorman intercepted a pass and returned it for a 35-yard touchdown. Sheeketski set up a Schwartz touchdown with a 32-yard pass to Kosky, Marchy tallying from the 11. The deep reserves constructed an 85-yard drive, with Carl Cronin running off tackle for a 35-yard touchdown.

Lake Michigan appeared to have encroached on Soldier Field when Notre Dame met Northwestern the following week. The teams sloshed and splashed to a 0-0 tie, marred by 17 fumbles, a battle Notre Dame won 9-8.

The 1931 team, the first since 1918 without Rockne.

Schwartz for a 59-yard touchdown; he accumulated 188 of Notre Dame's 388 yards of offense.

The Fighting Irish next trampled Penn 49-0. The starters scored three quick touchdowns, then the subs had fun. Schwartz scored first, untouched from 16 yards out. Other backs noted the gaping hole—Sheeketski went through the same place for a 49-yard touchdown. Schwartz fired a long scoring pass to Chuck Jaskwich. Sub scorers were Koken, Paul Host, Jim Leonard, and Carl Cronin.

Navy was coached by Notre Dame alumni Rip Miller, Christie Flanagan, and Johnny O'Brien. Notre Dame shut them out, 20-0, although the fullback position took a beating. Schwartz scored on a 17-yard run over the left side, escorted by six Irish players. Steve Banas, once the starting fullback, scored on a plunge. Navy's punter, Chung Hooh, rushed a punt; and Koken subsequently threw a touchdown strike to Emmet Murphy from the 32.

Ten million fans heard the Notre Dame-USC game on the radio. Melinkovich and Koken were hurt, but Notre Dame seemed superior for most of the game. Banas scored on a short plunge. Schwartz crashed in from the 10 for a 14-0 lead at the half. The teams sparred for the third quarter. The Irish knocked out the Trojan quarterback with a broken nose; coach Howard Jones shifted some personnel, and two touchdowns and a field goal later, USC won 16-14. Jones took his team to Rockne's grave after the game.

Whatever snapped in that fourth quarter did not mend quickly. Army shutout the Fighting Irish 12-0. A tired Irish team played heroically, especially Nordy Hoffmann on torn knee ligaments. Army's Ray Stecker won the game on a catch after a fake punt, good for a long gain to set up a touchdown, then iced it with a 70-yard touchdown run.

Schwartz, Kurth, Tommy Yarr, and Hoffmann made All-America teams.

1931 record: 6-2-1 (.722)
Record to date: 258-50-20 (.817)

The Fighting Irish recovered six fumbles, intercepted two passes, blocked one kick, and deflected another. Schwartz averaged 46 yards on his punts, a detail that might have saved a loss. Moose Krause blocked a kick and had several sacks.

The shutouts continued when Drake was annihilated 63-0. The Irish punted once; all other drives scored. Drake's best field position was the Notre Dame 46. Melinkovich scored two touchdowns, Koken three, and Bernie Leahy, Sheeketski, Jim Leonard, and Frank LaBorne one each. The best was Sheeketski's 45-yarder.

The shutout string ended against Pitt, but Notre Dame won 25-12. Jock Sutherland tried to stop Schwartz's running, so Marchy went to the air for two touchdowns. Melinkovich caught a pass for a 30-yard touchdown and also slammed in from the one.

Anderson took 115 players to face Carnegie Tech's 29. Still, Tech played a great game in a 19-0 loss, exactly reversing the 1926 score when Anderson subbed for Rockne. Leahy scored twice, a two-yard burst and a 13-yard run on a lateral. A fake spin play shook loose

1932

The Fighting Irish could start this season relatively untraumatized and unburdened. National media attention had diminished, and there was no streak to defend. The line was in great shape, especially with Kurth and Krause, but it would not be easy to replace two-time All-American Marchy Schwartz. Having a healthy Steve Banas would help.

Banas led the Fighting Irish to a 73-0 opening-season shutout of Haskell. His flashy running framed the win, with 54-yard and 74-yard touchdowns. In between he scored on a 10-yard run and with a 20-yard pass, while averaging 19 yards per carry for the game. Melinkovich scored three touchdowns, and Lowell Hagan scored one more to give the fullback position eight of 11 touchdowns. Al McGruff and Red Tobin added scores as Notre Dame racked up 673 yards.

Drake was the next victim, being trampled 62-0. Anderson had the team work on its passing game: the first score came on a 44-yard pass from Lukats to Ray Brancheau. Then Melinkovich ran 31 yards for a touchdown. Krause blocked a punt for a safety.

Carnegie Tech, in the early stages of what was to be a long football decline, lost 42-0, bringing the Irish score for the first three games of the year to an astounding 177-0. The 42-0 drubbing was the worst defeat for Carnegie Tech to that point. Mike Koken fumbled at Notre Dame's 10, but the Fighting Irish could not capitalize. Koken ran 58 yards for a touchdown on the next drive. He hit Norb Rascher with a 31-yard pass, and Laurie Vejar passed for the final nine yards to Sheeketski. Melinkovich scored from a foot out and Jaskwhich ran 66 yards for another. In the third quarter, Krause grabbed a fumble that led to a Brancheau score around left end. Lukats hit three different receivers on medium range passes and a 21-yard finale to Host. Banas wrapped it up when he scored from the one late in the game. Irish dominance was total 466 yards to 79 for Tech.

Pitt stopped the Notre Dame string of victories with its own shutout, a 12-0 upset (they had already beaten Army and tied Ohio State). The Fighting Irish seemed to be in control for three periods, driving well but not scoring. Pitt needed little more than one minute to win the game. Following an interception late in the fourth quarter, Sebastian ran 55 yards for another Pitt touchdown; another interception was also run back for a touchdown. The running games were about even, but Notre Dame hit only 10 of 29 passes.

Mike Koken, a speedster who backed up Marchy Schwartz for two seasons, then started at left half-back in 1932.

Notre Dame next went to Kansas and pounced the Jayhawks, 24-6. Kansas scored first through the air, which seemed to wake up the Fighting Irish. Lukats streaked 45 yards for a score and the extra-point conversion gave Notre Dame the lead. In the second period, Sheeketski ran 60 yards for another touchdown. Melinkovich scored on a 70-yarder in the third quarter. Koken wrapped it up with a three-yard touchdown dive.

Against Northwestern, Melinkovich took the opening kickoff 98 yards for a touchdown, taking the heat off the Fighting Irish ground game that was staring at the Wildcats's unusual 4-3-1-2-1 defense. Northwestern's defense was vulnerable to passes, however, and Notre Dame took advantage of that route. Kurth trapped their punter for a big loss to set up Koken's touchdown pass to Dom Vairo. On the next Irish drive, at the Northwestern six, Koken got the ball and did a double spinner before handing off to Kosky coming from around end, who lateralled to Jaskwhich, who had drifted wide as the Wildcats converged on Kosky, and sauntered in for the touchdown. Notre Dame won 21-0.

At Navy, Rip Miller scrapped the Midshipmen's wingback system and installed a Notre Dame offensive look. The Irish would be looking at a mirror image of themselves. Unfortunately, the game was played in a mudbath. The game was played in Sheeketski's hometown, Cleveland, and he scored twice before the field turned to Jell-O. He scored untouched from the 11 when he cut off a sweep to go inside. Navy's poor punting gave Notre Dame good field position and Emmett Murphy found Sheeketski alone in the right corner for a nine-yard touchdown pass. Later, Sheeketski intercepted a pass to stop a drive and cap his best day for the Fighting Irish.

The flu bug hit South Bend just before the game with Army in Yankee Stadium. The Cadets were favored, but had never beaten Notre Dame in consecutive outings. The Fighting Irish up-ended Army 21-0 in spite of the flu. The Irish defense stifled Army all day, while the offense twice drove to the Cadet five but stalled. The third time down, Koken faked a run and threw to Melinkovich for the touchdown. In the third quarter, Banas fired a 45-yard touchdown to Hugh Devore, who caught it with a broken hand. Guard Jim Harris scored on a busted punt snap to close the day. Devore continued his injured heroics with an interception and a fumble recovery.

USC was on a roll—18 straight wins. The Fighting Irish became number 19. Anderson had predicted a 13-0 USC win and that's what happened. Not since Nebraska in 1922 and 1923 had a team defeated Notre Dame in consecutive years. USC scored on a 31-yard pass play in the second quarter; in the third quarter Koken misplayed a USC quick kick to give USC great field position for a score seven plays later. Superior USC punting kept the Fighting Irish in the hole all day, and combined with good kick returns, the Trojans enjoyed a 200-yard advantage in that department alone. Otherwise, the teams were even.

Kurth, Krause, Melinkovich, and Kosky earned All-American honors.

1932 record: 7-2-0 (.777)
Record to date: 265-52-20 (.816)

1933

Not since 1888 had Notre Dame experienced a losing season. The success of Notre Dame football was breeding the difficult expectations that they would have a shot at the national title year in and year out. However, Anderson would steer the 1933 Irish to only three wins.

Following Rockne as he did, Hunk Anderson probably never had a chance and the 1933 season cinched it. The pool of Rockne's recruits was dwindling;

his last group were seniors in 1933. Recruiting was not going well. On paper, it was a good group, comparable to the 1925-1928 years. Moose Krause was the best college lineman. Wayne Millner, a sophomore, looked fine at left end. Don Elser, at 6'3" and 215 pounds, was the largest Notre Dame fullback since Eichenlaub. Lukats was solid at left halfback. The quality slipped at quarterback; Bud Bonar lacked speed. Two 1932 starters, Robinson and Melinkovich, were lost for the year because of illness, and Hanley was still out with a knee injury. Anderson's teams always played great defense (11 shutouts in 18 games), but the offense was suspect. In the four games where total scoring would be a touchdown or less, the Fighting Irish would win one, lose two, and tie one.

The season started with a 0-0 tie against Kansas. Notre Dame struggled to the Kansas 14 on the first possession, but could not score. That was it for the offense, but the defense played well. Kansas had only two scoring chances, both field goals; Notre Dame blocked one. A blocked Elser punt at the Notre Dame 13 gave Kansas another field goal try; but it was hurried as the offense was backing up before a Notre Dame line rush.

At Indiana, Notre Dame pulled out a 12-2 victory. Lukats had a fine run of 53 yards for a score in the second quarter, and Elser followed up a blocked punt for an 11-yard touchdown romp. Notre Dame's defense stopped the Hoosier running game, holding them to 30 yards,

Kitty Gorman, starting center and co-captain for the 1933 team.

USC's Cotton Warburton tries the Irish line in a Trojan shutout of the Irish in 1933. Wayne Millner (38) moves in.

while Notre Dame earned 223 yards. The Notre Dame passing game was invisible.

At Carnegie Tech, the Irish dug their own hole quickly when Red Tobin fumbled the opening kickoff at his 26. Tech scored on the next play, and the Irish never recovered. They reached the Tech 17 once, but misfired. Most of the game was spent in a punting duel. Notre Dame's passing was dismal: one completion in 10 tries for 12 yards.

Things got worse. Pitt dominated Notre Dame for a 14-0 win. The Irish offense was throttled: seven first downs to Pitt's 18, 97 yards rushing to Pitt's 251; and six of 16 passing for 96 yards. A Pitt interception set up a 78-yard touchdown, and another set up a 14-yard touchdown run. Notre Dame lost Brancheau with two broken ribs.

The Irish now had a scoreless streak of 10 quarters going, and Navy extended it to 14 with a 7-0 win. The Fighting Irish manhandled the Navy in all departments except the scoreboard. After the Navy score, Notre Dame put together an 85-yard march on two Banas passes, but an interception at the 15 ended the effort. The Fighting Irish held Navy to nine yards rushing for the game and only 37 yards in the air for an offensive production of 306 yards to 46, yet Navy won. In the turnover column, Navy dropped the ball five times but lost it only once; Notre Dame fumbled four times and lost three.

The scoreless streak reached 18 quarters when Purdue swamped the Irish 19-0. An intercepted Lukats pass earned a Purdue touchdown, and Purdue's offense

scored twice. Notre Dame reached the Purdue two-yard line late in the game but could not score.

Northwestern was next. Someone remembered the basic objective of the game as Notre Dame won 7-0. These points represented 20 percent of the scoring for

Bud Bonar, starting QB for the 1933 team, the worst offensive contingent in Irish history with only five TDs all season and 32 points.

the whole season. Krause blocked a Wildcat punt at their 13, Kitty Gorman recovered, and Andy Pilney took it in on two runs, the last an 11-yard reverse around the right end. The defense was merciless against Northwestern, allowing no pass completions and holding them to 46 yards on the ground.

USC beat Notre Dame 19-0 at South Bend. Cotton Warburton did most of the damage, gaining 95 yards on 18 carries for two short touchdowns early and late in the game. A short pass between his scores provided the final score. This was the first time since the Fighting Irish's humble beginnings against Michigan that a team had taken three in a row from Notre Dame.

Ten more scoreless quarters had passed before Notre Dame could score against Army. The Cadets were holding a 12-0 lead with five minutes to go; they were unbeaten and counting the votes for the national crown, when Moose Krause blocked an Army punt at the Notre Dame 48. Lukats ran to the 32-yard line, Millner picked up 13 yards on an end around; Millner gained the final 19 yards in four tries. Army had to punt again. Krause told Millner to stay put as he moved in tighter to the guard. Army read Krause as the "hot" man and left no one on Millner. Millner blocked the punt and scored a touchdown on the recovery. Red Tobin intercepted an Army pass to ice the 13-12 win. It was a magnificent win, but it was not enough to save Anderson's job. Officials announced that both Anderson and Harper resigned.

No one made an All-America team, but Krause should have.

1933 results: 3-5-1 (.388)
Record to date: 268-57-21 (.804)

1934

Elmer Layden, the quiet one of the Horsemen, was named head coach. He had played fullback at 160 pounds and helped beat Stanford with two long touchdown interceptions. He had coached at Columbia College in Iowa, and then Duquesne, where he compiled a 47-13-3 record in seven seasons. He also earned a law degree, but never used it.

At Notre Dame, he made some staff changes, keeping only Tom Conley and adding Joe Boland and Chet Grant. He stayed with the 1930s version of the shift. He also worked under a university-imposed limit on scholarships. He had a good mind for detail and a warm personality that wore well with the players. All in all, he was probably the right man for the job, even though Jimmy Crowley of Fordham, the jovial Horseman, also applied.

Layden had to rebuild the team's morale. At least he was not following a legend or coming on the heels

Texas's Hillard scores the winning TD of the 7-6 game in 1934.

of two undefeated seasons. There was less stridency for total Irish dominance. Layden was able to consolidate, much as Harper did in 1913.

His new team had more strengths than weaknesses, especially in the backfield. Fromhart looked good at quarterback, Elser was solid at fullback, Melinkovich was back at right halfback, and Bill Shakespeare was promising at left halfback. Moose Krause left a huge pair of shoes to fill. Millner was one of the best in the country at end. Overall, it was a larger team, with marginally better speed and good players in the pipeline.

Texas, coached by former Irish hero Jack Chevigny, came to the Dome and won a good game, 7-6. Layden wouldn't be burdened by ideas of instant success and the team did not look that bad in the loss. Gusty winds were a factor in both scores: Texas recovered a fumbled kickoff by Melinkovich and scored four plays later. In the second quarter, the Texas quarterback fumbled a punt, kicked it backwards, and dropped it again for John Michuta to recover near the goal. Melinkovich scored the touchdown three plays later, but Millner missed the conversion. The teams played even after that in a well-played game.

Missed conversions were instrumental in a lot of games at this time, but it should be noted that the kicker for the PAT came from the 11 men on the field at the time of the score. There was no wholesale changing of personnel (no special teams).

Jack Robinson, starting center in 1932 and 1934, played with severe eye problems, yet made All-American in 1934.

Layden broke into the win column the next week with an 18-7 triumph over Purdue. Three Irish touchdowns within a 10-minute span of the second quarter ruined Purdue's day: Melinkovich ran for a 60-yard touchdown; Fred Carideo intercepted a pass and ran it 70 yards for a score; and Melinkovich caught a 35-yard pass from Mike Layden and hammered twice from the three for the touchdown.

Beating Carnegie Tech 13-0 was a measure of the team's improvement in 1933. Shakespeare scored on a 56-yard run past right end. Andy Pilney hit Vairo with a 32-yard pass near the end zone just as three Tech defenders tackled him. He held on somehow and staggered in for the score. Pilney later broke up a Tech pass on the goal line to kill the only Tech threat.

Freezing sleet marred weather expectations for the last home game, against Wisconsin, but the Fighting Irish managed a 19-0 victory. Carideo scored off left tackle from the 10. In the third quarter, Melinkovich ran 38 yards for a touchdown around left end, and then a one-yard touchdown over left end again to end a drive. John Lautar preserved the shutout when he grabbed a Badger fumble at the Notre Dame 13.

Joe Sullivan replaced graduated Moose Krause at left tackle in 1934; died of pneumonia in 1935.

The 1934 backfield: from left, RH George Melinkovich, QB Bud Bonar (but Wally Fromhart would play most of the time), FB Don Elser (one of the largest Irish backs until the 1950s), and LH Andy Pilney.

Pittsburgh stopped the Irish momentum with a 19-0 win. Pitt's Nicksick scored twice, once on an interception return of 62 yards. Notre Dame's offense suffered a general breakdown—only 54 yards rushing and 34 yards passing. It was Pitt's third straight shutout of the Irish; they were closing in on Michigan's turn-of-the-century record of four straight.

The Irish once again pushed Navy all over the field in a losing 10-6 effort. Navy only had two scoring chances and made good on both, an early field goal and a pass for a 10-yard touchdown in the fourth quarter. To get the field goal, they blocked a Shakespeare punt. Their touchdown followed an interception and 35-yard return. Notre Dame moved at will between the 20-yard lines, but eight drives ended in Navy territory. They gained more than 300 yards total offense to Navy's 118 (with 47 on the ground). As Yogi Berra once said, more games are lost than won.

Northwestern was defeated 20-7. The Wildcats did well at first, although Notre Dame almost stopped them four times from the one. However, on the fourth down, Northwestern was able to push the ball across the goal line for the first score of the day. That was it for Northwestern. In the third quarter, Shakespeare's 24-yard throw to Melinkovich reached the 18, and two Melinkovich runs set up a short touchdown burst. A 17-yard pass from Pilney to Millner was followed by a 14-yard Pilney sweep for the touchdown. Melinkovich shook loose for a 40-yard gain to the four, and

Shakespeare rammed four times from there to end the scoring.

The following week, Shakespeare helped script a thrilling 12-6 win over Army with his first-quarter pass to Vairo for a 52-yard score. Pilney hit Hanley (playing for his third head coach) with passes for 48 yards, the second a 15-yard touchdown. It was a defensive game for both teams, with Notre Dame getting six first downs and Army only four. Superior Fighting Irish passing was the difference.

Passing again saved the day when Notre Dame beat USC 14-0. Shakespeare hit Layden with a 51-yard touchdown in the first quarter. In the next quarter, a long pass deflected off Warburton to Millner at the USC two, and Layden jammed it in. USC could not pass well, and that was the ball game.

It had been a quietly successful season, just what Notre Dame needed. Layden was building an effective operation rather than living off past merits. Jack Robinson returned from a missed year to earn All-America honors at center.

1934 record: 6-3-0 (.666)
Record to date: 274-60-21 (.801)

1935

Stabilized, the Notre Dame football program continued to come together, and Layden relied on the natural drawing power of Notre Dame in his recruiting. He was beginning to put together future dividends. There was a terrible loss in the spring when tackle Joe Sullivan died of pneumonia. The other tackle, John Michuta, would suffer a career-ending head injury in the third game. Millner was back to lead a solid line. The backfield was deep with talent and experience, and Layden's calm leadership kept competing players happy. Ohio State was added to the schedule.

Notre Dame opened with Kansas and was determined to avoid the 0-0 mishap of 1933. Layden's defense gave the Jayhawks only eight yards rushing and two pass completions in nine tries. Millner grabbed a fumble on Kansas's 26 and Carideo scored on a 15-yard sprint past a block by Millner. In the second period, Carideo had another 15-yard gain, followed by a two-yard touchdown plunge. Millner caught a 46-yard touchdown throw from Shakespeare and Notre Dame wrapped it up late in the game when Vic Wojcihovski concluded a 60-yard drive with a two-yard smash for the 28-7 final score.

Pitt Stadium had been the scene of Irish losses since 1931. The Fighting Irish let a Carnegie Tech 3-0 lead stand through the first half. Tech offered a tribute to Rockne at the half and maybe that helped the Irish. Shakespeare soon tallied a five-yard touchdown—the

Wayne Millner, three-year starter at LE, 1935 consensus All-American.

first Notre Dame score in Pittsburgh since 1931. In the fourth quarter, a 94-yard march of spinners, reverses, sweeps, and line smashes ended with a nine-yard score by Bob Wilke. Tech lost 14-3 and was held to 44 yards rushing and only 14 yards passing.

In Madison, Layden showed the Wisconsin Badgers an offense with as many tricks as possible (film was now a scouting tool). Passing earned the first two scores:

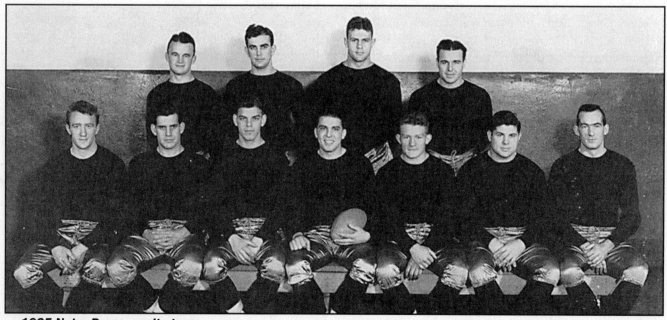

1935 Notre Dame varsity team.

Wojcihovski to Shakespeare for 19 and a touchdown, and in the second quarter, Pilney for five yards to Joe O'Neill. Then the Irish switched to a series of lateral passes before Carideo scored from the one. Pilney later scored, sprung by a Frank Gaul block, on a 40-yard sprint to close the scoring at 27-0. Millner earlier had blocked a punt and recovered the loose ball to help lead a defense that stymied the Badgers all day, allowing only 49 yards rushing.

A tough Pitt team visited the Dome, losing in a close 9-6 game. In the second quarter, Pitt scored first, on a two-yard plunge, but Millner showed them how to block a conversion try. Shortly after that, Shakespeare tied it up with a four-yard touchdown run. Later he rocketed an 86-yard punt to keep Pitt penned in. The teams went back and forth through most of the second half. With three minutes left, basketball player Marty Peters, made a 27-yard field goal. Fred Solari intercepted a Pitt pass in the final moments to end the game.

Pilney sunk Navy 14-0 with two second-quarter touchdown throws. He threw a long one to Frank Gaul, who had a convoy of Fighting Irish blockers, and later a three-yarder to Mike Layden, younger brother of Coach Layden. The defense kept Navy in home port the rest of the way.

Ohio State loomed next (in 1969, the centennial year of college football, this would be voted the "game

Bill Shakespeare, a two-time starter at LHB and a 1935 All-American, is best remembered as the man who threw the winning TD pass to Wayne Millner in the great 1935 win over Ohio State.

of the century" by the Associated Press). The 1935 Buckeyes were a razzle-dazzle team that used laterals almost indiscriminately—a very high-risk offense. They were very big, very physical, and had a bevy of fine backs. They manhandled the Fighting Irish in the first half. Their first score came when Antenucci intercepted a Layden pass and lateralled to Boucher, who was trailing the play; Boucher ran 65 yards for the score. Another interception started a 50-yard drive that ended in the second quarter when their brilliant sophomore, "Jumpin' Joe" Williams, slammed over for the score from the four.

Down 13-0 in front of 81,000 screaming Buckeyes, coach Layden quietly told his team to calm down, play steady ball, and announced that the second unit would start the second half. They were rested, determined, and experienced. He had faith in them.

Buckeye fans had spent the first half waving green hankies at the few Fighting Irish fans. But in the third quarter, Notre Dame's ends pinched down hard to the inside when they rushed so as to make the Ohio State laterals more dangerous to execute. Ohio State could not move, and when the quarter ended, Notre Dame was sitting on the Buckeyes's 12. Pilney got them there with a 28-yard punt return. Then he passed to Frank Gaul

Fred Carideo, cousin of Frank Carideo, started at FB in 1935.

to reach the two and Steve Miller took it in. But Notre Dame missed the point after for a 13-6 score. A later Fighting Irish drive ended when Miller lost a fumble. The Buckeyes eventually punted to the Notre Dame 20. There were three minutes to go.

Layden sent in the veterans. Pilney hit Fromhart, who had been open all day (because scouts said he was a blocking back), with a 37-yard pass. Pilney caught a nine-yard pass from Layden. Then Pilney passed to Fromhart to the 15, and again for the touchdown. But Notre Dame missed another conversion.

The Fighting Irish tried an onside kick but Ohio State retained possession. The Buckeyes fed the ball to Dick Beltz, who was "belted" between Danbom and Pilney. The ball went skittering toward the sideline where Notre Dame's Henry Pojman, subbing at center, recovered it. On the second play after the fumble, Pilney ran through a gap over center for a 30-yard gain to the 19. But Pilney was writhing with torn knee cartilage. He tried to watch from his stretcher.

Shakespeare replaced him. They had to pass and Beltz intercepted—but dropped it. There were 32 seconds left. Layden had a problem—he was out of subs, except for Jim McKenna (whom Layden had asked to pay his own way to the game). Layden sent him in with the play.

John Michuta, starting RT in 1934 and 1935, was injured in the third game of 1935 to end his career.

The ball was snapped to the fullback, who handed it off to Shakespeare on what appeared to be a reverse as the ends ran a crossing pattern. Then Shakespeare threw to Millner for the winning touchdown. Pilney missed it as they took him to the lockers. He heard the noise, though—81,000 gasps. True to form, the Fighting Irish missed the conversion, ending the game 18-13. The game was won on passing; Notre Dame hit 10 of 21 for 140 yards, while the Buckeyes managed only two of four for seven yards. The incredulous fans just milled around the silenced stadium.

The team returned to South Bend and found that students had been dismissed early from classes to vent their joy—for three days. But the team had to go on with its season, and Northwestern was next. The expected letdown came, and the Fighting Irish dropped this game, the first to the Wildcats since 1901, and dashed their emerging hopes for a national championship. Notre Dame scored first when Elser boomed in from the 13, but a penalty negated it. Fromhart later scored from the one-foot line. Northwestern, scoring in the second half, held on fiercely. Shakespeare shook loose on a 48-yard sprint to the 10, but holding brought it back. Fromhart lost a late fumble and that cinched the 14-7 Irish loss.

The following week against Army, the Cadets scored first on a 40-yard pass to Grove, and then hung on until late in the fourth quarter. Monk Meyer grabbed a Fighting Irish fumble and ran 50 yards, but Notre Dame stiffened and Army punted. From their own 15,

Andy Pilney, hero of the fantastic resurgent win over Ohio State in 1935.

Fromhart moved the Irish to the Army 29. Shakespeare threw to Millner, and an interference call put the ball on the Army one. With 29 seconds left, Danbom powered over for the touchdown. Fromhart missed the point after to conclude a great 6-6 game.

Finally, USC. The Trojans scored first from the six, after Elser fumbled the ball on his 18. The lead stayed that way through the half. The Irish opened up in the second half with Mike Layden throwing a 38-yard touchdown to Fromhart. Then Fromhart hit Millner with a 44-yard touchdown pass, caught on his fingertips. USC fired back with a 24-yard touchdown pass. Notre Dame was ahead 14-13. They exchanged possessions, then Fromhart iced the 20-13 win when he returned an interception 72 yards to the USC eight. Shakespeare scored from there. Layden sent in the limping Pilney for one play.

The Irish were back, only one bad game and a conversion away from being undefeated. Millner, Pilney, and Shakespeare made All-America teams.

1935 record: 7-1-1 (.833)
Record to date: 281-61-22 (.802)

1936

Layden had a few problems to solve in 1936. Two All-America left halfbacks (Pilney and Shakespeare) were gone. Millner was gone—and also seven others. John Lautar would anchor the line. There were some fine replacements: Joe Kuharich, Andy Puplis, and Joe Zwers. But overall, the Fighting Irish were too green.

Andy Puplis, starting QB for the 1936 and 1937 Irish.

Fortunately, the first half of the schedule would allow them some learning time before the heavyweights showed up.

Carnegie Tech lost 21-7, as did Washington University of St. Louis, 14-6. However, Notre Dame played an uninspired game against Washington University. Danbom hammered several times to score from the four and O'Neill caught a 12-yard touchdown pass from Bob Wilke. Washington University managed one score near the end.

The game with Wisconsin the following week started slowly; a Notre Dame touchdown in the first half was the only action. Wilke earned it on a 17-yard

The 1936 coaches: Joe Boland, Bill Cerney, Johnny O'Brien, Chet Grant, Elmer Layden.

Art Cronin, starter at RT for the 1936 Irish.

scamper to end an 80-yard drive. In the third quarter, Fred Mundee blocked a Badger punt and Wojcihovski scored two plays later. Third-string halfback George Kovalcik threw a 52-yard pass to Len Skoglund, who reached the Wisconsin four. Chuck Borowski, with the fourth string, banged in from there. The subs scored once more, and Ben Binkowski preserved the 27-0 shutout with an interception at the Notre Dame 10.

The Pitt Panthers demolished Notre Dame 26-0 in a game the Fighting Irish played poorly. They made their first first down with 15 seconds left in the third quarter. Pitt gained 310 rushing yards to Notre Dame's 58 rushing and 26 passing. Three Pitt drives were long, meticulous affairs led by Marshall Goldberg, a sophomore.

The Ohio State game started as a rerun of 1935, with the Buckeyes muscling Notre Dame all over the Fighting Irish home turf. They drove to the Irish three but Joe Gleason intercepted. Notre Dame stalled on the ensuing series, and its punt was blocked out of the end zone for a safety. The Fighting Irish didn't panic but used up much of the second quarter on a drive that ended with a Bunny McCormick touchdown. The second half was played in torrential rain that ruined the field. The two teams did not meet again until 1995. The Irish won this second meeting 7-2.

Notre Dame's offensive problems continued against Navy, where the Irish lost 3-0. The Irish reached the

Navy four, but fumbled three plays later. They reached the 12 but were intercepted. Navy played ball control and kicked well to win.

Layden needed a win over Army or the season would look very bleak. The defense saved the day in a 20-6 win. Army marched right away, 73 yards to the Notre Dame six, but Andy Puplis intercepted a pass. Army did the same a quarter later and reached the Notre Dame five, but could not score. Wilke led a 57-yard march for the Irish, hitting Puplis for a 36-yard gain, before taking it in from the two. After the half, Army came out with a combination of laterals and passes, but the Fighting Irish converted a fumble recovery and intercepted a pass for their last two scores. After Cronin fell on a fumble, Wilke scored on a fake reverse from the 15. Andy Puplis ran in from the three after Lautar grabbed a Cadet pass. Notre Dame's defense stopped Army's offense in the second half, allowing only six net yards (Army's Monk Meyer dashed 60 yards for their score on a punt return).

Northwestern came in ranked number one, but self-destructed for a 26-6 Fighting Irish win. Three Wildcat errors ended up as scores for Notre Dame. Wilke made carbon-copy touchdown runs of 30 yards in the first two quarters, and Joe O'Neill grabbed the loose ball after an Irish quick kick was muffed. Danbom scored three plays later. A six-yard shovel pass from McCarthy to Skoglund ended the Irish scoring in the fourth quarter. Notre Dame's defense did not allow Northwestern to complete a pass.

Hard-charging, speedy Larry Danbom, starter for the 1936 Irish at FB.

Joe O'Neill, starter at RE for the 1936 team.

Len Skoglund started at RE for the 1937 Irish.

Notre Dame had a modest two-win streak going over USC; neither had won three straight since the series started. A 13-13 tie kept it that way. The Fighting Irish scored on a 78-yard, 12-play drive, with Wilke scoring off tackle from the three. He had earlier hit McCormick with a 32-yard pass. USC scored on a busted play, a half lateral, half fumble that broke for 65 yards. The Fighting Irish drove right back to the USC nine. Puplis went for it all, but a USC reserve named Langley intercepted and took it 100 yards for a Trojan touchdown. In the third quarter, Notre Dame drove 88 yards in 12 plays, ending with Wilke's 15-yard touchdown pass to McCormick. Puplis missed a field goal a little later to ensure a tie. Notre Dame won the statistics: 18 first downs to one; 223 yards rushing to 24; 138 yards passing to 23.

John Lautar was the only player to earn All-America honors.

1936 record: 6-2-1 (.722)
Record to date: 287-63-23 (.800)

1937

Many question marks arose as the new season approached. There were no obvious stars, but the team looked sound. There were no game-breaking backs that the Notre Dame system demanded. The backs were smallish; Bunny McCormick was the smallest to start in more than a decade. Puplis was stable at quarterback. His backup, Joe Ruetz, made a strange switch from quarterback to left guard. Alec Shellogg would develop into a great tackle.

Notre Dame opened the season against Drake. Layden used 53 players in a 21-0 exercise. Jack McCarthy lobbed a five-yard touchdown pass to McCormick in the second quarter. In the third quarter, Kuharich

Alec Shellog, starter at RT for the 1937 team, had a twin brother playing for the reserves.

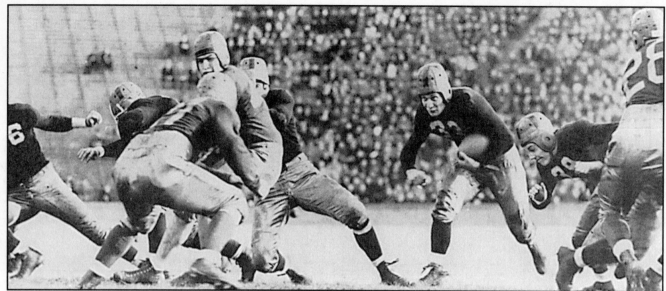

Fullback Joe Thesing finds a big hole in the 1937 USC game. Jack McCarthy (39) blocks to the right of the picture.

intercepted a pass deep in Notre Dame territory. McCarthy then ran 85 yards for the touchdown. He intercepted a pass later to set up Mario Tonelli's closing touchdown.

Illinois's Bob Zuppke, a great coach, innovator, and amateur artist, was celebrating his silver anniversary as the Illini mentor. The University of Illinois fought the Fighting Irish to a 0-0 tie. Illinois missed a 14-yard field goal, and Notre Dame missed on three passes from the 12. Beyond that, it was a dull game. Lou Zontini, a third-string back, led all runners with 40 yards.

Next, Carnegie Tech upset Notre Dame 9-7. The defense played the typical hard-nosed football that Layden's teams specialized in, and the offense accumulated good yardage but only scored on a 34-yard pass from McCarthy to McCormick. The Fighting Irish lost the game when a Zontini pass was picked off to set up the winning field goal from the 16. Notre Dame

Jack McCarthy, starting LHB for the 1937 team.

Bunny McCormick, the 1937 team's starting RHB.

fought to the Tech one in the fourth quarter, but for the fourth time in the young season, failed to score. Tech gained only seven yards on the ground and completed one pass, and still won. Carnegie Tech would drop football in only a few seasons.

The Fighting Irish offense continued to sputter against Navy, although they escaped with a 9-7 win. The game was played in snow; neither team threw any passes. The Middies dominated for three quarters, scoring on an Irish fumble. McCarthy got the only Fighting Irish touchdown on a 31-yard run. Puplis ran back a Navy punt 54 yards to the Midshipmen's eight, but a fourth-down fumble lost the ball. Moments later Navy had to punt; the snap was low and the kicker tried to run it out. Notre Dame's Chuck Sweeney engulfed him from his right end spot for a safety and the win.

Similar heroics led to a 7-6 win over heavily favored Minnesota. Sweeney did it again, blocking a Gopher conversion attempt. The Fighting Irish scored early and the defense had to hang on. Puplis scored on a 35-yard run to the Gopher 34 and then went in from the 2-yard line moments later. The Minnesota score came on a double lateral that turned into a pass for a touchdown. The Irish nullified the extra-point attempt to preserve the victory over Minnesota. It was not an artistic success, but the Fighting Irish defense was a force.

Jock Sutherland's powerhouse Pitt team crunched the Fighting Irish 21-6 for his 100th win, keeping them undefeated for the year. Notre Dame played well in the

first half and held the lead into the fourth quarter on a touchdown pass from McCarthy to Puplis. But in the fourth quarter, Goldberg rifled a 51-yard pass to set up a plunge for Pitt's first touchdown. Then they intercepted a wayward Irish pass, leading to a 22-yard touchdown run on a fake reverse. Pitt picked up the pace in its passing game, and Notre Dame's defense never recovered. A third touchdown put the game away. Pitt runners gained 328 yards, with Goldberg claiming 110 yards. The Fighting Irish defense had not been battered that way all season.

Notre Dame beat Army 7-0, scoring only the lone touchdown, despite six Irish ventures into scoring territory. The Fighting Irish scored first and then weathered the storm. Ed Simonich scored after Ed Beinor recovered a fumble on a botched Statue of Liberty play at the Army 14. Simonich took it in from the three-yard line. A penalty killed a drive to the Army six when the trainer was on the field without benefit of a timeout. They lost a sure touchdown when Thesing fumbled on a plunge from the Cadet one. The defense held Army to 99 total yards, with only 27 on runs.

If anything, the offense looked worse the following week against Northwestern. Notre Dame did not score, and neither did Northwestern. Chuck Sweeney beat Northwestern, it seems, by himself: he blocked a Wildcat punt and recovered it for the only score; he recovered a fumble; he intercepted a pass; he downed an Irish punt at the Northwestern one-yard line; and he teamed with Alec Shellogg to recover another fumble. It was Notre Dame's fourth shutout of the year.

The Fighting Irish sneaked past USC 13-6 in the season finale. The Trojans dominated the first half, and led 6-0 after a touchdown pass. Puplis scored in the third quarter following a 58-yard run in which he started right, reversed his field to pick up blockers, and then steamed down the sidelines. Tonelli ran 70 yards to the USC 13, and two plays later took it in on an eight-yard scamper. For once, Notre Dame's offense clicked, doubling USC's yardage (301 to 155 yards), with 26 yards on the ground.

Layden must have been relieved when the season ended. Sweeney and Beinor earned All-American recognition.

1937 record: 6-2-1 (.722)
Record to date: 293-65-24 (.798)

Joe Zwers captained the 1937 Fighting Irish, but did not start.

1938

The 1928 Fighting Irish had been a low-scoring team (4.2 points per game) with a good defense, and national championships followed. The 1937 season mirrored that of 1928, and the results would be remarkably similar. In 1929, the Fighting Irish averaged 16.1 points; Layden's 1938 Fighting Irish would average 16.5 points up from 4.3 the year before.

Layden had a solid core of veterans; Beinor anchored the line and was joined by future All-American Jim McGoldrick. Steve Sitko won the quarterback job. Lou Zontini and Harry Stevenson were halfbacks; the fullback position was stacked with Tonelli, Thesing, newcomer Milt Piepul, and dependable Ed Simonich.

Kansas, with future basketball coaching great Ralph Miller at the quarterback helm, opened the season. Notre Dame dismantled the Jayhawks 52-0 (this would be almost a third of Notre Dame's points for the year). Subs scored five touchdowns. Benny Sheridan scored twice and Bob Saggau had the best run of the day, a 51-yard sprint for a touchdown. The defense intercepted five Kansas passes. Tonelli started the scoring with a six-yard end run. In the second quarter, Sheridan sped 30 yards for a score, followed shortly by Simonich's 11-yard touchdown run. They kept up the pace in the third quarter: Zontini ran 25 yards for a touchdown; Earl Brown caught a 30-yard touchdown pass from Harry Stevenson; Sheridan went off tackle on a reverse from the 13. In the fourth, Saggau scored and Piepul went

Steve Sitko, starting QB for the Irish in 1938 and 1939.

in from the six. The ground game amassed 392 yards, the best in years.

The Fighting Irish went to Atlanta to meet a good Georgia Tech team and escaped with a 14-6 squeaker. Zontini's interception set up a 42-yard run and nine-yard touchdown by Tonelli. John Gubanich blocked a Tech punt in the fourth quarter, before "We The" Piepul rammed in from the one, and the Irish capitalized with runs of 17 and 10 by Sheridan. Both teams ran well but had difficulties with their passing games.

The 1938 Fighting Irish.

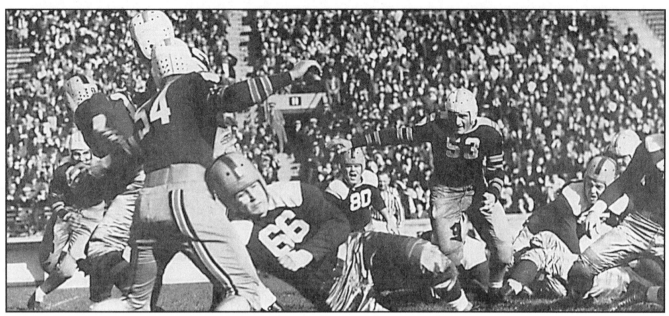

John Gubanich (66) blocks a Kansas player in the 1938 opener over Kansas.

Back home, the Irish met Zuppke's Illini and repeated the Tech score, 14-6, on good running and stern defense. Stevenson threw a 47-yard touchdown pass to Earl Brown for the first score, taking the lead into the third quarter. Then Sheridan intercepted an Illinois pass and streaked 68 yards for the score. The Illini blocked a punt and scored, but center Ed Longhi ended the Illini's hopes with an interception on the Irish nine. Notre Dame wasted three good drives on fumbles, but ran for 264 yards, while holding Illinois to 70 yards running, and only three completed passes.

Carnegie Tech's football program was not dead yet, dominating the Fighting Irish for three quarters before an official's error broke their momentum. With the ball on fourth down, the Tech quarterback asked about the down situation; the umpire said it was third down. Tech ran its play before the official recognized his mistake; he then had no choice but to give the ball to the Fighting Irish. Tech protested vigorously, but to no avail. The Irish had it at the Tech 36; Piepul ran to the 18. Sheridan ran for 10 more but fumbled; however, Bud Kerr recovered the ball for the Irish at the Tech 7. Kerr got the call for an end around and scored the game-winning touchdown. Both teams had played brilliant defense.

In the next game, Army tested Notre Dame's defense when it took the kickoff and executed a 73-yard drive, ending with a five-yard touchdown pass. Piepul brought the ensuing kickoff back 43 yards, but the Irish drive stalled, and despite John Kelly's recovery of a Cadet fumble, Army's 7-0 lead held into the second

half. In the third quarter, from short punt formation, Thesing took the ball up the middle for 34 yards. From the same formation, Saggau lofted a 46-yard touchdown pass to Brown, but Notre Dame missed the point after. Army stifled Notre Dame's next drive, but Saggau hit

Jack McGoldrick, captain of the 1938 national champions, and starting LG.

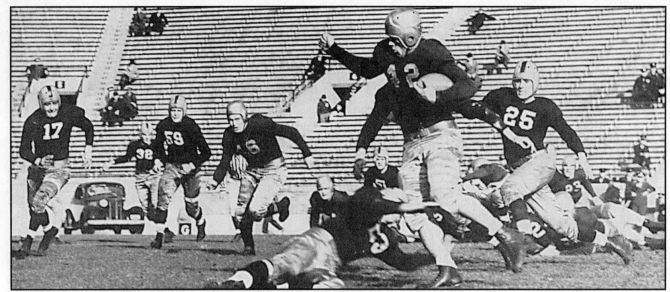

Carnegie Tech's Muha about to be finished off in a 7-0 Irish win in 1938. Zontini makes the first contact as Bossu (17), Stevenson (32), McGoldrick (59), and Brown (25) close in to end the play.

a 74-yard punt to keep Army on the defensive. In the fourth quarter, Bud Kerr blocked a punt, Bud Hofer recovered, and Sheridan slipped in from the half-yard mark for the second Irish score. Notre Dame wrapped it up with a Thesing touchdown of 48 yards. Good defense held Army to 49 yards to Notre Dame's 260 as the Irish prevailed 19-7.

The Fighting Irish defeated Navy next, 15-0. Saggau scored first, from the seven, to end an 80-yard drive on the ground. Johnny Kelly grabbed a Navy fumble in the third quarter, and Thesing converted it into an Irish touchdown. Subs tallied a safety in the fourth quarter for the final margin of victory.

Notre Dame's 300th win was against Minnesota, 19-0. Zontini started with an 84-yard run early in the first quarter. Minnesota never recovered. In the second period, Saggau found Brown open for a 48-yard scoring toss; and he hit Kelly with a 13-yarder in the final quarter. Notre Dame's pass defense allowed Minnesota only five completions in 18 tries for one yard.

Northwestern bowed 9-7. Bill Hofer insured the Notre Dame win with a 65-yard touchdown return on an interception in the second quarter, and a 20-yard field goal in the third quarter. Northwestern ran well, but the Fighting Irish did not pass well, which accounted for the close game.

The eight-game Irish winning streak ended when USC shut out the Fighting Irish 13-0. Notre Dame's offense choked, losing two fumbles and three interceptions. USC scored on a pass from Day to Krueger in the second quarter, and Anderson took it in from

the three after a Piepul fumble. Three interceptions late in the game spelled doom for the Fighting Irish. Their ground game never materialized. The loss cost them any hopes of an undisputed national title.

Beinor was a consensus All-American; Earl Brown and McGoldrick made honorable mention.

1938 record: 8-1-0 (.888)
Record to date: 301-66-24 (.800)

1939

The powerful Notre Dame backfield returned intact for the 1939 season. Thesing and Piepul powered the fullback operation while Sitko, Zontini, and Stevenson had good speed as a unit and plenty of experience. Three All-Americans were gone from the left side, so a strong running game was not likely.

Layden's fears were substantiated when Notre Dame hung on to beat Purdue 3-0 in the season opener. There was no passing game, and Notre Dame's running was modest. Third-string quarterback John Kelleher hit the winning field goal in the third quarter, but it was not a satisfying win.

Georgia Tech made the trip north the following week, and played tough football before bowing 17-14. Stevenson hit a field goal in the first quarter, the eventual winning margin, which served as a keynote for the year as the kicking game would have to work well for Notre

1939 Notre Dame Fighting Irish.

Dame to win. Tech blocked a punt in the next quarter and earned a touchdown to go ahead 7-3. Notre Dame responded with two scores when Saggau slammed in from the six-yard line and Thesing from the four-yard line on consecutive drives. The third period was dull, but Tech was learning that Notre Dame was vulnerable to the pass. Tech scored again to pull within three, and then watched as a last-gasp pass went off the fingers of an open receiver. The Fighting Irish offense had 246 yards running, but only five yards in the air.

In the third game of the season, the Fighting Irish twice had to overhaul the SMU Mustangs to win 20-19. SMU jumped on a Thesing fumble in the first quarter and turned it into a touchdown. Notre Dame came back with two passes, one netting an interference call and the other a 21-yard touchdown from Stevenson to Zontini. In the second quarter, the Mustangs drove 69 yards for a go-ahead touchdown. Notre Dame then went 67 yards the other way in 13 plays, with Piepul carrying seven times; he finally scored from the one-foot line. In the

The 1939 starting backfield: RH Zontini, FB Thesing, QB Sitko, LH Saggau.

Saggau rips for a TD in the 17-14 win over Georgia Tech in 1939.

fourth quarter, Piepul ran 10 yards around right end to cap another drive. Kelleher kicked the important point after. With two minutes to go, SMU blocked a punt at the Notre Dame two-yard line, and "Presto" Johnson scored, pulling SMU within a point. But SMU missed its conversion and Notre Dame won its third straight game on the strength of its kicking play.

Notre Dame won a 14-7 game over Navy to go 4-0 for the season. Notre Dame backs ran for 419 yards to Navy's 33. Sheridan opened the second quarter with a 26-yard touchdown thrust. A 64-yard drive, highlighted by Piepul's 22-yard burst, ended when Piepul tumbled in from the half-yard mark. Navy finally scored on a 64-yard pass late in the game. The Fighting Irish had another woeful passing day—one completion for 0 yards.

Bud Kerr, starting LE for the 1939 squad.

Ed Longhi, starter at center for the 1939 national champions and an All-American.

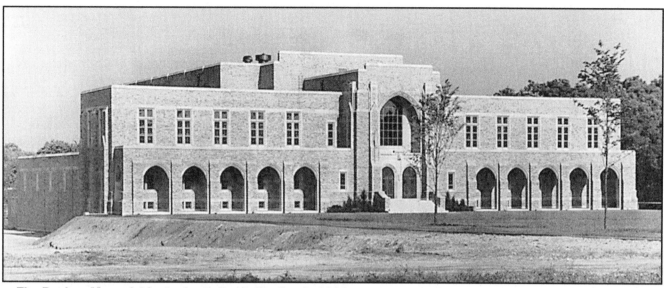

The Rockne Memorial just prior to its dedication in 1939.

Interior of the Rockne Memorial lobby.

Offensive consistency and balance were missing from the Notre Dame game.

Snow and Carnegie Tech in Pittsburgh were a tough combination. Notre Dame escaped 7-6, with the defense winning the game. A Tech runner was squeezed by a triple Irish hit, the ball went straight up, and an alert Bud Kerr picked it out of the air and scored from the 19. Zontini made the point after. In the fourth quarter, Tech was unstoppable on an 89-yard touchdown drive, but on the conversion kick, Notre Dame's center, John McIntyre, slammed through his blocker and took the ball in his chest to save the win.

Undefeated after five games, the Fighting Irish had outscored their opposition by a total of only 15 points. In their sixth game against Army, the Fighting Irish beat the Cadets 14-0, but the offense did not have that much to do with it. Both Notre Dame scores came from Cadet errors. A second-quarter fumble on Army's 31 was recovered by Notre Dame's Jack Finneran; Stevenson scored from the six-yard line on a sweep. In the fourth quarter, Steve Bagarus intercepted an Army pass and streaked down the sidelines for 45 yards and a touchdown, evading six Cadets.

Notre Dame next faced the University of Iowa, and Iowa standout Nile Kinnick, who was only weeks away from winning the Heisman. Kinnick scored on a four-yard plunge, and dropkicked the point after. Kinnick's score followed Sitko's interception, who then lost the ball to the Hawkeyes with an ill-advised lateral. Late in the third quarter, Piepul also tallied from the four, but Zontini missed the point after to clinch a 7-6 Iowa win.

Ed Beinor, two-year starter at LT, All-American in 1939 for the national champions.

Notre Dame managed a 7-0 squeaker over Northwestern to raise its season record to 7-1. It was a dull affair, punctuated only by Sheridan's non-scoring 52-yard run in the second quarter. In the third quarter, Bob Hargrave returned a punt 50 yards, and with 3:30 remaining Piepul went in for a five-yard touchdown. The defense held on for the win.

USC won the season finale 20-12. Trojans Lansdell and Schindler accounted for USC's three touchdowns, the latter on a 40-yard run. Piepul bulled in from the six and Sheridan jetted 60 yards to account for Notre Dame's scoring. A last-second drive by the Irish reached the USC seven but died there. The Fighting Irish almost sacked Trojan passers six times, but missed each time. Notre Dame had three fumbles and three interceptions, which was more than enough to offset 291 yards of offense to USC's 246. It was Notre Dame's 400th game.

Knowledgeable observers could see that change was needed to keep the Fighting Irish among the nation's elite teams. The old Notre Dame box and the shift could not operate as originally designed. The idea for the modern T was forming in Stanford's Clark Shaughnessey's head. It was only a matter of time before Irish football would have to make a clean break from the Rockne-influenced tactical past. Still, the 1939 season should be appreciated as a minor gem, with Layden the jeweler who knew how to make it shine more than it should have. Bud Kerr and Piepul won All-America honors to add to the luster.

1939 record: 7-2-0 (.777)
Record to date: 308-68-24 (.800)

1940-1949

1940

Administrative changes at Notre Dame may have portended the end of the "de-emphasis" of football under which Layden had worked. A new President, Fr. Hugh O'Donnell—the 1915 starting center—understood football as an insider. Still, the opinion about the Layden years was tending toward disillusionment. This "quiet one" of the Four Horsemen did not quite seem able to put the team over the top. But Layden still had a job to do.

He had to rebuild the line. Player turnover was high; he seemed to be getting only one to two years of starting time from them. Subs filled in the line's holes, except for sophomore flash Bob Dove at left end. The backfield had to be replaced, but the reserve backs had enjoyed more playing time, so the transition was easier. Piepul started at fullback, Saggau and Juzwik ran as halfbacks, and Bob Hargrave was quarterback.

The Irish first faced Amos Alonzo Stagg and his Pacific team. Stagg had coached four times against Notre Dame in the 1890s and never lost. He was in his 51st year of coaching. It was also "National Knute Rockne

Week," a promotional device for the soon-to-be-released motion picture starring Pat O'Brien and Ronald Reagan.

Pacific scored right away, using a mix of passes and trick plays on a 60-yard march, ended by a one-yard touchdown up the middle. But in the second period, Saggau threw to Juzwik for 40 yards to the Pacific 25. Piepul waited for an incompletion, then ran 18 yards to the seven. Juzwik faked a reverse and scored. Tied until the middle of the third quarter, Notre Dame blew it open with three touchdowns. Bernie Crimmins went in from the 16 with a run around end. Piepul ran 17 yards, starting right and then cutting back to the middle, to score. He then intercepted a pass on the Pacific 20, and Juzwik ran a cut back to score on the next play. Notre Dame had finally beaten Stagg, 25-7.

Georgia Tech, historically tough for the Irish, visited next. Notre Dame moved the ball well in the opening quarter but did not score. They scored in the second quarter on an 87-yard drive in seven plays, ending in a touchdown pass from Saggau to Hargrave. Two minutes later Saggau streaked off left tackle and ran 60 yards for another score. Saggau and Steve Bagarus traded passes to each other before Saggau scored from the five-yard line. Tech's John Hancock returned a kickoff

Layden's last coaching staff, 1940: Bill Cerney, Chet Grant, Elmer Layden, Joe Benda, Joe Boland.

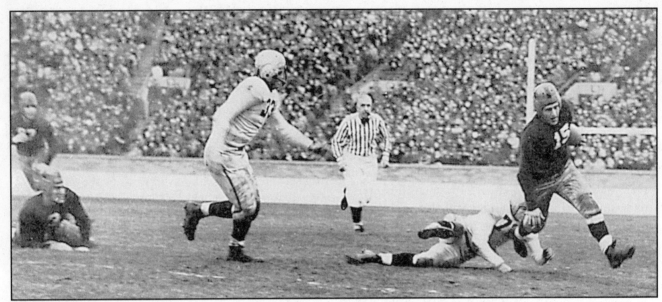

Steve Juzwik evades Iowa's Strauss as Enich moves in; Iowa won this 1940 game 7-0.

90 yards for a touchdown. Bernie Crimmins blocked a Tech punt, and Jim Brutz collected it in the end zone for Notre Dame's fourth TD of the day. Tech scored twice more in the fourth quarter, but Notre Dame held them off for the 26-20 win.

Carnegie Tech was sent packing 61-0, the largest score of Layden's years. Tech was helpless, entering Fighting Irish territory only in the third quarter against the fourth-string defense. Notre Dame scored nine touchdowns. Bernie Crimmins led with three, Piepul and sub Al Lee had two each, and Johnny O'Brien and Juzwik had one each.

Following the victory over Carnegie Tech, the largest crowd in 11 seasons met the Irish in Champaign for the game with the University of Illinois. Layden's subs struck, with Dippy Evans passing to Bagarus from the six for the touchdown. Late in the opening quarter, with the starters in, Juzwik rammed for 17 yards and then Saggau threw to him for a 29-yard touchdown. In the next period, Saggau threw a three-yard scoring pass to Crimmins. In the fourth quarter, Notre Dame wrapped it up with a 63-yard march crowned by Juzwik's six-yard run past left end for the final score, 26-0. The Irish ran for 262 yards to 26 for Illinois.

Army played inspired football to hold the Fighting Irish to a pathetic three yards of total offense in the first half, but the Cadets also made some big errors. With the ball about 15 yards from the right sideline, the Army quarterback tried to pass across the field to the wide side. Juzwik picked it off cleanly and headed for the end zone, but the Cadet quarterback had the angle on him.

Juzwik slowed a bit and the potential tackler overran the play. He then cut back to go 80 yards for the only score of the game. It was a replay of the Elder touchdown in 1929; even the sideline was the same. Army also missed a short field goal try, fumbled at the Notre Dame 14 (Dove recovering), and lost another interception in the third quarter to kill a drive. Army won the statistics as the Irish passing game earned 0 yards, but Notre Dame won the game 7-0.

Luck and good scouting beat Army; but it was Saggau who beat Navy the following week. In the first quarter, he passed to Dove for a 32-yard score and a 6-0 Notre Dame lead. Navy cruised to Notre Dame's 15 twice in the second quarter but could not score. The Midshipmen finally punched over a touchdown and took the lead on the extra point. This lead stood until the fourth quarter when Saggau scored from the seven behind great blocking. The offense was atrocious; good defense with three interceptions saved the day in the 13-7 Irish win.

After two ugly offensive outings, something had to give against Iowa. It did; the offense failed to materialize, and Notre Dame lost its first game of the year, 7-0 to Iowa. The loss was considered a giant upset, since Iowa had lost four straight while Notre Dame had won six straight. The defenses dominated a scoreless affair into the fourth quarter. Then, Notre Dame muscled a drive to the Iowa one but couldn't score. After an Iowa punt, Notre Dame drove again to the 10. Piepul coughed up one of his two career fumbles. Iowa drove, punted, intercepted a Saggau pass, moved to the Irish 25—and

Milt Piepul on his way to a gain around left end in 1940 action with Georgia Tech. Tech's Sanders (8) leaps over Bassas (66), Gubanich (69) and Hargrave (3).

missed a field goal. Notre Dame had the ball for only one play on the ensuing drive and fumbled. Two plays later Iowa scored. Notre Dame had self-destructed with four fumbles in the final five minutes.

The Fighting Irish troubles continued, as they were drubbed by Northwestern, 20-0. Bill De Correvont played a fine game for the Wildcats, throwing one touchdown pass and scoring from the four for another. Notre Dame had been shut out eight straight quarters.

Notre Dame would win the next close one, 10-6, over USC. The weather provided a broiling day; all the scoring was in the first half before everybody dehydrated. Sixteen USC players had been hospitalized with the flu the week of the game. Piepul made a first-quarter field goal. (Layden had four game-winning field goals kicked in his Notre Dame coaching career by four players who booted only once.) USC scored on a split buck play that broke for a 54-yard touchdown. Juzwik saved a touchdown, tackling a Trojan who had gained 45 yards. Notre Dame's winning drive started with Dippy Evans at quarterback, who fired a 46-yard pass to Ray Ebli; Piepul ended the scoring and his career with a three-yard touchdown moments later. Saggau intercepted a USC pass in the third quarter to save the win.

Two months later, Layden announced his resignation to become the NFL commissioner. He had won 47, lost 13, and tied three for a .770 percentage. He had also saved a deteriorating situation and consolidated matters under stringent Notre Dame rules.

Piepul earned All-America honors.

1940 record: 7-2-0 (.777)
Record to date: 315-70-24 (.799)

1941

When the 1941 season rolled around, times were tense, as world events gyrated out of control. As a result of WWII, life seemed to be lived with greater purpose in 1941. The decision to hire Frank Leahy to replace Layden (Buck Shaw withdrew) matched the intensity of the day.

Leahy was tough, shrewd, intense, and dedicated to a fault. A marginal player his first two years at Notre Dame, he started at tackle in 1929, and again in 1930, until injuries sidelined him. While with Rockne at the Mayo Clinic, he decided to go into coaching. He coached at Georgetown, Michigan State (with Jimmy Crowley), Fordham (where he coached Vince Lombardi and with Bud Wilkinson), and Boston College in 1939 and 1940 where he was undefeated, including an upset win over Tennessee in the Cotton Bowl. Leahy paid attention to detail—any detail, anywhere, any time. He later even kept a bed in his office at Notre Dame so he could collapse there rather than go home. He was almost as hard on his players as he was on himself, except that the players did not become physically sick, as he did, over missed assignments, busted plays, and—the worst of all—losses. They'd better come close to getting sick, though, or they didn't play for "The Man."

Leahy had the best and the worst of football in him. He could bend the rules in his favor and was blindly devoted to a game, seeing it as an end, letting it dominate his life and his players' lives for so long each year that their existence seemed one-dimensional. Yet, the players loved him for his drive, determination, dedication, and supreme willingness to encourage them to get the most out of themselves. He believed that one always strives for perfection, never slacks off, and never takes the easy way out. Rockne had preached the same message, but with humor that put things in a different perspective. Rockne enjoyed life—Leahy wrestled with it.

Leahy inherited a solid core. His best players were Bob Dove and Steve Juzwik; two fine sophomores were on hand in Angelo Bertelli and another of the Miller clan, Creighton. He moved Crimmins from fullback to guard and Dippy Evans from left half to fullback.

The Leahy era opened at home against Arizona, and the football world waited to see if Leahy's magic would transfer from Boston to Notre Dame. Bertelli, an unknown at the start of the season, threw seven passes in the first quarter and completed six. His last throw hit Bob Dove for a 16-yard touchdown. More passing led to the second Notre Dame touchdown, with the subs in, when Jack Warner found Bill Earley for a 22-yard scoring

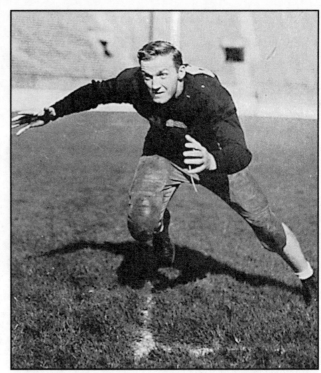

Three year starter at LE, Bob Dove was an All-American in 1941 and 1942.

strike. Arizona struck back with a 66-yard pass and run play for a 12-7 Irish lead at halftime. In the second half, Bertelli's passing got the ball to the Arizona nine-yard line, and Juzwik swept left end for the touchdown.

1941 Notre Dame lettermen.

The changing of the guard—Leahy's first coaching group: Ed McKeever, Frank Leahy, John Druze, and Joe McArdle.

Dippy Evans, on the next Irish possession, sliced past left guard, spun away from tacklers, and ran 78 yards for a touchdown. Sub Don Hogan scored a late touchdown and passed for another. Crimmins intercepted a pass to stop an Arizona drive as Notre Dame blasted Arizona 38-7. Four of six Notre Dame touchdowns came as the direct or indirect results of the passing game.

Notre Dame beat Indiana next, 19-6, with a balanced attack and a fine pass defense that allowed Indiana only two completions in 12 tries for 65 yards. Bertelli and Juzwik worked the ball to the Hoosier four-yard line, and Evans went in from there. Evans's punting kept Indiana in a hole and opened up a short drive in the second quarter with Evans piling in from the two. Evans earned all the yardage on a 48-yard drive in the third quarter, including his seven-yard run over right tackle for the final Notre Dame score. The lone Indiana touchdown came on a long pass and lateral.

The Fighting Irish went to Atlanta and beat Georgia Tech, 20-0, raising their season record to 3-0. Notre Dame's George Murphy blocked a Tech punt and later caught the resulting touchdown pass from Bertelli. For the next score, Evans got the snap and started to run towards Tech's left end, but he spun around and gave the ball to Juzwik, who stormed past the right end to

score standing up 67 yards later. In the third quarter, Dove smothered a Tech fumble, and after seven plays Juzwik scored from the four-yard line. The Irish ran for 221 yards and intercepted six of Tech's eight passes. After three games, the Fighting Irish also had 14 holding penalties called on them.

Carnegie Tech fell next, 16-0, in a rainstorm that almost prohibited the running game but did not slow down Bertelli's passing. He sparked a 74-yard march with passes and Juzwik ran in from the seven-yard line for the touchdown. The second unit drove 49 yards and Creighton Miller earned his first touchdown for the Irish from the one-yard line. Good defense and speed trapped a Tech back for a safety to end it.

The following week, Illinois bolted to an early lead after intercepting a Bertelli pass. This was answered by Juzwik's end sweep for a 12-yard touchdown at the end of the first quarter. The Fighting Irish scored twice in the next quarter: a Bertelli pass to Juzwik from the 13, and Evans ran in from the six for a 21-7 halftime lead. The Illini got back into it in the third quarter with a 65-yard scoring march, but a flagrant personal foul against Juzwik aroused the student body. The Fighting Irish slammed in four scores to turn it into a rout: Bertelli threw twice to Evans for touchdowns; Wally Ziemba intercepted a

Bob Maddox, starter at LG for the 1941 squad.

pass and Evans went in from the three; and Miller raced 40 yards with a Dick Creevy pass to score. The final score was 49-14.

Army played the Irish to a 0-0 tie. The weather was atrocious and Army punting kept Notre Dame in its back yard all day. On the last play of the game, Leahy called a triple wing back set for Harry Wright, Juzwik, and Bertelli as the ball was snapped to Evans. But the ball never reached him. It wobbled out of reach, and he chased it around with Cadets in hot pursuit until he literally slid out of bounds.

Undefeated Navy was next, and Bertelli beat them with three touchdown passes. Juzwik sparked the first score with an interception and a 49-yard run; Bertelli went for the jugular with a 42-yard pass to the two-yard line, and Evans slashed in from there. Navy came right back with a score, but Notre Dame offset that score with a Bertelli to Juzwik pass for an 18-yard touchdown. In the third quarter, Bertelli was intercepted for a touchdown, pulling Navy to within a touchdown. Bertelli kept passing in the fourth period to reach the eight, and Evans did the rest for a 20-13 hard-earned win.

A tired Irish team eked out a 7-6 win over Northwestern. This was basically the same Otto Graham team that had smashed the Fighting Irish the year before. A Crimmins interception let Bertelli pass on a short drive, hitting Matt Bolger with the winning touchdown.

Juzwik made the important point after. Northwestern marched right back with Graham scoring but Ziemba blocked the conversion try. Good defense stymied Graham the rest of the way for the Irish win.

USC was next, and the Fighting Irish were in the hunt for an undefeated year. USC blocked a quick kick and soon scored on a pass, but Ziemba again blocked a point after kick. Poor punting led to a Juzwik run of 23 yards to the USC six-yard line, from where Evans scored on a reverse. The Trojans fumbled on their next possession, and Bertelli fired three passes to Dove, good for 19, 10, and 16 yards to put the ball almost on the goal line. Juzwik rammed in from there, giving Notre Dame a 14-6 lead. USC scored, but John Kovatch blocked the conversion kick. In the third period, Bertelli flipped to Evans, who ran 18 yards for the last touchdown. USC scored again, but missed a pass for the conversion, giving Notre Dame a 20-18 victory.

Bertelli hit 13 of 21 passes for 156 yards and was 70 of 123 for 1,027 yards for the year—staggering statistics for those days. The Fighting Irish were ranked third behind Minnesota and Duke, Crimmins, and Dove earned All-American accolades. Notre Dame was back.

1941 record: 8-0-1 (.944)
Record to date: 323-70-25 (.802)

1942

Leahy knew that he had to change the obsolete Irish offense. The school's president gave him permission to scrap the time-honored Notre Dame box and what was left of the shift. Leahy tinkered with the pass blocking scheme in 1941 to help protect Bertelli. Next he proposed the T formation. He prepared diligently, interviewing the Bears's George Halas (who had just obliterated the Redskins 73-0 in the NFL title game using the T), Bears's quarterback Sid Luckman, and Clark Shaughnessy, architect of Stanford's great pre-war T-formation teams and the formation's major theoretician and proponent.

Bertelli may have been the slowest halfback ever fielded at Notre Dame. Putting him at quarterback would open up a halfback spot where speed mattered. He had a great arm—the best ever at Notre Dame to that point and one of the best of all time. Leahy's planning was so good, the T would stay at Notre Dame well into the 50s.

Football prior to the T was essentially a ground game, with an occasional pass to keep a defense honest, or thrown in desperation in a losing effort. But the T isolated the passing to the quarterback position, shifting it from the left halfback or even other backs, and left the quarterback to concentrate on the passing game

Leahy's new backfield had Bertelli at quarterback, Miller at right halfback, Bob Livingstone at left halfback, and Cornie Clatt at fullback (after a preseason injury ended it for Evans). The offensive line was a big, fast, mobile unit—precisely what the T called for.

Everything was ready for the grand unveiling against Wisconsin. The Fighting Irish took a train to Madison except for Bertelli, who was on the wrong train. He figured it out, changed trains, and reached the stadium just in time for the game. He must have left his passing game on the train, however, as the Badgers tied the Irish 7-7. Wisconsin's all-time great, Elroy Hirsch had a 35-yard touchdown run in the third quarter for the Badger's only score. Bertelli hit one of his four completions on the next drive, for 26 yards to Livingstone, and Jim Mello ran in from the three-yard line for the tying touchdown. Bad ball handling demolished Fighting Irish drives at Wisconsin's 27, 13, 16, 12, and 23.

Passing won the next game—Georgia Tech's passing. The Rambling Wreck scored on a short run after a Fighting Irish fumble, then cranked a 78-yard touchdown pass in the third quarter for the winning margin. Tom Miller scored for Notre Dame from the seven-yard line in the fourth quarter. Bertelli had three passes intercepted to offset Notre Dame's total yardage

superiority over Tech. Notre Dame lost 13-6.

The loss perhaps made Leahy sick; he did not coach the next few games (this was a pattern in Leahy's later years). Ed McKeever took his place for three weeks. During this time, the Fighting Irish went 3-0 against some tough foes. The first victory of the season was over Marchy Schwartz's Stanford team, 27-0, as Bertelli found the range: nine straight completed passes and all four touchdowns. In the second quarter, he connected with Dove for a 36-yard touchdown and later with Paul Limont for a 16-yarder. In the third quarter, Bertelli found George Murphy for a 26-yard score and Livingstone with a 15-yarder. He had 14 completions in 20 tries for 233 yards on the day.

Leahy was in the Mayo Clinic while the Fighting Irish whipped Iowa Pre-Flight 28-0, an upset since this was an all-star group. Bertelli threw to Livingstone for a 47-yard score, and 47 seconds later Cornie Clatt intercepted a pass and ran 37 yards to score. His backup, Gerry Cowhig, scored the other touchdowns on short runs.

Illinois was undefeated and was prepared to stop Bertelli, but three Notre Dame running scores downed the Illini, 21-14. Notre Dame trailed at the half and twice had to come from behind to win. Clatt followed up an Illini fumble to score from the five-yard line for a 7-7 first-quarter tie. In the third, down 14-7, Pete Ashbaugh ran 40 yards with a punt to the one-yard line, and Bertelli sneaked it in. Notre Dame won it in the fourth with a 77-yard march crowned by Cowhig's one-yard touchdown blast. The teams ran equally well; Bertelli's passing was the difference.

Leahy's 1942 coaching staff: Wayne Millner, Ed McKeever, Bob Snyder, Ed Krause, Frank Leahy.

George Murphy, captain of the 1942 Irish and a two-year starter at RE.

With Leahy back on the sidelines, the Fighting Irish shutout Navy 9-0. Bertelli hit a crucial pass of nine yards to Dove on the game's only touchdown march, then scored the touchdown himself from in close. John Creevey made a 17-yard insurance field goal in the fourth quarter. Bertelli helped the cause with an interception in the Notre Dame end zone in the first quarter. Both offenses were sluggish.

A solid Army team played the Fighting Irish even for the first half, but Notre Dame's power wore them out. Ashbaugh recovered an Army fumble at the Cadets's 25 to set up Creevey's 15-yard touchdown run for the first score. Near the end, Bertelli threw a 17-yard touchdown pass to Murphy for the 13-0 win. Notre Dame's 265 yards on the ground made the difference; Army had only 79.

After a hiatus of three decades, Notre Dame played Michigan again. Leahy worked hard to schedule the Wolverines. He even invited the retired Yost to watch the game. Yost, who had complained to Red Miller about calling his fair catches too late, would be watching Red's son, Creighton, starting for the Irish. Michigan won 32-20, the first team to score five touchdowns on Notre Dame since Army in 1916, and the first to score 32 points since Purdue in 1905. Notre Dame actually led 14-13 at the half. Bertelli hit Dove with a seven-yard touchdown throw. Michigan responded with a drive ended by a 14-yard quarterback run for the touchdown. Fighting Irish errors in the second quarter let Michigan off the hook—a fumble that the Wolverines grabbed led to a four-yard touchdown on a fake field goal play. But Michigan fumbled on its next possession, and Miller barged in from the three for a touchdown. The Wolverines owned the third quarter, scoring touchdowns on a 59-yard drive, a 25-yarder after Notre Dame fumbled the kickoff, and then an interception of a Bertelli pass led to a one-yard touchdown run. Miller scored on a well-executed Statue of Liberty play from the 14, but Irish mistakes were too much to overcome.

They redeemed themselves the following week against Otto Graham's Northwestern team, beating the quarterback of the decade, 27-20. The Wildcats had early leads. Clatt caught up with a five-yard touchdown buck and a one-yard scoring dive. Livingstone scored from the 14 on a drive in which Clatt netted 47 yards running. Clatt intercepted a Graham pass to set up a 31-yard touchdown strike from Bertelli to Miller. Graham won the quarterback duel, but the Fighting Irish ground game netted 295 yards to Northwestern's 95.

Leahy's team whipped USC for the third straight time, 13-0. The scores came from Bertelli's passing: a 48-yard pass and run play to Miller and an 80-yard march ended by a nine-yard touchdown pass to Livingstone. Again, Notre Dame's ground game dominated the offense, but the passes garnered the points.

Notre Dame played a "bowl" game against Great Lakes Naval Base at Soldier Field. The sailors had an all-star team and jumped out to a 13-0 lead on a strong running game. In the second half, Clatt ran 82 yards for a touchdown, and Miller had a 72-yard touchdown bolt. Great Lakes missed four field goals and Bertelli moved the Fighting Irish 62 yards in the last minute. But Creevey's field goal on the last play fell just short for a 13-13 tie.

The team matured nicely as they learned the T system, which could score from anywhere. Bertelli, Dove, and Harry Wright earned All-America honors.

1942 record: 7-2-2 (.727)
Record to date: 330-72-27 (.800)

1943

Once again a world war was impacting college football—and every other aspect of American life. Service call-ups had countless players shifted from one campus to the next. Arbitrary assignments sent players to schools where the military training matched their service. Notre Dame was a Navy center. In the next three seasons, several Notre Dame players would be seen playing against the Fighting Irish. Likewise, Notre Dame picked up some good players, notably Julie Rykovich of Illinois and John Perko of Minnesota Of the 1942 starters, only Pat Filley, Bertelli, and Miller returned. The line had to be rebuilt, but the backfield was in better shape with starters and good reserves. Bertelli's back up was a legend in waiting, Johnny Lujack.

Notre Dame opened the season against Pittsburgh and coach Clark Shaughnessy, who had been lured from Maryland after leaving Stanford. This opening matchup pitted Leahy's T against the master's. They sparred evenly until Pitt fumbled on their own 35, and the Fighting Irish quickly drove to the four-yard line. Miller ran in the first touchdown. For an encore, he sped past a Pitt defense on the next series for a 40-yard score. Bertelli scored an easy touchdown when he recovered a Pitt

fumble and stepped across the goal line two yards away. Rykovich tallied two touchdowns and Bob Palladino one to make the final score 41-0.

Georgia Tech had picked up several stars from other Southeast Conference schools, but Notre Dame's running game couldn't be stopped, ending in a 55-13 win. This was Georgia Tech's worst defeat since 1929. Notre Dame's backs ran 451 mostly unopposed yards for 24 first downs and eight touchdowns. Bertelli threw touchdown passes to Rykovich, Miller, and Ray Kuffel, while Mello scored three touchdowns on the ground. Bob Hanlon and George Sullivan scored for the subs.

Next was Michigan at Ann Arbor. The already strong Wolverines were even better with the addition of Wisconsin's Elroy Hirsch. This game would pit the top-ranked teams in the country. The Fighting Irish struck in the first six minutes when Miller went over left guard and cut right for a 66-yard score. Michigan came right back with a Bill Daley touchdown, but missed the point after. Four plays later, Bertelli found Earley loose and hit him with a 20-yard pass that Earley converted into a 70-yard touchdown. Moments later, Miller took off again, 57 yards to the end zone, but a penalty negated the apparent score. The Fighting Irish kept coming, driving to the nine-yard line, but stalled. Michigan had to punt and the Irish drove again; Jim Mello scored from

Notre Dame 1943 national champions.

Jim White, starting LT for the 1943 National Champs.

the four-yard line. In the second half, Rykovich returned a punt 40 yards and Bertelli scored on a short plunge. Then he fired a touchdown pass for a 35-6 Fighting Irish lead. Michigan scored a consolation touchdown on the last play. Miller had 159 yards on 10 carries. Even the Fighting Irish subs stopped Michigan's All-American backs twice from the one-yard line in a nice stand.

Notre Dame went to Wisconsin, who was coached by former Horseman Harry Stuhldreher. Wisconsin gained only five yards rushing all day and lost 50-0. Notre Dame scored within three minutes on a Rykovich run from in close. Then it was Mello's turn after a 52-yard drive, and then Miller continued the onslaught. The starters scored five touchdowns in the 22 plays they executed. Leahy emptied the bench, who scored three more touchdowns.

Leahy knew that his team, ranked number one, would soon be losing the services of Bertelli to the war effort. Illinois was next, and Leahy was looking for good spots to put in his future star, Lujack. Bertelli led the Irish in a 47-0 romp over the Illini. The opening touchdown was a 47-yard pass play from Bertelli to Rykovich. Other tallies went to Miller, Earley, and Lujack, among others.

Undefeated Navy was next. Notre Dame struck immediately—Bertelli to Rykovich for 50 yards and a touchdown. Then he tried a short pass to Miller, who ran 40 more yards for a touchdown. In the third quarter,

Bertelli fired another touchdown pass, then Mello intercepted one of Navy's 38 passes and lumbered to the Midshipmen's 12. Miller scored from there. After stopping a Navy drive, Vic Kulbitski exploded for a 71-yard touchdown. Bertelli scored from the eight for the 33-6 final, and his glorious career was over; he was called up by the Marines.

Having lost its star and eventual Heisman winner, Notre Dame faced another undefeated team—Army. Lujack, a sophomore, took Bertelli's place. The Fighting Irish opened the game with a drive to the Army three, where penalties and a gritty defense stopped the Irish. Army promptly punted and Notre Dame returned it to the Cadet's 31. Lujack struck, with a pass to John Yonakor for a touchdown. The Fighting Irish defense was playing well, too: Miller intercepted a Cadet pass and Bob Kelly picked off two; Jim White stripped Glenn Davis to set up the second touchdown. Lujack plunged for the third touchdown and Earley muscled in from the three for the final score, 26-0.

Northwestern played tough for a half, down only 6-0 on a Lujack to Kelly touchdown pass. Lujack and Kelly did it again in the third quarter, followed by scores from Miller and Rykovich. Northwestern's only score came when a lateral intended for Miller was intercepted to make it a 25-6 Irish win.

Yet another undefeated team—Iowa PreFlight, a team with several pro players—was next for Notre Dame. The Seahawks had a touchdown lead at the half,

John Yonakor, starting RE for the 1943 national champions and a consensus All-America pick.

but Lujack had hit them hard, including a 59-yard pass to Yonakor. In the third period, good Fighting Irish running got to the 17; Lujack hit Kelly for 13, and then Kelly took it in from there. The Seahawks used a fumble recovery to get their second touchdown, but a botched extra point eventually provided the margin of victory for the Fighting Irish. A long Notre Dame march garnered Miller a six-yard touchdown, and the successful extra point gave Notre Dame the win, 14-13.

The Great Lakes team was even better than Pre-Flight, but Lujack worked a long, patient drive and then on a sneak. The Bluejackets answered with two scores, the first one by Emil Sitko, playing against his old team. Dewey Proctor also scored for Great Lakes on a 50-yard run. The Fighting Irish responded with an 80-yard march in 18 plays; Mello picked up 54 of them. Miller threw the go ahead touchdown with 1:05 to play. But Great Lakes came right back and scored again on a five-yard pass for a 19-14 Irish defeat.

Leahy met Sitko after the game and said, "It's too bad we lost, Emil." Sitko, who had not forgotten his old school, replied, "Yes, coach, it is too bad that we lost, isn't it?" Nevertheless, the team was honored as national champions, Bertelli won the Heisman, and five made All-American: Miller, Yonakor, White, Pat Filley, and Herb Coleman.

1943 record: 9-1-0 (.900)
Record to date: 339-73-27 (.802)

1944

On May 1, 1944, Frank Leahy joined the Navy as a commissioned officer. Bertelli was already in the Marines, and Lujack was also in the service. Creighton Miller had graduated. Without a coach, and with its team weakened by the war effort and graduation, Notre Dame appointed Ed McKeever as interim head coach. He had a pool of talent with good size in the line and a somewhat smaller backfield. Frank Dancowicz at quarterback had excellent speed. Behind him were halfbacks Chick Maggioli and Bob Kelly, and lanky Elmer Angsman at fullback. The tackles and ends were big by 1944 standards at 6-5 and 210 pounds. Notre Dame would need all the help it could muster since both service academies were loaded with talent.

Chick Maggioli, starter at LH for the 1944 Irish, had his season interrupted by a service call.

The Fighting Irish conducted an offensive clinic in their season opener against Pitt, 58-0. In the first quarter Dancewicz passed to Kelly for a touchdown. Angsman started the second quarter with a fumble recovery on the Pitt 13; and Kelly caught his second touchdown pass. Moments later he scored from the five to end a drive started when Dancowicz intercepted a Pitt pass. Kelly, behind excellent downfield blocking, sprinted for an 85-yard touchdown. Two interceptions and two more fumbles led to more Pitt woes, with Zeke O'Connor, George Terlep, Joe Gasparella, and Mark Limont scoring. Kelly gained 137 yards on 11 runs and four touchdowns. The Fighting Irish offense produced 622 yards.

Against Tulane, the offensive barrage continued during a 26-0 Notre Dame win. After an even first quarter, Dancewicz fired to Kelly for a 6-0 lead. A second drive overcame penalties to have Angsman bang it in from the four-yard line. In the third quarter, Maggioli caught a pass from Dancewicz for 45 yards to get the Fighting Irish away from their goal, then ended the march smashing in from the three-yard line. Maggioli

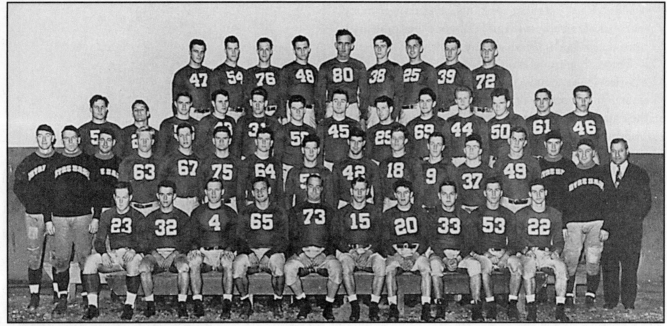

1944 Notre Dame varsity squad.

later shook loose on a sweep for 20 yards, followed by a 23-yard end run for the final score, 26-0. The Irish had 438 yards on offense for the day.

Kelly started the 64-0 rout of Dartmouth on the first play from scrimmage when he ran 52 yards past left end. Dancewicz scored on the next drive. Dartmouth showed occasional flashes of football savvy, but kept handing the ball to the Fighting Irish. Notre Dame's

Pat Filley, starter at LG, and captain of the 1944 team—an All-America pick.

other scorers were Terlep with two (his second from 32 yards out), and Kelly, Gasparella, John Corbisiero, Nunzio Marino (from 54 yards), Steve Nemeth (from 59 yards), and Ed Clasby with one each. Notre Dame had almost 600 yards of total offense, with 440 on the ground. They missed five conversion kicks.

After the first three games of the season, Notre Dame not only stood undefeated, but had outscored its opposition by an incredible 148-0. The winning streak would continue against Wisconsin the following week, although the Badgers would manage to score some points.

Against Wisconsin, the Fighting Irish started early; Kelly scored on a 51-yard streak on the second play. The Badgers dropped the ball at their 10 and Kelly scored again, prompting McKeever to play the subs in the second quarter. In the opening play of the third quarter, the Badgers's kickoff return man, Thompson, apparently did not like what he saw coming his way after fielding the ball on the two-yard line and calmly trotted into his end zone for a safety. Notre Dame received the ensuing kick, and Angsman scored on a 35-yard run. Gasparella later fired a 31-yard touchdown strike to Maggioli. Angsman lost a 75-yard touchdown run on a referee's mistake when the line judge saw Wisconsin offside and blew the play dead. The Badgers scored two meaningless touchdowns later, bringing the final score to 28-13.

Illinois won everything but the game, when Notre Dame escaped 13-7 with a sputtering offense. The Illini

Bob Kelly, starting RH for the 1944 squad.

Frank Ruggerio, a tough starter at FB for the 1944 Irish.

scored first and led until the fourth quarter. Fred Rovai helped the Irish with a fumble recovery on the Illini's 16; Kelly scored from the two. The Irish won on a hook and ladder play: Dancewicz's short pass to Kelly was lateralled to Maggioli—and he scooted 71 yards to win it. The Illini lost two touchdowns on penalties. They pounded the Fighting Irish defense with 343 yards running. Maggioli was called up a few days later by the Marines.

A fine Navy team exacted retribution for seven straight losses with a 32-13 victory. Kelly scored first for Notre Dame, but it was in the third quarter, long after Navy had built a big lead. He also scored on a three-yarder. The Fighting Irish watched former teammate Fred Earley kicking Middie conversions. Navy's blocking was superb and led to four touchdowns on the ground.

Army was next—it was the worst defeat ever for Notre Dame, 59-0. The Cadets had not won against Notre Dame since 1931. Army intercepted six Fighting Irish passes and ran at will. Glenn Davis scored three times and Doug Kenna ran for one, scored on an interception, and passed for one to lead the Cadets. An Army man named Travel intercepted a screen pass for another touchdown.

A week later, Notre Dame shut out Northwestern 21-0. Jim Brennan, future-coach Terry's older brother, scored two early touchdowns, one on a 41-yard scorcher, and the second a 29-yarder after a fumble recovery. Northwestern reached the Irish two-yard line on

penalties, but could not score. Marty Wendell ran seven yards in the fourth quarter to finish the scoring.

Georgia Tech was waiting in Atlanta for the Fighting Irish—Tech had beaten Navy and now wanted the Fighting Irish. Notre Dame disappointed Tech 21-0. Brennan scored an 11-yard touchdown on a lateral in the first quarter. There was no more scoring until the third quarter when Dancewicz passed to Kelly for 40 yards and a touchdown. Brennan later scored from the one to wrap it up.

Great Lakes was the last game. Great Lakes had stars galore, including Notre Dame's Jim Mello. The Sailors pushed the Fighting Irish around in the first quarter, but didn't score. Dancewicz rifled a 15-yard pass to Kelly for the halftime lead. In the third quarter, John Mastrangelo sacked Great Lakes' quarterback, causing a fumble. The fumble was kicked into the end zone, and Doug Waybright hauled it in for a touchdown. In the fourth quarter, Kelly punched out runs of 18, nine, and nine yards to reach the Sailors's three. The Sailors set up their defense for another run but Dancewicz passed to Skoglund for the touchdown. Kelly intercepted a later pass, and Dancewicz got the final score on a three-yard plunge for the 28-7 win.

The 8-2 record was a good one under the circumstances. The Fighting Irish showed resilience and courage after the academy routs. Pat Filley repeated as an All-American, and Kelly was also named to the honor.

1944 record: 8-2-0 (.800)
Record to date: 347-75-27 (.802)

1945

McKeever moved on to Cornell, although he had signed for another year with Notre Dame. Hugh Devore agreed to coach until Leahy returned from the service. Devore had begun his career as a coach at Notre Dame, before starting the rounds: Fordham, Providence, and Holy Cross. Leahy brought him back to Notre Dame in 1943. Two decades later he would serve as interim coach again, the only man to do so.

Devore took over a depleted squad. Only eight monogram men returned, and two of them would be shipped to Great Lakes (Szymanski and Wendell.) He had some talent; the problem was sifting through it. Only Fred Rovai returned on the line. There were some fine quarterback prospects behind Dancowicz: Gasparella was reliable, and Frank Tripucka (Kelly's father) and George Ratterman showed promise. Angsman moved to right halfback to make way for 5-8, 200 pound Frank Ruggerio. Phil Colella was at left halfback.

Colella won the season opener, 7-0, over Illinois with a 78-yard touchdown run. In the next game, Georgia Tech made it tough, for a while, with an early 7-0 lead before Notre Dame unloaded 40 points on them. Colella caught a short touchdown pass from Dancewicz to tie it, then Angsman capped a short drive with a 19-yard touchdown run. Gasparella came in for Dancewicz; he spotted Bill Zehler in the clear and hit him with a 54-yard touchdown pass. After the half, Tech was driving, but Terry Brennan intercepted a pass and returned it 42 yards. Angsman scored shortly afterwards. John Agnone and Emil Slovak finished the Fighting Irish scoring. Notre Dame had 560 yards and Tech 440, for an even 1,000 yards of offense for the game. In spite of the yardage, Tech was wrecked by a 40-7 margin.

Dartmouth fell short by 34 points, keeping the Notre Dame record unblemished at 3-0. Colella caught a Dancowicz pass and jetted 50 yards for a score on the first play. Devore called off the passing game and made the Fighting Irish do it on the ground. But the Irish couldn't stop entirely and threw a four-yard pass to Bob Skoglund and a score. In the second period, Zip Zehler had a 24-yard touchdown and Notre Dame led 20-0 at halftime. Later, Stan Krivik ran in from the three for a touchdown and then drop-kicked the point after. Joe Yonto wrapped up the Irish 34-0 shutout with a plunge from the two-yard line.

Pitt's football fortunes had been on the wane in recent years, and Notre Dame kept it that way, 39-9. Pitt fumbled early and Colella scored from the 23. A penalty killed Colella's run, so Dancewicz passed to him to the one. Ruggerio smashed over from there. Pitt tackled Brennan in the Notre Dame end zone for a safety. The game was pretty even until the last play of the half when Dancewicz threw a touchdown to Bill Leonard. Pitt tired in the second half: Angsman took a Dancewicz pass in the flat and scored from the 20; he also plunged for a touchdown in the fourth quarter. John Panelli went 19

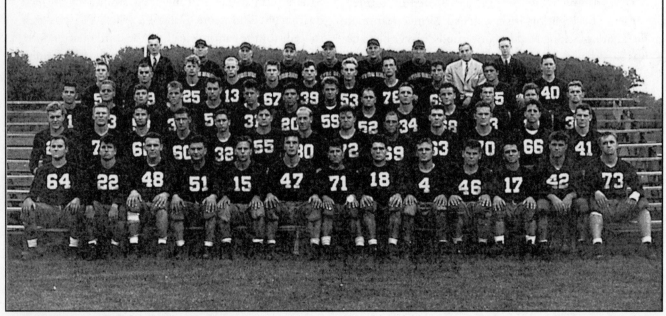

Notre Dame 1945 varsity football squad.

Pete Berezney, starter at RT for the 1945 Irish.

yards up the middle for a touchdown and Ernie Virok picked off an errant Pitt pass to go 40 yards for the final Irish touchdown.

Iowa was next. Devore saw a mismatch early on, let the regulars throw one pass in 11 minutes, and then pulled them out. Notre Dame blew out Iowa 56-0. Ruggerio and Angsman scored on offense, and Colella picked off an Iowa pass to score. In the second quarter, subs Bill Gompers, John Agnone, and Emil Slovak scored. Agnone intercepted a pass to set up his own touchdown. It was 41-0 at the half. Joe Yonto scored from 30 yards out, and Leon Traney dashed 51 yards, then scored from the 19 to cap the scoring.

The Fighting Irish were eager for Navy. Both teams were undefeated and looked evenly matched on paper. In the morning papers the next day, they were still evenly matched, 6-6. Notre Dame looked strong on its first series, with a 43-yard pass—but no drive emerged. Later Ruggerio intercepted a Navy pass and took it to the Midshipmen's 34. Four plays later, Ruggerio slammed in for a 6-0 lead. The Fighting Irish continued to dominate, when Navy's "Smackover" Scott scored the Midshipmen's only touchdown on an interception. On Navy's last drive, Notre Dame stopped the opposition's passes four times. Devore sent in Ratterman, who was sacked for 12 yards. Then he fired a pass for a 54-yard advance. Dancewicz, now in, threw to Colella. With

under a minute to go, Colella caught the ball and dove for the end zone. A Navy back tackled him and threw him sideways. Colella's feet crossed the plane of the goal line, but the officials said the ball hadn't. No score, and the game ended in a 6-6 tie.

There were distinct levels of football by this time. There were all of the colleges at a certain level (with Georgia and UCLA at the top), then a large gap before Notre Dame, then at the next highest level the NFL, and finally, at the top was Army. They really were that good. It has been said that Notre Dame had an NFL franchise from 1946 to 1949, but Army beat them to it in 1944 and 1945. Army wanted its 16th straight win; they were four-touchdown favorites over Notre Dame.

The Fighting Irish were banged up going into the Army game. Ruggerio had 13 stitches in his chin; Angsman and Colella were hurting. Angsman fumbled to Army on the third play at the Notre Dame 30. Davis whipped through on the second play for a 27-yard touchdown. In the second quarter, Davis caught a long pass from Arnold Tucker for another touchdown. Blanchard busted in from the one-yard line for a 21-0 halftime Army lead. Davis in the third quarter ran for a 21-yard touchdown. Blanchard intercepted a Ratterman pass and scored from the Notre Dame 36. Army's subs, who were good enough to have played in Canada's Gray Cup, scored after a 71-yard march. The last score came with 17 seconds left in the game—on a pass. The Fighting Irish would remember Red Blaik for that pass at the end of the 48-0 demolition.

Leahy was out of the service and watched the Fighting Irish play Northwestern from the press box. Northwestern played well at first but couldn't stop a 90-yard march by the Irish; Angsman ran for 50 yards and finished it off from the one. A Wildcat fumble in the second quarter was converted into a touchdown. Floyd Simmons scored on a four-yard run in the third quarter. Northwestern started passing carelessly; Gompers intercepted one and dashed 32 yards for a score. The Wildcats used a lateral for their only score, then Ratterman threw 42 yards to Gompers on the 10 who dragged a defender the rest of the way as Notre Dame won 34-7.

The Fighting Irish let Tulane score an early touchdown, but Mastrangelo blocked the conversion kick. The 6-0 score held until the third punt of the third quarter, when Brennan returned it for 30 yards, and made 52 yards and a touchdown on the next play. After a stalled drive, Angsman added another touchdown. Ratterman hit Brennan with a pass for the

Ed Mieszkowski, starter at LT for the 1945 team.

third touchdown. The Fighting Irish scored on an 84-yard drive, and on a Tripucka pass to Agnone for the 32-6 final score.

Great Lakes played its last game (because the war came to an end) against Notre Dame. They had former Irish quarterback George Terlep and a fullback better than Army's, Marion Motley. Living up to his reputation, Motley scored the first touchdown from the Notre Dame 10 in three tries. Ruggerio responded, after recovering a fumble, from the two-foot line. That would be it for the Fighting Irish. Terlep scored for a 13-7 halftime score. Notre Dame held Great Lakes scoreless until the fourth quarter. Then Aschenbrenner went wide for an 11-yard touchdown and Motley shrugged off five Irish tacklers as he ricocheted 44 yards for a score. The combination of Terlep to O'Connor scored again and a late interception led to the last touchdown and a 39-7 win for Great Lakes. It was a commendable season in view of wartime conditions and service academy manpower needs. Mastrangelo and Dancewicz earned All-America honors.

1945 record: 7-2-1 (.750)
Record to date: 354-77-28 (.801)

1946

Fighting Irish gridders from the good 1942 and the great 1943 teams were returning to campus after the war, eager to get on with their interrupted lives. There was a wealth of football talent surrounding Leahy. At quarterback, the Irish had Ratterman, Tripucka, and Lujack—the best trio at that position ever at the Dome. At left halfback were Terry Brennan, Cowhig, Livingstone, Coy McGee, Ernie Zalejski—all good enough to start anywhere. At right halfback were Emil Sitko, Frank Swistowicz, Gompers, Simmons, and at fullback, Mello, Clatt, and Panelli. Of the 15 backs, half were All-America material. The line had Jim Martin, George Connor, Ziggy Czarobski, and as a freshman sub, Leon Hart would never see Notre Dame lose a game in his four years. Mastrangelo was an All-American.

Notre Dame opened with Illinois, who was also loaded with talent. They played even for much of the first quarter until Lujack flipped a short lateral to Sitko, who went 83 yards before Rykovich stopped him. Livingstone scored from the three-yard line. Just before the half, the Irish scored on a quick drive: Mello for 30 around left end; Sitko for 11 to the 14; and Mello for the touchdown. The third quarter was scoreless, but in the fourth quarter, a fumble recovery by the Irish gave Brennan a chance to tally from the four-yard line. Swistowicz, who earlier had intercepted a 42-yard pass, intercepted another one and Clatt scored for the 26-6 win.

The following week, Notre Dame slept through the first quarter against Pitt. Finally, Lujack passed to Jack Zilly and then to Livingston for a 24-yard touchdown. A George Strohmeyer interception led to a touchdown run by Brennan from the seven-yard line. Pitt fumbled in the third quarter, allowing Lujack to throw a touchdown pass to Mello for a 19-0 lead. Mello scored once more and Brennan tacked on one for a 33-0 win. Notre Dame gained 468 yards in a lackluster day.

Purdue came out and played good football—until Livingstone was injured and carried off. This seemed to spark the Fighting Irish: Mello bulled 33 yards, Panelli gained 28 more on two runs, and Mello went in from the one-yard line. After a wasted fumble recovery, Brennan ran three times for 42 yards to the Purdue two-yard line; Clatt smashed in from there. The next drive was swift: Cowhig returned a punt 47 yards, Swistowicz for five, and Lujack to Brennan for a 28-yard touchdown pass.

1946 Notre Dame National Champions.

The halftime score was 21-0 in favor of Notre Dame. In the third period, Martin engulfed a fumble on Purdue's 18 and Panelli scored on a reverse. Shortly thereafter, Panelli ran for 42 yards and Lujack passed to Zilly for yet another Notre Dame touchdown. Purdue finally got on the scoreboard with a quarterback run of 52 yards. Notre Dame quickly responded with an intercepted pass for a touchdown, and Gompers ended the blowout with a 20-yard touchdown run with the subs.

Lujack struck quickly the next week against Iowa. In the third minute of the game, he found Brennan in the Hawkeye secondary for a 65-yard scoring pass. A fumble led to a Panelli score from the one-yard line. Lujack lost the handle on the ball on the next series, but recovered and ran 47 yards for a touchdown. Sitko led a Notre Dame march on the ground and scored from the three-yard line. Ashbaugh intercepted a pass, and Sitko scored from the 47 on three runs. Leahy sent in the subs. Gompers wrapped it up with a 20-yard scoring sprint for the 41-6 win.

Against Navy, Leahy wanted to keep it simple for Army's scouts. Playing a conservative offense, the Irish dominated 28-0. Cowhig scored first on a 31-yard end sweep. Floyd Simmons owned the next quarter, scoring two touchdowns. Gompers finished it with a two-yard burst in the last quarter.

Army players—two-time defending national champions with 25 consecutive wins—had never scored against a Leahy-coached Notre Dame team. The game was a titanic struggle, ending in a 0-0 deadlock. The only long drive belonged to Notre Dame, an 85-yarder that fizzled at the Army three-yard line. Both teams had runs of 21 yards, one by Brennan and one by Blanchard. It was Blanchard's run that decided the game's outcome; he was in the open and had a full head of steam, when Lujack made a picture-perfect tackle on the Notre Dame 36 to end the play and save the game. This was the only time in Blanchard's illustrious career that anyone had tackled him in the open field without help. The Fighting Irish survived the loss of two key fumbles, one by Sitko and the other by Brennan. Their finest moment followed a double fumble: Sitko intercepted but fumbled on his five-yard line, and Lujack recovered, only to have Cowhig do it again. The defense rose to the occasion and stopped Army's four plays. Notre Dame got the ball, punted it out of trouble, and Zilly sacked Army's quarterback, Tucker, who fumbled; Martin recovered. Neither team could move the ball after those defensive plays.

Northwestern seemed to always have the misfortune of playing Notre Dame following an upset or disappointment. True to form, Notre Dame dominated the game, 27-0. Sitko began the scoring, from in close, with a 34-yard run. Near the end of the game, Ratterman led marches of 43 and 59 yards for scores; Panelli tallied both. Tripucka led a drive that Slovak wrapped up with an 18-yard run past left end. Fighting Irish backs ran for 423 yards.

The Irish offense was in high gear against Tulane in New Orleans, 41-0. Mello and Zalejski both scored twice, and Brennan and McGee each once. A bruising defense made Tulane look all but inept.

Leahy's health failed him again, so assistant coach Moose Krause, soon to become athletic director, had the coaching honor against USC in the finale. He was high strung as the team prepared to go on the field; someone asked him who was starting. Moose replied in his booming voice, "Who are we gonna start? Why, we'll start everybody!" Notre Dame trampled USC 26-6. Coy McGee was the game's featured player: he opened with a touchdown on an 80-yard kickoff return, lost to a penalty; he scored on a 77-yard pass reception from Ratterman; and ran one in for 11 yards. In between, Ratterman threw a 22-yard touchdown pass to Leon Hart. Cowhig ran 15 yards through a cavernous hole to score the final touchdown. McGee, unknown to the press and the Trojans, gained 146 yards on only six runs.

Lujack, Connor, Mastrangelo, and Strohmeyer were honored as All-Americans. Navy beat Army to end the season, and Notre Dame won the national title.

1946 record: 8-0-1 (.944)
Record to date: 362-77-29 (.804)

1947

Almost everyone returned from the 1946 defending national champions. Three positions lost graduates (right guard, right end, and fullback). Leahy had his pick from a wealth of players. Leon Hart took over at right end and would be a three-time All-American. At fullback were three players who could start anywhere in the country—Panelli, Simmons, and Clatt. Lujack, Connor, Martin, and Hart must be considered as all-time Notre Dame players, and perhaps also Sitko. Then there were the mere All-Americans: Fischer, Czarobski, and Strohmeyer (who was a reserve).

Notre Dame opened the season by clobbering Pitt 40-6, in spite of it being Pitt's second game, in spite of losing six fumbles, and in spite of gaining only 209 yards rushing. Brennan scored first from the three-yard line after a Lujack pass to Martin gained 34 yards. Lujack sparked the second drive with an improvised 21-yard gain and a touchdown pass from the nine-yard line to

Waybright. In the third quarter, Lujack threw a 65-yard touchdown to Martin. And in the fourth quarter, he threw a touchdown pass to Hart. McGee scored on a run, and Lancaster Smith rounded out the scoring by running for a 17-yard touchdown.

Purdue played a tough game but lost 22-7. Lujack fired to Brennan for a 21-yard touchdown to start the scoring. Purdue scored soon after, a nine-yard touchdown pass by DeMoss. They made the point after, their first successful one against Notre Dame since 1945. After a fumble, Lujack threw to Larry Coutre, who took it to the Purdue 21. Lujack called a pass, saw it defensed well, and ran for the touchdown. Steve Oracko kicked the first Notre Dame field goal in five years, from the 18. McGee ran back a punt 43 yards with the reserves, and Simmons bulled in from the three-yard line to complete the win.

Fans had waited for the next game for 22 years—Nebraska. It was billed as a match of two great lines, but only one showed up—Notre Dame won 31-0. Panelli ended a 74-yard march with an eight-yard touchdown run. The Fighting Irish mixed runs and passes as Swistowicz hammered at their left tackle on a series of short runs for 22 yards; Tripucka threw to Brennan for 22 more. And Swistowicz ran three times from the 11 for the touchdown. McGee returned a punt 35 yards to the 50; Lujack fired to Swistowicz for a 36-yard gain.

George Connor, starting LT for the 1946 and 1947 Irish, twice a consensus All-American.

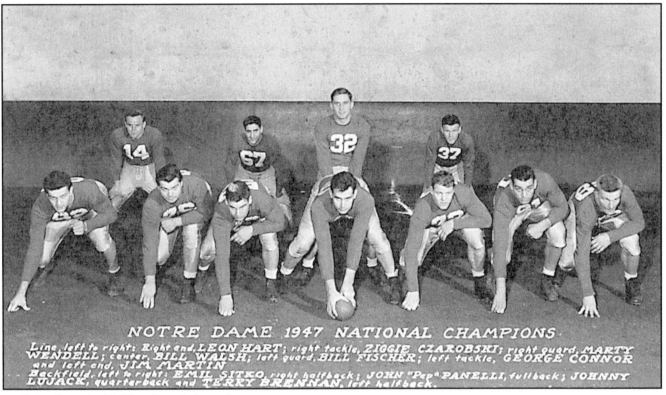

NOTRE DAME 1947 NATIONAL CHAMPIONS

Line, left to right: Right end, LEON HART; right tackle, ZIGGIE CZAROBSKI; right guard, MARTY WENDELL; center, BILL WALSH; left guard, BILL FISCHER; left tackle, GEORGE CONNOR and left end, JIM MARTIN

Backfield, left to right: EMIL SITKO, right halfback; JOHN "Pep" PANELLI, fullback; JOHNNY LUJACK, quarterback and TERRY BRENNAN, left halfback.

Notre Dame's 1947 national champions.

McGee scored from the 14 untouched. Waybright scored on a 14-yard pass from Tripucka, who later used a shovel pass to Sitko for a 10-yard score. The Irish gained 390 total yards to the Huskers's 153.

Iowa was next, coached by former Fighting Irish Eddie Anderson and Frank Carideo. Brennan scored the first Irish touchdown four plays after an Iowa fumble. On the next drive, McGee returned a punt to the 50, Sitko ran to the 18, and Brennan trampled four Hawkeyes for the score. Notre Dame's defense choked every Iowa possession except one, when Emlen Tunnell took a handoff, slipped between Connor and Martin and saw a hole—it was 65 yards before Lujack and Brennan could maneuver him out of bounds. The defense stopped the drive there. The last Notre Dame drive went for 98 time-killing yards; Coutre scored from the one-yard line for a 21-0 win over Iowa.

Navy was swamped 27-0. Lujack started it with a 29-yard touchdown strike to Brennan. Later, Lujack, on a pass play, ran 72 yards but fumbled. Tripucka spelled him and found Hart open for a 31-yard touchdown pass. Brennan slammed in on a short yardage play, and Livingstone finished it with an interception and a 42-yard touchdown. Hart also recovered two fumbles, Brennan's scores following each. Irish quarterbacks

passed for 308 yards. Tripucka was nearly perfect, hitting eight of nine for 136 yards.

Moose Krause shows how it should be done in a 1947 practice.

Four players enjoying themselves—Coy McGee, Emil Sitko, an unidentified player, and Frank Tripucka.

Army knew that its glory days would be hard to match now that the talent pool was equalized. With that in mind, the Cadets sought to end the series with Notre Dame. Army scouts knew of the great Fighting Irish passing, but the Cadets lost the game on Notre Dame's 361 yards rushing. Brennan opened with a 95-yard kickoff return for a touchdown. Army failed with its possession; a few plays later Notre Dame scored again on a Brennan touchdown. In the third quarter, Army blew a kickoff to give Notre Dame a 47-yard drive, with Livingstone scoring from the six-yard line. The Cadets scored but Notre Dame came back with an 80-yard march; Coutre's 11-yarder finished the 27-7 win.

The Fighting Irish went flat the following game against Northwestern, winning a close one 26-19. Panelli scored first from the nine-yard line to end a quick, decisive drive. Northwestern fumbled on the ensuing kickoff return, and the Fighting Irish had the ball on their eight-yard line. Lujack passed to Brennan for a three-yard touchdown. The Wildcats intercepted a Fighting Irish pass and got to the 15, then scored. Just before the half ended, Tripucka rifled a touchdown pass to Lancaster Smith, who made an acrobatic catch. In the third quarter, Northwestern scored on a pass play when Brennan slipped in the mud. Lujack put together a 62-yard drive, passing to Hart from the six-yard line for the score. The Wildcats intercepted for another touchdown, and Leahy responded by sending the starters back in to finish things.

Perhaps the purist in Leahy found the narrow win frustrating because he missed the next game. Moose Krause again took charge, and the Fighting Irish dismantled Tulane 59-6. The first quarter, which ended 32-0, was a blend of Tulane's incompetence and Notre Dame's talent. Tulane backs failed to field two kickoffs that led to quick Irish touchdowns—both in the first quarter. In the second quarter, Sitko scored twice, on a five-yard run and a 20-yard pass from Lujack. Brennan also scored twice, on an 18-yard run and a five-yard pass from Lujack. Gompers thrashed the Tulane defense for 37 yards and a score. Meanwhile, Fred Earley missed three conversion kicks. Tulane finally scored on an 83-yard drive. In the third quarter, Krause used everyone: Panelli, Livingstone, Clatt, and Jim Brennan (of the fifth backfield) all scored.

There had been no west coast games during wartime, so it was something new for many of the players to meet USC on the coast. With a perfect season in their grasp, the Fighting Irish beat USC 38-7. Earley kicked an 18-yard field goal after the USC quarterback lost the ball near his goal. In the second quarter, Sitko wrapped up an 87-yard march with a one-yard smash. In the third quarter, Sitko ran 76 yards for a touchdown behind Connor's blocking. Lujack intercepted a pass and Panelli scored from the five-yard line. After USC reached the Notre Dame eight-yard line and fizzled, Livingstone ran 92 yards for the score. A fifth-string tackle, Al Zmijewski, intercepted a USC lateral and lumbered 30 yards for the final score.

The win ended Leahy's fifth season at Notre Dame and brought him his third national crown. His record under the Dome stood at 41-3-4, an .895 winning percentage. There were five All-America selections: Lujack (plus the Heisman), Connor (1946 Outland Trophy), Fischer (1948 Outland), Czarobski, and Hart (1949 Heisman).

No other team in the history of the game has had that much talent on the field at one time. Leahy could have won the title with his second unit.

1947 record: 9-0-0 (1.000)
Record to date: 371-77-29 (.808)

1948

The Fighting Irish faced some big losses via graduation—Lujack, Connor, and Czarobski. The 1948 starters would be a good unit, but there was a drop-off in talent after that. The line was solid, and the backfield had Tripucka, Brennan, Sitko, and Panelli. Overall, Leahy had fewer options and more coaching challenges. It would be a while before another Notre Dame team could compare with that of 1947.

Two early touchdowns in the opener against Purdue bred some complacency as the Boilermakers came back strong only to lose 28-27. Sitko scored twice on short runs to cap short marches. Early on, the Fighting Irish seemed in complete control. Purdue fought back to a 12-7 halftime deficit, which they quickly turned into a 13-12 lead in the third quarter with a 70-yard touchdown drive. Jim Martin deflected a Purdue punt to Panelli who scored the third Fighting Irish touchdown. Oracko missed his third point after, but kicked a 23-yard fourth-quarter field goal to give Notre Dame a 21-13 lead. Purdue's quarterback brought them back again with a 50-yard touchdown pass. With two minutes to go, Zmijewski grabbed an errant Purdue pass and scored from the seven-yard line for his second career touchdown. Purdue kept coming, scoring at the very end to close the final score to within a single point. Purdue's offense worked well; Notre Dame won on the strength of two great defensive plays.

Notre Dame buried Pitt, 40-0. The starters played only the first half and gave the subs a 28-0 lead. After a Frank Spaniel interception and 30-yard return, Tripucka hit Hart for a 10-yard touchdown. In the second quarter, Sitko wrapped up an 84-yard drive with a two-yard smash. Bill Gay intercepted a Pitt pass, and Spaniel soon scored from the one-yard line. Jack Landry scored from

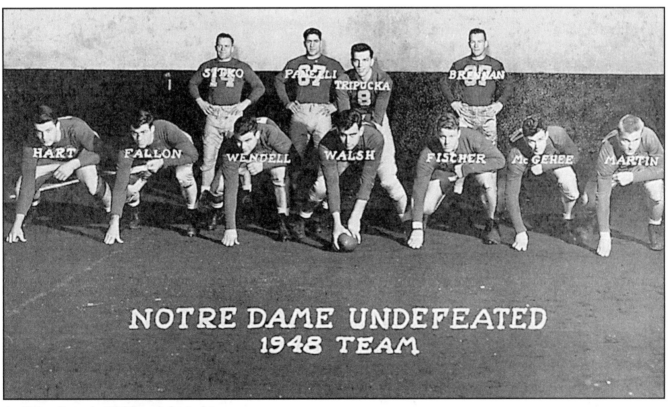

Notre Dame's 1948 undefeated team.

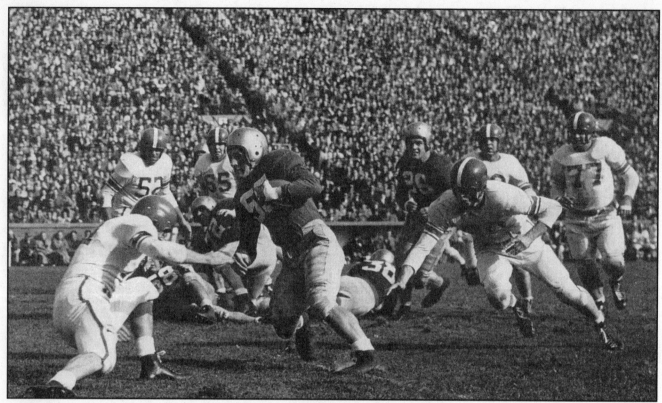

FB Mike Swistowicz cuts back in a 26-7 win over Michigan State in 1948.

the one-yard line for the 28-0 halftime lead. In the third period, Lancaster Smith returned a Pitt punt 85 yards for a touchdown. Leo McKillin ended the Notre Dame scoring with a nine-yard burst. Notre Dame seemed to be able to stop Pitt whenever the need arose.

After a 27-year hiatus, the Michigan State University Spartans (formerly the Michigan Agriculture College) showed up. They intercepted Notre Dame right away and LeRoy Crane later scored for the Spartans. The Fighting Irish struck back with a grinding 94-yard march ended by a Tripucka touchdown pass to Hart. Much of the second quarter was consumed with another lengthy drive by Notre Dame, a 96-yard effort, capped by Swistowicz's 12-yard run for the go-ahead score Brennan scored from the one-yard line in the third quarter as Notre Dame took the kickoff back on another meticulous series. In the fourth quarter, Gay intercepted a Spartan pass and returned it 35 yards to the Michigan State 11. Sitko rammed it in for the 26-7 win. The Irish running game chalked up 398 yards.

The Fighting Irish moved west to Nebraska, winning 44-13. Sitko scored twice in the first half, on runs of eight yards and four yards, while Panelli raced 74 yards past the Huskers for the second score in the opening period. Tripucka threw to Wightkin for a 28-

yard touchdown. Right after that, Groom intercepted a pass, which led to Landry's seven-yard score. It was 31-7 at the half in favor of the Irish. Gay kept it rolling in the second half with a 67-yard punt return, and Martin caught a 13-yard touchdown pass. The Huskers fumbled the ensuing kickoff; Coutre recovered and later scored

Bill Fischer, 1948 captain, three-year starter at LG, consensus All-American.

The chapel car in use during the long trip to play USC in early December, 1948.

from the 14. Nebraska scored on the last play of the game to close the scoring at 44-13.

Forty-seven seconds into the Iowa game, the Fighting Irish had the first score. Iowa fumbled the opening kickoff on their 34 and Tripucka used a "toss lateral" to Panelli for a quick touchdown. Fighting Irish runners would gain 372 yards on the day, but only one pass was completed for minus seven yards. The Hawkeyes recovered quickly from their opening mistake, answering with a 74-yard drive in six plays for the touchdown. Sitko took the ensuing kickoff 69 yards to the 11. No score resulted, but Iowa was pinned deep in its own territory. Hart recovered a fumble on the Iowa nine-yard line a little later in the second quarter and Gay sprinted in from the four-yard line for the touchdown. Tripucka and Panelli worked the toss lateral again for a 39-yard touchdown in the third quarter, and Coutre exploded in the fourth on a 35-yard touchdown run up the middle. Iowa scored off an interception for the 27-12 final. Panelli gained 154 yards on 12 runs and played a great game linebacking. A problem was emerging though—missing the conversions.

Navy was routed 41-7, bringing the Irish season record to 6-0. Sitko led Notre Dame with 172 yards on 17 carries. He ran 55 yards to set up the first touchdown, which he scored from the three-yard line. Navy fumbled and Notre Dame scored in three quick

plays: Tripucka passed to Hart who lateralled to Sitko for 18; Sitko for 11 more; and Panelli for 18 and the touchdown. After trading fumbles, Gay scored from the three-yard line. Navy fumbled again, on their 25, and quarterback Bob Williams tossed a lateral to Lank Smith for a one-play touchdown drive. It was 28-0 at the half. Coutre intercepted Navy in the third quarter, and Spaniel scored with a six-yard pass from Williams (after the referees killed two other touchdowns on the drive). Landry muscled in from the one-yard line for the last Notre Dame score.

The Indiana Hoosiers played against the Notre Dame starters for five drives and five touchdowns before Leahy relented in a 42-7 rampage. Sitko opened with a 23-yard score. The Hoosiers returned the kickoff to the Notre Dame seven-yard line, but the defense moved them back to the Irish   30. Tripucka struck again with a pass to Gay to the Indiana 15, and Landry scored from the three-yard line. In the next quarter, Panelli took a pitchout and followed a blocking clinic for a 51-yard touchdown. Tripucka opened up the passing game with touchdown strikes of 45 yards to Wightkin and 20 yards to Gay. The subs punched over a touchdown for the final Irish total, Landry going in from the one-yard line. Indiana threw a touchdown pass near the end.

The missed conversion syndrome almost caught up with the Fighting Irish when Northwestern played a fine

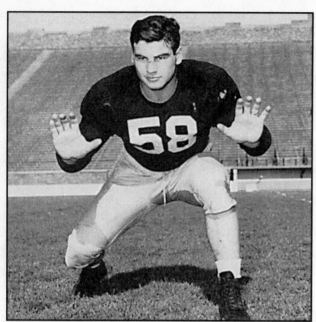

Marty Wendell, two-year starter at RG in 1947 and 1948, an All-American in 1948.

game, losing 12-7. After a surprise Northwestern drive to the nine-yard line, Notre Dame came back; Brennan ran for 22 yards and then 230-pound Hart smashed 13 yards on an end around to the Wildcat's one-yard line. Panelli did the rest, but Notre Dame missed the conversion. The Wildcats kept driving, only to falter around the Irish 30 twice. Leahy unveiled yet another variation—both Tripucka and Williams in the backfield.

The Wildcats made three interceptions in the second half to keep Notre Dame at half throttle. One interception was returned 90 yards for a Northwestern score and a 7-6 Wildcat lead. The Fighting Irish fumbled on the next series, but the defense got it back. Notre Dame worked carefully on a 63-yard drive, all on the ground, for the winning score by Gay. Four interceptions by the Wildcats almost ended the Irish winning streak.

Washington made the long trip from Seattle. The Fighting Irish decimated the Huskies 25-0 in the first quarter on the way to a 46-0 rout. The Huskies lost four fumbles close to their end zone. Panelli scored from the 12 after the first fumble, then Brennan on a 30-yard pass from Tripucka, Hart on an end around for a 19-yard score, and Hart on a 41-yard touchdown pass from Tripucka. That was the first quarter; in the second quarter, Washington lost the ball on their 14, and Tripucka threw to Wightkin for seven on the second play. In the third quarter, Gay was a one-man drive: he returned a punt 26 yards to the Washington 44; ran 38 yards to their six, and scored on a one-yard plunge. In

the last quarter, a Husky punt of 10 yards allowed Landry to score on a 30-yarder.

The fumble contagion spread to Notre Dame the following game against USC; the Irish lost six miscues, and USC tied them 14-14. Hart opened the scoring with a 35-yard pass from Tripucka. USC reached the Notre Dame one-yard line but was turned back. The Irish lost Tripucka as he tried to wedge the ball forward and was hurt in a pile up. Bob Williams replaced him. The half ended with Notre Dame leading 7-0. In the third quarter, Sitko fumbled on the USC 21 and Gay lost a punt return due to a clip. The mistakes were adding up, as Williams was intercepted at the end of the third quarter. USC went ahead 14-7 in the fourth quarter with two touchdowns by Martin. Gay returned the kickoff 87 yards, and a penalty moved the ball on the one. Sitko scored with 35 seconds left, and Oracko converted the point after to tie the score. Notre Dame recovered an onside kick a few seconds later, but time ran out before the Irish could score again.

Fischer won the Outland Trophy while Hart, Sitko, and Wendell made All-America teams.

1948: 9-0-1 (.950)
Record to date: 380-77-30 (.811)

1949

If any team compared favorably to the great 1947 squad, it was the 1949 contingent. There were five Notre Dame All-Americans in 1947, and four in 1949. Both teams produced a Heisman winner. Both teams threw 154 passes and completed 86, but the 1949 team gained more yardage and scored more points. The 1949 Fighting Irish were more dominant over the opposition, but they did not have Lujack as that intangible element. The rules changed to permit a defensive unit by 1949 (and would revert at least once more), whereas the 1947 team was made up of two-way players unless mass substitutions gave them a break. The 1949 offensive line was big and tough, anchored by Hart and Martin, the latter moved to tackle. The backfield lost three starters, but the depth of the 1948 squad filled out the new one with Williams at quarterback, Spaniel and Coutre as halfbacks, and Sitko at fullback. The defense also featured Hart, a fine group of linemen for support, good linebackers, and excellent speed in Gay and Swistowicz.

1949 Notre Dame national champions.

Indiana fell first. After some initial resistance, Notre Dame pieced together a 52-yard drive, thanks to a fourth-down pass from Williams to Coutre to the Indiana 17; Sitko scored the first touchdown on a short-long run. In the second quarter, Bob Toneff blocked an Indiana punt for a Notre Dame safety. The Hoosiers responded briefly and marched in for their only score of the day. Notre Dame fired back with a Williams pass to Gay, who made a contortionist's catch for a 28-yard touchdown. By the third quarter, Notre Dame touchdowns rained: Sitko had a six-yard touchdown, Gay's 50-yard punt return set up Coutre's 13-yard touchdown, Sitko scored on a six-yarder, and Swistowicz went in from the one-yard line in the fourth quarter. Quarterback John Mazur threw a 17-yard touchdown pass to Wightkin for the final tally in a 49-6 blowout.

The Fighting Irish returned Washington's visit and found themselves deadlocked 7-7 at the half. A Coutre fumble had led to the Husky score. West coast officials, unfamiliar with the Midwest's greater use of arms in blocking, made holding calls that stunted Irish progress. The Fighting Irish score came on a 21-yard pass from Williams to Hart. In the third quarter, Toneff again blocked a punt and the Fighting Irish were on the Washington 14. Sitko rumbled for six, then Hart scored an eight-yard touchdown on an end around as assorted Huskies tried to get out of the way. Another Husky fumble resulted in a 36-yard touchdown by Coutre. Hart separated a Husky from the ball at their 18 and took off

on another end around for 12 yards. Landry wrapped it up with a short run for the 27-7 win.

Having defeated Indiana and Washington, Notre Dame met its old nemesis, Purdue. Sitko opened the scoring with a 41-yard touchdown early in the game. At

Ralph McGehee, starting RT on the 1949 national championship team.

the end of the first quarter, Coutre raced for a 48-yard score, giving the Irish an early 14-0 lead. In the next period, a recovered fumble started a Notre Dame drive from its own 33. On good running the Fighting Irish reached the Purdue nine; Sitko hammered it in. Purdue tried more passing, but Gay intercepted and dashed 61 yards for a tally. In the third quarter, an interception by Notre Dame linebacker John Helwig led to Billy Barrett's six-yard touchdown run. Two Purdue touchdowns made the final score 35-12 in favor of the Fighting Irish.

Tulane's Green Wave was highly touted in 1949, but Notre Dame crushed them 47-6 for its fourth straight victory of the 1949 campaign. This game was over early, as Notre Dame led at the end of the first quarter 27-0. Coutre scored three touchdowns within the first 10 minutes: a 14-yard dash, an 81-yarder on a pitchout, and a two-yard burst after a long pass to Wightkin. Notre Dame also scored on a pass from Williams to Spaniel. In the second quarter, the Fighting Irish moved 83 yards quickly: Williams for 19 yards on a bootleg; a 44-yard pass to Wightkin; two runs to the 20; and a touchdown pass to Hart. Tulane scored its lone touchdown, but four plays later Notre Dame scored again on an 11-yard touchdown run by Spaniel. In the fourth quarter, Barrett ran 59 yards for the final score. The defense held Tulane to minus 23 yards rushing.

Notre Dame continued its onslaught with a 40-0 blowout over Navy. Quarterback Williams pleased hometown Baltimore when he threw to Zalejski for a 48-yard score to open. In the second quarter, Coutre

Leon Hart and Jim White let themselves hurdle Indiana in fall drills before the 1949 season.

outran the Middies for a 91-yard touchdown. Sitko ran 44 yards, followed by a 16-yard touchdown. Williams closed the first half's scoring with two passes to Zalejski for 46 yards and another touchdown. The Fighting Irish headed to the locker room with a 27-0 halftime lead over Navy. The subs played the second half: Landry racked up a 14-yard touchdown and Zalejski sped 76 yards for a touchdown. The win was Notre Dame's 33rd straight without a loss.

At East Lansing, the Michigan State game started as a punting seminar until Williams found Zalejski for Notre Dame's first score, a 19-yard touchdown.

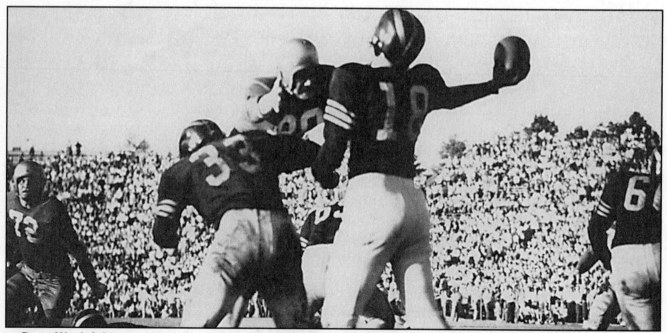

Doug Waybright menaces a Purdue passer in the 35-12 win in 1949.

The Four Horsemen circa 1949.

Moments later, Williams fumbled at his five, and the Spartans scored. Notre Dame answered with an 89-yard march, highlighted by Wightkin's 21-yard, fourth-down catch; Coutre scored on a short run. Notre Dame led 14-7 at halftime. The Fighting Irish took the opening possession of the second half 79 yards in eight plays, with Williams running the last 40 yards after a fake lateral to Sitko. On a later drive at the MSU 12, Sitko got the ball and faked MSU's Chandnois, an all-everything candidate, for the touchdown. Hart scored on a pass from Williams, giving the Irish 34 points. MSU kept trying and made the final score 34-21.

After Army declined to play Notre Dame, the Fighting Irish looked for someone else willing to play them in New York. North Carolina answered, losing 42-6. The Tarheels scored first, after an Irish fumble, and then watched the Notre Dame parade: Spaniel tied it with a 78-yard punt return; Williams threw long to Hart, who lateralled to Barrett for the score; Hart tackled a Tarheel for a safety; Williams threw touchdown passes to Spaniel and Barrett; Swistowicz ran 85 yards for a score on an interception; and Mazur threw 18 yards to Barrett for the final score.

Iowa tried next, but lost 28-7. Williams lobbed a high pass to Spaniel from the 20 for the first Irish score.

Iowa tied it after a fumble recovery in the second quarter, but Notre Dame came right back. Hart deflected a punt at their 22; Barrett scored from the eight for a 14-7 halftime lead. The third quarter was scoreless. Notre Dame consumed a lot of time in the fourth quarter with a 14-play, 95-yard drive, sparked by a 54-yard pass from Williams to Spaniel, who scored later. Hart grabbed a touchdown pass in the last minute to end it. Williams passed Bertelli's single-season passing marks.

Notre Dame had been waiting impatiently for more than a year to face USC. The 32-0 rout by Fighting Irish was certainly more pleasing than the 1948 tie. The Four Horsemen were honored guests on their silver anniversary. Leahy moved Hart midway through the game, (at 255 pounds) to fullback, a tactical enormity the Trojans hadn't expected; Hart started at end and caught a 40-yard touchdown pass from Williams. John Petitbon scored the second Irish touchdown with a 43-yard interception return. Up 14-0, Leahy made his move. After USC fumbled a punt, Barrett ran to the 11. Hart shifted to fullback, got the ball, and broadsided the USC line for seven yards. He lined up again at fullback, but as a decoy; Sitko scored untouched on an end run. Hart helped later with a 60-yard drive, and Spaniel went in from the two-yard line. In the fourth quarter,

Williams threw a 32-yard pass to Barrett to set up the final touchdown. Hart drove to the 15, Zalejski went for nine, and Barrett rammed in from the six-yard line. USC got only 17 yards rushing to the Fighting Irish's 312.

The game with Southern Methodist University, led by Kyle Rote (Doak Walker was hurt) was a classic, with Notre Dame prevailing 27-20. Notre Dame had a quick 14-0 lead on two Williams passes, a 42-yarder to Wightkin and a deflected pass to Zalejski for 35 yards. SMU scored on four Rote runs from the six-yard line. In the third period, a Zalejski fumble led to Rote running twice from the three-yard line to score. Jim Mutscheller, a budding Fighting Irish star, intercepted a Mustang pass and Barrett tallied from the three-yard line; Notre Dame was up 20-14. Rote tied the game after penalties and poor punting, but Groom blocked the point-after try. Leahy moved Hart to fullback on the last drive to preoccupy a tiring SMU team. The strategy worked, and

Barrett scored the winning touchdown from the two. But SMU drove to the Notre Dame five-yard line where a fourth-down Rote pass was intercepted by Groom and Bob Lally.

Leahy at Notre Dame had amassed 60 wins, three losses, and five ties, for a .919 winning percentage. Notre Dame was undefeated during the 1946-1949 seasons, compiling an astounding 36-0-2 record. Hart won the Heisman, one of only two lineman ever to do so. Sitko, Hart, Williams, and Martin made All-American teams. Twenty-nine players from this team were drafted by the NFL. Leahy and Notre Dame were at the height of excellence.

1949 record: 10-0-0 (1,000)
Record to date: 390-77-30 (.814)

Walt Grothaus, starting center for the 1949 national champions.

1950-1959

1950

Success does not always breed success. Leahy's talent pool was thinning. Two of the best Notre Dame players in its history were gone after the 1949 season—Hart and Martin. The rest of the offensive line was gone, too. Leahy brought up some good players, such as Bob Toneff and Jerry Groom, but overall it was not an overpowering bunch. The backfield was in better shape: Williams was back, with Petitbon and Barrett as halfbacks, and Landry replacing Sitko. Seven players on the starting offense had to go two ways as Leahy tried to get the most out of his personnel. The 1949 defensive line averaged 219 pounds; the 1950 group was 204. All Notre Dame linebackers returned, but they'd have their hands full.

North Carolina made its first visit to Notre Dame and fumbled the opening kickoff on its own 25; Notre Dame's Paul Burns recovered. Notre Dame was able to move on that series, and the Tarheels got the ball back only to fumble on the next play; Toneff recovered at the Tarheel 10. After three plays, Williams threw to Mutscheller from the three-yard line for the touchdown. Later in the first half, Barrett ran 52 yards, but the drive died. The Fighting Irish took a 7-0 lead into the locker room. In the third quarter, the Tarheels tied the game.

Jerry Groom, 1950 captain, and an All-American at center, leader of a tough Irish defense as MLB.

With only 2:40 left, Williams passed to Mutscheller for the winning touchdown, the 14-7 final score, and the 39th straight game without a Notre Dame loss.

Purdue shattered the streak with a 28-14 win. Notre Dame was never in the game, losing 21-0 at halftime. Purdue's defense held Williams to seven completions in

Leahy's inauguration of the 1950 campaign. Groom does the honors.

1950 Notre Dame varsity football squad.

22 tries for 46 yards. Purdue's running and a tiring Notre Dame defense were too much to overcome, although Notre Dame tried in the second half: Williams hit Mutscheller for a three-yard touchdown, and Petitbon dashed 10 yards for a score.

The Green Wave of Tulane gave the Fighting Irish all they wanted before losing 13-9 in the 500th game for Notre Dame. Tulane took the opening kick and drove 63 yards in five plays, exposing serious defensive flaws, scoring from the four-yard line. Notre Dame responded with an 80-yard scoring drive, which included passes to

Mutscheller for 23 yards and to Petitbon for the 58-yard touchdown. Similar passing in the second quarter set up Del Gander's 10-yard touchdown. In the second half, Tulane fumbled and the ball was recovered by Groom deep in Notre Dame territory. Tulane sacked Williams for a safety in the ensuing series, for the 13-9 score. The Notre Dame rushing attack gained only 34 yards to Tulane's 224. Bob Williams's passing won the game, with 16 completions for 225 yards.

Indiana beat the Fighting Irish the next week 20-7. Indiana scored first on a short pass, following a 51-yard punt return. Irish defenders were slow to react and the Hoosier quarterback had time to find the open receivers. Indiana went up by two touchdowns with another drive before halftime. As the second half opened, Robertson outran Fighting Irish defenders on an 83-yard streak on the second play from scrimmage in the third quarter. Del Gander got the only Irish score on an eight-yard run up the middle. Williams was hurt on the first play of that drive, and did not return for the rest of the game.

Michigan State, resurgent in the Big 10, won 36-33 at Notre Dame. The Fighting Irish scored first with a 19-yard pass from Mazur to Mutscheller. MSU roared into the lead with drives capped by a Pisano run of 15 yards and one by Grandelius for seven yards. A blocked punt was recovered by MSU for another touchdown. Early in the second quarter, the Fighting Irish responded with an 85-yard march, finished by Petitbon's five-yard touchdown plunge. Then the teams settled into a defensive draw, until MSU hit a 31-yard field goal in the third quarter. Notre Dame scored twice

Bob Williams—All America QB for Notre Dame in 1949 and 1950.

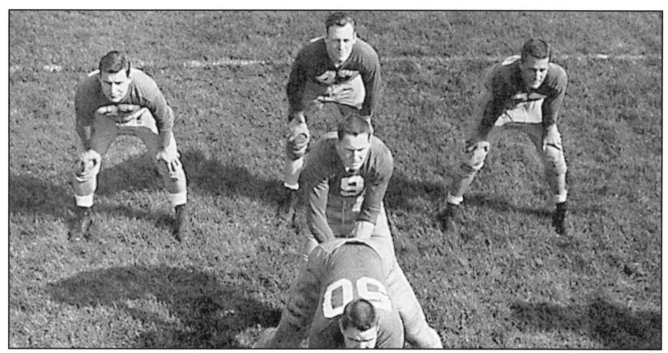

The T-formation circa 1950.

on touchdown throws from Williams to Mutscheller to go ahead 26-23 in the third quarter, but MSU fought back with touchdown runs by Grandelius and McAuliffe. Notre Dame came close at the end with a touchdown pass from Mazur to Gerry Marchand, but the Irish rally fell short. Petitbon gained 171 yards on 10 trips to pace the Irish's 526 yards.

Going into the Navy game, Notre Dame sported a sub-.500 record (2-3) for the first time in a long time. The Navy game did not start well for the Irish, as Navy took a quick 7-0 lead on an interception. Notre Dame's Dave Flood returned the favor and Landry sped 54 yards to the Midshipmen's 10; Williams passed to Gay for a five-yard touchdown and the halftime tie. Navy drove for a field goal and the lead in the second half, but Notre Dame responded with a six-yard touchdown pass from Williams to Ostrowski. Later, Groom blocked a punt, and Landry scored from the five for a 19-10 win.

Despite the Irish .500 record, Pitt still could not win a game from Notre Dame. The Fighting Irish scored first with a 15-yard pass from Williams to Mutscheller to conclude a 70-yard drive. Pitt fumbled the ensuing kickoff on its 38, and a half-dozen plays later, Williams fired a 12-yard touchdown pass to Petitbon. The defense then stopped a Pitt drive that reached the five-yard line; the Panthers came right back and scored on a 13-yard pass. The halftime score was 12-7. Notre Dame controlled much of the clock in the third and fourth quarters, and fashioned a touchdown drive boosted by

Landry's 22-yard run, and his three-yard touchdown plunge. The final score was 18-7. Williams hit 13 of 21 passes for 171 yards, surpassing Bertelli's 169 as a game high. Notre Dame was relieved to be back over .500 for the season.

Iowa tied Notre Dame 14-14 in the next game. The Hawkeyes threatened to win it with a 14-0 first quarter lead on interceptions and short marches. Mazur sparked a 63-yard, seven-play drive, featuring Landry's 43-yard run to the 20. Petitbon scored from the 11 on an end run. Before the half, Notre Dame used 20 plays on an 80-yard drive to tie the game. Williams went in from the one-yard line. Vince Meschievitz's conversion kicks were both good.

Leahy was ill for the USC finale in California. The 9-7 USC win did not make him feel any better. Crimmins handled the team in his absence, but injuries decimated attempts to sustain the effort. Seven starters and two subs were knocked out of action. USC won with a 94-yard kickoff return by Jim Sears and a safety on a blocked punt. Williams scored on a one-yard quarterback sneak. Notre Dame's defense held the Trojans to 70 yards on the ground and four in the air.

It was only the fourth time in 62 seasons that Notre Dame had lost four games. Williams and Groom earned All-America status.

1950 record: 4-4-1 (.500)
Record to date: 394-81-31 (.809).

1951

Leahy brought up some fine youngsters and good reserves to strengthen the team's weak areas: Ralph Guglielmi, Art Hunter, Neil Worden, Joe Heap, and John Lattner. Mazur took over at quarterback; Petitbon and Barrett were halfbacks, and Worden was the fullback. The defense would feature the hard hitting of Dan Shannon and the good linebacking of Dick Syzmanski, with fine defensive coverages from Lattner.

Indiana paid for its 1950 win over the Irish when Leahy's team pasted them 48-6. After conducting secret fall practices, Leahy showed an "I" formation with Petitbon, Barrett, and Worden lined up behind Mazur. The Hoosiers were confused, and Notre Dame moved 75 yards for the first score. Barrett logged the touchdown from the six-yard line. In the second quarter, Worden set a school record with four touchdowns: from the six-yard line, from the one after an Indiana turnover, from the five after a fumble, and from the 11 after Lattner's interception. Then Lattner scored from in close. Del Gander answered with Indiana's only score when he scored in the fourth quarter.

Notre Dame's first night game ever was against the University of Detroit in Briggs Stadium. The offense pulverized the Titans 40-6. Petitbon set the tone for the blowout when he returned the opening kickoff 85 yards for a touchdown. He and Barrett then worked a crisscross on a punt, with Petitbon scoring from 73 yards out. He tallied again from the Detroit 39 with a pitchout.

Neil Worden, three-year starter at FB, scored four TDs in the second quarter of his first game, the 1951 mangling of Indiana.

The scoring for the half ended when Mazur threw a 30-yard touchdown to Mutscheller. Detroit finally scored in the third quarter, but Lattner matched that score by intercepting a pass and returning it 32 yards for a Notre Dame touchdown. Guglielmi scored from the one after Walt Cabral fell on a Detroit fumble. Petitbon averaged 13 yards per carry to go with his long kick returns.

The Fighting Irish suffered the first loss of the season against Southern Methodist University, 27-20. SMU scored on a touchdown pass of 57 yards in the first

1951 Notre Dame starting eleven.

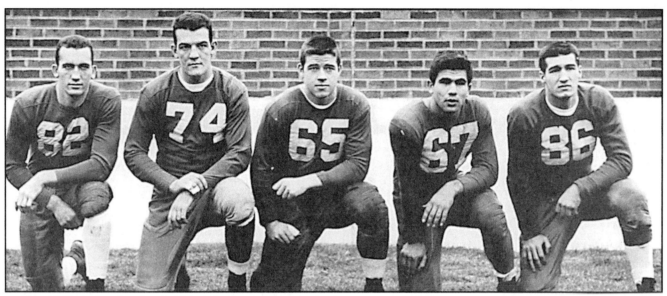

The 1951 defensive front: Bob O'Neil, Bob Ready, Jack Lee, Sam Palumbo, Fred Mangialardi.

quarter, but Paul Reynolds got it back on a crossbuck and cutback for a 33-yard touchdown run. SMU hit three quick passes for their next score, the last good for 37 yards. In the second quarter, SMU dropped a punt and Lattner recovered on SMU's 24. Mazur threw a 19-yard touchdown pass to Chet Ostrowski to tie it, 13-13. SMU's Benners hit two more touchdown passes; SMU picked off Mazur twice, and Lattner scored from the five as time ran out.

A look at how things went for Indiana as they lost to the Irish 48-6 in 1951.

Pitt had lost its best quarterback and receiver to early-season injuries before playing Notre Dame. Taking advantage of Pitt's misfortune, Notre Dame pounded the Panthers 33-0. Mazur started the scoring with a 10-yard pass to Barrett for a touchdown. In the second quarter, Mazur and Barrett repeated with a 28-yard score. Lattner, who started the second drive recovering a Pitt fumble, later grabbed an interception that led to a Mazur sneak from the one. Mazur did the same in the third quarter to finish an 80-yard drive. Syzmanski got an interception and Tom Carey looked good at quarterback on a 71-yard touchdown drive. Seven turnovers and a blocked punt completed the 33-0 victory over Pitt.

The first quarter was a sparring match between Notre Dame and Purdue. In the next quarter, Mazur fashioned a 75-yard drive, wrapped up by a fake to Worden and the score by Reynolds. Purdue took the lead following Irish fumbles with a field goal and a quick touchdown. Minnie Mavraides put Notre Dame back in front with a 10-yard field goal. Dan Shannon intercepted a Purdue pass to set up a Lattner touchdown run of 40 yards. Barrett and Mutscheller scored the last two touchdowns—on a one-yard slam and an eight-yard pass for a 30-9 Irish victory.

The Navy game was a punting duel, with 25 punts on a soggy day. The Middies kept it scoreless until well into the second quarter; Worden used a delay play to score on a 36-yard run. Shannon and Dave Flood grabbed a fumble and two plays later Mazur used a "split T sweep" to score from the 21. Winless Navy gained only three yards in the first half. In the second half, Barrett returned a punt 76 yards for a touchdown,

Joe Katchik at 6-9, 255, and Billy Barrett at 5-8, 180, at spring practice in 1951.

The set-up for publicity shots, circa 1951.

with Shannon blocking. Navy and the weather kept the Fighting Irish to 11 net rushing yards in the half, but the Irish managed to pull out a 19-0 win.

MSU routed Notre Dame 35-0, scoring the first touchdown with chicanery. With the ball on MSU's 12, the Spartans lined up but with the single wing backfield off to the right. A tackle looked left, over to an end, and said he wasn't lined up right. With that, the ball was snapped to the fullback, Dick Panin. The Irish never caught up with him on an 88-yard touchdown chase. Conventional football drilled Notre Dame after that: a one-yard dive, two short touchdown passes, and a touchdown off an interception. The Spartans smashed Notre Dame's defense with 353 rushing yards.

The Irish rebounded from the MSU game with a 12-7 win over North Carolina. Reynolds scored the first Notre Dame touchdown in the second quarter on a short run, and Worden went in from the four in the third quarter. The Tarheels's only score came on a 37-yard pass. It was Notre Dame's 400th win in 514 games. Leahy did not use most of his starting backfield, choosing instead to build experience for good young players.

Notre Dame tied Iowa 20-20 the following week, bringing the Irish season record to 6-2-1. The Hawkeyes scored first on a 58-yard pass. Notre Dame fired back; Worden scored from the nine, but the Irish missed the

point after. Iowa responded with a five-play drive that culminated in a 45-yard touchdown pass, giving the Hawkeyes the halftime lead. Iowa was using a spread formation during the first half that seemed to frustrate the Fighting Irish. Leahy made adjustments at the half to stop it; so the Hawkeyes used a straight T to move 62 yards, scoring from the seven on an end run. Down 20-6 in the third quarter, Notre Dame started its rally with a five-yard score by Lattner. This touchdown was set up by Guglielmi's passes of 31 yards and 44 yards to Reynolds and Lattner. On the next drive, Lattner completed a 23-yard pass to Mutscheller on fourth down from punt formation. Later, interference put the ball on the one and Lattner scored. Sophomore Bob Joseph kicked the point after with 55 seconds left to avert a loss.

After his strong second-half showing against Iowa, Leahy picked Guglielmi to start against USC, who boasted Frank Gifford and Leon Sellers. Gifford scored first from the eight. Notre Dame roared back with a 13-play, 78-yard drive that ended with Lattner scoring from the one. An interception led to a USC score, but Gifford missed his second conversion try, leaving the USC lead at 12-7. Leahy chose to use the youngsters in the backfield; Worden ran 39 yards, untouched, for the go-ahead score. Petitbon scored an insurance touchdown later for the 19-12 win.

The 1951 season was a satisfying return from the oblivion of 1950; Notre Dame's offensive output increased about 25 percent, resulting in 15 more touchdowns than the previous year. Toneff and Mutscheller were All-Americans.

1951 record: 7-2-1 (.750)
Record to date: 401-83-32 (.808)

1952

If the 1951 season represented a good comeback from 1950, the 1952 season earned back a strong measure of respect for the Fighting Irish. They were not quite a dominating team, but then few teams would ever dominate an era as the Irish had from 1946 through 1949. The 1951 season allowed talented youngsters to mature beyond their raw potential. The backfield was set with Guglielmi at quarterback, Heap and Lattner as the halfbacks, and Worden at fullback. This was a fast unit, with Lattner excelling in guile and instinct, and Worden in blocking. The line was adequate. Leahy shifted Art Hunter from center to left end. The defense was a bit undersized, although all three linebackers were back—Shannon, Syzmanski, and Jack Alessandrini. Lattner and Reynolds starred in the secondary (Lattner would play a substantial 422 minutes in the year).

The opener with the University of Pennsylvania ended in a 7-7 tie. The Fighting Irish started with an 89-yard march in 15 plays. Lattner blasted runs of 21 and 22 yards, and from the 11 he hammered three times for the touchdown. Notre Dame scored again shortly thereafter on a 44-yard pass to Heap, but a penalty killed the play, and eventually the win. Penalties killed another Notre Dame drive. In the third quarter, a secondary lapse let Penn score on a 65-yard pass for the tie. Notre Dame had

The studious Ralph Guglielmi.

one last chance if Guglielmi could move them 80 yards in two minutes. He almost did: he passed to Lattner for 21 yards, to Heap for seven, to Bob O'Neil for 15, and

The 1952 Notre Dame varsity.

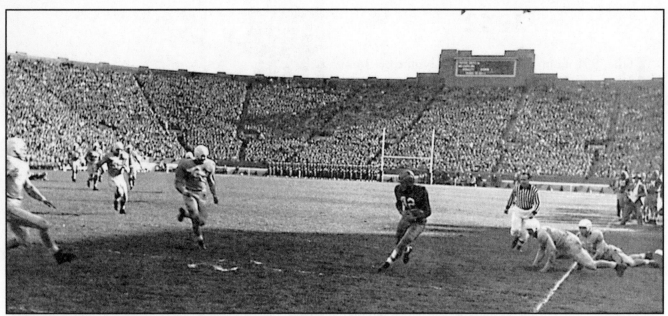

Joe Heap (42) wrapping up an 84-yard TD run against North Carolina to help the Irish win 34-14 in 1952.

to Lattner near the Penn 25, but the ball came loose as he spun away from the tackler, and Penn recovered to preserve the tie.

The Notre Dame-Texas series, last played in 1934, was resumed in Austin for the 1952 season. Texas started strong, driving to the Notre Dame two, but they fumbled and settled for a field goal. Their defense stifled Notre Dame's offense, allowing the Irish only 55 yards for the first half. In the third quarter, on the Texas 25, Guglielmi passed to Lattner in the flat. Lattner in turn threw to Heap for a gain to the one-yard line. Lattner scored on the next play. A fourth-quarter Irish punt hit the Texas returner squarely in the chest, and Shannon recovered the ball at the Longhorn two. Heap scored for a 14-3 win over Texas.

Notre Dame returned home and lost to Pitt 22-19. The Panthers struck first with a 79-yard touchdown on a pitchout to Billy Reynolds. Then quarterback Mattioli threw a 63-yard touchdown pass to end the first quarter, with Pitt leading the surprised Irish 13-0. Penalties and Pitt's gritty defense kept Notre Dame scoreless in the second quarter, giving Pitt a commanding 13-0 halftime lead. In the third quarter, Guglielmi put together a seven-play series of 78 yards; Worden scored from the 12. Several Irish penalties and a punt later, Mattioli scored from the Notre Dame two. Guglielmi drove the Fighting Irish again, scoring himself from the one-yard line. Then Heap returned a punt 92 yards for a score, drawing the Fighting Irish to within a point. However, they missed the point after, their second. More penalties,

a lost pitchout, and Guglielmi was caught for a safety—of such things are upsets made. Notre Dame lost 22-19.

As bad as the Pitt game was, the Irish looked even worse against Purdue in a fumbling derby (21 fumbles combined, 10 for Notre Dame). Nevertheless, the Fighting Irish won 26-14, largely because they recovered

Joe Heap latches onto a 10-yard pass from Guglielmi in the 1952 Pitt game.

One of the great Irish backfields: the 1952 quartet of Johnny Lattner, Neil Worden, Joe Heap, and Ralph Guglielmi.

15 of the fumbles. Notre Dame started quickly, scoring three plays after Purdue fumbled the opening kickoff. Even the Irish score involved a fumble, as tackle Joe Bush scored the touchdown when Lattner fumbled into the end zone. Purdue scored on a 27-yard pass, then Worden finished off a 68-yard drive by Notre Dame with a one-yard smash. Guglielmi threw a 47-yard touchdown to Lattner on the last play of the first half, giving the Irish a 20-7 halftime lead. In the third quarter, an Irish fumble led to a Purdue score. Notre Dame put together a solid drive, sans fumbles, that ended with another Worden score. Art Hunter keyed that drive with a 41-yard catch from Carey. Leahy was so upset by the fumbling of the talented Lattner, that he had a football taped to the halfback's hand for the entire week following the Purdue game.

A brush with polio had kept the North Carolina team hospitalized for three weeks; the Fighting Irish won the contest 34-14. A Worden touchdown opened it but a fumble let Carolina tie. A scrappy defense kept Notre Dame off balance until Leahy sent in Guglielmi. Guglielmi used two fourth-down gambles to keep moving, leading to a 10-yard touchdown to Hunter. After the half, Heap returned a kickoff 84 yards for a score. Sub Tom McHugh tallied twice, and the Tar Heels scored once more for the final result.

Navy had lost six straight to Notre Dame—the 1952 game made it seven. The Irish scored first, settling for a field goal after losing a halfback touchdown pass

on a penalty. Two other field goal kicks by Notre Dame were either blocked or goofed during the low-scoring first half. Worden ran for an eight-yard score, but the point after was missed, and the Irish headed to the locker room with a 9-0 lead at halftime. In the third quarter, another Notre Dame drive stalled; Bob O'Neil tackled Navy's quarterback for a safety. Later, Worden scored again and Navy salvaged six points from Guglielmi errors for the 17-6 final.

Leahy was concerned; the Fighting Irish were staring at the fourth-ranked Sooners of Oklahoma, led by Billy Vessels. This was one of the earliest nationally televised games, and he ran for 195 yards on 17 tries and scored three times. An early Irish drive stalled and the Sooners's quick drive ended when Eddie Crowder threw a 20-yard touchdown pass to Vessels. Notre Dame fought back with a 59-yard drive capped by a 16-yard touchdown pass from Guglielmi to Heap. Two minutes later, Vessels made a 62-yard touchdown run. Oklahoma led at the half, 14-7. The opening moments of the second half thrilled the national television audience: Notre Dame drove from its own 20 to the Oklahoma six, but fumbled. However, on Oklahoma's ensuing drive, Lattner intercepted a Crowder pass and returned it to the Sooner seven. Worden tried three times and scored, 14-14. Vessels three plays later ran for a 47-yard touchdown The Fighting Irish came back with a 79-yard drive, with a 36-yard halfback pass from Heap to Lattner reaching the 27. Worden ran seven straight

The 1952 Fighting Irish starting eleven.

times for the touchdown. Notre Dame kicked off to the six where Larry Grigg fielded it and ran to his 24; Dan Shannon met him going full speed, hitting him so hard that Grigg did a half loop in mid-air and lost the ball. Shannon lost consciousness. Al Kohanowich recovered for Notre Dame. Lattner ran it to the seven. Then the Irish shifted from the T into the Notre Dame box and the Sooners went offside. Worden went to the one-foot line, and Carey sneaked it in. A rejuvenated defense stopped Oklahoma over the final 13 minutes for the 27-21 win and an all-time great victory.

Next, the Fighting Irish faced Michigan State, ranked number one. Notre Dame lost seven fumbles and MSU beat them 21-3. The first two fumbles did not result in MSU scores, although they were deep in Notre Dame territory—the 34 and 15— but the Irish defense's efforts must have dipped far into their reserves of strength. The Irish grabbed the lead in the third quarter with a 14-yard field goal by Bob Arrix. Notre Dame's defense turned back the Spartans yet another time, but the offense fumbled. MSU's Willie Thrower kept firing the ball, Lattner intercepted on the Notre Dame 10, and Notre Dame promptly fumbled on its 13. A holding penalty moved it to the 1 and McAuliffe scored. One minute later, the Irish dropped the ball at their 21; and again they were called for holding—the ball

was on the one again. McAuliffe scored. The Fighting Irish managed a drive, with Lattner slashing for 36 yards and Heap catching a Lattner option pass for 24 yards. But Guglielmi was intercepted, and MSU drove for their third touchdown. Notre Dame outgained the Spartans across the board, but turnovers and penalties sealed the loss.

Leahy missed the next game against Iowa with the flu. Line coach Joe McArdle led them in a 27-0 win. Running from the right halfback slot, Worden led a 66-yard drive in 13 plays for the first score, going in from the four. Lattner seemed left out of things as a new backfield started with Worden: Carey, Heap, and McHugh. Iowa punted and Lattner returned it 84 yards for a touchdown. Officiating held Notre Dame scoreless in the third quarter. Then Worden scored from the two. Guglielmi sparked the last score with a fake for a 12-yard touchdown pass to Heap.

USC was undefeated and ranked in the top three. The Trojans hurt themselves to lead to Notre Dame's only first-half score when the Trojans's Jim Sears tried to gain more yardage with a lateral on a punt return, but no one was there and Mavraides grabbed the loose ball on the Trojan 19. Lattner scored a few plays later and Arrix added a third-quarter field goal for the 9-0 final score. The Fighting Irish defense stymied USC, allowing only

64 yards rushing and five first downs, while grabbing five interceptions.

The Fighting Irish had averaged one lost fumble per quarter of football. To make matters worse, the fumbles were bunched in key games. The quarterbacks hit only 93 passes in 205 tries, an unimpressive .453 rate. The interception to touchdown ratio was 4:1, far too high for a great team. Nevertheless, Notre Dame managed to upend highly-ranked Oklahoma and USC, and finished with a very respectable season record of 7-2-1.

Lattner was a consensus All-American, and O'Neil made the second team.

1952 record: 7-2-1 (.750)
Record to date: 408-85-33 (.807)

1953

Rule changes now mandated that a player could not leave the game and return in the same quarter—back to "Iron Man Football." Only Lattner had much two-way experience. Leahy shuffled his linemen around, moving Hunter from end to right tackle and Shannon to left end. This was a good group and some 1952 players found themselves backups. The backfield was set: Guglielmi, Heap, Lattner, and Worden, which was probably the best set of Notre Dame backs for the next decade.

Oklahoma was the opener in Norman. Lattner let the kickoff dribble out of his hands at the four, but Notre Dame retained possession. Worden fumbled on the fourth play, at the Notre Dame 23. Larry Grigg scored for Oklahoma on the eighth grudging play. Heap fumbled on the Sooner 23. Notre Dame's defense asserted itself, and took the ball back at their 42. Guglielmi threw to Lattner who reached their 12. Four short runs later Heap scored. Tied 7-7, punts dominated much of the first half until a long Oklahoma pass got to the Notre Dame 18. They scored. Frank Varrichione smothered one of their quick kicks on the nine and three plays later Guglielmi tied the game, for a halftime score of 14-14. In the third quarter, Guglielmi intercepted a Sooner pass and then threw a touchdown to Heap. The Sooners fumbled on their 38 in the next series; Don Penza recovered and Worden ran in from the nine a few plays later. Oklahoma returned a Lattner punt 60 yards for a touchdown, but he later intercepted a pass to cinch the 28-21 win for Notre Dame.

Notre Dame met Purdue in Lafayette and swamped the Boilermakers 37-7. Guglielmi looked sharp, got it started, and then watched the results. Mavraides on the second possession kicked a 22-yard field goal. Purdue dropped the ball two plays later on their 29. Worden slammed in from the 11 four plays later. The Fighting

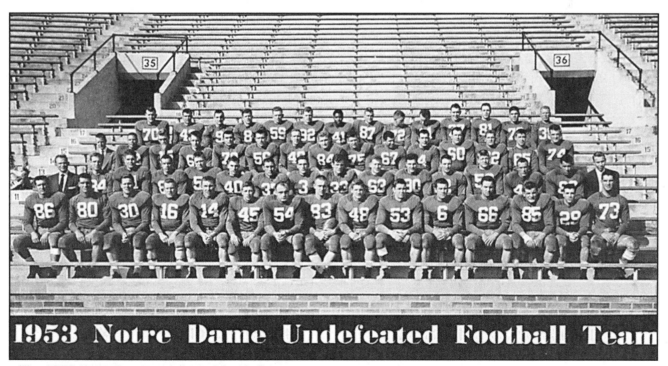

The 1953 Notre Dame undefeated football team.

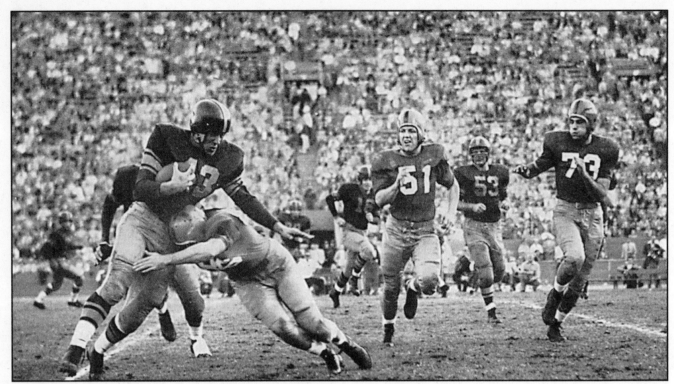

USC's Des Koch finds the going tough in the 1953 48-14 loss to Notre Dame.

Irish stalled on two series and Purdue threw a 75-yard touchdown. Lattner returned a kickoff for an 86-yard score. Late in the first half, Dick Washington ran 32 yards

Frank Varrichione held down the LT spot in 1952 and 1953, switched to RT in 1954, and made All-American.

for a touchdown and a 23-7 halftime lead. Purdue kept fumbling and Guglielmi scored from the five. Purdue punted to their own 17, and Worden scored from the 10 two plays later to cap the 37-7 win. Guglielmi completed seven of nine passes, and Irish backs ran for 302 yards.

Pittsburgh started with a 65-yard drive. The Fighting Irish came back on the next seven and put together a 67-yard march, with Worden scoring. Pitt intercepted and scored from the Notre Dame four. Pitt's 14-7 lead lasted into the third quarter when Varrichione tallied a safety. A fumble deep in Pitt territory gave the Fighting Irish the lead when Guglielmi sneaked over for a touchdown. Guglielmi scored the final touchdown from the Pitt nine in the fourth quarter for Notre Dame's 23-14 victory.

Georgia Tech, riding a 31-game winning streak, came to South Bend ranked number one. Notre Dame showed good concentration on the opening 80-yard drive, keyed by Heap's 33-yard run and Lattner's 21-yarder, that set up Worden's touchdown from the seven. Leahy sent in the subs after another long march, but they fumbled it away. The 7-0 score lasted into the third quarter, but Leahy didn't. An attack of gastroenteritis—an inflammation of the membrane lining the stomach and intestines—in the locker room sent him to the hospital. Tech tied the game after an interception. Heap started to take over, with a return to the 44 and a touchdown reception. Hunter scored by recovering a loose punt snap in the Tech end zone. Tech threw a 44-yard touchdown pass, but Lattner scored from the one for a 27-14 upset win over the nation's number one team.

Leahy stayed home and watched Notre Dame dismantle Navy 38-7. The defense gave up only eight yards in the first half to Navy while the offense staggered the Middies with four second-quarter touchdowns: a Heap plunge from the one, a long pass to Heap after a fumble recovery, a Guglielmi interception and 47-yard touchdown return, and a Tom McHugh dive. The regulars never returned to the game. Carey scored in the third quarter with a 27-yard keeper, and later threw a three-yard scoring pass to Dick Keller. Navy scored later on a lateral for the 38-7 final.

Penn was reported to be stronger than the team that tied Notre Dame in 1952, and they looked stronger when they scored on their first possession, 61 yards in seven plays. Lattner took the ensuing kickoff 92 yards for a touchdown, breaking three tackles on the way. After an exchange of possession, Notre Dame, in a 68-yard drive, scored on a three-yard run by Guglielmi. A Penn punt went to Heap, who handed off to Lattner for a 38 yard return. From the three, sub quarterback Don Schaefer scored to open the second quarter. Trailing 21-7, Penn drove for a score to start the second half. Lattner returned their kickoff 56 yards, and two plays later Guglielmi fired a 23-yard touchdown pass to Heap. Penn drove for another score, and threatened again, but Lattner intercepted in his end zone for a 28-20 victory.

The fullbacks took over against North Carolina; Worden and McHugh scored four touchdowns in a 34-14 win. Worden did most of the work for the first tally: Worden 14 yards to the Notre Dame 46; Worden 23 yards to the

Carolina 31; and Heap's lateral to Worden for a touchdown. Schaefer scored for the subs to start the second period. Then McHugh finished a drive with a two-yard touchdown slam. Carolina scored, the teams punted for a while, and Worden thundered for a 52-yard touchdown. In the fourth quarter, McHugh ended a drive with a one-yard scoring dive. The Tarheels scored later as Notre Dame prevailed.

Iowa came east to play Notre Dame. Iowa intercepted a pass and pieced together a 71-yard drive capped by a 12-yard touchdown run late in the first quarter. The Irish looked sluggish and Iowa looked sharp. A Fighting Irish drive to the goal line ended when a tipped pass went to a Hawkeye. Finally Lattner returned a punt to his 41; Heap caught a 22-yard pass to their 37; and Lattner ran for five. Time was running out in the first half. Worden grabbed a pass and went to the Iowa 25. A pass to Heap reached the 14, but there were no time outs left. Two seconds left—and time stopped. Notre Dame's Frank Varrichione groaned and collapsed, gripping the small of his back. The officials called an injury timeout. Varrichione was taken from the game, and Shannon scored with a pass from Guglielmi, making the halftime score 7-7. After a scoreless third quarter, Iowa scored on a pitchout that turned into a touchdown pass. Only 2:06 remained, and the Irish still

The 1953 Notre Dame starting eleven.

Art Hunter, 1951 center (later a consensus All-American at RT in 1953), gets ready to snap to QB John Mazur.

trailed 14-7. Worden returned the kick to the Notre Dame 42. Five plays later, the ball was on the Iowa nine, with 32 seconds left. Two incomplete passes wasted 26 seconds, and there were no more time outs. Suddenly, there were five Notre Dame linemen writhing on the ground, including a rehabilitated Varrichione, Penza, and Hunter. Guglielmi went to each and kicked them, telling them to get up. The referees called an injury timeout. On the last play, Guglielmi took the snap and faded to his left, then fired a pass across the field where Shannon caught it for the touchdown. Schaefer kicked the point after for the 14-14 tie, and the Fighting Irish were still undefeated. The NCAA authorities were none too pleased by the Fainting Irish. The controversy raged all week— resulting in an end to faked injuries—and Leahy was sent to bed by his doctor.

Notre Dame went to Los Angeles to meet USC. Notre Dame annihilated them 48-14. Lattner scored four touchdowns and gained 157 yards on 17 carries. Heap opened on a 94-yard touchdown kickoff return. Lattner scored from the nine with a pitchout. USC scored. Fighting Irish sub Ray Lemek intercepted a Trojan pass and the regulars came back in. Worden ran 54 yards to the three, and tallied. In the third quarter, USC fumbled; Lattner took a pitchout wide left from

the five. USC scored again. Lattner finished a quick drive with a one-yard touchdown. A Trojan back mishandled a handoff in his end zone, and Pat Bisceglia scored a touchdown on the fumble recovery. A USC fumble let Lattner run 50 yards up the middle for a touchdown. Later, disgruntled LA sportswriters complained that Notre Dame's jerseys tore off too easily.

SMU boasted one of the finest defenses in the country. Lattner and Worden combined for five touchdowns in their last game. Worden scored three to reach 29 for his career (Red Salmon had 36). Lattner threw a 55-yard pass to Shannon on the SMU four. Worden scored from the one. In the second quarter, Varrichione fell on a fumble for a touchdown. On the next Irish possession, Lattner scored on a 23-yard pass from Guglielmi. In the third period, he ran in from the five on a sweep. SMU finally scored with a pass. Guglielmi passed 42 yards to fellow quarterback Schaefer, to the 10. Worden hammered in from the one moments later. He scored again from the three after a Lemek interception. SMU scored once more to make it 40-14.

The Fighting Irish lost the national championship to Maryland. Lattner won the Heisman and the Maxwell trophies. Hunter and Penza earned All-America accolades.

Leahy was 45 years old with two years left on his contract. His teams had won 87 games, lost 11, and tied nine. The Fighting Irish had won national titles in 1943, 1946, 1947, 1949, and almost now in 1953. He had coached four Heisman winners. He had also missed six games due to illness over the years. His doctor advised him that the stress of coaching was killing him. Leahy's friends concurred. On January 31, 1954, his resignation was made official. And it was also announced that Terry Brennan, then 25 years old, would be the new head coach. Frank Leahy never coached another football game.

1953 season: 9-0-1 (.950)
Record to date: 417-85-34 (.809)

1954

Terence Patrick Brennan. His father, Joe, had been the backup center for the great 1909 Notre Dame team, but then transferred to Marquette. Terry had started at left halfback at the height of the glory years, 1946-1948. After graduating from Notre Dame, he

Notre Dame's Fighting Irish team of 1954.

coached Mt. Carmel High School to three straight Chicago city championships while earning his law degree at DePaul. He was the freshman coach for Notre Dame and worked the phones in the press box in 1953. President Hesburgh, who once had Brennan as a philosophy student, said that he'd been considered coaching material since his undergraduate days. He also advised Brennan to stick with older coaches since he had no experience as a head coach in college.

He inherited a great team. The entire line was made up of starters or former starters. Guglielmi and Carey were back, as was Heap. Jim Morse would try to fill Lattner's shoes, and Don Schaefer moved from reserve quarterback to fullback. Sophomore Paul Hornung subbed for him.

The Fighting Irish opened with a 21-0 shutdown of Texas. Varrichione saved the shutout on the fifth play of the game when he recovered a Longhorn fumble at his seven. Later, Guglielmi intercepted a Texas pass on his 19 and raced 42 yards to their 39. Shannon caught a 19-yard touchdown pass from Guglielmi early in the second quarter. In the third quarter, a 44-yard pass from Guglielmi to Heap keyed a 79-yard march. Guglielmi scored from the three. Lemek killed a Texas drive with a fumble recovery at the Notre Dame five and Varrichione recovered his second to keep Texas frustrated. Guglielmi scored again from the three to wrap up the game.

Purdue ended the euphoria with a 27-14 win behind two sophomores—former NFL player and Hall of Famer Len Dawson and Lamar Lundy. Dawson passed

Dick Szymanski, outstanding Irish linebacker and starting center in 1954 before an injury ended his season.

The Irish coaches under Brennan: Bernie Witucki, Bill Fischer, Jack Zilly, Terry Brennan, Bill Walsh, Jim Finks, and Jack Landry.

for four touchdowns and intercepted a pass, and Lundy rumbled 73 yards with a pass for his touchdown. Paul Hornung looked good on a 59-yard return of a free kick after a safety. Nick Raich scored from the one on the next play. Schaefer bulled in from the two after Shannon caught a 41-yard pass. Fighting Irish fumbles and Dawson's brilliance accounted for the loss.

Brennan's Irish recovered to beat Pitt 33-0. Carey threw a 24-yard touchdown to Sherrill Sipes. In the second quarter, Shannon caused a fumble that Sam Palumbo recovered; Guglielmi threw deep for 34 to Heap, and scored a few plays later on a sneak. After another fumble, Dean Studer took a pitchout and ran five yards for a score. Late in the third quarter, Hornung subbed at quarterback for a couple of drives, the second finished by his touchdown run from the 11. Later he intercepted a Pitt pass in his end zone and ran it back 22 yards. Carey scored with three seconds to go on an 11-yard touchdown strike to Jim Munro.

The Fighting Irish spotted Michigan State a 13-point lead before taking charge to win 20-19. Clarence Peaks scored first for MSU, then Earl Morrall threw a touchdown pass. Heap crashed in from the one to break the ice. In the second half, MSU drove to the Notre Dame 11 but fumbled. By this time the field was a mess due to steady rain. The Irish put together a long drive through the muck; Heap went around right end from the 16 for a touchdown. Early in the fourth quarter on a fourth-down play, Schaefer ran 30 yards

to the MSU 11. Paul Reynolds took a Guglielmi lateral from the eight for the winning points. The Spartans drove for a score but Bisceglia forced a bad conversion kick for the win.

Notre Dame barely escaped against Navy 6-0. Notre Dame should have mauled them. The Fighting Irish looked great in the first quarter; Navy had the ball for six plays. In the next quarter, Guglielmi threw to a streaking Morse for a 46-yard touchdown. Schaefer missed the point after. Navy had trouble getting out of their territory, but in the third quarter, they moved to the Notre Dame 12 where a penalty killed the drive. They intercepted an Irish pass and were at the 15. The Fighting Irish stopped them twice, and caused a fumble that Guglielmi recovered in the end zone. Guglielmi later intercepted a pass, as did Hornung, to save the win.

Brennan faced his first Ivy League team, Penn. The Quakers moved well in the first quarter but errors close to the end zone stopped them from scoring. Schaefer, from his three, ran 70 yards. Guglielmi finished the drive with a sneak from the four. Lemek intercepted a Quaker pass and Guglielmi hit Shannon with a 22-yard touchdown. The halftime score was 14-0. Penn kicked off to start the second half, and Notre Dame drove 95 yards in seven plays. Shannon scored on an 18-yard pass from Guglielmi. Penn scored but the Irish marched right back for one. Heap intercepted a Penn pass and ran it back to their 22. Two plays later, Carey found Studer open for a 20-yard score. Then Carey grabbed

Terry Brennan flanked by his 1954 co-captains, Paul Matz and Dan Shannon.

a fumble to set up Hornung's score from the three and the 42-7 final score.

Jim Morse opened the Irish blowout of the visiting Tar Heels of North Carolina with a 77-yard kickoff return, and Heap scored six plays later. Heap also scored the second touchdown, ending a nine-play drive of 50 yards. Heap gained 42 yards on a reception in an 82-yard drive, and Morse scored. Carey threw a 47-yard pass to Studer and a touchdown pass to Jim Munro. Hornung's subs, Frank Pinn and Jack Witucki, scored twice. The Tar Heels scored twice for a 42-13 final.

After last year's controversial game, Iowa had been waiting a year to play the Irish in Iowa. Evashevski's Hawkeyes were blasted 34-18. Notre Dame ran and passed at will, and the defense surrendered only eight yards on seven plays in the first quarter. Heap ran 43 yards to the six and Morse scored on a dive from the one-foot line. Heap scored on a dive. Iowa scored on a 47-yard pass in the second quarter but a fumble at mid-field in the third quarter stopped their momentum. Notre Dame's passing got the ball in close, and Schaefer scored from the three. The fourth Irish score came on a nine-yard pass from Guglielmi to right end Paul Matz. Carey threw from the Iowa 38 to Gene Kapish who scored. Iowa came back for a score on a rainbow pass.

Rain and mud met USC. The conditions also hurt the Fighting Irish, leading to nine fumbles and two interceptions; they still won 23-17. Morse "splashed" 179 yards on 19 rushes. A fumble on the fourth play of the game at Notre Dame's 14 let USC score early. The Fighting Irish looked bad on three more possessions and

they lost Lemek with a broken leg. Heap sprinted for 40 yards, took a pitchout, and fired a touchdown pass to Morse. USC drove for a field goal and a 10-7 lead. The Irish moved 80 yards in 20 plays, with Schaefer piling in from the two for the touchdown. The Trojans drove for another touchdown on a 21-yard pass. They led until the last seven minutes of the game, when Morse took a pitchout and ran 72 yards down the sideline for the winning touchdown. A safety for Notre Dame lifted it to 23-17. The Irish rushed for 373 yards.

Similar running helped Notre Dame beat SMU, 26-14. Heap drove in from the four to end an opening 60-yard drive, but SMU answered Guglielmi led a 12-play, 62-yard series, calling his own number from the three. Bob Scannell blocked a Mustang punt and recovered it for a touchdown and the 19-7 halftime lead. Heap concluded his career with an 89-yard run down the sidelines for a score. SMU rallied for one more score, but that was it. Brennan's first campaign ended with a number-four ranking, and his offense clicked for six yards per play. Guglielmi was a consensus choice for All-American while Varrichione and Shannon shared several postseason honors.

1954 record: 9-1-0 (.900)
Record to date: 426-86-34 (.811)

1955

In his first year, Brennan had produced outstanding results. However, the 9-1 record in 1954 would set a difficult standard to match. His most pressing concern was that six starting linemen had graduated and the sole returner, Lemek, had missed spring practice with surgery. Brennan came up with a starting unit that was one of the smallest in recent memory—the center and guards averaged only 5-10 and 200 pounds. Hornung was a capable replacement for Guglielmi, a better runner but a more questionable passer. Behind him were Jim Morse at right halfback, and tremendous speed in Dean Studer and Aubrey Lewis at left halfback. Schaefer was at fullback. Lewis, with world-class speed, and Dick Lynch were the best of the sophomores. Brennan had to hope for an injury-free season since this team had little depth.

The Fighting Irish started with SMU at home. Hornung led the rushing on the first drive, scoring a touchdown on an 11-yard keeper; he booted a 35-yard field goal later. The touchdown came on a third-and-10 in which his fake to Lewis fooled the Ponies. Lewis had two interceptions in the third period, the second leading to a 15-play touchdown drive. He also saved that drive on a fourth-and-16 play; he chose against the option pass, reversed his field, and ran to the SMU 19. Paul Reynolds scored on a fourth-and-long from the 14. The Fighting Irish defense played well: Larry Cooke grabbed a fumble and an interception near the end to save the

Wayne Edmonds, the first black letter winner at Notre Dame, started at LT in 1955.

shutout and Dick Prendergast recovered a loose ball, as the Irish won 17-0.

The smallish Notre Dame team had played well against SMU, but Indiana was a much larger group that would really test them, the critics said. Hornung opened the scoring with a fake pass and bootleg run around left end for a 33-yard touchdown. Indiana drove to the Notre Dame 15 but Hornung intercepted. The Hoosiers drove to the six in the second quarter but couldn't score and Notre Dame led 6-0 at the half. In the third quarter, Bob Gaydos hauled in a Hoosier fumble on their seven;

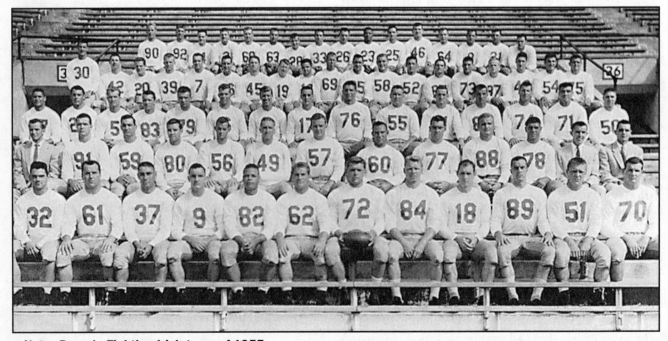

Notre Dame's Fighting Irish team of 1955.

Hornung intercepting a ball against Indiana in 1955.

Morse scored on an off-tackle run. Lewis set up the final score with a pass interception; Hornung passed to Prendergast from the seven for the 19-0 final score.

The Fighting Irish earned their third consecutive shutout win, 14-0, over Miami. Hornung threw two touchdown passes. On the first, two Irish receivers bracketed the Miami safety, forcing him to make a choice, and he chose the wrong one; Kapish caught an 11-yard touchdown pass. In the third quarter, looking at another fourth-and-long, Lewis zipped out of the backfield to catch Hornung's pass on the five to score and to complete a 32-yard play. Morse lost a 65-yard interception touchdown on a penalty. The Fighting Irish defense stopped Miami at the 13, 11, and two to save the shutout.

The euphoria ended in East Lansing against a powerful Michigan State squad. Clarence Peaks scored in the second quarter from the one to cap a long drive for MSU. (The Irish had played 196:48 minutes of shutout ball in the season to that point.) Notre Dame, meanwhile, ended three drives with fumbles. The only Fighting Irish score came on a 40-yard pass from Hornung to Morse; Hornung evaded three MSU pursuers to make the play. MSU scored on a short burst from the two and a sneak by Earl Morrall after an Irish fumble on their 16. The Irish out gained MSU's offense 374 yards to 367, but lost the game 21-7.

Brennan came up with an unbalanced line set—shifting interior linemen to load up on one side—that

befuddled Purdue for a 22-7 win. Purdue fumbled at the Notre Dame 39 on the first series. Morse picked up 23, and Studer gained 19. Schaefer scored from the two. A missed Fighting Irish pitchout gave Len Dawson a chance for a 13-yard touchdown pass. On his next series, Bob Scannell and Prendergast crunched Dawson and caused a fumble on the Purdue 26. Five plays later, Studer slashed in from the one for the lead.

Pat Bisceglia, starting LG foot the 1955 Irish.

Hornung closes in on a Tar Heel as the Irish whipped North Carolina 27-7 in 1955.

Morse stopped Purdue with an interception and Lewis sped in from the 10 for a 20-7 halftime lead. Hornung intercepted a pass in his end zone. Then inspired defense on a later drive earned three straight sacks for minus-27 yards and a fourth-and-52. The Purdue center snapped a rainbow on the punt play for a safety and the 22-7 win. The line helped Fighting Irish runners gain 325 yards to Purdue's 75, but Irish passing gained only eight yards.

Fumbles and punts took the better part of two scoreless quarters against Navy until Hornung led a 21-7 Irish victory. Hornung started the scoring by directing a 57-yard drive in 12 plays and his tally from the one. Both defenses played well, or the offenses didn't, with more fumbles and interceptions. Finally, Hornung recovered a Schaefer fumble; Lewis scored on a 12-yard

Don Schaefer, starting FB for the 1954 and 1955 Irish.

Ray Lemek, captain and RT on the 1955 team.

The 1955 Notre Dame starting eleven.

burst. Hornung intercepted yet another Navy pass and eventually threw to Kapish for a 14-yard touchdown. Navy scored later for the final 21-7 score.

Penn's Frank Riepl started the next game with a 108-yard kickoff return for a touchdown. In the hole, Fighting Irish fumbles stopped several drives. Finally, Morse went over from the five to complete an 80-yard drive at the end of the first quarter. Riepl fired an eight-yard touchdown pass in the second quarter. The Irish overcame some penalties on a 70-yard march; Kapish tallied with an eight-yard Hornung pass. Then Penn collapsed. Schaefer scored twice, from the three and the 24. Reserve Dick Fitzgerald bumped in from the one. Dick Shulsen got a Penn fumble and Carl Hebert threw a 24-yard touchdown strike to George Wilson for the 46-14 final score. Schaefer and Morse teamed up for 114 and 113 yards rushing, respectively.

The Irish allowed another weaker team, North Carolina, to play even for the first half. Notre Dame scored first, led by a 38-yard Schaefer run to the nine before Morse tallied from the two. The Tar Heels tied it in the second quarter on a 53-yard march. In the third period, Hornung patched together a 66-yard drive and scored from the two on a sneak. Sub Ed Sullivan took in a fumble on the North Carolina 27 and Lynch later scored from the two. Reserve tackle Lou Loncaric finished the scoring with an interception and a 75-yard touchdown, one of the longest on record for a modern Notre Dame lineman, as Notre Dame won 27-7.

It would be hard for the Irish to continue their poor play and beat Iowa. Prendergast's second-quarter fumble recovery on the Hawkeye 44 led to a one-yard score by Studer. Iowa tied it in the third quarter after driving 54 yards. Then they came right back, reaching the Notre Dame four; the Fighting Irish defense took over at the one-foot line. A poor punt brought Iowa back and they scored on a pass for a 14-7 lead. Ten minutes were left in the game. Hornung hit three passes for 47 yards on a 62-yard march, tying the game with a 16-yard touchdown pass to Morse and the conversion kick. Seven and a half minutes were left.

Great kickoff coverage penned up Iowa at their two; they punted and Notre Dame took over at the Iowa 43. Morse made a leaping catch at the nine. Notre Dame wanted to try a field goal after Iowa held them at the three. With 1:16 left to play, a kicking tee flew onto the field and a referee flagged it for "coaching from the sidelines." Hornung kicked the winning field goal anyway—for 18 yards—to win 17-14.

Brennan had been doing all this basically with 16 players. Only four were truly ambulatory for the USC game. USC blitzed Notre Dame 42-20. Jon Arnett outscored the Fighting Irish with three touchdowns and five point-after conversions. Hornung scored from the eight, fired a 78-yard touchdown pass to Morse, and scored from the one on a plunge. USC won going away in the second half.

Brennan had taken a relatively weak team and made the most of it. The weak passing game was one of the worst on record: only 846 yards all season and a .421 completion rate. Hornung was the only Irish All-America selection.

1955 record: 8-2-0 (.800)
Record to date: 434-88-33 (.811)

1956

The 1955 team had been overachievers. Brennan would be glad to have the same numbers for wins and losses in 1956. And that's what happened—but in reverse. This season would go down in the record book with those of 1933 and 1888—the only two losing seasons on record.

For starters, Brennan had Hornung, who seemed to do everything in 1955: second in rushing, first in scoring, first in passing, second in kickoff returns, first in punting, and first in interceptions. He could run, kick, play defense, throw, and provide a form of leadership that some mistook for cockiness. He was physically strong, hard to tackle, and could improvise with the best of them—a throwback to Gipp. He also had Gipp's flair for the dramatic. He was also plain, old-fashioned tough, as he showed when he played a game with two dislocated thumbs. He would win the 1956 Heisman, edging out Johnny Majors.

Lewis returned, as did Jim Morse. The fullback position was weaker, although a future star was there in Nick Pietrosante. However, the entire 1955 line was gone, along with some good reserves. He had to patch together five sophomores and gamble on their raw skills. Ranked third, the Fighting Irish prepared for SMU.

The Irish were upset by SMU 19-13, although they fought to the last second and had a chance to win. A 31-yard touchdown pass by SMU was the first score, but the Irish blocked the point after. SMU intercepted a Hornung pass but could not capitalize. They scored

after getting a Hornung fumble, when nine plays took Charlie Arnold to a one-foot touchdown sneak. In the third quarter, Morse caught a pass from Hornung for a 55-yard touchdown. Prendergast blocked a field goal try. To start the fourth quarter, Hornung ran from punt formation, faked to the trailing fullback, and dashed down the sideline for a 57-yard touchdown; the game was tied, 13-13. SMU twice gambled on fourth downs, earning a 14-yard touchdown; Prendergast blocked the point after. Al Ecuyer recovered a Mustang fumble on the Notre Dame 41 but only 28 seconds remained in the game. Lewis ran for 17 yards; Hornung sent everyone deep and heaved it. Morse caught it and was dragged down at the seven on the game's last play.

The Fighting Irish recovered, beating Indiana 20-6. Hornung led a 73-yard march, sparked by Jim Just's 19-yard run and Hornung's own 25-yard keeper, before he slammed twice from the five for the touchdown. In the second quarter, Hornung fired a 12-yard touchdown pass to Lewis. Indiana scored next. In the third quarter the Hoosiers were at the Irish one. Notre Dame held and took over on downs; they drove 99 yards to put it away. Lewis ran 25 yards to move away from the goal line, and then ran nine yards for the touchdown.

Purdue ran roughshod over the Fighting Irish 28-14. The Boilermakers's Mel Dillard rushed for 142 yards, scored twice, and had an interception to set up another Purdue touchdown. Purdue dominated with 27 first downs and ball control, running 86 plays to Notre Dame's 48. In spite of all that, it was tied 14-14 in the third quarter. Len Dawson and Erich Barnes powered Purdue on an 80-yard march, and Dawson passed for a 13-yard tally. Notre Dame fought back, lost a fourth-down gamble, and Purdue's Dillard scored from the eight, making it 14-0, Purdue. Hornung brought Notre Dame back on a 70-yard drive, in six plays, with 50 yards on passes. Dick Royer scored from the seven, ending the half at 14-14. In the third quarter, Notre Dame tied it when Frank Reynolds raced in from the 11. Purdue marched 75 yards, ending with a one-yard score. The final score was on a 28-yard pitchout from Dawson to Fletcher.

The long season got longer when Michigan State crunched Notre Dame 47-14. They intercepted a Hornung pass on the game's fourth play, but couldn't capitalize, allowing Notre Dame to score first, in the second quarter. MSU later showed it could score when it wanted. They scored on a long drive; then Peaks intercepted a pass meant for Morse at the MSU five. The halftime score was 7-7. Dennis Mendyk ran 62

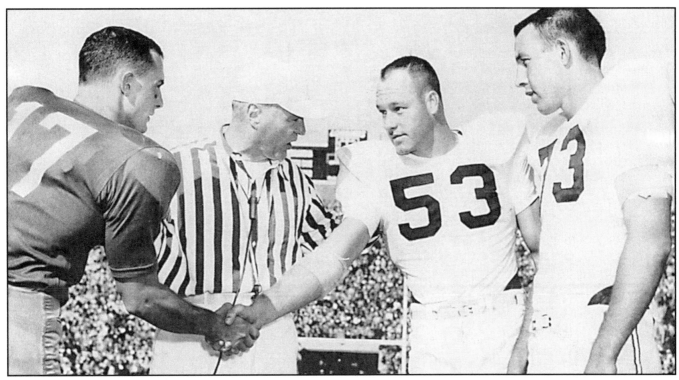

Captain Tubbs, meet Captain Morse—ND versus Oklahoma, 1956.

yards for a touchdown to open the third quarter. It was 27-7 before Sipes scored for Notre Dame from the three. Then Mendyk struck again, from 67 yards, for a touchdown. Five plays later, an Irish pass was intercepted and returned 35 yards for a touchdown. MSU's Don Arend scored the fourth touchdown of the final quarter on a 65-yard run, then the Spartans intercepted another Irish pass to finish things.

The Oklahoma Sooners, under Bud Wilkinson, had won 35 straight. At the end of the game, it was 36, after a 40-0 rout of Notre Dame. This was to be the only Oklahoma win over Notre Dame in eight games. Oklahoma played superb football on both sides of the line of scrimmage, moving the ball at will and stopping Fighting Irish drives with ease. Clendon Thomas did the most damage, scoring from the 11 on a run, catching a pass for 49 yards on a scoring drive, and scoring with an interception and a 36-yard touchdown return. Sooners John Bell, Jay O'Neal, and Tommy McDonald also scored. It was the first shutout of Notre Dame since 1951.

Navy added to Irish woes with a 33-7 win. The Midshipmen held Notre Dame's runners to a total of 50 yards; Hornung got 10 yards on six carries. The field was muddy, negating Lewis's strengths. He was held to minus-six yards. It was 0-0 until near the half when a Fighting Irish fumble led to a short scoring drive by

Navy. Lewis fumbled the first play of the new half and Navy scored in four more plays. The Irish scored in two plays after that: a 38-yard pass from Hornung to Lewis,

The story of the 1956 campaign—Morse, wide open, grabs for an Irish pass, but the ball eludes his grasp. The Irish were crunched by the Sooners 40-0, and won only two games all year.

The 1956 Notre Dame starting eleven.

and Bob Ward ran 27 yards for Notre Dame's only tally. The Middies came back with a touchdown after a 65-yard march, and an interception led to yet another touchdown. After another Irish fumble, Navy put in the reserves who scored in 12 plays.

Pittsburgh kept the losing streak going when it toppled Notre Dame 26-13. The first quarter was close, then Pitt drove 72 yards for a touchdown. After some punts, another drive ended with a Joe Walton touchdown. Hornung scored on a 50-yard run to make it 13-6. Pitt widened the gap with a 91-yard touchdown drive in the third quarter. A Fighting Irish pass was intercepted and returned for another touchdown. Bob Ward ran 84 yards with the kickoff for the final Irish score. It was Notre Dame's fifth straight loss, the worst string in the school's history.

This was the last chance for people to see The Golden Boy play under the Golden Dome. A 21-14 win over North Carolina made it special. Notre Dame was in trouble early. Lewis stole a pass on the 11 to dodge a threat, and Hornung ran 32 yards on fourth down to break out of trouble again. He passed 45 yards to Morse, who reached the seven. Three plays later Hornung scored from the one. Moments later, Lewis sprinted 78 yards to the North Carolina 15. Hornung scored on the third play. The Tar Heels used the next drive to go 63 yards

and score on a pass. In the third quarter, a Notre Dame fumble let the Tar Heels tie it up, 14-14. On a scoreless Notre Dame drive, Hornung hurt a thumb and was replaced by Bob Williams. The new backfield could not score, so Hornung went back in to direct a 63-yard drive, score again, and win the game. With 1:16 left on the clock, he scored from the one-foot line. He had scored all three touchdowns, rushed for 91 yards, made all three conversions, and completed four passes for 103 yards.

Iowa blasted Notre Dame, 48-8. Notre Dame's first drive netted minus 19 yards, and its second drive gained one yard. By that time, Iowa had the lead. The next Irish drive ended when Dick Klein intercepted a Bob Williams handoff and ran it back to the Iowa 37. The Fighting Irish got a safety and a touchdown on a pass from Cooke to Ward to avert the shutout. Iowa scored seven touchdowns with relative impunity. Hornung reinjured his thumb early in the game.

Hornung moved to left halfback for the USC game and played courageously. USC scored first after moving 66 yards. Notre Dame came back, using Hornung here and there, such as a nine-yard pitchout he took (with two dislocated thumbs) to the six; Williams scored. The Trojans marched right back, scoring with a 15-yard pass. Williams did the same, scoring with a throw to Bob Wetoska; USC led at halftime 14-13. The Trojans scored first in the second half on a 16-yard pass. On the subsequent kickoff, Hornung fielded it on his five, and started upfield, bulling through a wave of Trojans at the 25; he used his injured hands to ward off tacklers as he went 95 yards for the score. But USC scored again, on a 38-yard run, to win 28-20.

The Fighting Irish played with class and dignity in this 2-8 season. The opposition outscored Notre Dame 2:1. Notre Dame rushed for 1,000 fewer yards than last year; they scored only 67 percent of the previous season's touchdowns. The air game, however, improved by 50 percent, largely because Hornung had to play catch-up. Hornung accounted for 45 percent of the total offense, and led in rushing, passing, scoring, kickoff returns, punting, passes broken up, and was second in interceptions. And he did this for a third of the season with a dislocated thumb or two.

1956 record: 2-8-0 (.200)
Record to date: 436-96-33 (.800)

1957

Hope springs eternal. Hornung was gone, but Brennan was an optimist and decided to diversify the offense, rather than keying in on one man. His line now had good depth. Monty Stickles was a good addition at end, a prototype of future tight ends. Bob Williams was an adequate replacement for Hornung; George Izo was the backup. Frank Reynolds and Dick Lynch won the halfback jobs and Nick Pietrosante would show flashes of brilliance at fullback. So, Brennan had an improved line and a more balanced attack.

A modest 12-0 win over Purdue opened the season. The game started slowly. The Irish unveiled a halfback option pass, Lynch to Lewis for 22 yards. Later, Lynch took a pitchout and ran 22 yards around left end for the first score. Lewis missed the point after, but later intercepted a Purdue pass. Most of the third quarter was spent fielding punts, until Williams heaved one to Wetoska at the Notre Dame 45, who ran to the Purdue eight. Reynolds scored. Pietrosante led all runners with 62 yards on 10 carries as the Fighting Irish racked up 323 yards of total offense.

Notre Dame also started slowly with Indiana. Notre Dame finally put together a 54-yard touchdown drive that took some tough running from the seven. Lynch crashed in from the one. Indiana failed to move and a heavy rush made the punter shank the kick—Notre Dame's ball at the Indiana 27. Three running plays put the ball in the end zone: Chuck Lima for five, Izo for 21, and Lima for one and the touchdown. Just before the half, Williams scored on a short sneak and the 19-0 halftime lead. Most of the third period was dull. In the last quarter, Izo intercepted a pass; Lynch ran for 17; Just

The starting tackles for the 1957 squad: RT Bronko Nagurski and LT Chuck Puntillo.

finished it off with runs of 12, 14, and seven yards and the touchdown. Notre Dame won 26-0.

Army was next, after a decade's hiatus. Cadet Bob Anderson ended the shutout string when he took off on an 81-yard touchdown sprint for a 7-0 Army lead. Then Williams patched together a sporadic drive, letting Pietrosante do much of it, and his fullback rammed it in from the one to tie the game at 7-7. In the third frame, Pete Dawkins and Anderson scored for Army, using almost all of the quarter for a 21-7 Army lead. Pietrosante countered when he slammed over guard, brushed off two Cadets, and ran 65 yards for a score. Notre Dame stopped Army and got the ball on their 44. Lynch rolled for an 18-yard gain, then ran four times at the end before scoring from the one. Stickles missed the point after as Notre Dame took a 20-14 lead. Army elected to start passing. Geremia deflected a pass and Pietrosante caught it from a prone position. On a fourth-and-six, Stickles had to go for a field goal, something he'd never done before. He made it for a 23-21 lead. Army was then stalled by good defense to ensure the win.

The excitement carried over to a 13-7 win over Pitt. The Fighting Irish were tight—Gary Myers rescued two fumbles by Reynolds and Lynch. The first score came on a short run by Reynolds. Pitt scored in the second quarter on a quarterback keeper from the six. Late in the game, Williams and Lynch were ejected from the game when they disputed a punt call. Izo and Lewis replaced them. Moments later, Izo threw to the streaking Lewis, who won the game with a 74-yard touchdown. Pitt drove to the Irish 19 before losing the ball on downs.

Notre Dame jumped out to an early lead over Navy when Lynch intercepted a Middie pass and scored from the 46. Then Navy shut down the Fighting Irish to win 20-6. The Irish allowed a 79-yard touchdown run, a one-foot touchdown plunge, and a 36-yard screen pass for a touchdown, all scored by Wellborn. Irish penalties and an inspired Navy defense were the difference.

Michigan State whomped the faltering Irish 34-6. MSU scored on an 11-yard run in the second quarter for the halftime lead. The third quarter was the roughest as the Spartans moved 57 yards in 17 plays to go up by two touchdowns. The officials made a bad pass-interference call on Pietrosante to allow an MSU score, but it took them four plays to move the final five yards. Notre Dame drove back to the MSU 11, but a lost fumble started an 85-yard march highlighting Art Johnson's 50-yard touchdown run. Two more scores came on fumbles by Irish reserves. Al Ecuyer played a great game for Notre Dame—15 tackles, one pass broken up, and

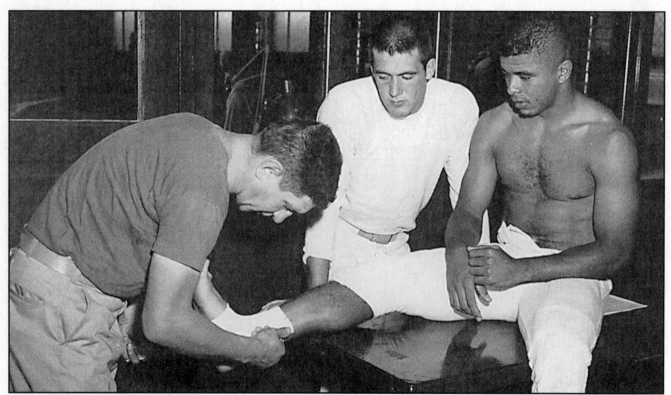

Longtime head trainer Gene Paszkiet tapes up the injured ankle of Aubrey Lewis as Ed Sullivan watches—just prior to the 1957 Indiana game.

The 1957 Notre Dame starters.

one intercepted. With the score 34-0, Williams tallied on a dive play.

The Fighting Irish rallied for one of their all-time classic wins, a 7-0 thriller over Bud Wilkinson's Sooners. Notre Dame went into the game as 19-point underdogs. Oklahoma had won 47 in a row (the Irish were the last to beat them, in 1953). Oklahoma reached the Irish 13 on their first drive, but that would be as far as they would get that day. In the second quarter, Notre Dame's pass rush made their quarterback drop the ball twice on one play, and Pietrosante recovered on their 49. Notre Dame drove to the one but lost it on downs, Oklahoma punted, and the Irish came back again. The Sooners intercepted a pass and the game stalled until the middle of the third quarter. After several punt exchanges, Notre Dame had the ball on its 20, still 0-0, in the fourth quarter. Driving carefully, Notre Dame moved to the Sooner 25 in 11 plays. Reynolds ran for one, Williams passed for 10 to Royer, Pietrosante rumbled for seven, Lynch ran to the four, Williams fumbled back to the eight, and after three runs Notre Dame was on the Sooner three.

On fourth-and-three, Williams faked to Pietrosante up the middle, then pitched to Lynch, who swung wide around his right end for the only touchdown of the game. There was only 3:50 left. The Sooners, held to 98 yards rushing, started using their passing game, and moved to the Notre Dame 36, but Williams intercepted a pass in the end zone. Oklahoma had not been shut out in 123 games. Defensive coach Bernie Witucki was awarded the game ball.

Iowa won the following week, 21-13. Pietrosante was hurt and missed the game, and it was frigid and windy. A Fighting Irish drive stalled at the Iowa 27, then an Iowa fullback scored on a powerful 36-yard run. They were ready to score again when Bob Scholtz recovered a fumble at the 13 (Notre Dame would stop them five times inside their 25). Iowa scored on a 24-yard interception return. Brennan put in Izo, who promptly found Stickles in the clear for a 55-yard touchdown. In the third quarter, Ron Toth grabbed a fumble caused by Royer, and scored from the 15. In the fourth period, Iowa ended a 51-yard drive with a 16-yard touchdown

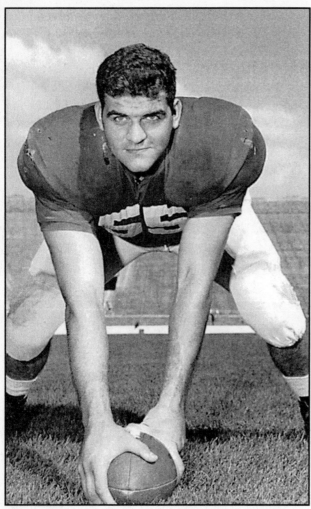

Bob Scholtz, starting center from 1957 to 1959.

pass—tipped twice by Irish defenders.

Notre Dame recovered to blitz USC 40-12, again without Pietrosante. Brennan showcased Pat Doyle and Jim Crotty. Two quick touchdowns gave Notre Dame a 13-0 lead: Toth followed a Williams interception with a three-yard score; Puntillo fell on a loose ball and Stickles caught a 17-yard touchdown pass. A series of fumbles let USC get a touchdown, they kicked off, and Doyle blasted through for a 92-yard touchdown return. In the third quarter, Notre Dame drove 66 yards to score in 13 plays, and USC ended its scoring with a ground drive (the 25-degree weather hurt their passing). Stickles, using the same play as earlier, caught a seven-yard touchdown pass. Izo threw an eight-yard touchdown to Prendergast for the final score. The loss closed USC's worst season at 1-9.

The Fighting Irish "stampeded" the SMU Mustangs 54-21. The Mustangs scored first on future Dallas Cowboy star Don Meredith's touchdown pass of 47

yards. The Fighting Irish banged fumbled and punted, but finally tallied on a Lima slam from the two. Lynch intercepted a Meredith pass to lead to Williams's four-yard quarterback option for a score. Williams grabbed an SMU pass, Toth ran, Stickles caught passes, and Williams scored on a two-yard keeper. Prendergast hit Meredith; the ball came loose and Nagurski recovered. Doyle shook loose for a 45-yard touchdown run on a pitchout for the fourth Irish score in nine minutes. The Fighting Irish kept the pressure on in the second half: Doyle ran for an 18-yard touchdown; Crotty returned a kickoff 70 yards; Toth scored from the three; and Norm Odyniec went in from the one.

Five opponents ended up in the top 10, so the 7-3 season was respectable. The defense played well all year and led Notre Dame to a ranking of ninth. Ecuyer was selected as an All-American.

1957 record: 7-3-0 (.700)
Record to date: 443-99-33 (.799)

1958

The Fighting Irish looked set for the new season. The sophomores who were mangled in 1956 were now seniors—more experienced, bulkier. The line was a known quantity, and Stickles and Wetoska were two of the best ends in the country. Williams and Izo were the quarterbacks, with Red Mack and Jim Crotty as halfbacks, and Pietrosante at fullback. There was excellent depth at all running spots.

Brennan's job had been on the line after the 2-8 season of 1956 when the Athletic Board wanted him replaced. Hesburgh overruled the move and Brennan got a one-year contract, then another after the resurgent 1957 year. The team would go 6-4 in 1958, and many would see it as a failure to get the best out of the talent on hand. Rumors abounded that a new de-emphasis on athletics was taking place, but, in fact, the school was in an early phase of much-needed academic, endowment, and physical plant improvements. Brennan must have known that disappointment was rife, and Leahy had been sniping from the sidelines. Conditions were not the best for the Fighting Irish football squad.

The Irish beat Indiana 18-0 in the opener, but the critics thought they lacked polish, a perception that stuck for the season. They also wasted 14 of 17 scoring opportunities. Indiana fumbled the kickoff at their 20

Co-captains Al Ecuyer and Chuck Puntillo psyching up for the Army game.

but Notre Dame did not score. Finally, on the fourth possession, the Fighting Irish tallied when Mack sprinted 11 yards. Dropped passes and fumbles plagued Notre Dame well into the third quarter. Williams managed to put it all together in a 71-yard drive, running it in from the 20. Near the end, Indiana handed over another fumble, to Stickles at the seven, who scored with a four-yard flip from Williams. Pietrosante led all runners with 75 of Notre Dame's 238 rushing yards.

An improved Southern Methodist University team awaited Notre Dame in Dallas. In the second quarter, Williams used Pietrosante for six runs and 41 yards on an 18-play march. Sensitive to the damage from fullback, SMU bit on a fake to him and Mack scored an 11-yard touchdown. In the third quarter, a good drive ended without a score; Meredith used a pitchout to score from the SMU 46. The Fighting Irish moved back deep but an interception stopped them. In the fourth quarter, Williams made a screen pass for 23 yards to Odyniec to spark a scoring drive that he ended with a sneak from the one for the 14-6 Irish win.

A resurgent Army squad, ranked third and featuring Pete Dawkins, who would win the Heisman, and the "Lonesome End," Bill Carpenter, came to Notre Dame for a 14-2 win. There were numerous turnovers created by good defense. Army scored first on a 16-yard touchdown pass. Stickles later stuck their punter with a safety. Several Fighting Irish drives were stopped with fumbles, bobbled snaps, interceptions, and penalties.

Dawkins scored a touchdown with seven seconds left. Brennan's tenure at Notre Dame began to slip away with this game.

Monty Stickles and Nick Pietrosante, Irish All-Americans in 1958.

The 1958 Notre Dame starters.

Against Duke, Notre Dame had nine penalties that nullified a touchdown and more than 200 yards of rushing, most on long gainers. Notre Dame squeaked through with a 9-7 win. Two potential touchdowns in the first three plays were lost on penalties. Eventually, Williams found Stickles for an eight-yard touchdown, but they missed a two-point conversion. Duke scored on its next possession. After a number of penalties, Stickles made a 23-yard field goal for the win.

The Fighting Irish started fast against Purdue—a Boilermaker fumble led to a 14-yard touchdown run by Williams. It was all Purdue after that until late in the game. Purdue's Jarus scored three touchdowns: from the one after a bad punt from terrible field position, from the one after a fumble, and from the five after an interception. A 26-yard touchdown run iced it for Purdue. Izo tried to throw Notre Dame back into the game; he hit Stickles for two touchdowns, one for 43 yards. Pietrosante scored a safety, but Notre Dame lost 29-22.

For Navy, Izo started out of a winged-T formation. It worked for a 40-20 win. Izo hit Mack with a five-yard touchdown pass, then Joe Bellino ran with a hand off on the kickoff for a touchdown to tie. Notre Dame took control: Pietrosante hammered in from the three; Izo threw to Royer for a touchdown; Notre Dame recovered

an onside kick and Izo threw to Doyle for a 38-yard touchdown; Mack returned a 65-yard punt return for

Red Mack, starting LH in 1958.

Jesse Harper accepts a Helms Hall of Fame award from Fr. Joyce at halftime of the 1958 Army game.

a touchdown. Bellino scored again when the Irish were up 34-6. Williams ended Notre Dame's scoring with a soft pass to Myers that he broke loose for a 74-yard touchdown. Navy subs scored after that.

Izo continued his hot hand against Pitt, with 332 yards passing (the best total in college ball since 1954), two touchdown passes, and two rushing touchdowns. Still, the Fighting Irish lost five fumbles and the game, 29-26. Pitt started its first drive from the Notre Dame two after a fumble. Ninety-seven yards later, they scored from the one. Three plays later, they intercepted Izo and scored for a 15-0 lead. The Irish fought back; Stickles scored from the 11 on an Izo pass. In the second quarter, they clicked for an eight-yard touchdown pass. Pitt led at the half, 15-14. Pietrosante caused a fumble in the third quarter and Izo scored. Pitt drove for a score from the 11. Notre Dame came back, but a fumble killed it at the eight. Izo later threw to Mack in the flat who ran 72 yards to Pitt's two. Izo sneaked it in for a 26-22 lead. Pitt turned Mike Ditka loose on a drive, and won the game on a quarterback roll out from the five with 11

seconds left. Izo used the last play to fire a 47-yard pass to Mack, who was tackled at the Pitt 15.

The Fighting Irish won a wild one back home in the mud against North Carolina, 34-24. North Carolina

Al Ecuyer, 1958 co-captain, starting RG, and two-time All-American.

Joe Scibelli works on the bag as captain Al Ecuyer watches in a 1958 practice.

scored a touchdown after Notre Dame fumbled for an early lead. Izo intercepted them moments later and the drive ended on a Pietrosante run from the two. A Tar Heel fumble led to another Pietrosante touchdown from the same spot. A poor North Carolina punt earned Mack a seven-yard touchdown run and a 21-6 lead for the Irish. The Tar Heels scored just before the half. Their momentum carried over to the first possession of the new half, a 65-yard drive and touchdown. Then they intercepted a pass and scored again. Crotty ran well on the return drive, getting 51 yards on four tries before Mack went in from the 15. Notre Dame had to stop the 235-pound Tar Heel fullback in a fourth-down situation, did so, and Izo scored from the three to end it.

Iowa, in beating the Fighting Irish 31-21, exposed all their weaknesses. In the first quarter, there were numerous punts, but Iowa was starting to move. They scored from the six to open the second quarter. Fumbles and interceptions eventually got the Hawkeyes a 36-yard touchdown. Notre Dame fought back with a 69-yard Izo-to-Stickles pass, highlighted when Stickles stiff-armed a Hawkeye into an early trip to the locker room. Iowa led at the half, 13-7. In the third quarter, a Fighting Irish drive died and Iowa moved 76 yards, capped by a one-yard touchdown. Izo stepped up the passing game: to Odyniec for 16, to Myers for nine, and to Scarpitto for a 52-yard touchdown. Iowa came back with a 53-

yard touchdown pass; they picked off a screen pass and slammed in from the one. Izo finished the scoring with a four-yard keeper.

Notre Dame earned a winning season with a 20-13 victory over USC in Los Angeles. Dave Hurd intercepted a pass and ran to their 43; Pietrosante scored from the four. USC answered with a 42-yard touchdown pass. Three interceptions later the Trojans scored again, from the one. Bob Williams led a 70-yard march, scoring from the 10. In the second half, Wetoska grabbed a 20-yard touchdown pass. Notre Dame's defense made a four-play stand at its two-foot line to stop the last USC threat.

Turnovers killed the Irish in 1958—45 turnovers. Brennan had coached his last game. Stickles, Pietrosante, and Ecuyer made All-America teams.

1958 record: 6-4-0 (.600)
Record to date: 449-103-34 (.795)

1959

The public learned of Brennan's departure four days before Christmas 1958. It was not an easy decision. He was universally recognized as a fine man. The press supported him, but the student body had hung him in effigy three times in 1958. He was probably too young and inexperienced to be running such a demanding college football program.

His replacement, Joe Kuharich, was born in South Bend and attended Fighting Irish practices as a child, watching Rockne. He played under Layden and coached at all levels: high school, college (he coached Ollie Matson and Gino Marchetti at San Francisco), and the NFL. He was the Coach of the Year in the NFL in 1955 for the Redskins. He brought "pro" football with him to Notre Dame: he emphasized passing, passing, and more passing, from complicated sets, motions, and shifts. The Fighting Irish would be exciting to watch—if they could just learn it all in time. And therein was the rub; close observers noted that Kuharich did not have the knack of teaching the game to those who still needed to work on fundamentals. He was accustomed to having pro players who knew it all.

He inherited only 12 monogram winners. There was some quality in the line: Stickles, Pottios, Buoniconti, and Joe Carollo, but they weren't a unit yet and injuries would hurt. Izo had a major-league arm but was slow and tended to fumble. Both he and Mack suffered knee injuries early in fall practice. Don White, a steady, dependable type, would get the nod at quarterback. George Sefcik and Scarpitto were the halfbacks, backed up by Angelo Dabiero. Gerry Gray won the fullback's job, with Crotty behind him. This was not an overwhelming group, without a game-breaker.

Against North Carolina, the Fighting Irish came out in the rain in new jerseys—dark blue with gold shoulder stripes (the helmet shamrock would come later). The first break came at the end of the first quarter when Notre Dame's Pat Heenan splashed his way to a loose ball. White threw to Scarpitto for 22, and Scarpitto slashed in from the two for a touchdown. Crotty tallied in the next quarter with a 19-yard run around end and scored again just before the half on a three-yard burst. In the third quarter, Stickles turned a Tar Heel punt into a safety and moments later Ray Ratkowski intercepted a pass and ran 43 yards for a touchdown. North Carolina scored a late touchdown. Notre Dame won 28-7.

Purdue was a different case. Jarus scored to end their first drive, a 76-yarder, going in from the five (his fourth career touchdown against the Fighting Irish). Then they put together a 77-yard effort, in eight plays, ending with a seven-yard touchdown pass. Crotty fumbled the kickoff and Jarus ran for his fifth touchdown. Purdue was up at the half, 21-0. Notre Dame scored on its first drive of the second half, pumped up by a 38-yard Stickles catch. Crotty ran twice from the four to score. Purdue's Jim Tiller raced 74 yards moments later for the 28-7 final.

Notre Dame beat California's Golden Bears in a costly 28-6 win. Pottios was lost for the year and Crotty, Gray, and Roy would be out for a few weeks. Notre Dame's John Powers grabbed a lost pitchout on Cal's first play; Izo found Scarpitto on Notre Dame's second play for a 27-yard score. On the second touchdown drive, Gray ran up the middle for 17 yards, White passed to Henry Wilke for 18 more, and Dabiero got 15 on a trap. White tallied from the one. A minute later, Cal fumbled and Heenan grabbed it. Nine plays later, Gray went in from the one-foot line. Cal had one good drive and scored, on a pass from the five. Irish subs ended it with a 45-yard touchdown pass from George Haffner to Les Traver. There were 158 yards of penalties against Notre Dame, including one for 25 yards (15 for roughing the passer and 10 for interference against the receiver).

Head coach Joe Kuharich.

An up-down, on-off, win-loss pattern was emerging (and would hold true for the Kuharich years) as Michigan State blanked Notre Dame 19-0. In the first quarter, there were five fumbles and eight changes of possessions. Eventually the MSU quarterback, Dean Look, ran 41 yards and set up a touchdown from the seven. This score held into the third quarter, which was marred by five more fumbles (Herb Adderly now had four) and interceptions. MSU's Look threw a touchdown pass to Fred Arbanas (legally blind in one eye) for 52 yards. MSU reserves tacked on a third touchdown.

Northwestern, coached by Ara Parseghian, knocked off Notre Dame 30-24 in South Bend. Their first drive dismantled the Fighting Irish secondary, using a down-and-out pass pattern for 14, 14, and 18 yards for a touchdown. The Fighting Irish only made it to their own seven before fumbling; Northwestern quickly scored for a 12-0 lead. Notre Dame drove to the three but lost it on downs, the Wildcats fumbled, and Scarpitto scored. Before the half, a fake into the line suckered the entire Irish secondary and Northwestern scored on a 54-yard pass. Northwestern led at the half, 18-7. Notre Dame closed it up in the third with an Izo-to-Sefcik touchdown pass, but Northwestern's John Talley fired a 78-yard bullet to Irv Cross for a score, then following a failed Irish drive, ran 61 yards for a touchdown when his man covered. White threw a deflected pass to Scarpitto for a late 52-yard touchdown. Stickles added a field goal to end it. It was a game Notre Dame could have won, except for their mistakes.

A week later, Navy quarterback Jim Maxfield sliced and diced Notre Dame's secondary with six straight completions on an 89-yard touchdown drive. Sefcik tied it up near the end of the first quarter with a 14-yard run. Scarpitto grabbed the ball when Bellino bobbled it on a pass and ran for a 52-yard touchdown, and Maxfield threw a 38-yard touchdown pass in response. The Fighting Irish fumbled and Maxfield went right to work: two quick passes, the second for a touchdown with no one near the receiver. An interception earned Navy a field goal a few plays later. Notre Dame tied it up when Williams led a drive that Scarpitto finished from the Navy two, then hit a two-point conversion, White to Rutkowski. Navy was unable to move and Notre Dame worked it down close. Bob McCuthan, Notre Dame's student manager, stepped on the field and threw out a tee. Flags went flying—"coaching from the bench." Stickles had to make a 33-yard field goal with 30 seconds left. It was good for a 25-22 win (Stickles's third game-winning field goal in his career), but Navy had shown how weak the secondary was.

The modest progress seen against Navy disappeared against Georgia Tech, where, once again, turnovers and penalties mangled Notre Dame's chances. Stickles made a 41-yard field goal in the first half; he caught a 43-yard touchdown pass from White and booted the point after for all of Notre Dame's scoring. But Tech scored two touchdowns to win—from the one-foot line and from the six, both by the reserve quarterback. Tech did not pass much, but Notre Dame gave them seven turnovers to lose 14-10.

On to Pitt and a complete mud bath. The Fighting Irish ground game stayed in South Bend, although Pitt ran for 248 yards in a 28-13 win. Pitt scored first on a 64-yard punt return. Later, Fred Cox (who was a good

Angelo Dabiero, 1958 and 1959 starter at RH.

kicker as a halfback) lurched for a 44-yard touchdown. In the third quarter, White's fake freed up Scarpitto for a 58-yard touchdown pass. Other drives faltered until the fourth quarter when Notre Dame simply dropped the ball on its own five. Two plays later, Pitt scored. Their last score came on a 72-yard drive, scored from the three. Izo tried to fire back; Scarpitto scored on an eight-yard Izo pass, but it was too late.

Iowa's Evashevski tried to become the first coach to beat Notre Dame four straight times, but Izo foiled him. In a 20-19 upset win, Izo passed for 295 yards and three touchdowns as the Fighting Irish came from behind twice. Iowa had been rampaging for 400 plus yards per game, but an alert Irish defense shut them down. Iowa scored after an interception, but used nine plays to go 22 yards. Six plays later, Izo hit Stickles with a touchdown pass. Iowa grabbed another pass to set up Bob Jeter's touchdown run. Notre Dame punted in the next series, and Iowa ran it back for a 19-7 lead. Izo used a third-and-one situation to suck in the Hawkeyes before throwing a pass to Heenan for a 55-yard touchdown. Iowa stopped a drive at their four, but Izo later threw

Jim Crotty, starting RH for the 1959 squad.

a 58-yard touchdown pass to Sefcik. Stickles made the winning point after, and Sefcik got an interception to wrap up Kuharich's biggest win of the year.

Kuharich avoided a losing season by beating USC 16-6. Stickles deflected a punt, and Gray overcame his own fumble to score from the three. USC intercepted a pass. The Trojans's passing was suspect and they lost two good opportunities. Their running game wasn't working either. Notre Dame scored when Gray smashed in from the 10 after a Stickles reception. On the second half kickoff, USC's Angelo Coia ran it out to the 18, drifted backwards, and Gray tackled him in the end zone for a safety. Gray also scored Notre Dame's final touchdown for the 16-6 win.

The 1959 Fighting Irish were 5-5 in a season where their running game did not work well, they committed 40 turnovers, and their passing game disappeared. Stickles earned All-America honors.

1959 record: (5-5-0) (.500)
Record to date: 454-108-34 (.790)

1960-1969

1960

Kuharich had two problems to overcome—losses due to injuries and losses via graduation. The line was in fair shape but the quarterback situation was clouded: the returners did not have much experience and sophomores were potential problems at the helm. Daryle Lamonica, blessed with a great arm, would take most of the snaps but would not be used much in the passing game. The halfbacks were Sefcik and Dabiero; the fullback was Mike Lind. Injuries to Mack and Gray basically kept them sidelined.

Notre Dame started with a 21-7 victory over California. Carollo recovered a fumble and Scarpitto ran eight yards for the touchdown. Cal tied it up with a 76-yard drive, using mainly passes. In the third quarter, Scarpitto returned the kickoff 44 yards, and a few plays later, saw a lane open up for a 33-yard touchdown run. Cal had earlier tried a quick kick; when Nick DePola saw the same formation, he split the blockers and literally took the ball off the foot of the kicker for a 15-yard touchdown.

The Fighting Irish suffered their worst home defeat in history when Purdue demolished them 51-19. The Irish fumbled too much, failed to tackle well, and played poor pass defense. Purdue's scores came in: a 44-yard touchdown pass, a 78-yard touchdown run that broke three tackles, another touchdown pass, a 34-yard field goal after an Notre Dame fumble, a touchdown run after an interception, a touchdown pass after a Notre Dame fumble, a 65-yard punt return for a touchdown, and then Purdue subs scored a touchdown. Scarpitto got the first Irish touchdown on a 64-yard run, Dabiero tallied with a George Haffner pass from the 24, and the subs got one. Ironically, each team had 358 yards of total offense.

Another setback awaited Notre Dame—North Carolina. The first quarter was a display of incompetent football—interceptions, fumbles, stalled drives, and penalties. The Tar Heels had the first sustained drive, a 74-yard effort ended by a 47-yard touchdown pass. Then they intercepted a pass from Clay Schulz and took it 42 yards for their other touchdown. The Fighting Irish kept playing poorly in the second half. Scarpitto eventually scored from the two, but the game was one of the worst displays of major college football to be seen as the Tar

Kuharich and his 1960 QBs: Ed Rutkowski, George Haffner, and Daryle Lamonica.

The 1960 Notre Dame starters.

Heels won 12-7.

Michigan State was Notre Dame's 600th game. Kuharich juggled his quarterbacks to find the right combination. Notre Dame kept the game scoreless for 23 minutes until a Spartan deflected a pass and ran it back for a touchdown. The Fighting Irish defense put on a great pass rush next time out. However, MSU's coach, Duffy Daugherty, called for a screen pass and the Spartans broke for a 52-yard touchdown. The Irish kept trying to come back, but bobbles, interceptions, and incomplete passes ruined each effort. Herb Adderly scored the final MSU touchdown on a 22-yard reception for the 21-0 win.

The Irish offense solved its problems of killing its long drives against Northwestern—they did not have any to kill, as they failed to gain a first down for two quarters. The Wildcats got their only touchdown following a punt return to the Notre Dame 41; 10 plays later Elbert Kimbrough scored on a three-yard run. The Irish improved in the second half by reducing their problems to one—penalties. The only Fighting Irish score came on a 25-yard pass from Haffner to Jim Sherlock. After that, penalties killed two promising drives. Notre Dame lost 7-6.

Notre Dame's next opponent, Navy, had the eventual Heisman winner in its lineup—Joe Bellino. Bellino dominated the opening drive, as he returned

the kickoff to the 19, gained 43 yards around left end, gained 18 yards over left tackle to the 19, and scored from the 12. Meanwhile, two Fighting Irish drives ended with a fumble and a sack. Bellino also fumbled, leading to a Dabiero touchdown from the three-yard

Joe Carollo, starting RT in 1960 and 1961.

Coach Joe Kuharich with the 1960 Captain Myron Pottios and the Irish mascot of the day, Clashmore Mike.

line. Moments later, offensive pass interference in the end zone killed a drive for Notre Dame. The Fighting Irish kept plugging away, with a blocked Navy field goal try and a 69-yard pass to Scarpitto that reached Navy's 14. Good defense kept it there. Navy won, 14-7, when a Haffner pass was intercepted and Bellino scored from the half-yard line. Irish drives had ended at Navy's 22, 14, and twice at the five.

Pittsburgh kept the Irish losing streak alive by beating Notre Dame 20-13. Their second play from scrimmage went to Mike Ditka, who was caught at the Irish 30, but just kept lumbering along with a struggling Dabiero hanging from his shoulder pads for 22 more yards. Notre Dame held for three plays, but they scored from the one-foot line. For the first half, Notre Dame accumulated more yards in penalties, 55, than in total offense, 50. Haffner had completed one pass. Fred Cox, a good kicker for a halfback, intercepted the ball and ran to the Irish two; he scored on the next play. Two Fighting Irish possessions went nowhere; Pitt sauntered 73 yards, mostly on end runs, for their third score. The Irish went down to defeat in a flurry of passes. It was the sixth consecutive defeat.

Number seven came against Miami, a 28-21 cliffhanger. Miami ran a draw play that gained 56 yards on the pass-conscious Irish, then scored from the one on a dive. Notre Dame fumbled on its first drive, but then put together an 80-yard effort in seven plays; Dabiero led the charge on a 43-yard run. Lind tallied from the one. Miami answered with a 60-yard touchdown drive in the next quarter. Notre Dame moved well again and scored to end a 77-yard march when Kuharich's ninth fullback for the year, Bill Ahern, went in from the five. A two-point conversion pass by Lamonica made it 14-14 at the half. Miami took the lead in the third quarter using a long pass to Bill Miller, then two short runs for the touchdown. Lamonica teamed with Scarpitto on a 37-yard pass and a drive reached the one; Lamonica took it in for a 21-21 deadlock. A Notre Dame drive was killed by a penalty, Perkowski missed a long field goal, and Miami went on to win. A quarterback keeper broke for a 49-yard advance, then they muscled it in from short range.

The Fighting Irish fumbled on their first play from scrimmage against Iowa. Iowa went 28 yards in six plays for a touchdown, winning eventually 28-0. Iowa also scored on a 28-yard pass, a run from the Notre Dame three, and a two-yard run. Fighting Irish drives ended usually by interceptions. The losing streak now reached eight.

Notre Dame had the pleasure of giving USC's John McKay a losing season when they beat the Trojans 17-0 to end the season. Notre Dame dominated the whole game, driving well enough on its first series to salvage three points on Perkowski's, kick from the 21. This was their first lead in a game since September 24 (this game was played on November 26). Lamonica intercepted a Bill Nelson pass and scored a few plays later from the one. With 10 minutes to go in the second quarter, Scarpitto shrugged off several hits to score from the USC nine. Good defense kept the Trojans out of the end zone for the whole game, and the win kept this team from being the worst Notre Dame squad of this century.

The real story of the season was in hospital bills. Virtually every starter lost playing time—some most of the season, some all. The defense often played well but the offense was wretched. The passing game gained 37 percent less yardage than in 1959. Pottios was the only All-America pick.

1960 record: 2-8-0 (.200)
Record to date: 456-116-34 (.780)

1961

Things had to get better this year, and they did, at least marginally. Kuharich had eight starters from 1960 and two from 1959. The backfield was the same, although Lamonica hoped not to be in a revolving door as the quarterback. There were some excellent sophomores in Bob Lehmann, Frank Budka, Jim Kelly, and two behemoth running backs, Paul Costa (6-4, 230) and Jim Snowden (6-4, 235). They indicated good recruiting skills for Kuharich, but Snowden and Costa would both play their NFL careers as offensive tackles, so perhaps there was a problem knowing where such talent should line up.

The Fighting Irish opened with Oklahoma. The Sooners moved well, but when they tried a field goal Buoniconti blocked it so hard at the 22 that Dabiero recovered on the 41. Sefcik carried for eight; Dabiero broke loose for a 51-yard touchdown run—a nine-point swing in three plays. Oklahoma drove 72 yards for a four-yard touchdown. Notre Dame's answering drive ended with a 23-yard touchdown for Mike Lind. The game was a 13-6 standoff until halfway into the fourth quarter when Dabiero ran for 23 yards, to the two, and Lind punched in for the 19-6 final score. The Fighting Irish rushed for 367 yards, 176 of it from Dabiero.

The Fighting Irish avenged the previous year's blowout by Purdue with a 22-20 victory over the Boilermakers. Purdue scored first, using nine plays for 74 yards, ending with a quarterback sneak from the one. The Irish fired back with a 73-yard drive; Dabiero gained 32 yards and Lind scored from the 27. Purdue scored from the Notre Dame four. A bad punt snap led to a Purdue field goal from the 26. An Irish field goal failed but Lamonica soon had them back at the two, where a Purdue linebacker tried to stop the 235-pound Snowden and didn't. Purdue led at the half, 20-13. A failed onside kick led to a Purdue field goal. Near the end of the third

quarter, Snowden ran for 11 and 16 yards; a few plays later, Jim Kelly caught a Lamonica pass for a touchdown. A two-point conversion failed. Kuharich sent in an all-sophomore backfield to pummel a tiring Purdue team. Costa ran 29 yards. Perkowski won the game with a 29-yard field goal. Two later Purdue drives failed.

USC was next; the weather was frigid and the Trojans skated to a 30-0 loss. Fighting Irish backs ran for 322 yards to USC's minus-four, the first time such an indignity had happened to USC in 69 seasons. The Irish defense sacked quarterback Bill Nelson for minus-128 yards. The Irish scoring was: Lamonica around right end for a 12-yard touchdown; Lamonica to Kelly for a 17-yard touchdown; quarterback Ed Rutkowski around left end for a six-yard touchdown; Lamonica on a one-yard sneak; and Perkowski with a 49-yard field goal. Dabiero ran 43 yards to set up Rutkowski's touchdown and Carollo recovered a fumble before Lamonica's sneak. It was the fifth straight win over USC and the second consecutive shutout. It was probably the high-water mark of the Kuharich years.

Another big rival was next, Michigan State. The Fighting Irish scored on a 68-yard drive, with Lamonica going 22 yards on a fourth-down play and then two yards for the touchdown, giving Notre Dame a 7-0

Joe Perkowski, famous for his "overtime" kick that beat Syracuse in 1961.

QB Lamonica handing off to FB Mike Lind on 1961 photo day.

the Wildcats recovered. They scored on a broken screen pass; the receiver darted around long enough for blocking to form and then ran 50 yards for the touchdown. Perkowski kicked a 36-yard field goal for a 10-6 Irish lead. Northwestern scored the go-ahead touchdown on a short pass play and then tried to stop the Irish with eight minutes to go. Behind 12-10, Budka moved Notre Dame to the Northwestern 28, passed to Traver for a short gain, and handed off to Snowden to set up a good field goal angle to try to win the game. But Snowden lost the ball and the ball game with a fumble.

Navy added another loss, 13-10, even though the Fighting Irish seemed to have the better team. Perkowski scored first with a 45-yard field goal, then Navy came back with a 72-yard drive that scored on a one-yard run and a later field goal. Dick Naab, another Kuharich fullback, tied the game at 10-10 from the one in the third quarter. In the fourth quarter, Lamonica tried to throw a long pass but the ball slipped out of his hands and Navy recovered at the Irish 10. They settled for a 22-yard field goal and the 13-10 lead. Two late Irish drives ended on downs and a fumble.

Kuharich went with Budka for the Pitt game and Notre Dame won 26-20. The first touchdown came on a 59-yard touchdown pass from Budka to Traver. Fred Cox hit a field goal in the second quarter, giving Notre Dame a 7-3 halftime lead. Then Cox scored in the third quarter after a Naab fumble for a 10-7 lead. Budka intercepted a Panther pass and geared up a 72-yard march, keyed by his 40-yard pass to Traver to the two. Naab scored Marty Olosky fell on the Pitt fumble of the kickoff at their 12, and Sefcik scored around right end from the eight. Cox hit a 52-yard field goal. Reserve halfback Charlie O'Hara got the winning touchdown on a 53-yard run over tackle before Pitt made the last score of the game on a pass.

Sometimes, timeless games and incidents come out of nowhere, and that's what happened in this game with Syracuse, won by the kick. Everybody eventually was involved—the school's administration, the NCAA, and the media. But it started out like any other game; it was a tight defensive match, until Budka sent out Dabiero into territory defended by Ernie Davis, soon to be the Heisman winner. Angelo put some moves on Davis that left him open; Budka threw to him for a 41-yard touchdown for a 7-0 Irish halftime lead. In the third quarter, a punt hit a Syracuse lineman and Gene

halftime lead. After being held scoreless until late into the third quarter, MSU exploded for 17 points in the final 18 minutes of the game. The scoring began when a Budka pass was intercepted at the MSU eight. Another interception followed. George Saimes scored from the 24 on a pitchout. The tide had turned. Another interception and Saimes scored a 25-yard touchdown behind great blocking. A failed Irish drive led to an MSU field goal for the 17-7 victory. The Spartans became the only team to beat Notre Dame six straight times, but they had been held scoreless for 42 minutes.

Parseghian always had Northwestern ready for Notre Dame—he never lost to the Irish in four tries. The Fighting Irish stopped Northwestern and then Lind scored from the 14. The 7-0 lead held into the second half, although three injured Irish starters were out (Hecomovich, Lind, and Kelly). Northwestern started getting some breaks—a whistle stopped a Notre Dame fumble recovery, a punt touched an Irish lineman and

Viola recovered. Les Traver tallied a 25-yard touchdown on a Budka pass against Davis, pushing Notre Dame's lead to 140. Syracuse's John Mackey scored on a 57-yard pass, they got two points, and drove 53 yards, scoring on a pass from the three, taking the lead, 15-14. Interceptions killed drives by both teams until Notre Dame took over on downs at their 30, with 17 seconds left. Budka tried to pass, saw nothing, and ran 21 yards before going out of bounds. With eight seconds left, Sefcik caught a pass for 10 yards and went out of bounds. Three seconds. Perkowski would have to try a 56-yard field goal, Sefcik held. Walt Sweeney rushed the play from his end position, crashed through his blocker and into Sefcik, annihilating the kick. Head linesman F.G. Skibble called a roughing-the-kicker penalty. They moved the ball 15 yards and Perkowski made a 41-yard field goal for an Irish win, 17-15.

Syracuse pointed to Rule 3, Section of the NCAA Football Rules Interpretations, which stated that a foul during the act of kicking does not call for another down or extension of time that may have expired. Notre Dame asserted that the infraction happened before time ran out and before the ball was dead. A strict construction of the rules would have allowed total mayhem on similar plays since no penalties could have been called or enforced. Some called for Notre Dame to forfeit. The Irish never did, rightly so.

Continued fumbling doomed the Irish in a 42-21 loss to Iowa. Iowa got five scores in the first half as the partial results of three Irish fumbles and three interceptions: a 43-yard touchdown pass after an interception, a quarterback sneak for a touchdown after a penalty, a one-yard touchdown sneak after a fumble, a 45-yard touchdown pass after Notre Dame's only drive failed, and a 104-yard touchdown runback of a kickoff. In the third quarter, Notre Dame drove deep but Lind fumbled on the Iowa one; they came back to score on a drive, started with a 37-yard pass. Two Fighting Irish scores came on a 16-yard run by Sefcik and Dabiero's 42-yard interception return within the game's last minute. Notre Dame outgained Iowa 365 yards to 337.

Against Duke, Dabiero ran 54 yards down the sidelines for a touchdown on the first series. Duke came back with a quarterback sneak for a touchdown. In the second quarter, Duke intercepted a Budka pass on their 30 and scored on a 21-yard pass. The Fighting Irish

Tom McDonald, excellent defensive back for the Irish in the early 1960s.

came back: Costa to the 38, Lind for 15, Budka to Tom Goberville for 19, Budka to Sefcik for 20, and Lind on a one-yard touchdown plunge. Duke drove on a 43-yard pass and a 16-yard touchdown pass for a 20-13 halftime lead. In the second half, Duke added a field goal and two touchdowns. The Irish collapsed and Duke won 37-13.

Turnovers and terrible pass defense ruined chances for a winning season. And the offense had its own miscues. This was not a season when a few close calls would have changed much. There were growing doubts about the quality of the coaching. Buoniconti was the lone player who made All-American.

1961 record: 5-5-0 (.500)
Record to date: 461-121-34 (.775)

1962

Don Hogan, starting RH on the 1962 squad.

This was Kuharich's last season. He left as the only Fighting Irish coach with a losing career record. The pro-style passing offense never fully materialized. He did not win the hearts of his players; there was too much shuffling of personnel at key positions. Two things stood out: an inordinate number of injuries, undetermined as to cause—bad luck or bad conditioning, and excellent recruiting. But with all this talent, why not win more? Could he have turned it around with the maturing of an excellent sophomore group? It's doubtful. The 1962 record of 5-5 would be the end of the Kuharich years.

There were holes to fill in the line, but good players moved up, especially Jim Carroll and Bob Lehmann. Lamonica would start most of the time. His halfbacks were Ron Bliey, one of the fastest men to play for Notre Dame, and Don Hogan, a runner with much promise. Lind never recovered from surgery and Gray was not completely healthy. It was a big team and promised much in its offense.

The Fighting Irish opened the season in Oklahoma, and they muscled two touchdowns over the smaller Sooners for a 13-7 win. Rutkowski scored on a drive he led with rushing, scoring from the seven and kicking the point after. Oklahoma's Paul Lea ended a 58-yard drive with a one-yard touchdown. The Irish wore out the Sooners with an 89-yard drive in the third quarter that took 11:35. After 18 plays, Ahern went in for an eight-

Lamonica, long before he became known as a "bomber," gets set to throw long against Iowa in the 35-12 1962 win.

The Notre Dame first team in 1961.

yard touchdown. The Irish stopped the Sooners's last drive and were pleased to get out of Norman with a win.

Purdue came to South Bend and beat Notre Dame handily. The Fighting Irish had reverted to their old form—untimely penalties and fumbles. Purdue spent much of the first half in the vicinity of Notre Dame's goal. They finally capitalized with a 17-yard field goal after a short punt and run back. Notre Dame lost the ball on downs and Purdue marched 63 yards, capped by a 25-yard touchdown pass by Ron DiGravio, with Purdue up at halftime, 10-0. In the third quarter, another Irish possession ended at Purdue's 42; Purdue's DiGravio put together a 58-yard drive, capped by his one-yard sneak. Denny Murphy lost an interception and a 55-yard touchdown return on a penalty (and the Fighting Irish would lose another touchdown with a penalty). Kuharich put in Denis Szot for Lamonica. Szot fumbled the snap on his 20 and Purdue scored on the next play. Szot fired a 17-yard touchdown pass to Hogan, but it was too late. Purdue won easily 24-6.

At Wisconsin, Notre Dame ran into an emerging media darling, Ron VanderKelen, who would play a magnificent Rose Bowl game against USC. Vandy got the Badgers in range for an opening field goal and a 3-0 lead. Notre Dame could not move, punted, and Vandy threw a 20-yard touchdown pass to Pat Richter.

Wisconsin fumbled away its next two drives but the Fighting Irish did nothing, ending the half at 10-0 in favor of Wisconsin. In the third quarter, the Irish dropped the ball on their five, and Vandy took it in three plays later. Szot put together a touchdown drive in a lost cause, 68 yards in eight plays with Hogan scoring the touchdown. Jack Snow caught a two-point conversion pass. The Badgers won 17-8.

Michigan State won easily 31-7; George Saimes rushed 153 yards for the Spartans, scored three times, and played great defense. Saimes sprinted 54 yards for his first touchdown on MSU's fifth play. Sherm Lewis ran 72 yards for a touchdown on their 10th play. Szot and Joe Farrell led the Fighting Irish back to score, with Farrell going in from the two. Then Saimes took charge: he intercepted a Lamonica pass at the Notre Dame 22 and scored from the 16; and later he cruised 49 yards for a touchdown. In between, MSU scored on a pass play. It was Daugherty's seventh straight victory (still unequalled) over Notre Dame.

Northwestern's Tommy Myers was the next hero. The Fighting Irish fumbled on the first play. Eight plays later, Northwestern scored. After trading turnovers, Myers found Paul Flatley alone for a 23-yard scoring strike and a 14-0 Wildcat lead. They blocked an Irish punt and scored on the ground for a 21-0 halftime lead.

Ron Bliey, starting LH in 1962.

Notre Dame turned the ball over again in the third quarter and Myers found Flatley for 40 yards and for a seven-yard touchdown. Lamonica threw for 39 yards to Sherlock, then to Kelly for 10 to set up Farrell's three-yard touchdown. The Wildcats closed it out, 35-6, with a score from the six. Notre Dame was 1-4.

Next was Navy and their new quarterback, Roger Staubach. Notre Dame won, 20-12. The first Notre Dame drive reached the Navy 13, where an interception killed it. Navy could not move, punted, and Hogan ran 16 yards to the one; Lamonica scored. The 7-0 lead lasted through the half as Notre Dame stopped Navy's offense, allowing no first downs, no pass completions, and only three yards of total offense. The Middies switched to delayed traps and draws to hold off the Fighting Irish rush in the third quarter, and they scored a touchdown but missed a two-point conversion. Staubach took advantage of a fumble to sneak in from the one for a 12-7 lead. The Middies's kicker topped the ball on the kickoff and a reserve Irish tackle ran to the Navy 45. Lamonica threw deep to Denny Phillips; it was tipped, but Phillips hauled it in for a 13-12 lead. On the next

drive, Budka appeared at flanker and made a catch at the Navy two. Lamonica used a jump pass to Kelly for the final score.

The Fighting Irish beat Pitt 43-22 with great performances from Lamonica and Kelly. They clicked on passes of 14 and 11 yards to set up Hogan's six-yard touchdown for the first score. Pitt punted and Lamonica used a jump pass to Kelly from the five for a touchdown. Pitt fumbled and Bliey ran in from the seven on an end sweep. Moments later, Tom Goberville blocked a punt and Lamonica went to Kelly for another touchdown. Pitt then used a double reverse for a 56-yard touchdown. The halftime score was 21-6. After intermission, Lamonica hit Stephens for a 40-yard touchdown. Kelly caught another touchdown pass, a 13-yarder from Lamonica, before Pitt added a 93-yard kickoff return for a touchdown. Lamonica completed 11 passes to Kelly and tied Bertelli's record of four touchdowns.

The defense played well in the 21-7 win over North Carolina. The Tar Heels scored first, helped by a tipped pass that Ken Willard caught at the Notre Dame five. The Carolina defense kept the Fighting Irish bottled up throughout the first half, so good defensive play was needed. Tommy MacDonald helped with three interceptions, tying Bertelli's record of eight for a season. Farrell scored from the one after the second interception. Right after that, he grabbed his third and raced to their eight. Farrell went in from the six to take the lead. Gray then intercepted a Tar Heel pass and returned it to the Notre Dame 28. Hogan capitalized with a 59-yard touchdown run to end the scoring. Notre Dame fought back to .500, 4-4.

Lamonica looked good as he led the Fighting Irish to a 35-12 win over Iowa. Hogan scored first with a 29-yard run. Notre Dame had a 7-0 halftime lead. Iowa scored in the third quarter, but it was all Irish after that: a six-play drive of 71 yards ended with Minik's 19-yard touchdown; a Lamonica touchdown on a fake pass and a 27-yard run; a Minik touchdown set up by a Lamonica run; an Ahern touchdown after a Budka interception. MacDonald also picked up his record-setting ninth interception. The win pushed Notre Dame's record over .500 for the first time since the season opener over Oklahoma.

Any chance for a winning season, however, seemed doomed by the final opponent—USC, who was trying to win a national title for McKay's third season at the school. The Fighting Irish did not play well against USC's backs, Ben Wilson and Willy Brown, and three quarterbacks, Pete Beathard, Bill Nelson, and Craig

George Bednar, starting RT in 1962.

Fertig. The Trojans shut out Notre Dame 25-0. It was Kuharich's last game as Notre Dame's head coach.

The 1962 Fighting Irish never developed much of a running game; rushing yardage decreased 38 percent from 1961. They did stop the negative turnover ratio of previous seasons. The passing game was marginally better, with the statistics padded in the three games where Lamonica couldn't miss. They simply never put together all the parts of a successful season, which was true for all four years under Kuharich. He had been a superb recruiter and left behind a fine core of talent. Jim Kelly was the sole All-America selection.

1962 record: 5-5-0 (.500)
Record to date: 466-126-34 (.771)

1963

Kuharich left Notre Dame on March 13, 1963, to become the NFL's head of officials. The recruiting season was almost over. The administration felt it had insufficient time to do a proper search and decided to go with an interim coach. Hugh Devore was on hand, having made all the stops after his one interim season for Notre Dame in 1945. Devore recruited one of the best classes of football players ever at Notre Dame, a group that would have seven All-Americans. The team bequeathed to him was loaded with talent—seven more eventual All-Americans. He made several adjustments in the line, switching the positions for about half of the players. Budka was quarterback and Farrell moved to left halfback. Don Hogan was injured in an auto accident and would never play football again. Devore used Jack Snow at right halfback and Joe Kantor at fullback. This was, on paper, a fine group of players.

Budka was still recovering from a leg broken in the 1962 USC game, so Szot started against Wisconsin. Snow scored on a pitchout, which he took for a 24-yard touchdown. John Huarte kicked the point after. Goberville blocked a Badger punt for a safety and a 9-0 lead. In the second quarter, Wisconsin's Hal Brandt found Jimmy Jones for a five-yard touchdown pass. Good defense stopped Badger drives in the third period, but the Fighting Irish were tiring. Wisconsin won 14-9 when Jones intercepted a pass and Ralph Kurek smashed over from the one. It was only the third Irish loss in an opener in 75 tries.

Purdue was next. In the first quarter, Purdue tried a field goal that missed. Huarte came in and fired to Alan Loboy for 39 yards and to Kelly for a 15-yard

Bill Pfeiffer, defensive specialist in 1963.

1963 Notre Dame Fighting Irish.

touchdown. But Huarte injured an ankle on the play, tried a two-point conversion pass, and missed. The ankle would be a large factor as the season progressed. Purdue came back for their only touchdown, in the fourth quarter, on a seven-yard pass from DiGravio to Bob Hadrick. They made the point after, giving Purdue a 7-6 lead. Huarte limped out and cajoled the Fighting Irish to the Purdue 10, but a field goal try missed, preserving the Boilermakers's 7-6 victory.

Budka started against USC, the third quarterback in three games. MacDonald intercepted a Beathard pass in the first quarter and sped 62 yards to score. The Trojans immediately advanced 74 yards in nine plays. Beathard scored from the three. Sophomore Bill Wolski returned the kickoff to the 37, then ran twice for 39 yards, blocked on a Budka run, and ran 22 yards for the touchdown and a 14-7 lead. The Trojans showed their championship quality: Beathard to Bedsole for 43 yards;

1963 Notre Dame coaching staff: (l to r) kneeling: John Murphy, Dave Hurd, Gus Cifelli, head coach Hugh Devore, Lou Stephens, Bill Daddio; standing: Jerry Stoltz, Brad Lynn, and George Sefcik.

ditto for 13 more; and Beathard to Mike Garrett for a 24-yard touchdown. Good defense kept USC scoreless in the third quarter. Ken Ivan kicked a field goal from the 16 for a 17-14 Notre Dame lead with 6:30 left. The defense, led by Bill Pfeiffer, then hog-tied the Trojans for the upset win. Pfeiffer made 17 tackles on the day.

Budka and Notre Dame whipped UCLA 27-12. He lofted a screen pass to Kantor from the 11 for the first touchdown to end a 72-yard drive. A shanked UCLA punt led to a four-yard touchdown run by Wolski. A UCLA drive reached the Irish 27 but Pfeiffer caused a fumble. The Bruins scored using a tackle eligible play, Larry Zeno to Mitch Johnson for 12 yards. In the third quarter, Notre Dame went 54 yards in six plays, with Kelly blasting through two deep backs for a 17-yard touchdown pass. Budka scored from the four after Charlie O'Hara set him up with a 33-yard run. UCLA scored later on a pass. The Irish went to Stanford. Notre Dame scored first after a fumble, on a one-yard Budka sneak. An interception set up a Stanford touchdown from the Irish four; they hit a field goal later for a 10-7 lead. On the return drive, Budka threw a 10-yard touchdown pass to Dave Pivec. But that was it for the Fighting Irish. Stanford scored twice for a 24-14 victory. Notre Dame killed a good drive with penalties and was unable to stop Stanford on a consistent basis.

Roger Staubach was in his Heisman-winning year and led Navy to a 35-14 win that exposed some previously undetected problems. A bad punt snap gave Navy the ball at the Notre Dame 18; Staubach used four runs before using play action on a three-yard touchdown pass. The Fighting Irish put in a behemoth backfield of Costa at 235 pounds, Pete Duranko at 220, and Kantor to jam the football for a Budka score from the two. Staubach hit three passes for another touchdown and the lead. Navy scored from the two in the third quarter. Middie Gary Kellner intercepted a Notre Dame screen pass and scored, then Staubach outpaced a lunging defense to throw a last touchdown pass. A Navy fumble let Kantor rumble in from the 10 to end it. Notre Dame's Bob Lehmann made 20 tackles.

Four Irish quarterbacks were not enough against Pitt, losing 27-7. A Tom Longo interception led to a Budka sneak from the one, but Pitt ran away with it after that: a 92-yard touchdown kickoff return by Paul Martha; a one-yard touchdown plunge; a touchdown run of 10 yards after an interception; and a penalty-assisted touchdown.

Michigan State continued its dominance over Notre Dame with a 12-7 win, its eighth victory over Notre Dame. The Fighting Irish got inside the MSU 30 four times and inside the 15 twice, but failed to

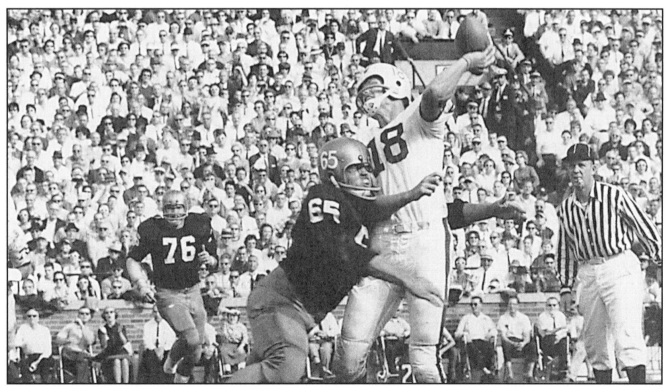

Captain Bob Lehmann interrupts Badger Hal Brandt's plans for a completion. Tommy MacDonald intercepted the throw in the 1963 opening 14-9 Irish loss.

score. MSU completed one of eight passes for 0 yards; MacDonald intercepted his 14th career pass, a Notre Dame record at the time. Following a Spartan fumble, Denny Phillips went for a touchdown from the 11. The Fighting Irish could not move in spite of bad MSU punting and an interception. Spartan Sherm Lewis scored from the three but a two-point try failed. In the fourth quarter, a bad punt gave Notre Dame the ball at the MSU 18—no score after three runs and a pass. Longo intercepted an MSU throw on their 11—no score after three runs and a pass. Lewis won the game for MSU with an 85-yard touchdown run.

The assassination of President Kennedy cancelled the Iowa game, and Notre Dame went a week later to Yankee Stadium to play Syracuse. The Irish took an early lead, and then faltered. Syracuse scored first on a six-yard touchdown pass, but Dick Arrington blocked the kick. Lehmann blocked a field goal try. Sandy Bonvechio pitched out to Budka, who then threw to MacDonald for a 20-yard touchdown. In the fourth quarter, MacDonald intercepted his 15th career pass. Pfeiffer got one, as did Lehmann. Notre Dame's Ken Maglicic grabbed a fumble. Finally, Syracuse scored on a 47-yard pass to win it 14-7.

There were not many signs of life in the Fighting Irish offense all season. They gained 1,980 yards of total offense all year (Vagas Ferguson would come within 500 yards of that by himself in 1979). There were only 54 completions all year for a scant 654 yards, the kind of statistics Joe Theismann would generate in two games. The defense played well and gave the offense numerous chances. Kelly and Lehmann made All-American teams.

1963 record: 2-7-0 (.222)
Record to date: 468-133-34 (.763)

1964

On December 3, 1963, Notre Dame officials announced that for the first time in half a century they would turn over the school's football fortunes to an outsider—Ara Parseghian of Northwestern. He immediately made a promise to the students, "Notre Dame's players will be in shape in the fourth quarter of their games." Parseghian had a firm sense of dedication, quiet dignity, and a burning desire for excellence. There were no short cuts. He was a brilliant football tactician who had Northwestern playing over their heads for years.

His football mentors were Paul Brown, Sid Gilman, and Woody Hayes. He had been the head coach at Miami of Ohio and Northwestern. There he had beaten Notre Dame four times, using inferior football talent to do it. At Notre Dame he would have talent but the task would be motivational. He found a marvelous group of players who had lost faith in themselves. It's often easier to take an average player and have him play beyond his capacity than it is to make a psychologically wounded star play to his potential. There are hidden obstacles and resistances; they've heard all the pep talks, but they still break down at crucial moments. Ironically, his 1964 seniors had met as a group earlier in their careers and promised that they would win a national crown. Most observers were hoping for a 6-4 season.

Two-platoon football was back as a result of an NCAA rule change; Ara could make instant use of the large talent pool and hone skills for specific jobs. He insisted on getting the country's best group of sophomores on the defense where they would have an immediate impact. Huarte was quarterback, hoping that complete rest would solve a shoulder problem instead of surgery—it worked. Huarte had an uncanny ability to make fakes, very quick feet, a calm confidence, and a good throwing arm with a peculiar three-quarter sidearm motion. The halfbacks were Bill Wolski and Nick Eddy, who had brilliant speed and fine hands. Joe Farrell won the fullback's job. Jack Snow was a wide receiver. The line was technically solid, with good tacticians, led by Dick Arrington. The defense was led by Jim Carroll at linebacker, Nick Rassas as a deep back, and Kevin Hardy and future NFL Hall of Famer Alan Page on the line. Page would prove to be an all-time player, both in college and as a pro. He had unbelievable quickness. This group was an unknown quantity as a team, with good size, excellent speed in the right places, good leadership, and talent.

Wisconsin was blown out 31-7. Huarte and Snow combined for 217 yards in passing (33 percent of the 1963 season total). Wisconsin's running game was held to minus-51 yards. Tom Carey intercepted a Wisconsin pass and Ken Ivan kicked a 31-yard field goal. The first touchdown came on a 61-yard bomb from Huarte to Snow. Another field goal stretched the lead to 13-0 at the half. Wisconsin scored on a 45-yard pass. Kantor went in from short yardage for a touchdown, Wolski banged in from the two, and Snow ended the scoring with a 42-yard catch and run on a Huarte pass.

Bob Griese led Purdue to a score in 75 yards on 12 plays, capped by his sneak from the one. A Fighting

Irish drive misfired with a failed field goal, but Huarte charged back, throwing to Snow to set up Wolski's three-yard touchdown burst. In the second quarter, Longo intercepted a Griese pass and Notre Dame went 47 yards in seven plays, Snow scoring on a two-yard touchdown reception. In the third quarter, Hardy blocked a Purdue punt to Page, who sprinted 57 yards for a touchdown, losing a Boilermaker running back in the footrace. Purdue could not drive, punted, and Notre Dame marched 76 yards; Pete Andreotti scored from the 23 with a pitchout. Snow later rocketed a 70-yard quick kick; it hit a Purdue player, and Phil Sheridan recovered at their three. Huarte threw to Rassas for the touchdown. Purdue scored against the reserves to end it 34-15. Jim Carroll led the Irish with 21 tackles.

The Irish flew to Colorado to play Air Force; the Falcons scored when a Huarte pass was intercepted and returned for a 25-yard touchdown. Huarte led Notre Dame back with a ground game and Eddy zipped outside for a seven-yard touchdown. The next score also came from a battering ground game; Huarte faked to Farrell; while the Falcons tackled him, Huarte went in for the touchdown. The Fighting Irish had to overcome penalties before Wolski caught a 19-yard pass for another score. A Carey interception led to Huarte's touchdown sneak in the third quarter; Rassas intercepted a Falcon aerial and returned it to the Air Force seven. Huarte faked to Wolski up the middle, then lobbed a pass to Snow for the touchdown. The Fighting Irish defense mangled the

Norm Nicola, starting center for the 1963 and 1964 teams.

Falcon running game, holding them to 38 yards as they soared to a 34-7 win.

The Fighting Irish defense under coach John Ray was allowing less than one yard per carry and now faced the country's offense leader, UCLA's Larry Zeno and sophomore star Mel Farr. The result was Ara's first Notre Dame shutout win, 24-0. Wolski blasted in from

The great 1964 defensive front: Alan Page, Kevin Hardy, Tom Regner, and Don Gmitter—who helped the Irish register four shutouts and give up only 77 points in the season.

Tom Regner prepares to unload on a Spartan back in the 34-7 1964 win.

the one-foot line for the first touchdown. After a missed Notre Dame field goal, Zeno marched UCLA to the Irish 37 where Carey intercepted the ball. Huarte threw a 37-yard touchdown pass to Sheridan for a 12-0 halftime lead. In the second half, Zeno lost the football on his 16 after a crushing hit. Huarte threw a touchdown pass to Snow. Alan Page tackled Zeno and Costa recovered another fumble. Farrell scored the final touchdown.

Stanford played good football for nearly two quarters before Ivan drilled a 28-yard field goal for the Irish. Stanford punted and the onslaught began with a 54-yard touchdown strike from Huarte to Wolski. The Fighting Irish scored again in 53 seconds and seven plays after a Carey interception; Eddy went in from the one on a pitchout. In the first half, Stanford had 31 yards of total offense, failed to move the sticks, and failed to complete a pass. Wolski pounded in a touchdown from the one-foot line in the second half. The Indians made a first down midway into the third quarter, but linebacker Ken Maglicic intercepted their next pass. Wolski scored on a six-yard run and Stanford scored against the subs for Notre Dame's 28-6 win. Huarte completed 21 of 37 passes, eight of them to Snow, who already had the season record for receiving yards in five games. Wolski tripled Stanford's total offense with 102 yards rushing and 60 yards receiving. The 1963 Heisman winner, Staubach, met the "winner to be" in Huarte. The Fighting Irish demolished Navy 40-0. Notre Dame had 504 yards of total offense and scored in inventive ways: Eddy on a 74-yard touchdown screen pass; Snow with a 55-yard touchdown pass; 68 yards on three passes, and Wolski from the one; Farrell on a 20-yard touchdown run; a one-yard Huarte touchdown pass to Snow; and Denny Conway from the two. Huarte had thrown 12 touchdown passes for the year; Snow had equalled Kelly's total catches, 41, in the 1962 season.

Jim Carroll, Parseghian's first captain, two-year starter at LG and RG in 1962 and 1963, then starting MLB in 1964, and an All-American for Ara's wonder team.

Three All-Americans: Bob Lehmann, Roger Staubach, and Jim Kelly, before a 1964 basketball game.

Pittsburgh lost 17-15 in the first real test for the Fighting Irish. Notre Dame scored on an 80-yard march with Farrell slashing in from the two. On their next series, Huarte and Eddy hooked up for a 91-yard touchdown. But an Andretti fumble led to a Pitt score and a 14-8 scoreboard. Joe Azzaro kicked a 30-yard field goal to make it 17-8 at the half. Pitt used up much of the third quarter on a series that scored in the fourth quarter, 17-15. The Panthers made their move late in the game but Carroll and Tom Regner stopped a fourth-down run at the Notre Dame 16; some strategic punting by Snow and a fumble recovery by Tom Kostelnick wrapped it up.

Notre Dame had not beaten Michigan State since 1954; this year they came away with a 34-7 win. Ara had the offense line up in a double wingback set, and Eddy dashed 61 yards with the first play for a touchdown. Farrell scrapped for the next score: three runs for 15 yards, a 22-yard reception, and a 13-yard touchdown reception. MSU backed the Irish up to the 14, but Huarte calmly brought them out: a 20-yard pass to Snow, a 26-yard pass to Bob Merkle, some Eddy runs for 33 yards, and Eddy in a five-yard touchdown burst for the 20-0 halftime lead. In the third quarter, Eddy lost a 78-yard touchdown run on a penalty; the Spartans scored on a 51-yard touchdown pass play by Gene Washington. Carey intercepted a Spartan pass; Huarte fired a 16-yard scoring pass to Snow, and Eddy caught a two-point conversion pass. Carroll grabbed a fumble on their 15 Andretti scored from the two to wrap it up.

When it was over, Duffy said he wouldn't want to play a better team than Notre Dame.

A bitterly cold day slowed down the passing game against Iowa but the ground game led to a 28-0 win. Wolski jammed it in from the three for the first score. After Arunas Vasys recovered a fumble. Huarte found Snow open for a 66-yard touchdown. Iowa stayed cold in the third quarter, but Eddy scored on a sweep from the seven. Notre Dame scored in the game's final minute for their 9-0 record.

With the national championship within their grasp, the Fighting Irish headed to Los Angeles for the Thanksgiving day matchup with USC. Unfortunately, USC spoiled the Irish championship dreams with a 20-17 victory. Ken Ivan kicked a field goal from the 15 after Maglicic caused a Rod Sherman fumble. From the Notre Dame 26, Huarte passed to Snow for 23 yards, then to Sheridan for 13, and Snow ran 10 yards on a draw play to the USC 35. Huarte froze USC's defense with two fakes, followed by a 22-yard touchdown pass to Snow. Wolski scored from the five to end a 72-yard drive. In the second half, Mike Garrett scored from the one. Notre Dame's Joe Kantor scored from the half-foot line, but a holding penalty took the score away. Notre Dame was unable to score after that. This was a crucial turn of events; USC scored on a 23-yard pass from Fertig to Fred Hill. USC's defense held the Irish; the Trojans drove for the winning touchdown, a 15-yard pass to Sherman, with 1:34 left. The Fighting Irish managed

Ara congratulating John Huarte after the Heisman Trophy award in 1964.

two drives, one; but couldn't score.

Ara had taken a doormat team to a possible national title. In 1963, total offense was 1,980 yards, but in 1964, it increased to 4,014—from 654 yards passing to 2,105, from 15 touchdowns to 41, from 159 opposition points to 77. Snow almost doubled the 1963 passing total with his 1,114 yards. Huarte won the Heisman. Ara was Coach of the Year. Huarte, Snow, Carroll, Hardy, and Carey were All-Americans.

1964 record: 9-1-0 (.900)
Record to date: 477-134-34 (.765)

1965

Huarte's graduation stripped the Irish of their devastating passing game. They'd sink or swim with the run in 1965. Parseghian adjusted with a much larger offensive line, from the 1964 average of 217 pounds to 226, end to end, actually 233 from tackle to tackle. Regner switched from defense to left guard and Sheridan and Tom Talaga were essentially a double tight end set. Bill Zloch, a dependable runner but not a great passer, was quarterback. Behind him were Wolski and Eddy, who had teamed for 1,629 yards of offense in 1964. Larry Conjar was at fullback with fine blocking

and excellent speed. The defensive line was solid with Harry Long, Duranko (whose fullback's quickness was an asset as a lineman), Arrington, and Page. Kevin Hardy's season was curtailed by an injury in the Purdue game. Jim Lynch led the linebackers and all three deep backs returned. This was a fair team, not outstanding at the skill positions, and thus without the quick-strike capability of the 1964 team.

Bill Zloch, starting QB for the 1965 Irish.

The strengths and weaknesses were evident immediately in the 48-6 trampling of the University of California. Fighting Irish running gained 381 yards but the passing game only 68. Notre Dame had control of the game from the outset: an 80-yard march for Ivan's 28-yard field goal; a Rassas interception followed by Zloch's three-yard touchdown sneak; a Page fumble recovery to set up a Conjar touchdown; Rassas for a 65-yard touchdown punt return; a Cal score offset by Zloch's 11-yard keeper for a tally; a third quarter drive of 74 yards in six plays, Eddy scoring with a 24-yard pass; a Wolski touchdown run from the six after a Cal fumble; and a Dan Harshman touchdown scored with the reserves. Parseghian showed concern over linebacking errors and pass completions in the secondary.

Bob Griese and Purdue awaited the number-one Irish. Griese completed 19-of-22 passes for 283 yards and three touchdowns in a 25-21 Purdue win. He also punted to keep the Fighting Irish penned deep. Notre Dame led 21-18 with only moments to go after Wolski ran 54 yards for a score and Ivan hit a field goal. Griese hit three passes on the game's concluding 70-yard march, and then used a fullback plunge for the winning tally. He did this in the face of a tremendous pass rush, throwing completions a half dozen times as Irish defenders clutched at his jersey. Many completions went into a vulnerable area just behind the linebackers. The defense lost a star when Hardy went down with a bad back.

Notre Dame recovered to beat Northwestern 38-7, although Northwestern had the halftime lead at 7-6. Wolski scored the first touchdown, then an interception of a Zloch pass went back for a 50-yard touchdown

Dick Arrington, starting LT in 1963, starting RG in 1964, starting RG in 1965, and consensus All-American in 1965.

return. Eddy went out with an apparent concussion, and Wolski was bruised badly, so the defense would have to stop Northwestern. They created five turnovers in the second half. Rassas atoned for a fumbled punt when he took a pass away from Woody Campbell and ran 92 yards for the go-ahead score. He broke it open with a 72-yard punt return for another tally seven minutes later. Two more fumbles and another interception let sophomores Paul May and Rocky Bleier score the final touchdowns.

1965 Notre Dame Fighting Irish.

Parseghian and staff for 1965: kneeling—George Sefcik, Joe Yonto, Tom Pagna, Paul Schoults; standing—Brian Boulac, Doc Urich, Ara Parseghian, John Ray, and Dave Hurd.

Sophomore Tom Schoen started against Paul Dietzel's Army team in a night game at Shea Stadium. He threw a touchdown pass to Don Gmitter for starters.

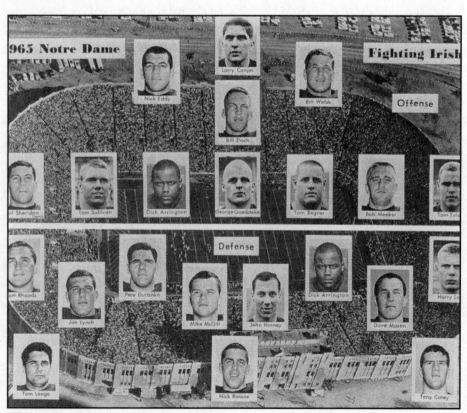

The 1965 starting offense and defense.

That score held into the third quarter when Tom Rhoads deflected a pass and recovered it to set up Eddy's end sweep for a tally. Larry Conjar, on a 12-play drive, ran 10 times, eight in a row, to get Ivan in field-goal range for the 17-0 win.

It had been building since spring practices. The ruined Thanksgiving dinner, the lost perfect season, the game won until the last 94 seconds—each Notre Dame student and player knew to *remember*. That word was repeated at Notre Dame thousands of times in the weeks and days leading to the USC rematch. The student body had to wait two weeks after the win over Army; 3,000 students jammed the practice field two days before the game and chanted *"Remember!"* The avenging Fighting Irish held USC's Garrett to seven yards in the first half on their

The great defensive backfield of 1964 and 1965: Tony Carey, Nick Rassas, and Tom Longo.

way to a 28-7 win. Wolski and Conjar led a 45-yard scoring drive, with Conjar scoring the first of four touchdowns for the greatest day of his career. The Trojans were penalized on a roughing call and Conjar scored his second touchdown. He kept up the pace in the second quarter gaining most of the 67 yards on a drive for a 21-0 lead. When USC went back on the field after halftime, they were met by the Notre Dame student body who had made a tunnel for the Irish players. Conjar led a carbon-copy 67-yard drive for the four-touchdown lead. USC scored but spent the rest of the day in reverse. Conjar gained 116 yards for the day, 42 more than the USC team. Each starting Irish back

had more yardage than Garrett.

Navy jammed the scrimmage line with nine defenders and kept two deep. They nursed a 3-0 lead into the last 14 seconds of the half when Zloch lofted a swing pass to Eddy, who ran for a 55-yard touchdown. In the third quarter, Zloch and Conjar tallied to finish long drives. Rassas returned another punt, this one for 66 yards and a score for the 29-3 win.

Against Pittsburgh, Wolski scored five touchdowns to lead Notre Dame in a 69-13 rout. Eddy scored first on a 26-yard touchdown run. Other scores were: Conjar for 43 yards up the middle after a fumble; Eddy for 56

The halfbacks for 1964 and 1965—Nick Eddy and Bill Wolski.

yards with a pass; Gmitter for 30 yards with a pass; and singles by reserves May, Bleier, and Conway. Wolski's five touchdowns came on only 54 yards rushing. Zloch completed six of seven passes for 184 yards.

North Carolina held Notre Dame scoreless until the fourth quarter. Ivan kicked a 38-yard field goal. Eddy sped 34 yards on a sweep past right end for a touchdown halfway into the quarter. Mike McGill intercepted a Tar Heel pass and Eddy capitalized with a three-yard touchdown. It was a 17-0 win, but the Fighting Irish were not operating smoothly on offense.

The number-one Spartans boasted a tremendous defense with Bubba Smith, George Webster, and 320-pound nose guard Harold Lucas. Ivan hit a field goal early after a Michigan State fumble. Two other turnovers, however, were wasted by the Irish. MSU's Dwight Lee and Clinton Jones scored touchdowns; MSU harassed Zloch with its defense to win 12-3.

The Fighting Irish played Miami to a 0-0 standoff. Miami used the Navy ploy of a stacked defense with nine men near the line of scrimmage. They pressured Zloch into six of 20 for 60 yards. Ivan missed two field goals. The Irish defense, however, stopped Miami's offense. Notre Dame finished its season 7-2-1.

There was a 59 percent drop in passing yardage in 1965 compared with 1964. Overall, the offensive output fell 25 percent, although scoring was about the same. They failed to capitalize on a couple of crucial turnovers. The big task was to do something about the passing game. Arrington, Regner, Rassas, and Lynch made All-America teams.

1965 record: 7-2-1 (.750)
Record to date: 484-136-35 (.765)

1966

At the end of the 1965 season, Parseghian had been watching film of the Pennsylvania Big 33 game, that state's annual high school all-star game, when a player caught his eye as a deep back. Ara told the assistant coaches to "get him." Eventually, he showed up and blended in with hundreds of other aspirants.

Ara coached from a tower above the practice fields. Word filtered up to him during the 1965 season that he had a couple of fine prospects as freshman quarterbacks. One was Coley O'Brien, and the other was the kid he'd seen on the film, Terry Hanratty. Every now and then

John Horney, diminutive starting LB in 1965 and 1966.

Ara would catch a glimpse of hard-thrown, flat passes zinging out of the backfield—some by Hanratty, some by O'Brien. Then he'd see this tall, rangy kid with a middle distance runner's stride and Paul Warfield's hands—Jim Seymour.

He could turn them loose in 1966. There were other sophomores who could help, especially George Kunz, the most dominating tackle ever seen by assistant athletic director Brian Boulac, and Bob Kuchenberg at the other tackle. Hanratty edged out O'Brien for the starting quarterback job. Eddy moved to left halfback and Bleier moved up. Conjar stayed at fullback. On defense, Tom Rhoads moved up to start with Duranko, Hardy, and Page. Lynch led a good group of young linebackers. Ara had to replace the entire secondary, so he switched Schoen to safety and made him a two-time All-American. Jim Smithberger and Tom O'Leary worked the corners. Overall, this was a young but talented team, with good depth in most places.

Jim Lynch had studied Purdue's offense until he knew it better than Griese. He kept a binder filled with flip cards of their sets on one side and the appropriate Fighting Irish defense on the other. He memorized it. Griese set up for Purdue's first play, and Lynch hunched just across from him. The Purdue quarterback looked at the Irish defense, checked off, and called a new play. Lynch checked off; the Irish adjusted. Griese checked

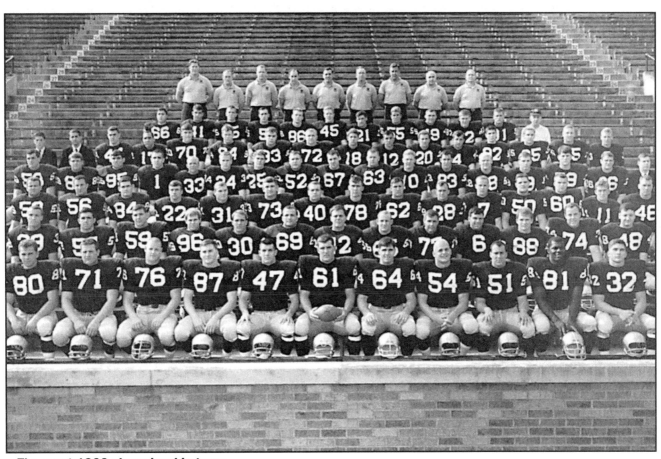

The great 1966 championship team.

to a new play. Lynch checked off; the Irish adjusted. Frustrated, Griese stood up behind center and called time out. Griese knew then it would be a long day. And it was—26-14. Leroy Keyes speared a fumble in mid-air and jetted 95 yards for a Purdue touchdown. They kicked off. Eddy fielded it, hesitated, started to his right, got past the first wave, and cut right again. He was gone—97 yards to the end zone. There had been two plays and two touchdowns. On the next Fighting Irish series, Hanratty threw a 42-yard pass to the loping Seymour. On the next Notre Dame series, with third-and-14 at their own 16, Hanratty threw to Seymour for an 84-yard touchdown. In the second half they connected again for a 39-yard score. Purdue scored, but Notre Dame scored on a seven-yarder for the final score. Although Purdue would go to the Rose Bowl that year yet, Notre Dame's sophomores made 13 completions, 276 yards, and three scores.

Northwestern came up with the idea of crashing the ends in on Hanratty and double-teaming Seymour. It was marginally successful but left other spots vulnerable; Notre Dame exploited them and won 35-7. Conjar plunged for the first touchdown. In the second quarter, the Fighting Irish survived a deep thrust and Eddy shook loose on a long distance score. Bleier scored, untouched, on a short run. Schoen scored twice, but lost the first to a penalty, and kept the second on an

George Goeddeke, starting center in 1965 and 1966.

The 1966 defensive front and linebackers. They helped the Irish record six shutouts in 1966, giving up a mere 38 points in the undefeated season.

interception. Northwestern's tactics held Seymour to nine catches and 141 yards.

Army was next in a mismatch. Bleier ran from the two for the first score, set up by Seymour's 19-yard catch. Duranko fell on a fumble and Hanratty showcased Seymour for a touchdown. Hanratty scored on a keeper, and Eddy tallied twice for a 35-0 halftime score. The starters gained 323 yards in the half; the subs played the rest. The score did not change.

North Carolina ran into problems when they found themselves using a fullback as quarterback within a span of four plays because injuries had decimated their quarterback corps. Conjar capped marches of 73 and 55 yards with touchdowns from one yard out. Hardy engulfed a fumble; and Hanratty went to Seymour for a 56-yard touchdown play. In the third quarter, Eddy ran 52 yards for a touchdown. Bob Gladieux took an O'Brien pitchout five yards for a score to end a 67-

Conjar "pro" football catches a pass against Duke in 1966.

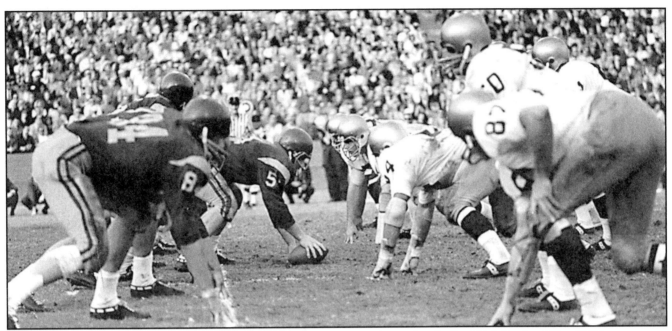

Hardy, Duranko, and mates dig in as USC tries to get something going in the 51-0 finale of the 1966 season.

yard drive by the reserves. Notre Dame kept its modest shutout string with a 32-0 win.

Undefeated Oklahoma was next; it was a typical Southern team for that era—light, quick, aggressive, and great at "pursuit." They were unprepared to meet men 50-70 pounds heavier who were just as fast. The Fighting Irish shut them out, 38-0. A great linebacker led the Sooners, Granville Liggins, but he was injured. Notre Dame scored 17 points in the second quarter: Eddy and Hanratty both had two-yard end runs after drives, and a field goal followed an injury to Seymour. There were three more touchdowns in the third quarter: Eddy, Bleier, and O'Brien. When it was over, all of the Fighting Irish wide receivers were hurt.

With a crippled passing game, Notre Dame scuttled Navy 31-7 with a running attack. Linebacker John Pergine intercepted three Navy passes. The Navy defense scored on a blocked punt; their offense was 28 yards passing and 36 yards running. Hanratty scored twice, Conjar and Gladieux once each, and Azzaro kicked a 42-yard field goal. Jim Lynch tipped a pass, which went to Pergine, and then Lynch tackled him just to be sure. It was the last tackle of a Notre Dame player by a member of the Lynch family (his brother, now the Naval Academy's Superintendent, had played for Navy in 1963).

Pitt folded 40-0, but held Notre Dame scoreless for the first 25 minutes. Hanratty scored

from the three. In the third period, Eddy zoomed 85 yards with the kickoff for a touchdown. Schoen returned a punt 63 yards to score. Eddy hurt a shoulder at the end of a 51-yard trip, so Ara started shuffling in strange

The starting running backs for the 1966 national champions: Bleier, Conjar, and Eddy.

combinations for the opposing scouts: Hanratty and O'Brien, or two fullbacks, May and Conjar. Conjar scored and May scored two.

Duke, another quick, small team, trailed 43-0 at the half and 64-0 at the end. Eddy on the second play ran for a 77-yard touchdown. John Horney intercepted a pass and tossed a lateral to O'Leary, who scored from the 25. Bleier scored twice, Conjar once, and a healed Seymour followed Hanratty's 50-yard run with a 43- yard touchdown catch. Dave Haley, O'Brien, and Frank Criniti scored for the reserves. The defense had four interceptions, two fumble recoveries, and one touchdown. The defensive line from 1964—Gmitter, Hardy, Regner, and Page—went in for one nostalgic play and stuffed it to a standing ovation. Ara played 64 men, 29 of them seniors.

Michigan State—more marriages were broken by this one game than any other in the century. The networks still show it as they count the anniversaries of this classic contest. Eddy reinjured his shoulder getting off the train in frozen East Lansing. Bubba Smith wiped out Hanratty in the first quarter. Center George Goeddeke sprained an ankle two plays later. O'Brien had been recently diagnosed as diabetic; his insulin intake had not yet been regulated. Ara had a surprise—275-pound Kevin Hardy did the punting, seemingly putting it above the second deck of the stadium. The center-quarterback units stayed the same, O'Brien worked with Tim Monty after Goeddeke's injury. Gladieux had a good day in Eddy's spot. He had the lone Irish touchdown. MSU scored on a plunge by Regis Cavender, and a barefooted Dick Kenney kicked a field goal. O'Brien was chomping

Pete Duranko, starting LDT in 1965 and 1966, All-America in 1966.

on candy bars to keep his blood sugar up. The Fighting Irish scored a touchdown on a 34-yard pass, O'Brien to Gladieux. It was 10-7 at the half. In the third quarter, a long drive got Notre Dame close and Azzaro tied the game with a 28-yard field goal to begin the fourth period, 10-10. Moments later, Schoen intercepted a Michigan State pass and ran it to their 18. Two runs didn't work;

Jim Lynch and Kevin Hardy dressing for a 1966 game.

Alan Page, three-year starter as RDE from 1964 to 1966. Consensus All-American in 1966.

Jim Lynch, an all-time great for Notre Dame as a three-year starter at LB. Captain and consensus All-American in 1966.

O'Brien tried a pass to Seymour, but it missed. With 4:39 left, Azzaro tried a 42-yard field goal into the frigid wind. It missed to the right by less than a foot. The Fighting Irish stopped the next MSU possession and got the ball back on their own 30 with less than three minutes to go. Ara saw that O'Brien was really tired; Schoen was the only other experienced quarterback but he wasn't prepped. MSU was in a prevent defense. Notre Dame ran three plays for nine yards. The third was a draw play by Conjar. Now fourth-and-one, O'Brien took the snap and got two. MSU called a timeout. Ara tried an option play but Bubba smeared it. There was time for one more play; O'Brien ran into the line. Tie game. MSU had not crossed Notre Dame's 45 in the second half.

Still time to *remember*. This was the poll bowl, USC and Notre Dame. The Trojans were humiliated, 51-0. O'Brien hit 21 of 31 passes for 255 yards. Seymour caught 11 for 150 yards and two touchdowns. Conjar scored after 17 grinding plays. Schoen ran 44 yards with an intercepted Trojan pass for a score. Azzaro kicked a field goal. O'Brien unleashed a 66-yard drive of passes. Seymour scored from 13. And again from the 39. It

was 31-0 at the half. USC fumbled on their second play. Danny Harshman, Eddy's replacement, scored a 23-yard touchdown. Eddy slanted in with a seven-yard score. Linebacker Dave Martin intercepted a pass and went in from 33 yards out.

This national championship team has to be considered for all-time status. It had 11 All-Americans (and five others too young in 1966). Ten of the starting offensive 11 played pro ball, as did eight defenders. They trampled the opposition 362 points to 38. They had six shutouts. The All-America list included Eddy, Lynch, Regner, Page, Duranko, Hardy, Seymour, Seiler, Goeddeke, Schoen, and Conjar.

1966 record: 9-0-1 (.950)
Record to date: 493-136-36 (.768)

1967

The 1967 team was stuck at the outset with the number-one rating. The sophomores were maturing and were a real threat on offense. Behind Hanratty, there was a decline in the quality of the backs—Bleier and Harshman were dependable, solid players but lacked game-breaking speed. Jeff Zimmerman, at fullback, was not quite a Conjar. Seymour remained as a deep threat. On defense, Page, Duranko, and Lynch had to be replaced. The defensive line had Hardy and Kuechenberg, with Mike McCoy as a good reserve. Most linebackers returned and all of the secondary, who had enough speed to handle all but the fastest deep threats.

Notre Dame, as a 35-point favorite, beat the University of California 41-8. Hanratty went 15 for 30; Seymour caught six, one a nine-yard touchdown. Bleier caught another Hanratty touchdown pass. O'Brien threw a 14-yard touchdown to Gladieux.

Harshman and Azzaro accounted for the rest. Cal's passing was inept—two of 20. Linebacker Dave Martin intercepted as many of their passes as Cal caught.

Purdue's Mike Phipps led an inspired team to a 28-21 upset. Hanratty threw 63 passes, completed 29, for 336 yards and one score, but four were intercepted. Purdue scored on the kickoff and intercepted a Hanratty pass on the return drive at their 19. The Fighting Irish scored, Hanratty tallying on a one-yard plunge. The second quarter was frustrating for Notre Dame as they had 32 snaps but no score. Purdue's Perry Williams scored and they made a two-point conversion for a 14-7 lead. Bleier tied it in the third quarter with a one-yard run on a 94-yard march. Leroy Keyes scored from the five to answer. Hanratty threw three passes and a touchdown to Paul Snow from the 27. Purdue drove; a face mask penalty led to a touchdown pass by Phipps from the Notre Dame 31. Keyes defensed Seymour in key situations and took him out of the game.

The Irish rebounded against Iowa, 55-6. Hanratty had a 35-0 first half, hitting nine of 10 passes. The scoring was: a Hanratty rollout touchdown from the two; Zimmerman from the two; a 22-yard pass to Bleier; a Schoen interception of an Ed Podolak pass returned 34-yards for a touchdown; Zimmerman for a 14-yard touchdown. The reserves tallied three more times.

Headaches for the 1967 opposition—Coley O'Brien, Terry Hanratty, and Jim Seymour with Ara.

USC and O.J. Simpson beat the Irish at home, 24-7. It started out well enough as Notre Dame intercepted three USC passes and held O.J. to 41 yards in the first half. Hanratty scored from the three in the second period for a 7-0 lead. But the Irish fumbled a kickoff on their 18. McKay used O.J. on six of seven plays for the score. A USC interception led to O.J.'s 36-yard touchdown burst, and a poor punt led to a USC field goal. USC had seven interceptions and put Hanratty out with a concussion. Simpson scored again after a Mike Battle interception. Seymour, with two dislocated fingers, caught passes good for 170 yards.

The Fighting Irish dumped Illinois 47-7, decimating their running game with minus-four yards on the day. Azzaro hit two field goals; and Notre Dame scored six touchdowns: a punt return by Schoen led to Zimmerman going up the middle for a seven-yard score; an 18-yard Hanratty-to-Seymour touchdown; Gladieux on an end run; and a Hanratty-to-Seymour touchdown pass just before the half. In the second half, Tom Quinn and Bob Gladieux each scored. The Illini used one of their four interceptions to score. Hanratty was now trying to force the ball to Seymour more than he should have, probably because it worked better than the running game.

MSU, a star-depleted team, was also minus six players suspended for curfew violations. The Fighting Irish won 24-12, due to Duffy's defense of Seymour, who was held to one catch. That opened up Zimmerman, who scored all of the Fighting Irish touchdowns on runs of seven and 47 yards to go with a 30-yard scoring pass from Hanratty. Azzaro kicked a field goal. Dwight Lee managed two late touchdowns. Zimmerman hammered the Spartans for 135 yards; they in turn ran 91 yards all day.

A few snowflakes turned into a blizzard and Navy scored two touchdowns. But by the time they scored, Notre Dame had wrapped up a 43-14 win with five first-half touchdowns shared among Zimmerman, Bleier, and Hanratty. The Irish ran for 313 yards.

The Fighting Irish shut out Pitt, 38-0. Hanratty scored two first-half touchdowns and Zimmerman another, as Notre Dame built a big lead early. O'Brien led a scoring drive in the second half, and Dave Haley went in from the one-foot line. O'Brien ran for two points as Notre Dame tried to impress the polls. This was done without Seymour, who was home with a leg injury. Schoen set a new interception return record with a 40-yard runback.

Georgia Tech, the 500th victim of Notre Dame, had a 3-0 lead and played well for a quarter until Notre Dame's size and talent wore them out. Hanratty led a 77-yard scoring drive, capped by a 38-yard strike to Gladieux. Bleier's Notre Dame career ended a game early with ligament damage, but he scored two touchdowns before he told anyone about it. Zimmerman scored a first-half touchdown and Gladieux chipped in with one in the second half. A field goal made the final score 36-3.

Bleier was out and Hardy was hobbled when the Fighting Irish visited Miami. They pulled out a tough 24-22 win over a determined Miami team. Azzaro kicked a 22-yard field goal. Hardy's punts were ineffective and Miami had good field position, leading to a nine-yard touchdown on a pass. Harshman fumbled the kickoff, Miami recovered and scored its second touchdown 18 seconds after its first. Those were the only touchdowns against the Irish all season in the second quarters of games. Smithberger intercepted a Miami pass and Hanratty went to work: a 14-yard pass to Seymour, a 39-yard flare pass to Zimmerman, a keeper for nine, and Ed Ziegler ran in from the one. Azzaro made a field goal, but Miami answered with its own for a 16-10 halftime score. In the third quarter, Notre Dame scored using 11 runs, with Zimmerman for five of them in a

row for 36 yards. Azzaro's point after put Notre Dame up 17-16. John Pergine deflected a field goal and later he intercepted a pass; Gladieux ran twice from their 38 for the final Notre Dame score. Miami scored again; linebacker Bob Olson preserved the win when he broke up their two-point try.

The Irish overcame a .500 start to come in fifth nationally. The running game matured by midseason to surpass the 1966 total. The defense, however, allowed 17 touchdowns. Three players were repeat All-Americans: Schoen, Seymour, and Hardy. They were joined by McGill, Pergine, Swatland, and Smithberger.

1967 record: 8-2-0 (.800)
Record to date: 501-138-36 (.768)

1968

Hanratty, Seymour, and Kunz were seniors. The offense was in pretty good shape. However, three linebackers and all of the secondary had to be replaced. Ara switched O'Brien to left halfback; his running mate was Gladieux. Hanratty's backup was Joe Theismann. The defense was anchored by Mike McCoy, one of the most impressive physical specimens (6'5", 270, 56" chest) ever to play under the Dome. Bob Olson was

George Kunz, an all-time lineman for the Irish, played some TE in 1967, was a consensus All-American in 1968.

Terry Hanratty zips through the snow and the Middies in a 43-14 rout in 1967.

the only returning linebacker. Everyone else behind the line would have to learn his assignments quickly. The offense would be a constant scoring threat. The defense would be able to stop the run and hope that the young secondary could handle the passing game.

Dick Swatland, starting RG in 1966 and 1967, All-American in 1967.

Oklahoma had not changed much since 1966, they were still small and quick. The Sooners faced an offensive line that averaged 233 pounds and a defensive line that went 246—and all of them were fast. Oklahoma lost 45-21. Gladieux scored on a one-yard blast; the Sooners hit Eddie Hinton for a 72-yard touchdown, and Steve Zabel for a 16-yard touchdown pass. The second quarter belonged to Hanratty and Seymour for two more scores. In the second half, Gladieux scored twice and Zimmerman ate up the clock with many of his 17 runs for the day. Chuck Landolfi ran for a six-yard touchdown. Notre Dame amassed 357 yards in 69 runs.

It was a bad sign that all of Oklahoma's scores came on passes. Phipps knew what to do; Purdue won 37-22. The defenses gave up a combined 55 first downs and 933 yards. Hanratty threw 43 times, completing 23 for 294 yards and two touchdowns, but three were intercepted. Notre Dame started with a patient ground game, scoring on Denny Allan's five-yard slant outside. Phipps used key passes to move the sticks, and Keyes ran past Irish deep backs for a 16-yard touchdown. The Fighting Irish gave them the game in the next four minutes with a Hanratty interception and a Gladieux fumble, both converted to touchdowns. Hanratty threw a 13-yard touchdown to Tom Eaton. Other drives misfired; Gladieux missed a touchdown pass; Notre Dame also missed a field goal. Purdue scored two more touchdowns in the fourth quarter. The Irish kept trying and scored on an eight-

Mike McGill, tough LB for the Irish from 1965 to 1967, All-American in 1967.

yard flip from Hanratty to Denny Allan. Three turnovers turned into Purdue scores; three more killed Irish drives.

Iowa started out with a 38-yard touchdown pass, but Notre Dame answered; Hanratty pushed it over from the three. After a punt, Gladieux ended a 67-yard march with a touchdown catch. But Iowa tied it with their next possession. Hanratty used the last moments of the first quarter on a 69-yard bomb to Gladieux, and Allan went in over left tackle from the two. Notre Dame tallied five more touchdowns to Iowa's two for a 51-28 win. Hanratty and O'Brien scored, and subs racked up three more.

Northwestern played tough but submitted 27-7. Hanratty scored on a seven-yard run. In the second half, Gladieux scored twice and O'Brien caught a touchdown pass. The backs gained 308 yards to the Wildcats's 93.

In a 58-8 win over Illinois, Hanratty surpassed Gipp's career yardage record of 4,110. Notre Dame amassed 673 yards of total offense. Hanratty passed for 212 yards and three touchdowns—to Seymour, Gladieux, and O'Brien. Ron Dushney, O'Brien, and Theismann scored on the ground. The Fighting Irish rushed for 461 yards on 67 plays, 6.8 yards per try.

Duffy Daugherty told reporters he'd open up with an onside kick if he had the chance. He did and Michigan State recovered, winning the game 21-17. They scored on that first drive and it was the difference. Kuechenberg scored on a fumble recovery, Gladieux

tallied once, and Hempel kicked a field goal. MSU added two more touchdowns. Hanratty had the team on the MSU two with a first-and-goal; three runs failed; he went to Seymour on fourth down. Seymour was turning to grab the touchdown pass when he was hit by Spartan Al Brenner. No flag—the official who should have called interference had fallen down and missed the play.

The Irish won easily against Navy, 45-14. Hanratty completed 14-of-21 passes for one touchdown, to Seymour, and directed his backs to 337 yards rushing. Gladieux ran 117 yards and scored twice; Hanratty ran for another. Hempel kicked a field goal and the subs tallied twice. Navy tried running 26 times, gaining only 66 yards.

Hanratty went down for the season with a knee injury in a scrimmage. Theismann, with three days' preparation, led the Fighting Irish against Pitt. Notre Dame obliterated Pitt 56-7. The first drive was 55 yards in four plays, and Gladieux scored. Theismann passed twice to Seymour, for 20 and 29 yards, on the next series before he took it in himself from the 10. The third drive was a clone of the second; Theismann fooled the Panthers with a bootleg play for a tally. Eric Norri scored a safety for 23 points in the first quarter. O'Brien owned the second quarter with two scoring receptions and a touchdown run. The reserves, led by Bob Belden, added the final score when Landolfi scored from the one. Theismann went seven for 10 for 153 yards and the touchdowns to O'Brien.

Bob Gladieux, starting RH in 1968, had one of the best seasons on record that year.

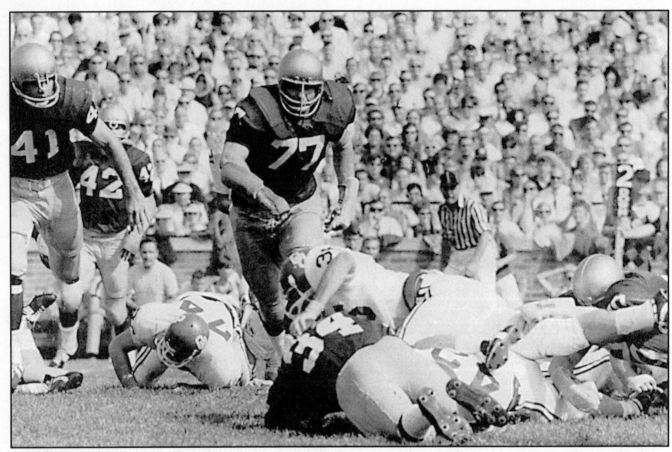

DE Mike Kondria has just finished off a Sooner runner in the 1968 Irish 45-21 win as McCoy (77), Lavin (41), and Kelly (42) make sure that it's over.

Theismann orchestrated a 34-6 Fighting Irish win over Georgia Tech in terrible weather. Gladieux scored two touchdowns, and Ron Dushney ran for 87 yards

Bob Olson, three-year starter at LB from 1967 to 1969, All-American in 1969.

on 16 carries, while Theismann slithered around in the mud for another 51 yards and a touchdown. Subs scored twice.

USC and O.J. in Los Angeles—the defending national champs and the Heisman winner-to-be. The Fighting Irish had their great defense and a wounded offense led by a sophomore quarterback. Notre Dame rose to the occasion and held O.J. to 55 yards on 21 carries. Gladieux outpaced the Trojans with 121 yards on 19 runs and one touchdown; Dushney added another while gaining 72 yards. Ara ran a six-man front with two linebackers in tight. USC scored on a pass interception, and Theismann responded with an 86-yard march capped by Dushney's three-yard touchdown. Gladieux took a pitchout and ran 57 yards for a second touchdown. Theismann scored on a 13-yard pass from O'Brien. USC started passing in the second half and tied it 21-21, the final score. Notre Dame missed two field goals, and USC just missed a touchdown on a dropped ball.

This was the best offensive team Ara had produced—5,044 yards on 3,059 yards running and

1,985 passing. They scored 53 touchdowns and had the fourth-rated rushing defense in the nation, although pass defense was weak all year. Hanratty finished third behind O.J. Simpson in the Heisman race. Kunz, Hanratty, and Seymour for the third time were All-Americans.

1968 record: 7-2-1 (.750)
Record to date: 508-140-37 (.768)

1969

Ara had two major concerns for his 1969 team—no returning starters in the backfield (Theismann had been a replacement) and improving the pass defense, which was 81st in the country in 1968. The coaches had confidence in Theismann, but there were no game-breaking backs waiting to move up. The backfield would be rather slow: Ed Ziegler, a two-year sub at fullback,

Mike McCoy, three-year starter at DT from 1967 to 1969, a consensus All-American in 1969.

started at left halfback; Denny Allan moved to right halfback. Bill Barz would be the fullback for two seasons. Seymour was gone but Tom Gatewood was a fine receiver. Two great players toiled in the trenches—tackle Jim Reilly and guard Larry DiNardo. The defensive line featured McCoy and two sophomores, Walt Patulski and Mike Kadish. Three veteran linebackers were on hand, and Clarence Ellis moved into the secondary. For it to work, the backs had to help out Theismann, Gatewood had to mature quickly, and the deep backs had to learn on the job.

For Theismann, the opening moments of the Northwestern game were a nightmare when the Wildcats jumped out to a 10-0 lead on a field goal and an interception. He brought the team back for two first-quarter scores, his own five-yard run and Ziegler's 18-yard rumble. Northwestern held Notre Dame scoreless for two quarters. Theismann fumbled and had another interception. Irish walk-on Brian Lewallen scored on a 44-yard punt return; Barz broke loose for two touchdowns, of eight and two yards, for the 35-10 Irish win. Theismann's passing was six of 12 for 88 yards, with Gatewood catching only one.

In mid-week, doctors told Zimmerman that he had a kidney ailment that needed treatment. And then came Mike Phipps and Purdue. Phipps was the first quarterback to go undefeated in three tries against the Fighting Irish; Purdue doubled the Irish score, 28-14. Phipps burned a blitz with a 37-yard touchdown pass in the first quarter and on a second-quarter drive, he made third-down conversions along the way to a three-yard touchdown by Stan Brown. Theismann led a 79-yard march, ended by a 10-yard pass to Ziegler for Notre Dame's first score. In the third quarter, Notre Dame forced two Purdue punts and then drove to the 26. A bad call, a motion penalty, blunted matters; Theismann was sacked; Phipps scored on a quarterback sneak and Brown scored a touchdown. Gatewood ended the scoring with a 20-yard touchdown catch. Phipps made 12 of 19 third-down plays; Theismann had an average day, 14 of 26 for 153 yards.

Notre Dame beat a declining Michigan State team, 42-28. Barz bobbled a touchdown catch from their 11. MSU scored after a Fighting Irish quick kick failed to get past a

The Northwestern quarterback encounters Mike Mc-Coy in the 1969 game won by Notre Dame 35-10.

linebacker's chest. Theismann brought the Irish back on an 85-yard drive in 17 plays, with Barz banging in from the one. MSU's Don Highsmith exploded for a 15-yard touchdown. Theismann directed a go-ahead drive with 2:09 left: from his 29, he went around right end for 13 yards, pitched to Barz for 16, and to Gatewood for 13. From the 29, with MSU in man-to-man formation, he saw Ziegler isolated on a linebacker and Gatewood crossing underneath— he hit Gatewood for the touchdown. Notre Dame controlled the game after that: Theismann on a seven-yard touchdown, a pass to Gatewood for a 23-yard tally, and Barz for a one-yard blast. Theismann completed 20-of-33 passes for 294 yards, and the backs rushed for 225 yards.

Army went down 45-0. Hempel started the Notre Dame scoring blitz with a 20-yard field goal. Gatewood ran in a 55-yard touchdown; Theismann scored on a four-yard run after an interception; and he threw a seven-yard touchdown pass to Gatewood for the 24-0 halftime score. Barz scored from the one; and then the bench scored—Andy Huff from the one and Jim Yoder from the 16. Army's runners gained 47 yards in 29 tries. Notre Dame's backs controlled the game with 365 yards on 80 runs.

The Fighting Irish controlled another great USC runner, Clarence Davis, to earn a 14-14 tie with the number-one Trojans. Davis gained only 75 yards on 30 carries. It was 0-0 at the half; Notre Dame had dodged

several scores thanks to Trojan penalties and fumbles. USC had held the Irish offense to 35 yards. In the third quarter, Theismann fired pinpoint passes to move Notre Dame 74 yards in 11 plays; Barz went in from the one. USC went 75 yards on 10 plays, with a 19-yard touchdown pass; they opened the fourth quarter with an interception, returning the ball to the Notre Dame 15, and scored on pass play. USC punted from their 33. When the ball was snapped, two Trojan linemen were assigned to 274-pound Mike McCoy. Upback Mike Berry was obliterated, and fullback Charlie Evans was removed. The ball was leaving the punter's foot; nine inches later, McCoy's face mask altered the ball's intended path. Patulski recovered at the seven. A minute later, Denny Allan scored from the one. On a later drive, Notre Dame got to the 16, but a questionable clipping call moved them back to the 31. Hempel tried a 48-yard field goal. He knew he had hit it dead center and he had—right into the middle of the crossbar; it bounced back. Ara's decision to move Ellis upfield to CB to cover USC's best receiver may have been the saving decision, allowing tight man-to-man coverage.

Tulane folded 37-0. Ziegler ended a two-drive drought with a touchdown from the two; then the Irish

Larry DiNardo, an all-time player for the Irish, three-year starter at LG, consensus All-American in 1969 and 1970.

Jim Reilly, two-year starter at LT, All-American in 1969.

a 29-yard Theismann touchdown pass to Gatewood concluded a 95-yard march, a 10-yard touchdown pass to Huff, an Allen slant for a three-yard touchdown, a three-yard touchdown pass to Gatewood after a botched fake punt by Pitt, an 18-yard touchdown run in the third quarter by Allan, and a 26-yard Etter touchdown dash accounted for the scoring.

Notre Dame pulverized Georgia Tech with 31 opening points. Theismann threw a 16-yard score to Gatewood, then ran 18 yards for another touchdown. Ellis intercepted a Tech pass and charged 70 yards to score. John Gasser did likewise, for a 57-yard runback, resulting in a Hempel field goal of 25 yards. Ralph Stepaniak intercepted a pass and ran it back 51 yards to set the stage for Huff's one-yard dive. Tech's Bill Ford intercepted a Theismann pass and ran 100 yards for a touchdown. Theismann scored an eight-yarder in the third quarter. Tech kept trying and scored two more touchdowns to make the final score a 38-20 Notre Dame victory.

For the first time in many years, the Irish "had to win" against a service academy opponent—Air Force—when school officials revealed that Notre Dame would

scored 17 points in the second quarter: a McCoy-caused fumble led to a Huff touchdown from the four; a 69-yard march and a Huff touchdown from the one; an Ellis interception set up Hempel's 33-yard field goal. Allan scored from the one in the second half to close it out. Sub quarterback Bill Etter led all runners with 81 yards on eight carries.

Navy gave up a record 720 yards to the Fighting Irish offense in a 47-0 losing effort; of that 597 yards came on 91 runs. Theismann was held to 123 yards passing on three completions. In the first quarter, Gatewood caught a 35-yard touchdown pass. In the second quarter, Notre Dame scored 26 points: Allan from the one, Theismann on a rollout for a 46-yard touchdown, Allan recovering a Theismann fumble for a touchdown, and Huff for a seven-yard touchdown. In the second half, Etter made a 79-yard touchdown run and a 15-yarder. He led all runners for the second week in a row with 140 yards on 11 carries.

Notre Dame then squashed Pitt 49-7. Theismann completed 9-of-11 passes for 126 yards and three touchdowns to complement 335 yards of rushing. Allan sprinted past left end for a four-yard touchdown,

A walk-on who made good—Mike Oriard, starting center for the 1969 squad, an All-American, and a Rhodes Scholar nominee.

go to a bowl if they won. Injuries were mounting, and perhaps a little tight over pending prospects, Notre Dame squeaked out a 13-6 win. Allan followed precision blocking for a 39-yard touchdown run. Hempel kicked field goals of 22 and 25 yards. After that, the Fighting Irish held on as Air Force added two field goals in the last quarter. The Falcons only managed 77 yards of total offense.

After a 45-year absence, Notre Dame returned to postseason bowl play—against the number one Texas Longhorns in the Cotton Bowl. The Fighting Irish opened with an 82-yard drive resulting in Hempel's 26-yard field goal after six minutes. Theismann in the second quarter called on Gatewood to delay at the line, then go deep after the secondary had committed themselves—a 54-yard touchdown. The Longhorns's Bertelsen tallied from the one. The third period was scoreless, but the Texas wishbone was working fairly well. In the fourth period, Texas drove again, Worster pounding hard, until Koy scored from the three. On the return drive, Theismann ran for 14 and 11 yards, threw for 11 yards to Allan, and for a 24-yard touchdown to Jim Yoder. Texas won it on a 75-yard march, making two crucial fourth-down plays, to score from the one. Their wishbone, good for 331 yards, taught Ara a lesson he would repay in a year. Theismann set a Cotton Bowl record with 279 yards of total offense.

This was a lineman's year for All-America honors: McCoy, Reilly, DiNardo, Olson, and Oriard reaped various awards.

1969 record: 8-2-1 (.772)
Record to date: 516-142-38 (.768)

Larry Schumacher, two-year starter at LB in 1968 and 1969.

1970-1979

1970

Ara had six starters return to the offense and five starters on defense. There were good replacements at all positions. Theismann would have a season some claim was the best ever by a Notre Dame player. Gatewood's first campaign was almost a carbon copy of Seymour's sophomore year. The offensive line was led by DiNardo and the defensive line had Patulski and Kadish. Linebackers were solid and the deep backs were at least adequate. Ellis moved up to the corner from safety. Overall, team speed was better, the defensive line would be a great one, and the offense would be as good as Theismann.

Northwestern lost 35-14. Allan scored from the six; Gatewood put it there with a 39-yard reception. Theismann ran a bootleg play for a nine-yard touchdown. Fighting Irish errors led to two Northwestern scores—a Barz fumble and a punt runback. Notre Dame struck

back—Allan scored from the three and Barz with a 17-yard flip from Theismann. In the third quarter, Allan scored his third touchdown on a one-yard burst.

Notre Dame unloaded on Purdue 48-0, the worst beating in the rivalry to that point. Even though Purdue fielded virtually the same defense as in 1969, Theismann orchestrated 633 total yards to 144 for Purdue. He completed 16 of 24 passes for 276 yards and three Gatewood touchdowns. The Fighting Irish defense grabbed three fumbles and three interceptions. The scores were: a Hempel field goal of nine yards, Allan on a four-yard touchdown burst, a screen pass touchdown to Gatewood after a fumble on their 15, a touchdown pass from the seven to Gatewood, a 20-yard touchdown pass to Gatewood in the third quarter, and a Hempel field goal. Subs Darryll Dewan slammed in from the four and Larry Parker sped 63 yards for a touchdown.

No Fighting Irish team had beaten Michigan State at Spartan Stadium since 1949. Theismann's troopers

The 1970 Fighting Irish.

The 1970 coaching staff.

changed that, 29-0, in the 700th football game for Notre Dame. Barz ended a 79-yard drive with a one-yard touchdown. Theismann ran around for 37 yards to set up a Bob Minnix score from the one. Gatewood caught a Theismann pass for 39 yards, and Gulyas went in from the two; Theismann made a two-point conversion. Parker capped it with a four-yard touchdown sweep with seconds left. Notre Dame's offense netted 513 yards.

Army surrendered 51-10; Notre Dame scored 30 points and gained 345 total yards in the first half. Theismann scored from the seven; he later fired a 40-yard touchdown strike to Minnix; Gulyas scored from the six to end the quarter. Patulski got a safety, and Gatewood went in from the 29 with a touchdown pass. In the third quarter, Theismann found tight end Mike Creaney open for a four-yard touchdown. Subs continued—Dewan cruised for 10 and Pat Steenberge tallied on a four-yard quarterback keeper. Cadet runners gained 16 yards for the day. DiNardo was injured and his play was curtailed for the rest of the season.

Missouri fumbled twice and gave away two passes. Hempel put Notre Dame up 3-0, but a bad punt led to a Missouri touchdown by Mel Gray from the 11; the Fighting Irish trailed for the first time all season. Barz caught an 18-yard pass in a third-and-nine situation and Gatewood regained the lead with a five-yard touchdown.

Missouri attempted an interception; Gulyas caught the pass for a 30-yard touchdown. He also scored on a one-yard plunge for the 24-7 Irish win.

Navy lost 56-7. Gulyas was hurt; Dewan took his place and ran well on the first drive, carrying six times for 30 yards and a touchdown from the five. Navy tied it, but Notre Dame's backs scored five more touchdowns with 408 yards of rushing; Gatewood scored twice. Barz scored from the two and then the one, Gatewood tallied on two passes from Theismann, Allan chipped in with a three-yard touchdown, sub John Cieszowski ran 30 yards for a touchdown, and Minnix ran in from the five.

Pitt played two ball games—one in which they led 14-13, the other in which they disintegrated, losing 46-14. In only the seventh game of the season, Theismann surpassed Hanratty's total yardage mark. Allan scored from the three, then Barz from the three in the second quarter. Pitt used an Irish fumble and an interference call to get its scores on short runs. They tried to intercept a Theismann pass, tipped it twice, but Allan caught it and ran 45 yards for the touchdown. Pitt fumbled two plays after the kickoff and Theismann struck quickly, freezing their safety with a fake before he hit Allan with a 54-yard touchdown pass. He hit Gulyas for a 35-yard touchdown and Mike Creaney for a 78-yard score, one of the longest on record for an Irish tight end. Cieszkowski

Ara and Joe Theismann ponder a point.

bulled in twice in the fourth quarter. Notre Dame gained 606 yards on the day.

Perhaps the Irish read too many clippings about their high ratings in the polls, beating Georgia Tech only 10-7. Tech held the Fighting Irish scoreless in the first half. Theismann could not get the team deep into Tech's territory until late in the third quarter, missing 11 third-down conversions. Tech also shut down Gatewood. Tech loaded their linebackers towards the tight end and brought a safety over on Gatewood. Ara countered with the plan of running two tight ends with Gatewood angling across the middle against the flow—somebody had to be open. Scott Smith hit a field goal in the third quarter for Notre Dame, then Tech burned Mike Crotty on a 66-yard touchdown pass. Theismann lost a possible touchdown when Tech intercepted at their goal. The Irish held and Tech was forced into its 11th punt. Starting from the Notre Dame 20, Theismann worked the crossing pattern for a 46-yard pass to Gulyas, and Allan ran into the Tech line five times to score the winning touchdown. Ellis stopped their final threat with an interception on his 27. Tech's running game managed only 36 yards all day.

The game with LSU was even tighter, with Notre Dame prevailing 3-0. Great defense by both teams was

the story of the game. Notre Dame's running was throttled to 78 yards. Only aggressive defense and multiple sacks kept the Fighting Irish in the game. Hempel finally made a 24-yard field goal with 2:54 left in the game for the winning score.

For the second time, USC ruined a perfect season for Ara when they beat Notre Dame 38-28. On a sodden field that had suffered many college and pro games in recent weeks, Theismann scored from the 25 in the first quarter. A Hempel field goal missed by inches a bit later. USC scored two quick touchdowns on short spurts by Clarence Davis. The field was now a quagmire. USC's Sam Dickerson scored, literally taking it away from Clarence Ellis. USC hit a field goal, and Cieszkowski intercepted a Theismann pass from the nine for a touchdown. In the third quarter, Dewan fumbled on his 19. USC scored, but it took one of their tacklers to recover it. Forty-two seconds later, Theismann lost the handle on the wet, slimy ball; USC scored. Theismann fired to Parker, who dashed 46 yards for a touchdown; he then used 17 plays to score again, on a quarterback sneak from the one. Conditions and bad luck conspired to produce three interceptions. When the splashing was over, Theismann had completed 33 passes in 58 tries for 526 yards. Poor running cost the game; Notre Dame gained a miserable 31 yards. It was the fourth time that USC had foiled Notre Dame in a bid for an undisputed national title.

There was still Texas to play in a rematch of the previous year's Cotton Bowl. The Longhorns were number one; no one had beaten them in 30 games. Parseghian came up with what he called a "mirror defense" against their wishbone. He had a linebacker shadow each Longhorn back and force them to make a decision to go upfield or run into the sidelines. Forcing the wishbone runners to make the decision nullified the wishbone's predication of making the defense commit itself. If they changed to quick-hitting plays, then it wasn't the wishbone anymore and would be handled accordingly.

Ara's plan worked flawlessly. The Longhorns, who ran 333 yards in the 1970 Cotton Bowl, were held to 216. The wishbone is a high-risk offense; Texas mishandled the ball nine times. All of the scoring happened in the first half. Texas kicked a 23-yard field goal after Happy Feller gained 63 yards on an option play. Three minutes later Notre Dame drove 80 yards in 10 plays, capped by a 26-yard Theismann pass to Gatewood. Texas fumbled the next kickoff and Tom Eaton recovered on their 13. Six plays later, Theismann scored on a keeper. In the second quarter, a 53-yard drive resulted in a 15-yard touchdown run by Theismann. Hempel wrapped up the scoring with a 36-yard field goal. In the second half Texas was unable to handle the mirror defense. The Fighting Irish won 24-11. The win put Notre Dame second (AP) and fifth (UPI) in the national rankings.

Theismann accounted for 2,801 yards of the total 5,105 yards gained for the year, easily one of the best individual performances in Fighting Irish history—and not done at the expense of the team. DiNardo, Ellis, Theismann, and Gatewood made All-America teams.

1970 record: 10-1-0 1(.909)
Record to date: 526-143-38 (.770)

1971

This is the year that might have been. A number of quality players returned, especially on the two lines. The big loss was Theismann. Ara would have to emphasize defense and hope someone would emerge as the offensive leader. The fact that his teams never lost more than two games in a season is a testament to his coaching and motivational skills. He would need it all in 1971. Bill Etter was slated to start and did until an injury in the fourth game ended his career. He was a gifted runner, with the best speed at quarterback since Frank Dancewicz. In 1969 he had led the team in rushing average with 10.7 yards gained per run, but he had missed all of 1970 with an injury. When he went down, Cliff Brown stepped in, another good runner who lacked great passing skills. There were good, not great, backs, so the weak passing game would eventually allow defenses to stack against the run. Gulyas and Minnix ran as halfbacks and Andy Huff returned from a year's absence to start at fullback. This was a faster backfield than the 1970 unit but lacked the extra dimension Theismann had contributed. The offensive line was solid; Gatewood and Creaney had real potential, but they needed someone to throw to them. The defensive line was awesome, with Patulski and Kadish at 260 each, Greg Marx, almost their equal in skill, and Fred Swendsen. The linebackers were solid, led by Eric Patton and Jim Musuraca. All starting deep backs returned. It was the most experienced defense Ara had fielded.

Cliff Brown, starting QB for most of the 1971 season.

Northwestern managed only a touchdown while Notre Dame posted 50 points. The Fighting Irish defense scored two touchdowns; Northwestern surrendered two fumbles, seven interceptions, and a blocked punt. Gulyas scored from the three after Patulski blocked a punt; Minnix tallied from the four in the second quarter; Steenberge passed to Gatewood for an eight-yard touchdown; Bob Thomas kicked a 36-yard field goal; Cieszkowski slammed in from the four for a 30-7 halftime score. Stepaniak and Crotty scored with interceptions from 40 and 65 yards, and Greg Hill ran in from the four. It was Ara's highest-scoring opener.

The pace shifted radically against Purdue under copious amounts of rain and mud. The Fighting Irish won 8-7 in a comeback. Otis Armstrong scored for Purdue on a 26-yard screen pass from Gary Danielson. The intense rain slowed everyone down, until a low punt snap in Purdue's end zone sent their punter running; just as he tried a desperate kick, he was hit and Swendsen scored a touchdown. Steenberge passed to Creaney for the two-point conversion. The defense won the game.

The defense put in a stellar performance in a 14-2 win over Michigan State. The offense scored early and then disappeared, but the defense rocked the Spartans all day. Minnix scored from the one to end an eight-minute, 80-yard drive. He tallied again, from the five, after Musuraca recovered a fumble at the MSU 17. MSU

Larry Parker cuts upfield in the 1971 Irish win over Tulane.

scored two points when Etter wisely fell on Parker's fumble in his end zone. The second half was composed of lost opportunities. MSU held them to 92 yards passing. Spartan runners gained only 32 yards on the ground.

Miami lost 17-0, but Notre Dame lost Etter in the second quarter (a knee injured in the MSU game finally gave out). Cliff Brown came in and moved the team; Thomas kicked a 38-yard field goal. In the third quarter, Brown moved the team 66 yards, with Huff scoring on a 16-yard run. Brown ran 33 yards, and Dewan scored on a six-yard touchdown run. Notre Dame passed for 35 yards, but the defense allowed only 60 yards rushing and 51 yards passing.

Bob Thomas put up three field goals as the first scores in the game against North Carolina. Ellis saved the shutout when he dodged six blockers on a kickoff to tackle the runner; he got an interception on the next play. Kadish deflected a field goal try in the third quarter. Gatewood scored on a four-yard pass from Brown in the last quarter. Notre Dame still had not hit the century mark in passing. Final score: 16-0.

McKay and USC took it to the defense, winning 28-14. An interception led to a 31-yard touchdown pass. Gary Diminick returned the kickoff 66 yards and Huff piled in from the one to tie. USC scored almost immediately: a long kickoff return and a 24-yard touchdown pass. Sam Cunningham scored in the second quarter from the one. Brown tried to pass the

Fighting Irish into contention but USC intercepted him and returned it 53 yards for their last touchdown and a 28-7 halftime lead. Cieszkowski got the only second half score, a four-yarder.

The Fighting Irish won a boring game against Navy, 21-0. Gulyas scored from the one to end a 78-yard first-quarter drive; Minnix scored twice in the second quarter, from the one and the 10. Navy couldn't move, and the Fighting Irish muddled along in the second half.

The offense finally jelled against Pitt, 56-7. The running game exploded for 464 yards and seven touchdowns. Gulyas scored three times from the one-yard line. Gatewood went in for an eight-yard touchdown, and Larry Parker scored from the nine and the six. Willie Townsend tallied from the 12 and Dewan crunched in from the five. Pitt had only 113 yards of total offense. Patulski hurt a knee and was taken away on a stretcher.

Notre Dame won 21-7 over a mediocre Tulane team. The Green Wave scored first and led through halftime. Brown finally scored from the one to tie. Creaney tallied with an eight-yard pass after Gatewood caught an 18-yard pass. Brown scored from the five in the fourth quarter to end a 20-play, 75-yard, 9:13-minute drive. The passing yardage went up to 154 yards for the day.

LSU ended the season on a sour note with a 28-8 win, the worst defeat for Ara to that point. Future NFL

Mike Creaney, three-year starter at TE.

Walt Patulski, All-America defensive end in the early 1970s when Ara had a dominating defensive line.

star Bert Jones threw touchdowns of 36 and 32 yards, and scored from the five himself. They attacked the defense, ran for 143 of their 299 yards, and set up the passing game well. Notre Dame did not respond except with yardage—323 total yards.

For the season, total yardage fell off 34 percent, from 5,105 yards to 3,329. The passing game dropped a precipitous 60 percent, which led to a 35 percent decline in touchdown production. The team fell out of the top-10 ranking, a first in Ara's era. Patulski, Ellis, Kadish, and Gatewood made All-America teams.

**1971 record: 8-2-0 (.800)
Record to date: 534-145-38 (.771)**

1972

The Fighting Irish were in a holding pattern in 1972—consolidating, gaining experience, and assessing personnel. Interior linemen were needed, three on each side of the ball—and a quarterback. When the shuffling was done, the offensive line was solid; Willie Townsend was an adequate replacement for Gatewood. Tom Clements, a talented sophomore with quick feet, a fair arm, and an excellent football mind, won the quarterback job. The starting backs were Darryll Dewan, Gary Diminick, and Andy Huff.

This was the first year of freshman eligibility; Steve Niehaus of Moeller High in Cincinnati would immediately help the defensive line (although he was out after the fourth game). Greg Marx returned and reserves moved up. Ara stuck with the 4-4-3, and the linebackers were a good group, especially Musuraca and Drew Mahalic on the outside. The linebackers were quicker, as were the deep backs. There were some fine reserves—especially Eric Penick, Art Best, Wayne Bullock, Mike Fanning, Jim Stock, and Greg Collins.

Northwestern looked tougher than usual, having lost to Michigan only 7-0. The Fighting Irish left

Greg Marx, three-year starter on the defensive line in the early 1970s.

The 1972 coaching staff.

Evanston with a 37-0 win. Dewan scored from 30 yards out, and Cieszkowski slammed in from the two. In the second quarter, Thomas hit field goals of 23 and 26 yards. Jim O'Malley intercepted a Wildcat pass, Townsend ran a reverse for 30 yards, and Huff piled in from the one. Thomas made it 30-0 in the first half with a 47-yard field goal. The reserves played the rest of the way; Penick gained 87 yards on the day and scored the final touchdown.

A star-studded Purdue team, led by Darryl Stingley and Dave Butz, had lost twice already. The Fighting Irish held them off 35-14, gaining 636 yards of total offense. Penick ran 133 yards on 12 carries. Clements completed 17 of 24 passes for 287 yards. At the end of the first half, the Irish had 403 yards to Purdue's 39. Creaney scored on a 39-yard pass from Clements and set up another touchdown with a 30-yard catch before Penick dashed in from the 14. Clements threw a 62-yard touchdown pass to Willie Townsend at the beginning of the second quarter. In the third quarter, Diminick ran 42 yards, and Cieszkowski blasted in from the one. Huff scored from the one after an 84-yard clock-killing drive. Later Purdue scored two touchdowns.

Michigan State was running a primitive wishbone. Their defense, led by Brad Van Pelt, held Notre Dame to two field goals until the last five minutes. The Fighting Irish defense held off MSU eight and picked off enough passes to halt MSU drives. Thomas kicked his third field goal in the fourth quarter and Huff scored from the one after a Ken Schlezes interception for Notre Dame's 16-0 victory.

Notre Dame nailed a seventh straight win over Pitt, 42-16. Huff scored in the first half with bursts from the one and the four; Pitt closed in with a third-quarter touchdown and two-point conversion. They were threatening again, but Mahalic intercepted a pass and ran 56 yards for a touchdown. Later, Penick scored and Art Best scored on a 56-yard run, his first carry for Notre Dame.

Missouri upset things with a 30-26 win over the Fighting Irish, even though Nebraska had routed them 62-0 a week earlier. They ran 77 plays to Notre Dame's 63. They scored first after an interception of a Clements pass. Clements directed a 66-yard drive with Huff scoring from the one. Missouri pounded back, especially up the middle (Niehaus was hurt), and scored again. Cieszkowski tied it from the one after an 81 yard return drive. The next Mizzou touchdown was right out of the Charles White method—with the runner over the goal line but the ball suspended in the air about five feet above and behind him. Notre Dame fumbled a punt and a kickoff to let the Tigers score two field goals, then they hit another one. Clements and Huff scored touchdowns for the final result.

Andy Huff, starter at FB in 1971 and 1972.

Ara's teams never lost back-to-back games in the regular season. Texas Christian University lost 21-0. During the week they had denigrated the Fighting Irish defense. So, while Notre Dame amassed 522 yards of offense, TCU managed only 70 on the ground and 62 on passes. Jim Roolf scored first, on an 11-yard pass from Clements, following a Schlezes interception. Irish turnovers stopped further scoring until the third quarter when Best broke loose for a 57-yard touchdown. In the fourth period, Roolf ran an end around for 36 yards, and Penick jetted 11 yards for the last touchdown. On the day, Penick made 158 yards on 16 carries.

Although Navy had its best team in a decade, Notre Dame won easily, 42-23. Diminick ran 84 yards for a touchdown on the opening kickoff. After that, Notre Dame gained 597 more yards of offense. Clements moved the team 85 yards on the next drive and scored from the 18 with a keeper. His four-yard touchdown in the next quarter made it 21-0. Schlezes ran a punt back 46 yards, and Penick made a 27-yard touchdown. Diminick capped a drive with a seven-yard touchdown run for a 35-0 halftime score. The Middies scored twice, and Al Samuels scored from the four with the reserves to end it.

The Fighting Irish grounded Air Force, 21-7. The referees could have been the deciding factor in a closer game when they blew a "play" dead— a Clements fake to Penick into the line—when the real play was a 35-yard pass to Townsend. The Falcons boasted a superior passing game so Ara switched to a 4-3 and held them to eight completions in 25 tries, while intercepting four passes. In the second quarter Diminick scored from the seven and Townsend caught a 13-yard Clements touchdown pass. Air Force scored on a 51-yard run and played a good game until they fumbled late in the fourth quarter, allowing Huff's touchdown run of 13 yards.

An Orange Bowl bid depended on a win over Miami, which Notre Dame earned 20-17. It was almost negated when someone threw a snowball during an Irish field goal try that ruined the kick. Miami scored a field goal, but Clements masterminded a 90-yard return march and finished it with a 10-yard touchdown to Townsend. Miami fumbled the kickoff and Huff scored from the one moments later. Clements scored the last Fighting Irish touchdown on a one-yard sneak in the third quarter, but Miami tallied twice more and then barely missed a field goal try.

This young Fighting Irish team met USC in Los Angeles. Anthony Davis racked up six touchdowns, something never done before to the Irish. Ara used his speediest kickoff coverage people, but they overran Davis, who took it all the way. Notre Dame came back for a Thomas field goal. Davis scored again from the one after an interference call. Penick fumbled on the nine and Davis scored after two tries. Clements threw a five-yard touchdown pass to Townsend. In the third quarter, a USC interception led to another Davis touchdown, so Clements clinched a touchdown with an 11-yard swing pass to Diminick. Mike Townsend intercepted his 10th pass of the season, a record, to lead to a Clements touchdown pass to Creaney, who made a career-best catch, for a 25-23 score, USC up. Davis then ran another kick back 96 yards for a touchdown. Deflated, the Irish watched two more USC scores, another by Davis and one by Cunningham. Final score: USC won, 45-23.

After that, Notre Dame had to face Heisman winner Johnny Rodgers and the supporting cast from Nebraska in the Orange Bowl. It was Ara's worst defeat, 40-6. Rodgers scored four touchdowns and threw for another. Pete Demmerle scored Notre Dame's only touchdown on a five-yard pass from Clements. The Huskers gained 560 yards of total offense to Notre Dame's 207.

As a young team, it had won some games it should have lost, lost when it could have been in the game, and was beaten by its betters. Greg Marx and John Dampeer were the All-America selections.

1972 record: 8-3-0 (.727)
Record to date: 542-148-38 (.770)

1973

The offensive line Ara fielded produced one of the most devastating rushing attacks in Notre Dame history. The line was led by tight end Dave Casper, moved from tackle, Frank Pomarico, and Gerry DiNardo. Clements returned at quarterback, and halfbacks Art Best and Eric Penick were both capable of scoring from any spot on the field. Wayne "The Train" Bullock was fullback. It was probably the best backfield Ara coached at Notre Dame, with the possible exception of 1966. Hanratty was a better passer, but Clements was the better ball handler. The 1966 offensive line was more

Al Hunter, first Irish player to rush for 1,000 yards.

dominating, and Eddy had an ability to exploit seams that other backs never saw; the 1973 backfield was faster. The 1973 defensive line was awesome, starting with Ross Browner, perhaps the best player in cleats, even as

Four members of a great defensive line in 1973: Willie Fry, Mike Fanning, Steve Niehaus, Ross Browner.

Art Best turns the corner against Air Force in the 48-15 blowout near the end of the 1973 championship year.

a freshman. Then came Niehaus, Mike Fanning, and Mike Stock, whose specialty was sheer speed on his pass rush. The linebackers were solid; Collins and Mahalic as outside linebackers had excellent range. The secondary had excellent speed and a fine talent in freshman Luther Bradley. This was a dominating team in almost all areas.

Although Northwestern had already beaten Michigan State, Notre Dame shut them out, 44-0. Browner blocked a punt for a safety. Penick scored on a 16-yard run, and Demmerle caught a nine-yard touchdown pass from Clements. Ron Goodman slashed in for a nine-yard score in the second quarter; three minutes later, Clements sneaked in from the one. He passed for another touchdown to make the halftime score 37-0. Northwestern had minus eight yards rushing. The last touchdown was Diminick's, a 21-yard sprint.

Purdue played a good game but lost 20-7. Best set up a Thomas field goal with a 64-yard run; Purdue scored on a 64-yard pass play to Larry Burton. Best scored from the nine to regain the lead through halftime. In the third quarter, Bullock slammed in from the one and the reserves moved well enough for Thomas to hit a 42-yard field goal. Purdue's running was held to 33 yards all day.

Michigan State was in a slow recovery from mediocrity and played well enough to blunt early Fighting Irish drives. Twice in the first quarter long

field goal tries failed. Finally, Notre Dame put together an 80-yard drive, all on runs, with Bullock muscling in from the one. Later in the second quarter, Clements struck quickly with a four-play, 63-yard drive, started with a 30-yard screen pass to Casper and ended by a 10-yard touchdown pass to Demmerle. In the third period, a fumble led to an MSU field goal; then an interception was run back for a Spartan touchdown. A sequence of

Tom Clements on the loose against USC in 1973.

fumbles killed time MSU needed, and Rudnick saved the 14-10 Irish win with an interception on the last play.

The Fighting Irish were underwhelmed to play Rice, and played poorly in the early going. A Rice fumble picked up by Stock led to a Bullock touchdown blast. Penalties marred the second quarter, but Clements threw a 21-yard touchdown pass to Casper. Good running by Best and Diminick in the third quarter led to Bullock's smash from the one. The defense held Rice to minus 14 yards for the second half. Cliff Brown ended the scoring with a 38-yard touchdown run for the final 28-0 score.

Army was defeated 62-3. Notre Dame was scoreless in the first quarter, but Penick scored early in the second quarter. After that, the Fighting Irish rolled: Casper on a 34-yard touchdown pass; Best on a five-yard scoring run; Casper for a three-yard touchdown pass from Brown; Penick scored from the six; and Brown to Al Hunter for a touchdown after an interception. Reserves scored the rest; the best play was Tim Simon's 73-yard punt return for a touchdown.

USC was next, only a tie with Oklahoma blemishing their record. Rudnick deflected a punt and Thomas turned it into a 42-yard field goal. Rather than risk a Davis touchdown return, the Fighting Irish squibbed the kick. The Trojans scored anyway, Davis going in from the two. Another bad USC punt led to a Thomas field goal of 43 yards. For the third time, USC had a bad punt and the Fighting Irish finally moved in for a touchdown, helped by two Demmerle catches and ended by Clements over left guard. Reserve quarterback Frank Allocco had been watching the Trojan coaches as they signalled plays; he thought he had figured out their blitz call. In the third quarter, Notre Dame had the ball on its 15. The Trojans blitzed and Clements pitched out to Penick in motion to his left, who turned upfield behind blocking by DiNardo and Pomarico, and ran for an 85-yard touchdown. This single play was one of the most electrifying moments in recent Notre Dame football history. USC returned a drive, with Lynn Swann scoring from the 27. Clements fumbled but it was recovered by Russ Kornman; Thomas kicked a 32-yard field goal. Luther Bradley stopped a late drive with an interception. Great rushing defense won the game; USC made only 66 yards all day, while the Irish ran for 316 yards in their 23-14 victory.

Father Joyce, Ara Parseghian, and Moose Krause with the MacArthur Bowl in honor of the 1973 championship.

Mike Townsend, consensus All-American at FS in 1973.

Navy was next and they played well for most of the first quarter until a good punt return led to Penick scoring from the 11. Al Hunter scored in the second quarter from the three after plays by Demmerle, Clements, and Hunter set it up. In the third period, a Greg Collins interception reached the Navy 19. Demmerle made a circus catch at the one, and Clements tallied. After Potempa recovered a fumble, Al Samuel scored from the seven. Mahalic intercepted a Navy pass on the Notre Dame 34. Subs scored two more touchdowns: a nine-yard touchdown from Brown to Townsend and a Parise run. Stock earned a safety to wrap up the scoring and 44-7 win. Twelve Irish runners rushed for 447 yards.

Pitt's Tony Dorsett in eight games had run for 1,139 yards. He would make a career of running well against the Fighting Irish, starting with 209 yards in 29 runs in a losing effort, 31-10. The Panthers fumbled three times early, and the third led to Bullock hammering three times from the 24 to score. Before the half ended, a deliberate drive ended in a Thomas field goal; Pitt kicked one as well. In the third quarter, Notre Dame's defense started to create situations rather than wait for Pitt errors. Collins intercepted a Pitt pass and returned it to the Notre Dame 42. Bullock took over again, gaining 32 of 58 yards plus the score from the nine. A long Diminick kick return set up Bullock's third touchdown to end it.

Penick led a touchdown parade as Notre Dame swamped Air Force 48-15. He scored on runs from the four and the six as Notre Dame set off a 21-0 first-quarter avalanche. Air Force was unable to move—they even tried a 62-yard field goal in exasperation.

Notre Dame jumped out to a 24-0 lead over Miami. They scored on a Demmerle touchdown run from the 21 and a 24-yard field goal by Thomas in the first half. Demmerle scored two touchdowns to start the second half, with catches from the 15 and the seven. Cliff Brown led a touchdown drive with the reserves. The Fighting Irish dominated both sides of the ball. Ten Notre Dame runners amassed 477 yards. The 44-0 win gave Notre Dame its first perfect season since the Leahy era.

The Sugar Bowl against Alabama pitted two offensive machines against each other (Notre Dame was ranked third, and Alabama was ranked first), as well as a wishbone team against a great Fighting Irish defense. In the first quarter, the defense held the wishbone to 0 yards in 12 plays. Clements used Demmerle on receptions of 19, 26, and 14 yards to lead to Bullock's six-yard touchdown; the point after was missed. Alabama went ahead 7-6 with a six-yard touchdown run to end a 52-yard march. They kicked off and Al Hunter flashed his 9.3 speed on a 93-yard touchdown return. Clements fired a two-point conversion to Demmerle for a 14-7 lead. Alabama kicked a field goal; the halftime score was 14-10. Alabama took the lead on a 93-yard touchdown drive in the third quarter. Both teams missed field goals. Mahalic grabbed a mid-air Crimson Tide fumble at their 12. Penick scored on a counter play behind a Casper block. Alabama scored when quarterback Richard Todd drifted away from a play to get lost behind the flow and then threw a touchdown pass. They missed the point after but led 23-21. The Irish worked a patient drive; Thomas kicked a field goal for a 24-23 lead. Fans watched breathlessly as a third-and-eight developed deep in Notre Dame's territory; Clements threw from his end zone to tight end Robin Weber and cinched the 24-23 win and the national championship.

This undefeated season was a total team effort—great offense and great defense. Only two players made All-American, Casper and Mike Townsend.

1973 record: 11-0-0 (1.000)
Record to date: 553-148-38 (.774)

1974

It's always difficult to defend a national crown. Casper, Pomarico, Mike Townsend, and Rudnick had to be replaced due to graduation. Four more, however, were lost for the year due to a controversial dorm violation (females were present in their rooms beyond curfew): Browner, Bradley, Hunter, and Fry. Penick, Quehl, and Simon suffered injuries. Still, Notre Dame had plenty of good players returning. Clements and Demmerle, Best at left halfback, Al Samuels at right halfback, and Bullock at fullback all returned. But Best would break his jaw and not fully recover. Others would have to fill in and develop quickly.

The defensive line was awesome again, featuring Niehaus, Fanning, and Stock. Mahalic and Collins returned and Tom Eastman started in the middle. Reggie Barnett led a largely untried secondary. The offensive backfield was weakened, and there were enough losses in personnel to cause some worry about depth.

Georgia Tech scored first to open the season, but Notre Dame then scored 31 unanswered points. Bullock tied it with a 14-yard touchdown run after a Tech fumble. The Fighting Irish took the lead in the second quarter on a 22-yard Dave Reeve field goal and a seven-yard touchdown pass from Clements to Demmerle. In the second half, Bullock scored from the one and Samuels slashed in from the eight on a sweep. The national telecast caught a great play when Steve Sylvester blindsided a pursuing Tech lineman as he chased Clements on a broken play.

Notre Dame dropped four fumbles in the first half and Northwestern held the Irish to a 14-3 halftime lead. The first Fighting Irish score followed a pass to Demmerle that reached the Northwestern two; Kornman scored. Bullock scored for the second touchdown after a Northwestern roughing penalty boosted a drive. Ron Goodman ran 62 yards to score on the fourth play of the new half. Clements followed a fumble recovery with a drive and a 14-yard touchdown pass to Weber. Frank Allocco scored a keeper after another fumble. Reserves Mark McLane punched over an 11-yard touchdown and Terry Eurick a two-yarder. Future All-America tight end Ken MacAfee (6'5" and 245 pounds) made his freshman appearance. Notre Dame won 49-3.

Purdue stopped the winning streak at 13 with a 31-20 victory. The Fighting Irish self-destructed with early fumbles and interceptions. Purdue enjoyed a 21-0 lead after only 11 plays. Their scores came on a one-yard

Jim Stock, starter at DE in 1973, then as a LB in 1974 and 1975, cat-quick specialist in pass rushing.

quarterback keeper around end, a 52-yard scoring sprint, and a 21-yard interception return. Notre Dame shanked a punt and Purdue nailed a 47-yard field goal. Bullock scored early in the second quarter. At the half, the score was 24-7, and Notre Dame had 208 yards to Purdue's 168. Bullock scored on a short run in the third quarter after a busted punt play. Two scoring opportunities were wasted with loss of possession on downs and an ineligible receiver penalty. Purdue intercepted a pass and made a six-yard follow-up touchdown. Clements hit Demmerle late with a touchdown pass, too late to change the final outcome. The Fighting Irish beat themselves with offensive mistakes, although they outgained Purdue 407 yards to 270.

The Fighting Irish came back against Michigan State, winning 19-14. In the first quarter, Kevin Nosbusch recovered a fumble caused by Stock and Fanning. Clements almost got a touchdown out of a pass play to Weber; Bullock plowed in for the score. The Spartans fumbled at their 10 and Bullock scored on the next play. Reeve made a field goal from 38 yards after a bad Spartan punt. He added a 32-yarder in the last period. The Spartans drove 99 yards for their first

Wayne Bullock, 1974 fullback.

touchdown, scored again, but Randy Payne intercepted a pass to kill their last good chance. Bullock ran the ball against MSU 36 times, a new record.

Rice, normally a patsy, went down by the surprising score of 10-3. Notre Dame spotted Rice an early field goal and spent the rest of the game searching for their missing offense. In the second quarter, the Fighting Irish were flagged for illegal procedure; a referee claimed that the linemen's posteriors were not on the same horizontal plane, within an inch's variance. Ara protested with all he had, only to add to the penalty. After five futile drives, Reeve kicked a 45-yard field goal. Rice was kept in check for the rest of the game. In the fourth quarter, Notre Dame used 20 plays to execute an 80-yard drive. Bullock scored from the two around left end.

Army was again mismatched, 48-0. Bullock scored from the six to lead Fighting Irish backs to 525 yards rushing and 30 first downs, a new record. Bullock scored the second touchdown as well. Clements ran a seven-yard keeper before halftime for a touchdown and a 20-0 score. In the third period, Russ Kornman scored twice, from the seven and the four, and Al Samuels went 35 yards on a pitchout to score. Tom Bake scored the same way in the fourth quarter, from the six.

Miami was 4-1 and had stars Rubin Carter, Dennis Harrah, and Mike Archer. The Fighting Irish won 38-7. Demmerle caught a 53-yard touchdown in

the first two minutes of the game. Miami later fumbled on a 69-yard punt, at their nine; Bullock rammed in to score on the next play. Reeve made an 18-yard field goal after MacAfee set him up with a 24-yard pass play. Randy Harrison intercepted a pass and ran it back 44 yards for a touchdown. Clements scored on a keeper from the Miami eight, and MacAfee made a four-yard touchdown catch. Clements was 13 of 19 for 154 yards and two touchdowns.

The 14-6 win over Navy was a turning point in Notre Dame football history; on the flight back from Philadelphia, a weary Ara Parseghian decided he would leave football. He had important family considerations and constant pressure; the fun was gone. The Fighting Irish probably played down to the Middies. Goodman fumbled a punt early in the game and Navy kicked a field goal. They added another in the second half for a 6-0 lead. The only decent Fighting Irish drive to that point ended in a missed field goal. The defense turned it up, forced a punt, and Goodman took it back to their 28. Surviving a bad snap at the five, Clements found Demmerle for a touchdown. Randy Harrison made an interception and returned it 40 yards for a touchdown. It was an ugly win and Clements had his worst day, five of 22 with two interceptions.

Pete Demmerle nears the end zone with a Clements pass in the 38-7 rout of Miami in 1974.

Robin Weber, best known as the TE who caught the game-saving pass from Clements in the great 24-23 win over Alabama in the 1974 Orange Bowl.

They would have to play much better against Pitt and Dorsett if they expected to win. Notre Dame looked proficient on the first possession and Bullock scored from the seven. But then they had to wait until the fourth quarter. In the interim, Pitt kicked a field goal and scored from the one. Notre Dame had stopped a Pitt scoring attempt after a blocked Irish punt—this proved to be the game-saver. With eight minutes left, and 55 yards away from the goal, Clements used Bullock for 32 yards on line smashes, and hit Demmerle with a three-yard touchdown pass for the win. Bullock's 25 runs gave him 193 for the year to break Worden's old record. The Irish won 14-10.

Notre Dame handed Air Force its ninth straight loss of the year, 38-0. Kornman, in for an injured Bullock, scored from the one, but Parise got it there with a 62-yard jaunt. Parise scored in the second quarter from the 11, and Clements scored from the nine. Allocco scored on a keeper from the one for the 28-0 halftime score. In the second half, Reeve booted a 33-yard field goal and Allocco hit Kevin Doherty with a 25-yard touchdown pass.

USC was the final game. The Fighting Irish blew a two-touchdown lead as USC scored 55 points in a strange game. Mahalic intercepted a Haden pass, and Bullock scored from the two to end the short drive. Clements threw to Demmerle for a touchdown from the USC 29. Reeve hit a field goal, and McLane scored from the nine with a draw play. Anthony Davis scored from the eight with a swing pass but they missed the point after. They then hammered Notre Dame for 49 unanswered points in the second half. Davis ran the kickoff back 102 yards for a touchdown, scored from the six, and then the four. J.K. McKay caught an 18-yard touchdown pass, and a 44-yarder. The Fighting Irish fumbled, and Diggs caught a 16-yard touchdown pass. A long Clements pass was returned 58 yards for the final touchdown. USC won 55-24.

After that shock, and knowing it was Ara's last game, the Fighting Irish ruined Alabama's national title hopes with a 13-11 Orange Bowl win. A Crimson Tide fumble at their 16 ended in a Bullock score from the four. Notre Dame rolled on a long drive, mostly running, and McLane scored from the nine in the second quarter. The point after was missed. An Irish fumble earned Alabama a field goal. The third quarter was scoreless. The Crimson Tide scored on a 48-yard pass play in the fourth quarter and made a two-point conversion. The wishbone had foundered on the Notre Dame defense, so they had to pass. It was their undoing. Barnett intercepted a pass and zigzagged all over the Orange Bowl for the win. The wishbone gained 62 yards all evening. The Fighting Irish players carried Ara off the field and into history.

He had done a great coaching job under tremendous personal and team adversity. He had also set a new standard of excellence for both Notre Dame and college football. All Fighting Irish fans must be thankful that Ara Parseghian led their fortunes for 11 seasons. He was 95-17-4 (.836), just behind Leahy's .855. The All-Americans were Demmerle, Fanning, DiNardo, Clements, Collins, and Niehaus.

1974 record: 10-2-0 (.750)
Record to date: 563-150-38 (.774)

1975

The university had wanted Dan Devine in 1964, and 10 years later they still did. Devine, like every Fighting Irish coach since 1913, was a son of the midwest. He was born in Wisconsin and grew up near Duluth, Minnesota. He played college football at Minnesota-Duluth, coached an unbeaten high school team in Michigan, and was an assistant coach at Michigan State. His first head coaching position was at Arizona State in 1955, where he gave the school its first undefeated season and bowl bid while compiling a 27-3-1 record. In 13 seasons at Missouri, he won 93 games, second best in the school's history. He had done fairly well at Green Bay, but the situation had deteriorated. Whereas Parseghian had struck more than a few Irish players as a "Napoleonic figure," no one could make that claim of Devine. He was low key, although intense competitive fires burned within. This seeming lack of intensity may be why Devine was not going to be fully accepted into or by the Notre Dame family, as had Ara.

He had a well-earned reputation as a top-notch recruiter. He needed it to rebuild the offensive line, since six starters had graduated. Reserves would move up, including Steve Quehl who had survived a nearly fatal work accident. Ernie Hughes moved in as a sophomore at right guard. MacAfee became a fixture at tight end. Most of the interior men were technicians; only Hughes was a dominating player. Rick Slager started in the backfield, beating out a kid named Joe Montana. Hunter, who had returned from the suspension, was a breakaway threat at all times. Mark McLane was at right halfback (Best had transferred to Kent State). Jerome Heavens would get most of the starting time at fullback. There was great speed in this group, but it would need to jell. The defense had outstanding players in Ross Browner and Niehaus, with Jeff Weston and Willie Fry not far behind. Fry and Browner might have been the best pair of defensive ends in Notre Dame history. Jim Stock moved to outside linebacker, paired with Doug Becker, flanking a burly freshman, Bob Golic. The secondary had plenty of speed, especially with Bradley and Mike Banks.

The first game under Devine was against Boston College. Fighting Irish authorities had been reluctant to schedule other Catholic schools in recent years, to prevent a parochial, inbred reputation. Both teams were tight and made little headway in the first quarter. Notre Dame stopped a Boston College threat at their 23 in the second quarter and McLane ran 41 yards to Boston College's nine, where the drive stalled. Reeve kicked a 30-yard field goal for an early lead. Boston's Fred Steinfort answered with a 45-yarder; the 3-3 tie held through the half. The second half began as a repeat of the first with fumbles and penalties. Notre Dame took advantage first and moved 40 yards for Jim Browner's 10-yard touchdown run. In the fourth quarter, Randy Harrison grabbed a Boston College pass to set up Hunter's 24-yard dash for the last Irish score. With that, Devine had a 17-3 win over a tougher-than-expected team.

The Fighting Irish blanked Purdue 17-0. Reeve scored with a 29-yard field goal. Old-fashioned, tough football dominated play throughout. Notre Dame missed a field goal in the third quarter, and Purdue sped 66 yards in five plays, reaching Notre Dame's four. The huge Irish line stopped them; Purdue tried a pass back to the quarterback, as Alabama had in the 1973 Sugar Bowl. The pass went for a touchdown once again, but it was Luther Bradley's on a 99-yard interception return, the longest on the books for Notre Dame. A few minutes later, Al Hunter ran in from the one to end the scoring.

Devine had won two games in five days due to the voracious demands of television. They faced an undefeated Northwestern team, who fell readily, 31-7. Northwestern scored first, and Notre Dame unloaded: with Slager hurt, Montana led a 46-yard drive with Hunter scoring from the four; Jim Browner scored

Rick Slager, Irish QB in 1975 and 1976.

from the 10 after Fry blocked a punt; Montana fired his first Fighting Irish touchdown pass to McLane from the Wildcat 14. In the second half, Reeve nailed a three-pointer and Montana rolled right for a six-yard touchdown.

Michigan State broke the winning string with a 10-3 win. The Fighting Irish offense was tamed most of the day and a defensive lapse let the MSU fullback loose for 76 yards, which led to their only touchdown. Montana had a pass intercepted in the MSU end zone. Several fumbles also killed drives. The only Irish score came on a 35-yard field goal. Devine lost five players for part or all of the season during the game.

The game against North Carolina began the legend of Montana as "The Comeback Kid" when he overcame earlier team mistakes to overtake a 14-0 Tarheel lead. Slager had taken Notre Dame to the eight but a fumble ended that threat. With two minutes left in the third quarter, Slager moved the offense well enough for Hunter to score from the two. The two-point try missed. With 6:04 left in the game, Montana came in and launched a five-play scoring drive. Hunter scored from the two and Montana passed for a two-point conversion to tie. The Tar Heels then missed a 42-yard field goal. With 1:15 left, a draw play was called, but Montana audibled when he saw his split end facing only loose coverage. He was supposed to catch it and step out of bounds, but Burgmeier ran for an 80-yard touchdown to win the game. Montana had thrown four passes and completed three for 129 yards, one touchdown, a two-point conversion, and the win.

Air Force scored first with a 45-yard field goal, and converted a Heavens fumble into a 16-yard touchdown. Slager responded with a drive that earned a field goal; Montana went in and was intercepted. Air Force kicked a field goal for a 13-3 lead. Heavens shook loose for a 54-yard touchdown run in the third period, but Montana had another pass intercepted on the next series. Air Force turned that into a touchdown from the one for a 10-point lead. They made it worse with another field goal. Heavens fumbled and Air Force fired a touchdown pass for a 30-10 lead. Montana scored from the three on a bootleg play. Ten and a half minutes remained. The Falcons intercepted a third Montana pass but they fumbled. Montana hit McLane for 66 yards to the seven, and fired to MacAfee for the score. Five and a half minutes were left. The defense forced a change of possession and Hunter gained 45 yards before Heavens tallied from the two and a 31-30 victory. Fighting Irish

Great defensive player Jim Stock.

rushing gained 320 yards to Air Force's 90.

Fighting Irish fans were relieved to see Anthony Davis was gone, but USC always seemed to come up with something—this time it was Ricky Bell. The Irish scored first with an Al Hunter run of 52 yards, but USC went ahead 7-6 on a touchdown pass. Bradley deflected a Trojan punt for Lopienski's touchdown recovery. But a penalty killed the play, so Bradley deflected the next punt and Lopienski scored again. USC tied it in the third quarter after an interception, with Bell scoring from the two. Reeve kicked a field goal. USC ran for a touchdown and hit a field goal for a 24-17 win. Bell gained 165 yards on the day. Montana was three of 11 for 25 yards.

Next, Navy lost to the Fighting Irish 31-10. A face-mask penalty helped the Middies get a field goal in the first quarter. Browner blocked a punt and scored the touchdown with his recovery. Montana fired another interception. Browner recovered a fumble at the Middie 30 and three plays later MacAfee took a Montana pass and a Middie into the end zone for a touchdown. In the third quarter, Slager replaced Montana (who found out he had a broken finger) and Navy closed the gap with a touchdown. The Fighting Irish defense intercepted another pass but the offense stalled. Defensive tackle Jeff Weston stole a pass and ran 53 yards for a touchdown.

Hunter scored after another interception. Nevertheless, Navy had held Notre Dame's runners to 80 yards on 44 runs. Against Georgia Tech, Heavens made 148 yards on 18 carries for a 24-3 win. Heavens's rushing yardage was greater than Tech's; they also failed to complete a pass. Slager pitched out to Heavens even though he was flipping through the air after a hit. The score came from the Tech 16. A Reeve field goal made it 10-0 at the half. In the third quarter, Heavens broke it open with a 73-yard touchdown. Dan Knott scored for the reserves.

Pitt was next and Dorsett was having his usual fantastic year. The Fighting Irish didn't stop him; he ran for 303 yards, including a run of 57 yards to set up a Matt Cavanaugh score, 71 yards for a touchdown, and a 49-yard touchdown to go with 71 yards receiving. Notre Dame scored with two Reeve field goals, a Slager sneak from the one, and a 10-yard touchdown pass from Slager to MacAfee. Pitt won 34-20.

Miami was more adept at fumbling than Notre Dame. They lost five in a 32-9 loss. The teams traded field goals, and Browner grabbed a fumble at their 12. Heavens scored from the two. Browner crashed into Pitt's punt formation to surprise the punter, who was intent on passing the football, for a safety, the second of his career. Becker grabbed a Miami miscue, and MacAfee scored two plays later. Hunter scored from the four after another Miami bobble and Restic took a pitchout to throw to MacAfee for a 10-yard touchdown.

The 8-3 record was not seen favorably in all quarters; it was indicative of the inconsistent play through the season. The offense's production dropped 24 percent, the defense gave up 27 percent more yardage, and touchdown production fell 26 percent. Notre Dame was unranked by AP and 17 by UPI. Niehaus, MacAfee, and Bradley were All-Americans.

1975 record: 8-3-0 (.727)
Record to date: 571-153-38 (.774)

1976

Devine had a strong group, even with Montana out for the year with a shoulder injury. The basic backfield personnel were all returning; the line was solid, especially with MacAfee and Hughes. Tackles Woebkenberg and Steve McDaniels were the largest tandem on record at 269 and 279 pounds. At quarterback, Slager would

Ross Browner, an all-time great, four-year starter at LE on defense, consensus All-American in 1976 and 1977, Outland Trophy winner in 1976.

be alternating with Rusty Lisch and Gary Forystek. Hunter and McLane would start as halfbacks, until McLane was suspended for violating team regulations. Heavens shared the fullback position with freshman Vagas Ferguson. This was a sound, solid offense but not a great one—not yet.

The defense faced serious losses in the line, with Niehaus graduated and Weston lost with an injury after the first game. Browner and Fry were the two ends. The linebacking corps was led by sophomores Golic and Steve Heimkreiter; who posed serious problems for opponents. Doug Becker also worked at outside linebacker. Bradley switched from right to left corner and Burgmeier moved from split end to right corner. Jim Browner moved to strong safety. Joe Restic was the free safety and punter. Of this group, the only concern would be for the young, smallish tackles, Mike Calhoun and Ken Dike.

Pitt with Dorsett was the opener. The Panthers (who would be national champions) won, 31-10. The Fighting Irish scored on a 25-yard touchdown from Slager to MacAfee. Dorsett ran 61 yards on Pitt's first play; six plays later he scored from the five. Pitt intercepted a Slager pass and scored from the Notre Dame two. They repeated this pattern for their next

1976 Notre Dame Fighting Irish.

touchdown, an interception and a one-yard touchdown run. Reeve kicked a 53-yard field goal for a Notre Dame record. Pitt answered with a field goal and a touchdown following a bad Irish punt. Dorsett had 181 yards on 22 carries and 754 total rushing yards in four games against Notre Dame.

The Fighting Irish wasted two drives and then Reeve kicked a 39-yard field goal to take the lead against Purdue. After trading mistakes, Slager pitched out to Hunter, who threw a 33-yard touchdown pass to McLane. As the half ended, Randy Harrison was lost with a broken arm. Purdue penalties and fumbles kept the Irish supplied with opportunities, and Slager scored from the one. Burgmeier stopped a drive with an interception and a run to midfield. Hunter scored for the 23-0 final score.

In the final scheduled game of the series with Northwestern, Notre Dame won 48-0. The scoring, after a slow start, went like this: Hunter for a 16-yard touchdown in the second quarter, Slager to Willard Browner for an 8-yard touchdown, Slager to Tom Domin for a 70-yard score, Hunter for 37 yards and a tally, and Slager to MacAfee for a seven-yard touchdown. In the final quarter, Rusty Lisch scored from the four and Bobby Leopold ran 57 yards with a Wildcat pass to score. Slager set a new record with 12-of-14 passes completed for an .857 mark, breaking Bob Williams's 1949 record.

Against Michigan State, Hunter ran 23 yards to set up Reeve's 47-yard field goal, and scored a touchdown from the six moments later. Slager threw a 20-yard

touchdown pass to Terry Eurick. Late in the fourth quarter, Slager threw a one-yard touchdown pass to MacAfee. MSU kicked two field goals as a stifling Irish defense stopped MSU cold on its way to a 24-6 win.

Oregon gained no rushing yardage as Notre Dame shut them out 41-0. Slager scored on a keeper from the one, and he threw an 11-yard touchdown pass to McLane. Hunter ran nine yards for a touchdown. The Ducks fumbled the kickoff and he scored again six plays later from the six. Oregon's passing game failed in the second half; Notre Dame intercepted three. Hunter ran a 31-yarder in the third quarter and Ferguson bolted over from the two.

Solid defense aided a slim 13-6 win over South Carolina. The first Fighting Irish drive went 80 yards in 10 plays concluded by a 10-yard touchdown pass to Willard Browner; Reeve later kicked a 37-yard field goal. In the second quarter, he booted a 30-yarder to pass Bob Thomas for career field goals. The Gamecocks kicked a field goal with two seconds left in the half with the help of penalties. They kicked a fourth-quarter field goal. Fry sacked their quarterback and Jim Browner intercepted to stop the last drive.

After disappearing from the second half of the South Carolina game, the Notre Dame offense didn't show up for the beginning of the Navy game. Reeve kicked a 47-yard field goal at the end of the first quarter, and the defense kept Navy off the board to set a record of 21 straight scoreless quarters, surpassing the 1946 record of 20. In the second quarter, Navy used an interception

Steve Heimkreiter, Irish LB from 1976 to 1978.

to set up a touchdown pass for a 7-3 lead. They passed for another touchdown. Slager threw a 58-yard touchdown pass to Kelleher, the defense halted Navy, and Hunter scored from the from. After a Middie fumble, Slager threw a 28-yard touchdown pass to Hunter for the 24-14 halftime score. Navy scored from the one. Reeve hit another field goal and Dave Waymer stopped a late threat with an interception; Luther Bradley intercepted a pass in the Irish end zone on the last play. Notre Dame won 27-21.

Georgia Tech took advantage of Irish flaws to win 23-14, and then commented that the Notre Dame players were too fat and too slow. Tech took the lead on a second-quarter field goal. Hunter scored from the two, and he scored again when a Tech punt never got off, thanks to Ross Browner. Tech came back with a 48-yard run and an eight-yard touchdown dash. Two second-half touchdowns and paralyzing Notre Dame penalties finished the game.

Alabama, vengeance-minded, came to South Bend. Notre Dame won 21-18, in spite of mangling two scoring chances in the first quarter. Slager threw a

56-yard touchdown pass to Kelleher. Alabama was not moving against the Fighting Irish defense; Slager used Ferguson to set up a Hunter score from the two. Alabama scored on a one-yard quarterback keeper. Slick passing on the next Irish drive led to Ferguson's 17-yard run around right end to score. The Crimson Tide intercepted and kicked a field goal; Ozzie Newsome tallied with a 30-yard pass in the fourth period. Lisch replaced an injured Slager, used up the clock on two drives, and Jim Browner intercepted an end zone pass. It had probably been Bryant's best chance to beat Notre Dame.

Miami fell, 40-27. Reeve kicked a 31-yard field goal; Willard Browner threw Notre Dame's third option pass of the year to Kelleher for a four-yard touchdown. Heimkreiter grabbed a fumble, and Lisch threw a 42-yard touchdown to Kelleher. Lisch tallied from the seven for a 23-0 lead as the defense held Miami to three yards rushing and three completions. Lisch scored on a keeper in the third quarter, and Miami broke a kickoff return for a touchdown. Lisch passed sparingly, killing time, and Reeve hit a field goal in the fourth quarter. A Miami fumble allowed Hunter to score from the 14. With the win, Notre Dame accepted a Gator Bowl bid to meet Penn State.

Questionable officiating helped USC win. USC scored with a six-yard pass to Sheldon Diggs, and made it 14-0 with a 63-yard touchdown pass. In the fourth quarter, Lisch found Ferguson for a 17-yard touchdown pass; a bad call on Bradley for interference led to a Trojan field goal. Lisch scored from the one to make the final score read USC 17, Notre Dame 13.

In the Gator Bowl, Penn State opened with a field goal, but Eurick returned the kickoff to their 35; Hunter converted a fourth-down play, and then scored from the one. A Heimkreiter tackle of a Penn State runner led to a fumble and a 23-yard Reeve field goal. Hunter scored again from the one and Reeve booted another 23-yard field goal. Penn State scored on a Fusina to Suhey pass for the final score of a solid 20-9 Irish win.

The 1976 Irish passed for 45 percent more yardage than in 1975, and the defense made the running game even tougher for opponents. A solid group of runners developed, and the core of the defense gained valuable experience. Ross Browner won the Outland Trophy and was joined by fellow All-Americans MacAfee, Bradley, and Fry.

1976 record: 9-3-0 (.750)
Record to date: 580-156-38 (.773)

1977

Joe Montana was back after a year's recuperation—buried in the third team. The offensive line was a record 256 pounds per man. MacAfee was back for a third year as an All-American, and Kris Haines provided good speed and great hands as the split end. Lisch started at quarterback; behind him were Ferguson at left halfback and Dave Waymer at right halfback. Heavens was fullback. When Montana was in, this was an outstanding backfield, with great speed, good size, and good hands. On defense, Browner and Fry were back. The tackles and linebackers all returned, as did the entire secondary. This was a strong team with no apparent deficiencies.

Nevertheless, the Fighting Irish did not have a strong showing against a Dorsett-less Pitt, winning 19-9. A Lisch pass was intercepted and Matt Cavanaugh threw a 25-yard touchdown pass. Cavanaugh, however, never saw the pass being caught because he was hit by Willie Fry just as he threw; the big end and Cavanaugh landed together and the fall broke Cavanaugh's wrist. A few plays later, punter Joe Restic missed the snap and Pitt earned a safety. Pitt intercepted another Lisch pass, but without Cavanaugh, their offense lacked direction. Lisch found MacAfee for a five-yard touchdown, but the point after was blocked. Although behind 9-6 at the half, Notre Dame, from the point of Cavanaugh's injury, had allowed Pitt a total of six yards. Golic grabbed a Pitt fumble on their 16 and Reeve tied it with a field goal. Ross Browner rounded up a bad pitchout and Reeve made his second

field goal. Jim Browner picked up a fumble after a pass reception and Eurick scored from the four.

Mississippi beat the Fighting Irish 20-13. The only score in the first quarter was an Ol' Miss field goal. In the next quarter, Heavens blasted in from the two, after a Jim Browner interception, for a 7-3 lead. The Rebels fought back, going 75 yards in six plays, scoring on a nine-yard pass play. Jay Case grabbed an Ol' Miss fumble and Reeve kicked a field goal. Another fumble, another Reeve field goal, and a 13-10 lead. But the Irish offense was misfiring badly. A new Rebel quarterback executed a five-play, 80-yard drive, and finished it with a 10-yard touchdown pass. Notre Dame later fumbled, and Mississippi kicked a field goal.

Purdue's freshman quarterback, Mark Hermann, directed his team to a touchdown on its first possession. Becker picked off a Hermann pass on their next series. Lisch threw to Eurick for Notre Dame's first score. Purdue scored a field goal and two more touchdowns on Hermann passes, while Notre Dame managed only one more touchdown before the half. The defense took command in the third quarter, and Forystek moved the team well until his collarbone was broken on a rollout. Montana came in, but no miracle—just a field goal. Hermann kept passing. Bradley intercepted, and the Irish were at their 48. Montana fired to Haines and MacAfee, finally scoring with a 13-yard throw to MacAfee. Purdue was shut down on offense; Montana got the ball at his own 30 with three minutes to go. Sixty yards and four passes later, the Fighting Irish were on the Purdue 10. Dave Mitchell ran it in from the five for a 31-24 win,

The 1977 Notre Dame Fighting Irish.

Dan Devine and staff in 1977.

the third comeback victory in Joe Montana's career.

Devine gave the start to Montana against Michigan State. A fumble and interception stopped two Notre Dame drives, and MSU scored a field goal. Heavens dropped a perfectly thrown pass, but Notre Dame salvaged a field goal. Waymer fumbled; Reeve missed a field goal. But the defense was hammering the Spartans. A Golic interception led to a 40-yard Reeve field goal, and a Restic pick netted another field goal. The Spartans later kicked one to end it at 16-6 in favor of the Irish.

Against Army, Heavens became the first modern Fighting Irish runner to gain 200 yards on the ground (John Farley had once run for 464 yards in the 1890s). Penalties, fumbles, and poor passing meant a scoreless first period. A bad Army punt gave Montana the chance he needed; he directed a 47-yard drive in five plays. Heavens picked up 43 of the yards and scored from the three. In the third quarter, with a scant seven-point lead, Notre Dame kept the ball for 10 minutes. After six straight runs by Heavens, Reeve kicked a 29-yard field goal. Mike Whittington intercepted an Army pass and Montana moved in for the kill. Eurick ended a 75-yard drive with a two-yard touchdown burst, and later scored from the three. The final score was 24-0.

For USC, Devine concocted a ploy to add more charge to his players. After their pregame warmup, they returned to the lockers to find new kelly green jerseys with gold numbers. The locker room went nuts at the sight. Fans went berserk when the team came back out. The Trojans's first drive ended with a missed field goal, and Notre Dame's offense did what it was supposed to do—take it right to the other team, control the line of scrimmage, and make no mistakes. Heavens ran well and Montana looked sharp; Dave Mitchell scored with a four-yard run. USC missed another field goal, but Eurick fumbled and USC scored an easy three-yard touchdown. Charles White coughed up the ball on his 14, and Montana sneaked in from the one six plays later. A bobbled point-after snap ended up as a two-point conversion for the Fighting Irish. Bradley intercepted a USC pass, the 16th in his career. The Irish seemed stopped, but Burgmeier called a fake field goal and moved the sticks. Montana tossed a 12-yard scoring pass to MacAfee for a 22-7 lead. Golic blocked a punt and tackle Jay Case scored on a 30-yard runback. In the third quarter, Montana put together a good drive and a one-yard touchdown lob to MacAfee. The teams traded touchdowns, Montana's on a one-yard keeper. Lisch threw a four-yard touchdown pass to Kevin Hart for the 49-19 final score. Years of frustration seemed redeemed by this win.

That victory helped the offense start playing with intensity and competence. Navy went down 43-10. Heavens scored a 49-yard touchdown. Reeve kicked

Joe Montana, one of the most famous Notre Dame graduates.

three field goals in the second quarter. Montana scored from the one on a sneak and later threw a seven-yard touchdown to Mitchell. Reserves scored the last two touchdowns: Jim Stone on a 58-yard sprint and Leopold with an interception and a 50-yard return.

The next game was a grudge match for Notre Dame's linemen—Georgia Tech, who bragged in 1976 that the Fighting Irish were slow and fat. Georgia Tech lost 69-14. There was no scoring for more than a quarter. Notre Dame then rained touchdowns: Montana from the one (followed by a kickoff return for a score), Eurick with an eight-yard touchdown pass, Haines with a 19-yard touchdown pass; Waymer with a 68-yard touchdown pass, Heavens from the two, Ferguson from the one and from 56 yards out, Jim Stone from the 21 and 24, and Speedy Hart with a 31-yard pass from Tim Koegel. The Fighting Irish offense exploded for 667 yards.

The Fighting Irish nipped Clemson 21-17. Joe Montana pulled out a win. Heavens scored from the five, but early in the second quarter Irish drives fizzled. Clemson kicked a field goal, and their quarterback shook loose for a 10-yard touchdown run. In the third quarter, Clemson showed their "12th man" play; referee W.R. Cummings "threw" a good brush block to spring their tailback for a two-yard touchdown. A Clemson fumble at the Notre Dame 16 gave Montana what he needed. Montana scored from the one after a drive in which

he faced a second-and-31 on penalties. Mike Calhoun recovered his second fumble, and Montana wrapped it up with a quarterback sneak from the one.

After that narrow escape, Notre Dame beat Air Force 49-0. Ferguson ran for a 56-yard touchdown on the first play. Ferguson scored again from the nine. A 13-yard Falcon punt set up a Heavens score from the one. In the second quarter, four gains set up Ferguson's touchdown from the two. Haines capped the first half with a 33-yard touchdown pass from Montana. Reserves finished it: Eurick from the one and Steve Schmitz on an 11-yard touchdown pass from Lisch. Notre Dame gained 680 yards to the Falcons's 102. Notre Dame accepted the Cotton Bowl bid to play Texas and Heisman-winner Earl Campbell.

Miami was dispensed with 48-10. Fry welcomed its freshman quarterback with two sacks. Golic grabbed a fumble after the first sack and Ferguson scored from the 11. The second led to Leopold's third career touchdown from the 17. Miami scored its 10 points in the second quarter. Montana fired back with a 23-yard touchdown pass to Haines. In the third quarter, Montana decimated Miami's defense with three long drives. MacAfee caught touchdown passes of three and four yards. Mitchell scored between those two from the four. Lisch went in from the one. Notre Dame gained 404 total yards, while Miami gained only 28 yards on the ground.

Ernie Hughes, starter at RG from 1975 to 1977, ready to unload on a Georgia Tech defender in the 1977 rout.

Texas was hot, and Campbell reportedly was unstoppable. But he mishandled a pitchout on their fifth play, and Browner recovered the ball. Reeve kicked a field goal. The Longhorns got to the Irish 13 on good runs, but then they started to pass and their quarterback was sacked twice. They kicked a field goal to end the first quarter tied 3-3. Montana led the Fighting Irish back to the six; Eurick scored on the first play of the second quarter. Moments later, the Texas quarterback dropped the ball and Fry recovered. Eurick ended a short drive with an eight-yard touchdown blast. Texas intercepted a Montana overthrow, but Texas quarterback McEachern threw a pass right to Becker on the 40. He ran to the 17 and three plays later Montana threw a touchdown pass to Ferguson. It had been a disastrous quarter for Texas. Golic and Bradley blocked a field goal but Texas scored a touchdown with no time on the clock for a 24-10 Longhorn deficit at the half. In the third quarter, Heimkreiter intercepted a pass, and Ferguson ran for a three-yard touchdown. Ferguson scored from the 26 in the fourth quarter for a 38-10 triumph. Campbell gained 116 yards on 29 carries, which was remarkable since Golic was on him all day. For Notre Dame, Heavens gained 101 yards and Ferguson 100. The Fighting Irish won the national championship with their convincing win over an undefeated number one team.

Ross Browner won the Maxwell Award and the Lombardi Award. MacAfee won the Walter Camp Award. Other All-Americans were Bradley, Hughes, Golic, Fry, and Burgmeier. It's a shame that Montana was not similarly recognized, but perhaps it's even worse that he never reached that collegiate height.

1977 record: 11-1-0 (.916)
Record to date: 591-157-38 (.776)

1978

Devine had to replace key personnel—the right side of the offensive line, both defensive ends, and the left corner. Five were All-Americans. There were capable replacements, but it's hard to fill in for All-Americans. The backfield, newly configured with a pro-style flanker, featured Montana, Ferguson, Heavens, and Pete Holohan as the flanker. There was excellent potential for scoring. The defensive linemen were slightly smaller than those on the offense; the premium on defense was placed on quickness and mobility. Weston and Calhoun

Jim Browner, starter at FB and at SS, specialized in blitzing for the 1977 and 1978 Irish.

were experienced tackles, but the ends were new to starting. The linebacking corps was in fine hands with Golic, Heimkreiter, and Leopold. Waymer switched from offense to fill Bradley's shoes. The safeties were Jim Browner and Restic. Overall, the defense probably would be vulnerable to the run.

The defense of the national title started with two losses, a pattern not seen in two decades under the Dome. The first loss was to Missouri, 3-0; Notre Dame had not been shut out since the 0-0 tie with Miami in 1965. Against Mizzou, missed opportunities were the story: a fumbled snap at the Missouri 18; a Montana fourth-down run stopped short at the Missouri 11; failure to convert a recovered fumble on their 17 into points; a personal foul at the four moving the ball back to the 19; a muffed field goal snap and a misfired pass to the "hot" player (the player who is supposed to go for the ball). With 13 minutes left in the game, Missouri moved from its 14 to the Notre Dame 16 and scored the game's only field goal. Notre Dame had three more chances: a fourth-down run by Heavens was stopped short at their 28; with 3:31 left, Ferguson fumbled on their 25; and Harrison fumbled a punt with 1:15 left. Devine blamed his coaching for the loss in not taking his chances with the field goal sooner. It was the most embittering loss of his Notre Dame career.

The next loss was to Michigan; the series had been renewed after a 35-year hiatus. The Wolverines defeated Notre Dame 28-14 in South Bend (as had Missouri). A fumble on the kickoff led to a Montana six-yard touchdown pass to Dennis Grindinger, his tight end, for an early lead. The next two Fighting Irish drives were ended by a penalty and a dropped pass, followed by a missed field goal. The Irish were on Michigan's 33 but lost a pitchout. Michigan put together its own drive, with Rick Leach going in from the four. The Irish helped out with two offside penalties. Montana brought Notre Dame back and Ferguson scored from the four. In the third quarter, a Fighting Irish drive died at the Michigan 24. More adversity—two interceptions—led to two Wolverine touchdowns from Leach to Clayton of five and 17 yards. They also scored Michigan's last touchdown, a 40-yarder. Montana was nailed for a safety. The bright spot was Golic's 26 tackles, a new Irish record.

The Fighting Irish nipped Purdue 10-6. The offense was uninspired, but the defense was stifling. Purdue led at the half on two field goals. The Irish offense asserted itself on a short drive of 46 yards; Heavens scored from the 27. Joe Unis kicked a 27-yard field goal halfway into the third quarter. Heimkreiter made 24 tackles and intercepted a Purdue pass at the Notre Dame 21 in the last two minutes.

The offense showed more signs of waking up in a 29-25 win over Michigan State. The Spartans scored on a 25-yard Morten Anderson field goal. Heavens scored from the one, set up by a Montana to Haines pass of 35 yards. MSU passed for a 59-yard gain to set up another field goal. The next Fighting Irish drive, of 78 yards, was the first of the year in which the offense dominated its opponent. Done basically on the ground, Montana ended it with a one-yard sneak. Greg Knafelc passed to Nick Vehr for a two-point conversion. The last score of the half came when Jim Browner stripped a receiver of the ball and ran 45 yards for a touchdown. MSU scored in the third quarter, making it 22-13. The Fighting Irish drove 81 yards in 11 running plays. Ferguson scored from the 11. MSU scored twice but failed with both two-point conversions.

Pitt went down 26-17. Heavens opened with a two-yard smash to end a drive begun by Tom Gibbons's interception. That was it for Notre Dame's scoring for more than two quarters. Pitt tied it with a second-quarter drive of 79 yards, capped by a three-yard touchdown run. They scored a 33-yard field goal after Jim Stone fumbled. Pitt scored a quarterback keeper in the right corner of the end zone. Montana led an 86-yard drive and finished it with an eight-yard touchdown pass to Haines The two-point try failed, and Notre Dame was down 17-13. Pitt was stopped after one first down, and Montana was 59 yards from a win. He hit Haines for 29 yards, and Dean Masztak for 22. Eventually, Montana wiggled in from the one. With seven minutes left, Pitt fumbled; Case recovered at their 29; Montana flipped a three-yard pass to Ferguson for the insurance touchdown. Heavens gained 130 yards on 30 carries and surpassed Gipp's all-time running total of 2,341 yards.

Notre Dame was playing well, and beat Air Force, 38-15. Chuck Male kicked a field goal of 42 yards. Restic intercepted an Air Force pass and Ferguson scored from the 24 for a 10-0 lead. The Falcons scored after Notre Dame botched a reverse, but Montana tallied on bursts of one and four yards for a 24-7 halftime lead. Haines increased it with a 56-yard touchdown reception, and Grindinger scored with another Montana pass from the nine. Air Force scored a touchdown and a two-point conversion.

Notre Dame needed an impressive win against Miami to keep the bowl committees interested. Little happened in the first quarter; then Heimkreiter tackled a tight end, who fumbled. Golic recovered on their 30. Six runs later, Ferguson scored from the four. Male hit

Dave Huffman, Irish starter at center from 1976 to 1978.

a 47-yard field goal after a Restic fumble recovery in the third quarter. Ferguson added another touchdown with a three-yard blast, and Waymer intercepted a pass to set up Male's 37-yard field goal. Miami never was able to get Ottis Anderson into scoring territory as Notre Dame prevailed 20-0.

Navy was number one in total defense and number two in rushing defense; they were undefeated in seven games. Notre Dame won 27-7. Ferguson rushed for 219 yards, the best single-game effort in the modern era (to give Notre Dame its top two single-game runners in the same backfield). Montana flipped a 20-yard touchdown pass to Haines after Weston recovered a Middie fumble. Four plays later, Case picked up a loose ball; Male kicked a 38-yard field goal. Heavens started a drive with a 39-yard sweep and finished it with a three-yard touchdown run. Navy fumbled, and Ferguson sprinted 80 yards for another touchdown and a 24-0 lead. Three later Fighting Irish drives were stopped at the one, two, and 12. Male hit another field goal in the third period, and Navy scored with 12 seconds left in the game.

Tennessee was defeated 31-14. Male kicked a 24-yard field goal. The Volunteers came back with a six-yard touchdown on an option play. A bad Tennessee punt in the second quarter led to another Male field goal for a 7-6 halftime score. Freshman Bob Crable blocked a punt at the Tennessee 16 and freshman Pete Buchanan muscled in from the two for the touchdown. Montana hit Holohan for a two-point conversion. Waymer returned a punt 46 yards to their 30; Male kicked his third field goal, another 37-yarder. A good Restic punt put the Volunteers in trouble at their three; they tried passing, but Calhoun tackled their quarterback, who lost the ball. Hankerd recovered at the three, and Montana took it in from the five, moments later. The Volunteers scored on a 73-yard pass when Restic and Waymer eliminated each other on the coverage, but Restic later intercepted and ran back a 30-yard touchdown.

Georgia Tech ended the Irish seven-game winning streak, 38-21. Ferguson ran 68 yards on the second play from scrimmage to set up Male's 23-yard field goal. Ferguson's running kept Georgia Tech off balance in the second quarter; Montana threw a 20-yard touchdown to Pete Pallas. Ferguson ran for a 20-yard touchdown. Tech scored on a 10-yard pass play for a 17-7 halftime score. In the first half, Ferguson gained 188 yards. Most of the third quarter was a defensive standoff, but Montana moved Notre Dame 52 yards and went over from the one to score. He found Haines for a five-yard touchdown in the fourth quarter. Tech scored on a 64-yard pass

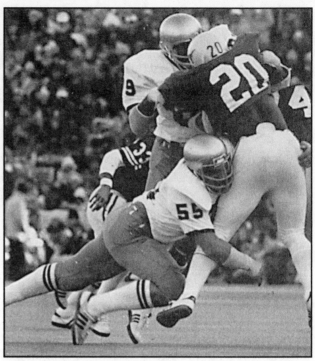

Ross Browner and Bob Golic do a number on Earl Campbell in the 1978 Cotton Bowl win over Texas that clinched the national title for the Irish.

play. Jim Stone racked up a score from the five with the reserves. Tech got the last score on a six-yard pass. Ferguson gained 255 yards, a single-game record, and Montana hit 10 consecutive passes to tie Bertelli's record. The Fighting Irish accepted a bid to play Houston in the Cotton Bowl.

But USC was first; it was one of the all-time great games, with 949 yards of total offense in a 27-25 Trojan win. For three quarters, Notre Dame only had two Male field goals and trailed 24-6 going into the last period. USC had scored on a 30-yard pass, a 35-yard pass, a 39-yard field goal, and a one-yard touchdown by Charles White. A Notre Dame drive died when Montana fumbled at the USC one; the Trojans killed the clock with a 96-yard drive that ended in a missed field goal. That time was crucial, as it turned out. Montana spotted Haines in a soft spot in the USC coverage and threw a 57-yard touchdown pass. The Trojans drove to the Notre Dame 38 and punted to the Irish two. Less then seven minutes were left. Montana passed for 81 yards: four throws to Haines of seven, 18, 19, and 20 yards, one to Masztak to the 17, and his own run of 15 to the three. Buchanan slammed in over right guard to make it 24-19.

After a poor USC punt, the Irish took over at the Trojan 43. With 1:35 left, Montana passed and ran, throwing a two-yard touchdown to Holohan. Notre

Dame led, 25-24. The two-point try failed. USC "won" the game when a Weston hit and fumble recovery was ruled an incomplete pass, allowing a USC field goal with seconds left. (In the Rose Bowl, White would "score" a touchdown without the ball on another official's error.) Montana amassed 358 yards on 20 of 41 passes. Haines caught nine for 179 yards and one touchdown.

The Cotton Bowl was played under bizarre conditions. There were 39,500 fans imitating empty seats because of bitterly cold temperatures and ice that forced people to stay home. The game itself got off to a Marx Brothers's "Duck Soup" start when both kickoff teams lined up and faced each other—eventually, the Cougars kicked off to Notre Dame. Randy Harrison made a 56-yard return on the ice. After slipping and sliding, Notre Dame scored on a 66-yard drive, with Montana skating to a touchdown in the right corner from the three. Crable recovered Houston's kickoff fumble, and Buchanan bulled in from the one six plays later. Both conversions were missed. Then a referee ruled that a punt had touched Waymer, so the Cougars got the ball on the Notre Dame 12. Houston scored for a 12-7 game. In the next quarter, moving into the unpredictable, bitter wind, a Fighting Irish fumble gave Houston another score. A fluttering Montana pass was intercepted, and Houston kicked a field goal. Another interception gave them another field goal. In the third quarter, with no sign of Montana, the Cougars put together a short drive and scored on a two-yard quarterback keeper. Houston blocked an Irish punt and scored three plays later for a 34-12 lead.

By this time the soup was beginning to work—given to Montana at halftime for hypothermia. There were only five minutes left in the third quarter when Montana arrived. Notre Dame had not moved past its 21 in his absence. His second play was an interception. Montana had the wind to his back in the fourth quarter and went to work on the 22-point deficit. He started with yet another interception, but Houston did not get a first down in the last quarter, and the ball came right back. Tony Belden blocked a Houston punt and Steve Cichy scored with the deflection after a 33-yard return. Montana made a two-point conversion; the score was 34-20 with 7:25 left. Houston had to punt again. Good passing and an interference call got Montana to the two; he scored on a rollout and threw a two-point conversion to Haines. Waymer broke up a third-down pass moments later, and Houston had to punt. Montana, with 2:25 left, got to the Houston 20, but fumbled. The Irish got the ball back with 28 seconds. Montana threw into the

right corner to Haines, but he just missed. He tried it again, and it worked. The score was 34-34. A penalty on the kick made Unis kick again, and it was good—35-34, Notre Dame's 600th victory. This finish might rival the 1935 win over Ohio State.

There was no justice for Joe Montana. After his great personal feats in 1978, he was once again not elected to an All-America team. Golic and Dave Huffman earned the honors, and deserved them.

1978 record: 9-3-0 (.750)
Record to date: 600-160-38 (.775)

1979

All the Irish needed in 1979 was a replacement for "The Comeback Kid." Rusty Lisch, the 1977 early-season starter, was on hand, with capable replacements in the wings. Ferguson was back. John Sweeney was at least adequate as fullback. Freshman split end Tony Hunter provided good speed and great size. The line was solid, with veteran leadership and excellent size. This offense would have a one-dimensional running game and a serious deep threat in Hunter, but lacked the sparkle that Montana provided.

The defensive line came in at 235 pounds per man (as opposed to 255 pounds for the offensive line). The linebackers were also smaller than the previous group, but faster. Crable held down the middle, flanked by Whittington and Leopold. Waymer led a young group of deep backs.

This young team, with no proven leader, went to Ann Arbor for its maiden outing against a loaded Michigan team. They did not score a touchdown and gave up 306 yards to Michigan's offense while they gained only 179 yards, completing five-of-12 passes. They also won, 12-10, on Male's four field goals, a defense that kept Michigan penned up in the second half, and Crable's block of a field goal with six seconds left in the game. Ferguson carried 35 times (63 percent of the offensive plays and 77 percent of the running plays). Michigan kicked a field goal of 30 yards. Male hit a 40-yarder after Anthony Carter fumbled a punt. In the second quarter, the Wolverines drove 80 yards, scoring from the one. The Irish kicked a 39-yard field goal for a 10-6 halftime score. In the third quarter, the Fighting Irish drove 65 yards for a Male field goal. Less than five minutes later, he kicked a 39-yard field goal and

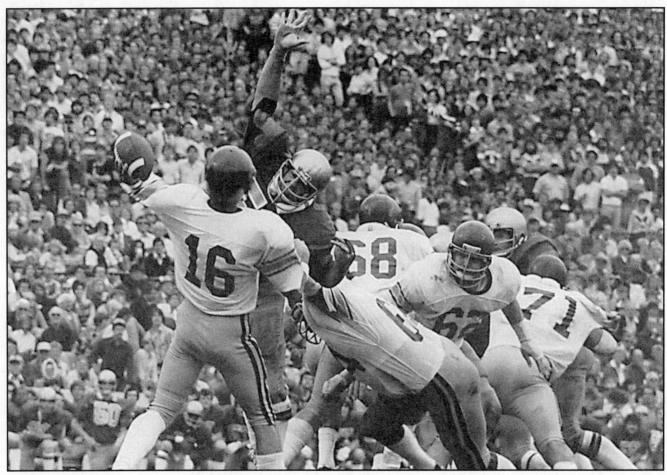

Heimkreiter disturbs USC's Paul McDonald in 1979 action.

Notre Dame led 12-10. In the fourth quarter, Michigan intercepted a pass to start its final drive, which Crable ruined with his block.

Nineteen Irish players were injured when the game with Michigan was over. Devine called for some trickery at the first opportunity against Purdue—a fake field goal try at the Boilermaker 17. It worked and Greg Knafelc found Masztak for a touchdown pass. Purdue tied it 12 plays later on a 15-yard pass. Male hit two field goals in the next quarter, the second set up by a fake flanker reverse which turned into a 34-yard pass from Holohan to Hunter. The Fighting Irish moved well in the third quarter on a 62-yard drive ended by a Koegel to Nick Vehr touchdown pass from the four. Purdue made a long drive and scored from the one, and then intercepted a pass and converted it into a touchdown. The Irish never made another first down and a fourth-quarter Purdue touchdown won it 28-22. It was Notre Dame's 800th game.

The seventh-ranked Michigan State team opened the home season for Notre Dame, losing 27-3. They could not move the ball well and two drives spent in their half of the field eventually earned Hunter a 14-yard touchdown pass from Lisch. Two drives later, Male booted a 49-yard field goal. Michigan State punted badly, and Male kicked a 36-yarder. MSU finally booted a 53-yard field goal, equal to any ever kicked in the stadium. A hard hit on their only ambulatory quarterback by Hankerd turned their punter into a quarterback. Ferguson scored on a 24-yard run, they punted, and Ferguson ran 48 yards down the sideline for the last touchdown.

Against Georgia Tech, Dave Duerson, replacing the injured Waymer, intercepted a Georgia Tech pass on their 41 and ran it back to the eight. Ferguson scored from the three. Tech scored on an 80-yard pass when their quarterback bobbled the snap just long enough for the deep backs to read a running play. A Scott Zettek tackle led to another Duerson fumble recovery; Ferguson gained more yardage, and Ty Barber ran it in from the four. Tech hit a 41-yard field goal in the second quarter. In the fourth quarter, Tech lost a lateral to Crable and Ferguson scored on a 17-yard run for the 21-13 Notre Dame win.

The 1979 tri-captains, Tim Foley, Dave Waymer, Vagas Ferguson, and Coach Devine.

Notre Dame bombed Air Force 38-13, with scores on each of the first three possessions: a Ferguson blast from the five, a 43-yard Male field goal after a Leopold interception, and a Lisch sneak from the three. The defense was now missing five starters. Air Force scored a touchdown, and the Irish came back, led by a 59-yard pass to Holohan; Vehr gained the last 17 yards on two receptions and scored. The Falcons dropped the ball on the kickoff, Dan Stone recovered, and Ferguson ran it in. The last Fighting Irish touchdown went to Hunter twice—an 80-yarder lost to a penalty and a 75-yarder.

USC won 42-23 as the teams amassed 1,128 yards of offense. Early in the game, Ferguson became the all-time rushing leader on a 79-yard run. Notre Dame failed to score and USC drove 99 yards for a touchdown. Ferguson tied it with a one-yard slam just before the half. In the third quarter, USC rolled against the Fighting Irish defense; Charles White scored from the three. Ferguson led the Irish back, but Lisch fumbled. White scored from the one. Lisch's passing set up a 21-yard touchdown burst by Ferguson, but USC exploited the Irish secondary for a 12-yard touchdown pass. Hunter caught two from Lisch for 66 yards and Stone scored from the two. USC burned the deep backs again with a 46-yard pass, and White scored from the one. The Irish answered with a 42-yard field goal. An interception set up White for another one-yard touchdown run. For the game, White carried 44 times for 261 yards and four touchdowns to Ferguson's 25 runs for 185 yards and two scores. White averaged almost six yards per carry, and Ferguson almost 7.5. USC's quarterback, Paul McDonald, passed for 311 yards to Lisch's 286.

Notre Dame beat South Carolina 18-17, winning in the last 42 seconds. Notre Dame kicked a field goal in the first half, and then watched the Gamecocks score 17 points in the third quarter: a 62-yard pass, a 49-yard run, and a 39-yard field goal. Ferguson made a 26-yard touchdown near the end of the quarter. After a nine-minute South Carolina possession, Lisch had 1:36 left, trailing 17-10. He completed three passes and grabbed a deflected pass for a short gain. From their 14, he fired to Masztak for a touchdown and a 17-16 score. Lisch threw to Holohan in the left corner of the end zone; he juggled it but brought it in for the conversion and the 18-17 win. It was Lisch's finest hour as an Irish quarterback.

The Fighting Irish barely beat Navy, 14-0. Lisch led a 73-yard drive and scored from the one early in the game, followed by lost opportunities until Ferguson rammed in a three-yard touchdown in the fourth quarter to finish a 70-yard, six-run (all his) drive. The Irish defense held Navy in check throughout.

The Irish were in the running for a Sugar Bowl bid, but Tennessee destroyed that with a 40-18 win. Ferguson scored from the one. The Volunteers went ahead 7-6. Tennessee scored 23 points in the second quarter: their second-string fullback ran for three touchdowns and Lisch went down for a safety. Ferguson answered with a two-yard scoring run. In the third, Tennessee scored another 10 points on a fullback touchdown and a field goal. Ferguson scored from the 10 to end it. The Volunteers ran for 352 yards, much of it up the middle.

Clemson nipped the faltering Irish 16-10 in South Bend. Clemson was ranked 14th, but Notre Dame beat themselves with turnovers. Male booted a 42-yard field goal. Freshman Phil Carter made a good showing on a second quarter drive to help divert attention from Ferguson, who scored from the two. A dropped punt led to a 33-yard field goal by Clemson; they controlled the ball, keeping it for 22 minutes in the second half. A second field goal made it 10-6, but a Ferguson fumble on the Notre Dame 20 gave Clemson an easy touchdown. Hunter tipped a pass at the three and Clemson recovered.

A 6-4 Notre Dame team went to Tokyo to play Miami on a marshy field. The Japanese would have liked a better record from the Fighting Irish, but Notre Dame won 40-15 anyway. Ferguson slushed 35 times for 177 yards, and Waymer scored twice on interceptions. Ferguson scored a two-yard touchdown, and Waymer picked a Jim Kelly pass at the three for a touchdown. Miami drove for a touchdown. The Fighting Irish came back all the way to the one but did not score. Crable blocked a punt for a safety, and Male hit his 13th field goal of the year, a new record. Ferguson ran twice from

Dean Masztak, starting TE in 1979 and 1980, in a 18-17 squeaker over the Gamecocks.

the 18 for a touchdown, and scored again from the one in the fourth quarter. Waymer's second interception went for 37 yards and his second touchdown before Miami scored with four seconds left.

Ferguson ended his year with a record 1,437 yards running, 17 touchdowns, and 3,472 career rushing yards. The second leading 1979 rusher for Notre Dame, Ty Barber, had 172 yards. This was the worst Notre Dame season in 16 years. Ferguson and Tim Foley earned All-America honors.

1979 record: 7-4-0 (.636)
Record to date: 607-164-38 (.773)

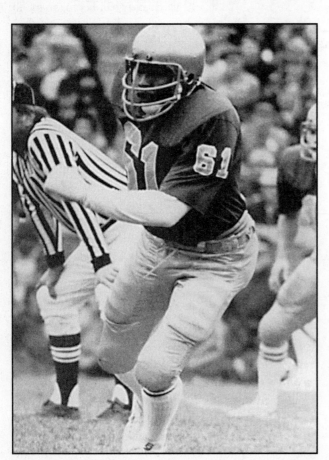

Bobby Leopold, speedy Irish LB in 1978 and 1979 scored two career TDs on interceptions.

1980-1989

1980

On a Saturday in fall practice, Devine revealed that this would be his last season at Notre Dame. He was not being pressured by anyone; he enjoyed the support of the administration, there was team unity, and there was no undue alumni pressure. His wife's deteriorating health was the deciding factor. He had agonized over his commitments to players and family. The tri-captains (John Scully, Bob Crable and Tom Gibbons) spoke to the team alone and emphasized playing for the institution, not the coach.

The team came together and played as they should. Hunter was back as a deep threat; the line had some excellent players, especially Tom Thayer, Tim Huffman, and Dean Masztak, Devine's favorite tight end. Mike Courey started as quarterback for two games, but freshman Blair Kiel would take over. Phil Carter was the wave of the near future—a fast, small back with great leg drive and lateral mobility. Jim Stone was behind him. Sweeney returned at fullback from a broken ankle. Holohan returned as flanker. This was a large, fast offensive outfit.

The defense had three returners on the line and a combination of speed and size. The linebackers were a strong contingent—Crable, Mark Zavagnin, and Joe Rudzinski. The deep backs lost Waymer, but Stacy Toran would hold the job for four years and Duerson returned. This was a good squad with some heavy hitters in key places.

The first test was against Purdue, and the Fighting Irish passed 31-10. Mike Courey shredded the Purdue secondary with 10-of-13 passes for 151 yards and a

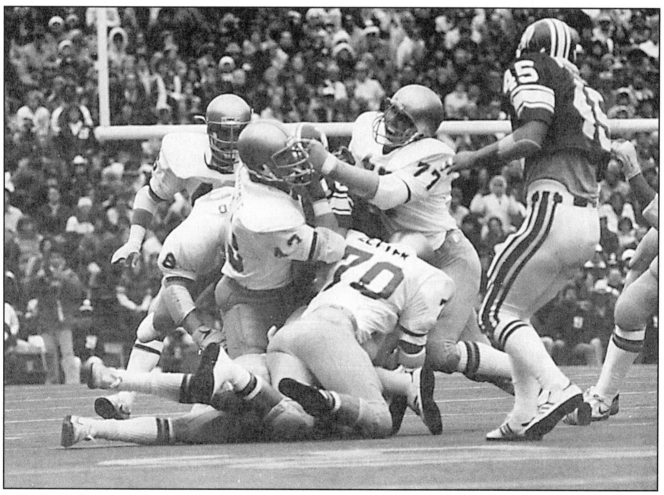

Crable, Zettek, and Marshall showing a Spartan how it's done in the 1980 Irish win.

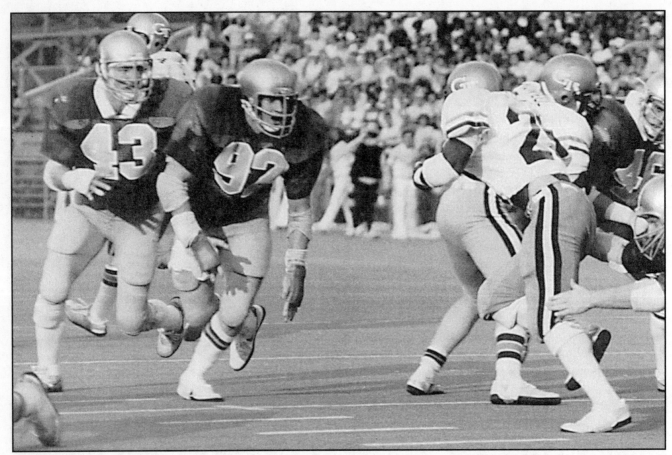

Crable and Gramke prepare to interfere with Eddie Lee Ivery's plans in a 3-3 game with Georgia Tech.

touchdown. Carter led the runners with 142 yards on 29 carries. Harry Oliver kicked a 36-yard field goal, and Courey led the team on a return trip of 57 yards, running and passing well; Rob McGarry went in from the two. Purdue was unable to move for the third time and Masztak caught a 28-yard pass from Courey and Carter slammed in from the one. Purdue drove 74 yards but stalled at the Irish nine; they booted a field goal. The Fighting Irish fumbled and Purdue scored a touchdown from the four. In the third quarter, Courey and Hunter conspired on a drive, highlighting it with a 57-yard play that left the deep backs baffled; Hunter scored from the nine. The Irish defense clamped down, getting minus-54 yards in sacks. Courey closed the scoring with a 14-yard run in the fourth quarter.

After waiting two weeks, Notre Dame met Michigan. The Wolverines drove but a field goal try missed. In the second quarter, a 16-play drive ended when Phil Carter ran in from the six. Michigan couldn't move and punted. Courey threw a 16-yard pass to Hunter and a 10-yard touchdown pass to Holohan. Michigan scored. Michigan intercepted a pass at midfield to set up the tying touchdown, a nine-yard pass

with half a minute to go in the half. In the third quarter, Anthony Carter returned the kickoff 67 yards and they rammed it in from the two. The Fighting Irish offense stalled, but John Krimm intercepted a pass and returned it 49 yards for a touchdown. Oliver missed the point after. A Michigan fumble was recovered by Crable. Hunter threw a 31-yard pass off a fake reverse and Phil Carter ran in from the four for the 26-20 lead. Michigan came right back, led by Butch Woolfolk's running, for a touchdown pass from the one. A two-point try missed and they led 27-26. Devine sent in Kiel at quarterback, his first college experience, with the ball on the Notre Dame 20 and 41 seconds left. With fitful passing and a penalty, Kiel coaxed the Irish to the Michigan 34 with four seconds left. Oliver came in for a 51-yard field-goal try, with Koegel holding, against a 15 mph wind. His longest try had been a 38-yarder in a junior varsity game. Oliver made the kick for a dramatic 29-27 Irish victory. Devine was so choked with emotion afterwards, he was unable to speak to the media.

The Fighting Irish beat Michigan State 26-21. The Spartans took the early lead on a Morten Anderson field goal, and drove 60 yards in 10 plays for a touchdown

Phil Carter goes into a cavernous hole between Sweeney and Foley in the 1980 Sugar Bowl action with Georgia.

and a 9-0 lead. Oliver kicked two field goals, 44 and 49 yards, for a 9-6 halftime score. Notre Dame took the lead in the third quarter with a 51-yard march and Carter's 12-yard touchdown run. The defense stopped MSU and the Notre Dame scored another field goal, from 27 yards. The Spartans used four plays to score.

Blair Kiel, first four-year starter at QB since Dorais.

With the score 16-15, Jim Stone scored from the one. Oliver booted another field goal. Carter ran the ball 40 times, a new record, for 254 yards, but he was injured and Stone would take his place.

Miami was led by a quarterback who had been recruited by Penn State as a linebacker, Jim Kelly. Oliver made a field goal early in the second quarter. A good punt return by Duerson set Kiel up on their 29 and he scored from the four a few plays later. Rick Naylor recovered Miami's fumble of the kickoff and Oliver kicked another three-pointer. In the third quarter, another Oliver field goal followed yet another fumbled kickoff. Kelly hit a touchdown pass early in the fourth quarter. Gibbons intercepted a Kelly pass and ran it in for a 53-yard touchdown. Kelly threw a 37-yard touchdown pass to make it 22-14. Oliver hit another field goal, and Stone ran in a 27-yard touchdown in the final seconds. Stone carried 38 times for 224 yards to lead all runners.

Army lost 30-3. Stone scored from the four in the second quarter. Oliver kicked a 49-yard field goal, and Zavagnin recovered a blocked punt in the end zone for a touchdown. Army scored in the third quarter; Kiel scored on a one-yard keeper. Army tried to play catch up, but Zavagnin intercepted a pass, and Ty Barber scored from the one. Stone again led all runners with 122 yards on 25 carries.

The Irish slipped by Arizona 20-3. Kiel used half of the first quarter to engineer the first score, his own from the one. Arizona kicked a field goal in the second quarter. Kiel ran on a fake punt—for an 80-yard touchdown. Oliver finished with two field goals. Stone passed the century mark for the third game, with 105 yards on 29 carries.

Navy fell 33-0. Navy backed up Notre Dame to its eight, but Stone broke out for a 73-yard gain. Barber scored from the nine. Navy fumbled the kickoff on their 21, and Tim Marshall recovered. Six plays later, Pete Buchanan slammed in from the three for a 12-0 lead. In the second quarter, Stone scored a 13-yard touchdown and Dave Condeni threw to Vehr for a two-point conversion. Navy fumbled at their 15. Zavagnin recovered. A disgusted Navy defense played well and Oliver kicked a field goal for a 23-0 lead. He booted one more and Notre Dame held a 26-0 halftime lead. In the fourth quarter, with Courey at quarterback, Greg Bell ran for a 27-yard touchdown. Stone set a record with his fourth consecutive 100-yard plus game: 33 runs for 211 yards.

Georgia Tech tied 3-3. Notre Dame was ranked number one while Georgia Tech had won one game. Tech booted a field goal in the second quarter. Notre Dame lost five fumbles and had to contend with a tough Tech defense all day. With less than five minutes to go in the game, Oliver hit a 47-yard field goal after a Stacy Toran interception. Stone was held to 85 yards.

Alabama promised to be tougher—much tougher. Zettek slammed Alabama's Major Ogilvie hard on the first play for a two-yard loss (Ogilvie ran for four yards all day). In the second quarter, Hankerd recovered a Crimson Tide fumble at their 12, but Kiel muffed a snap and lost it. Zettek recovered another Alabama miscue

at their four. Four tough, crunching plays later, Carter dove for the game's only score. Oliver missed a field goal when he slipped, but Crable stopped an Alabama fourth-down play and Bear Bryant had lost his fourth and final game to the Irish by a 7-0 margin.

An improved Air Force team played a tough game but lost 24-10. They staked an early lead on a field goal; in the second quarter Oliver kicked one after a fumble. In the third quarter, the Fighting Irish took command, led by Carter's 13 runs on a 14-play drive, gaining 71 yards, and scoring from the two. Stone scored after the Falcons were stymied again. Air Force threatened in the fourth period with an interception and a follow-up touchdown, but Notre Dame killed the clock with an 80-yard drive. Stone scored a two-yard touchdown. Carter ran 181 yards on 29 carries; Stone chipped in with 71 yards on 18 runs.

The new head coach was announced before the next game—Moeller High's Gerry Faust. It was a distraction during the days prior to the USC game. The Trojan defense kept Notre Dame from moving the sticks until the last 10 seconds of the first half. An Irish fumble at their 31 led directly to the first USC score, a six-yard run by their fullback. They followed it with a field goal. Oliver booted a field goal following a Trojan fumble at their one-yard line, which Notre Dame could not convert into a touchdown. In the fourth quarter, USC made a 17-yard field goal and scored another touchdown for the 20-3 final score.

The Georgia Bulldogs were number one and

An exalted Devine after the 7-0 win over 'Bama in 1980.

had freshman phenomenon Herschel Walker for the Sugar Bowl game with the Irish. To start the game, the kickers did the scoring: Oliver with a 50-yarder and Robinson with a 46-yarder. Their ensuing kickoff was the turning point when Jim Stone called for Barber to take the kick, but Barber didn't hear the call and the ball bounced around near the goal as Georgia players ran toward it. Stone saw the ball too late, and Georgia had it at the one. Two plays later, Walker bulled in for the touchdown. Another Notre Dame fumble, at their own 22, led to another easy touchdown for Walker. Good Georgia defense kept Notre Dame from scoring until the third quarter, when Carter went in from the one. A final interception in the fourth quarter wrapped it up for Georgia, 17-10. Notre Dame outgained Georgia 328 yards to 127 and demolished their passing game (one of 12 for seven yards). Walker had 36 carries for 150 yards. One more time, too many Irish mistakes cost the game.

The passing game fell off 57 percent from 1979. The running game worked better. The defense improved greatly, but the story of this year was trying to get by with a freshman quarterback. Devine was leaving behind a good team for Faust. Scully, Crable, and Zettek were the All-America choices.

1980 record: 9-2-1 (.791)
Record to date: 616-166-39 (.774)

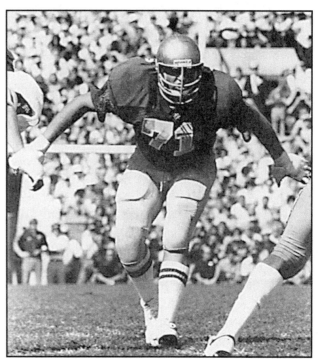

Phil Pozderac, 6'9" and 270 pounds, started at RT in 1980 and 1981.

1981

Gerry Faust brought an incredible record from Moeller High in Cincinnati: 174 wins, 17 losses, and two ties for a .907 winning percentage (70-1 from 1975-1980). He was a demanding coach who preached excellence and commitment. He had an abiding love for Notre Dame, and the admiration was reciprocated. He had sent many players to college ball from Moeller—at one point when Notre Dame met Michigan, a dozen starters for the two teams came from Moeller. He thrived on pressure.

The big question was whether Faust would be able to make the adjustment to the college game. Notre Dame's experience with Brennan in the mid-1950s was potentially analogous, although Brennan was not much older than the seniors he coached. There may be disparities in the skills of players in college, but coaching skills are more widely and uniformly excellent in college than in high school. Great coaches, their chosen systems, and their chosen talent meet in big games. If there

are failures over many years in any variable, either the coach changes or departs. It is rare for college coaches to be "outcoached" on a consistent basis. This general concern—the ability to coach at the college level—would be watched carefully by those closest to the program.

Faust inherited a good team, perhaps on the verge of becoming a great one. It had good size and excellent speed. Kiel could throw to Hunter (who was moved three times, ending at tight end) or to freshman Joe Howard. The interior line was the largest on record, 260 pounds, with the right side gargantuan for this era—Mike Shiner at 6'8" and 270 pounds and Phil Pozderac at 6'9" and 270 pounds. Phil Carter was at tailback and Sweeney returned at fullback. The defensive line was all new and tipped the scales at 245 pounds per man. It was vulnerable to the run. The linebackers returned as a unit and the secondary had two fine players in Duerson and Toran. Both units would face some difficulties in making the transition to different coaching and theories, and all would suffer a morale problem as the high promise of the preseason disintegrated into the first losing season in 18 years.

The first score of the new era followed a Rudzinski hit on the LSU quarterback. He fumbled, Kevin Griffith recovered at the LSU 20, and Kiel hit Moriarty with a seven-yard touchdown. Faust's first Fighting Irish touchdown happened within three minutes. About four minutes later, the Irish had another touchdown after Greg Bell ran 41 yards down the sideline and Carter scored from the one. In the second quarter, Hunter scored from the one on a wingback run. Toran intercepted a touchdown pass in his end zone, and Crable smashed a drive with three straight tackles; LSU fumbled on fourth down at the Notre Dame two. LSU kicked a field goal after a Kiel pass was intercepted. At the end of the third quarter, Koegel fired a six-yard touchdown pass to Condeni. LSU scored in the final seconds as Notre Dame won 27-9.

Ranked first in the country, the Fighting Irish went to Ann Arbor and lost 25-7. Michigan moved 74 yards on the ground before missing a field goal. The Irish drove back to the Michigan four. Condeni tried a pass from a fake field goal formation, throwing to Hunter, who was tackled at the four for no field goal, no touchdown. Michigan stormed back with four unanswered touchdowns: a 71-yard bomb to Anthony Carter, a 15-yard strike to Carter, a one-yard smash by Lawrence Ricks, and a six-yard quarterback keeper. Koegel found Masztak for an eight-yard touchdown completion, but it was too late. The Wolverines manhandled the defense for 304 yards on the ground, to only 70 for Notre Dame.

The Purdue team did not look as strong. After a scoreless opening quarter, a Fighting Irish drive launched Chris Smith for a one-yard touchdown, set up by Koegel's passing. In the third quarter, Oliver missed a 51-yard field goal, and Purdue tied. Late in the fourth quarter, Carter scored on a 30-yard run and put Notre Dame ahead. They had used 50 seconds and left Purdue with almost three minutes. A badly underthrown pass missed its target, but a nearby Boilermaker made a great diving catch at the Notre Dame one. The defense pushed them back, but on a fourth-down play they scored with a seven-yard pass and made a two-point conversion, with 19 seconds left, to win 15-14.

The Irish reached .500 with a 20-7 win over Michigan State. Greg Bell scored after Griffith recovered a Spartan fumble on their first play. Bell scored again from the 30 on a run up the middle. In the second quarter, MSU exploited a lapse in coverage for a 63-yard touchdown pass. The Fighting Irish kicked a 38-yard field goal. The defense played tough the rest of the way. Griffith grabbed another fumble, MSU missed a field goal, and Oliver made one for the 20-7 final score. Bell had 165 yards on 20 carries, but lost a 75-yard touchdown run on a penalty.

Against Florida State, the first Notre Dame drive ended in an Oliver field goal. The halftime score was 3-3. Zavagnin intercepted a Florida State pass on the first play of the second half, at their seven. Notre Dame kicked a field goal. Florida State ran 53 yards in two plays and scored on a 17-yard pass play. Notre Dame kicked another field goal. The only Irish touchdown came on an 80-yard drive and a one-yard hurdle by Bell. Florida State intercepted a Kiel pass at the Notre Dame 31 and scored five plays later with a five-yard pass. Seven minutes remained, but the Fighting Irish were unable to move and lost 19-13. The Notre Dame air game was absent: 38 yards on six completions.

Faust had two weeks to get the Irish ready for USC. Kiel played the whole game for stability; Hunter went to split end to cover for an injury. The Fighting Irish played well: Carter outgained Marcus Allen, 161 yards to 147, and the Trojan passing game was a mere 46 yards. But they lost to USC 14-7. The first half was scoreless, although Notre Dame reached the USC two where a field goal try backfired. In the third quarter, USC scored on three runs, with a touchdown from the Notre Dame 14. Four minutes later, Notre Dame scored after an 80-yard drive; Carter went in from the five. In the fourth quarter, a good USC punt nailed Notre Dame at their four. This bad field position resulted in a short Trojan drive, capped by a 26-yard counter play for the touchdown Joe Howard returned the kickoff 56 yards, but the drive died and the final possession ended with a Kiel fumble.

Navy had high hopes, but Notre Dame brushed them aside 38-0. Hunter was at tight end; Howard moved to split end. These changes invigorated the passing game to end up with 249 yards. Kiel scored from the one after a 34-yard strike to Howard. Howard scored on a reverse of 13 yards, with the key block made by Kiel. Hunter scored on a 27-yard pass from Kiel, and Kiel found Howard with a pass that he turned into a 52-yard touchdown and a 28-0 halftime score. In the second half, an Oliver field goal followed a Rudzinski fumble recovery, and Koegel threw a touchdown pass to Moriarty. Navy ran for 38 yards on the day.

Notre Dame registered a 35-3 win over Georgia Tech. Tech kicked a field goal to open, and later punted to the Irish seven. After losing yardage, Kiel dropped back into the end zone, found Howard, and threw to him at the 46. Howard completed the longest-ever pass play for Notre Dame, a 96-yard touchdown. Tech held the Fighting Irish for three series, but in the second quarter

Dave Duerson following the prescribed strength conditioning.

Kiel threw to Howard for a 58-yard score. In the third quarter, three wingback reverses sparked an 80-yard march and a 20-yard score by John Mosely. To start the last quarter, Crable intercepted a pass and returned it 33 yards to the Tech 26. Koegel passed to Mosely for a 14-yard tally. Duerson intercepted another pass, and Koegel lofted a 10-yard scoring pass to Tim Tripp.

Air Force fell next; Carter led the way with 156 yards on 27 runs and two touchdowns. Kiel ran for 31 yards, and Carter sped in from the nine. In the second quarter, Joe Johnson grabbed an Air Force fumble at their 19. Carter ran five times, scoring from the two, for the 14-0 halftime lead. No one scored in the third quarter, but Air Force started a drive that ended later with a touchdown run from the nine. Carter gained 41 yards, and Bell ran around right end for a 17-yard touchdown. With Howard double-teamed, Hunter shook loose for an 18-yard reception to set up Moriarty's five-yard touchdown. Freshman Mark Brooks scored from the 12 to wrap up the 35-7 win.

For the first time in more than 50 years, Penn State and Notre Dame met in the regular season. Penn State won 24-21, even with injured Curt Warner seeing very limited action. Jon Williams ran for 192 yards. They

took the kickoff to midfield, Williams ran for 39 yards, and for four more for the touchdown. Kiel answered with a 40-yard strike to Howard, and Carter scored on a one-yard dive. Duerson dropped a punt on his 12 and Penn State scored a touchdown seven plays later. The Nittany Lions made a field goal. Kiel threw a 17-yard score to Hunter. In the third period, Crable intercepted a pass at their 32 and ran it to the five. Kiel found Sweeney for a touchdown from the four. Penn State intercepted a pass at mid-field, and Blackledge scored after good running by Williams got him to the one. Notre Dame had the ball twice more but could not score.

Miami beat Notre Dame 37-15 and guaranteed the losing season. Bell scored for Notre Dame when he ran 98 yards with a kickoff return. Oliver hit a field goal, and Duerson ran 88 yards for a score on an interception. The rest was Notre Dame punting and Miami's Jim Kelly passing for touchdowns. Miami racked up 462 yards of offense to Notre Dame's 200. A pattern also emerged of the Fighting Irish defense tiring in the late stages of a game.

The season showed a Notre Dame team that could score fairly well, blow out weak teams, stay close to the stronger teams, and look bad too often. The rushing defense allowed 37 percent more yardage than in 1980, the running game declined too much for consistent ball control, but the passing game increased substantially with a maturing Kiel and the emergence of Howard. With this losing season, a more realistic view of Faust began to prevail. Crable and John Krimm earned All-America status.

1981 record: 5-6-0 (.454)
Record to date: 621-172-39 (.769)

1982

No one was more surprised by the 1981 results than Gerry Faust. Four close losses turned the season into ashes: Purdue, 15-14; FSU 19-14; USC, 14-7; and Penn State, 24-21. One field goal and three touchdowns distributed in these games would have made a 9-2 year. Four losses were to Top 20 teams. So Faust recruited a superb class, tried to delegate matters better, and hunkered down to do the extra work that might pay off.

The offense was talented: Hunter and Howard as receivers, Kiel in his junior campaign, Carter at tailback, and Moriarty at fullback. Allen Pinkett, a freshman, backed up Carter. The receiving corps plus tailbacks would be among the fastest in recent memory. The line

was massive, strong, and quick. The defensive line was an improved version, and had some very promising youngsters, such as Mike Gann, and in the wings Eric Dorsey. Bob Crable was gone, but Zavagnin, Rudzinski, and Naylor were back, with Mike Larkin also available (although injuries nagged his career). In the secondary, Toran and Duerson led the list. This appeared to be a marginally better defense than the 1981 group, although Duerson was vulnerable on deep throws.

The first night game at Notre Dame was played against Michigan. Nose guard Jon Autry welcomed them with a fumble recovery at their 12, and Mike Johnston booted a field goal 2:22 into the game. In the second quarter, Zavagnin picked up a loose ball, and Moriarty scored from the Michigan 24. The rest of the quarter was a punting clinic until the Fighting Irish broke loose on a 65-yard drive, capped by Johnston's 37-yard field goal with two seconds left in the half. Anthony Carter scored in the third quarter on a 72-yard punt return, but he was hurt later and taken out. Johnston kicked another field goal of 41 yards. Bell scored a touchdown from the 10. Michigan scored a field goal and a touchdown later for the 23-17 Irish victory. Notre Dame hammered a good Michigan defense for 419 yards of total offense.

Against Purdue, Moriarty scored a touchdown from the two, helped by his run of 30 yards and catches by Hunter and Howard. The Fighting Irish struck for

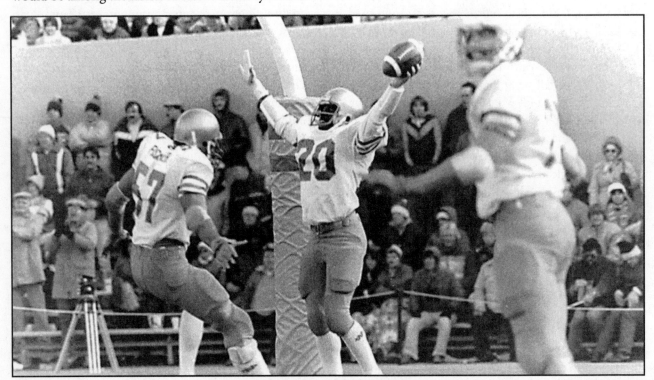

Allen Pinkett exults after a 76-yard TD burst to help beat Pitt in 1982.

Head coach Gerry Faust confers with All-American Tony Hunter in 1982 action.

yard touchdown pass. Moriarty broke loose on a 21-yard run and Mike Johnston kicked a 29-yard field goal. Miami took a 14-10 lead with a 79-yard touchdown pass play. Notre Dame booted a field goal, but another drive died at the Miami six. There were less than three minutes left. The defense stopped Miami and Notre Dame got the ball back on its 30. Kiel used a blend of runs and passes to get to the Miami 15 with 11 seconds remaining; Johnston kicked the winning field goal.

The modest winning streak of four games died with a last-second Arizona field goal in a 16-13 loss. Johnston kicked a 22-yard field goal on the opening drive, and Pinkett made a darting 25-yard touchdown run. Arizona came back in the third quarter with two Max Zendejas field goals, both from turnovers. Mike Golic fell on a loose ball at the Arizona 35, and Johnston converted with his ninth straight field goal. The Arizona return drive chewed up 79 yards and more than five minutes. They jammed it in from the one to tie, 13-13. The Notre Dame offense couldn't move, punted, and watched as Arizona's Zendejas booted a 49-yard field goal with no time on the clock.

Oregon tied the Fighting Irish, 13-13, holding Notre Dame to 80 rushing yards. Oregon fumbled at its 30; Pinkett ran for 24 yards and then scored from the six. The Ducks made a field goal in the third quarter. After an interception, Johnston made a 42-yard field goal for a 10-6 lead. The Ducks took the lead with a touchdown plunge from the one. Kiel used the remaining time in a good passing show to get to the Oregon 18. Three passes missed, and Johnston kicked the tying field goal with 11 seconds left.

The Fighting Irish beat Navy 27-10 on 328 yards of offense. In the first quarter, Johnston missed his first field goal in 14 tries. In the second quarter, Kiel led a drive with six completions in six throws, capped by a three-yard flip to Chris Smith for the touchdown. Navy was unable to move, and Johnston booted a 40-yard field goal. Jack Shields recovered a Middie fumble and Johnston kicked another field goal four plays later. In the third quarter, Navy trapped Kiel for a safety. A Zavagnin interception led to an 18-yard scoring pass to Moriarty. Fifteen seconds later, Duerson stole one and took it to their 12; Pinkett scored. Navy scored a touchdown late in the game. Pinkett led the rushers with 129 yards on 27 carries.

another score, a three-yard smash by Moriarty. Purdue marched 80 yards, finishing with a two-yard touchdown pass, and then tied the game with a five-yard touchdown pass. Notre Dame scored two more touchdowns to win: Carter from the six and the 10. Unfortunately, Greg Bell broke a leg. The offense gained 403 total yards. Notre Dame won 28-14.

Michigan State went down next, 11-3—the first game without a touchdown by either team since 1906. Gann registered a safety in the first quarter when he split the blockers and tackled an escaping Spartan quarterback in his end zone. Johnston scored field goals of 33, 29, and 42 yards. The Notre Dame defense manhandled the Spartan running game, allowing 19 yards for the day, but the Irish offense worked for only 280 total yards.

The Fighting Irish running defense allowed Miami only 67 yards on the ground to help in a 16-14 win. Gann grabbed a loose ball on their 12, and Kiel scored from the six. Miami ended a 74-yard drive with a one-

Irish DT Mike Gann and LB Mark Zavagnin against Michigan State.

Notre Dame beat the number-one team, Pitt, 31-16. The Panthers hit field goals of 48 and 22 yards in the opening quarter, answered in the second quarter by Johnston's 38-yard effort. Pitt was stopped, punted, and Kiel fired a 30-yard pass to Moriarty, who scored later from the three. Pitt QB and future NFL star Dan Marino led a 98-yard scoring drive in the third quarter. Carter threw a 54-yard touchdown pass to Howard. Pitt drove again for a 48-yard field goal. After an exchange of possessions, Pinkett bounced out of three tackles for a 76-yard touchdown run. Pinkett scored again with a seven-yard touchdown for Faust's best victory.

Standing 6-1-1, Notre Dame closed out the season with three losses. Against Penn State, Kiel was out with a shoulder injury. Ken Karcher led a first-quarter touchdown drive, throwing to Chris Smith for the score from the eight. Penn State's Todd Blackledge scored on a quarterback keeper from the one. A missed pitchout gave Penn State the ball and a field goal at the end of the half. In the third quarter, Pinkett ran 93 yards with a kickoff for a go-ahead touchdown. In the fourth quarter, Penn

State's Curt Warner scored with a 48-yard pass. On the kickoff, the Fighting Irish returner's knee touched at the Notre Dame one, and Pinkett was trapped for a safety. The Irish later missed a field goal, and Penn State made one for the 24-14 final score.

Air Force's 30-17 win was the low point. Their wishbone kept the defense befuddled for 366 yards. A Hunter fumble at the Notre Dame 35 led to a Marty Louthan score from the Notre Dame two; a Karcher pass was intercepted, and they scored again for a 14-0 lead. Air Force hit a field goal for a 17-0 halftime score. Notre Dame opened the new half with a field goal. Louthan saw the Irish linebackers split wide and took a quick snap for a 55-yard run. The Falcons scored from the three.

Two Falcon field goals in the fourth period kept the score distant. Jim O'Hara threw two late touchdowns for the Irish—a 28-yarder to Moriarty and a 55-yard score to Howard. The Falcons ran for 296 yards against Notre Dame. It was after this game that rumors circulated that Faust could be outcoached—that he was not a good field strategist.

Kiel was back for the USC game and led a 74-yard touchdown drive after USC missed a field goal. Moriarty slammed in from the two for the score. In the second quarter, Johnston kicked a 40-yard field goal, answered by a 35-yard Trojan effort. In the middle of the third

Tony Hunter, instant starter for the Irish in 1979, All-American in 1982.

quarter, Johnston booted a 47-yard field goal for a 13-3 lead, but USC came back in eight plays for a five-yard touchdown run. A Fighting Irish drive stalled; Karcher threw from a fake field goal play, but the touchdown dribbled off the receiver's fingers. So did the game—USC marched back and the referees signalled a touchdown although the ball was snugly in Kevin Griffith's hold at the Notre Dame two. The USC runner dove over the goal without the ball. The score stood as a 17-13 Irish loss.

Only the loss to Air Force was a blowout. Faust's Irish played well against Penn State, could have won the Arizona game, and should have beaten USC. Duerson, Hunter, and Zavagnin made All-America teams.

1982 record: 6-4-1 (.590)
Record to date: 627-176-40 (.767)

1983

After three excellent recruiting years, Faust had more of the best football prospects than any other school in the country. The Fighting Irish were big, fast, physical, and well-conditioned. But allegations were mounting, especially from a disgruntled former assistant coach in Colorado, that Faust did not understand how to use the hashmarks in play-calling and that he underestimated the need for total team speed. The players nitpicked about little things—the presence of Faust's youngest son in team meetings and too much praying by the head coach—revealing an unhappy state of affairs. Faust claimed, rightfully so, that the team had been "that close" (fingers about 1/8-inch apart) to outright success. Bert Metzger had said 50 years earlier that Rockne "coached in inches." If it took inches, they weren't coming under Faust often enough. There seemed to be some lurking, hidden flaw eating away at the team's potential for success.

The 1983 Fighting Irish squad was loaded with talent. Kiel, threatening to break some longstanding records, was the first four-year starter at quarterback since Dorais (though Steve Beuerlein would get the starting nod later in the season) Pinkett shattered Salmon's 1903 point total and Gladieux's total offense mark. Joe Howard was at split end. Mark Bavaro replaced Tony Hunter. The offensive line was the most massive on record, coming in just under 275 pounds (and with only 12 percent body fat). The defensive line was solid, led

by Gann and Mike Golic. Eric Dorsey and Jon Autry shared nose tackle. The linebackers were a quick, young group, but lacked a hammer. The secondary had Toran for only part of the year, and a good hitter in Joe Johnson.

The explosive offense showed in a 52-6 obliteration of Purdue. The offense clicked: a nine-yard touchdown pass, Kiel to Bell; Bell for a two-yard touchdown; a Johnston field goal of 31 yards after a Mike Golic fumble recovery; a Bell touchdown from the two after a Golic-caused interception; and a Tony Furjanic interception led to a Bavaro touchdown catch from the 17. At the half, Purdue's offense had been held to 33 yards. In the third quarter, a 61-yard pass to the Purdue one led to a Pinkett touchdown; Bell scored from the six after Tim Marshall picked up a fumble; Hiawatha Francisco gained 81 yards on nine carries and Byron Abraham tallied a three-yard touchdown. The Irish offense pounded Purdue for 522 yards—339 running and 183 passing.

Unfortunately, the momentum did not carry over to the Michigan State game. The Spartans, not a great team, played a great game to win 28-23. Bavaro scored on a two-yard pass from Kiel. Three plays later, MSU tied it with an 81-yard scoring pass after two Fighting Irish deep backs knocked each other out of the play. After trading punts, Bell sprinted 50 yards down the sidelines for a touchdown, but MSU intercepted a pass and scored two plays later. Five minutes later, Daryl Turner made a second touchdown catch. Kiel tied it 21-21 at the half with a 13-yard pass to Howard. MSU's defense fended off the Irish for the third quarter; the Spartans used an interception and 42-yard run to earn a five-yard touchdown. MSU gave up a safety with four seconds left. The Notre Dame offense, good for 446 yards, could not overcome four fumbles and three interceptions.

Miami, the eventual national champions, shut out Notre Dame 20-0. Two turnovers gave Miami easy first-half touchdowns. They kicked two second-half field goals. Three Fighting Irish turnovers were directly involved in the scoring. Notre Dame's offense outgained Miami's 335 yards to 296, but Miami's quick defense held Pinkett to 65 yards on 15 tries. It was bad enough that the players decided to hold a team-only meeting, choosing to have some fun and play for themselves.

It worked well enough for a 27-3 win over Colorado. With Steve Beuerlein at quarterback, Pinkett scored from the Colorado 10 on the opening drive. Colorado answered with a field goal, and then it was all Irish: a Johnston field goal after a 58-yard Beuerlein-to-Howard pass; a 31-yard Mark Brooks touchdown run; a Chris Smith 29-yard touchdown run; and a fourth-

Steve Beuerlein passed for 1,000-plus yards as a freshman.

quarter 39-yard field goal by Johnston. Notre Dame gained 494 total yards, 334 of it on the ground.

The Fighting Irish next beat South Carolina 30-6. After a 53-yard Pinkett run, Johnston booted a 49-yard field goal. Beuerlein fired a 29-yard touchdown to Chris Smith. Johnston hit a 27-yard field goal after an interception and a 41-yarder after a fumble recovery. Beuerlein made it 23-0 at the half with a 58-yard scoring pass to Pinkett. The Gamecocks converted a turnover into a touchdown. Pinkett wrapped it up with a two-yard touchdown near the end.

Army surrendered 42-0. Half of the scoring occurred in the first quarter: Mike Kovaleski intercepted a Cadet pass at their five, and Pinkett scored; Pinkett gained 45 yards on two runs, and Beuerlein hit Bavaro with a 22-yard scoring strike. After another punt, Pinkett broke three tackles on an 11-yard touchdown run. Army changed its coverages, and the passing game slowed down in the second quarter. In the second half, Pinkett ran twice for 29 yards and a touchdown; 235-pound Mark Brooks demolished Cadet tacklers on a six-yard score. Kiel led some freshmen on a 79-yard march in the fourth quarter and scored when he turned to handoff, saw no one, and ran over some Cadets for the touchdown.

Faust used every motivational trick he could muster for a win over USC (mired in NCAA-rules violations for academic malfeasances): he taped photos on the Irish lockers showing the "winning touchdown" in 1982 (USC runner in the end zone, ball several yards upfield, and referee calling touchdown); he played a Pat O'Brien rendition of a Rockne pep talk; and he reverted to green jerseys. It worked for a 27-6 victory. Pinkett rolled with an option pass to Bavaro that went for 59 yards to the USC 21. Pinkett scored on an 11-yard touchdown run. He struck from the nine to end a 55-yard drive. Naylor intercepted a Trojan pass and Johnston made a 30-yard field-goal try for the 17-0 halftime score. A wilting USC defense allowed huge chunks of yardage in the third quarter after another Naylor interception. Pinkett ran in from the 11. An interference call set up an easy touchdown for the Trojans. Johnston booted a 39-yard field goal for the final score. Pinkett gained 122 yards on 21 carries, tying Stone's record of four consecutive century games.

Pinkett broke the record the next week against Navy, as the Fighting Irish defense handled Navy star Napoleon McCallum. The first score followed Howard's 30-yard end around; Beuerlein fired a five-yard pass to Milt Jackson for the touchdown. Howard threw a touchdown to Jackson, a 29-yarder. Navy kicked two field goals in the second and third quarters, while its defense sparred with the Irish. Pinkett broke it open with a six-yard touchdown run. He fumbled and Navy scored. Pinkett wrapped it up with a touchdown from the Navy three for Notre Dame's 28-12 win.

Pittsburgh won a close game, 21-16. To open, Pitt scored two touchdowns, one on a 44-yard pass and the other on a 10-yard run after Pinkett fumbled deep in Notre Dame's territory. The Fighting Irish, on two long drives in the third quarter, settled for Johnston field goals. Pitt scored an 80-yard touchdown in the fourth quarter. Two Pitt interceptions killed Irish drives; too late, Kiel threw a touchdown pass to Pinkett of nine yards. Pitt gave up a safety to round out the scoring.

Penn State defeated Notre Dame 34-30. The Nittany Lions started the scoring by kicking a first-quarter field goal; Notre Dame hit one to start the second quarter. The Nittany Lions came back with an 80-yard drive, capped by an 11-yard scoring pass. Pinkett turned it on with great outside running to set up his own 17-yard touchdown. Paterno's team went ahead 13-10 with a field goal late in the half. In the third quarter, Beuerlein converted a third-down situation with a pass to Bavaro, and Pinkett tallied from the 16. Penn State scored a

46-yard touchdown on a screen pass to regain the lead. Starting from their six, the Fighting Irish drove 94 yards; Pinkett scored from the one. Penn State made a 29-yard scoring pass to go ahead again. Notre Dame marched 77 yards and Pinkett blasted in from the one. Penn State's quarterback ran for an eight-yard touchdown with 19 seconds left. Faust would be haunted by a quarterback sneak call at the end of the first half, which ended a drive at the Penn State one. In spite of 526 yards of offense, it was another Irish loss.

Air Force won a 23-22 squeaker. The Irish wasted a first-quarter drive. The Falcons hit a three-pointer in the second quarter, and intercepted a Kiel pass for a quick touchdown. Pinkett ran 41 yards and seven yards for a touchdown. In the third quarter, his 37-yard run set up Johnston's tying field goal from 37 yards out. Pinkett caught a 46-yard pass from Kiel to set up Milt Jackson's nine-yard touchdown catch. The conversion was blocked. Early in the fourth quarter, Kiel hit Howard for a 67-yard score, but the two-point conversion misfired. The Fighting Irish muffed an a interception, and the Falcons scored on a 48-yard Louthan pass. A clipping penalty negated Alonzo Jefferson's touchdown

Mike Kovaleski started as a LB as a freshman in 1983.

kickoff return. Stuck at their five, Notre Dame punted and gave up a touchdown on a long drive. The Falcons missed the point after—but Notre Dame was offside and Air Force made it on a replay. Kiel got the Irish within field-goal range, but the Falcons deflected the ball on the game's last play.

Despite its 6-5 record, Notre Dame accepted a bid to meet Boston College in the Liberty Bowl, a family affair in that its director was a Notre Dame grad. Boston College's Flutie threw a 13-yard touchdown pass to end their first drive, but they missed the point after. The Fighting Irish offense showed a new wrinkle—the backs were split farther apart and Smith ran more to confuse Boston's keys on Pinkett. Both men gained 100-plus yards as Notre Dame won 19-18. Notre Dame took the lead after Pinkett ended an 87-yard drive with a one-yard blast. After Gann blocked a Boston College punt, Kiel threw to Alvin Miller for a 13-yard score, but that point after was blocked. Pinkett jammed in from the three midway through the second quarter. Doug Flutie got two more scores on passes, but Boston College couldn't convert either two-point try.

Faust's offense in 1983 was 30 percent more productive (4,713 yards to 3,640 in 1982). Pinkett gained 1,394 yards as a sophomore. The Fighting Irish were still that 1/8-inch away from the pinnacle of college football, but excuses were wearing thin. Pinkett and Larry Williams made All-America teams.

1983 record: 7-5-0 (.583)
Record to date: 634-181-40 (.764)

1984

The key administrators were not giving Faust strong votes of confidence, so the overall mood under the Dome was not the best. Players, fans, and alumni were not fully supportive of Faust, either. Injuries would keynote the season, starting with Pinkett's ankle injury in spring drills. The offensive line on paper was a devastating group, but it did not work together as a unit. The backfield was in good shape: Beuerlein was a mature sophomore, All-American Pinkett, and fullbacks Smith and Brooks. Bavaro was all-world in the opinion of football enthusiasts, and Tim Brown, a freshman, was at flanker. The defensive line featured Gann and Wally Kleine (6-8, 278 pounds), the largest man there since Mike McCoy or Steve Niehaus. Mike Golic was

1984 Fighting Irish.

there, too. Injuries hit the linebackers hard. The deep backs were a bit small and green, but they had good speed. Francisco moved over there from the crowded tailback spot.

Purdue started the season (one that would see seven Irish opponents go to bowl games). Tim Brown fumbled the kickoff at the Notre Dame 12 and Purdue converted it to a 31-yard field goal. The Fighting Irish dominated the rest of the quarter with two long drives; Pinkett scored an 11-yard touchdown and Brooks went in from the three-yard line. Jim Everett closed the gap with a six-yard touchdown pass in the second quarter. A Purdue interception led to another field goal; Notre Dame led 14-13 at the half. Brooks fumbled on the Purdue three to begin the third quarter (one of five for the day). The Boilermakers marched 92 yards and kicked another field goal. Everett passed for a touchdown in the fourth quarter. Beuerlein hooked up with Milt Jackson on a 26-yard pass on the return drive, and Pinkett scored from the six. But a Beuerlein pass was picked off, dooming the Irish to a 23-21 opening loss. Everett completed 20 of 28 for 255 yards.

The Fighting Irish trailed Michigan State 17-0 at the end of the first quarter. MSU's first score, a 15-yard run, came through hard work and good passing. After an Irish fumble, the Spartans ran 23 yards for a touchdown; six seconds later Notre Dame fumbled again and MSU kicked a field goal. John Carney made a 42-yard field goal to make it 17-3 at the half. After stopping the Spartans in the third quarter, Beuerlein threw a 40-yard touchdown pass to Pinkett, but MSU hit a field goal for a 20-10 lead. The Fighting Irish scored on an eight-yard pass from Beuerlein to Jackson. Mike Haywood blocked an MSU punt and Beuerlein pitched to Pinkett for a five-yard touchdown. Notre Dame won, 24-20.

A Colorado team, saddened by the brain injury

to their great tight end Ed Reinhardt, lost 55-14. The Fighting Irish exploded for eight unanswered scores in their first 10 possessions. Pinkett scored with runs of one, four, and 13 yards; Alonzo Jefferson scored twice from the Buffalos's three; Milt Jackson caught a nine-yard touchdown pass from Beuerlein; Brooks ran for a nine-yard touchdown; and Notre Dame made two field goals. Gann and Greg Dingens grabbed fumbles, and Haywood intercepted a Colorado pass.

The Fighting Irish beat Missouri 16-14 when the Tigers missed a field goal at the end. The defense stopped Mizzou at the Notre Dame 1 on the first possession, but surrendered 433 yards on the day. The Tigers trapped Pinkett for a safety on Notre Dame's first play from scrimmage, but they fumbled three plays later and Carney kicked a field goal. After a Tiger punt, Beuerlein threw a 74-yard touchdown bomb to Reggie Ward, the longest of the season. Missouri punted and Carney kicked another field goal. In the third quarter, Missouri drove 76 yards, scoring on a 15-yard pass. Pat Ballage broke up their two-point try. The final Irish points, a 37-yard Carney field goal, followed a Gann hit and a Kleine fumble recovery. Mizzou intercepted a Beuerlein pass and scored, but failed to make their two-point try. Their last-minute field goal try just missed.

A disastrous mid-season slump started with a 31-13 loss to Miami and QB Bernie Kosar. Pinkett's ankle had been sore, and he was starting a slow decline. Notre Dame had a 10-7 halftime lead on a safety, a four-yard touchdown pass from Beuerlein to Jackson, and Jefferson's two-point conversion run. Early in the third quarter, John McCabe grabbed a Miami fumble, and Carney booted a 39-yard field goal. It was all Miami after that, as Alonzo Highsmith creamed the Irish defense for three short touchdowns on two runs and a pass. A field goal wrapped it up.

Beuerlein had bruised a shoulder and Pinkett was in pain; for the first time in history, Notre Dame lost a third consecutive game to a service academy when Air Force won 21-7. The Fighting Irish were at least 40 pounds bigger per player, just as fast, and would send at least a dozen men into the NFL, but Air Force's wishbone worked for 371 yards. The Falcons scored on runs of five, one, and five yards. Notre Dame's score came on a two-yard pass from Scott Grooms to Milt Jackson. The Falcons held Notre Dame to 90 yards rushing (Pinkett was limited to 76 yards with his ankle) and 117 yards passing. "Oust Faust" bumper stickers were seen around campus.

South Carolina beat Notre Dame in South Bend, 36-32, although it was an exciting game. The Fighting Irish gained 415 yards of offense, and Pinkett reached the 100-yard mark for the first time in the season. Following an Irish fumble, Allan Mitchell scored on a one-yard plunge. Notre Dame scored 17 points in the second quarter: Pinkett's six-yard touchdown run to crown an 80-yard drive, Bavaro's six-yard scoring pass from Beuerlein after a Troy Wilson interception, and Carney's 48-yard field goal. South Carolina scored a two-yard touchdown as well. In the third quarter, Mike Golic recovered a fumble, and Carney kicked a 47-yard field goal. Gann pulled in a loose ball, and Beuerlein scored with a six-yard pass from Pinkett. The two-point try failed. A 10-minute period in the last quarter spelled doom in spite of the 26-14 Irish lead. After an Irish punt, South Carolina drove 76 yards for a touchdown from the one. They scored another from the Irish 33 on a run. Another Fighting Irish fumble led to a four-yard score. Pinkett came back with a one-yard touchdown, but Beuerlein had his last pass intercepted.

This misery at home continued on the road as the Fighting Irish travelled to play the sixth-ranked LSU Tigers. Dalton Hilliard scored the first touchdown after a Fighting Irish fumble at midfield. They missed a field goal after an interception, and Notre Dame made the next four scores: Pinkett rammed in from the one to end a 79-yard drive, Carney kicked a 44-yard field goal, Pinkett ran in from the LSU two after a 48-yard march, and Carney kicked a 37-yard field goal. LSU intercepted a pass, and Hilliard ran 66 yards for a touchdown; Carney booted another field goal after a 15-play drive. The Fighting Irish defense stopped a fourth down play at their 28; Brooks pulverized some tacklers as he went in from the three. LSU scored late in the game for the 30-22 win. Pinkett picked up 166 yards on a record-tying 40 carries—in awful heat.

Mike Golic, 1984 defensive end.

The usual ho-hum game with Navy turned into a serious scare before Notre Dame won 18-17. Pinkett slashed in from the Navy one, but Navy used three turnovers for three scores, getting two touchdowns and a field goal to take the lead at 17-7. Pinkett charged back on an 83-yard march, hurtling in from the one. Howard grabbed a two-point pass from Beuerlein for a 17-15 deficit. With one minute to go, the Fighting Irish had to get Carney into field-goal range. After five plays, Carney made a 44-yarder with 14 seconds left.

Notre Dame annihilated Penn State, a team known for its defense, 44-7, staggering Paterno's team with 543 yards of offense. The teams traded touchdowns in the first quarter; Pinkett scored on a one-yard blast. Then the Fighting Irish attack decimated Penn State in the second quarter with 24 points: Pinkett stepped around right end for a 17-yard score, and ran for a 66-yard tally; Carney nailed a 28-yard field goal after an interception; Pinkett slipped in again from the Penn State one. Carney kicked two more, and Jefferson went in from the one to end it. Pinkett gained 195 yards on 34 runs, and Beuerlein completed 20 of 28 passes for 267 yards.

The last time the Fighting Irish beat USC in Los Angeles was in 1966. Notre Dame needed a win to clinch a bowl bid. It was a mudbath. USC committed six turnovers, five of them on lost center snaps. The first quarter was uneventful, except for players adjusting to an absence of footing. USC struck on a three-yard touchdown lob. Notre Dame marched 76 yards, with Tim Brown catching an 11-yard touchdown pass from Beuerlein. Rick DiBernardo fell on a loose ball at the USC 44 to set up a Pinkett touchdown from the Trojan three. In the second half, Carney kicked two field goals. The Fighting Irish won 19-7. Faust had his seven wins, as he had predicted in a *Sports Illustrated* article. The bowl bid followed, to meet SMU in the Aloha Bowl.

Notre Dame entered the game ranked 18 against 10th-ranked SMU, the college team with the most wins at that point in the decade. As it turned out, it was the best team money could buy and their program received the NCAA's death penalty not long after this game. SMU went up 14-0 on an eight-yard run and a 12-yard pass. Brown returned the second kickoff 53 yards, and Notre Dame scored in seven plays. Pinkett ran for a 10-yard gain and scored on a 17-yard pass from Beuerlein. More sharp passing led to Carney's career-best field goal of 51 yards. SMU kicked one as the half ended. In the third quarter, Brooks ran in from 11 yards out. Though injured, SMU's Reggie Dupard twice made fourth-down conversions that kept a drive alive. A quick whistle overturned an Irish fumble recovery, and SMU kicked a field goal. Dupard scored again, and Carney hit a 31-yard field goal. With Pinkett gone due to a shoulder separation, Beuerlein used the passing game; his last one went off Milt Jackson's fingertips, who was open in the end zone. SMU won 27-20.

The running game declined dramatically in 1984 due to injuries, changes in the line, and Pinkett's bad ankle early in the season. Only nine touchdowns were thrown, but 19 interceptions were taken away—a very bad ratio. Three straight home losses in mid-season soured the campaign, and continued mediocrity threatened to end Faust's tenure at Notre Dame. The All-Americans were Bavaro, Larry Williams, Mike Kelley, and Gann.

1984 record: 7-5-0 (.583)
Record to date: 641-186-40 (.762)

1985

This was the last year of Faust's contract. What kind of a season would he need to renew? Most observers put the minimum number of wins at eight, as well as a strong bowl showing. The sharks called for 9-10 wins. It would be difficult because talent was spread more evenly around the country. Faust's .554 won/loss percentage was more than 200 points below the school's average after nearly 100 years of football. The critics were not in a reasonable mood.

Pinkett and Beuerlein returned on offense, followed closely by Tim Brown. Frank Stams, a 6'4", 229-pound sophomore, was fullback. Milt Jackson left school due to an illness, so Alvin Miller and Tony Eason filled in at split end. Bavaro went on to pro ball; Tom Rehder, a 1984 defensive lineman at 6'7" and 243 pounds, replaced him. The entire starting offensive line was made up of seniors, and the hope was that they could avoid the crippling injuries suffered in 1984. There were no truly dominating players, but a steady group of linemen. The defensive line lost Mike Griffin early in the year and Eric Dorsey took over at nose tackle. Wally Kleine was the other known quantity. The linebackers had experience, but there were no dominant players. The same was true of the secondary, although Ballage was a hitter in the mold of Joe Johnson. Problems included getting production from the fullback spot, keeping the defensive line healthy, and avoiding the drive-killing errors of recent years.

The Fighting Irish met Michigan in Ann Arbor and once more scored only field goals, as they had in 1979; Michigan won, 20-12. Carney scored the Irish points on boots of 34, 41, 47, and 25 yards. Pinkett was contained, gaining 89 yards on 22 carries. Notre Dame led 9-3 when Alonzo Jefferson fumbled a kickoff (and was lost for the year with an injury). Michigan scored with a quarterback draw play, and then they scored just enough to put it out of reach while fending off Notre Dame. The loss revealed that the team was not sharp, especially in the line play that allowed six sacks.

Faust tried to improve morale by suiting up 117 players for a home game with Michigan State. The first half was a 7-7 affair. MSU's Lorenzo White scored from the Irish four. The defense held him in check after that,

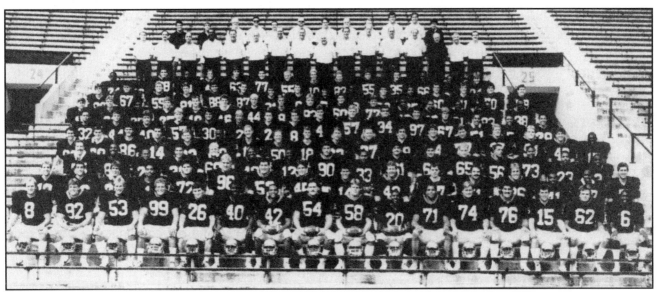

1985 Fighting Irish.

and Tony Eason scored a touchdown on a 17-yard pass from Beuerlein. In the second half, Tim Brown ran 93 yards on a kickoff return through the clutching Spartans for a touchdown. MSU hit a field goal. Brown victimized MSU on a 49-yard pass play and Pinkett made a two-yard touchdown—his 674th career run, a new record. Stams lurched in for a touchdown from the five for a 27-10 win. Pinkett earned 116 yards on 25 carries, the 16th time he had gone more than 100 yards.

Before the Purdue game, athletic director Gene Corrigan was seen having coffee with an old friend from Virginia, Lou Holtz, who was coach at Minnesota. Notre Dame lost 35-17. Beuerlein completed seven-of-25 passes for 88 yards, but Terry Andrysiak looked sharp in relief. Purdue's Jim Everett had a record 368 yards on 27-of-49 passes and touchdowns of 15, 12, and 32 yards to go with their one-yard touchdown run and a 30-yard interception return for a tally. Pinkett was targeted by the defense and gained only 45 yards on 21 tries. He scored in the fourth quarter on a three-yard run and Hiawatha Francisco scored from the Purdue one. Carney kicked a 48-yard field goal. With this loss, opponents were averaging nearly 350 yards per game against Notre Dame's defense.

After three straight losses to Air Force, the Fighting Irish allowed a 77-yard touchdown off a blocked field goal try for another loss. Air Force's wishbone gained 412 yards; quarterback Bart Weiss was uncanny in his decisions. Thirteen Irish penalties for 97 yards contributed to the 21-15 loss. Carney hit field goals of 28 and 33 yards, and Weiss completed an 80-yard drive with a 24-yard touchdown pass. Air Force kicked a field

goal, and Carney booted his third, a 40-yarder. In a display of poor planning and poise, with 18 seconds on the clock in the second quarter, Carney's field goal team tried to line up without a time out. They lost the race and were behind 10-9. DiBernardo recovered a fumble and Pinkett scored from the two, but Joel Williams dropped the two-point conversion pass. The Falcons made a field goal and scored on a blocked field goal play in the fourth quarter. They made the two-point play. Falcon linebacker Terry Maki not only deflected the field goal try but made 19 unassisted tackles and was in on 11 others for a total of 30. The Falcons became only the fourth team this century to defeat the Irish four times straight.

The Fighting Irish beat Army 24-10 in a good showing, lacking fumbles and drive-killing penalties. An early Army fumble led to Pernell Taylor's four-yard touchdown. On their next possession, Notre Dame scored with a 19-yard pass to Brown from Beuerlein. An Army 37-yard pass play and a lateral for four more yards made it 14-7 at the half. A Pinkett run in the second quarter put him atop all Irish runners with 3,472 yards. He iced the game with a leaping, twisting effort from the Army one, and Carney tacked on a field goal.

This up-down team demolished USC, 37-3. George Streeter put a tremendous hit on the opening kickoff returner and the Fighting Irish took over at the USC 12 after the Trojan left on a stretcher. Pinkett scored from the two. Beuerlein scored his first Notre Dame touchdown on a keeper from the USC six. Carney booted a 26-yard field goal in the second period. Andrysiak led the reserves on a 55-yard march, and Stams pounded in from the five. Carney hit another field goal for a 27-0 halftime lead. Faust had the green jerseys ready for the second half. The teams swapped field goals in the third period, and Andrysiak fired an eight-yard touchdown to Joel Williams in the last quarter. It had been nearly a quarter of a century since Notre Dame had beaten USC three straight times.

The Fighting Irish made Navy and McCallum the next victim. McCallum scored on a one-yard dive, but then Notre Dame amassed 544 yards of offense in a 41-17 rout. Andrysiak started and went into the record books with five straight completions, for 10 in a row from the previous games. Pinkett scored from the Navy two to tie. Pinkett's second tally was sparked by freshman Mark Green's 40-yard dash. Navy hit a field goal, and Pinkett ran 43 yards to set up Stams's one-yard touchdown. After a McCallum fumble, Andrysiak hit Reggie Ward for 17 yards, and Pinkett scored on a 29-yard run. In the fourth quarter, Tim Brown shredded the deep backs for a 48-yard touchdown pass play from Andrysiak. Francisco later scored on a 15-yard burst and Navy scored. Pinkett had his fourth 100-yard game against Navy—this time 161 yards on 27 runs. The Fighting Irish had never looked this good over a period of time under Faust.

They kept it up against Mississippi with a 37-14 victory. Andrysiak started, but Beuerlein went in after three listless possessions. Meanwhile, the Fighting Irish defense was manhandling the Rebels, allowing only five

first downs well into the third quarter and no scoring until halfway into the last period. Carney scored a 41-yard field goal in the first quarter. In the next period, Steve Lawrence ignited a drive with an interception and Pinkett closed it out with a two-yard touchdown run. Beuerlein followed that up with a 73-yard drive, featuring passes of 16 and 14 yards to Brown, the latter for a touchdown. At the half, Mississippi had minus-five yards passing. In the third quarter, Lawrence snatched a fumble in midair and ran 79 yards to the Rebels's five. Pinkett ran in from the two, his 52nd career touchdown. Andrysiak threw a 22-yard touchdown pass to Rehder. Mississippi worked for two touchdowns near the end and Corny Southall scored an eight-yard touchdown for the Irish.

A mudbath contributed to Penn State's 36-6 win, a game in which Notre Dame looked so bad that it had to seal Faust's fate. Penn State intercepted three passes, blocked a punt, and grabbed a fumbled kickoff for 19 points. An early Fighting Irish field goal try was a comedy of errors, and the Nittany Lions came back to score on a 21-yard pass. Their kicker booted three field goals, and they added a two-yard touchdown to make it 23-0 at the half. In the third quarter, an interception led directly to a quarterback sneak for another Penn State score. Yet another interception and a blocked Irish punt kept their kicker busy with two more field goals. Francisco averted a shutout with a two-yard touchdown run.

Linebacker Mike Stonebreaker.

1986

The Fighting Irish looked better against LSU, but the Tigers won 10-7, keeping the Irish from having an unblemished slate of home wins. It was the final nail—Faust resigned on Tuesday, November 26. Fighting Irish errors helped LSU: the Tigers blocked two Carney field goals, tipped another, and killed two Notre Dame drives with interceptions. Pinkett became the first Irish runner to have three consecutive 1,000-yard seasons, and surpassed the 4,000-yard mark by the end of the game. This was offset by LSU's passing game, which decimated the Irish secondary for 294 yards on 31-of-42 passes. Near the end of the game, Eric Dorsey stripped a Tiger runner of the ball, but a Beuerlein pass hit Brown in the chest and he dropped the ball. Brown scored earlier on an 18-yard end around. LSU scored with a 27-yard field goal, their kicker's first in college. In the fourth quarter, the LSU tailback jammed in a touchdown from the Irish two.

Faust told the press conference that he wanted the school to have a good chance in the recruiting season and that he wanted the seniors to have a "chance to go out in style against a real good opponent in Miami." Hiawatha Francisco observed that Faust "needs a rest." Everyone agreed that he was a nice guy and deserved better. Lou Holtz was named head coach on November 27.

A demoralized team lost one of the worst games Notre Dame ever played, 58-7, as Miami ran up the score. The Fighting Irish made every mistake possible. Pinkett asked his younger teammates to remember the humiliation. He scored his last touchdown on a three-yard play when Notre Dame was behind 20-0. Miami was still throwing long passes in a 21-point fourth quarter.

The Fighting Irish were outscored for the year, 234 to 230, but the two blowout losses made up most of that. They lost three close games. In his five years, Faust's teams lost 15 games by eight points or less, but won only eight such games. Pinkett was an All-American and Tim Scannell made second-team All-America. Faust left Notre Dame with a 30-26-1 record, a .535 percentage. He became the head coach at the University of Akron.

1985 record: 5-6-0 (.455)
Record to date: 646-192-40 (.758)

Lou Holtz had his work cut out for him, but that seemed to be the way he liked things. Perhaps the consummate overachiever, he was a fireman who took over programs on the downside and turned them around. Self-deprecating—a trait perhaps necessitated by his physical dimensions beside the football giants—he considered himself not very smart and not very impressive; however, tremendous competitive fires burned within, very much like Rockne. Holtz was a child during Leahy's glory years after the war, and he was impressed by the glamor and mystique of Notre Dame. His high school years were unimpressive, and he went to Kent State for college. He played two years as an undersized linebacker and left the game following injuries. But he was a keen student of the game and hung on in coaching circles, including a 1964 stint at South Carolina where Paul Dietzel kept him on the staff although he had to cut his pay to the bone. If not for that gesture of good faith, Holtz would not have gone on to be the head coach at William and Mary, then North Carolina State. He achieved greater distinction at Arkansas and Minnesota, but it was his work at William

Tim Brown, holder of many Notre Dame records.

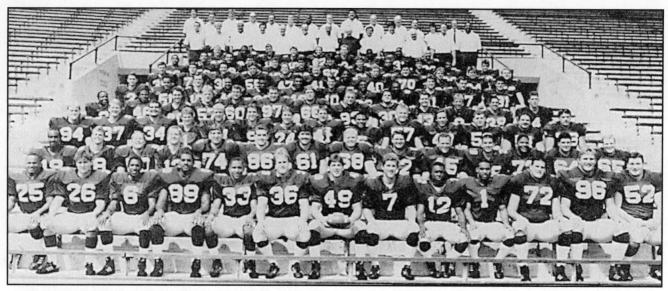

The 1986 Fighting Irish team.

and Mary that caught Gene Corrigan's attention, then with Virginia in the ACC. Corrigan was impressed with how much Holtz got out of his undermanned squads. What might he be able to do with a program that automatically interested the best players in the country? If he could win 116 games and lose only 65 at places that were relative backwaters, and do it without compromise, then he might be the man to turn the Notre Dame program around.

Holtz liked option football, but the Fighting Irish had never been an option team and the personnel showed it. The players had been recruited to fit a classic passing attack; he would have to make the best of it. For starters, he had Beuerlein and Tim Brown on offense. Beuerlein had a great arm, but he did not have the quick feet needed to make the option run as designed. The basic problem, however, was in front of Beuerlein: few of the 1985 starting linemen returned; Rehder moved from tight end to left tackle, and Heffern moved to right guard. Some others moved up and the coaches held their collective breaths. Pinkett was gone and sophomore Mark Green got the call. Frank Stams, the 1985 fullback, would be hurt and lost for the year; he would later switch to defense. Brown was a constant threat, but Holtz knew he was playing with a hand he had not dealt.

The defense was in slightly better shape. Faust left few down linemen and Banks was moved to try to rectify that. Wally Kleine provided some stability, but there was no depth behind him. The linebackers were led by Cedric Figaro and Mike Kovaleski (in his fourth year as a starter). The secondary had George Streeter in his sophomore year, a safety who was one of the hardest

hitters on record, and Steve Lawrence in his second year as a starter. Stan Smagala and Pat Terrell were in the wings. As a group, this was a fair bunch of players, but there was not a dominant force.

Hopes were high that Holtz would get the bugs ironed out, but most recognized that this was going to be a jury-rigged endeavor until Holtz had the personnel he preferred to coach.

The maiden outing was against Michigan. The Fighting Irish showed plenty of spunk and they did a little of everything—from the power "I" to the wishbone (a trait that Holtz would show in remaining years). Michigan prevailed 24-23, but they knew they had been in a game. Indeed, they lost everything but the score. The Fighting Irish handed it to them with numerous non-scoring drives, two fumbles inside the Michigan 20, an interception in the Michigan end zone, a missed point after, a narrowly missed 45-yard field goal, and tight end Joel Williams's apparent touchdown being ruled out of bounds. Beuerlein passed Theismann's career passing yardage as he hit 21-of-33 passes for 263 yards. Tim Brown scored on a three-yard run, but the Wolverines drove back for a Jamie Morris touchdown. Mark Green scored in the second quarter with a one-yard run, and Michigan booted a 23-yard field goal for the 14-10 halftime lead for the Irish. The Wolverines took command in the third period with two Morris touchdown runs, offset by a touchdown pass from Beuerlein to Williams—but Carney missed the point after. In the fourth quarter, Williams lost the touchdown reception on an out-of-bounds call. Carney kicked a 25-yard field goal for the final score. The Fighting Irish gained 455 yards of total offense against the third-ranked team in the country.

Michigan State won 20-15 in East Lansing. Again, Notre Dame prevailed in total offense, but most of the Irish yardage came on passing; only 82 yards were earned on the ground. Lorenzo White blasted Notre Dame for 147 yards on 41 carries. Carney kicked a 27-yard field goal, but the lead lasted about five minutes before the Spartans's Todd Krumm intercepted a Beuerlein pass and ran 44 yards for a touchdown. An MSU field goal ended the first-half scoring. The Spartans kicked another field goal in the third quarter, and Notre Dame answered with a 38-yard touchdown pass from Beuerlein to Williams. MSU took command in the fourth quarter with a five-play 80-yard drive, capped by a 40-yard touchdown pass. Anthony Johnson ran in from the five for the final Irish tally. Beuerlein's two tries for two-point conversions failed, as did his attempt at a quick-kick, which dribbled 19 yards. Krumm sealed the loss with an interception in

Cedric Figaro, three-year starter at LB.

the final moments. Although the interceptions looked like the problem, it was really the failure of the running game. Holtz wanted a ball-control offense built around successful running and long drives. If that worked, then the rested defense could dominate when they were on the field. The Irish defense held MSU to 13 points, but they didn't get the help they needed from the offense.

Purdue lost 41-9. The Fighting Irish hammered out five scoring drives before the Boilermakers could respond. The defense held Purdue's running game to 54 yards on 22 carries. It was a vindication of Holtz's plans. Pernell Taylor ran for a two-yard touchdown, Carney kicked a 42-yard field goal, Johnson went in from the two, Milt Jackson caught a 35-yard touchdown pass from Beuerlein, Carney kicked a 49-yard field goal, Johnson scored on a 13-yard burst, and Green ran in from the 27. The Irish gained 478 yards of offense, and Holtz had his first Notre Dame win.

Alabama stuck the Fighting Irish for a 28-10 loss. After four straight Irish wins, the Irish were going into a heated atmosphere, literally and figuratively. Notre Dame lost three interceptions and two of four fumbles. Beuerlein suffered a concussion when Cornelius Bennett blindsided him. The Irish gained 324 yards to Alabama's 354, but good drives were killed by turnovers. Tim Brown scored with an eight-yard pass from Beuerlein, and Carney added a 22-yard field goal. Two Crimson Tide scores came via long-distance routes—a 66-yard punt return and a 52-yard Mike Shula pass.

More mistakes combined to give Holtz a fourth loss—this time to Pitt, 10-9. Notre Dame almost had it won, but Pitt blocked a punt with less than three minutes to go and made a field goal with 1:25 left. The defense had to keep Notre Dame in the game; five sacks almost did the job, too. All Notre Dame scores came on Carney field goals, of 35, 48, and 20 yards. He missed a 38-yarder in the closing seconds. The defense held Pitt's runners to 23 yards on the day. Pitt's passing game, however, worked for 310 yards and set up a quarterback sneak for their touchdown. This loss made it the worst Fighting Irish start since the days under Kuharich in 1962, certainly not what Holtz wanted.

The Fighting Irish next faced Air Force and their troublesome wishbone. The Falcons were averaging nearly 30 points a game and amassing impressive yardage, but Notre Dame stopped them, 31-3. The defense disrupted Air Force's offensive flow. After an Air Force field goal, Notre Dame attacked with impunity: Tim Brown for a 95-yard kickoff touchdown return, a one-yard Beuerlein run, a 27-yard Carney field goal, a one-yard Taylor smash, and a one-yard Johnson plunge. The Irish gained 356 yards, with 237 yards on 61 runs.

The Fighting Irish beat Navy, 33-14. Beuerlein's 248 yards passing, on 15 of 22 for two touchdowns, made him the all-time offensive yardage leader for Notre Dame. Cedric Figaro led the defense, which held Navy in the first half to one yard rushing; Figaro also recovered his sixth fumble of the year, a new record. The Irish led 28-0 at halftime on a two-yard touchdown pass from Beuerlein to Williams, a 77-yard bomb from Beuerlein to Brown, an 11-yard Pernell Taylor touchdown blast, followed by his one-yard touchdown slam. Carney added a field goal in the third quarter from 19 yards out before Navy scored. The Irish tacked on a safety, and Navy scrapped for another touchdown on a 21-yard pass. Notre Dame had 480 yards of total offense to Navy's 211.

The Fighting Irish obliterated SMU 61-29. Tim Brown gained 235 offensive yards; the Irish used 10 running backs for 322 yards on the ground, scored on 11 of 15 possessions, and gained 615 yards of total offense. Freshman linebacker Mike Stonebreaker led the team with 10 tackles. Brown scored two touchdowns—a 15-yard run and an 84-yard strike from Beuerlein; Carney kicked four field goals—38, 40, 30, and 22 yards. Anthony Johnson, Pernell Taylor, Aaron Robb, and Andrysiak also scored touchdowns.

Against the third-ranked Nittany Lions, the Fighting Irish did everything but win the game. Critical errors nullified an otherwise stellar effort on both sides of the ball: on a first-and-goal play, the second-string tight end failed to get on the field, and Penn State stopped the ensuing play; Tim Brown lost a 97-yard kickoff return for a touchdown on a clipping call. Penn State won 24-19. The Fighting Irish offense gained 418 yards to Penn State's 314. Beuerlein was 24-of-39 throws for 311 yards and two touchdowns; Brown scored both on passes of 14 and eight yards. Carney hit field goals of 20 and 38 yards. The Irish had a final chance with less than four minutes to go. They drove to the Penn State six-yard line, but Paterno turned loose two blitzes for a loss and a sack; and a touchdown pass glanced off Joel Williams's fingertips. A fourth-down pass was completed short of the goal. Penn State went on to the national title.

Eighth-ranked LSU nipped the Fighting Irish 21-19. This loss guaranteed the first back-to-back losing

seasons for Notre Dame since 1888. In the first quarter, LSU gained 178 yards and two touchdowns before the Irish offense got its first snap in the 14th minute of the quarter. Tim Brown sandwiched a 96-yard kickoff return for a touchdown in between the LSU scores. Carney booted a 49-yard field goal, but LSU was whistled offside before the kick. Carney then missed a 44-yarder. In the second half, Carney added field goals in each quarter, and D'Juan Francisco caught a 14-yard touchdown pass from Andrysiak with less than four minutes to go in the game. LSU's defense held Notre Dame to 270 yards of total offense.

Notre Dame won its fourth consecutive game against USC on Carney's 19-yard field goal on the game's last play. His kick, set up by Tim Brown's 56-yard punt return, capped a come-from-behind win for the Fighting Irish, who went into the fourth quarter trailing 37-20. Carney's kick was his 21st field goal for the season, a new Irish record. Beuerlein ended his career with four touchdown passes and 18 of 27 passes for 285 yards. Mark Green gained 119 yards on 24 carries as the Irish amassed 490 yards of total offense. Beuerlein's touchdowns went to Andy Heck for five yards, to Braxston Banks for 22 and five yards, and to Milt Jackson for 42 yards. He threw another—to Trojan

Lou Holtz, the 25th Notre Dame head football coach.

Lou Brock, who went for a 58-yard touchdown. Carney added field goals of 33 and 32 yards, as Notre Dame slipped past USC 38-37.

The last games were a microcosm of the season—occasionally thrilling offense, sometimes suspect defense, costly errors, and the ability to score long-distance touchdowns. Offensive output increased 23 percent, mainly from a passing game that picked up 2,444 yards (53 percent of the total offense). Scoring increased from 230 points to 299, and opposition scoring fell, as did opposition yardage. The team had one of the worst starts on record, corrected itself in mid-season, and then lost two heartbreaking games to top-ranked teams. Holtz's squad lost five games by a total of 14 points. Tim Brown, Wally Kleine, and Cedric Figaro earned All-America honors.

1986 record: 5-6-0 (.454)
Record to date 651-198-40 (.754)

1987

Would those hopeful glimmers from 1986 become the glowing center of rekindled football proficiency in Holtz's second year, Notre Dame's centennial year for football? The all-time passing yardage and total offense leader, Beuerlein, had graduated. It would be difficult to replace the experience of any 39-game starter, but the problem was magnified when it was the quarterback. Terry Andrysiak was a possibility, and there was an unknown quantity—Tony Rice, who was more in the mold of an option quarterback, but who had not been able to practice his freshman year due to Proposition 48. Tim Brown was the Heisman front-runner. He finished 1986 ranked third nationally for all-purpose yardage production. He had to be more than a well-known diversionary figure. Veterans returned for the line, as did most of the backfield.

The defense was a different matter. Only one of the top seven tacklers returned; Figaro and Griffin missed spring ball. The kicking game would be with new players, and no one threatened to be confused with Carney. Wes Pritchett led a group of untried linebackers. Stonebreaker was lost for academic reasons. George Streeter and Brandy Wells headlined the secondary; Stan Smagala moved up and added blazing speed on the right corner. Mike Griffin overcame back surgery to lead a light, relatively untried defensive line. In sum, the team had a

solid core, but the question marks were major, especially at quarterback and the defense in general. At least the players knew the system better than before.

The Fighting Irish stunned Michigan 26-7 in Ann Arbor, Schembechler's first-ever home opener loss. The Irish were ready, and the Wolverines weren't. Notre Dame recovered three fumbles and made four interceptions. Andrysiak played well, completing 11 of 15 passes for 137 yards and an 11-yard touchdown pass to Brown, who made the catch in between two defenders. Braxston Banks ran in from the one to end a 55-yard drive. Freshman Ricky Watters ran 16 yards following an interception by Corny Southall to score. Ted Gradel had opened the scoring with a 44-yard field goal after Figaro's interception, and added a 38-yarder in the fourth quarter.

The Fighting Irish returned home to smash Michigan State 31-8. Tim Brown became the first player in college football history to return consecutive punts for touchdowns, both in the opening quarter, the first from 71 yards and the second from 66. On the opening kickoff, Spartan Blake Ezor took the kick, surveyed what was headed his way, and stepped back into his end zone for a safety. Notre Dame's defense recorded eight sacks, grabbed two fumbles, and made two interceptions. Linebacker Ned Bolcar recovered a fumble and made an interception; freshman Todd Lyght made the other interception. Andrysiak made nine-of-17 passes for 105 yards. Anthony Johnson went in from the MSU three for a third-quarter touchdown, and Gradel kicked field goals of 27 and 37 yards. Jeff Kunz tackled the Spartan quarterback for a safety to round out the Irish scoring. MSU's Andre Rison caught a 57-yard touchdown pass in the fourth quarter for MSU's lone score.

Purdue lost 44-20. The score is misleading, because the Fighting Irish took an early lead, lost it, and had to roar back. Notre Dame mounted a 10-0 lead in the first quarter on a 25-yard Gradel field goal and a six-yard Johnson touchdown. In the second quarter, Purdue scored 17 unanswered points with two touchdown passes and an 18-yard field goal. With only 36 seconds left in the half, Johnson scored from the Purdue one to make it 17-17. In the third quarter, Purdue kicked another field goal. Notre Dame took control as Johnson scored his third touchdown, from the Purdue eight, and Brown went 49 yards with an Andrysiak pass. In the fourth quarter, Gradel added two field goals of 28 and 44 yards, and Southall intercepted an errant pass and ran 57 yards for a touchdown. Holtz had used the fourth offensive

Tim Brown, Notre Dame's seventh Heisman Trophy winner.

series to showcase the option game with Tony Rice for a 74-yard march that ended in a Mark Green fumble. Notre Dame gained 476 yards of offense to Purdue's 263.

Unbeaten and ranked fourth, the Fighting Irish went to Pitt and lost a tough contest 30-22. Pitt led 27-0 at halftime, and Notre Dame lost their starting quarterback on the last play with a broken collarbone. The Panthers scored on a 31-yard pass, a 260-pound Craig Heyward touchdown from the Notre Dame one, a quarterback touchdown run from the two, and another Heyward run from the one. Tony Rice made his starting debut in the second half, hitting Brown with a 25-yard pass on his first play, and eventually scoring from the 16. In the final quarter, Braxston Banks slammed in from the one after Lyght blocked a punt, Pitt hit a 20-yard field goal, and Mark Green scurried in from the 17 before Brown scored a two-point conversion run. Pitt's defense held Notre Dame to 296 yards, and Heyward ran 42 times for 132 yards and two touchdowns. In addition to losing Andrysiak, Southall also went down with severe ligament damage (he was out for four games and was replaced by Brandy Wells).

The loss of Andrysiak made Holtz turn to the basics. Against Air Force, the Fighting Irish kept the ball on the ground for 69 time-consuming, energy-sapping rushes as Notre Dame gained a season-high 354 yards on the way to a 35-14 victory. The Irish were both bigger and faster than the Falcons. Their quarterback, Dee Dowis, however, turned in a good individual performance. Tony Rice garnered the first two touchdowns for Notre Dame, using his reading abilities to score from the one and the four in the first quarter. Air Force answered with a four-yard touchdown in the second quarter. Irish fullbacks took over the third quarter when both Anthony Johnson and Banks slammed in from the one for touchdowns. Dowis led a fourth-quarter drive of 78 yards, capped with a one-yard touchdown run, but Tim Brown returned a 57-yard punt for his third such touchdown of the season. He also lost a 74-yard touchdown reception on a penalty call.

Ranked tenth, the Fighting Irish defeated USC for the fifth straight time, 26-15. The running game was the deciding factor; Irish runners gained 351 yards. USC scored first, and quickly, on a nine-yard Rodney Peete pass. The next five scores were Notre Dame's: a 26-yard Gradel field goal, a Rice option for his own 26-yard touchdown, a five-yard Tim Brown run, and a 32-yard Gradel field goal with two seconds left in the first half. In the second half, Mark Green scored from the USC 11. The Trojans punched over a late touchdown against Irish reserves. Linebacker Ned Bolcar led an aroused Fighting Irish defense with 13 tackles, a fumble recovery, and an interception. With this win, there were no Trojan football players on that squad who had beaten Notre Dame.

Notre Dame beat Navy easily, 56-13. The Fighting Irish trampled the Middies with 630 yards of total offense (406 rushing and 224 passing). The defense played as if they could take the ball away with impunity—and did on several occasions. Holtz went into the fourth teams on both sides of the ball. Among the starters, Anthony Johnson scored four touchdowns on six carries. Mark Green made nine carries for 102 yards and a touchdown, and Tony Brooks ran 82 yards on 12 carries and had one touchdown. Tim Brown added to his Heisman-nominee laurels with a 51-yard touchdown catch from Kent Graham.

Boston College played Notre Dame on nearly even terms for much of the next game before the Fighting Irish ground game took command for a tough 32-25 victory.

Gradel opened with a 25-yard field goal following a Kent Graham strike to Brown for 58 yards. Boston College fired back with a drive and a three-yard touchdown pass. Gradel hit a 21-yard field goal in the last minute of the quarter. Boston College took the lead in the second quarter with a 31-yard field goal, and extended it with an 11-yard touchdown after an interception. In the third quarter, Green sprinted 33 yards for a touchdown. Boston College's Darren Flutie caught a 31-yard touchdown pass, and the Eagles made a two-point conversion for a 25-12 lead. Wes Pritchett recovered a fumble, and eight plays later Anthony Johnson boomed over a one-yard touchdown. The defense asserted itself the entire fourth quarter, and Boston was unable to move the sticks. Banks scored from the one and Green made eight consecutive runs, the last a two-yard touchdown. He led all runners with 152 yards and two touchdowns on 23 carries, as Notre Dame compiled 454 yards of total offense.

The Fighting Irish avenged the 1986 loss to Alabama, 37-6, amassing 465 yards of offense to the Crimson Tide's 185, the 11th-ranked team in the nation. Alabama scored a 34-yard field goal. Gradel kicked a career-best field goal of 49 yards. After an exchange of possessions, Rice ran 12 yards for a touchdown. Heck caught a three-yard touchdown pass from Rice, and Gradel hit a 21-yard field goal before Alabama scored its second one. Gradel boomed one more in the third quarter, from 22 yards, while the Irish defense kept Alabama from converting a third down the entire quarter. In the fourth quarter, Green and Watters ran 74 and 75 yards down the sideline stripe. Tim Brown gained 225 all-purpose yards and became the all-time career reception yardage leader for Notre Dame with 2,371 yards.

Ranked seventh, and with national championship thoughts, the Fighting Irish met Penn State and lost a thriller 21-20 when a two-point try fell short with 31 seconds left in the game. The Nittany Lions ran well and played gutsy defense, as did the Irish. Both teams gained 312 net yards, both lost a fumble, and both had an interception—although Penn State's interception killed an Irish scoring threat. Penn State followed up a fumble recovery of a punt for a 10-yard touchdown run. Rice ran 32 yards for a score. In the second quarter Blair Thomas scored on a one-yard run. Rice matched that with a touchdown from the 11. Penn State used an interference call to keep a drive alive, although it took

three runs to go the final three yards. Notre Dame used its last possession to get Johnson in close for a touchdown try from the one—he made it, but a good Penn State defense stopped Rice just short of the victory. It was Penn State's sixth win in the seven most recent games against the Irish and Notre Dame's 200th loss.

Notre Dame went to Miami to play its 900th game, losing 24-0. The offense did not materialize; Miami kept Notre Dame to 169 yards total and sacked Irish quarterbacks six times. Miami's Melvin Bratton scored two short touchdowns, Leonard Conley scored from the six, and a field goal rounded it out as the 'Canes gained 417 total yards.

With its 8-3 record, Notre Dame met Texas A&M in the Cotton Bowl. Texas A&M had all of its starting linebackers in the decade drafted by NFL teams. The Fighting Irish ground game was held to 74 yards on 36 runs, and 203 yards passing did not make up the difference as the Aggies amassed 407 yards of total offense. Tim Brown scored on a one-yard pass from Andrysiak, but the defense could not stop A&M after that. Gradel added a 36-yard field goal in the second quarter. The final score was 35-10 in favor of Texas A&M.

Total offense for the year, compared to 1986, fell off marginally but the passing game was more than 1,000 yards less and 10 fewer touchdowns. The running game carried the team to a more successful season since opponents gave up 2,773 yards, roughly 33 percent more yardage on the ground, a vindication of Holtz's theory of a ground game controlling the clock, keeping the opponent's offense off the field, and resting one's defense.

Clearly, the Irish had turned a major corner. Tim Brown became Notre Dame's seventh Heisman Trophy winner and was a consensus All-American. Others earning All-America honors were Chuck Lanza, Ned Bolcar, and Cedric Figaro.

1987 record: 8-4-0 (.666)
Record to date: 659-202-40 (.753)

1988

Although some fine players returned from the 1987 team, two matters were readily apparent: it would be hard to replace a Heisman winner who had been involved in so many phases of the offense, and the entire starting offensive line was gone. The defense was big, strong, fast, and especially talented in the linebacking corps and the secondary. Since 1987 had shown that Notre Dame could run like Holtz wanted (and all top rushers were back), the whole theory could now be applied—the controlling ground game augmented by a dominating defense. It looked good on paper.

Holtz made some personnel adjustments—Heck from tight end to tackle, and Watters to flanker. Only Tim Grunhard had more than 15 minutes of offensive line experience. The others had potential. Rice returned at quarterback, Green at tailback, and Johnson and Banks as fullbacks. Tony Brooks and Rodney Culver looked promising as running backs. Rice, however, did not have a major league arm; he had thrown for only one touchdown in 1987. However, he could move the ball on the ground as an option quarterback; he had a sense of when to keep or pitch and when to cut upfield or swing wide. Many defenders, frozen in indecision, would attest to his skills.

The defensive line was reworked and had some talented youngsters, especially Chris Zorich at nose tackle. Frank Stams had made the switch successfully to defensive end. The linebackers were among the best ever assembled at Notre Dame: Pritchett and Stonebreaker started and All-American Bolcar relieved them. Pat Terrell switched to free safety, and veterans Streeter, Smagala, and Lyght teamed with him to make this an impressive and very fast group.

Overall, the defense had to play great football in the early part of the season to give the offensive line time to jell as a unit, Watters had to grow into his new position, and Rice had to develop an improved passing game so that opponents would not be able to load up against the run. Holtz had been recruiting speed, speed, and more speed at virtually every position (no starter slower than 4.8). And in the speed department, the coaching staff took immediate notice of freshman Raghib Ismail, the fastest player ever in pads at Notre Dame.

Part of the plan worked well in the first quarter against Michigan. Watters returned a punt return for an 81-yard touchdown. But Rice came up empty on his first nine passes. The Fighting Irish ground game

worked well and the defense stopped a highly touted Michigan ground game. Notre Dame's new kicker, Reggie Ho booted a 31-yard field goal near the end of the first quarter, and added a 38-yarder in the second quarter before Wolverine Leroy Hoard ran in for a touchdown. Michigan took the lead in the third quarter on another short run. Ho kicked a 26-yard field goal in the fourth quarter, and Michigan booted a 49-yard field goal. With 1:13 left, Ho won the game with a 26-yard three-pointer. The Wolverines drove back, only to miss a field goal on the last play. The stats showed a glaring deficiency—only 40 yards on three completed passes, but the Irish won 19-17.

A similar pattern emerged as Notre Dame defeated Michigan State 20-3 in East Lansing. The Spartans kicked a 39-yard field goal but the Fighting Irish defense allowed only 89 yards on 35 carries. But Rice hit only two of nine throws for 50 yards. The Irish won it with good defense and running, especially in the second half when they dominated MSU with 195 yards on the ground. Mark Green led the runners with 125 yards on 21 carries, but Notre Dame lost both Banks and Johnson to injuries; Brooks took over. Ho kicked field goals of 31 and 22 yards, Rice made an eight-yard touchdown run, and Stonebreaker scored after an interception and 39-yard return.

The Fighting Irish defeated the Boilermakers 52-7. Touchdown passes from Rice to Derek Brown and Ismail showed that Holtz had been trying to improve this phase of the offense and also revealed the tremendous talent just waiting to get on the field. It was 42-0 at the half as Notre Dame gained 468 yards of total offense. The scoring was: Rice on a 38-yard touchdown run, Rice to Brown for an eight-yard touchdown, Rice to Ismail for a 54-yard strike, Green for a seven-yard touchdown scamper, Watters on a 66-yard punt return, Brooks with a 34-yard touchdown pass from Steve Belles, Billy Hackett for a 44-yard field goal in the third quarter, and Culver for a 36-yard touchdown in the fourth quarter.

Against Stanford, Rice tied a Fighting Irish record for consecutive completions (with the first four coming against Purdue) when he completed his first six of the game. He ended the day with 11 of 14 for 129 yards and one touchdown, as the Irish gained 467 total yards for a 42-14 victory. The ground game worked as diagrammed for 332 yards on 61 carries. Rice also ran well and handled the option game with flair; he scored the first touchdown on a 30-yard dash in the first quarter. Mark Green ran in from the one in the second quarter. Rice

Todd Lyght, starter at CB for 1988 National Champions.

and scored with a one-yard run. The Panthers booted another field goal, but Mark Green capped a drive with an eight-yard scoring run.

Perhaps the close score of the Pitt game was the result of Notre Dame being preoccupied with thoughts of undefeated Miami. Certainly Frank Stams had terrible recollections of the 58-7 defeat suffered by Notre Dame in his first season. Stams played his heart out in a 31-30 win over Miami The defense planned to pressure Miami's quarterback Steve Walsh to cut down his reading and reaction time—Stams was the man, rushing Walsh from the outside. He had Walsh on the run much of the day, tipped a pass that went to Terrell for an interception and a 60-yard touchdown, recovered a fumble, and caused a crucial fumble in the fourth quarter. Walsh still managed to pass for 248 yards in the first half and a 21-21 halftime score. Rice scored on a seven-yard run; Miami tied it in the second quarter on an eight-yard pass. On the next Fighting Irish drive, Ismail caught a 57-yard pass from Rice and Banks scored on a nine-yard pass. Stams tipped a Walsh pass and Terrell ran the interception in for a score. Walsh closed out the half with two touchdown passes. In the third quarter, Miami gambled with a fake punt that Notre Dame stopped and Pat Eilers scored from the two after a short drive. At the end of the third quarter, Jeff Alm intercepted a Walsh pass to lead to a Ho field goal and a 31-21 lead. Miami scored twice after that, but Terrell batted down a Walsh throw for a two-point conversion with 45 seconds left in the game. In spite of giving up 481 yards of offense to Miami, this all-out defensive effort must be counted among the top two or three in Irish football history.

Notre Dame sustained the intensity against Air Force, 41-13. The Falcons and their wishbone had been running for big yardage with impunity, but they hadn't played anyone like Zorich and Stonebreaker. The defense dismantled their wishbone in the first half, allowing only 39 yards. Air Force made it a game, however, trailing only 20-13 at the half. They scored first with a 22-yard field goal, but Mark Green scored from the seven after a 71-yard return march. The Falcons hit another field goal, but Notre Dame drove back and Rice made a touchdown from the four. Johnson tacked on a four-yard touchdown before Air Force tallied a three-yard score for the half. Irish speed and passing took over—Brooks scored on a 42-yard strike from Rice; Watters caught a 50-yard

ran for a two-point conversion to make it 14-0. Tony Brooks made a five-yard touchdown next. Stanford came back on a 68-yard drive, capped by a one-yard touchdown. Ismail took the kickoff back 35 yards, and Anthony Johnson later made a touchdown from the one. In the third quarter, Rice threw a three-yard touchdown pass to Derek Brown, but Stanford drove for a second touchdown. Rice scored on a six-yard run in the fourth quarter to wrap it up.

Notre Dame won a tough game 30-21 in Pittsburgh. Pitt took the early lead on a 42-yard touchdown pass. Rice led Notre Dame for a tally four plays later, due in part to Brooks's 52-yard run; Rice scored from the two. After a Pitt punt, the Fighting Irish drove 86 yards and Johnson scored from the one. Pitt scored a touchdown on a 33-yard pass. Ho kicked a 37-yard field goal seven plays later to make it 17-14 at halftime. Pitt tied it midway through the third quarter with a 44-yard field goal. Braxston Banks caught a 30-yard pass from Rice, option play bomb from Belles for a touchdown, and a 28-yard touchdown pass from Rice.

Notre Dame beat Navy 22-7. The defense held Navy to two first downs and 46 yards of total offense in the first half. In the first quarter, Rice followed up a Navy fumble with a 10-yard touchdown strike to Derek Brown. Culver scored on a 22-yard dash. Ho tacked on a 29-yard field goal to end the half. In the third quarter, Mihalko went in from the one to end a 67-yard opening drive, and then the offense disappeared for the rest of the day. The Navy quarterback shook loose for a 22-yard touchdown run near the end of the third quarter.

Holtz put the team through some serious self-examination and tough drills after the uninspired game with Navy. Notre Dame then demolished Rice 54-11. The Fighting Irish gained 439 yards of total offense. Holtz used 12 different running backs to generate 294 yards on the ground. The Owls scored first when they took the kickoff back 70 yards in 10 plays and kicked a 23-yard field goal. The next six scores were by Notre Dame: Ismail streaked 87 yards for a touchdown with the kickoff, Mark Green gained 40 yards to set up Johnson's two-yard touchdown, Johnson scored again from the two after Brown set it up with a 41-yard reception, Brooks scored from the one and Johnson made the two-point conversion, and Hackett kicked a 42-yard field goal. In the third quarter, Pritchett grabbed a fumble and Culver launched himself 19 yards for a touchdown. The Owls booted a 45-yard field goal, and Notre Dame scored three more: Ismail returned the kickoff 83 yards for a touchdown, Hackett kicked a 28-yard field goal, and Joe Jarosz ran for a six-yard touchdown after Steve Roddy recovered a fumble. The point after was blocked and a Rice player ran it back for two points, the first time this happened to Notre Dame under the new rules.

The 21-3 blitz of Penn State guaranteed Penn State its first losing season in half a century. The Nittany Lions played a gritty game but still gave up 502 yards of total offense. Rice made a 31-yard run to spark a drive that ended in his own two-yard touchdown. Green broke loose for a 22-yard touchdown run near the end of the half, but Penn State kicked a field goal on the last play of the period after a face mask penalty. In the third quarter, Ismail streaked down the sideline and Rice hit him with a pass for a 67-yard touchdown.

The game between the two top-rated teams in the country, Notre Dame and USC, took a back seat to Holtz's sending Watters and Brooks home for disciplinary reasons—they had been too late for team

meetings too often. He'd done it before at Arkansas in a bowl game, and other players picked up the slack for the upset win. Something like that would have to work in this case, because these players were important elements in the total package. The team pulled together and the offense clicked when it had to. On Notre Dame's first play from scrimmage from their own two, Rice went to Ismail for a 55-yard gain that would have been a touchdown had "Rocket" not lost his balance. On their next possession, Rice took an option play outside left and found himself and a running back isolated on a single defender. After the shake and bake, Rice streaked to a 65-yard score. Rodney Peete worked a careful drive in the second quarter to garner a one-yard touchdown by Scott Lockwood. A Fighting Irish possession got nowhere, and Peete fired a pass to his left but the receiver had fallen down. Smagala intercepted it, and took off down the right sideline, avoiding a USC lineman, to score on a 64-yard return just before the halftime gun. Peete hurt his shoulder attempting a tackle after Stams blindsided him. In essence, the game was over. In the third quarter, USC kicked a 26-yard field goal. In the fourth quarter, Green stepped in for a one-yard touchdown. Rice ran for 86 yards and passed for 91 more as the Irish won their sixth straight game over USC, 27-10. In an attempt to stir up victory juices, a clip from the 1964 USC upset win was shown on the Coliseum's big screen, but it was not to be.

Undefeated and ranked number one, the Fighting Irish went to Tempe, Arizona, to meet undefeated, third-ranked West Virginia in the Fiesta Bowl. The Mountaineers experienced a clinic in team speed, losing 34-21. Notre Dame had a perfect 12-0 season and an undisputed eighth national championship. The Irish jumped out to a 15-0 lead before a Notre Dame penalty gave West Virginia their initial first down—in the second quarter. Hackett kicked a career-best 45-yard field goal. After a futile possession by West Virginia, a Fighting Irish drive resulted in Johnson's one-yard touchdown. In the second quarter, Culver made a five-yard touchdown run before the Mountaineers tallied a 29-yard field goal. Ismail used his speed for a 29-yard pass play and an Irish touchdown. Another West Virginia field goal made it 23-6 at the half. In the third quarter, Ho kicked a 32-yard field goal after a Pat Terrell interception. West Virginia got their first touchdown on a 17-yard pass In the fourth quarter, Rice threw a three-yard touchdown pass to Frank Jacobs. The Mountaineers scored at the end. Notre Dame had 455 yards of total offense to the

Mountaineers's 282; Rice was named Offensive Player of the Game and Stams was named as his defensive counterpart.

For the year, the Irish averaged 108 more yards per game of total offense than did their opponents (388 to 280) and increased the offensive production in both rushing and passing. The average scoring differential increased from 13.3 in 1987 to 20.3, nearly a three-touchdown differential against the 1988 opponents. The 1988 team ran the ball superbly, passed it competently, and played excellent defense. Overall team speed made this a tough team to play against. It was probably among the top four or five teams ever produced under the Dome. Stams, Heck, and Stonebreaker were consensus All-Americans, while Zorich and Pritchett also earned All-America accolades.

1988 record: 12-0 (1.000)
Record to date: 671-202-40 (.756)

1989

Defending national champs quickly learn that every opponent wants to take their shot at dethroning them. The Fighting Irish also faced the prospect of playing five of their first six games on the road in 1989. Seven starters were gone, including Green and Heck on offense, and Stams, Streeter and Pritchett on defense. The team was in good shape at most spots, but the 1989 team would be unable to sneak up on people. It was an established fact that Holtz was a marvelous coach, had had four great recruiting classes, and that his brand of football worked at Notre Dame. The Fighting Irish under Holtz were no longer an unknown.

On offense, most skill position people returned, although there were several position changes. To get Ismail into the action, he took over at flanker; Watters replaced the departed Green at tailback, and Eilers went to split end. Rice was at quarterback—the first Irish quarterback since Hornung in 1956 to lead the team in rushing (121 carries for 700 yards and nine touchdowns in 1988). He had good runners behind him—Johnson, Culver, Watters, and Ismail. In Derek Brown and Ismail, he had two dominating players as his receivers. Four starting linemen returned to make this offensive unit a potentially more explosive one than the 1988 squad.

The defense was in good hands in important spots, especially among the linebackers and secondary.

The flanks on the line would have to be replaced, and filling Stams's shoes would be a tall order. That job fell to Scott Kowalkowski. Zorich and Alm returned, and Donn Grimm and Andre Jones joined Bolcar to make the linebackers a solid group. The deep backs added D'Juan Francisco to Lyght, Smagala, and Terrell for a fast, smart group.

The Fighting Irish and their 12-game winning streak met Virginia and their five-game streak in the Kickoff Classic at the Meadowlands. In the first half, the Irish defense dominated: the Cavaliers rushed for scant yardage and missed nine-of-12 passes with two interceptions, while Notre Dame rang up a 33-0 halftime score. Lyght's interception to end Virginia's first series led to a Watters's touchdown of two yards. The Cavaliers could not move the ball and Rice led the Irish back for a touchdown by Johnson from the one-yard line. Thirteen of the first 15 plays had been runs for the Irish. After another futile Cavalier possession, Rice fired to Ismail for a 52-yard advance, and Culver jetted over from the two for a 19-0 lead. At that point, the Cavaliers had two first downs. In the second quarter, another long drive, sparked by a Rice-to-Ismail pass for 24 yards, ended with a one-yard Johnson blast. Rice completed a 30-yard pass to Watters to set up a three-yard Rice touchdown. The third quarter passed uneventfully as Holtz looked over junior personnel. Virginia's Shawn Moore threw for two touchdowns in the fourth quarter before Hentrich

Mike Stonebreaker, 1988 consensus All-American.

Raghib Ismail, 1989 Consensus All-American.

hit a 32-yard field goal near the end of the game for the 36-13 final score. The Irish ran for 300 yards using 11 backs. Their total output for the day came to 477 yards to the Cavaliers's 231.

Notre Dame went to Ann Arbor to face an aroused Wolverine team and nearly 105,000 fans. Holtz played the game conservatively: Rice threw only twice and the Fighting Irish ground game ran 54 times for 213 yards. The Michigan line, as big as the Redskins's famous Hogs, was able to open holes for only 119 yards. Speed was the difference—"Rocket" Ismail returned two kickoffs for touchdowns, both in the second half, the first for 89 yards and the second for 92. The first Irish score came on the only pass completion for the day, a six-yarder from Rice to Johnson. Michigan threw a nine-yard touchdown, but the conversion kick failed. Ismail opened up the second half with his 89-yarder and Hentrich added a 30-yard field goal. In the fourth quarter, Elvis Grbac made his appearance as the Wolverine quarterback. He passed five- and four-yard touchdowns to make a game of it. In between, Ismail made his 92-yard touchdown. The 24-19 score was Holtz's third straight win over Schembechler, a first against him.

The Fighting Irish played their third game as the home opener and squeaked out a 21-13 win over Michigan State. Mistakes were the order of the day—two interceptions and a fumble by Rice helped an opportunistic MSU defense led by linebacker Percy Snow. Watters scored on a first-quarter two-yard run and a second-quarter 53-yarder that started, ironically, when Rice fumbled the snap. A fumble by Culver led to an MSU field goal and an interception let the Spartans have a second field goal for a 14-6 halftime score. The Spartans gained only 75 yards rushing for the day. In the third quarter, their second interception led to a 30-yard touchdown pass. Anthony Johnson made a one-yard touchdown blast, and the defense took over again. MSU would not kick to Ismail, with the inevitable tradeoff of good field position for Notre Dame.

Purdue turned the ball over eight times in a 40-7 Fighting Irish win. Holtz played the starting offense only into the second quarter, used 12 running backs, and amassed 530 yards. Johnson ran for a six-yard touchdown shortly after Smagala smothered a Purdue fumble. Rice added a four-yard touchdown a few minutes later for a 14-0 first-quarter lead. Tackle Jeff Alm intercepted a Purdue pass and used his 270 pounds to chug 16 yards for the third touchdown. Terrell intercepted a Purdue pass in his end zone. Rice found Derek Brown for a 38-yarder, and Johnson slammed in from the one. Watters wrapped up the first half scoring with another one-yard run. Hentrich hit two field goals in the fourth quarter, and Purdue finally found the end zone with a touchdown pass.

The Fighting Irish went to the Bay area and beat Stanford 27-17 for their 17th consecutive win—but it wasn't easy. Stanford, from the films, knew what to expect for a run defense. So they threw and kept throwing—Steve Smith heaved the ball 68 times, completing 39, for 282 yards and one touchdown. The Irish picked off three and two led to scores. Stanford kicked two field goals in the first quarter to take a 6-0 lead, but Rice optioned for a 38-yard gain to set up Johnson's seven-yard touchdown in the second quarter. After exchanging some punts, Francisco intercepted a wayward pass and Culver tallied a two-yard touchdown. Stanford scored a third-quarter touchdown on a two-yard pass and a two-point conversion run. They kicked to Ismail, who made a 66-yard runback. Johnson pounded in from the one to put Notre Dame in front again. Notre Dame booted two field goals to one for Stanford; Terrell's interception set up the second Irish field goal.

The undefeated Fighting Irish met undefeated Air Force. Notre Dame gained 149 yards to Air Force's 11 in the first quarter. It was 21-0 before Air Force moved the sticks. The defense crunched Air Force's wishbone so Air Force threw for 306 yards and two touchdowns. Johnson scored on a one-yard blast. Watters scored on a five-yard run. Ismail sped 56 yards on a punt return for a touchdown. The Falcons fired back with a 61-yard touchdown pass. The Irish bounced back, flashing Ismail out of the tailback spot, and Johnson caught a 27-yard touchdown from Rice. Air Force quarterback Dee Dowis hit a 26-yard touchdown pass, but Ismail closed out the half with a 24-yard touchdown run. Hentrich added two field goals, the second after a Lyght interception, and Air Force scored two fourth-quarter touchdowns on the ground for a 41-27 final score. The teams amassed 929 yards of offense on the day, 455 for Notre Dame and 474 for Air Force. Ismail accounted for 180 yards of all-purpose offense.

USC came to Notre Dame and nearly beat the Irish behind the leadership of Todd Marinovich, their lefty quarterback. The Fighting Irish pulled out the win, 28-24, but found themselves in the hole on two uncharacteristic fumbles by Ismail— one on the opening kickoff and the other on a punt at the end of the first quarter. USC converted both turnovers into touchdowns on Marinovich passes. Ismail returned a kickoff 58 yards to set up Rice's seven-yard touchdown run. The Trojans hit a 28-yard field goal in the second quarter for a 17-7 lead. Rice led a good drive in the third quarter, running 24 yards to set up Watters's two-yard touchdown. In the fourth quarter, on a third-down play at the USC 35, Johnson got the call for a fullback dive but he broke it for the score. USC drove back on the next series to tally

Tony Rice, 1989 All-American and tri-captain.

Chris Zorich, 1989 consensus All-American.

on a 16-yard pass. Rice led a careful 80-yard drive to win the game, capped by his own 15-yard touchdown burst. Marinovich tried a long pass for the win, but it fell incomplete.

Pitt came to Notre Dame undefeated and ranked seventh, but went home sadder and wiser after a 45-7 drubbing. They scored on an eight-yard pass, and then the roof fell in on them. In the first half, Notre Dame scored a safety when Pitt's quarterback slipped in the end zone; an Ismail-led drive ended in a one-yard Culver touchdown; and Terrell returned an interception for a 54-yard touchdown. In the second half, Watters scored from the two after Kowalkowski recovered a fumble; Ismail ran for a 50-yard touchdown; Culver scored from the one after a Francisco interception; and Steve Belles ran 13 yards for a touchdown after a Lyght interception. The Irish kept it simple with 57 rushing tries for 310 yards, a 5.4-yard average.

Navy succumbed 41-0 as Holtz kept the Fighting Irish on the ground, this time with 60 runs by 13 ball carriers for 414 yards, an unstoppable 6.9-yard average. The victory tied the Irish record, set under Leahy, of 21 consecutive wins. It was Holtz's 150th career win. Watters led with nine carries for 134 yards, including

a 43-yard run on the game's first play from scrimmage and a second-quarter touchdown run of 48 yards. His first long gain set up a Rice touchdown run of six yards. Ismail broke loose for a 30-yard gain, but suffered a groin pull and sat out the rest of the game. Culver scored from the 11. Billy Hackett followed Watters's touchdown with a 27-yard field goal to make it 24-0 at the half. He added a 39-yard field goal in the third quarter, and reserves Dorsey Levens and Ted McNamara wrapped up the shutout with touchdown runs of two yards and one yard, respectively, in the fourth quarter.

SMU, who was trying to rebuild its program after their NCAA death penalty, was not much of a challenge. SMU lost a half yard on each of 13 rushing tries for minus-seven yards for the day. They did complete 30 of 59 passes for 206 yards. Holtz had told his charges to run at will (54 carries for 362 yards) but not to score unnecessarily, so the final was 59-6. The win set a new record for Notre Dame with 22 consecutive victories. The scorers were: Watters for a 35-yard touchdown, Pete Graham on a one-yard sneak, Andre Jones for two points on a blocked point after SMU had scored on a five-yard pass), Hackett with a 34-yard field goal, Watters on a 97-yard punt return, Johnson for a four-yard touchdown burst, a safety when a reserve SMU quarterback stepped out of his end zone, and Walter Boyd for a 14-yard touchdown. In the third quarter, reserve Rusty Setzer added a touchdown from the SMU two, and Hackett kicked a 32-yard field goal. In the fourth quarter, Rick Mirer threw a 33-yard pass to Mihalko to set up Rod West's one-yard touchdown. Ismail gained 135 all-purpose yards on 10 attempts.

Penn State fell victim to Notre Dame's ground game, 34-23. The Irish showcased their runners 71 times for 425 yards, a record against Penn State. Rice and Watters both ran for more than 100 yards, and Ismail was just behind them. Penn State's defense simply wilted against the insistent Notre Dame ground game. Blair Thomas scored midway into the first quarter on a two-yard blast. Rice used up much of the rest of the quarter to lead a drive capped by his five-yard touchdown burst. Penn State earned a field goal, but Notre Dame took the lead with two touchdown drives, the first completed by Watters with a 12-yard run and the second by Johnson's one-yard slam. The Irish defense forced a fumble, which Smagala recovered at the Penn State 14; Rice took it in from the one moments later. Thomas, who made 133 yards on 26 runs, scored from the Irish three. Hackett booted two field goals in the last quarter and Penn State got a five-yard touchdown pass.

The winning streak ended at 23 games against Miami, 27-10. Miami did not break, not even on a third-and-44, which they converted just moments after they had recovered their own fumble that had passed through the hands of Notre Dame defenseman Devon McDonald. Those two plays turned the tide. Miami scored for a 24-10 lead in the third quarter, and Notre Dame never recovered. They had come back from a 10-0 first-quarter deficit when Hackett kicked a 22-yard field goal and Bolcar intercepted a Craig Erickson pass and ran 49 yards for a touchdown. But the Irish offense was bottled up all day by an aroused, speedy Miami defense; Miami allowed only 142 yards on 45 carries, about three yards per run below the average of previous games. Rice completed seven of 15 for 106 yards, and the kick return game was also held in check.

Notre Dame rebounded to drill top-ranked Colorado 21-6 in the Orange Bowl. Having beaten nine bowl teams and winning 12 games, Holtz staked a claim on the national crown, but Notre Dame came in number two when the votes were counted (Miami was number one). The first half was scoreless. Colorado's star running back, Eric Bieniemy, broke loose from the Irish 35 and threatened to go all the way, but he dropped the ball at the Irish 18. In the third quarter, the Fighting Irish scored in seven plays, with Johnson drilling in from the two for the touchdown. Ismail made a 35-yard touchdown on a reverse. Colorado answered with a 39-yard touchdown run by Darian Hagan. In the fourth quarter, Johnson led a long, time-consuming drive and scored from the seven for the final 21-6 score.

The Irish improved their ground game by nearly 20 percent, and scoring went from 359 points in 1988 to 406. The passing game produced about the same yardage, but the Irish scored primarily on the ground in 1989, a testament to their faith in the offensive line. Lyght and Zorich were consensus All-Americans, and Rice, Ismail, Bolcar, Alm, and Grunhard also won All-America honors.

1989 record: 12-1-0 (.923)
Record to date: 683-203-40 (.759)

1990-1999

1990

When Tony Rice graduated, the Fighting Irish lost a quarterback who had directed them to a 28-3 record as a starter. A glance down the chart located two sophomores—Rick Mirer and Jake Kelchner. Kelchner went down with a broken right collarbone in the first quarter of the spring game. Mirer had passed for 3,973 yards and 30 touchdowns in his senior year at Goshen, Indiana. As a reserve behind Rice, he got mop-up duties in eight games in 1989, carrying 12 times for 32 yards and completing 15 of 30 passes for 180 yards and one interception. Holtz tried not to put too much pressure on him, but Mirer had been assigned the No. 3 jersey, Montana's old number. In Mirer, Holtz had a quarterback closer to the classic dropback mold of Montana or Beuerlein rather than the option running dimension Rice had provided.

Two starters returned to the interior offensive line, and the backfield boasted Watters, Tony Brooks (back after a year of working on academics), Culver, Ismail, Mihalko, Dorsey Levens, and Jerome Bettis. The receivers were led by Derek Brown and Ismail. This group had more than enough speed and good size while the line had fine size and mobility. Mike Heldt, Tim Ryan, and Mirko Jurkovic led the workers in the trenches.

The defense had some returning stalwarts, notably consensus All-Americans Zorich and Lyght. Stonebreaker and George Williams returned from a year away from football. The linebackers also included Kowalkowski and Demetrius Dubose.

The team's strength was in its runners and receivers on offense, and the nose tackle and linebacker spots on defense. Lyght, in the secondary, was a proven All-American, but the rest of the deep backs were untested. The offensive line had to mature to provide

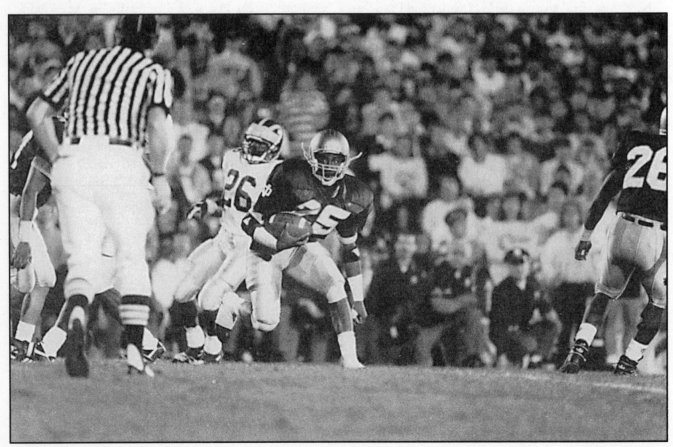

Raghib Ismail vs. Michigan.

the sophomore quarterback enough time to read the complicated defenses.

Michigan provided the first test, and the Fighting Irish almost flunked. Elvis Grbac was back, assisted by Jon Vaughan as a running back. Vaughan ran 22 times for 201 yards. The Irish won 28-24, their fourth straight win over the Wolverines, when Mirer hit Adrian Jarrell with an 18-yard touchdown pass inside the two-minute mark of the fourth quarter. The sophomore opened the scoring with a two-yard run, capping a short drive after Greg Davis recovered a Michigan fumble. The Wolverines kicked a field goal, and Tony Brooks ran for a two-yard touchdown to end a long answering drive. Future Heisman winner Desmond Howard tallied in the second quarter on a 44-yard pass from Grbac; the score at the half was 14-10. Michigan owned the third quarter; they put together a long drive that ended in a one-yard touchdown run, and Howard scored on a 25-yard pass from Grbac following a Tony Brooks fumble. Notre Dame won the game in the fourth quarter with two long drives, the first capped by Culver's one-yard run and the Mirer-to-Jarrell pass for the second. Howard returned a kickoff to the Wolverines' 41. Reggie Brooks cinched it with an interception of a Grbac pass. The Wolverines both ran and passed for more yardage than did the Irish; the difference was the Irish converted an early fumble into a touchdown and then stopped Michigan's final drive with an interception. In between, there were plenty of scares for the Irish faithful.

Michigan State took Notre Dame all the way, only to lose 20-19; the offense brought Notre Dame back from a 19-7 deficit. Watters dashed in from the five late in the first quarter and showed the Spartans to be a very determined group. They played the best quarter of defense to be seen in the whole season and stopped Notre Dame without a first down in the second quarter. Meanwhile, the Spartans scored 12 points on a 43-yard field goal, a safety on a blocked punt, and a touchdown from the one, seven plays after the free kick. Tico Duckett scored a one-yard touchdown after the Fighting Irish failed to convert a fourth-down try. The offense struck in the fourth quarter—first on a Ricky Watters touchdown from the one; Stonebreaker grabbed an interception but the team stalled, and then scored on a Culver smash from the two. A Mirer pass deflected off the pads of a Spartan and Adrian Jarrell grabbed it at the MSU two. The tight score was reflected in the teams' yardage figures—311 for Notre Dame, 313 for MSU.

An assertive Fighting Irish defense, sparked by Kowalkowski (one fumble caused, one recovered, and constant pass-rush pressure) led Notre Dame to a 37-11 win over Purdue. The offense sputtered to two Hentrich field goals in the first quarter, answered by a Purdue field goal. In the second quarter, Notre Dame scored 21 unanswered points. Mirer tallied from the 12 on a run to end a five-play, 66-yard drive. After Zorich recovered a fumble caused by Kowalkowski, Ismail ran 64 yards on a reverse for another touchdown—the drive's only play. Then a 15-play drive helped kill the clock, capped by Culver's two-yard score. In the third quarter, Kowalkowski grabbed a Purdue fumble at their 33; Shawn Davis later scored from the one. Hentrich added his third field goal as Notre Dame dominated much of the game for the win, allowing a late Purdue touchdown and two-point conversion. Two passes took up most of that drive, a 58-yarder and a 37-yard scoring throw from Eric Hunter to Curtis McManus. The Irish ground game made 65 carries for 362 yards.

Three disastrous fumbles in the kicking game led to Stanford's 36-31 upset win. Ismail was out of the game with a deep thigh injury, and his replacements, Watters and Jarrell, dropped two and one punts, respectively. Stanford scored following two of those turnovers. Although Tommy Vardell scored four Stanford touchdowns, it took a Mirer pass slipping off Derek Brown's fingertips in the end zone on the game's last play to seal Notre Dame's fate. The Fighting Irish had a 24-7 lead in the second quarter on a Mirer touchdown from the one in the first quarter, a Hentrich field goal of 29 yards, an 11-yard Tony Smith touchdown reception from Mirer, and another Mirer to Smith touchdown from 15 yards. Good defense set up Smith's scores; Devon McDonald grabbed a fumble to set up the first and Rod Smith blocked a punt to create the second opportunity. Vardell cut into that lead with a one-yarder for a 24-15 halftime score. He did it again halfway into the third quarter, but Culver answered with a one-yard bolt Vardell scored at the end of the third quarter from the one, and once again in the fourth quarter, for the final 36-31 score. Mirer moved the Irish 47 yards in the last 30 seconds, only to see the touchdown pass fall to the ground as Brown stretched to bring it in. Irish mistakes built Stanford's confidence, and tough inside running by Vardell (13 carries for 37 yards but four touchdowns) caused Notre Dame to lose its number-one ranking.

Air Force lost 57-27, due in large part to breakdowns in their punting game. Mihalko blocked consecutive punts that led to touchdowns. Their punter, perhaps a bit disoriented, was tackled for a safety as well. The Fighting Irish gained 542 yards of total offense and Mirer had an

Quarterback Rick Mirer.

excellent passing day, hitting 11 of 15 for 253 yards and two touchdowns The Irish scores were: a Hentrich field goal of 28 yards, two Dorsey Levens touchdowns of two and five yards, an Ismail touchdown of 52 yards on a Mirer pass, and a Mirer to Brown touchdown pass of five yards for a 31-7 halftime score. Mihalko's punt blocks led to Levens's first touchdown and Brown's touchdown. In the third quarter, Lamar Guillory tackled the punter for a safety and Hentrich added a 26-yard field goal. The Irish added three touchdowns in the fourth quarter to two for Air Force—Watters slammed in from the four and the one and Jeff Burris scored from the one. Ismail had six catches for 172 yards.

Now ranked sixth, the Fighting Irish faced Miami, also once beaten and ranked second. When the cheering subsided, Notre Dame had won 29-20. Defense did it with two interceptions, one in the fourth quarter, and two crucial fumbles recovered in the fourth quarter. The first quarter was a 10-10 deadlock: Miami recovered an Irish fumble and drove 25 yards for a touchdown. Hentrich kicked a 25-yard field goal. Miami's Huerta booted a 23-yard field goal, and Ismail zoomed 94 yards with the kickoff for a touchdown. Greg Davis intercepted a pass and Hentrich boomed a 44-yard field goal. Miami replied with an 80-yard drive and a one-yard touchdown by quarterback Erickson. Hentrich

hit his third field goal with four minutes left in the half; Miami led 17-16. In the third quarter, Hentrich entered the record books when he hit two more field goals of 36 and 35 yards. George Williams recovered a Miami fumble to set up the first kick. The defense played inspired football to hold Miami to minus-eight yards rushing for the third quarter. Miami closed the gap to two points when Huerta kicked a 25-yard field goal. The Irish dominated the rest of the quarter. Mirer capped it with a pass play, which had literally been invented at the team breakfast that morning, for a 21-yard touchdown to Culver, who dragged a Miami deep back the last five yards into the end zone. The 'Canes fumbled at the Irish 23, and Stonebreaker recovered the loose ball with 4:44 remaining.

Emotionally drained, the Irish stumbled to a 31-22 win over Pitt in Pittsburgh; Zorich hurt a leg in the third quarter. Pitt's quarterback, Alex Van Pelt, hit 37 of 51 passes for 384 yards and two touchdowns, not enough to offset their 84-yard ground game. Devon McDonald recovered a Pitt fumble at their 16; Brooks scored from the two four plays later. Lyght made an interception in the Irish end zone; Brooks capped it with a 28-yard touchdown blast. Pitt scored on a nine-yard pass near the end of the first half. In the third quarter, Hentrich kicked a 39-yard field goal. Ismail, early in the fourth quarter, made a 76-yard touchdown run from scrimmage, the longest such run in his career. Pitt's passing game set up a one-yard touchdown plunge. They tried an onside kick, but Tony Brooks smothered it. Six plays later, aided by an Ismail run of 18 yards, Mirer ran in from the one. With under a minute to go, Van Pelt threw his second touchdown pass.

Notre Dame tangled with Navy in a surprising 52-31 win, one that saw the teams gain 859 yards of combined offense. The Fighting Irish were taken aback when Navy opened up in a wishbone, having prepared for a wide-open passing attack. Jerome Bettis smashed over from the one near the end of the first quarter. Navy tied it, using a 44-yard pass from quarterback Alton Grizzard to set up a one-yard score. Hentrich kicked a 31-yard field goal to end the next series. Navy tied with 14 seconds left in the half with a 27-yard field goal. Notre Dame scored 42 second-half points: Culver for a seven-yard touchdown on the opening drive, Watters on a two-yard slam, and Mirer on a 30-yard touchdown sprint. An Irish fumble at their 19 led to Grizzard scoring on a six-yard run. In the fourth quarter, Mirer hit Ismail for a 21-yard gain and Brooks ran the last two yards to make it 38-17. Navy pulled to within two touchdowns on a 19-yard touchdown pass by Grizzard. Mirer floated a pass to Ismail, who made it a 54-yard touchdown. Grizzard fired a seven-yard touchdown pass. Navy tried an onside kick; Lyght recovered just as two Middies zoomed past him. Looking up and seeing no one, he ran 53 yards for his first touchdown.

Again ranked number one, the Fighting Irish were still not favored to beat Tennessee on the Volunteers' home turf. In the first quarter, Tennessee bracketed an Irish touchdown with field goals. The Notre Dame score came on a 41-yard pass from Mirer to Culver. The second quarter was slow-paced, and Hentrich kicked a 26-yard field goal. Tennessee took the lead in the third quarter on a Carl Pickens circus catch for a 33-yard gain, which set up a 10-yard scoring run. Watters took a handoff and hit the middle, broke an arm tackle and ran past the secondary, all of whom took bad angles to catch him. Tennessee's Andy Kelly threw to Alvin Harper for a 32-yard score, and the Volunteers led 20-17. Hentrich tied it six seconds into the fourth quarter with a 20-yard field goal. Tennessee mounted a 12-play drive that netted a 45-yard field goal. After an exchange of possessions, Mirer floated one to Culver who broke it for a 20-yard gain; Watters scored from the 10. Donn Grimm intercepted a pass, and Ismail rocketed for a touchdown

on a 44-yard reverse play. Tennessee came back for a 23-yard touchdown pass from Kelly with less than two minutes to play. The Volunteers stopped Notre Dame from running out the clock, but Rod Smith intercepted Kelly to secure the win. The Irish won 34-29, but Kelly had riddled the secondary for 399 passing yards.

Looking at Penn State, Holtz opined the day before the game that no one outcoaches Joe Paterno. Not even when Paterno is down 21-7, the halftime score. Up to that point, Notre Dame made Penn State look miserable. Watters scored a 22-yard touchdown and Brooks a 12-yarder. Penn State's Tony Sacca threw a 32-yard touchdown pass near the end of the quarter. In the second quarter, Penn State had the Irish on their eight-yard line with a good punt. Mirer used 16 plays for 92 yards, scoring himself from the one. With mere seconds left in the half, Hentrich missed a field goal. The Fighting Irish had pounded Penn State for nearly 300 yards of total offense, but Ismail reinjured his thigh and did not play in the second half—a fact Paterno admitted he did not notice until halfway through the third quarter. Notre Dame did not score again, and Penn State won 24-21 when a Mirer pass was intercepted in the last minute of play. The winning field goal came with only four seconds on the clock. Without Ismail—or even the threat he represented—Notre Dame's offense never left its end of the field in the second half.

USC was next. They had beaten Penn State early in the season. Having lost seven in a row to Notre Dame, and under the leadership of Todd Marinovich, USC was primed for the game. Oddsmakers had Notre Dame as the underdog. The defense had, in losing to Penn State, allowed 20 or more points for seven consecutive games for the first time in Notre Dame history. But the defense had the final say this time—a 10-6 win, five sacks of Marinovich, and Notre Dame's eighth straight victory over USC. The Trojans scored two field goals, one in the first quarter and one in the third; the Fighting Irish scored on a 30-yard Hentrich field goal in the second quarter, and a Tony Brooks touchdown of one yard on an option pitchout in the third quarter. USC's runners made 29 yards on 28 carries, with Marinovich's sacks chopping off about 50 yards of their total.

In the Orange Bowl against top-ranked Colorado, Notre Dame beat itself with five turnovers and a questionable clipping penalty on what appeared to be Ismail's game-winning kickoff return in the last minute. In the third quarter, the Fighting Irish lost three turnovers in four snaps. Colorado played a good, steady game, refusing to panic when their starting quarterback was lost to a knee injury. In fact, the defense seemed out of synch as they had to adjust to a new quarterback. Colorado scored a 22-yard field goal early in the second quarter. On the next Notre Dame possession, Watters scored a two-yard touchdown, but Hentrich's point-after kick was blocked. The Irish nursed a 6-3 lead at the half. Hentrich made a 24-yard field goal on the first possession of the second half but an Irish fumble on their own 40 eventually led to a one-yard touchdown by Bieniemy for Colorado's 10-9 win.

The two regular-season losses, to Stanford and Penn State, were by a total of eight points and came within the combined last 40 seconds of those two games. The common denominator was that Ismail was not able to play. With him out of the lineup, the quick-strike offense became a plodding affair; defenses were less distracted by his scoring threat. The same held true, in a way, in the Orange Bowl loss to Colorado when his touchdown was wiped out by the penalty call.

The 1990 team's rushing game fell off about 37 yards per game, compared with 1989, although the passing game increased about 53 yards per game. The 1989 team allowed opponents only 295 yards of total offense per game, but the 1990 defense allowed opponents 390, which accounts for the average opponent's score of 22.6 points per game in contrast to 15.3 in 1989. Ismail, Lyght, Stonebreaker, and Zorich were consensus All-Americans, and Mike Heldt also earned All-America accolades. Zorich won the Lombardi Trophy, and Ismail was named the Walter Camp player of the year.

1990 record: 9-3-0 (.750)
Record to date: 692-206-40 (.759)

1991

Some great players graduated after the 1990 season. Chris Zorich returned to his home from the Orange Bowl game to find that his mother had passed away. Zorich's loss led to Ismail's decision to forego his final season of college ball for a multimillion dollar pro contract in Canada. Like Zorich, Ismail was very close to his widowed mother and decided to make his contribution to her well-being as soon as possible.

Losing four two-time consensus All-Americans, three on defense, and the other the leading candidate

Lake Dawson, always a deep threat, one of the best WR to play for the Irish.

for the Heisman in 1991, crimps a coach's plans. With the exception of Ismail's departure, the offense posed no major problems for Holtz. It was on the defense where he would be hard-pressed to fill vacancies.

The backfield returned virtually intact—Mirer, Culver, Tony Brooks, and Bettis. For sheer talent among runners, this unit ranked with the very best—excellent speed and size, superb blocking, and good receiving. The flanker's position required a talent search, but Lake Dawson prevailed as a capable deep threat to complement Tony Smith. Derek Brown returned for his fourth year as the starting tight end. The line had good returning personnel in Mirko Jurkovic, Gene McGuire, and Justin Hall.

The entire defensive line had to be replaced. Troy Ridgely returned from a year's absence (academics) to provide some maturity and savvy. Untried youngsters had to learn the ropes quickly. The linebacking corps was in better shape with DuBose and Devon McDonald. Sophomore Pete Bercich had to grow quickly into the middle linebacker spot. Talented, speedy Willie Clark switched again to help at free safety. Jeff Burris, Tom Carter, and Rod Smith rounded out the secondary—short on experience but long on speed. Injuries kept Holtz from starting the same defensive unit in back-to-back games the entire season.

The Fighting Irish opened up at home against Indiana, a team they had not played since 1958. The usual clunkers and jitters plagued the offense on its opening three possessions. Likewise, the defense had its problems throughout the game, in spite of making four interceptions, in allowing a mediocre Hoosier team to make 25 first downs and 418 yards of total offense. Finally, 10 minutes into the first quarter and behind 3-0, Demetrius DuBose intercepted a Hoosier pass and ran 49 yards for a touchdown. Hentrich missed a second-quarter field goal, and Indiana marched 79 yards to score on a five-yard quarterback run. Culver answered with a 19-yard touchdown run to put Notre Dame ahead 17-10. The Hoosiers gained 60 yards on four throws to grab the lead again. Mirer, with the blocking help of Adrian Jarrell who took out the Hoosier corner, made a 46-yard touchdown run to recapture the lead. Indiana tried an onside kick, but the Irish grabbed it and Tony Brooks scored a 13-yarder. In the third quarter, Indiana booted a 29-yard field goal. Mirer executed a 12-play drive, hitting passes to Lake Dawson and Derek Brown, before running in from the six. Rod Smith intercepted a

Hoosier pass. Reserve tight end Irv Smith got loose in the Hoosier secondary, caught a Mirer pass at the IU 28, and dragged three Hoosiers the rest of the way for a 58-yard touchdown play. In the fourth quarter, the teams traded touchdowns, an Indiana pass and a Mirer one-yard plunge, for the 49-27 Irish victory. Other than Smith's touchdown, it had not been pretty; the secondary looked vulnerable and the defensive line had not dominated. Rod Smith led the team in tackles with 11.

Michigan's Elvis Grbac had never really had a bad day against the Fighting Irish, even though he had lost both prior games. With the help of a large offensive line and eventual Heisman winner Desmond Howard, the Wolverines ended Notre Dame's regular season four-game winning streak with a well-played 24-14 victory. Grbac played a nearly perfect game, completing 20 of 22 passes for 195 yards and the back-breaking 25-yard touchdown throw to Howard, who made a catch fully stretched out in the end zone. An interception led to Michigan's opening score, a field goal in the first quarter. Howard added a 29-yard touchdown on a reverse play in the second quarter. An Irish fumble shortly after that led to a 16-yard touchdown run by Ricky Powers. With 17 seconds left in the half, Mirer hit Bettis with a three-yard pass. In the third quarter, Mirer fired a strike to Tony Smith for a 35-yard touchdown to make it 17-14. With 9:02 left in the game, Grbac called the

Jerome Bettis in action against Tennessee in a tough '91 home loss.

Bryant Young, All-American in 1993.

touchdown play, pump-faked, and Howard opened up a tiny seam for the touchdown catch and the win. The Wolverines' 428 yards of total offense confirmed Notre Dame's defensive problems. Michigan's Ricky Powers hammered the Irish for 164 yards on 33 carries; Notre Dame's running game was held to 78 yards.

Michigan State had already been beaten by Central Michigan, but the Fighting Irish knew that each game was critical. They came out running—76 carries for 433 yards as they smothered the Spartans 49-10. Seven players scored touchdowns and Mirer fired three touchdown passes. The scorers were: Reggie Brooks for a two-yard touchdown burst, his first touchdown for the Irish; Tony Smith with a 29-yard touchdown pass from Mirer; Derek Brown for a 55-yard touchdown pass and run from Mirer. MSU made a field goal and a 48-yard touchdown pass to Courtney Hawkins for the 21-10 halftime score. The third quarter belonged to Notre Dame—Irv Smith with a two-yard touchdown pass from Mirer, Tony Brooks with a nine-yard touchdown blast, and Mirer with a 12-yard scoring run. In the fourth quarter, Willie Clark ran in from the one-yard line to make the final score 49-10. The Fighting Irish gained 650 total yards.

Purdue lost 45-20 as Bryant Young played a "career game" with two fumble recoveries, three tackles behind the line of scrimmage, and six other tackles. Mirer was nursing bruised ribs, so freshman Paul Failla started; Mirer took over completing 12 of 14 passes for 139 yards and two touchdowns. Purdue scored on a one-yard run, but four Irish scores followed: Mirer on a 29-yard run, Bettis on a six-yard blast after a Young fumble recovery, Derek Brown on a five-yard touchdown catch after another Young fumble recovery, and Bettis plowing over from the two. Purdue scored on a 19-yard pass, but two more Irish scores slammed the door on their comeback: Hentrich hit a 33-yard field goal, set up by Tony Brooks's 57-yard run, and Mihalko powered over for a one-yard touchdown.

The torrid scoring pace of 39 points per outing kept up in a grudge match against Stanford, 42-26, the first time since 1943 that Notre Dame had exploded for four 40-point games in the first five. Lake Dawson scored on a 27-yard touchdown pass from Mirer. Bettis followed up a DuBose fumble recovery with the first of his four touchdowns for the day, this on a three-yard burst. Early in the second quarter, Bettis ran 28 yards to the one, and slammed over for the touchdown on

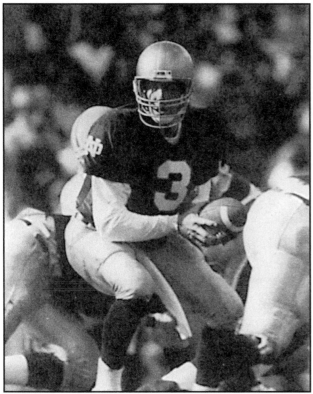

Rick Mirer, career total offense yardage leader for Notre Dame when he completed his career.

the next play. Mirer ended the next drive, sparked by Bettis and Tony Brooks, when he slipped over from the one. Down 28-0, Stanford scored on a Vardell run of 27 yards for the 28-7 halftime score. Stanford got two more Vardell scores in the second half and a touchdown on a quarterback keeper, but Bettis scored twice, once in the third quarter with a 13-yard touchdown pass from Mirer, and after a Rod Smith interception in the fourth quarter with a one-yard run. He led all rushers for the day with 179 yards on 24 carries; Tony Brooks added 122 yards on 17 carries.

Against Pitt, the Irish kept up the scoring pace with a 42-7 rout, although Pitt held them to a 0-0 affair in the first period. Early in the second quarter, Irv Smith recovered a fumble after a punt; Bettis slammed over from the one seven plays later. Pitt was unable to move, punted, and Reggie Brooks returned it for a 26 yard touchdown. Notre Dame scored twice in both of the remaining quarters: Irv Smith with a two-yard touchdown pass from Mirer and Mirer with an eight-yard keeper in the third quarter. Pitt's Van Pelt fired a 51-yard touchdown after an interception. Bettis ran for 66 of 80 yards on the next drive, scoring with a bruising 40-yard run. Reserve quarterback Kevin McDougal made a five-yard touchdown keeper.

Air Force played a good game, losing 28-15. They ran the ball 75 times, gaining 354 yards. Still Air Force was able to get into the end zone only once. The Fighting Irish picked up 420 total yards to control the outcome. The Falcons scored a field goal but couldn't stop the return march. Bettis powered in from their seven to make it 7-3. Air Force kicked a field goal in the second quarter, stopped Notre Dame, came back, and missed a field goal. Mirer hit Tony Smith with an 83-yard touchdown bomb on the next play. Troy Ridgley grabbed a fumble on their 36; Bettis ran it in from the three to end Notre Dame's first-half scoring. The Falcons kicked another field goal on the last play of the half. They tried an onside kick to open the second half, it backfired, and Bettis ran 19 yards for a touchdown moments later. The Falcons scored a touchdown in the fourth quarter to make it 28-15. Two defensive linemen went down with bad ankles—Bryant Young and Eric Jones. Irish players complained that Air Force used illegal cut blocks to do the damage.

Injured and somewhat suspect on defense, the

All-time punting leader for the Irish, Craig Hentrich.

Reggie Brooks (41) running loose in Navy's deep secondary in '91 action.

Fighting Irish faced USC. The Trojans were spoiling for a win—and almost got it, though Notre Dame prevailed 24-20. Holtz tinkered with personnel to patch together a defensive line. Bettis surprised the Trojans with his speed and strength on a 53-yard touchdown run to start his day's work of 178 yards on 24 carries. In the second quarter, Bettis ran 23 yards to set up a 14-yard touchdown pass from Mirer to Brooks for a 14-0 halftime cushion. In the third quarter, USC's Deon Strothers made a 29-yard touchdown run. Bettis killed a drive with a fumble. Following a DuBose fumble recovery, Bettis ended an 89-yard drive with a one-yard touchdown blast. The Trojans forced a Mirer fumble on a sack at the Notre Dame 20, and Mazio Royster converted the turnover with a 14-yard touchdown run. Hentrich kicked a 34-yard field goal, and USC scored a touchdown on their next drive. They tried an onside kick and Irv Smith came away with the ball; the Irish killed the clock for the ninth consecutive win over USC.

Winless Navy succumbed 38-0, following a week in which Holtz put the Fighting Irish through their most strenuous workouts of the season to sharpen the team for Tennessee and Penn State. Mirer threw three touchdown passes to earn the single season all-time touchdown passing record with 17. Derek Brown caught a two-yard touchdown, after a 22-yard strike to Tony

Smith. Hentrich booted a 35-yard field goal and Bettis caught a nine-yard scoring pass from Mirer. In the third quarter, Mirer threw a 13-yard score to Smith. Bettis slammed over from the one in the fourth quarter and Reggie Brooks made a 65-yard run to set up his three-yard touchdown. Mirer threw for 303 yards on 17 of 23 attempts. Devon McDonald led a solid defensive effort with one sack and two other tackles for losses.

The high-water mark for the Fighting Irish occurred in the first quarter of the Tennessee game when they held a 21-0 lead. However, the Irish lost the game 35-34 to see their chances for the national crown blasted. The Irish stunned Tennessee with three scores in the first quarter: a 12-yard touchdown run by Brooks, a 79-yard touchdown run by Tom Carter with an interception, and a 10-yard run by Mirer. In the second quarter, the Volunteers made a touchdown pass. Hentrich kicked a 24-yard field goal. Bettis made it 31-7 with a two-yard run. With only 14 seconds in the half, the Volunteers blocked a Hentrich field goal try and took the ball in for an 85-yard score. In the melee, Hentrich went down with a sprained knee. Coach Johnny Majors could see that Notre Dame was having its way on the ground, with 233 yards in one half. He strangled the run in the second half, forced a milder passing game, and Tennessee picked off three Mirer throws. When it was over, Tennessee scored three more times on short drives. Walk-on kicker, Rob Leonard, saw his 27-yard winning field goal attempt deflected at the line of scrimmage. The Fighting Irish won the stats, but Tennessee won the game.

Defeated, deflated, and nursing some lingering injuries, the Fighting Irish went to Penn State, losing 35-13. In a lackluster performance, they gained only 90 yards on the ground, and gave up 239 yards running and 151 passing. Penn State racked up a 21-0 first-quarter lead. Bettis scored in the second quarter on a two-yard effort, and William Pollard caught a 38-yard touchdown pass from Mirer in the third quarter. Holtz was so distressed he admitted that he wanted to practice right there at Penn State just hours after the loss.

Two weeks later, and about six time zones across the world, the Fighting Irish faced the University of Hawaii and piled up 499 yards of total offense for 48 points—and they still almost lost the game, 48-42. The defense was nearly in total disarray due to innumerable personnel changes on the line. Only Tom Carter's two interceptions and a fumble recovery by Troy Ridgley staved off a strong first-half performance by Hawaii. By that time, Notre Dame led 28-10. Culver made a three-yard touchdown run to convert Carter's first interception. Ridgley's fumble recovery led to Tony Brooks's 13-yard touchdown run. In the second quarter, Culver ran 52 yards to set up a touchdown run of 11 yards by Mirer. Hawaii scored on a touchdown pass, and Brooks tallied again after a 47-yard screen pass to Culver set it up. Hawaii ended the half with a field goal. Bettis scored twice in the second half, on four- and two-yard runs, for a record 16 touchdowns on the ground for the season. Hawaii hammered away at the Irish defense on their way to 473 yards of total offense, and the highest point total against Notre Dame in an Irish win. Bettis missed a 1,000-yard season when he was held to 31 yards on 12 carries.

Notre Dame had redeemed itself some with a strong final game, but critics said the 9-3 record was unworthy of the Sugar Bowl and third-ranked Florida. However, Holtz, given enough time to do a thorough coaching job, would always keep the Fighting Irish in a game. He used his time wisely and retooled the defense so that steady pressure and good containment forced a hobbled Gator quarterback to throw into no fewer than six defensive backs. The odd defense, a 3-2 look with six backs deep, initially looked porous. The Gators opened up a 10-0 first-quarter lead with a 15-yard pass for a score and a 26-yard field goal. They added another field goal in the second quarter before a quick strike of 40 yards from Mirer to Dawson scored. The Gators kicked another field goal at the end of the half. Trailing 16-7, the Fighting Irish closed the gap in the third quarter with a 23-yard field goal by a kicker recruited from the soccer team, Kevin Pendergast; Hentrich had reinjured himself in the first half. Irv Smith filtered into the end zone on a play-action pass to score with a four-yard pass from Mirer. Florida booted two more field goals in the fourth quarter, but Bettis made three touchdown runs. The first capped a patient drive and gave Notre Dame its first lead. The Gators tried to jam the line of scrimmage and Bettis scored on runs of 49 and 39 yards on almost identical plays. The Gators scored on a pass, but it was too late. Holtz's "bend but don't break" defense allowed 511 yards, but Bettis led a dominating ground attack and Mirer completed 14 of 19 passes for the 39-28 win.

Notre Dame finished 12th in the nation, even though they had beaten some teams ranked ahead of them. The 1991 Fighting Irish set records with 59 touchdowns scored, 425 points, and 5,466 yards of total offense. The first two records had lasted for nearly eight decades, shattering records set when Rockne was in his junior season, 1912. The defense, however, allowed 1,103 more rushing yards than in 1990, while also allowing opponents to run more total plays and maintain longer ball possession.

Holtz signed a new five-year contract, a relief after earlier rumors that he was headed to the Minnesota Vikings. There were some immediate concerns, not the least being the status of his starting quarterback, Mirer, who was considering turning pro (weeks later, Mirer decided to return for his senior year). And he certainly knew that the defensive line would need a major infusion of talent. Brooks and Culver were gone from the backfield, as was Derek Brown after four years as the starting tight end (although Irv Smith looked quite capable).

1991 record: 10-3-0 (.769)
Record to date: 702-209-40 (.759)

1992

The '92 Irish certainly would have to execute a gut check, especially in light of the shattering defeats in '91 to Penn State and Tennessee when Notre Dame

Notre Dame's fifth 1,000-yard runner, Lee Becton.

speedy Lake Dawson, as well as Ray Griggs, and Mike Miller. (Of this stellar offensive group, Mirer, Bettis, and Brooks would turn into NFL starters almost immediately). Tight end Irv Smith, complemented by Oscar McBride, gave the Irish an impressive tandem at this position, although Irish tight ends seemed underutilized throughout the Holtz years. The O line would be led by Aaron Taylor (well on his way to earning the '93 Lombardi Trophy), Lindsay Knapp, Justin Hall, and Tim Ruddy. The five interior starting linemen would tip the scales just a slice of lean turkey under 290 pounds.

Minter's defense had some emerging luminaries—Jim Flanigan had beefed up enough to leave his spot as a reserve linebacker to take over as nose guard, although at 247 pounds he was often facing opponents 60 pounds heavier. Next to him, Bryant Young lined up, with tremendous quickness and fast moves—a nightmare to block. Demetrius DuBose was the leading linebacker, although a small scandal of sorts dealing with supporters at home in Seattle cost him a suspension for the first two '92 games. Blazing speed in the defensive backfield abounded especially with do-it-all player Jeff Burris, but also Tom Carter, and bright newcomer Bobby Taylor. Notre Dame had been ranked a miserable 84th in the country against the run in 1991, so these defenders had their work cut out for them. All-purpose kicker Craig Hentrich returned for his final year, but the special teams had not yet really found a reliable replacement for the Rocket.

The maiden voyage for the '92 Irish took place after a short jaunt to a South Bend suburb, Chicago, where they renewed the series with Northwestern at Soldier Field. Notre Dame had not seen the Wildcats since 1976. Their new head coach, Gary Barnett, had high hopes of turning the 'Cats into something more than the patsies they had been for decades. When the dust settled, the 'Cats had generated 408 impressive yards of offense to go with 26 first downs—but they were still on the short end of the score, 42-7. The Irish bested these figures with 561 yards of offense, 28 first downs, and twin TDs by Oscar McBride on five-yard passes from Mirer and Kevin McDougal, Lee Becton's two-yard TD slant to the left, a 70-yard bomb from Mirer to Mike Miller, a 25-yard TD rumble by Jerome Bettis, and a 72-yard TD sprint by Reggie Brooks after breaking two

played poorly at crucial times, as well as the Hawaii scare. Rick Minter signed on as defensive coordinator, fresh from assembling an impressive defensive record at Ball State. Whether he would be able to step it up from that level of college football to the pressure and intensity of Notre Dame's plateau remained to be seen. It would also be difficult to maintain the offensive pyrotechnics that had highlighted the '91 campaign, although Holtz would enjoy having many of the key personnel. It would all start with Rick Mirer's return for his senior season, during which he would threaten to obliterate virtually every passing mark in ND's record book. Mirer would have some of the finest backs in the country to give the ball to: Jerome Bettis, who could run against Third World countries—and tireless, determined Reggie Brooks. Among his receivers he could count on elusive,

Derrick Mayes, Notre Dame's leading receiver for career yard-age gained. **Photo by Br. Charles McBride**

tackles at the line of scrimmage. Brooks blasted the 'Cats for 157 yards on a mere nine carries; Bettis hammered them for another 130 yards on 19 carries. Mirer had a less-than-overwhelming day, with eight completions in 17 attempts, for 165 yards and the two TDs, with one interception.

Season openers are supposed to be opportunities to iron out the team's wrinkles and test new faces. But opening with a Northwestern can hardly prepare a team for the likes of a Michigan, a juggernaut aiming for its fifth consecutive Big Ten title. Back from the suburbs, the Irish strapped on their helmets and prepared to meet the Wolverines' Elvis Grbac, Heisman hopeful Tyrone Wheatley and their supporting cast of behemoths. The jitters and hard-hitting showed up early, on ND's first drive, when Dawson snagged a Mirer pass but coughed

it up at UM's 33. Michigan showed its mettle by going for it on fourth down after a drive of nine plays, but Notre Dame held and came right back for more. Reggie Brooks capped the 67-yard return drive with one of those plays that deserve to be bronzed and mounted—scoring on a 21-yard option play that ended with the diminutive running back busting between two crashing Wolverines near the goal line, splitting them, then falling, apparently unconscious, into the end zone as he clutched the ball. The next two series ended with punts, then Tom Carter snagged a Grbac pass in the Irish end zone to end a Wolverine drive of 80 yards. The Irish drove to the UM 22, sparked by the persistent running of Brooks, Bettis, and another B, Lee Becton, but Holtz turned a little too frisky with a call for a reverse to Miller that ended in a fumble (one of three fumbles the Wolverines would benefit from this day). Michigan took advantage and used most of the remaining two minutes in the first half to drive back and tie the game, 7-7. Wheatley broke a tackle on the way to a 28-yard TD with a Grbac pass down his left sideline. In the third quarter, Michigan stuffed a Hentrich field goal try of 48 yards to end ND's first drive, then turned the tables, on a drive starting at their 39, with their own 27-yard field goal. Both teams held on the ensuing possessions, then a Bettis fumble killed the next Irish drive at midfield. Grbac struck immediately with a 16-yard pass, a Wheatley run, then a 30-yard TD pass to Derrick Alexander for a 17-7 lead early in the fourth quarter. Three Irish turnovers had given UM 14 crucial points in a tight game. The Irish weren't finished, though—Mirer roped a pass to Dawson for 22 yards, Bettis atoned with a 17-yard run off a brilliant cutback... and on fourth and 11 at the UM 26, Holtz passed up a field goal and went for the first down, Mirer hitting Dawson for the needed yardage. A pass interference call put the ball at the two, and Bettis slammed it in from there on a dive. Hentrich's PAT made it 17-14 with 11:23 remaining. The teams traded punts, then Brian Rattigan intercepted a Grbac pass at the UM 20. Notre Dame couldn't move it in for the touch, and Hentrich tied it at 17-17 on a 32-yard field goal with 5:28 left. Michigan stormed back, reaching the Irish 30, but Greg Lane blitzed Grbac from the corner, hurried the throw, and Burris grabbed the third Irish interception of the day, with 1:20 left on the clock. After mounting a great comeback, with the ball now on the Notre Dame 12, and Michigan with all its timeouts, Holtz chose to try Bettis up the gut, then a Brooks run, then a long-pass attempt down the right side to Dawson. With seven seconds left, UM's Corwin Brown broke up Mirer's last pass of the day. The 17-17 result obviously called up memories of the monumental 10-10 tie in 1966 with another team from Michigan, the Spartans. But this was a bit different—the Irish were at home, in good weather, with a healthy QB. Holtz probably did the right thing—deep in his territory, Bettis up the middle had the potential to break loose for a big gain, and UM had control of the clock if Mirer threw errantly into Michigan coverage expecting a pass. Times like this certainly make a coach earn his salary. Nevertheless, there were boos from the home crowd soaring to the skies as the exhausted teams left the field—unjustified boos, in view of one of the great games in college football having just gone into the history books.

Would the Irish be able to put their disappointment behind them and put up a fight against that other Michigan nemesis—MSU? Holtz saw an early spark of life as Mirer led his mates on a 65-yard scoring drive the first time the team had the ball. Lake Dawson's 43-yard reception served early notice to the Spartans, then Mirer finished off the drive with a masterful fake to Bettis, followed by a four-yard TD flip to TE McBride on a delay. Hentrich made good his 123rd consecutive PAT for the 7-0 lead. MSU fought back and kicker Jim Del Verne made good a 44-yard field goal. After that—an Irish deluge, three unanswered TDs and a field goal: Clint Johnson's 53-yard kickoff return led to a seven-yard TD pass, Mirer to Dawson; a 59-yard bomb from Mirer to Dawson set up a four-yard TD pitch from Mirer to Becton; Tom Carter's interception of a Spartan aerial sparked a drive completed with a fake reverse and a 39-yard TD pass from Mirer to Griggs; a John Covington interception let Notre Dame eat up some clock and garner a 26-yard FG by Hentrich. The Spartans fought back after that, with Jim Miller capping a 74-yard drive with a one-yard TD flip to fullback Tony Rollin, making the score 31-10. Lee Becton promptly dashed Spartan hopes with a brilliant 78-yard kickoff return for an Irish TD. In the second half, Notre Dame piled up two more scores, Reggie Brooks's third-quarter six-yard TD burst, and a 38-yard TD pass from Kevin McDougal to Dawson on the first play of the fourth quarter. The hapless Spartans registered three TDs against Irish reserves, but couldn't make the final score

any better than 52-31. Mirer ended up with 260 yards on 13 completions in 25 attempts, good for three TDs, as the powerful Irish offense kept up a hectic pace good for 506 total yards.

With that tune-up, Notre Dame shifted into high gear and demolished Purdue 48-0. The first half was misleading, with Notre Dame going into the locker room nursing a meager 13-0 lead, built upon a five-yard Bettis TD burst and a Mirer TD run of six yards, capped by a missed Hentrich PAT attempt. He had made 130 straight, but the field was wet and the snap was off the mark. Holtz must have used the halftime wisely because the Irish roared into action with three TDs in the third quarter: Brooks on a thing of beauty good for 63 yards (followed by Becton's run for two points), then a slam by Bettis of 24 yards, followed by another Brooks score—three broken tackles and a TD 20 yards later. John Covington's interception brought Brooks back on the field moments later, and he promptly took off for another score, with three more broken tackles and the TD 80 yards later. Kevin McDougal ended the Irish scoring feast with a 15-yard TD run, then the Irish defense stopped a "never-say-die" Purdue drive at the Notre Dame one-yard line. The Irish racked up 580 yards of total offense. Reggie Brooks earned the first 200-yard game since Allen Pinkett's 1983 heroics against Penn State. For his busy day, Brooks carried 15 times for 205 yards, three TDs, and a robust 13.6 yards per carry.

The Irish had not enjoyed their usual luck in all of their recent home contests—the thunder had not been called down consistently from the sky. This trend unhappily continued when Bill Walsh and Stanford visited the Dome. Holtz was smarting from comments Walsh had made about his coaching decisions in '91 losses, so there was an element of involvement not often seen in Irish games, in spite of the pressures that were always there. Stanford came into the game with a great defense and an all-purpose threat in flashy Glyn Milburn, not to mention their usual cerebral type at QB, Steve Stenstrom. But early in the game, Mr. Stenstrom met Mr. DuBose—in Stanford's end zone, for an Irish safety. Mike Miller's return of their free kick put Notre Dame in good shape near midfield, then Bettis shredded Walsh's vaunted defense with a 13-yard run that stopped only after seven defenders had jumped him. So much for tackling drills. Brooks capped the drive on an option play with a pitch to the right side, good for an 11-yard TD zip and a first-quarter Irish lead, 9-0. The Irish didn't know it, but they had scored more than half of the points they would score that day. The first period ended on an up note when DuBose forced a fumble, Germaine Holden recovering. Notre Dame kept the pressure on in the next quarter when Burris, operating out of the full T, took a pitch right for a two-yard TD. That was it for ND's scoring—it is entirely possible that Walsh outcoached Holtz the rest of the way, as Stanford steadily chipped away. The sky began to fall on the Irish when Ray Griggs fumbled after a long pass completion; Milburn scored, they missed a two-point try and went into halftime down by 10. In the second half, Mirer seemed to miss Dawson, who had injured his ribs in the first half, but Mirer was overthrowing his targets in any case. Early in the third quarter, Stenstrom fired another TD pass, for eight yards, but the Irish still had the lead. On the next drive, Bettis took a screen pass and rumbled 32 yards, but fumbled. The Irish began to look for toes to shoot after that and did a good job of it. Stenstrom hit another TD pass, the Irish self-destructed with an interception thrown from the Stanford nine-yard line, then Stanford sandwiched a Milburn TD run between two FGs. When the shooting was over, the Stanford defense had given up a lot more yardage than it was accustomed to, but Irish production fell off the previous level of 500-plus yards to a mortal 349 yards. Four lost fumbles and the disastrous interception spelled ND's doom—self-destruction added up to 11 yards of total offense in the second half.

All-American center Tim Ruddy.

Later, Lou Holtz would surmise that ND's fourth and fifth games were annually their toughest, thanks not to the opposition, but due to midterm exams. Players are tired, practices lose key personnel, the general rhythm is disrupted. Academics have the priority—but Stanford's players must also face the same rigor—and they have all the distractions of the Bay area rather than South Bend.

Notre Dame tried to put this bitter loss behind them, but with the season standing at 3-1-1, self-doubts had to be creeping into their thoughts. The week of practice had a certain emphasis on the running game, but ND's first series showed not much improvement, ending with a missed 38-yard field-goal try. The Panthers then patched together a patient 16-play drive, blunted by Jeff Burris when he broke up a third-down pass in the Irish end zone. Sean Conley hit on a 21-yard FG to round it

off. The Irish came back, 66 yards on four plays, Bettis scoring off the left side out of the full T, rumbling nine yards to pay dirt. Pitt ended the first period's scoring with a 48-yard FG. Notre Dame then turned serious—putting Bettis at tailback with Zellars at fullback, they slashed and burned on an 80-yard drive until Mirer looped a two-yard TD pass to McBride, passing Joe Theismann's career mark of 31 TD passes. After a punt on the next series, Holtz tried out Kevin McDougal at QB, who promptly took his charges 65 yards in five plays, capped by a 31-yard TD pass to Derrick Mayes; McDougal's excellent mobility helped him escape a good pass rush on the play. Irish DB Tom Carter kept the pressure on when he grabbed an interception from a lateral and a pass play, but the Irish failed to convert the play to a score. The Irish closed out the quarter with a Bettis TD smash of three yards, again out of the full house backfield, making the score at halftime 28-6. The Panthers came out firing in the second half, Alex Van Pelt throwing a five-yard TD pass and picking up a two-point conversion on a run by John Ryan. The Irish, however, answered with a 77-yard drive in 10 plays, with Bettis rumbling 15 yards off the right side for a TD. Jeff Burris stopped the next Pitt drive with an interception off a tipped pass; Mirer used three plays to zip downfield, with Mayes latching on to a TD pass covering 69 yards. Pitt cut the score in half with a seven-yard TD pass from Van Pelt to Chad Askew, making it 42-21. The Panthers tried an onside kick, but Adrian Jarrell alertly claimed possession near the Notre Dame 40; a few plays later Hentrich kicked a 25-yard FG. Dean Lytle recovered the fumbled kickoff and Paul Failla wrapped up the scoring with a three-yard TD run on a keeper to the left side. Soccer refugee Kevin Pendergast booted the PAT for the final score of 52-21. The Irish were back in business, with 533 yards of total offense for the day's work, averaging more than eight yards per play.

The pressure to perform well back at home must have been mounting—Holtz responded at the Friday night pep rally by promising no more home losses in the season. This, the night before meeting BYU's aerial circus. But the defense took the challenge seriously: After initial inconclusive possessions, DuBose got the Irish on the scoreboard when he recovered a BYU fumble for a TD. BYU persisted on a drive that garnered an 18-yard FG. The teams exchanged punts (BYU's punter was 6'7", 280 pounds and blasted 50-yarders with regularity, so an exchange of punts was not in ND's best interests). In the second quarter, the Irish racked up a TD on a two-yard pass from Mirer to Irv Smith. BYU tacked on two FGs for a halftime score of 14-9, but their running game had been snuffed, for minus-24 yards in the half. They traded TDs in the third quarter, Ray Griggs scampering 54 yards to paydirt on a middle screen with a Mirer pass; BYU responding with a five-yard TD pass. The Irish running game iced the game in the fourth quarter as Bettis pinballed for an 18-yard TD early in the quarter. Jeff Burris snitched an interception and Bettis slanted in from the full T formation for a five-yard TD. Burris had more in him after that—Tom Carter hauled in an interception and Burris got the touch with a one-yard scoring run, then, moments later, Irish DT Brian Hamilton tipped a BYU pass, and Burris brought it in for his second interception of the day. The Irish ground game racked up 291 yards to BYU's three. The Cougars'

339 yards of passing could not sustain long drives in the absence of a running game; Notre Dame's three interceptions demolished other chances.

The Irish went east to meet Navy, and they would have to do it without Bettis and McBride. Jeff Burris subbed for Bettis at fullback and did well enough to garner the game's first score—a five-yard burst midway into the first quarter. The fleet sunk in the second quarter as Notre Dame scored 24 unanswered points: a 32-yard FG by Hentrich, a 24-yard TD pass from Mirer to Brooks, Brooks again on a four-yard TD burst, and Irv Smith with a three-yard TD flip from Mirer. The third quarter was a scoreless affair, and most of the fourth quarter as well. The Middies managed to avoid the shutout when QB Jason Van Matre tossed a 22-yard TD pass. Lee Becton returned the favor with a nine-yard TD scoot up the flailing middle of the Navy defense to end the scoring for a yeomanlike 38-7 Irish win, their 29th consecutive win over Navy.

The Irish, ranked eighth, next had to face the undefeated, ninth-ranked Golden Eagles of Boston College. BC boasted the seventh-best rushing offense behind Chuckie Dukes and his seven straight 100-yard games. Glenn Foley, the BC QB, brought back memories of Doug Flutie, coached a decade earlier by head coach Tom Coughlin. Well, all these paper credentials meant little as Notre Dame crushed the Golden Eagles 54-7 (in the process perhaps garnering some ill will that would haunt the Irish in future seasons). The humiliation was total: 576 total yards to 176, 26 first downs to nine, a throttling 340 yards on the ground to 55. There was no drama to relate, just a drubbing: in the first quarter, Mirer had a hand in three scores—a nine-yard TD pass to Becton, a 37-yard TD rope to Bettis, and, following Brian Hamilton's fumble recovery, his own 16-yard TD scamper on an option play run left. In the second frame, Brooks scored on a one-yard option play, then rambled for a 73-yard TD; Hentrich's 37-yard FG just before the half made it 37-0. At that point, the Irish defense had caused BC to fail to convert on seven third-down plays. The first Irish series in the third quarter earned Holtz some BC enmity, although he was probably just giving Penn State and USC something to think about: On fourth and one, Hentrich ran for 11 yards out of punt formation, leading to a Mirer pass of three yards to Burris for a TD. Hentrich tacked on a 42-yard FG to end the scoring at 47-0 in the third frame. Dean Lytle wrapped it up in the fourth quarter with a three-yard TD run set up by passes of 14 and 40 yards from McDougal to

Mayes. BC tallied a consolation TD in the final minute to put the game in the books at 54-7.

The Irish next faced Penn State, a game that would wrap up the series for the time being as the Nittany Lions were joining the Big Ten. It turned into a tight-scoring affair, with Notre Dame scoring only three Hentrich field goals in each of the first three quarters, countered by a Richie Anderson dive from the one for a TD in the second quarter. Bobby Taylor, in an extraordinary effort, blocked the PAT kick, letting the Irish take a 9-6 lead into the fourth quarter. But Penn State racked up 10 points in the fourth quarter, a 22-yard FG and a 13-yard TD run by Brian O'Neal with 4:25 left in the game. Mirer stayed steady under the pressure of the moment, finding Bettis through increasing snow flurries for a 21-yard gain, then scrambling 15 yards. Mirer followed that up with a 17-yard strike to Ray Griggs, before Brooks and Mirer worked some careful runs to the Penn State four. On fourth and goal, Bettis hauled in a Mirer pass for a TD. There were 20 seconds left in the game and the stadium was literally shaking as the crowd went ballistic. The Irish went for the win, lining up with three receivers wide to the left. At the snap, Mirer surveyed the trips left and saw good coverage then spotted Reggie Brooks angling to the right corner. He lofted a pass to Brooks who hauled it in as he dove into the corner—good for two points and a 17-16 win! This incredible win has to be ranked in anyone's list of top ten Irish triumphs.

For their finale, the Irish were next tasked with keeping alive their decade-long streak over USC's Trojans. Their job was not made easier due to a flu outbreak that hit half of the Domers, including Reggie Brooks, ruining a planned team outing to Disneyland. That's OK, as long as they could beat the Trojans. It wasn't easy, but the flu-afflicted Irish did win, 31-23. The Trojans tallied a score first, a Cole Ford FG from 35 yards out. Notre Dame took the lead on the next series, a 74-yard affair featuring 69 yards shared between Brooks and Bettis, with the big fullback taking a pitchout wide right from Mirer for 12 yards into scoring territory. USC turned the tables with their own drive, capped by a one-yard TD blast by Deon Strother. Mirer, who had a terrible day passing (five of 14 for 75 yards), then tossed an interception (although replays revealed it to be a bad call, the ball was trapped) to kill the next drive. USC tried to put the hammer down with a fourth-down trick play but Burris did the right thing and grabbed an interception, a major swing in the game. As the first half ran out, the action picked up—Notre Dame struck for

a Hentrich FG of 37 yards and a 10-10 tie, then USC drove back for their own 38-yard FG, making it 13-10. With under two minutes to go in the half, Brooks gave the Irish some hope with a 55-yard TD blast. USC hit one more FG to make the half-time score read 17-16, the Irish up. The teams traded TDs in the third quarter, a 44-yard run by Brooks and an 18-yard TD pass by Rob Johnson, who seemed to have abandoned the Trojan running game in the face of great Irish D (USC's runners ended up about as bad as Mirer's passing—36 carries for 78 yards). Midway through the last frame, Bettis barged through three Trojan tacklers for a nine-yard TD blast, then Notre Dame held on for the win. QB Johnson was sacked six times in the second half alone, making sustained drives difficult at best. On the next to last play, Devon McDonald nailed the final sack, and Tom Carter wrapped it up with an interception in the Irish end zone on USC's last throw.

The Irish ended up ranked fifth in the country, scheduled to meet undefeated (12-0), fourth-ranked Texas A&M in the Cotton Bowl. The only common opponent of the two had been Stanford; the Aggies had nudged them 10-7 in the season opener. Maybe the Irish loss to Stanford lulled A&M with an unrealistic sense of superiority, but the Aggies were simply manhandled by the Irish, dominated in any meaningful category you can think of, including the 28-3 score being A&M's worst losing margin ever in its long history of bowl games.

The game itself started out as a scoreless deal in the first quarter, thanks mainly to a Reggie Brooks fumble deep in A&M territory. But the signs of dominance were there if anyone was looking carefully—especially A&M's inability to sustain a drive, not registering their initial first down until the first quarter had all but expired. The second quarter was almost more of the same, until Holtz had the feeling that the Aggies were sure to blitz so called a middle screen to Dawson and, sure enough, "here comes everybody" on a blitz, and there goes Dawson with a 40-yard TD pass from Mirer, leaving 37 seconds in the half. In the third quarter, Mirer found Bettis lingering in the backwash of hotly pursuing Aggies, hit him with a pass, and let Jerome do the rest for a 26-yard TD play and a 14-0 lead. After that, Notre Dame showed who was boss, letting its dominant offensive linemen shove the smaller, weaker Aggies all over the place—no passes, just runs, option football all the way, including 33 straight running plays that simply annihilated the clock. Bettis scored twice more, from one and four yards out, sandwiching the consolation FG kicked by the Aggies. When it was over, their proud defense was in total shambles, giving up 439 yards to Notre Dame compared to an anemic 165 yards (78 running, 87 passing) gained by their offense.

For the year, the Irish had overcome early adversity in the tie and loss to Michigan and Stanford, Holtz had made good on his promise to win the remaining home games, they had continued their winning ways over USC, and demolished an overrated Texas A&M team (and in the process making thoughtful observers wonder even more about the accuracy and role of the "rankings"). Holtz said that they were the best team playing at the end of the season—who knows, short of a playoff? Ask A&M.

For his career, Mirer took over the second spot in Irish annals, just three yards short of 6,000 for passing yardage, with 377 completions in 698 attempts, for 41 TDs (a new Irish career record) and only 23 INTs, for 15.9 yards per completion. Jerome Bettis turned pro a year early, having stormed through opposing defenses for 1,912 yards in only 22 starts (2,164 yards counting his three Bowl games). Reggie Brooks had the third best season ever for an Irish back, with 1,343 yards in 167 carries for a sparkling 8.0 yards per carry—the only other Irish back to do better was George Gipp in 1920. The Irish D cut the rushing yardage against them in half, from 2,458 yards to 1,222 yards, reducing the total yardage against them from 4,588 yards to 3,599, a 22 percent decrease. So, the '92 Irish had been explosive on offense and fairly stingy on defense. Facing a great Irish run defense, opponents could not count on time-consuming drives to ice a game. The Irish had dominated in most games, had played a classic game against Michigan, and had only the one stinker, the loss to Stanford. The players who had put in their four years through '92 had won 41 games, lost eight, tied one—a winning percentage of .830, one of the best for any comparable group of Irish players. Aaron Taylor achieved All-America status.

1992 record: 10-1-1 (.875)
Record to date: 712-210-41 (.760)

1993

Sometimes being a head coach can be thoroughly enjoyable, at other times extremely frustrating, but it's always interesting. For the 1993 season, Lou Holtz had this to contemplate: three-fourths of his starting

backfield gone, as well as seven of the 11 starters on offense, and five of the starting 11 defensive players. If coaches are teachers, then Holtz would have plenty of teaching ahead of him.

Actually, his starting backfield would be in pretty good shape, with plenty of latent talent: Ray Zellars at fullback to replace Bettis—smaller, quicker, explosive; Lee Becton at TB—larger than Brooks, not as quick or explosive, perhaps faster once in the open field, elusive for his size; Lake Dawson switched from SE to FL, with great hands, good size, and game-breaking speed; and, finally, Kevin McDougal for Mirer at QB—some 49 minutes played under center for three seasons; good accuracy in passing (14 of 21 for 233 yards, three TDs, one INT); and acceptable running skills (16 carries for 74 yards, one TD). He would need lots of help reading defenses, and more help in the finer points of running Holtz's favorite option plays. He would also have to grow into a leadership role, perhaps change his public persona of being a bit shy and quiet. In the line, Aaron Taylor, Tim Ruddy, and Lindsay Knapp shuffled around a bit, but they had enjoyed solid seasons in '92. Mark Zataveski and Ryan Leahy rounded out the starting interior linemen, with Oscar McBride leading a strong group of TE candidates. This interior line had beefed up over the '92 edition, coming in at 293.4 pounds on average as the Irish, as with many major college teams, flirted with the 300-pound average.

On D, Jim Flanigan, Brian Hamilton, and Bryant Young returned, flanked by Thomas Knight as LE. Flanigan, at 276 pounds, had added nearly 30 pounds to his frame (and would later impress the NFL combine folks by benching 250 pounds 39 times). Anthony Peterson would be in and out with injuries as a linebacker, so the linebackers were essentially all new as starters—Bert Berry, Justin Goheen, and Pete Bercich. The DBs were mainly a veteran group back from '92, with John Covington being added to the group as Greg Lane took over Carter's vacated LCB spot. Bobby Taylor played opposite him, moving up from FS; Jeff Burris switched to FS. Mike Miller, Jeff Burris, and Clint Johnson would be the primary kick returners. The punting chores switched to a committee—Rob Leonard, Adrian Jarell, and Brian Ford, with Kevin Pendergast handling the FGs. The defense would be charged with keeping the offense from having to play catch-up while it matured as a unit. The run defense looked solid; opposing QBs would be probing the pass defense for weaknesses, trying to isolate receivers on the linebackers.

That seems to be what Northwestern had in mind

Ray Zellars, fine Irish fullback, looking for someone to run over. **Photo by Bill Panzica**

on its first play from scrimmage in the '93 season, but a hustling Pete Bercich hugged the pass to his chest and lumbered 21 yards for a gift TD. The game settled into a dull affair until the waning seconds of the first half, when the 'Cats capped a 79-yard drive with an eight-yard TD pass from Len Williams to Dennis Lundy. They missed the PAT, so the Irish nursed a 7-6 lead into the third quarter. McDougal mishandled the center snap for a fumble early in the third quarter and NU struck quickly after recovering it deep in Irish territory, with Lundy registering an 11-yard TD scamper. They tried and missed a two-point conversion. McDougal atoned on the return drive with a 23-yard pass to Clint Johnson, then Becton set up a TD chance with a 16-yard burst up the middle. Zellars took it in from the six for the go-ahead TD and a 14-12 lead. McDougal found Miller wide open for a 50-yard gain on the next Irish possession, setting up Pendergast's 29-yard FG. Northwestern had experienced its high tide, and the Irish tallied two fourth-quarter scores to survive the scare—a 27-yard

Pendergast FG, then a fumble caused by Greg Lane led to a Jeff Burris TD from two yards out. The 'Cats gained more yardage than the Irish, 319 to 308, a measure of the basically conservative play calling by Holtz as he schooled his quarterback. The 27-12 score hid the fact that the Irish had been in a tougher ball game than they were used to with NU.

The Irish traveled to Ann Arbor to meet the Wolverines and try to undo the tie from '92. Kevin McDougal didn't waste much time in the game before he flashed speed and elusiveness not seen in an Irish signal caller since Tony Rice when he took off on a keeper down the left side and scored 43 yards later. The rest of that first quarter saw the teams trade FGs, a 32-yarder for UM's Peter Elezovic and a 24-yarder for Pendergast, set up by 32-yard strike from McDougal to Dawson. The Irish really rolled in the second quarter—Miller zipped 56 yards to a score with a Michigan punt and McDougal threaded his way for 11 yards on a scramble for another TD. In between those scores, powerful Tyrone Wheatley blasted for a one-yard TD to close a Wolverine drive of 89 yards and leave the halftime score at ND 24 to UM 10. Pendergast added a FG in the third quarter, a 19-yard chip shot, a gift from Burris's earlier INT. The Wolverines had plenty of fight left, scoring twice in the final frame, a Wheatley TD run of four yards to cap an impressive 99-yard drive, and a 13-yard scoring strike from Todd Collins to the aptly-named Mercury Hayes. The Irish foiled a two-point conversion with 34 seconds left, preserving their 27-23 triumph before 106,851 fans in the cavernous Michigan stadium. In winning on the road, the Irish showed a decisive, opportunistic offense, still on the conservative side, combined with a grudging, rock-ribbed defense. This team was beginning to define itself as more than a caretaker operation.

When the MSU Spartans visited ND, Holtz took the opportunity to showcase a TB recruit, Randy Kinder, who had played his high school ball in E. Lansing right in front of MSU's recruiters. The youngster responded in kind, darting for a game-high 94 yards on 12 runs, showing great acceleration turning the corner and running loose in the backfield. But the Spartans drew first blood, a one-yard slam by Craig Thomas after a patient drive covering 74 yards in 14 plays. MSU also scored the final TD of the game, a five-yard pass from Jim Miller to Mill Coleman. Everything else was done by the Irish: the Irish duplicated MSU's long drive in the second quarter with a 14-play, 75-yard march, with a TB sub, Robert Farmer, slamming in for a one-yard TD. This was followed by a Pendergast FG of 26 yards before Zellars closed out the half with a four-yard pass from McDougal. The Irish QB showed real flair on that drive, hitting crucial passes three times to his TE to keep the drive alive. In the third quarter, Pendergast tallied two FGs, set up by Irish TBs, then freshman fullback Marc Edwards bulled into the end zone from a yard out to make the score 29-7. McDougal teamed up with Becton near the end of the game for a 12-yard TD pass. MSU's second TD made the final score 36-14. This game showed that Holtz was starting to get a better sense of the possibilities of a talented stable of running backs, eight of whom ran the ball more than twice each as ND outgained MSU with 471 total yards to 251.

For the Purdue game, Becton was out with an injured hamstring, so it was a good thing that Holtz liked what he saw in his running backs. On a muddy field, Zellars and the new TBs picked up the slack in a workmanlike shutout win over Purdue, 17-0. The first half was a desultory affair, with no scoring. The Irish did not seem to be outgunned by Purdue, but they weren't moving the ball crisply. Bobby Taylor was the only highlight of the first half with a block of a Boilermaker FG try. The game's first score happened when Burris

Pete Bercich, rugged ILB in 1993 Northwestern game.

sacked Purdue's QB on a safety blitz, causing a fumble that DE Brian Hamilton alertly ran 28 yards for a TD. The fourth quarter was almost exhausted before Pendergast booted a 34-yard FG. Purdue fumbled the ensuing kickoff and the Irish ate up the remaining clock with seven plays, Marc Edwards ploughing in from the one for a TD. Stout Irish defense held the Boilermakers to 51 net yards rushing. Holtz took no chances with the passing game on the wet field, with only 10 Irish passes called for all day.

More than 10 passes *per quarter* were the norm for Stanford's Steve Stenstrom in the next game, but the Irish withstood the onslaught to hand Bill Walsh a 48-20 loss. Holtz kept the passing game under wraps again, with exactly 10 passes attempted again for the whole game, but this time they worked for 221 yards. Willie Clark garnered the first TD of the day, a nine-yard slash shortly after McDougal had lofted a 46-yard pass to Mike Miller. Stanford responded with a FG of 23 yards. McDougal eluded Stanford tacklers in the next quarter on a 17-yard TD jaunt on an option play, and Stanford came back with another FG for a 20-6 halftime score. In the third quarter, the Irish worked their first drive for more than five minutes, McDougal saving the drive with a third down pass of 24 yards to Dawson before scampering 19 yards on an option for an Irish TD. Stanford's Ellery Roberts tallied their first TD on the next series with a one-yard run, setting the stage for Clint Johnson's highlight-film 100-yard KO TD return (to go with an earlier 79-yard KOR). Stanford tried to pick up the pace, now down 34-13, and Stenstrom fired a 30-yard TD pass to Brian Manning to put them back in the game. But ND closed it out just as quickly with a six-play drive punctuated by a Becton TD run of eight yards. While McDougal shook out some cobwebs, Paul Failla added to his stats early in the fourth quarter with an 80-yard TD bomb to Derrick Mayes, ending the scoring at 48-20. Stenstrom had operated for 321 passing yards; great Irish D stuffed the Cardinal running game for 74 yards on 28 rushing attempts.

The next game turned into a total mismatch as Pittsburgh, under old nemesis Johnny Majors, expired at the Notre Dame Stadium 44-0. The Irish managed only two scores in the first half, but then scored at will. Starting with their first possession, Lee Becton tallied with an eight-yard TD run. Early in the second half, Greg Lane hauled in an INT and scooted 29 yards with it. Zellars slammed in from the 19 on the next play. ND mishandled the PAT snap, settling for a 13-0 run. Pendergast added to that with a 44-yard FG, then Lee Becton slashed seven yards for a commanding 17-0 Irish lead at the end of the first quarter. BYU mustered a drive that ended in futility with a missed FG, then Holtz unveiled the Irish air game with a 66-yard TD fling from McDougal to Miller as he slanted into the middle of the BYU defense. Jeff Burris killed another Cougar drive with an INT and FB Marc Edwards muscled his way into the end zone six plays later from the five, running the score up to 31-0. BYU avoided total ignominy with a two-yard TD pass at the end of the half from Tom Young to Eric Drage. Late in the third quarter, an Irish drive seemed to have stalled at the BYU 33, but McDougal saved the situation with a great 25-yard pass to Dawson on fourth and eight, setting up the baby bull fullback, Edwards, for a one-yard TD slam. BYU's Young added to their scoring with a three-yard TD run in the fourth quarter, but Paul Failla led a 73-yard drive with a 16-yard strike to Miller before wrapping up the day with a 35-yard TD strike, again to Miller. It was clear by this

Jeff Burris, stellar Irish free safety, bringing down another opponent. Burris also made signigicant contributions to the Irish offense.

halftime lead. Pitt had struggled to five first downs in the first half, but that would be their final total as the Irish D hammered them mercilessly in the second half. Pendergast booted a 27-yard FG early in the third frame, and Zellars converted a Bobby Taylor INT into an 11-yard TD romp. Early in the fourth quarter, McDougal spotted Mayes loose on the left sideline and fired a pass that Mayes hauled 55 yards, setting up a subsequent 31-yard TD jaunt by Kinder. After a three-yard TD run by another Irish TB, Robert Farmer, Jeff Burris sailed 60 yards to paydirt with a Panther punt to close out the scoring. Holtz used two different kickers on the final PATs, Drew Marsh and Stefan Schroffner. The Panthers could muster only 122 yards of total offense, eclipsed by ND's 539 yards, 371 coming on the ground. The Irish now had a 13-game winning streak.

Notre Dame flew out to Utah to meet BYU and whatever passing fancy was running the Cougar show. When it was all over, BYU had only 140 net yards of passing in a 42-20 loss to the Irish. The Irish offense, meanwhile, romped over and through BYU for 535 total yards, 307 of it coming on the ground in a running clinic. Ray Zellars led the way, around ND's massive right side, for the first score of the day with a 29-yard TD

A dominant force in the Notre Dame secondary, Bobby Taylor. **Photo by Br. Charles McBride**

point in the season that Holtz had certainly not lost his teaching touch.

USC came to South Bend with former head coach Johnny Robinson back at the helm hoping to end the 10-year-long drought. The Irish were up to the task, even without Kevin McDougal running the offense, and raced to a 28-7 halftime lead. USC kicked off and two plays later Lee Becton zoomed 70 yards for a TD. Later in the fourth quarter, the Irish took their time on a drive of 67 yards, executing 15 plays in nearly eight minutes, capped by a signature fullback TD blast of two yards by Edwards. In the second quarter, USC put together a modest drive but it stalled and they tried a 22-yard FG—but Jeff Burris blocked it, starting an 80-yard TD drive capped, appropriately enough, by a four-yard TD burst by—Jeff Burris. Trailing 21-0, USC fought back again on their next drive, marching 80 yards to a score, a 13-yard TD strike from Rob Johnson to Deon Strother. Now inside the last two minutes of the half, Clint Johnson took the USC kickoff and blasted 40 yards with it. Failla followed up with a 23-yard strike to Miller, setting up a middle screen to Zellars, but USC had it defensed. No matter, Zellars smashed

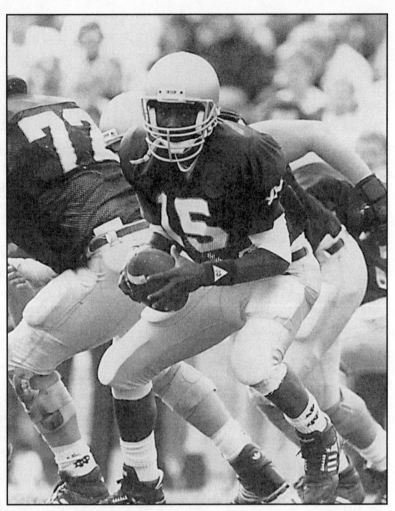

Record-setting quarterback for the 1993 team, Kevin McDougal.

through three Trojan tacklers, then hurdled a hapless DB to turn it into a 29-yard TD play. In the second half, ND settled for a 43-yard Pendergast FG at the end of the third quarter, and USC scored its final TD with an eight-yard TD pass from Johnson to Johnny McWilliams to make the final score read 31-13. The Irish ground game worked for 305 yards to USC's anemic 69 yards. The Trojans—famed as "Tailback U" and for "student body left and student body right" found themselves in the odd predicament of having to throw 46 passes. (In fact, in the '92 and '93 games, USC had gained a *total* of 144 yards on the ground, but had fired 87 passes. Notre Dame's corps of running backs, meanwhile, had smashed Trojan defense for 635 yards on the ground in those two games).

The Irish next met Navy at Veterans Stadium in Philadelphia, coming away with a 58-27 blowout win—but only after Navy had taken a 24-17 halftime lead against an apparently lackadaisical ND effort. Becton was most of the running game in the first half, gaining

124 yards—and would be lost with an injury in the second half—while Navy had mixed up its offense well enough to keep the Irish D hesitating when it should have been active. Navy scored first, a 38-yard FG, matched by Pendergast's 32-yarder. Navy came right back and took the lead with a 31-yard TD pass from Jim Kubiak to Damon Dixon. In the second quarter, Edwards finished a drive for ND with a three-yard TD burst. But Navy fired right back with a one-yard run by Brad Stramanak. Holtz knew a good thing when he saw it and insisted with Marc Edwards again who kept the Irish in it with a 10-yard TD run, his longest of the season so far, but Navy persisted with a 53-yard scoring pass from Kubiak to Jimmy Screen, a play where the Irish D looked almost inept. At the halftime, the ND players might have pondered the absurdity of losing this game just two weeks before facing number one Florida State. With renewed resolve and determination, the Irish came out and showed Navy just who was in command here,

slashing through the Middies' defense for 296 rushing yards. Lake Dawson made the first impression in the second half when McDougal scrambled to find him open enough to fire a 44-yard TD pass, making the score 24-24. Navy's offense failed to move, they punted, and Irish TB Randy Kinder almost immediately exploded up the middle on the second play for 70 yards and the go-ahead TD. The Irish nailed one more TD in Navy's coffin in the third quarter, set up by Marc Edward's longest run of the year, 27 yards, and tallied by a slashing Robert Farmer with a nine-yard run. Navy kept trying, earning a 34-yard FG, but ND pounded in three more scores in the fourth quarter, a Jeff Burris run of three yards, then yet another TD by Edwards, from the one, and a Bobby Taylor INT followed by his 31-yard return run for the score. When it was over, the Irish had overcome their bumbling in the first half to steamroll Navy for 604 yards of total offense. Becton ended up with 128 yards rushing and Kinder added 114 yards. Irish fullback Marc Edwards racked up 97 yards, almost completing an Irish trifecta.

Every now and then, college football has the fortunate scenario of a one-two matchup late in a season, and this unlikely Notre Dame team found itself hosting Florida State in that very manner. Notre Dame was facing a truly high-powered operation in FSU's team—

with offensive stars such as eventual Heisman winner Charlie Ward, Kez McCorvey, Tamarick Vanover, TB Warrick Dunn, and FB William Floyd operating the Seminole "fast-break offense" and a defense fired up by the likes of Derrick Brooks, Derrick Alexander, Jon Nance, and Toddrick McIntosh. Both teams were riding 16-game winning streaks, both had great team speed, high-powered offenses and intimidating defenses—your basic dream matchup. FSU's Ward struck first, hitting Kevin Knox with a 12-yard TD pass to end an 89-yard march. The Irish, butterflies dismissed, came right back on the next possession and used some trickery to use FSU's quickness and aggressive pursuit against them—Adrian Jarrell angled in for a TD on a 32-yard reverse play. The second quarter belonged to the Irish, with Becton slanting left for a 26-yard TD followed shortly by a John Covington INT to lead to a Jeff Burris six-yard TD burst. Leading 21-7 at the half, ND kept up the pressure in the third quarter with a 47-yard FG by Pendergast. FSU got back in the game with its next drive, an 80-yard affair, capped by a six-yard TD pass from Ward to the impressive freshman, Warrick Dunn. FSU kept up its effort in the fourth quarter with a 10-play drive that earned them a 24-yard Scott Bentley FG. The game's winning margin came courtesy of Jeff Burris, scoring from the 11—but leaving the Seminoles

1993 Lombardi Trophy winner, two-time All-American Aaron Taylor.

nearly seven minutes with which to operate. The teams exchanged punts, but the 'Noles worked a 45-yard drive late in the fourth quarter, with Ward firing a pass that was tipped but caught by McCorvey for a 20-yard score. Under two minutes, the Irish gave some hope to FSU when Jarrell did the almost impossible—a five-yard punt. The 'Noles had 51 seconds, one timeout, and Charlie Ward. He was almost up to it—completing four passes, including gains of 19 and 18 yards, putting the ball on the Irish 14 with 10 seconds left. On the last FSU play of the game, Shawn Wooden had a clear view of Ward's intentions, waited for the opportune second, then came up to bat the ball away from the intended receiver. With that play, Notre Dame clinched a 31-24 victory that saw their defense hold FSU to 96 yards rushing, including two big sacks of Ward by Bryant Young. Lee Becton ran for 122 yards on 26 carries to lead the jubilant Irish.

Ranked number one, standing at 10-0, with a 17-game winning streak, the Irish were once again on top of the collegiate football world. Against Boston College, they would pile up 427 yards of offense, score five TDs, including 22 points in the final eleven minutes—and lose a national championship on the last play of the game, 41-39. It was both an incredibly courageous performance, and a stunning, bitter defeat, with no love lost between the two teams, going back at least partially to the fake punt ND had run against BC while holding a 37-0 lead in the '92 contest. The Irish had the first scoring opportunity, a Pendergast 47-yard FG attempt, but BC's Stephen Boyd both blocked the try and then located the loose ball to return it to the ND 15. This took place halfway through the first quarter; it's hard to look into a game's final moments, but this represented a six-point turnaround, crucial to the game's outcome. The Irish drove back to BC's 39-yard line, but couldn't convert a fourth down play; BC took the opportunity to go all the way, using nine plays, ending the drive with a four-yard TD pass from Glenn Foley to Ivan Boyd, taking a 10-point lead into the second quarter. The teams traded four TDs in the second quarter—Zellars tallying with a 39-yard pass down the left sideline from McDougal, Boyd again from Foley with a 36-yard TD pass, followed by Jeff Burris ricocheting past left guard for a one-yard TD run, the teams' scoring burst completed by Pete Mitchell's three-yard pass from Foley in the final seconds of the half, BC leading 24-14. Matters grew even darker for the Irish when BC racked up another TD in the third quarter, a 21-yard zip by Darnell Campbell. Notre Dame could only muster a 29-yard Pendergast FG in response. Early in the fourth quarter, BC put the hammer down with an INT of a McDougal pass followed by a one-yard TD pass from Foley to Pete Mitchell, making the score a gloomy 38-17. All but out of the game, Notre Dame pulled off what would be a miraculous 22-point comeback for any other team. Having been ranked number one for less than a week, the Irish played like the champions they had worked so hard to be the rest of the game: McDougal throws a neat 22-yard pass to Derrick Mayes, leading to Becton's 29-yard TD jaunt, punctuated by a two-yard conversion pass play from McDougal to Becton; Jim Flanigan recovers a BC fumble, and six plays later

Zellars smashes in from the four for a TD; with 1:09 left, Notre Dame takes the lead with a TD pass of four yards from McDougal to Lake Dawson. Ahead 39-38, what happened to the Irish next was stunning—a personal foul called on Jeremy Sample for a late hit out of bounds on the kickoff gave BC the ball at their 25 rather than the 10. Somehow, Foley managed to work seven plays in the seconds remaining—including a pass incompletion that Pete Bercich nearly intercepted, then BC kicker David Gordon killed Notre Dame's national championship with a 41-yard FG with no time left in the game. BC QB Foley was allowed to play an unruffled game—no sacks, no appreciable hurries, as a somewhat passive (tired?) Irish defense couldn't muster the kind of pressure it had put on Charlie Ward a week earlier. Foley ended up completing 30 of 48 passes for 315 yards and four TDs—although a case could be made that kicking game woes hurt the Irish as much, if not as spectacularly. Lee Becton gained 122 yards on 14 carries to become the first 1,000-yard rusher for ND since Pinkett in '85—small consolation in light of what was lost as Gordon's FG floated through the goalposts at the north end of the desolated ND stadium.

Life goes on—Cubs fans prove that. The next chapter for the '93 Irish looked like an old chapter—the Cotton Bowl again and Texas A&M again, still with Corey Pullig as QB. This would be a "Poll Bowl" for the Irish—although in the final analysis, the voters almost predictably turned against Notre Dame anyway and voted Florida State the national title. (A strong case could be made that fickle wire service voters, on a fairly consistent basis, underrate ND when they are doing well and penalize them more harshly than others following losses or performances deemed to be insufficient—until the Gold and Blue are needed to round out the national slate of Bowls. The voters know that fans will come in droves and watch in tens of millions to see Notre Dame [1] win or [2] lose. So, the newswire voters appear to be tough on the Irish during the regular season, but need them nevertheless, the team everybody loves or loves to hate). In the '94 Cotton Bowl, beating A&M 24-21 apparently wasn't enough to overcome the desire to smite the Irish.

In the game, ND took the lead on a 19-yard McDougal TD run to end a beautiful 91-yard drive, but that was basically it for the rest of the half as A&M played great defense, holding the struggling Irish to 32 yards the rest of the half, while they scored the next two touchdowns. A&M's outstanding runner, Greg

Adrian Jarrell, reliable wide receiver for the Irish from 1989 to 1993.

Hill, sped eight yards for a TD near the end of the first quarter, then near the end of the second quarter, Pullig fired a 15-yard TD strike to Detron Smith for a 14-7 halftime lead. The Irish coaches and players had had some practice when it comes to using halftime to bring themselves to the higher pitch needed for the remaining half, and this was no exception. First, Lee Becton turned on the rushing jets that had been absent before the half to power a short third quarter drive that Ray Zellars ended with a two-yard TD blast. A&M's Rodney Thomas got that score back with a one-yard dive after an 80-yard drive. Following an 18-yard pass from McDougal to Zellars, Edwards tied the game at 21-21 with a characteristic two-yard TD smash, his ninth TD of the campaign. As proof of the existence of poetic justice, Pete Bercich doomed an Aggie drive with a clutch INT early in the fourth quarter. Then, with only 1:38 on the clock, Kevin Pendergast kicked the winning points with a 31-yard FG, thanks largely to a Mike Miller punt return of 38 yards to A&M's 22-yard line. On the ensuing ND kickoff, Jeff Burris really popped Aggie returner Rodney Thomas, causing a fumble that Bobby Taylor nabbed. The Aggies, however, had used up only eight lives—they still managed to get the ball

back. This time, however, they resorted to trickery—a lateral on a hook and ladder play, a lateral that went awry, recovered by an Irish LB. For their troubles, the Irish ended up the number two team in the country—perhaps one of the most cherished such rankings, since no one had seriously envisioned such eminence for this team. Lou Holtz proved to be a great teacher, especially of his senior QB, Kevin McDougal, whose season became a new Irish standard, setting three records that will be difficult to break: [1] the single-season pass completion percentage, .616 (98 completions in 159 attempts) [2] ND's career pass completion percentage, .622 (112 completions in 180 attempts) [3] best career passing efficiency mark—154.41, surpassing Mirer's previous QB career mark of 138.9 [4] career leader for passing yards gained per attempt—9.58 yards (180 for 1,726 yards). These marks are complemented by his season's mark of yards gained per pass attempt (9.69 yards per attempt for '93, 1,541 yards in 159 attempts), second only to John Huarte's 1964 campaign, and his INT avoidance mark, second best among all Irish QBs, .0333 (six career INTs in 180 attempts), just a notch behind Mirer's standard of .0329. In directing McDougal's senior season, Holtz and his staff showed a mastery of detail, excellent play selection in light of a player's gifts, of knowing a player's limitations, and of emphasizing a player's strengths. The Irish as a team had only 10 lost miscues (five fumbles, five INTs) in 798 opportunities (561 runs, 185 pass attempts, 29 punt returns, 23 KO returns). The defense chopped off even more of the opponents' total rushing, from the 1,222 yards allowed in '92 to an impressive 985 yards. In sum, the 1993 Irish campaign was a classic case of overachievement nearly resulting in a national championship—but for a questionable penalty call, a missed INT, and a FG on the last play of the BC game (all in one drive), this team would have entered the pantheon of Notre Dame immortals. Aaron Taylor and Jeff Burris earned All-America honors, with Bobby Taylor getting impressive recognition as well.

1993 record: 11-1-0 (.916)
Record to date: 723-211-41 (.762)

1994

From the standpoint of expectations, oddly enough, the 1994 Notre Dame season bore some similarities to the 1981 campaign. In 1981, Irish players and fans had been excited by the bright promise brought to the program by new head coach Gerry Faust. His unbelievable record and incredible work ethic at Cincinnati's Moeller High had all leprechauns everywhere ecstatic with dancing visions of national championships running through their dreams and thoughts.

That was then—overwrought expectations about a coach. In 1994, however, the expectations were largely grounded on a player, a sophomore with skills reminiscent of previous greats. With a brilliant high school career from a region of Pennsylvania that had produced classic All-America quarterbacks for decades, blessed with good size and a strong arm, Ron Powlus as the heir apparent raised the expectations of Irish fans everywhere. No one doubted his arm and his competitive desire. The real question, as with any newcomer to the position, involved whether he would be able to do the multiple tasks Holtz asked of his QBs, especially running the option, not to mention reading the more complicated defenses he would face in college football. How would Powlus react when flushed from the pocket? Above all, perhaps, how would he handle the pressure of being Notre Dame's starting QB? There are precious few roles in life for young adults that demand the balance of composure, maturity, leadership, charisma, intelligence, and toughness that characterize the demands faced by those who play QB for Notre Dame. All of this remained to be seen in the case of the youngster who would follow the record-setting years of Rick Mirer and Kevin McDougal.

On paper, Holtz's offense looked at least adequate—fair experience and size in the line, a good complement of backs and receivers. But looking at this team is to try to analyze a moving target; the offensive line, for instance, had nine different sets of starters in twelve games. Powlus would be dealing with two different centers—Dusty Zeigler and Rick Kaczenski. He would be giving the ball to three different backfield units, led by 1,000-yard runner Lee Becton and sophomore Randy Kinder at TB, with Zellars and sophomore Marc Edwards (whose eight TDs as a freshman had set an Irish record) at FB. All of this because of an unbelievable, excruciating sequence of injuries that afflicted Holtz's Irish throughout the '94 season. The starting interior

Paul Grasmanis started at nose guard for the Irish in '94 and '95.

line for the season's first game averaged 284 pounds—but the starting lineup in terms of time played per position comes in at a rather light 273 pounds. Those 11 pounds are merely symbolic—more important is the fact that the changing cast of characters meant constant adjustments, constant interruptions in a team's basic character, constant alterations in team chemistry, and a constant struggle to learn basic assignments and gain the right feel for the work of your teammates. Mixing nine different starting interior lines with three different sets of running backs is a sure formula for frustration and, occasionally, disaster. Several linemen had to play two positions over the course of the campaign as Holtz patched here and tinkered there, especially with Ryan Leahy, Dusty Zeigler, and various underclassmen. The only consistency on the '94 ND offense would be found in the QB and SE Derrick Mayes, who started all 12 games, and TE Oscar McBride, who started 11 games.

The musical chairs routine did not stop with the ND offense. The Irish D played precisely one game with the first game's starting unit; after that injuries and personnel changes led to a unit that had six different looks in the remaining 11 games. Most of the problems

Ryan Leahy, solid offensive lineman for Holtz, grandson of coach Frank Leahy.

struck the Irish flanks—the outside linebackers and ends played in eight different combinations in the 12 games. This was on top of making the adjustment to a new defensive coordinator, Bob Davie, who made the big switch from Texas A&M to ND, and from ND's 4-3 look in '93 to his preferred 3-4 set. Davie placed a premium on overall team speed, but even more than usual for the linebackers, giving the Irish some of the A&M look for blitzing and aggressiveness. Oliver Gibson at NG and Paul Grasmanis as one of the ends gave Davie a good pair to start with on his D line, while Jeremy Sample and Justin Goheen would try to hold the fort as the inside linebackers—probably not exactly the model Davie's scheme demanded—as seen in the fact that FS Brian Magee would lead the Irish in tackles for the season. Still, Sample and Goheen would be consistent troopers in the '94 campaign. The DBs were led by Bobby Taylor and Shawn Wooden on the corners, with Taylor in his third season as a starter, and Magee and Travis Davis as the safeties. Playing for their third coach in four seasons, this defensive group's putting it all together might prove to be difficult.

On special teams, Holtz would basically spend the entire year trying to find the right combination for his punter and FG kicker. Holtz would have a pretty good pair of kick returners, led by Mike Miller, but they were not really game breakers. In short, the kicking game would not measure up as the season progressed. Two seasons after Hentrich's departure, no one had really stepped up to replace the All-America kicker.

In sum, this looked like another transition year—a transition into a new QB with new potential and a new type of on-the-field leadership, and a transition into a new defensive scheme. In fact, the season would prove to be an adjustment into a trench mentality, waiting for the next disaster to hit, trying to learn how to handle adversity coming at the team in waves.

It didn't start out that way. Ranked third nationally, the Irish met Northwestern and rocked the Wildcats 42-15. QB Ron Powlus, in his first game for ND, joined the record books and Irish luminaries named Bertelli, Lamonica, and Beuerlein when he ended the day with four TD passes—arguably the best first-game performance ever by a new Irish QB. The Irish started out the game using an unbalanced line, a wrinkle they would largely abandon as attrition later struck their personnel. In the first quarter, Bobby Taylor snagged a pass by NU and returned it 38 yards, but the Irish failed to capitalize on the opportunity. In the second quarter, the QB found Mike Miller open but his pass was underthrown; Miller made a good catch anyway and hauled it 42 yards deep into NU territory. Three plays later, Powlus found Derrick Mayes in the end zone corner and hit him with a nine-yard TD pass. The 'Cats came back to try a 22-yard FG, which was tipped by Taylor, but it corkscrewed through the posts anyway. The Irish owned the rest of the quarter—a flanker reverse to Miller good for 14 yards set up a 46-yard TD pass on a post pattern to Miller, then Shawn Wooden hauled in an INT that led to Zellars catching a two-yard TD pass. In the third frame, Zellars made a fantastic one-handed catch on a screen pass, then rumbled 20 yards to the NU 7. Lee Becton wrapped it up with a sweep right for a two-yard TD play and a 35-3 Irish lead. Powlus inscribed his name in the QB record books in his first Notre Dame game with a fourth-down TD pass of 36 yards to Mayes. In the fourth quarter, NU scored on a five-yard run by Dennis Lundy but Travis Davis stopped a later drive by NU deep into ND territory with an INT. Backup QB Tom Krug then got into the act with a seven-yard TD before Tim Hughes scooted nine yards to paydirt for the 'Cats to make the final score read ND 42, NU 15. In his first game, Holtz's new starting QB had gone 18

for 24 with 291 yards and four TDs, nearly 10 percent of Rick Mirer's career total of TDs.

The blush came off the Irish rose a week later when Michigan beat the Irish 26-24 on the strength of a last-minute FG. The Wolverines served an early notice of some sorts by refusing to be the first team out on the field for the opening kickoff. Powlus showed good judgment and maturity when he broke an arm tackle on the first drive, stepped up into the pocket and found Zellars in the right flat for a 14-yard gain. Stefan Schroffner made a 32-yard FG for ND's 3-0 lead. The Wolverines used the next drive, their first of the game, to reach a dramatic turning point—Walter Smith returned the Irish KO 46 yards to set up a 29-yard FG try by Remy Hamilton, but a great Irish D blocked the kick—unfortunately, however, FB Che Foster snagged the rebound and advanced it for a first down. Reinvigorated, UM took it on in from there, Zaire's Tim Biakabutuka ramming it in up the middle from the ND 10. The PAT made it 7-3, the four-point swing in Irish misfortune being more than enough to cover the game's final margin. But no one could see that outcome halfway through the first quarter. Lee Becton got the TD back after an 80-yard march in response, although it took the Irish four tries from within the one-yard line, Becton snagging a one-yard TD pass. In the second quarter, Becton lost the handle on a pitch from Powlus; Remy Hamilton tied the game at 10-10 with a 33-yard FG a few moments later. In the third quarter, the Irish scored midway through when ND's bruising Marc Edwards rambled eight yards untouched through the middle of the UM team for a TD. Michigan tied it 17-17 on its next drive with a three-yard TD pass from Todd Collins to TE Jay Riemersma. Scant moments later, Becton fumbled again and Hamilton capitalized with another FG, this one from 35 yards out, for a 20-17 UM lead. The first score of the fourth quarter, a 32-yard FG by Hamilton, also came off another Irish fumble. ND took the lead, however, when Powlus fired a seven-yard TD strike to Derrick Mayes. With 46 seconds left in the game, the Wolverines geared up for another drive and made it work well enough for Hamilton to drive the final nail in the coffin with a 42-yard FG. Two seconds were left on the clock. Time wasn't the big problem for Notre Dame this day—turnovers were the story, with three lost fumbles in this one game as opposed to 10 turnovers in 12 games in '93. Furthermore, the option play that Holtz favors so much did not work smoothly; Ron Powlus is obviously not Tony Rice coming down the line of scrimmage. Rice made the play work crisply with incredible foot quickness

Jeremy Sample, starting ILB for the Irish, makes his decision on run or pass in '94 action.

and impeccable decisions. Rice could make you miss a tackle or an assignment; Holtz's offense would have to make do with a QB who more or less lumbers along, pretty much an easy target for a defender.

The Irish had handled MSU's Spartans the year before 36-14. In 1994, however, ND would squeak past a persistent Spartan team 21-20, another measure of the difficulty this Irish team would face all season. The win would give Holtz a new ND record—16 straight road wins (a stat that is misleading, for the Irish had stumbled at home just often enough in recent seasons to cause some disgruntlement). Some key Irish players were hurting—Derrick Mayes with a bad ankle, Ryan Leahy likewise, and Lee Becton with a hurt foot (followed by a groin pull in the second half). Mayes and Becton would contribute, but not as well as they would have liked. The Irish D knocked MSU off stride on the first drive, with timely blitzes and sacks by Justin Goheen and Jeremy Nau. Jeremy Sample nailed a third sack on their next drive, forcing a punt but Miller fumbled it at his 20, allowing MSU to kick a 31-yard FG. The Irish offense stayed stalled into the second quarter, and Mill Coleman kept the pressure on with a 30-yard TD burst on a flanker reverse. Mayes got that one back with a 29-yard TD pass from Powlus. Spartan QB Tony Banks scored on another three-yard TD run and kicker Chris Gardner tacked on a 24-yard FG for an Irish halftime deficit of 7-20. Irish drives were being killed by INTs in the meantime. But the last MSU FG was it for the Spartans, and ND won the game with a third-quarter 37-yard TD run by Becton on a fake trap to the FB followed by an option play and a fourth-quarter 15-yard TD pass to TB Robert Farmer off a flanker screen as a decoy. Steffan Schroffner kept the Irish kickers from being completely in the dog house when he made the two needed PATs. Holtz had eschewed kicking a FG from the MSU 25 in the third quarter, a good indication of his mistrust in that department. Powlus had a horrible day—10 of 30 for 161 yards and the one TD, but four costly INTs. Sophomore TB Randy Kinder saved the day for the Irish ground game, subbing for the injured Becton with 104 yards on 18 carries. After three games, it was apparent that the kicking game was a potential weakness, the option play was not going to be the core of the offense, Powlus could be streaky completing passes. None of this was good news for the Irish.

Shawn Wooden's strong defensive play in '94 helped turn the ball over to the Irish offense on numerous occasions.

The injuries that would mar the season kept Becton and Leahy, among others, out of the Purdue game. The kicking game resulted in a blown drive, the first of the game for ND, when Schroffner's 22-yard try glanced off the right goalpost. On their next possession, it became clear to keen observers that Powlus was not at his best when he was flushed from the pocket and had to throw downfield on the run. But the Irish D kept Purdue and their big fullback, 235-pound Mike Alstott, in check until Holtz's offense could get untracked. The Irish broke the ice with a 31-yard FG near the end of the first quarter. In the second quarter, the QB enjoyed the luck of the Irish when he floated a pass into double coverage, caught by Charles Stafford anyway for a 15-yard TD. The Irish kicker, perhaps pumped by his earlier FG, promptly shanked the PAT try, but Purdue was offside. An impatient Holtz yanked the hapless kicker, and Schroffner tallied the PAT for a 10-0 Irish lead. A forgiving Holtz then had his chastened kicker try a squib kick on the next KO. Purdue was still stymied and

Schroffner capped the next Irish drive with a 27-yard FG. Purdue closed up the gap with an answering drive of 64 yards good for a two-yard TD run off the left side by Joe Hagins while Irish defenders were mesmerized by Alstott slamming into the middle. Notre Dame came right back on the next drive, marched 75 yards, and tallied when Kinder followed an explosive Oscar McBride block for a three-yard scoring run. A two-point run try failed and ND led at the half 19-7. The Irish D stopped the first two drives by Purdue, first with a Grasmanis sack and later an INT by Sample off a Taylor tip. Ray Zellars swept left for 35 yards to set up a Schroffner FG of 23 yards. Travis Davis snagged an Alstott fumble on the next drive and Schroffner racked up a 33-yard FG for a 25-7 lead. Bobby Taylor caused a fumble on Purdue's next drive, the Irish recovered it, and then Zellars executed a one-man highlight film TD run of 62 yards on a sweep, including turning a hapless Purdue DB into road pizza. Kinder tallied a one-yard TD in the fourth quarter, then ND hung on while Purdue scored twice for the 39-21 final score. Zellars and Kinder annihilated the Boilermaker defense with 156 and 146 yards rushing respectively and Powlus was given a homework assignment to improve over his MSU miseries, which he did with nine completions in 14 tries for 111 careful yards. Notre Dame's ninth straight win over Purdue revealed a gap in total yards of 547 for the Irish to 266 for Purdue.

With starter Lee Becton still nursing his ailments, Kinder added to ND's woes when he sprained a foot jumping over a fence during the week before the game with Stanford. Meanwhile, Bill Walsh's QB, Steve Stenstrom, was zipping passes for 300-plus yards per game and he did not disappoint this time either—hitting 37 of 59 passes for 360 yards and two TDs. Walsh had beaten the Irish on their home turf twice in a row; no one had won three in a row in more than 30 years. In spite of Stenstrom's heroics, the Irish prevailed 34-15 in Walsh's final visit as Stanford's coach to the Dome. Stanford worked a 14-play drive on its first possession to earn a 34-yard FG and the only lead they would enjoy for the day. Near the end of the first quarter, following a Stanford fumble recovered by an Irish reserve WR, the Irish struck with a 15-yard TD pass from the QB to Stafford. Schroffner came out of the kicking committee and tacked on the PAT for the 7-3 lead. Stanford answered with a 20-yard drive but they missed a FG try. The Irish tallied in the second quarter with a FG set up by a Zellars romp of 58 yards in which he absolutely dusted four would-be tacklers. Stanford was winning the

clock at the half, holding the ball for 22:07 to ND's 7:53, a pattern that didn't change dramatically in the second half as ND used five and six DBs to contain the threat without allowing a full-scale barrage of points. Stanford had no answer to three Irish scores in the third quarter. The Irish had Powlus in command on the first drive of the second half: finding Mayes for 20 yards on a great catch, then Zellars for 17 yards before coming back to Mayes, rolling right, for a 10-yard TD strike. After some inconclusive possessions, Powlus geared it up again and found Miller, after a play fake, open for a 47-yard TD strike. Shawn Wooden grabbed a Stanford fumble, and sophomore ND kicker Scott Cengia stepped up for a 32-yard FG and a 27-3 Irish lead. Marc Edwards wrapped up Notre Dame's scoring with one of his patented one-yard TD slams out of the full-T backfield. Stanford scored on a nine-yard TD pass but Travis Davis blocked the PAT, then they scored on a 23-yard pass, but Sample turned a two-point try into an Irish INT to make the final score read 34-15 for Notre Dame. Stanford ran a staggering 95 offensive plays to 50 for ND, but the Irish averaged 7.7 yards per play. Powlus hit 11 of 14 attempts for 166 yards and three TDs; Stenstrom went 37 for 59 for 360 yards and two TDs.

Ranked eighth, the Irish looked to be capable

Oliver Gibson turned in a commanding performance in a close loss to FSU.

of overcoming their shortcomings and injuries, and appeared to be jelling as a team as they looked to play Boston College. Their 4-1 record, however, would prove to be the high-tide point of their season: all the wheels fell off against BC as the Golden Eagles prevailed 30-11 in a game where the Irish didn't seem to have their hearts in the contest. After enjoying a carefully crafted passing game against Stanford, Powlus backslid horribly, nagged by a groin pull, to a mere five completions in 21 attempts for a miserable 50 yards, two INTs and no TDs. With Becton and Zellars out with injuries, and the line depleted with Leahy's absence, the Notre Dame offense mustered only 210 net yards, led by the Kinder's 148 yards on the ground. Boston College's DE Mike Mamula hounded Powlus throughout. BC, meanwhile, used a good ground game, led by Justice Smith's 147 yards, and trick plays such as a fake field goal play and a pass off a fake reverse to keep the Irish on their heels. The Irish scored first on a Schroffner 27-yard FG, then watched as BC scored on three TD runs and a FG before Kinder jetted in on a 15-yard TD run. BC tacked on another rushing TD to make the final score 30-11 in their favor. The Irish offense had not looked this inept in many, many years.

Unbelievably, the wheels did not get back on the Notre Dame offense in time to beat BYU a week later at home. The Cougars kept up the defensive pressure on Powlus, with four sacks, to go with nine other ND plays stopped behind the LOS. The constant pounding led to a concussion for Powlus and a seat on the bench in the fourth quarter. Irish kickers muffed three FGs—more than enough to have won the game. It started out well enough for ND, however, when Kinder rocketed through the Cougars for a 41-yard TD run to cap the opening possession of the game. BYU mustered an answering 49-yard FG at the end of the first quarter, then tallied another halfway into the second quarter before Jamal Willis hauled in a 19-yard TD pass from John Walsh—set up by a Notre Dame gift fumble (a botched center snap) recovered by BYU at the Irish 45. Derrick Mayes countered that score with 34 seconds left in the half when he scored from the BYU 7 with a pass, following a 55-yard aerial gain. The third quarter was scoreless, but not without ND reaching the BYU three-yard line before driving backwards—two runs stopped, then an 18-yard loss on a sack of Powlus, all capped off lamentably by a blocked FG. In the final frame, BYU tacked on eight more points with another Willis TD on a two-yard run, and a two-point conversion. ND had nearly the whole quarter to operate but kept misfiring.

BYU tried to help out with a fumble and a turnover, leading to a 37-yard run by Edwards to help the Irish reach BYU's 14. Powlus suffered his concussion on this drive, a fitting preface to Schroffner's missed 32-yard FG try. On the last Irish drive, reserve QB Tom Krug completed his first two passes, then missed his final four throws to put the final sad punctuation to a tough day for Notre Dame.

Somebody would have to step it up pretty soon or the season could become a total disaster. Notre Dame found a hero just in time, Emmett Mosley, a 5' 9" kick returner and WR, who turned on the jets long enough to rack up four TDs against Navy as ND blitzed the Middies 58-21. Holtz shifted the speedster from flanker to tailback and Mosley met the challenge to lead a host of Irish runners with 84 yards on 15 carries (Becton (groin) and Zellars (ankle) were not yet ready to play). The five interior offensive line positions saw three new starters as well—Jeremy Akers, Mark Zataveski, and Mike Doughty—as Holtz did what he could to spark the team out of its doldrums. Navy scored first, a 32-yard TD pass from Jim Kubiak to Ross Scott, but the sky fell on them in the form of 51 unanswered points: in the first quarter, Mosley scored on an 11-yard TD slant to the right, then a 38-yard FG; in the second quarter, Mosley, really enjoying himself, on a 19-yard TD zip, then Mayes with a 60-yard TD pass, Alton Maiden with an INT and a 44-yard TD return, then a Mayes encore with a 20-yard scoring strike; in the third quarter, Mosley burned the Middies again with a 24-yard TD run; in the final frame, an Irish LB clutched a Navy KO fumble and Mosley, the WR-turned-TB hero, ploughed two yards over the right side out of a full-house T for his final TD of a big day. Navy tallied a consolation TD before TE Leon Wallace hauled in a 15-yard TD pass from sub QB Gus Ornstein, ending a TD drought for Irish TEs that went back to the '92 season. The makeshift line and Holtz's committee of runners managed 267 yards on the ground to Navy's 28. Mosley's all-purpose yardage for the day came to an impressive 206 yards—a welcome boost for the beleaguered Irish. QB Powlus was kept reined in—eight attempts, four completions, two TDs, 126 yards.

With the season becoming a shambles, Holtz and the Irish had two weeks to prepare for Bobby Bowden and his eighth-ranked Seminoles, winners in seven of their eight games. This would allow time for the nagging injuries to heal, for newly assigned players to become more familiar with their positions, and for the Irish to do a serious gut check. Ever the tinkerer, Holtz

Travis Davis, part of a strong Irish defensive effort against Stanford.

yards. His run led directly to a second FSU FG, a 30-yarder. Things looked dark indeed for ND on the next possession when Powlus rolled right and threw into a gaggle of Seminoles, six to be precise, giving Derrick Brooks an INT. Bobby Taylor redeemed the offense's error when he hammered Kanell from the blind side on a blitz, recovered the ensuing fumble, and rumbled 57 yards to the end zone—one of the genuine highlight plays of the '94 season. But FSU showed their mettle with a drive to end the half that garnered yet another FG, a 19-yard boot set up by another Rock Preston run to daylight. In the third quarter, a patient drive netted an Irish FG and a 10-9 lead—but a scrambling Powlus missed seeing an open Oscar McBride in the FSU middle. Preston came back to haunt the Irish at the end of the third quarter when he jetted straight up the Irish middle on a 28-yard TD run. The Irish tied the game at 16-16 when Derrick Mayes scored with an 11-yard TD pass, tying Jack Snow's record of nine TD catches in a season, but the PAT kick bounced off the left post, yet another dud kick in a long tale of such woes this season. FSU earned the win with 2:53 left in the game when old nemesis Warrick Dunn scored on a five-yard TD run off the left side. Irish NG Oliver Gibson nearly had the elusive Dunn on the play, another big if in a long season of such plays. In two remaining possessions, Powlus threw four incompletions and was sacked once—just not enough firepower to win the game. Preston and Dunn rushed for 165 and 163 yards respectively, far too much for ND to be able to control the clock and the game's tempo. The Irish kicking game must have left Holtz kicking himself in frustration. And Powlus had not been exactly scintillating—nine of 22 for 83 yards, one TD, and two INTs. In spite of this, Notre Dame might still have won the game, but the breaks, the supposed "luck o' the Irish," just did not go their way.

The 5-4 Irish next had to face the 7-3 Falcons of Air Force, operating out of their slightly weird "Wing Bone" (nice pun, right, for Falcons) which set halfbacks out on the flanks, angled in towards the center. Variations on the Bone hid personnel deficiencies, maximized strengths, and often gave the Irish fits. With Beau Morgan at QB—a pretty slick customer, blessed with great speed, a keen mind for option reads, and plenty of sheer guts for a little guy—Air Force was staring at the

made two more switches in the line (Akers and Chris Clevenger) and decided to go with his sophomores as his backs, although Becton would play much of the time. So, taped up, jury-rigged, bashed by delighted critics, the Irish played a whale of a game against the loaded Seminoles, but lost in a great effort, 23-16. The game's first break came when the D forced a fumble, recovered at the FSU 30. The Irish couldn't move, tried a 45-yard FG, but the kicker missed to the left—yet another blot on the '94 season's kicking game. The Irish operated with six DBs in obvious passing downs and FSU QB Danny Kanell was having a hard time reading the coverages, giving ND's pass rush some good shots at him. After a couple of possessions, Powlus made the mistake of firing into triple coverage, Stafford tipped the pass, and FSU hauled in the INT. The 'Noles used the freebie to notch a 20-yard FG for a 3-0 lead, a six-point turnaround given the failed ND FG. The Irish were unable to sustain a drive, punted, and then flailed at tailback Rock Preston when he took the snap in the shotgun and zipped 46 chance to doom the entire ND season. They came out and tried to take charge, going 60 yards before settling for a 23-yard FG. Perhaps the Irish players had taken stock of their plight, or the 3-0 score energized them, whatever, but they slammed the door on the Falcons then and there, with five unanswered TDs: Derrick Mayes made a fantastic catch over the middle for a 45-yard gain, then Zellars slammed in for the TD from the AFA three. In the second quarter, Mayes broke Snow's record when he caught a 25-yard TD pass, his tenth of the season. Moments later, Kinnon Tatum, an alert Irish LB, recovered a Falcon fumble on an option play and the offense went back to work, Mayes tallying with a seven-yard TD pass, Powlus's 18th of the season, tying Mirer's record. In the third quarter, the opening drive saw ND drive deep, survive a QB fumble, then rack up a one-yard Zellars TD, giving Notre Dame a 35-3 lead. The Falcons, with no quit in them, closed the gap considerably by tallying the next three scores: Morgan fired a 51-yard TD strike, then scampered 21 yards for another score; in the fourth quarter, Morgan sparked another score with a 35-yard pass, with Nakia Addison registering the TD on a one-yard run. Lee Becton, back in action, closed ND's scoring with a 10-yard TD burst on an option play. Morgan struck one final time with a six-yard TD run to make the final score 42-30. Becton looked to be back in good form with 115 yards on 19 carries. Ron Powlus bounced back to hit 13 of 18 attempts for 227 yards and the two scores. But the Irish surely had to have generated some respect for the scrappy Falcons and their diminutive QB.

If Holtz could beat USC, the Irish would have their 12th straight win over Troy and Holtz would have his 200th career win. John Robinson's team boasted the third-ranked passer in the country in Rob Johnson. Holtz would not earn his personal win, however, the win streak over USC was not exactly broken, just marred a bit with a disappointing 17-17 tie. Using a quick pitch option, the Irish maneuvered 68 yards in 12 careful plays, Schroffner earning the honors with a 29-yard FG. In the second quarter, Powlus spotted a wide-open Stafford roaming unregarded in the middle of the Trojan secondary and hit him with a perfectly thrown pass, but the receiver failed to complete the connection and the Irish lost what appeared to be a sure scoring opportunity. The Irish drive went clunk again when Oscar McBride dropped a pass good enough for a first down on the next play. USC took advantage of the break to score on their next possession—although

the TD was registered by Johnny McWilliams while he was unceremoniously seated in the ND end zone. Notre Dame kept up the pressure with a nice drive of their own just before the halftime, marching 80 yards in 10 plays, with Zellars hauling in an 11-yard scoring pass, a play that broke Mirer's single-season TD pass record, giving the Irish a 10-7 halftime lead. In the third quarter, Trojan punter Cole Ford blasted a 65-yard punt to end their first possession, the Irish couldn't respond, and USC tied the game with a 23-yard FG by Ford. Notre Dame came right back, scoring 10 plays after a 65-yard drive, sparked by Becton's 29-yard scamper and capped by a one-yard QB sneak. Good pass defense by the Irish kept USC bottled up the rest of the third quarter. Kicking game woes struck ND in cruel fashion in the fourth quarter having started at their 20, the Irish had negotiated to the Trojan 23 where Stefan Schroffner's attempted FG was blocked and recovered for a 56-yard runback by Sammy Knight. Capitalizing on a drive conveniently starting at ND's 16-yard line, Shawn Walters slammed in for a one-yard TD run and the 17-17 tie. The Irish had the ball for two more possessions but were unable to score. The tale of the game was the fact that USC's 17 points were earned on three "drives" totaling 74 yards. Notre Dame's 17 points came after drives that rolled for 213 yards, a nearly criminal contrast to SC's good luck. Becton had roamed through the Trojans for 158 yards on 26 carries and the Irish passing game had clicked well enough—Powlus hitting 13 of 22 for 115 yards and a TD. A key to the outcome is found in the difference in the punting game: six punts for ND for a 32.5 yard average, in contrast to USC's five punts for an average of 48.8 yards, a terrible yardage exchange for the Irish. This stat, combined with the woes in the FG department and the gifts of three short drives, proved to be too much of a deficit to overcome for a win.

Unranked, standing 6-4-1, the Irish met Colorado in the 1995 Fiesta Bowl. The Buffs, fourth-ranked, with Heisman winner Rashaan Salaam, do-everything QB Kordell Stewart, and only one loss looked too strong for ND. Holtz would be missing Kinder and Bobby Taylor (who had, in fact, played his last game under the Dome). This time, appearances matched reality and the Irish bowed to the talented Buffaloes 41-24. The Irish D contained Salaam, holding him to 83 yards on 27 carries, but Stewart ran them ragged on option plays, with a mere seven carries for 143 impressive yards. Powlus compared favorably to Stewart in passing, with three TDs on 18 completions in 34 attempts good for 259 yards (to Stewart's 12 or 21 for 227 yards and one TD). Holtz likes the option and he had to like what he saw—except it was the other team doing a Veg-a-matic on his defense. At least he'd have the game films to use to show his QBs how it ought to be executed (which would be cruel anyway since Powlus is really a classic dropback QB, in the Dan Marino mold, not a nimble-footed option motor scooter). Colorado would sack Powlus seven times, leading to a net of 149 yards on the ground for ND, well under their usual net yardage. The Buffs took the early lead and never lost it: they tallied a 33-yard FG to cap their first drive, then used two big plays, a Stewart run of 29 yards and a Stewart pass for 37 yards, for a quick drive ended by a one-yard TD run. The Irish settled for a 29-yard Cengia FG near the end of the first quarter to break into the scoring column. In the second quarter, Colorado slammed the door with three TDs—Stewart on a nine-yard run and Salaam for a pair of one-yarders. Mayes snatched a 20-yard pass followed by a seven-yard TD to make the halftime score read 31-10, Buffs up. Mayes hauled in a 40-yard TD strike in the third quarter, but CU tallied a 48-yard FG. Salaam racked up a five-yard TD run in the fourth quarter, and Irish TE Leon Wallace (perhaps modern college football's version of a lonesome end) wrapped up the scoring with a seven-yard TD pass from Powlus. The 41-24 outcome was not ever really in doubt once the game began, and the Irish performance did not mollify those who thought the team did not deserve to be in the Fiesta Bowl. They did not, however, embarrass themselves—they were simply outclassed by a more talented team.

The 6-5-1 record could have been significantly better had Notre Dame enjoyed some of the luck that often blessed the team in other seasons. The kicking game was particularly snake-bitten—the blocked FG that contributed to the two-point loss to Michigan, three missed FGs in the seven-point loss to BYU, a missed PAT and a missed FG in the seven-point loss to FSU, and the blocked FG in the USC tie. Ron Powlus's performances had been streaky, he was clearly not a whiz trying to run the option, and he tended to try to force completions when harried and scrambling. Total offense dropped off nearly 500 yards from '93 to '94, down from 4,725 yards to 4,230, with most of that loss happening in the running game, down from 2,868 yards in '93 to 2,372 yards in '94, with injuries to starters the primary culprit. Not highly mobile, Powlus proved to

be a tempting target for pass rushers; the Irish had lost 241 yards in '93, but proved porous enough in '94 to lose 408 yards as the hapless starter absorbed 25 sacks. In '93, the Irish had made good 14 of 19 FG tries; in '94, they could manage only 11 of 18, but gave up 16 to opponents, double the '93 figure. Kick returns fell modestly, from 859 yards to 822, but punt-return yardage almost dried up, from 293 yards to 89, down from a 10-yard average return to 4.9 yards per return. The Irish were minus-one in turnovers in '94, but had been plus-13 in '93. Powlus clearly represented a serious passing threat; in his first season as a starter, he had fired almost half of the career TDs Mirer had thrown in more than three seasons. The defense gave up considerably more rushing yards in '94 than in '93—1,538 yards allowed on the grounds in '94 compared to 985 yards the prior season. The scoring differential changed dramatically, not in ND's favor: the '93 Irish scored 403 points and allowed 194, but the '94 team fell to 318 points and allowed 239. Bobby Taylor earned the only recognition as an All-American for Notre Dame in '94—but someone should have been paying attention to Derrick Mayes.

1994 record: 6-5-1 (.541)
Record to date: 729-216-42 (.759)

1995

After the disastrous '94 season, the '95 campaign looked like a rebuilding project. Holtz would have to find and school replacements for Lee Becton and Ray Zellars, Mark Zataveski and Oscar McBride, but the real problem was on the other side of the ball, where seven '94 starters were gone: NG Oliver Gibson, three linebackers in Justin Goheen, Jeremy Nau, and Jeremy Sample, and half of the DBs—Travis Davis and Bobby Taylor. Much of the starting offensive line returned, led by Ryan Leahy, and Irish QBs could look again to Derrick Mayes and his great hands to keep the passing game clicking, with help coming from the TE Pete Chryplewicz and WRs Emmett Mosley and Charles Stafford. Holtz had impressive runners with Edwards at fullback to go with veteran Randy Kinder and freshman Autry Denson at TB. On defense, Paul Grasmanis inherited the NG spot, Renaldo Wynn held down one end spot, and Shawn Wooden and Brian Magee provided stability in the defensive backfield.

Clearly, a good number of players from the defensive depth chart and the newcomers would have to step up to the task. Talented athletes Lyron Cobbins and Kinnon Tatum took over at the inside LB spots, while a freshman speedster, Kory Minor, joined veteran Bert Berry at the OLB positions. Sophomore Allen Rossum, the fastest prep sprinter in the U.S. in '93, replaced Taylor at CB. Magee moved to SS and LaRon Moore took over at FS. Another freshman, Hunter Smith, took over the punting duties. NCAA recruiting restrictions over the years now meant that almost any team could show up thin in spots and for the '95 Irish this would mean NG and TB. This aggregation, on paper, looked to be a pretty good mix of veterans (especially on offense) with some bright but untried hopefuls. Team speed was at least adequate, with some real jets lining up on the defense. Ron Powlus had a year's experience under his belt and many hours getting his timing down with Mayes.

Holtz took the team to nearby Culver Military Academy in August where "nothing" became a team theme—nothing to do, nothing for distractions, nothing to break the heat, nothing but practice football.

Perhaps some of the Irish players had nothing to worry about after Culver, as they looked at their opening opponent—Northwestern, 28-point underdogs. But the Wildcats would disabuse anyone of that oversight by playing a great game to beat ND 17-15 and send the entire team into a drastic tailspin. The Irish got off to a stumbling start when Kinder fumbled at midfield to kill the first ND series. The Wildcats capitalized, led by the strong running of Darnell Autry, as he ripped the defense for gains of 16 and 14 yards, through gaping holes, setting up a seven-yard TD pass on a timing pattern between QB Steve Schnur and WR Dave Beazley. Later in the first quarter, after some punts, it was clear that Holtz knew he was in for a game, that this was not the type of Northwestern team that had lost 14 straight to ND in the previous 33 years. Surveying the damage done so far, he called for a pass on fourth down, needing seven yards, but the toss to the TB netted only five yards. On the next Irish series, Holtz went ballistic when the WRs looked confused ... no wonder, the QB had them in the wrong formation. The Irish overcame that little quandary to keep the drive alive, reaching the Northwestern 24. There, on a second-down play, the Irish persisted in their ongoing effort to keep option football alive: the big Irish QB took the snap and lumbered along the line to the right but was noticed

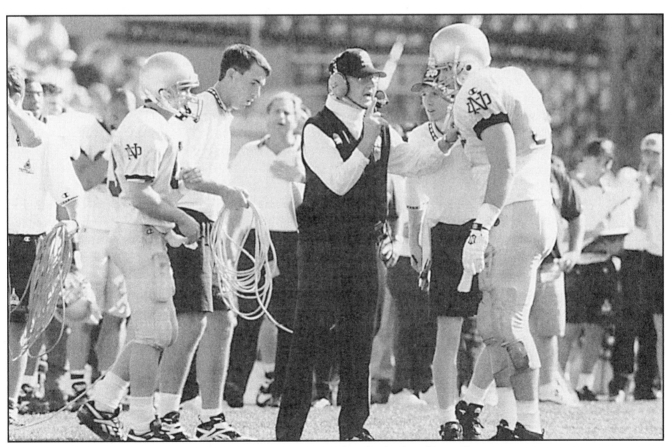
Lou Holtz giving a play during 1995 action, a season when he had major neck surgery.

QB Tom Krug helped the Irish finish the '95 season with an impressive win over Air Force and led a valiant effort in the 1996 Orange Bowl.

by alert NU defenders who promptly stopped him for no gain. Notre Dame overcame this to keep the drive going for four more plays, but all they could get out of it was a 35-yard FG. Northwestern answered that with its own FG for a 10-3 lead. The Irish were beginning to show signs of life—they started at their 20 and patched together their best drive of the day, capped by Robert Farmer's five-yard TD burst. The woes of the '94 kicking game were revived for the PAT try—a bad snap by the center, a bad hold by the holder, and a missed conversion kick, to keep ND in a 10-9 deficit. On the next series, just to compound matters, NG Paul Grasmanis broke his right wrist (but would play the rest of the season anyway with a cast). In the third quarter, the Irish D showed that it had not figured out Autry as he zipped along for 29 yards, sparking a 54-second drive for a TD, tallied on a 26-yard scoring pass from Schnur to D'Wayne Bates and a 17-9 lead. Time for a gut check, but the Irish could only manage a standoff for the rest of the quarter and half of the fourth. Powlus spent most of his time as a passer looking for Mayes, but NU usually had him doubled (he would end up with eight passes for 94 yards, but no TDs). Finally, Kinder

finished off a 45-yard drive with a two-yard TD dive. With 6:26 left, ND tried a two-point conversion to tie the game, but the center stepped on the Powlus's foot after the snap and the big guy unceremoniously hit the turf, along with Irish hopes. Autry took over from there as NU played keepaway, getting the win the hard way and starting them on the road to the Rose Bowl. Autry had dominated the Irish D for 160 yards on 33 carries. In '94, the Irish QB had joined the immortals with four TD passes against the 'Cats, but they shut him out this day. In retrospect, the Culver "beast barracks" experience looked like nirvana compared to this.

Notre Dame had now lost four of its last eight home games. They had just run into a Northwestern team with its own destiny shaping up—now the Irish would have to regroup. Before they did that, however, Jeremy Akers was injured in practice and Dusty Ziegler shifted over from C to the LG spot—shades of the position juggling in '94. Rick Kaczenski, who had been deep on the depth chart, moved up to start at C the rest of the season. With his patched-up line, Holtz took the Irish to Purdue to see if they could break into the win column. They did, but it was an ugly win, 35-28. Purdue scored first, on a 42-yard TD run by Corey Rogers, with a generous assist from poor Irish tackling. In the second quarter, fans saw that the Irish passing game was coming back from hibernation, Powlus hitting Kinder with a 30-yard swing pass for a TD. Shawn Wooden helped out with an INT and return to the Purdue 40, setting up a TD pass of 12 yards to Derrick Mayes. Purdue closed the gap to 14-10 with a FG with six seconds in the half. Notre Dame kept the pressure on in the third quarter on its opening drive when Powlus fired over the left side to WR Scott Sollmann for a 15-yard TD pass. (It was apparent that Mayes was being used as a decoy on this drive—a good sign after the brainlock of the Northwestern loss.) Purdue wasn't quitting and persevered for a 77-yard possession capped by a 21-yard FG by Brad Bobich, although good Irish D at the end of the drive averted a Boilermaker TD when Wynn made a great tackle to blunt a threat and a LB tipped a pass deep in ND territory. Holtz showed that he could still pull off some magic when he had Powlus fake in to the line, then fake a reverse, before Mosley shook loose from coverage to grab the ensuing pass for a 51-yard TD play. With this TD pass, Powlus had just tied the Irish record of four TD passes in one game for the second time. The next two scores were Purdue's: a 13-yard TD run by Edwin Watson and a 54-yard INT TD return by Derrick Brown, this tying the game at 28 each. Randy Kinder ended the day's scoring on the next

Bob Davie works the Irish sideline in the one-point victory over Army in 1995.

play from scrimmage—a 52-yard burst during which he broke three tackles and showed great balance. Walk-on Irish defender Mark Monahan, recently awarded a scholarship, made a genuine contribution with an INT to kill the next Purdue possession, but kicker Kevin Kopka failed to take advantage when his FG effort sailed wide left. Purdue continued to hammer back at the Irish, their comeback reaching the Irish 15 before the aroused Irish D blunted their final drive. Good pass defense kept Purdue stymied at the ND 13-yard line, and two Irish DBs put a good stick on the Purdue TB at the five-yard line on fourth down, two yards short of the first down. It was not exactly an artistic success, but there was some hope to be found: Kinder's 142 yards on 10 carries, Powlus's four TD passes, and freshman speedster, Autry Denson, just moved over from the defense, looked promising at TB with nine carries for 72 yards. The Irish D had redeemed itself on the last series, but they had given up 478 yards of total offense to the Boilermakers, including 275 yards on the ground. Some fine tuning was in order there. It was Holtz's 200th win as a head coach in college.

Three days after this win, Lou Holtz had major surgery at the Mayo Clinic, correcting a spinal condition involving a bone growth pressuring his spinal cord, a potentially dangerous situation if ignored. He named defensive coordinator Bob Davie the interim head coach. The announcement of his impending surgery was a 6 a.m. shock to the Monday team meeting. Other Irish coaches had faced medical emergencies—Rockne's phlebitis and Leahy's gastroenteritis come readily to mind—and many observers consider the Irish head coaching job there to be one of the most demanding, draining positions in American public life. Like Rockne, Holtz seemed to thrive on the pressure, putting in incredible hours, constantly in public demand, always facing the daunting expectations of Notre Dame's fans. The job had worn down some of the best in the business. Holtz was already the oldest head football coach ever to serve under the Dome; the surgery and its outcome promised to be a terribly rough period for the Holtz family, the team, and the coaches. Holtz nevertheless came through the procedure in pretty good shape, returning to South Bend a few days after the surgery, then seeing the team little more than a week later. He had not missed a team practice at any time in the 33 years of his coaching career. Even though Holtz would make a fairly quick recovery, times like this always put things like mere football games into proper perspective.

Sports are, in the final analysis, mysterious experiences. Who could tell how a team in ND's situation would react in light of the head coach's precarious situation? Vanderbilt found out how this team responded—a 41-0 blowout win for the Irish. Kinder got it started with a six-yard TD run, accompanied by a couple of Commodores who hung on for the ride. The Irish D stuffed Vanderbilt all day, so moments later it was the turn of Mayes to impress fans—making a brilliant one-handed catch of a pass. His theatrics were nullified by two QB fumbles on this one drive, but ND managed to boot a FG, a 38-yarder. Denson tacked on a five-yard TD burst to make it 17-0, but that score was promptly changed when the special team reaped an eight-yard TD, scored by Jarvis Edison's return of a fumble on the ensuing kickoff return, the fumble courtesy of a Mark Monahan hit. Kopka drilled another FG just before the end of the half for a 27-0 lead. At the end of the third quarter, Marc Edwards showed great effort on a one-yard TD explosion when he carried a Vandy LB with him into the end zone for a 34-0 lead. Brian McGee ended the quarter with an INT and a nifty 41-yard return to the 18. Edwards kept up his good work on the short drive, capping it with a great one-yard TD run that saw him slam into the pile, then spin right and reach pay dirt. Powlus also had a good day: 13 of 18 for 200 yards, but even more important was the fact that he distributed his passes evenly—five to his wide receivers, four to running backs, four to tight ends. Notre Dame abused the Vanderbilt D for 493 yards; The Irish D allowed the Commodores only 94 yards of total offense, nearly complete domination in all phases of the game. Interim coach Bob Davie thus earned a Gatorade shower and was carried off the field. Meanwhile, an antsy Lou Holtz followed the game at home.

Given some leeway by his physicians, Holtz made it to each practice the next week for 90-minute visits, but he'd stay in the press box for the game with the visiting, undefeated Texas Longhorns. The Irish started the scoring with a 27-yard Kopka FG to end their first drive. Moments later, Emmett Mosley fielded a Longhorn punt and blasted through their flailing special team for a 64-yard TD punt return. Texas had plenty of fight in them and came back for a TD pass to their TE, Pat Fitzgerald, off a misdirection play, but early in the second frame Derrick Mayes snagged his 100th career pass, an 11-yard lob pass, for an Irish TD and a 17-7 lead. Texas knew a good thing when they saw it

and drove right back to garner another TD to TE Pat Fitzgerald, on a middle screen for a 16-yard scoring play. On the PAT try, Irish NG Paul Grasmanis ploughed through the blockers and blocked the kick with an elbow. An alert Allen Rossum picked up the careening ball and scooted 98 yards for a two-point PAT return and a 19-13 ND lead. On the next Irish drive, the kicker would miss a FG try, but the drive was worth watching for an incredible one-handed catch by Mayes in the right flat for a 35-yard gain. An opportunistic Irish D stopped the ensuing Texas drive with a recovered fumble, but Texas kept pace when a Powlus pass was intercepted by a Texas LB, although they squandered the opportunity when a bad snap on a FG try killed the scoring opportunity. In the third quarter, Texas took the lead at 20-19 with a one-yard TD pass to Steve Bradley, yet another TE running around without much coverage on him. The Irish couldn't move the ball, punted, and Texas went for the jugular with a long pass into the middle of the ND secondary, but it was picked off by LaRon Moore, perhaps the turning point of the game. Mayes snagged a pass for a 53-yard gain to set up three-yard TD run by Kinder. Edwards then bulled in from the three for a two-point conversion and a 27-20 Irish lead. On the next Texas possession, ND's DE put on a great pass rush and the ensuing throw was snatched by Shawn Wooden. Marc Edwards scored again in the fourth quarter from the three, to give ND a 14-point

LaRon Moore started at FS for the '95 Irish and played with two broken bones.

lead. Texas shot themselves in their boots again on their next possession when Irish LB John McLaughlin put a good hit on the scrambling Longhorn QB, then also recovered the loose ball. Powlus promptly threw a 12-yard TD pass to his unbelievably open fullback to capitalize on McLaughlin's excellent play to start the drive. The Longhorns finally stopped the turnovers and drove back for a score, yet another TD pass, a 20-yarder, to TE Pat Fitzgerald, for a 41-27 Irish lead. The next Irish drive averted disaster when a Longhorn just missed making an INT on an inexplicably long pass down the right side, but the offense kept their wits about them long enough for Edwards to show his great balance as he almost went down just past the LOS on a 27-yard scoring run. His heroics gave Notre Dame a 48-27 lead with less than two minutes in the game. Moments after this clincher, Holtz appeared on the sideline to the wild support of the fans throughout the stadium, then Rossum turned out the lights entirely for UT with an INT and a 29-yard INT TD return. Kinder played a steady game for Notre Dame, with 29 carries for 129 hard-earned yards, his third straight game over 100 yards, the ninth in his career, just behind Jerome Heavens and George Gipp. The Irish racked up 511

total yards in a game that cranked out a total of 933 total yards between the two teams. And the Irish D is still looking for the Longhorn TE.

Ohio State had not been answering phone calls from Notre Dame for 60 years, so embittered were they by the results of the teams' prior meetings in 1935 and 1936, both narrow Notre Dame wins. The 1935 game had been voted, on several occasions, the REAL "Game of the Century" and had taken its rightful place in the lore of college football. When the '95 Buckeyes took the field for the long-awaited rematch, they ran through a cordon of 500 Buckeye football alums. . . including veterans from those earlier games. It must have crossed the minds of the Notre Dame players and coaches that they were playing in a crusade of sorts against a whole state. The Buckeyes were undefeated and were led by eventual Heisman winner, TB Eddie George, the number three QB in the country, Bobby Hoying, a dangerous receiver in Terry Glenn, a rock-solid offensive line led by Orlando Pace, and the usual stout Ohio State defense. Lou Holtz was on the Notre Dame sideline, helping to set the scene for high drama. And that's exactly what happened—for most of the game, a contest that almost matched the wild Texas game for total

Construction adding 20,000 seats to the stadium began in 1995.

yardage, with the Irish and Buckeyes romping around for 980 combined yards. The second quarter alone matched the point total of the famous 18-13 Notre Dame win in 1935. The first quarter was a probing affair, scoreless, as the teams looked for weaknesses and settled nerves. ND's Kevin Kopka tallied the first points with a 20-yard FG very early in the second frame, then Kinder staked the Irish to a 10-point lead with a two-yard TD run, behind a crushing block by reserve FB Jamie Spencer. The Buckeyes drove back, scoring on a seven-yard slant pass from Hoying to Glenn. Notre Dame maintained the 10-point lead after a 65-yard march in eight plays, with Kinder doing the damage again, scoring over the right side from the seven after a great fake to the left had the Buckeyes fooled. Near the end of the half, Ohio State drew closer with a TD pass to Dimitrious Stanley, a 17-yard affair in the right corner of the end zone. The Irish kept the heat on in the third quarter as they tacked on a 22-yard Kopka FG to make the score 20-14. Notre Dame's defense stymied Ohio State on the next possession, forced a punt, and then the sky fell—the Irish punt returner muffed the punt and the Buckeyes set up camp at the ND 19. Three plays later, Hoying hit TE Rickey Dudley with a 14-yard TD strike. Holtz had Powlus go deep to Mayes on the next series, good for a 56-yard advance thanks to a great catch by Mayes, then he called for an option play to the left. Result: the relatively immobile Powlus was sacked for minus-three yards. On third and 10, Powlus lofted a pass on a fade pattern (but Mayes cut in) and Shawn Springs grabbed the gift INT. Hoying capitalized by hitting Terry Glenn on a curl pattern to the left, the defender slipped, and Glenn was off to the proverbial races, for an 82-yard TD catch and run. The Irish finished the job on themselves on the next series when the snap was fumbled, with Ohio State regaining possession at the ND 14—the third turnover in three possessions. Eddie George slammed in from the six for the TD three plays later. Two of the Buckeyes' three scoring drives in the second half required a grand total of 33 yards of offense, a situation much like that in the '94 USC tie when ND gifted the opponent with short scoring opportunities. The Irish had been in pretty good shape until this turn of events, but playing in Columbus, against a talented team, the adversity was too much to overcome. Leading 20-14, within a matter of five minutes, the Irish found themselves holding the short end of the stick at 35-20. But the Irish weren't through yet—they used two minutes to drive 65 yards,

Kinder earning the scoring honors again on a 13-yard TD sweep. They tried to go for two points but the predictable call, an option to the right, garnered the predictable result—Powlus was stopped two yards short of the line. Ohio State counterpunched with an 80-yard drive done in less than two minutes, George tallying on a three-yard TD run. In 13 offensive plays, the Buckeyes had scored four TDs. They wrapped it up with a 35-yard FG to win the game 45-26, the most points allowed by a Holtz team at Notre Dame. Kinder had his fourth straight century mark game, with 28 carries for 143 yards and three TDs, but George countered this with 207 yards on 32 rushes, the mainstay in Ohio State's 533 yards of total offense.

A lesser team might have folded up its tent then and there. Notre Dame, ranked 23rd, had to travel west, to Seattle, where the encountered the 15th-ranked Washington Huskies. Lou Holtz, reflecting the effects of a medical setback, was not on the sidelines for the game, but returned to the coach's box. The Irish scored first, on their second possession, after Mayes made an incredible catch for a 39-yard gain. But at the UW five, the Irish had to run the obligatory option play, with Powlus trundling to his left, but the Huskies sniffed it out for a five-yard loss. Mayes came to the rescue on the next play, making up for the botched option with a 10-yard TD catch. On their first series, the Huskies had unveiled their backup TB, Rashaan Shehee, seemingly a clone of Napoleon Kaufmann. Shehee proved to be a tough runner—quick and powerful—and brought the Huskies into a tie with a one-yard dive for a TD on the next series. The second quarter was scoreless, although the Irish came close enough to miss a 30-yard FG try. Washington took the lead in the third quarter when Damon Huard found Andre Desaussure for a 13-yard TD in the right corner of the endzone. Powlus had a drive destruct when he tried a pass while falling down on a rollout, the throw errant enough for UW to intercept it. Mayes, who spent most of the day unattended by any DBs in the middle of the UW zone, tied the game with a catch for a 30-yard TD. Tallied on a slant and up route off a pump fake, it was Mayes's 20th career TD, a new Irish record. Shehee put UW back on top when they moved downfield with alacrity—due mainly to wide splits in the line and the TE set wide. Shehee jetted in for a 22-yard TD to cap a great personal effort of six runs for 65 yards on the drive. With the clock running down, the Irish had to do something, so they turned to Mayes, who caught a 12-yard pass but fumbled it away, sinking Irish hopes with 3:53 left in the game. Notre Dame's defense came to the rescue, with good tackling and pressure by Shawn Wooden and the LBs to slam the door on a conservative Husky offense. John Wales, the backup UW punter, mishandled a punt snap and was downed by Wooden. The Irish got the ball on the Husky 17 and Denson, in for the injured Kinder, took a pitch to the right side in for a seven-yard TD play. On the next play, one of the strangest situations ever came along for ND: lined up in a weak set, Holtz had Mayes and Mosley set out wide left, but there was only one defender on them. Mosley went into motion—and the defender followed him, leaving Mayes totally alone! Mayes cautiously (sheepishly?) waved to his QB, who spotted the UW oversight and threw Mayes the easiest pass of his illustrious career, for the two-point conversion, and a tenuous 22-21 lead. In the game's final minute, the Huskies drove back, hoping for a FG to win the game, but the speedy Rossum snagged a floating Huard pass from a shotgun formation, then zoomed 76 yards for the clinching TD in an exciting 29-21 Irish win.

From this excitement the Irish literally went coast to coast (a Rockne innovation) across the country to Giants Stadium to meet Army. The Irish had won 10 in a row over the Black Knights going back to 1958, including six shutouts, often by ridiculous margins. After Joe Namath's big contract with the Jets in 1964, few blue-chip athletes planned on attending the service academies. The Irish seldom had to face a player at a service academy they had recruited heavily. The result was often a physical mismatch. To offset the disadvantage, the academies played variations on the wishbone. To its great credit, Army played a great game this time, and could have won, but came up one point and one foot short, losing a thriller 28-27. The Irish started out in control, with the freshman Denson ending a short drive with a two-yard TD burst. Ron Leshinski tied it up on the next Army possession with a short TD pass reception from Ronnie McAda. Army showed that they could sustain a long drive and that McAda could make accurate reads on his various options. Notre Dame moved 70 yards in response, with 31 yards gained on a pass to Mayes, before Edwards rumbled in from the two for a 14-7 lead. In the middle of the second quarter, Army fumbled the ball to ND and Mayes and Powlus worked their magic again, a 47-yarder this time. Denson capped the drive with ND's third two-yard TD run of the day. Early in the third quarter, Notre Dame unveiled a new weapon—their fullback as a TD threat with a pass—when Edwards took

Kirk Doll coached defensive end and special teams for the '95 Irish.

a delay and rumbled 46 yards to the Army end zone, giving the Gold and Blue a 28-7 lead. The rest of the game pretty much belonged to Army—John Conroy, who started the season mired on their fifth-string, scored a TD from five yards out, then scored again late in the fourth quarter from the three. The Irish, who might have been sleepwalking, fumbled the ball on the snap moments later and McAda saw his opportunity, firing a seven-yard TD pass to Leon Gantt with less than a minute in the game. Army chose to go for two and McAda swung a pass to his big TE, Ron Leshinski. Just as he caught the ball, the 240-pound Leshinski was hit by a diminutive Irish DB, Ivory Covington, on the left side, who read the play perfectly and dropped the TE like a tall tree, even though Covington was 80 pounds lighter. With his great tackle, ND escaped with a 28-27 win. Army had used the wishbone to a textbook-perfect 365 yards rushing. It's a pretty safe bet that they won't take Army lightly any time soon.

If the Irish could just barely handle an upstart Army team, what would they do with undefeated, fifth-ranked USC? For starters, they didn't listen to the well-publicized self-dramatizations of Trojan All-America WR

Keyshawn Johnson, who pretty much had ND whipped with hot air. They did respect the Trojan's run defense, number three in the country, allowing only 81.2 rushing yards per game. They also had to pay attention to the simple fact that this was not the classic "Tailback U" any more—coach John Robinson emphasized the passing game much more than he had formerly, even to the point of running a two-QB system, dividing the playing time between Brad Otton and Kyle Wachholtz. The Irish D took all this seriously enough to keep USC bottled up into the second quarter. After forcing a punt to end the first Trojan series, Holtz's offense crafted a meticulous drive—14 plays, 80 yards—with Edwards careening off the left side, breaking three tackles, for a nine-yard TD run, but they failed on the PAT. The Trojans came right back, reaching the Irish three, to set up a play that deserves to be on any Irish highlight film: Operating from the I formation, Otton was handing off to his TB, Delon Washington, but Irish ILB Kory Minor had read the play and blitzed, leaping over the lunging FB, then slamming with total abandon into the surprised runner, who promptly surrendered the football. Notre Dame recovered the loose ball and USC could only contemplate the wreckage of a wasted 70-yard drive. In the second quarter, the Trojans benefited from a fumbled punt at the ND 17; Wachholtz promptly pitched a 17-yard TD pass to Keyshawn Johnson, they converted the PAT, and took a 7-6 lead. Notre Dame kept up the offensive pressure and drove 60 yards for a score, another TD by Edwards (an emerging offensive force) scored untouched from the two-yard line. For the two-point conversion, Holtz tried some trickery: Powlus pitched out to Edwards, who "scrambled" left, then shotputted a pass of sorts back to Powlus, who was waving, in the left corner of the end zone. The next Trojan drive fizzled on a failed fourth down play, courtesy of a good defensive play, then ND used nine quick plays in little more than a minute to set up a TD by Denson, a four-yard run, for a 21-7 lead with 41 seconds left in the half. The Irish tipped a USC pass deep in ND's territory just before the halftime to stop a threat. To start the third quarter, the Trojans got an early INT that garnered a FG. In the fourth quarter, with USC backed up to their 10, Minor continued his heroics for ND with a great rush to drop Wachholtz for a safety and a 23-10 Irish lead. Pete Chryplewicz was the beneficiary of the ensuing free kick when he tallied a two-yard TD with a pass—the first for an Irish TE in '95—before Edwards continued his heroics with a three-yard run to the left for another two-point conversion, making the score 31-10. Two Notre Dame defenders

helped the cause, one tipping a pass on the next USC series to another for an INT at the Trojan 12. The Irish fullback put an end to the abuse of the Trojan D with a one-yard TD burst and the final score of 38-10. Near the end of the game, ND's ILB Lyron Cobbins just missed hauling in his third INT of the game, so dominant was the play of ND's linebackers all day. On offense, Notre Dame stunned the Trojan defense for 191 yards rushing, with Edwards scoring three times, catching four passes, and helping out on both two-point conversions—not to mention his clutch blocking throughout the game. (For trivia buffs, Ronald Reagan was in his second year as U.S. President when the Trojans last defeated an Irish team).

Other trivia experts would know that Boston College owned a two-game winning streak, both games depressing for Irish fans, but for very different reasons: the '93 loss cost the Irish an untainted claim for the national title, while the '94 loss was one of those desolating losses, a total team collapse. So there was a sense of intensity among the players and coaches as they prepared for BC. Taking over as a team leader, Marc Edwards would have a career day against the Golden Eagles—167 yards on 28 hammering carries—to lead ND to a 20-10 victory. He led the way on the first scoring drive for the Irish, gaining 65 of the drive's 70 yards, and scoring with a 17-yard TD screen pass over the middle. LaRon Moore, in spite of wearing a cast on his left hand, intercepted a pass on the ND 20 on the next series, but a QB fumble deep in BC territory scotched the opportunity. BC's Omari Walker tied the game 77 yards later with a two-yard TD run tallied after he bounced off an Irish tackler. Holtz was still looking for a consistent kicker and had reinstated Cengia earlier, who broke the tie with a 22-yard FG near the end of the second quarter. In the third quarter, BC missed a 49-yard FG try, setting up a 68-yard Irish drive capped by a three-yard TD run by Edwards, his 12th of the year. The Eagles drove back to hit a 41-yard FG, and were on their way again early in the fourth quarter when Cobbins made an INT at their two. His effort both killed a threatening drive and led to ND's taking nearly 10 minutes off the game clock, as they methodically drove 83 yards to set up a 26-yard Cengia FG for the 20-10 final score. Notre Dame's dominating fullback was the main weapon for ND, his 167 yards on the ground representing his first 100-yard game. BC had shut down the passing game, but never figured out ND's Marc Edwards.

The Irish would have to win their next two games, against Navy and Air Force, to be considered for a top-flight bowl. Given ND's problem dispatching Army, none of this was a sure bet. Navy showed why, too, in the first half as they galloped to 301 yards of offense with their version of the wishbone. Navy scored first, a 15-yard TD run on an option toss to Ross Scott. Notre Dame came right back, however, with Powlus targeting Charles Stafford for a 38-yard gain, then TE Leon Wallace for the touch with an eight-yard toss. In the second quarter, Navy's QB, Ben Fay, ran the 'bone to perfection, leading the way on a 51-yard drive to rack up a TD on a three-yard keeper to the right and a 14-7 Navy lead. Notre Dame's Powlus evened things up by tallying on a one-yard keeper of his own (his first of the year) with little more than a minute in the half. But that was enough time for Navy to move in close enough for Brian Graham to hit a 21-yard FG as time expired in the half. The second half, however, was a totally different story. The Irish D played with an intensity that yielded a mere 14 yards to the Middie running game. The offense suffered a massive jolt, however, when Navy LB Fernando Harris sacked Powlus for a nine-yard loss, the force of the fall breaking the QB's left humerus, ending his season. His TD pass to Wallace in the first quarter had tied him with Joe Theismann at number two in career TD passes with 31, and that's where he would stay in the books until the '96 season. Backup Thomas Krug would lead the Irish to three TDs and dominance in the second half: a 42-yard bomb to Mayes near the end of the third quarter, then a three-yard TD flip to Mayes after Cobbins tipped a pass and intercepted it (after recovering a fumble early in the third quarter). The next series saw the Irish defense stuff Navy on three key plays: Grasmanis sacked Fay, then Minor played the option pitch perfectly, sacking Fay for a six-yard loss, then sacked Fay again on play action for minus-three yards, before another LB stopped a fourth-down run to give the ball back to the Irish. Seven plays later, Denson turned on the jets on a great run for a 24-yard TD to make the final score read 35-17. Navy kept self-destructing, LaRon Moore hauling in a fumble and Rossum closing out the D's day with an INT. For the game, Denson had zipped and darted for 116 yards on 16 carries; Krug had hit five of eight throws for 90 yards and two TDs. With the starting QB gone, the fate of the Irish would largely be in Krug's hands the rest of the way.

Holtz would have two weeks to groom Krug before ND would meet Air Force. Krug lacked the overall polish of the injured starter, but he might have had quicker feet and an equally quick pass release. The difficulty, as always in such situations, came down to reading defensive coverages in the midst of the action—the

2-3 seconds after the snap, with a blur of bodies and motion, reading blitzes, reacting on timing patterns—all the subtleties that become routine for a starting QB. And Air Force would not be easy to defense; QB Beau Morgan had rushed and passed for more than 1,000 yards each, evidence that the Falcons did not run a one-dimensional attack out of their modified wishbone. Perhaps the Irish linemen on both sides of the ball knew that Krug could use a boost, but they rose to the occasion and played textbook football, providing the Falcons a clinic in blocking and tackling, as ND outclassed a hapless AFA 44-14. Holtz showed a new wrinkle early in the game when Edwards lined up as a TE, but it was the running game, with both Kinder and Denson, that accounted for the first score. Notre Dame seemed intent on proving who was in charge as Holtz called 10 consecutive runs on the first Irish possession; Denson ripped a beauty with a 24-yarder from the ND 36, and Kinder punctuated the drive with a 17-yard TD run. On the next series, good Irish D forced a fumble that led to Krug throwing a seven-yard TD pass to his TE, but a penalty killed the play. The Irish settled for a 30-yard FG and a 10-0 lead after one quarter. The Falcons were unable to get airborne on their third possession, missed a FG try, and ND kept up the pressure. A Krug pass to Mayes for 32 yards ignited a nine-play drive of 80 yards, with Denson rocketing through a gaping hole in the middle of the line for a three-yard TD tally. Notre Dame finished the first half's scoring with a 26-yard Cengia FG. In the third quarter, they picked up where they left off, Cengia booting a 27-yard FG for a 23-0 Irish lead. The Falcons then capitalized on a roughing the kicker penalty as Morgan fired an eight-yard TD pass to Nakia Addison. Notre Dame's Denson led ND right back, showing tremendous balance and scintillating moves on a six-play, 71-yard drive, fulfilled with his 23-yard TD run/ballet. Air Force was unable to move and Holtz kept showing new plays to whatever coaching staff would be studying the game for a Bowl encounter. On their next drive, he had his Edwards run wide around end for six yards—surely unfamiliar territory for this fullback, then called a reverse for WR Scott Sollmann, netting 17 more yards. Kinder ended the show with a five-yard TD burst. Less than a minute later, following Cobbins's fifth INT in four games (tying a record for Irish LBs), a reserve fullback, Marcus Thorne, tallied a five-yard TD for the good of all walk-on players at Notre Dame. To close the scoring, Morgan threw an 11-yard pass to Matt Brooks. For ND, the TBs had 121 and 109 yards, while Morgan was held to 40, with only nine yards coming in the first half. Krug hit eight of 13 passes for 96 yards; AFA netted only 63 total passing yards for the game.

Defeating Air Force gave the nod for the Irish to meet Florida State in the Orange Bowl (after the Bowl Coalition's various mating rituals were completed). Bobby Bowden and Holtz had met more than two decades earlier. The Seminoles had some glittering credentials—10 straight Bowl wins, 71 TDs scored over the season, number-three rank in total yards per game (551.6 yards) and also in passing yards per game (328.7 yards). Both teams entered the game at 9-2, and the charged atmosphere of rivalry hung heavy in the humid air over the Orange Bowl, the stadium hosting its last such game. The Irish were the biggest underdogs of the major bowl matchups, a reflection of the fact that the absence of the injured Powlus and Kinder being suspended for disciplinary reasons meant that 59 percent of their season's offensive production had been the work of those two absent players.

Nevertheless, the Irish came out like gangbusters—Denson ran off the right side for a 38-yard gain, followed by Edwards and a slam over right guard for another 28 yards. After two short runs, the 'Noles blinked when the Irish lined up in a five WR set, then called time out. Krug went into a shotgun at the 7 but he was sacked, then Notre Dame missed a 35-yard FG try. FSU cranked it up briefly, but Shawn Wooden hauled in an INT when Danny Kanell lofted a pass into a gaggle of Irish DBs. FSU lost LB Sam Cowart for the game when he made the mistake of leg whipping the powerful Edwards on a shovel pass, then Krug showed good quickness and a fast release when he fired a 39-yard TD pass to a wide-open Mayes. The 'Noles got it going on the next drive, using a screen pass to their 280-pound FB, Pooh Bear Williams (at his size, call him whatever he wants), and slashing runs by Warrick Dunn, before Kanell threw a 15-yard TD pass to Andre Cooper. Notre Dame came back, using 14 plays to grind out 62 yards before Cengia, guilty of being wide right the first time, tried a 20-yard FG ... this time hitting the *left* cross bar, but the kick landed luckily for the Irish and toppled in for a FG and a 10-7 lead. The first quarter ended with an Irish KO to Dunn, who slipped at the four on turf that had been a problem for both teams. There had been no punts by either team, an indication of the offensive intensity by both squads. The Irish had demolished the first quarter clock, holding the ball 11:03 minutes to FSU's 3:57, a ratio not likely to hold the rest of the game. In the second quarter, Wynn mangled FSU's hopes on their first drive

Joe Moore created dominating lines for the Irish.

when he sacked Kanell, who was escaping great pressure by ILB Kory Minor. Derrick Mayes returned the ensuing punt for a 53-yard TD but there was a flag for a block in the back—a devastating turning point for the Irish—the third time since the '91 bowl game with Colorado in which a crucial call at a key moment meant the difference against ND (the other the penalty call on the last Irish KO against BC in '93). The Irish drive fizzled and they punted to FSU. Good Irish defense kept Kanell bottled up, especially a Shawn Wooden play in the ND end zone, batting away a Seminole TD hope, then a 13-yard QB sack by LB John McLaughlin. An FSU punt to the ND one-yard line worked to keep the Irish offense bottled up, then the 'Noles took advantage with a possession starting on their own 40. The ensuing drive saw Warrick Dunn zip around for 36 yards on assorted runs before Kanell found the 6-2 Cooper isolated on ND's 5-8 Rossum. Cooper made a great catch of a 10-yard TD pass in spite of determined, tight defense by Rossum, FSU taking the lead at 14-10. Krug led a drive back in the final moments, but FSU snagged an INT when Krug was hit as he threw from their 39-yard line. In the third quarter, FSU could not move on their first possession, but ND took the lead

17-14 when an alert Mayes grabbed a tipped pass in the end zone for a 39-yard TD completion. Another Irish DB ended FSU's next drive with an INT, but the Irish did not capitalize. FSU came back on a long drive but a 42-yard FG try went wide left. The Irish threatened to score on their next series, but Krug and Mayes didn't connect on a long pass, Mayes took the wrong route, and ND settled for a punt to the FSU one-yard line. On their first play, Kanell stepped out of the end zone for a safety and a 19-14 Irish lead. Holtz kept the pressure up with the possession following their free kick—turning loose TB Robert Farmer for a brilliant 51-yard run to set up Krug's five-yard TD flip to Chryplewicz. This was the high tidal point for the Irish, having so far doubled FSU's running game, 228 yards to 110 yards. Bowden didn't panic, however, and FSU came back to earn an 11-yard TD pass from Kanell to E.G. Green, making the score 26-21. The next Irish drive went nowhere and FSU took the lead on a questionable non-call when Cooper, drifting across the back of the end zone, stepped out of bounds right in front of the official but was allowed to catch a TD pass for a 29-26 FSU lead. The Irish were moving crisply on the next drive but Edwards lost the handle on the ball and FSU regained possession. The 'Noles kept picking on Rossum covering Cooper, but he played his heart out with great defense to keep FSU from earning a TD after they reached the ND three. On the last Irish possession, with two minutes left in the game, Krug was pressured and called for intentional grounding in the end zone resulting in a safety and the final score of 31-26. (Thomas Krug, unfortunately, played no more for ND after a spinal condition cut short his career in spring drills). Notre Dame had played a great game, as had the Seminoles, and the expected blowout never materialized. The Irish running game bruised FSU for 256 yards; Krug completed 14 passes in 24 tries for 140 yards and two TDs. The two teams cranked out 903 yards of total offense. Irish mistakes and the official's failure to see Cooper step out of bounds proved to be the difference in the game.

The 1995 season was a significant turnaround from the miserable '94 campaign. This was a considerably stronger offensive unit—scoring improved from 318 points (28.9 per game) in '94 to 366 points (33.3 per game) and total offensive yardage likewise increased from 4,230 yards to 4,619 yards. The running game improved from 2,372 yards to 2,572 yards while the aerial game went up from 1,858 yards to 2,047 yards. Irish opponents scored less, about a FG per game, although the Irish D

gave up more yards in the running game, 560 yards more in '95 than in '94 (Ohio State's Heisman winner, Eddie George, accounted for about half of this yardage). Notre Dame went plus-10 in turnovers for '95, an impressive improvement over the minus-one of '94.

1995 Record: 9-3-0 (.750)
Record to date: 738-219-42 (.759)

1996

For the 1996 Irish edition, Holtz would have to find nine new starters, but his backfield of Powlus, Denson and Edwards remained intact, with Jarious Jackson installed as the heir apparent behind Powlus. Perhaps the hardest man to replace would be Derrick Mayes, with his silky moves and great hands. Holtz gave Denson a look at WR, but eventually settled him at TB. Malcolm Johnson took over the SE spot. Jeremy Akers moved up to fill the LG position; massive Mike Rosenthal took over for the departed Ryan Leahy at RT.

On defense, three-fourths of the Irish secondary had to be replaced, with only Allen Rossum still on patrol. Ivory Covington started at LCB, opposite Rossum. Jarvis Edison held down the FS position, with Benny Guilbeaux his running partner at SS, the two providing good size and hitting skills. Coach Bob Davie switched his starting OLBs, with Bert Berry going over to the right side and Kory Minor to the left. Alton Maiden returned from an injury to start at NG; Melvin Dansby, capable of some impressive plays, lined up beside him at RE. Lyron Cobbins returned to ILB after an excellent '95 season; his partner in linebacking mayhem, Kinnon Tatum, also returned for the Irish. In sum, the '96 Notre Dame edition entered the annals as a potentially explosive team, with veteran leadership at key spots, and more of the speed the Irish had been looking for on the defensive side of the ball.

For Notre Dame's 1,000th game, the Irish opened the season against Vanderbilt on the road, a potential patsy, also Holtz's 122nd Notre Dame game, tying Rockne's record. The Commodores damned the torpedoes, however, and under the influence of Rod Dowhower's defensive theories, played a tough game, bowing to ND by a narrow 14-7 margin. The game started slowly for both parties: with Denson at WR, Robert Farmer got the call at TB, but he fumbled to

Vandy on the first series. No problem—Jarvis Edison intercepted a pass, only to fumble it before Cobbins regained possession. Notre Dame took the opportunity to piece together a patient drive, but Cengia shanked a 38-yard FG try to end the effort. Good Irish defense kept Vanderbilt off the scoreboard in the first half, with Renaldo Wynn almost earning a safety on a sack. Marc Edwards fumbled to stop another drive, but snagged a screen pass for a 23-yard gain to set up Jim Sanson's 33-yard FG with nine seconds left in the half.

NCAA record holder, defensive back Allen Rossum.

To start the third quarter, ND ran the ball 13 straight times, overcoming fumbles by Edwards and Farmer, setting up Sanson's 32-yard FG. The next two Irish drives were stopped by fumbles by Edwards and Farmer, the latter giving enough hope to Vanderbilt for a 50-yard TD pass and a 7-6 lead, making the point spread of 22 look ridiculous. The Irish clawed back on their next drive, a 75-yard affair, showing grit and determination by running Edwards from the TB spot for a three-yard TD blast, then Edwards again for a two-point conversion and the 14-7 win.

After that inauspicious season debut, the Irish flattened Purdue 35-0. Allen Rossum turned on the jets with the opening kickoff for a 99-yard TD return. Two drives later, ND worked over the Boilermakers for a 92-yard drive sparked by Mosley's 16-yard gain on a reverse, and capped by Denson's 12-yard TD run off the right side. Denson continued the Irish dominance in the second quarter with a 34-yard gain on a Powlus pass; Edwards ended the 90-yard drive blasting over the right guard for a one-yard TD. With two seconds left in the half, Powlus hit Denson on a middle screen for a 10-yard TD pass and a 28-0 halftime lead. Denson continued his heroics in the third quarter when he wrapped up the scoring with an option pitch to the right side, breaking a tackle and juking the FS for a two-yard TD burst. The Irish combined nine sacks, Rossum's TD run, and 459 yards of total offense to dominate their long-time

Purdue nemesis.

The sixth-ranked Texas Longhorns promised to provide stiffer competition for Notre Dame, now ninth-ranked. Sure enough, Texas scored early, 11 plays after the Irish KO, with a three-yard TD pass to Mike Adams. The Irish came back strong, led by Kinder's 28-yard run to the Texas five; Jim Sanson booted a 20-yard FG to get his team on the scoreboard. Texas scored on its first possession of the second quarter on a Priest Holmes three-yard TD run, taking a 14-3 lead. But Robert Farmer cut into the lead on the next Irish possession with a brilliant 18-yard run. The Irish D stopped Texas, and Denson dashed 23 yards to the Texas three, setting up Edwards's three-yard TD rumble with 27 seconds left in the half. Texas tied the game at 17-17 with a 47-yard FG after an Irish drive was stymied. The Texas D kept ND in check until late in the fourth quarter; in the meantime, future Heisman winner Ricky Williams had slashed for a 30-yard gain before pounding in from the one for a 24-17 lead. Irish LB Lyron Cobbins picked off a Longhorn pass as the fourth quarter waned, giving ND good field position on the Texas 34. Eight plays later, Denson careened in from the six for a TD; Sanson's PAT tied it at 24-24. With less than three minutes in the game, Notre Dame's D kept Texas out of scoring range and the Irish took possession with 59 seconds. With only 14 seconds left in regulation, Powlus fired a

Kory Minor.

13-yard pass to Malcolm Johnson. On the game's last play, with no time left on the clock, Jim Sanson redeemed the kicking corps with a 39-yard FG to win the game, 27-24, for Notre Dame. Denson led all runners with 160 yards on 24 carries; Ricky Williams garnered 108 yards on 17 runs.

Next up for the number five Irish were the fourth-ranked Ohio State Buckeyes, loaded with talent—Orlando Pace at tackle, Joe Germaine at QB, LBs Greg Bellisari and Andy Katzenmoyer, and DB Shawn Springs. Even the loss of Heisman winner Eddie George did not seem to have slowed down the Buckeye juggernaut. Their talent showed on the opening KO as Dimitrius Stanley exploited a seam in the Irish KO team for an 85-yard return. Four plays later, Ohio State scored on a Pepe Pearson TD run of three yards. The PAT snap went awry and the Irish felt fortunate to be looking at a 0-6 deficit. It was the 11th scoring drive in three games for Ohio State to be done in under two minutes. The first two offensive series for the Irish quickly demonstrated that the Buckeyes' D had plenty of speed and would be able to stack up ND's runners with near impunity. The Irish D helped out admirably though when Lamont Bryant tipped a pass to Kinnon Tatum at their 15. Notre Dame took the lead 7-6 when Marc Edwards hauled in a three-yard TD pass from Powlus. The Buckeyes picked

up the pace on their next possession, using a mere 2:28 to sail 80 yards to a three-yard TD pass to their fullback, Matt Calhoun. They tried a two-point conversion, but it failed.

Trailing 7-12, the Irish opened up with a fake reverse and later a long pass to Mosley in which a DB seemed to have crashed into him early—but no call ensued. Apparently baffled by the Buckeye D, ND began to hope for breaks in the kicking game. Hunter Smith booted a towering punt of 54 yards. When the first quarter was over, Ohio State had racked up 127 yards of offense to ND's 19.

As if that weren't bad enough, the second quarter began inauspiciously when Kinder fumbled to the Buckeyes at the Irish 35. Notre Dame tightened their chin straps, holding Ohio State to three yards on three plays before Benny Guilbeaux blocked a 48-yard FG try. Holtz picked up the pace a bit—an option, a draw, a scramble, a pass towards Malcolm Johnson, who slipped and fell on a deep route, then another pass in the face of a terrific blitz . . . but Johnson did not read the blitz and Luke Fickell snagged Powlus's pass. Pepe Pearson spearheaded a drive resulting in a FG and a 15-7 Buckeye lead. The Irish were unable to sustain their next drive, and Pearson came right back again, including a 26-yard

One of the best Irish fullbacks, Marc Edwards.

gain on a slant pattern to the Irish one, before he capped it with a one-yard TD run and a 22-7 Ohio State lead at the half. Holtz had to be shocked to see the stats in the locker room: Denson had 13 yards on six carries to Pearson's 104 yards on 20 carries and two TDs.

Jim Sanson got ND going with a 26-yard FG to end the first possession in the third quarter. The teams traded brief drives, then Ohio State struck quickly, using Pearson on three of the drive's six plays leading to a 13-yard TD pass to their TE, D. J. Jones, and a 29-10 lead.

The Irish seemed stalled and Denson had a broken finger to make it even worse. But Pearson fumbled early in the fourth quarter, Covington recovering. Powlus fired a 42-yard pass to TE Kevin Carretta; Edwards dashed in for a TD from the nine on a draw play, but the PAT was blocked, leaving ND in a 29-16 hole. Moments later, Denson hauled in a punt and streaked cross country for a long TD run, but a penalty dashed Irish hopes. The final stats seemed to reveal a closer game than the final score, but stats could not demonstrate the sheer quickness of the Buckeyes that stymied the Irish for most of the game.

How a team responds to a handling like that can make for an interesting next game. The Washington Huskies made their first trip to South Bend in nearly 50 years and, ranked 16th, they had high hopes to find the Irish in their cups. Instead, ND bounced the Huskies hard, 54-20. Denson led the way with 141 yards on the ground on 14 carries, including the game's opening score on a 34-yard run featuring a brilliant cutback move; Irish QBs

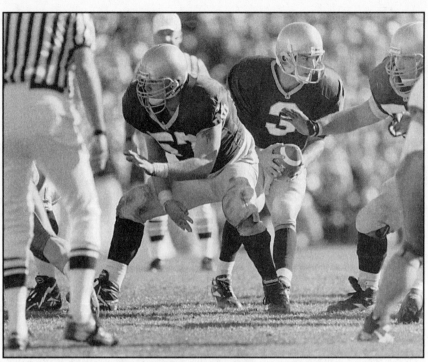
Ron Powlus, Irish quarterback, holds numerous passing records.

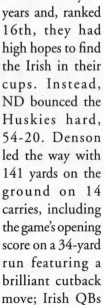

Ivory Covington.

Powlus and Jarious Jackson combined to complete 11 of 16 passes for 222 yards and four TDs. Leading 26 to 14 at the half, ND kept the Huskies in the dog cage with a 21-point third quarter, the damage coming through the air with two TDs to TE Pete Chryplewicz and one to Malcolm Johnson. Meanwhile, Huskie QB Brock Huard, the highly-touted lefty, managed a mere eight completions in 26 tries, and spent much of the game on the sidelines looking dazed as Irish DBs snagged three INTs. When the dust settled, ND's offense had rebounded from the week before to rack up 650 total yards to UW's 257.

The pesky Falcons of Air Force, unranked, next met the eighth-ranked Irish. Navy had defeated the Falcons the same day that ND was pounding the Huskies, but AFA boasted the best running game in the country, averaging more than 354 yards per game. Beau Morgan, yet another diminutive AFA QB, had perfected the "duck" part of the triple option, ducking behind the line in order to be lost to the defenders. The starting offensive line for the Falcons was smaller than the Irish freshman team's line, but they played with tremendous intensity and eventually copped a 20-17 Falcon win in overtime, a crushing blow to rising Irish hopes for the season.

Allen Rossum tallied the game's first score when he picked up a Falcon fumble and scooted 57 yards for a TD. Air Force then pieced together a 66-yard drive to allow barefooted Dallas Thompson to kick a 21-yard

Pete Chryplewicz.

FG. Morgan got the Falcons into the lead in the second quarter, scampering 30 yards to the ND seven before scoring on a five-yard run (but the refs missed his knee being down). Jim Sanson, properly shod, tied the game at 10-10 with a 27-yard FG just before the half ended. But the action wasn't over yet: the Irish cobbled together a final drive and Powlus fired an apparent 13-yard TD pass to Raki Nelson, who made a brilliant fingertip catch—but the refs called it incomplete. Marc Edwards sparked a scoring drive in the third quarter with an 11-yard run that demonstrated his unbelievable balance, capped by his run and jump TD from the one-yard line. Air Force tied it up on a 26-yard option pitch to Tobin Ruff on the next drive. The 17-17 score held up for the rest of the game, setting up the overtime period. Air Force won the toss and chose to defend. With the ball at the 25, Powlus took the snap but Air Force knew what was coming and what they were going to do about it—they had called an all-out blitz, sacking Powlus who fumbled on the play. With the ball, the Falcons played it safe, using a face-mask penalty call on ND to get close to the end zone. After careful play calling, they asked their bare-footer to do the job, even though he was only 50 percent on FG tries for the season. Thompson hit it twice (a penalty nullified the first one), and Irish eyes weren't smiling to see AFA LB Alex Pupich ecstatically

snapping pictures on the field with a little camera.

All day long, the Irish offensive line had been having trouble blocking the Falcons, partially because of the loss of RG Mike Rosenthal to a broken ankle. In the OT, it was imperative to come out and take command. For Holtz, in light of the blocking problems, that meant a pass play. AFA must have sensed this, called the blitz, and won the game as a result.

Two weeks later, ND met Navy in Dublin, Ireland, at Gaelic football's venerable Croke Park before 38,651 true Irish men and women, most of whom had only rudimentary knowledge of the game of American football. With the extra week, the Irish players had plenty of time to lick their wounds and recompose themselves. Navy was enjoying its best season in many years, entering the game with a 5-1 record. Their enjoyment was short-lived, however, as ND put it all together in a 54-27 blowout. It started slowly, as ND had two possessions with no fireworks to show for it. But Navy eventually had to punt from its end zone, giving the Irish a short field to play on. Denson found a seam after a few plays, ripping off 15 yards, then Edwards busted into the end zone from five yards out, moving the whole pile for a TD. Navy couldn't move, punted again, and Rossum zipped around for a 41-yard punt return, setting up a five-yard TD pass to a wide-open Chryplewicz. Navy came back, used a

A big target for Ron Powlus—tight end Pete Chryplewicz.

fake punt to complete a pass, and worked hard enough for a six-yard TD run by Omar Nelson. Just before the half ended, Denson took advantage of a gaping hole on the left side and dashed 33 yards to paydirt for a 21-7 halftime lead. Early in the third quarter, Renaldo Wynn sealed Navy's fate with a 24-yard TD fumble return, but the Middies kept fighting back, trading TDs with the Irish, Denson zipping 23 yards for his second score of the quarter. The fourth quarter belonged to the Irish ground game, with Edwards busting in for two TDs from the one, and Jamie Spencer using Robert Farmer's stunning 58-yard blast to slam in from the two for the final Irish score. It was Notre Dame's 33rd consecutive win over Navy, an NCAA record.

A few days before the game with Boston College, head coach Lou Holtz called a meeting of his staff and told the assembled coaches that they were free to pursue other coaching opportunities. Suddenly, the rumor mill went into overtime as the media chased down any available source. Athletic director Mike Wadsworth gave Holtz a vote of confidence, but also managed to leave the press hanging as to the future.

The high-flying Irish kept up their scoring pyrotechnics against Boston College in Boston, blasting the Golden Eagles 48-21 on 426 bruising yards of rushing. Denson led the charge with 155 yards on 23 carries, but Robert Farmer also impressed with 98 yards on only three carries, including an 81-yard TD romp in the third quarter, followed by an 11-yard TD rumble barely two minutes later. Farmer's 81-yarder was the longest run from scrimmage for ND since Eric Penick's dramatic run against USC in 1973. Marc Edwards chipped in with a single TD, as did Randy Kinder and Jamie Spencer. The win cost the Irish the services of Marc Edwards, who went down with a ligament injury in the second quarter.

In spite of the distractions caused by the rumors involving Holtz, a seemingly invincible Notre Dame team dismantled the Pitt Panthers 60-6. Pitt, a mere shadow of its former glory with Dorsett and Marino, offered little resistance, especially in the second quarter, during which ND almost set an all-time school record for scoring in a quarter when they exploded for 40 points based on three cross-country punt returns—two by Rossum, of 55 yards and 83 yards, the third by Denson a minute later while spelling a winded Rossum, as he zipped 74 yards into the end zone. Joey Goodspeed, Robert Farmer, Jamie Spencer, Randy Kinder, and Kevin Carretta also tacked on scores as the Irish humbled

Notre Dame's head coach from 1986-96, Lou Holtz.

the Panthers. Farmer and Denson both went over the century mark in rushing.

On November 10, Holtz ended the rumor-mongering at a press conference during which he simply said of his resignation, "It's the right thing to do." He admitted that he had thought of this as far back as February, and the thought had been with him ever since. Once told, the players had tried to talk him out of it. He told the press that he hoped the new coach would come from the current staff (and he would, Bob Davie, the defensive coordinator). TV types wondered if Holtz's 99 wins at ND and the thought of surpassing the immortal Rockne's 105 wins sometime in the 1997 season might have proven to be too much of a burden to contemplate. Holtz remained somewhat coy to the end: "I do not feel good about this at all. It's the right thing for the players." Clearly, Holtz was torn and anguished, but the source of that was never made clear.

His last home game was against Rutgers, and the juggernaut just kept rolling as ND shellacked the Scarlet Knights 62-0. (In light of the final score, perhaps Scarlet referred to something else in this case.) The Irish did not

Notre Dame's all-time leading rusher, Autry Denson.

explode for a 40-point quarter, but they never scored less than two TDs in any quarter. Farmer and Denson both rushed for more than 100 yards again; Powlus fired four TD passes, giving himself a career total of 42, surpassing Rick Mirer's record. Farmer racked up two TDs; singles were registered by Denson, Joey Goodspeed, Spencer, Chryplewicz, Johnson, Mosley, and Nelson. Holtz's offense amassed 648 yards of total offense; Bob Davie's D throttled Rutgers' ground game for minus-six yards and gave up a total of 43 yards in the game. Rossum and Guilbeaux speared Scarlet Knights passes; Carretta blocked a punt that Goodspeed scored with. It was the first time since 1932 (whose seniors had played for Rockne) that Notre Dame had scored 60 or more points in consecutive games. As he left the stadium, observers noted Lou Holtz choked up with a welter of powerful and possibly conflicting emotions.

The day after the victory over Rutgers, November 24, 1996, Notre Dame announced the hiring of its 26th Head coach—Bob Davie. Even with that announcement, the team still had to focus on the task at hand—the USC Trojans.

Ron Powlus had been playing football in the schoolyard in the second grade when a Notre Dame team last lost a football game to USC. But in 1996, barely more than a week after Notre Dame was rocked by the loss of its head coach, the dominance of their 13-game win streak vanished in a flurry of fumbles, penalties, a missed PAT, poor execution, and frustration. The 27-20 OT loss would also cost ND a lucrative Bowl Alliance berth.

USC garnered a 30-yard FG by Adam Abrams on their first drive, a 39-yard affair, but QB Brad Otton was injured on a Kory Minor blitz. The Irish could not get untracked on their next two possessions, the second one ending when Emmet Mosley was stripped, giving the Trojans another short field, with the ball at the ND 10. Great Irish D backed them up 13 yards, but Abrams tacked on another FG for a 6-0 Trojan lead. The Irish came back, however, with an 11-play drive covering 65 yards, capped by Jamie Spencer's one-yard scoring burst. Jim Sanson made the PAT kick for a 7-6 lead. The defenses dominated the rest of the half (although USC ran 24 of their 32 plays from Irish territory) and most of the third quarter. Near the end of the third frame, Powlus scrambled around to buy some time, then found Cikai Champion open for a 25-yard TD pass and a 14-6 lead. Powlus had the Irish posed to take a commanding lead with a long pass to Malcolm Johnson, but he fumbled and the Trojans took possession on their own one-yard line. They punted, but Rossum fumbled, hampered by an injured arm, and USC set up shop on the Irish 12. Otton, back in the game, hit Chris Miller with a five-yard TD pass, but the Trojans missed a two-point pass

Lou Holtz says goodbye to Notre Dame in 1996.

Notre Dame's defensive coordinator, Bob Davie, became the head coach in 1996 after Lou Holtz resigned.

and ND hung on to a 14-12 lead. It was no consolation, however, that USC's three scoring drives had given them the ball with a total of 61 yards to move.

The Irish didn't waste their next opportunity, moving steadily on a 65-yard drive in nine plays, Denson getting the scoring honors on a 10-yard TD jaunt off the right side. On the prior play, he had broken four tackles on a stunning 12-yard run. Sanson, however, missed the PAT, a crucial turning point, even though ND led 20-12 with 3:52 left in the game.

It was too much time. For the umpteenth time in this great series, a team fought back from the void, USC using barely more than two minutes to negotiate 67 yards, Delon Washington weaving to his right through a tiring Irish defense for a 15-yard TD run. The Trojans used their last timeout before the conversion try. Good idea—Washington ran the ball in, through a missed tackle, and the game was knotted at 20-20. The teams then each had possessions that failed to break the tie in regulation time. The Irish won the toss and chose defense. The Trojans made good on their only

possession—a pass for 15 yards, a run for no gain, a pass for a five-yard TD, plus the PAT. A defender ran into the kicker, so ND got the ball on the 30, a sign of things to come. Powlus completed his first pass, then Denson was stopped for minus-three yards, a pass to Mosely fell incomplete, and on fourth down a Powlus pass was knocked down by a Trojan defender.

The incredible victory string was over. . . Irish hopes for a bowl were dashed. . . and the Holtz era of ND history ended somewhat ignominiously as Powlus's pass fluttered to the ground.

The season's statistics reveal some impressive achievements: an increase from 4,619 yards of total offense in '95 to 5,096 in '96, to go with a sharp decline in the opponents' total offense, from 3,984 yards to 2,970. The ground game for ND improved from 2,572 yards to 2,965; the passing yards were about the same, 2,047 to 2,131. Scoring was up, from 366 points to 407, with points allowed cut dramatically, from 216 to 181, the result being an increase in the margin of victory of a full touchdown, from 14 points in '95 to 21 in '96. Denson led the runners with 202 carries for 1,179 yards. Powlus hit 133 passes in 232 attempts for 1,942 yards, 12 TDs, and only four INTs. Turnovers were something to worry about, however, going from a plus-six in '95 to -21 in '96, with an alarming 23 fumbles lost. The Irish made only six of 10 FG attempts, and missed eight PATs, continued evidence of a decline in the kicking game.

Lou Holtz's 11-year record included coaching the most games ever under the Dome: 132; the second most wins: 100; one Heisman Trophy recipient: Tim Brown in '87, and the 1990 Heisman runner-up, Raghib Ismail; one national championship in '88; and nine consecutive bowl appearances, from '87 through '95. He was instrumental in the careers of Powlus and Denson, who would alter the Irish record books before their collegiate careers would be over.

1996 record: 8-3-0 (.727)
Record to date: 746-222-42 (.759)

1997

The beginning of the Bob Davie era at Notre Dame would seem to bring back memories of the other times in recent Irish football history when the school took the chance of elevating someone to the top position who had never experienced a head coaching job at a major football power. Notre Dame's choices of Terry Brennan and, later, Gerry Faust, should have taught some lessons to those who paid attention to these matters. Bob Davie does not quite fit this mold. His apprenticeship years at Pittsburgh and Texas A&M, under Jackie Sherrill and R.C. Slocum, placed him in the presence of head coaches who had made significant impacts on the college game. His three years under Holtz also included several games in which Davie was the de facto head coach, at least on the sidelines, during Holtz's recovery from surgery. He knew the Irish personnel well, had extensive recruiting experience in places that Notre Dame needed to mine well, and had seen the kinds of pressures that regularly came with the job under the Dome.

In spite of his awareness of the exalted, perhaps unrealistic, expectations most Irish fans have for yearly success, Davie did not instantly verbalize his own sanguine hopes for a national championship. He had good reason to be circumspect; he would have to find new starters for half of the starting 22, five on offense, six on defense, including two linemen and both ILBs. The offense would also have to learn some new things under a new offensive coordinator, Jim Colletto, the former head coach at Purdue (where he lost six times to ND, three of them shutouts). The departure of Marc Edwards left a major void at the FB spot, and the Irish would not easily find a replacement. Powlus and Denson gave the Irish a great one-two punch in passing and the ground game. And the renovation project on the stadium was finally complete, adding more than 20,000 spectators to one of the most raucous crowds visiting teams would ever face.

Ranked 11th and celebrating the dedication of the new stadium, ND's opening opponent in the Davie era was Georgia Tech, quarterbacked by the dangerous Joe Hamilton. After the KO, the Irish came out in a two-minute, hurry-up offense, but the drive fizzled. Tech couldn't move, and the Irish moved relentlessly towards the goal, mixing up the offense well, setting up a Denson TD of four yards. Out of the full T backfield, Denson ran right, broke outside contain, and juked a defender to the ground to get to the end zone. Sanson booted the PAT for a 7-0 lead. The Irish blunted the next Tech drive with a Rossum INT, but Hamilton later shook loose for an 11-yard TD run, spinning out of a poor tackling attempt at the three to knot the score at 7-7. Tech took the lead 10-7 with a 33-yard FG; Sanson brought the Irish into a 10-10 halftime tie with an answering 28-yard FG with no time left on the clock.

The third quarter saw ND make a much-needed adjustment to stymie the Tech option, but Hamilton's frenetic scrambling nullified any blitzes. Benny Guilbeaux intercepted a pass near the ND end zone to demolish the first Tech drive of the second half. The Irish wasted a great play by Denson—in motion to the left, he was picked up by a Tech LB; Powlus threw a perfect pass as Denson distanced himself from the defender, then put on some fancy moves for a 48-yard gain. The drive came down to a fourth-down play in the red zone, but the try failed and Tech put together a patient 84-yard drive, culminating in a 32-yard FG and a 13-10 Tech lead. Two Tech INTs kept the issue in doubt after that, but Tech also missed two FG tries. After the second misfire, Denson ran seven times on an 11-play, 70-yard drive. Tim Ridder snagged a Denson fumble to keep the drive alive. On the Tech one yard line, the Irish lined up in the full T, with Denson hauling the mail for the winning TD. DE Melvin Dansby made a crucial sack for minus-13 yards on Tech's final possession, and Davie savored his first triumph as the head coach of legendary Notre Dame.

Head coach Bob Davie.

Allen Rossum (15), outruns Pittsburgh defenders while running for a touchdown.

Whatever euphoria existed after the Tech game did not last long, however, for ancient nemesis Purdue burst the bubble with a 28-17 upset win. New head coach Joe Tiller brought a fancy passing offense from Wyoming and turned around the 11-game ND winning streak. In the process, assistant coach Jim Colletto, former head coach at Purdue, became the lightning rod for criticism.

Even though Powlus had his best game ever for the Irish (31 completions in 43 attempts for 293 yards) and the ground game picked up a respectable 164 yards, the Irish were never able to take command at any point in the game. Purdue struck first, after a Hunter Smith punt put them on their own one. QB Billy Dicken hit five passes in an 11-play drive, with TB Edwin Watson slipping in from the ND one for the first TD and a 7-0 lead. In the second quarter, Powlus hit four passes on an Irish 11-play drive, with Sanson's 34-yard FG putting ND on the scoreboard. The Irish kicked off, only to see a 33-yard return and a penalty set the Boilermakers up

at midfield. Five plays later, Watson scored again for a 14-3 lead. Perhaps sensing that the game was slipping away, ND came back, with Denson scoring on a 16-yard run to cap an 84-yard drive, making the halftime score 14-10.

The teams traded blows in the third quarter, with no advantage to either. In the fourth quarter, after Purdue had missed a FG try, Powlus was rolling to his right as a screen pass developed, but DE Roosevelt Colvin rocked him from behind, caused a fumble, alertly recovered and run in for a TD by Safety Adrian Beasley. Purdue kept the pressure up, but missed another FG try. Powlus and Denson teamed up on some pitches and catches on a late drive, with a one-yarder for a score to make it 21-17 for Purdue. With only 1:47 left in the game, the Irish had a chance, but they let Purdue score. A prevent defense somehow allowed a 38-yard completion from Dicken to Vinny Sutherland, and then a two-yard TD run by Kendall Matthews to seal

ND's fate. Summing up the disaster, Davie said, "We're embarrassed as a coaching staff ... we're embarrassed as a team."

The 17th-ranked Michigan State Spartans, under Nick Saban, maintained the embarrassment with a 23-7 win at Notre Dame. Sedrick Irvin and Marc Renaud both rushed for more than 100 yards while the stultifying Spartan D gagged Irish runners for a mere 61 yards on the ground. With no ground game to respect and conservative Irish pass patterns that failed to stretch the defense, State racked up a 17-0 lead before Powlus found Bobby Brown open for a seven-yard TD pass with 27 seconds left in the first half.

More of the same took place in the third quarter. On a second-and-27 play, Powlus was reduced to throwing to FB Joey Goodspeed as an outlet receiver for a three-yard gain. To the contrary, MSU had total control of the line of scrimmage, and averaged five yards on their first-down plays. They kept the pressure on with a FG to end their first possession, mounting a 20-7 lead. Powlus managed to throw enough safe passes to hit 11 in a row but the depth of ND's desperation was found in a pass thrown off a fake FG try by high school QB Hunter Smith, the holder, to Joey Goodspeed. The pass was incomplete and (Murphy was an Irishman, right?) Goodspeed separated his right shoulder in his courageous attempt to catch the football. In the fourth quarter, MSU tacked on another FG for the final score of 23-7. Perceptive Irish fans noted that on two separate occasions in the game, third-down pass play routes and completions for ND ended up short of the necessary first down yardage.

With a scoring offense ranked 105th in the country, ND had to try to recover from the abyss in Michigan Stadium. On their second drive, the Irish showed that they were more willing to go deep, with a 32-yard strike from Powlus to Malcolm Johnson setting up a 15-yard TD pass to Bobby Brown, who made an incredible catch while falling and twisting towards the ball. In the second quarter, Wolverine QB Brian Griese marshaled his team down the field for a 66-yard drive, crowned by TB Clarence Williams's untouched four-yard run up the middle of the defense. The Irish took a 14-7

Ivory Covington, Irish DB, saved the '95 win over Army with a great goalline tackle.

lead into the halftime as they crafted a 98-yard drive in 11 plays, sparked by FB Ken Barry's 22-yard run into and through no less than five would-be Wolverine tacklers. At the UM two, ND came out in a full T backfield with an unbalanced line to the left. Tony Driver, an impressive freshman TB, took the handoff and angled right, untouched, for the go-ahead TD.

Michigan took control of the game in the fourth quarter with a 41-yard TD pass from Griese to Tai Streets, as Rossum went for the INT but missed, and a 14-yard TD run by Chris Floyd. In the fourth quarter, LBs Lamont Bryant, Ronnie Nicks, and Jimmy Friday all snagged Wolverine fumbles in UM territory, but in each case ND was unable to take advantage of the turnovers. Beset by inopportune penalties (10 of them—enough to stall many of the dozen or so drives a team expects to have in a game) and unable to move the ball at will, a gallant effort by Notre Dame thus ended up in a 21-14 loss, their third in a row. The critical voices making themselves heard noted that Holtz had never lost three scheduled games in a row.

The Irish could only hope that a weak Stanford defense would give them a break. The Cardinals had just come a cropper in a 58-49 loss to the Oregon Ducks, so they looked vulnerable. Instead, the nightmare continued for Notre Dame as Stanford's coach Tyrone Willingham put an offense on the field that romped for 322 yards on the ground, ground out 34 first downs, and 514 yards of total offense in a 33-15 win. The Irish got off to a strange start, with FB Ken Barry at one point moving in the wrong direction and slamming into Powlus during a handoff, but eventually Sanson garnered a 45-yard FG. Stanford fired right back, with TB Mike Mitchell scampering over the collapsed left side of the Irish D for a 15-yard TD run and a 7-3 lead. Powlus and Denson brought ND back—94 yards in 11 plays, with freshman TE Jabari Holloway running a TE drag route to the right for an 11-yard TD reception. The PAT went awry and the score stood at 10-9 with Stanford up at halftime.

Stanford ran amok in the second half, piling up 303 yards of total offense against a hapless Irish defense and taking command of the game. For the fifth consecutive game, the Irish were blanked in the third quarter. Stanford's touchdowns all came on the ground: Miller on a three-yard run, Anthony Bookman on a 58-yard sprint, and Bookman again on a four-yard run. The only ND response was a 27-yard TD pass from Powlus to Bobby Brown; the two-point effort failed. The final ignominy struck when LB Kailee Wong tackled Powlus for a safety. Mitchell and Bookman both ran for 100 yards or more, a phenomenon the Irish had recently seen. For the game, ND ran 56 plays; Stanford cruised with 91.

With all this adversity, Pittsburgh came along at the right time for ND. Pitt seemed to offer a pass defense Powlus could exploit, but ND's run defense was 67th in the rankings. None of this came into play, however, on the opening Pitt KO: Rossum fumbled it, grabbed it, started left, was hit, stopped, then spun right and sprinted 91 yards for a TD. After the Irish KO, Pitt was unable to move and ND took over on downs. On the fourth play for the Irish, Denson took a handoff and started right, looked up, and saw nothing but turf and blocked Panthers lying all over it. Fifty yards later, he scored. The 14-0 score held into the third quarter;

Hunter the Punter—Hunter Smith, second all-time for ND.

Sanson broke the third-quarter drought for the Irish with a 22-yard FG. Pitt scored a TD on the ground but Jamie Spencer got that back with a 23-yard TD run off the left side to end the drive on which Denson became the fifth leading rusher in Notre Dame history, surpassing the immortal George Gipp. The teams traded TDs again, Denson scoring from the two with Jarious Jackson at QB with a Full T backfield. Pitt squeezed a TD pass between two Jackson TDs—a three-yard option keeper and a 40-yard bolt with an onside kick attempt—for the final score of 45 to 21. The win stopped ND's worst losing streak in 36 years.

Coming out of the darkness, the light at the end proved to be unranked, 3-3 USC, in South Bend for their midseason contest. The light went out for ND as they lost 20-17—the same score to the same team that cost the Irish an undisputed national title in 1964. Except this loss had no national implications other than the fact that two of the country's premier football programs were wallowing in mediocrity—or worse. The Irish came out strong as Rossum turned on the jets for a KO return of 56 yards on the game's opening play. Five plays later, Denson scored on a two-yard burst. USC came right back to tie the game on the ensuing drive, DeLon Washington slamming in from the three. The track meet continued as ND took the Trojan KO and marched 82 yards in 12 plays, with Tony Driver getting the TD honors with a one-yard run. In the second quarter, USC held up their end of the deal with yet another answering drive, R. Jay Soward catching a John Fox pass for an eight-yard TD. It was about time for a momentum shift and the Irish kicking game obliged as Jim Sanson's next two second-quarter FG attempts missed, killing Irish drives. He hit his third try, just before the halftime, and ND nursed a 17-14 lead at the intermission.

The futility marking earlier Irish third quarters returned in full bloom: this time, against USC ND's ground game amassed a mere two yards as the offense ran six measly plays. Sanson missed a third field goal later in the game, although USC managed to tie the game with an Adam Abrams FG from 42 yards out, then won the game with an Abrams FG after an INT by Mark Cusano put the ball on the ND 29. The Irish were not horrible—they did win some stats, such as Hunter Smith's two punts for a 60-yard average, 24 first downs to 14 for USC, only seven penalties to 15 for the Trojans. But this is not how games are won. There is also that definitive stat: the score. And this score led to an ugly moment as the disheartened team left the field when unforgiving, mean-spirited fans were seen spitting on Ron Powlus.

The Jekyll and Hyde nature of the '97 Irish was evident against Boston College as ND blasted the Golden Eagles 52-20. Benny Guilbeaux got it started with an INT and TB Tony Driver scored on a short run to open the rout. Powlus hooked up with Malcolm Johnson on a 36-yard pass to set up their four-yard TD hookup for a 14-0 lead. Davie shook things up a bit in the second quarter when he inserted Jarious Jackson at QB, who led an 83-yard drive to his own three-yard TD run. Denson zipped in for an eight-yard TD run after Powlus hit TE Jabari Holloway with a 32-yard pass. The doldrums for the Irish in the third quarter were not too bad this time; Scott Cengia's 20-yard FG after a 44-yard Powlus pass to Raki Nelson was sandwiched between two BC TDs. Three fourth-quarter TDs for ND wrapped it up: Bobby Brown's 10-yard TD catch, Rossum's 80-yard KO return, and Jackson's one-yard TD run after directing a 90-yard drive. ND romped for 526 yards on 83 plays, reminiscent of the dominance of the '96 routs.

Perhaps the Irish could not stand prosperity for long. With Navy up next, you'd think that they could settle in and have another blowout. Not this group, though. Navy came out and ran up 399 yards of total offense, averaged nearly six yards per play, caused three fumbles, had three sacks, and nearly won the game but for an amazing play by Allen Rossum. Middie QB Chris McCoy showed that he knew how to operate the QB duck play, a la AFA, gaining 27 yards on his first option play, setting up his own nine-yard TD option run to the left. ND punted to end their first drive, but Kory Minor made up with an INT and runback to the Navy 16. Two plays later, Powlus spotted Bobby Brown in the right flat and fired a 14-yard TD pass, his 51st career TD pass. Cengia put the thrill back in the PAT try when he hit the left upright with a kick that fell the right way. The teams traded INTs, with Navy coming out ahead with a 22-yard FG, but misfired on a FG try near the end of the half to take a 10-7 lead over the Irish into the intermission.

On the fourth play of the second half, Denson took a deep pitch down the right sideline for a 48-yard TD romp. Navy used an INT by Rashad Smith to get McCoy into the end zone again, a two-yard run after a good fake to the FB, to take a 17-14 lead into the fourth quarter. Benny Guilbeaux slammed the door on a Navy drive with an INT in the Irish end zone, setting up a 17-play, 93-yard winning TD drive, Denson getting the scoring honors with a cutback run over the right side from five yards out. With less than six minutes, the Irish D stopped Navy's offense, giving the ball back to Powlus and mates with 3:27 left. The Irish worked the clock and the downs until they felt they could start kneeling for the win—but they miscalculated the time needed and Navy got the ball at the Irish 29 with three seconds left. McCoy threw into a crowd, the ball caromed off Deke Cooper's helmet to Middie Pat McGrew who snagged the ball and exultantly lit out for the territory! But Rossum had alertly trailed the play, saw the impending disaster, turned on the afterburner, and tackled McGrew on the one-yard line to end the game. Worth mentioning were the 18 tackles made by DE Melvin Dansby, 26 percent of Navy's plays.

A week off gave the Irish time to recover from the theatrics of this win, but they were facing the 11th-ranked LSU Tigers in Death Valley. Not having defeated a ranked team in '97, Davie and the team used their break wisely and ND played an outstanding game to defeat LSU 24-6, an effort that included no penalties and no turnovers. The Tigers won the coin toss, and that was about it. They deferred, so kicked off to Rossum, who scooted 43 yards to give Powlus great field position. The Irish promptly exploded for 17 first-quarter points, a deficit LSU never overcame. Denson finished the first drive with a nine-yard TD run, Cengia added a 29-yard FG, and Clement Stokes ended the first-quarter rout with a six-yard run following an A'Jani Sanders INT and 26-yard return. The second quarter found LSU forcing passes as their running game stayed in low gear. Guilbeaux intercepted one of their prayers, and another drive ended with an incompletion thrown into double coverage. In the third quarter, an LSU FG try clanged into the upright; ND answered with a 79-yard drive, Stokes slamming in untouched from the one to make it 24-0. In the last quarter, Kevin Faulk scored from the two and a two-point conversion failed. This time, the Irish took the knee to end the game in proper fashion. It was the first time since 1981 that a Notre Dame squad had played a game without a penalty.

The next opponent, West Virginia, had lost to the same BC team the Irish had dominated earlier in the season. But the Mountaineers had Famous Amos Zereoue, who was averaging 140 yards per game on the ground. He wouldn't disappoint as he cruised into, around, and through the Irish D for 234 yards on 32 busy carries, good for two TDs. But ND scored three TDs and stopped WV when they had to. Zereoue scored

Hunter Smith.

the game's first TD, an 11-yard affair that held up until Stokes answered early in the second quarter, with a one-yard burst. Zereoue showed his mettle on the next drive, a 60-yard explosion up the left sideline followed by a six-yard TD. After 12 carries, he had cruised for 111 yards. A fumble ended ND's next drive, but WV soon had to punt. Davie put in Jarious Jackson, obviously with an eye to future campaigns, who mixed up option plays with some passes, one of which went to Malcolm Johnson, who made a super over-the-shoulder catch for a 46-yard gain deep in WV territory. Two plays later, Jackson went back to Johnson for a seven-yard TD and a 14-14 tie. The third quarter passed by without any scoring, as ND worked on containing Zereoue, but Rossum had left the game earlier with a concussion, replaced by Ty Goode. In the last quarter, WV seemed to be picking on Ivory Covington, who responded in splendid fashion, defensing several passes and grabbing an INT on the ND six, returning it 15 yards. Davie knew that this was the time to put the hammer down: Denson took a pitch and ran left for 36 yards, helping to set up a TD pass from a shotgun, Powlus to Bobby Brown for 11 yards and the 21-14 score. But WV had nearly five minutes to work with; they would have two possessions. On their first drive, Minor had a sack and Covington stopped a scramble short of a first down. On the second possession, the Mountaineers stayed in a shotgun and reached the ND 27 with 15 seconds left. QB Marc Bulger threw into the end zone, where Goode met the challenge with an INT to end the threat. Denson, with 144 yards rushing, and Zereoue, with 234 yards, combined for 378 yards on the ground in a tremendous display of the runner's art.

Improbably, in spite of their horrific start to the season, the Irish could earn a bowl bid with a win over Hawaii. Even though the Rainbows had only three wins, it's never easy to win a game played in Honolulu, as the '91 Irish could attest with their 48-42 shootout. There are too many distractions to count, and the reffing can be hard to take.

Rossum got the Irish on the scoreboard with an INT and a 37-yard TD return on UH's first play from scrimmage, setting a new NCAA record with his ninth career score on a return (three each for KOs, punts, INTs). Early in the second frame, the Rainbows stitched together an 89-yard drive, capped by Charles Tharp's dive off the left side from the one. The PAT was wide left. The Irish came right back, driving 80 yards, Denson slashing right, then cutting back to the left for a 12-yard TD run. Cengia made the PAT kick and the Irish led 14-6. Hawaii cut into that lead with an Eric Hannum FG near the end of the half, the beginning of four unanswered scores.

Hannum hit two more FGs in the third quarter, then added a PAT in the fourth quarter after Charles Tharp scored from the ND eight. With that, the Irish were looking at the short end of a 22-14 score. Notre Dame fought back, Denson leading the way with a 42-yard cutback run that took the ball to the UH nine. Working from an I formation, Powlus pitched the ball on a toss sweep to Denson, running to the right, who scored from the three, closing the score to 22-20. With 11:36 on the clock, the teams traded possession no less than six times, but the Irish had the ball with 5 seconds left for a Cengia FG try, set up by a great 47-yard pass from Powlus to Raki Nelson. Cengia hammered the 20-yarder for a 23-22 lead. He still had to KO, though, and what followed look like the old tapes of the Cal-Stanford game in which the runner ran into the marching band, but ND escaped with no further harm and the win.

The Irish received a bid to play LSU in the Independence Bowl, the second time in a month and a half that they would have to face the Tigers in Louisiana. It's always a difficult task to take on an opponent twice in such short order. Early on, the Irish had noticed that Kevin Faulk, the Tiger TB star, had gone out of the game.

They didn't know much about his sub, Rondell Mealey, but they would know plenty before the game was over. The game started out as a FG clinic, Cengia hitting two, LSU's Wade Richey the same, his second coming in the third quarter. By the time Richey tied the game, ND had seen plenty of Mealey—and had wasted all but one play of the third quarter without gaining a first down. To start the drive that ended with the LSU FG, Sanson kicked off to Mealey, then LSU called his number eight straight times for 45 hard-earned yards.

The game's first TD came on an eight-play drive covering 49 yards; Mealey hauled the mail on five of those plays, though the score was a 12-yard pass from Herb Tyler to Abram Booty. Cengia responded with his third FG (finally, perhaps ironically, the Irish had some reliable point production in the kicking game) to make it 13-9. But Mealey took control, doing all the work on an 80-yard drive, with a 78-yard burst and a two-yard TD, with his final TD coming on a one-yard blast following his 26-yard set-up scamper. When it was all over, Rondell Mealey had carried 34 times for 222 yards, more than the entire ND running game.

The season had to be seen as a significant disappointment for all concerned. To his credit, Bob Davie told it straight; he seldom offered excuses. The team could have folded after the loss to USC, but it turned it around in time to avoid a worst-case scenario—though this is not the kind of claim Notre Dame football teams want to be making. The season's statistics reveal a sharp drop in offensive production from the 1996 campaign: total yardage dropped 15 percent from 5,096 yards to 4,323 yards, primarily from a 30 percent drop in the ground game, from 2,965 yards in '96 to 2,099. The passing game increased modestly, from 2,131 yards to 2,224 yards, although the Irish both threw more passes and completed more than any other Notre Dame team. One really positive note was the dramatic improvement in the turnover ratio; the '97 Irish turned in a plus-five, vastly better than the minus-21 from '96. The offensive downturn was also reflected in the team's scoring: whereas the '96 Irish beat up on people by an average margin of 21 points, the '97 edition scraped by with a three point margin, a scary prospect given ND's recent kicking woes. Scoring fell from the 407 points racked up in '96 to 273 in '97. The kicking game ended up hitting more FGs than in '96, eight of 15, but the percentage fell; there was somewhat more consistency in PAT kicks.

Denson led the runners with 264 carries for 1,268 yards and 12 TDs. Powlus capped a fine career with

182 completions in 298 attempts for 2,078 yards, seven INTs, and nine TDs. For the first time in ND's storied history, the Irish boasted two receivers with more than 40 receptions each: sophomore Bobby Brown with 45 and junior Malcolm Johnson with 42.

1997 record: 7-6 (.538)
Record to date: 753-228-42 (.756)

1998

Head coach Bob Davie could look at his returners in '98 and rely on a bit more experience and continuity than the personnel shuffle he encountered in '97. He could count on seven returning monogram winning starters on offense and six on defense. He would have to develop the skills of Jarious Jackson at QB after four seasons with the same QB, Ron Powlus. Jackson, an excellent athlete who had been considered as a LB early in his career, would give the Irish more mobility, better quickness, and better option skills at QB than Powlus offered. The unknowns were his pass defense reading skills, his throwing accuracy, and leadership qualities. Jackson would have the pleasure to be handing off to Autry Denson, whose senior campaign found him on the verge of breaking Allen Pinkett's rushing record from the early and mid-'80s. Jamie Spencer would help solidify matters at the FB spot. Malcolm Johnson and Bobby Brown returned as the receivers. Sophomore Jabari Holloway, a truly big target, held down the TE spot, but the Irish had not been making great use of this position in recent seasons. The interior line was a veteran unit, led by pre-season All-American Mike Rosenthal. Luke Petitgout could be counted on, and Jerry Wisne was showing much promise. Tim Ridder moved over from TE to the strong guard spot, and a new center took over that spot, John Merandi. Overall, averaging 6' 6" and 310 pounds, this group would appear to be positioned to make an improvement in offensive production, to have a good chance at ball control, and be able to offer good protection to Jackson as he honed his QB skills.

The defense would be led by the returning quarter of LBs—Kory Minor and Lamont Bryant on the outside, fireplug Bobbie Howard and Jimmy Friday on the inside—a group with good size, range, and speed. An impressive freshman, Anthony Weaver would lead the way at left DE, and the '97 starter there, Brad Williams,

Mike Rosenthal.

would move to RE; junior Lance Legree moved up from the second unit to start at NG. The question mark for the Irish D rested with the potential for two new players and a starter moved from FS: only Guilbeaux returned to the SS spot he held down in '97. Deveron Harper moved to LCB from '97 starting spot as FS. Brock Williams took over the RCB spot vacated by the talented Allen Rossum and senior A'Jani Sanders moved over from the number two SS to work the FS spot. Defensive coordinator Greg Mattison saw a good mix of talented youngsters, steady veterans, impressive experience at the LB spots, and some personnel in the secondary who would be tested by opponents' passing games.

Other matters lingered on the periphery of Irish consciousness: the mid-season possibility of ND's joining the Big Ten (eventually voted against), an embarrassing age-discrimination case and trial brought by a former coach, and allegations of illegal gifts to players and hints of a scandal leading to those gifts. The staff and players had to attend to these matters as best they could, then put them out of their minds in order to concentrate on football. Taken together, however, these latter matters were new territory for the Notre Dame family, an institution that takes great pride in running an absolutely clean program.

The usual demanding schedule faced Davie and the

Dependable Irish defensive back A'Jani Sanders.

Irish in his second year. He had survived a tough first year and looked forward to his team responding better to the rigors of the season. It started with ancient opponent Michigan, defending national champs, at the Dome. The Wolverines took it to the Irish from the start, controlling more than two-thirds of the game clock in the first half, running 54 plays to ND's 22. The first quarter ended in a 3-3 deadlock, although UM missed two other FG attempts. Irish spirits were lifted by Denson when he took a pitch and rambled to his left for a 57-yard gain, leading to Sanson's 33-yard tying FG. In the second quarter, Davie opened up the offense a bit, with Jackson rolling out and looking for open receivers, but many of his throws were too high, often a problem for a new QB trying to pass on the move. Jackson did better on the drive that brought ND into a second tie at 6-6 when he faked an option, stopped, dropped into the pocket and took a long look where he found Raki Nelson open for a 32-yard strike. Sanson's tying FG was not a thing of

beauty, but it counted. UM took the lead a third time when QB Tom Brady bounced off a Bobbie Howard hit into the end zone for a one-yard TD run and the 13-6 halftime score. In spite of the Wolverines' ball-control game, this was their high-water mark, as a deluge of five unanswered ND scores hit them.

Jim Sanson banged in a FG after the UM KO, then ND worked for its first TD after recovering a Michigan fumble, the score coming off a fake option that turned in to a four-yard TD pass to wide open TE Dan O'Leary. Michigan fumbled to ND on their next possession and Jackson instantly converted the error into a Notre Dame TD with a 35-yard pass to Raki Nelson for a 23-13 Irish lead. The wheels kept falling off the UM offense on their next drive when Irish LB Jimmy Friday blocked a 40-yard FG try. Denson kept up the pressure in the fourth quarter with a great four-yard TD run, showing tremendous balance and strength as he powered through two would-be tackles. If there were any wheels left for UM, they lost them with their third missed FG after back-to-back QB sacks. The Irish then drove for their last TD, a one-yard Denson special, before the Wolverines got a consolation TD on a pass to Jerame Tuman. In the 27 prior games, the Irish had averaged 14 points per game, so the 36 scored here were an impressive team record. Denson made a strong opening statement for his senior campaign with 24 carries for 162 yards and two TDs. Jackson hit only four of 10 passes, but managed two TDs anyway.

The common coaching wisdom has it that a team makes the most improvement between the first and second games of the season. If that is the case, then MSU's 45-23 demolition of the Irish in Spartan Stadium indicated a serious lapse in the Irish program. Davie's Irish literally could not get anything done right at all until the outcome was a foregone conclusion. The Spartans scored the first three TDs before Sanson could contribute a FG. The first score came on a blocked punt. Then MSU poured on three more unanswered TDs; the halftime score was 42-3. Denson scored on a two-yard run in the third quarter and Deke Cooper recovered a Spartan fumble and took off on a 96-yard TD return. Subs garnered the last Irish score in the waning moments. Jackson was forced into a passing frenzy as the score mounted; 10 attempts had sufficed against UM. . . this time he had to go downtown 30 times. The Irish had eight penalties, lost two INTs and one of four fumbles; the D gave up 451 yards to MSU, including an 86-yard TD pass, the longest in history against a Notre Dame team. Enough said.

The Irish looked so inept—Davie took full responsibility—that many fans wondered if this was déja vu all over again, the loss the beginning of another four-yard losing skein. Well, it was the start of something, as ND had an extra week to prepare—but this time it turned into an eight-game winning streak.

The streak started with a heart-stopping 31-30 win over a talented, hungry Purdue team led by a great QB, Drew Brees. But the Irish started in a deficit, as usual, when a pass deflected off a DB's helmet into the hands of a Purdue receiver coming back on the field of play from out of bounds. Got that? Adding to the adversity, Brees tallied a two-yard TD run for a 14-0 Purdue lead. Having seen enough, Denson took over on the next drive, with several impressive runs, finished by a 14-yard sprint up the middle plus a good cutback. The Irish D forced a fumble recovered by Deke Cooper, but ND couldn't capitalize. Purdue's Travis Dorch kept the pressure on with a 37-yard FG, but Jackson hooked up with his sophomore TE twice, once for 16 yards, the second time for a 10-yard TD following the big guy's shucking a potential tackler. Brees came right back with a 65-yard drive with a TD pass to Isaac Jones that looked all the world like a fumble and an Irish recovery.

On the second ND possession in the third quarter, Holloway snagged a 51-yard pass from Jackson on play action to set up a five-yard TD run by Denson who passed Vagas Ferguson to become the number two ND rusher. The Irish D was beginning to take control, holding Brees to a three-and-out drive, but the answering drive fizzled when a Sanson FG try sailed way right. Travis Dorch, however, banged a 40-yard FG into a stiff wind to make the score 27-21 for Purdue, then he hit another one, a 47-yarder, for a 30-21 lead with 7:52 left in the game.

Jackson gathered his troops and started an amazing comeback, highlighted by a 15-yard pass to Jay Johnson that set up a 17-yard TD pass to a jubilant Holloway. Sanson hit the PAT and the Irish were back in it, 28-31, with 3:36 left. Purdue tried two runs, then went into a shotgun formation on a third-and-15; Tony Driver, who had made the switch from TB to SS and earlier caused a Purdue fumble, came away with the Purdue pass and ran it 37 yards to the Purdue five with 1:39 left. The Irish

used Denson three times, then Sanson kicked a 17-yard FG for ND's first lead in the game, 31-30. Brees came back in the shotgun formation and, unbelievably, Driver intercepted his second pass within a 1:02 time span, sealing one of the great comeback wins for Notre Dame.

The Irish kept up their momentum with a steady, well-executed 35-17 win over Stanford. Jackson had one of the great multi-threat games for an Irish QB: 18 rushes for 100 yards (the first century mark for an Irish QB since Hornung) and three TDs, to go with 11 completions of 15 passes for another 163 yards. His spree started on the eighth play of the game when Jackson ran out of a double wing set for a 22-yard TD. Denson followed this up on the next ND drive with a two-yard TD jaunt. Deveron Harper wreaked havoc on the next Cardinal drive with a blitz, stripping the ball from the QB for Brad Williams to recover. Jamie Spencer made short work of the opportunity: a 10-yard blast off the left guard, then a seven-yard TD run on a similar play to give the Irish a 21-0 lead in the first quarter. Stanford fought back with a FG, but Jackson ran an option keeper for a seven-yard TD in the second quarter, then repeated the play in the third quarter for a five-yard scoring run. Stanford scored two late TDs for the final 35-17 score.

The Irish played Arizona State in Tempe[rature =120 degrees] on the playing field, fully aware of the great offensive potential of J.R. Redmond, Tariq McDonald, and QB Ryan Kealy. Jackson was nursing a bruised shoulder, so Joey Goodspeed played up to his

Bobbie Howard.

name and had 100 yards rushing on four carries, one a 60-yard ramble. Good Irish D picked off an ASU pass and Jackson went to work, hitting Malcolm Johnson for a seven-yard TD in the first quarter. The D did it again when A'Jani Sanders hauled in a tipped pass and sprinted 25 yards to pay dirt. ASU drove for a FG and the 14-3 halftime score. Denson scored twice in the second half on short runs, the second set up by Goodspeed's long run. ASU could only muster a J.R. Redmond TD in the fourth quarter as ASU went down 28-9. The Irish had 13 penalties to make further scoring difficult, but Hunter Smith awed everyone with a 79-yard punt from his end zone to help keep ASU in the hole.

Army visited ND and nearly copped a victory, playing a great game in a 20-17 ND win. They used a blocked punt to put up a FG midway into the first quarter. Sanson responded five minutes later with a 39-yarder, then Denson put the Irish up with a five-yard TD run early in the second quarter. On the next Irish possession, Denson hauled in a 33-yard pass from Jackson, who threw it with Cadets draped all over him, but the drive snagged with a missed 49-yard FG. Army's Bobby Williams ran a counter off an option for a three-yard TD to make it 10-10 at the half. Most of the third quarter was spent in futility by ND: another missed FG, an INT to kill a drive. But Jackson did hit Bobby Brown with a 36-yard pass that Brown broke for a TD—except he fumbled near the end zone and Johnson claimed the

Luke Petitgout.

TD. Army's Craig Stucker, who seemed to be making a living with bruising FB runs up the middle of the Irish D, did just that and scored on a 19-yard untouched blast, tying the game at 17-17. As the fourth quarter passed away, the teams traded punts. Finally, ND moved 46 yards in 10 careful plays to give Sanson a shot at avoiding OT with a 49-yard FG. He made it, a career-best, then the D held on until Sanders hauled in an INT with 8 seconds left to ensure the surprisingly tough win.

For the first time in nearly three-quarters of a century, the Irish met Baylor. With the Bears possessing the 92nd-ranked rushing defense, you can pardon the Irish backs' salivating over the possibilities. For Autry Denson, they came true: 24 caries for a career-high 189 yards rushing, 12 more than Baylor's total offense in a 27-3 spanking. The teams traded first-half FGs, and then everything went ND's way (except for a rare fumble by Denson). With Denson running for sizable chunks of real estate at every opportunity, the Irish broke the tie, with lineman Mike Gandy lined up at FB, when Denson jumped over the pile for a one-yard TD in the second quarter. Baylor punted back, Denson shook loose for 48 yards, then seven yards, before Jackson fired to Malcolm Johnson for a 24-yard TD. The second play from scrimmage in the third quarter was a 66-yard bomb from Jackson to Bobby Brown. While the Irish were thus cavorting, Baylor kept misfiring on FG attempts. The last Irish score followed a QB draw that worked to perfection for 43 yards; shortly thereafter, Sanson racked up a 21-yard FG for the finale.

Ranked 13th, ND went to Boston to meet Boston College. The Golden Eagles boasted the fourth-ranked runner in the country, Mike Cloud, averaging 153.4 yards per game. Although BC was having a down season, with only two wins and five straight losses, the Irish had come to expect a tough game from them. This would be no exception.

Notre Dame took charge right away, with Denson scoring a one-yard TD on a trademark cutback move to end the first drive. The teams sparred for the rest of the quarter, but Cloud scored from an unbalanced line set on an 11-yard blast. Notre Dame showed good poise on a six-play, 64-yard drive, when Jackson saved the situation on a second and 20 play by firing a 28-yard TD pass to sophomore WR Joey Getherall on an inside post route. BC, not to be denied, used a 28-yard KO return for good field position, then worked in for a 23-yard TD pass from Scott Mutryn to Anthony DiCosmo. The Irish tightened their chin straps and forced BC into two long

FG tries for the rest of the quarter; Kicker John Matich succeeded on the second one to give BC a 17-14 halftime lead.

Davie had coached the team into a complete third-quarter turnaround compared to the '97 disaster, outscoring opponents 53-3 to this point. This game followed the new pattern as ND put up 10 points to earn the lead: a Sanson FG and a Jackson pass to Johnson following a Bobbie Howard INT. On their next drive, BC sent Matich in to try a 50-yard FG, but his kick went wide right. He made good on a 35-yarder following an Irish fumble, making the score 24-20. The Irish had to do something decisive and, on their own five-yard line, third and 22 (courtesy of two great defensive efforts by Dennis Hovan), Jackson scrambled around, pointed, and threw a pass to Johnson for a crucial 68-yard gain. From the BC 26, Denson gained 10 and then eight yards, Spencer rumbled for six more, and Denson skipped in from the two to give ND a 31-20 lead with 9:23 left. Not to be denied, BC turned loose Mutryn and Anthony DiCosmo, hitting him three times with passes worth 45 yards on a 68-yard drive, the finale a seven-yarder. BC went for a two-point conversion, but Ty Goode intercepted Mutryn's pass and took off for a long runback to preserve the 31-26 score.

Inspirational leader for Notre Dame, linebacker Bobbie Howard.

The Irish were unable to sustain their next possession and punted back with about four minutes left, setting up one of the most stirring, thrilling finishes to a game any fan could want. BC started at their own 23; after a bumpy start, Mutryn hit two big passes—24 yards to Dennis Harding, then 27 yards to Rob Tardio (enough to make you want to ditch any form of the prevent defense). With the ball at the ND four, Sanders had to leave the game with an injury, but in the excitement no one replaced him, so the Irish called a TO. With 1:01 left, Mike Cloud gained two yards on first down running the middle, then BC insisted again with Cloud up the middle, but Bobbie Howard stopped him for a short gain. With the ball near the one-yard line, BC put in two TEs; from a one-back set, Cloud ran left, but Friday met him at the pass and dropped him with a great tackle. BC took a TO with 11 seconds left. On fourth down, with BC's fans going nuts in Alumni Stadium, they came back in the one-back set, then ran Cloud slightly to the left where Deke Cooper came through unblocked and hit him with all he had for no gain! The Irish ran one very careful keeper with Jackson to seal the win. BC had gained 491 total yards of offense, but not gaining the 492nd yard meant all the difference.

After all that excitement, one could understand a bit of a letdown, but ND took on Navy and laid a shutout on the Middies, a 30-0 win that revealed pretty much a total domination of all phases of the game. Denson used the opportunity to gain 107 yards to become ND's all-time leader in rushing and 100-yard games (22). Jackson hit 12 straight passes, close to Powlus's record. In workmanlike fashion, the Irish put up a score in each quarter: Jamie Spencer slammed in from the four shortly after hauling in a 10-yard pass, then Denson showed great field vision and his cutback skills on an eight-yard trip to pay dirt in the second quarter. Denson hauled the mail for an 18-yard score in the third quarter, and Johnson ended the third quarter with a 16-yard TD strike from Jackson. Sanson wrapped it up with a FG in the last frame for the 30-0 win.

In recognition of his fine work in the season, Bob Davie had been announced as the recipient of the prestigious Walter Camp Coach of the Year award. With that done, for the third time within a calendar year, 10th-ranked ND faced the LSU Tigers. Two college teams simply could not become more familiar with each other than these two had in that span. The game got off to a strange start when the refs noted that some Irish players did not have their uniform pants reaching a certain point below their knees. Once that little problem was solved, LSU's Mark Roman intercepted a Jackson pass and steamed 53 yards for a TD and a 7-0 Tiger lead. The Irish answered with a 44-yard pass to Brown, followed by a great play—in a double-wing set, Jackson showed option right, but there was a fake reverse LSU had to honor, allowing freshman WR David Givens to score on a 22-yard run. LSU scotched the next ND drive by tipping a Sanson FG try, then drove 92 yards for a 16-yard Kevin Faulk TD, but the PAT was tipped away when the entire right side of the LSU collapsed before the Irish charge. The Irish patched together a good drive from their own 20, but a Sanson FG try drifted wide left. On the next play, Faulk ran to his right where OLB Lamont Bryant stood him up, stripped the ball, recovered it, and rumbled 13 yards for an Irish TD. Still stinging from that play, Faulk showed his mettle on the next play when he took the KO back 88 yards for a Tiger TD and a 21-14 lead.

The teams both scored two TDs in the third quarter and both missed a PAT, as the kicking game for both seemed to have slipped a notch. Denson scored on a three-yard run to end the first ND drive, Sanson's PAT was blocked, then Herb Tyler found Abram Booty open for a 27-yard TD strike and a 27-20 lead after the right side collapsed again and the D blocked another PAT effort. ND came right back on a 78-yard, eight-play drive, featuring a 22-yard Jackson pass to Johnson, and then an eight-yard TD pass one to the other on a timing pattern for the 34-27 LSU lead. In the fourth quarter, LSU marched methodically to the ND 11 where Bobbie Howard read a Tyler pass perfectly, intercepted it, and hauled it 89 yards for a TD, but the PAT kick was blocked to leave ND on the short end

of the 34-33 score. Howard continued his heroics by tipping an LSU FG try on their next possession. Jackson then led ND on the game-winning drive, hitting Raki Nelson with a crucial 24-yard pass before finding him again for an 11-yard TD pass. A two-point try missed and the score stood at 39-36. LSU drove back to the ND 31, lost the ball on downs, setting up a kneeling scenario that once again nearly backfired, forcing the Irish to try to waste the last seconds with Jackson running around in his end zone for a safety, but a Tiger LB slammed into him before he could get out of bounds, damaging his MCL. ND executed its free kick with three seconds left and then defensed a long pass for an incompletion and the win, a costly one after it was revealed that Jackson would be out for at least a month.

Within a two-week period, Notre Dame's 1998 team had played two of the most stirring games on record—its thrilling goal-line stand to stop BC and this great come-from-behind win over a determined LSU squad, with enough ups and downs and ditzy plays for an entire season.

Without Jackson, who had grown during the season

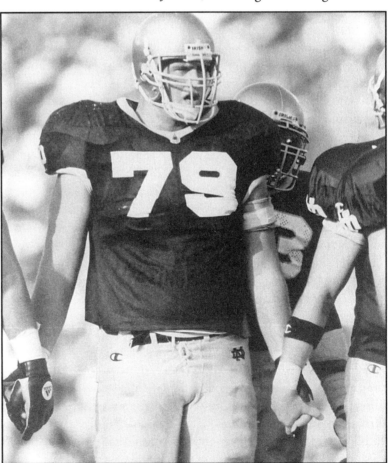

Mike Rosenthal, three-year starter on the offensive line for Notre Dame.

into the kind of offensive force that drove defenses crazy, the Irish would have it tough with the USC Trojans. Ranked ninth, but lacking a significant portion of their offense with Jackson out, and with QBs who had not enjoyed many reps in practices during the regular season and very little game time, the Irish were shut out for the first time in more than a decade, 10-0, in a game that few would recognize as a match-up of these two old rivals. The first half was a scoreless affair, with inexperience, mistakes, and defenses dominating. USC got a two-yard run from their freshman QB, Carson Palmer, for a TD and a FG, both in the third quarter, for all they needed. The Trojan defense committed nine men to the LOS, holding Denson to 46 yards on 19 carries. Arnaz Battle, a freshman QB for ND, broke four tackles on a great run that reached the USC two-yard line, but he fumbled on his way down, a cameo moment for the entire ND effort.

The loss to USC cost the Irish a bowl championship bid, the second such loss within three seasons. The '98 ND team accepted a Gator Bowl bid to play Georgia Tech, still boasting the impressive Joe Hamilton at QB the Irish had seen in the '97 season opener.

The teams played to a 7-7 first-quarter tie. ND had a good opportunity in Tech's territory with Holloway open by 15 yards on a delay route, but Jackson didn't see him. Tech scored first on a halfback pass from Joe Burns to Joe Hamilton, his first catch of the year. The Irish came right back with six quick plays, Denson juking and cutting for a nine-yard TD run.

Tech took command in the second quarter, Hamilton running a QB draw play that looked remarkably like the AFA QB duck play. Phillip Rogers scored their second TD by diving over the pile for a three-yard score. For two possessions, ND failed to get into scoring territory, but Tech was able to move in close enough for a TE crossing pattern to work for a nine-yard TD pass from Hamilton and a 21-7 halftime lead.

Denson began ND's return from the depths by scoring to end the first possession of the third quarter, a one-yard burst. Tech fumbled soon thereafter and the Irish maneuvered 26 yards in eight plays, with Jackson scoring on a keeper from the three. Tech blocked the PAT to keep a 21-20 lead. The Irish were clearly back in the game and Hamilton responded in splendid fashion, firing a 44-yard TD pass to Dez White on an out-and-up pattern. ND responded in kind, an 88-yard drive in 11 plays, Denson scoring from the one, his third of the game, tying a Gator Bowl record. Jackson hit Bobby Brown for a two-point conversion and a 28-28 tie. Tech

Irish assistant coach Greg Mattison.

continued the track meet, Hamilton finding White again for another long-distance score, a 55-yarder, for a 35-28 lead with 7:55 left. The Irish had two more drives, both marred by fumbles, and Tech kneeled their way through the final seconds to the win. The Irish had converted only two of nine third-down plays, gave up 242 yards passing, and gained only 309 total yards to Tech's 436.

With the Irish going from a 7-6 in '97 record to a 9-3 in '98, one would expect some improvements. The difference appears to have been mostly on the defensive side: ND allowed only 213 points in '98, an 11 percent decrease. The Irish choked off opposing runners dramatically, a 30 percent decline, from 2,217 yards to 1,560. Opponents seem to have picked on the Irish secondary roughly the same as in '97: 193 completions, down one from '97, for a four percent increase in yardage, from 2,164 to 2,259 yards, good for 11 TDs, more than double the '97 total of five. On the offensive side, the total yardage for ND (surprisingly) declined 4 percent—due mainly to the anemic offensive production of the shutout loss to USC, from the '97 figure of 4,323 yards to 4,207 yards. Irish running jumped 11 percent, from 2,099 yards to '98's 2,338 yards. The yardage total for the Irish passing game dropped 16 percent, from 2,224 to 1,869 yards, although Jackson's QB efficiency rating was better than Powlus's '97 figure: 124.92 for Powlus to 149.5 for Jackson. The Irish went to the air more than 100 fewer times in '98 than in '97, reflecting a carefully controlled passing game philosophy. The turnover ratio remained the same, plus five, but there was a drop in PAT efficiency, from 94 percent to 86 percent, although the Irish FG game was considerably better, hitting 11 of 15 in '98, up nicely from the '97 figure of eight of 15. Oddly enough, the Irish committed 78 penalties in the season, the most since 1980. For the third year in a row, Denson surpassed 1,000 yards rushing, carrying the ball 251 times for 1,176 yards and 15 TDs, becoming Notre Dame's all-time leader in the process. Jackson had a serviceable year at the QB spot, hitting 104 passes in 188 attempts for 1,740 yards, 13 TDs and six INTs. Average yards per catch increased 46 percent, from 11.4 yards per catch to 16.73 ypc. Malcolm Johnson had another consistent year as a pass receiver, snagging 43 aerials, but Bobby Brown went off the chart, from 13 receptions in '97 to 42 in '98, perhaps reflecting Jackson's process of learning his progressions.

Mike Rosenthal earned All-America recognition, and Hunter Smith capped his career as the second-leading punter for the Irish, at 41.2 yards per punt just a shade behind Craig Hentrich's career figure.

1998 record: 9-3 (.750)
Record to date: 762-231-42 (.756)

1999

There are many mysteries involved in sports. Ultimately, it is nearly impossible to understand precisely how an individual or a team wins or loses. In football, there are split seconds in the individual's athletic effort on a given play that are decisive for the success or failure of that effort—footwork, leverage, quickness, strength, explosiveness, determination, conditioning, and technique are just some of the important factors that all come into consideration. It is extremely difficult to isolate one factor out of the mix and identify it as the problem in a failed effort. In a team sport such as football, the interlocking relationships of the members of the team create an infinity of possibilities. Between evenly matched opponents, it is equally difficult to identify that moment when a drive turned to dust, or a game turned to a loss. The same may be said of a

season. In addition to the physical and technical aspects of athletic success, there is also a large component based simply on an athlete's or team's psyche or morale.

The Irish seemed to have turned around the disappointment of '97 to be on the verge of an outstanding season in '98. The media constantly reminded fans and players that this was the third year of the Davie era, a reference to the championships won by Leahy, Parseghian, and Holtz in their third campaigns. Aside from that, the task facing Bob Davie and his staff (with the significant addition of Kevin Rogers as the offensive coordinator, fresh from Syracuse and coaching Donovan McNabb) would be yet another major rebuilding job: they would have to find 13 new starters, seven on offense, six on defense. On offense, the most pressing needs the Irish would have to meet would be bringing up four interior linemen and a replacement for Autry Denson and his 5,327 yards of career offense and experience at tailback. (Within a span of two seasons, ND lost the services of two players, Denson and Powlus, who had produced nearly 13,000 yards of total offense and 99 TDs between them in their careers, something to consider if you are contemplating joining the college football coaching profession). On the line, only the starting center, John Merandi, returned. Elsewhere, Bobby Brown switched to SE from FL, Raki Nelson moved up to take the FL position, TE Jabari Holloway returned, underclassmen would operate at TB as a committee, led by Tony Fisher, although a brilliant freshman, Julius Jones, would emerge by mid-season, Joey Goodspeed would start at FB, and Jackson returned as the QB. Jim Sanson would handle the placekicking chores; freshman punter Joey Hildbold hoped to take over where Hunter Smith left off.

On defense, Greg Mattison made the change from a 3-4 to a 4-3, kept two people in their original positions (LT Anthony Weaver and LCB Clifford Jefferson), moved three, and filled six positions with new starters. One lineman, Brad Williams, all three LBs—Rocky Boiman, Anthony Denman, and Ronnie Nicks—and DBs Clifford Jefferon and Deke Cooper moved up the chart to starting roles.

The opener for the 1999 season had been Michigan, but ND booked Kansas in the Eddie Robinson Classic to give their young line a chance to jell a little before playing the Wolverines in Ann Arbor. Ranked 18th, Notre Dame came out of the blocks fast, scoring 20 unanswered points in the first quarter: Kansas fumbled to ND to end their first drive; Jackson ducked a sack on the third Irish play, then scrambled for a 38-yard TD run. Deveron Harper intercepted a pass on the Jayhawks' first play from scrimmage and rambled 22 yards for the second Irish TD in a 17-second span. In the quarter's final minute, TB Tony Driver darted in from the one for the third score of the quarter. Kansas woke up enough for Zac Wegner to fire two TD passes in the second quarter to make it 20-13 at the half. Notre Dame owned the second half: in the third quarter, another young TB, Tony Fisher, scored a two-yard TD from the wishbone and LB Anthony Denman took a Kansas fumble 31 yards for a TD. In the fourth quarter, Fisher broke loose for a 46-yard TD dash and Jackson's sub, sophomore Arnaz Battle, broke three would-be tackles on his way to a 74-yard TD run. The Irish ended up with 363 yards gained on the ground and did not have to go to the air often. Two areas were sub-par: missed FGs and PATs along with a 33.3-yard punting average.

So, a fairly young and inexperienced ND team invaded the home of the seventh-ranked Michigan Wolverines in a game that set an NCAA record for official attendance (111,523). UM started the affair with two first-quarter FGs by Jeff Del Verne. In the next frame, ND took the lead on a fancy play after the Irish faked to the FB up the middle then ran an option play to the short side of the field. With the ball on the wide hashmark, Davie's charges set up in an I formation, put a wing man in motion left, ran a fake option to the right, then reversed the ball to Getherall, who ran it in for a four-yard TD, completely baffling the UM defense. Sanson's PAT made it 7-6 for ND. The Wolverines were still searching for their first TD and settled for another FG to regain the lead. At the end of the first half, Jackson scrambled for a 12-yard TD run behind a super block by FB Joey Goodspeed, taking a 14-9 halftime lead. The Wolverines came out in the third quarter and finally established that they could run their 221-pound TB, Anthony Thomas. After an 80-yard march, Thomas bulled in for a two-yard TD. The Irish fumbled on their next drive but they held off the Wolverines and blocked the ensuing FG try. Their next drive stalled and UM drove back for another FG and a 19-14 lead. On the next drive, a shaky ND offense showed that it needed more seasoning when a Jackson option pitch went to no one in particular, although a quick-witted back did pick up the loose ball and gain five yards anyway.

Jackson led the Irish to a fourth-quarter lead with another stunning play: at the UM 20, fourth and short, ND came out in a wishbone, then broke the bone with motion left, reversed the motion, Jackson rolled right but then passed left to Holloway who was in splendid

Jarious Jackson.

isolation for a 20-yard TD. Jackson then hit a two-point conversion with a pass to Bobby Brown, who was flagged for too much celebrating. It was an ominous penalty, combining with a late hit penalty a few plays later to give UM a short field to work on, Thomas thundering in on the seventh play from the one for a 26-22 lead. Jackson brought a gallant ND team back, hitting Raki Nelson with a 36-yard pass, then just missing a first down with the ball close to the end zone, six inches short of a first down when time ran out, a heartbreaking loss but one that showed the mettle of the '99 Irish.

That mettle would be severely tested by ND's various errors in a gut-wrenching 28-23 loss to Purdue. Sanson broke a FG drought with a 20-yarder early in the first quarter, then A'Jani Sanders reeled in a pass deflected by Brad Williams, setting up Jackson's 15-yard TD run for a 10-0 lead. Drew Brees, one of the best QBs in the Big Ten in many years, led his team back 74 yards, scoring on a nine-yard QB draw. The Irish blocked a Purdue punt on their next possession, Jackson took advantage with a 28-yard strike to Holloway, then used a QB sneak to score from the one but the PAT hit the upright. Brees cut the Irish lead to 16-14 when he found WR Randall Lane for a 29-yard TD pass. From their 20, the Irish drove to the Purdue 35, but with only 21 seconds left, had an illegal procedure penalty; Jackson fired a pass to Givens for a 16-yard gain. As the final seconds waned, the Irish couldn't get anything done right—no spike, no FG effort—a harbinger of things to come. Notre Dame came right back in the third quarter and moved the ball well to midfield then fired another round into a foot with a fumble. Antwon Jones, however, made a great effort and tipped Travis Dorch's FG try moments later to maintain ND's two-point lead. Brees took over, hitting Chris Daniels with a 40-yard look-in pass, then pitching to Jay Crabtree for a one-yard TD followed by his own keeper for a two-point conversion and a 22-16 lead. Jackson showed he could play as well as Brees on he next drive, hitting Raki Nelson with a 12-yard pass and TE Dan O'Leary with a 23-yarder before finding Bobby Brown with a seven-yard scoring toss and a 23-22 lead at the end of the third quarter. Purdue hit two FGs and intercepted an Irish pass in the fourth quarter, but ND replayed its confusion from the end of the first half to lose the game with the ball once again near the opponent's goal-line. This time, in addition to poor clock management, the coaches may have outthought themselves by calling a fake checkoff with 16 seconds left on third down with the ball at the Purdue one, but some players took the fake call as the only call and fired out on that basis; with the busted play, Jackson was ignominiously sacked to end the game— surely one of the most bitter defeats on record, a game Notre Dame should have won—but for its own play.

Notre Dame, somehow ranked number 24 even with its 1-2 record, could be said to be mere inches away from a very different season. How the team would react to its situation was a major concern, especially with Michigan State on deck. So far, the Irish defense had been carrying the team. The offense did not seem to have found an identity for itself in the absence of Autry Denson; the option game in particular looked ragged.

Having said all that, the Irish played a great game against Michigan State, staying even with the Sparts until the middle of the fourth quarter. State scored first, an eight-yard TD pass to start the second quarter. The teams traded punts for the rest of the quarter until LB Anthony Denman caused a fumble that Jackson turned into a 14-yard TD pass to Bobby Brown for the 7-7 halftime score. Like the first quarter, the third frame was scoreless, although Jackson got the Irish close to a score until an endzone INT ended the threat. ND took the lead in the fourth quarter with a 33-yard Sanson FG, but MSU responded with two FGs of their own, then Sanson knotted the score at 13-13 with a 34-yard FG.

Then lightning struck in the form of an 80-yard TD pass from Bill Burke to Gari Scott, a 33-second drive. The Irish were unable to sustain a drive, punted, and MSU ate up the clock before closing the scoring with another FG for the 23-13 final score, the first time since the early '60s that they had won three in a row over Notre Dame. The Irish stayed in the game for 55 minutes, but the sky fell in the form of 236 yards of MSU offense in the fourth quarter.

Mercifully, ND's players enjoyed an extra week before their next game, versus Oklahoma and its top-ranked offense, averaging 536 yards per game, and QB Josh Heupel, completing 71 percent of his passes. The Sooners may have had the headlines, but the Irish D stonewalled them, at least statistically. Nevertheless, Jackson and his mates would need to mount a great comeback to snatch a 34-30 victory against an honored foe. Jackson opened the scoring with a 10-yard TD scramble, building on a 55-yard sprint Tony Fisher. The Sooners didn't let anyone celebrate too long as Brandon Daniels zoomed 89 yards with the Irish KO for a TD. The second quarter saw the Sooners get a safety on a bobbled punt snap and wrap two TD passes around an Irish TD pass, the latter a 58-yarder from Jackson to Getherall, for a 23-14 Oklahoma halftime lead. In the third quarter, Heupel hit his third different receiver for another TD, a 15-yarder (he completed 22 passes to eight different receivers in the game), creating a 30-14 deficit for the Irish. They proved to be up to the task; Jackson hit receivers with 26- and 23-yard passes, setting up a 15-yard TD strike to Holloway. The Irish intercepted a pass on the second play from scrimmage, then patiently moved 56 yards for a one-yard TD burst by Tony Driver. In the fourth quarter, Jackson hurt Oklahoma with a 23-yard scramble and a 29-yard aerial to Getherall before Driver slammed in from the one again for the winning score.

Notre Dame's D cut Heupel's pass completions down to 55 percent; ironically, it was Jackson who hit 71 percent of his passes—15 of 21 to Heupel's 22 of 40. Irish runners cavorted for 317 yards and Jackson and Arnaz Battle added 282 yards of passing for 566 total yards to Oklahoma's 237, less than half of what they had been running up. It was the best Irish comeback in more than a decade and showed what this team could do when it set its mind to it.

Jarious Jackson was beginning to inscribe his name in the Notre Dame record book: the only Irish QB ever to pass for 240 yards and rush for 100 yards in the same game and the first Irish signal caller ever to pass for

240 yards or more in four consecutive games, although he'd be without Raki Nelson, out for a month with an MCL injury. Arizona State was aware of the threat Jackson posed and played a strong first half to contain him. The teams traded punts to start the game, but LB Ronnie Nicks whacked J.R. Redmond to cause a fumble recovered by Deke Cooper. ASU was well-prepared for the ND ground game, and Jackson's passing wasn't cranked up yet; ND's 33-yard FG try was wide right. Deveron Harper stopped the next Sun Devil possession with an INT, but once again the Irish could not convert the opportunity to points. ASU plugged away with a patient drive, but they missed their first FG try, early in the second quarter. Jackson was beginning to pull his game together and started hitting his receivers in big chunks: 15 yards to Joey Goodspeed, 23 yards to Bobby Brown on a fade pattern, then 42 yards to Brown, who broke a tackle and scored. ASU's next drive went glimmering when A'Jani Sanders gathered in an INT and returned it 28 yards for a TD and a 14-0 lead. Bad luck struck ASU again when TE Todd Heap caught a Kealy pass but LE Grant Irons popped him hard and Deke Cooper recovered in the ND end zone. The Irish offense was hitting on all cylinders by now: an option play for 25 yards, Jackson 44 yards on a roll out, a six-yard TD pass to Dan O'Leary. Unbelievably, Deke Cooper crushed ASU hopes even further with yet another INT and a 33-yard runback. Jackson hit Getherall with a 25-yard TD pass on the next play, but ND missed the PAT. In the third quarter, ASU tried to work a fourth-down run to Redmond, but ND held; two plays later, Jackson churned 48 yards for another TD and a 34-0 lead. Later in the quarter, Jackson fired a 34-yard pass to Tony Fisher, then Julius Jones jetted 13 yards for his first Irish TD. ASU finally got on the scoreboard when Gerald Green dove over the pile for a one-yard TD. The final Irish score came on the twelfth play of a 74-yard march when Jackson found Jay Johnson open on the right side and fired to him, but Johnson was hit hard just as he caught the ball, knocking off his helmet, but he scored anyway on the 31-yard play, surely the last Irish player ever to score while not wearing a helmet. ASU added a FG and a TD for the 48-17 final score. Jackson's four TDs were the seventh time that feat had been achieved in ND history. Irish walk-on TB Tim O'Neill, at 5' 5" and 163 pounds, had his moment in the sun with two carries for five yards.

A sign that a certain shift in college football power had been taking place was found in the fact that neither ND nor USC was ranked in the Top 25 when they met a week later at Notre Dame. The Trojans had won four in a row against the Irish and they took a commanding 21-0 lead before an Irish FG with a minute left in the second quarter. The Trojans scored with a 23-yard pass to Windrell Hayes, a one-yard run by Chad Morton, and a 12-yard pass to R. Jay Soward. USC tacked on a 29-yard FG in the third quarter. Halfway through that quarter, the Irish began to chip away at the deficit. Jackson found TE Dan O'Leary for a seven-yard TD strike following set up passes of 19 and 16 yards to WRs, the first ND TD against the Trojans in 10 quarters. Early in the fourth quarter, the Irish D forced a Trojan fumble and Tony Driver slanted right eight plays later for a two-yard TD run, making it 24-16. USC ran four plays but managed only an 11-yard punt. ND earned a 33-yard FG with 8:07 left, down now 24-19. The Trojans had another inconclusive drive, punted again, and Jackson did his thing again—a 28-yard pass to Fisher, a 10-yard aerial to Holloway, then a scramble toward the end zone, 17 yards before being hit and fumbling, but an alert Holloway was right there and recovered the loose ball for a TD and ND's only lead of the game at 25-24 after a two-point try failed. The teams next swapped fumbles, but USC had time for a score on their last drive before ND's Irons tipped a fourth-down pass attempt, ending the threat. It was the biggest deficit the Irish had to overcome in some 20 years.

A'Jani Sanders.

Earlier in the season, the second-string Irish QB had been dismissed from the team. Before the Navy game, a junior TB and a senior DB were suspended for unspecified dorm infractions. Fortunately, other personnel were able to step up, but Irish fans knew that the NCAA ruling on a university-reported case of infractions was looming and these latest issues perhaps boded ill for both team morale and the good reputation of Notre Dame.

Morale did not seem to be too low as ND prepared for Navy, but some players showed poor judgment just before the game by making some smart remarks overheard by some Middies, who came out really fired up. The Irish took the early lead with a 31-yard TD pass from Jackson to Bobby Brown, and padded that after Terrance Howard scored on a one-yard run following Jones's 28-yard run. But Navy tallied twice in the second quarter, earning their scores with the QB's 11-yard option run and with a blocked punt recovered for a TD. The third quarter had four possessions in a row that ended these ways: Navy's first possession ended when ND recovered a fumble; then Navy's Bas Williams intercepted an Irish pass; then Deke Cooper made a crushing tackle, causing a fumble recovered by a LB; finally, Navy's Davede Alexander snagged a Jackson pass and returned it 21 yards for a TD and a 21-14 Navy lead. Jackson quickly put the Irish back in the game with a 57-yard TD run coming off an option keeper. The Middies blocked an Irish FG try, and Alexander attempted to advance the ball before being run out of bounds. Navy went ahead 24-21 with a 33-yard FG with 5:56 left in the game. Notre Dame used more than five minutes to drive 59 yards in 16 plays, capped by Jackson's game-winning 16-yard TD pass to Jay Johnson. The defense kept Navy bottled up for the remaining 36 seconds to ice the win. Jackson accounted for 200 yards passing and 74 yards running of the 524 total yards for ND. Julius Jones nearly set a Notre Dame record with 146 yards rushing, just two yards short of the record set by Jerome Heavens in 1975. It was a gutsy performance for ND, but their composure wasn't completely steady, as evidenced by 13 penalties for 130 yards.

The Irish would need all the composure they could muster in their next game, against defending national champ Tennessee on their home turf. The coaches decided to throw everything possible at the Volunteers. It would seem that this was a good decision because the Vols had the greatest team speed the Irish had seen since the '96 Ohio State squad and they went out to a 10-0 lead with a first quarter FG and a 21-yard TD pass from Tee Martin to Donte Stallworth. The smorgasbord approach worked well enough for ND on the ensuing drive, a 12-play, 81-yard affair. At one point, the Irish lined up in a gun, showed an option run to the left, then faked a shovel pass, finally turning it into an option keeper for Jackson—all that for a two-yard gain. Notre Dame kept the drive alive with a fake FG play, Getherall running left for a five-yard gain to set up a four-yard slant run for a TD by David Givens. The starting LT, sophomore Jordan Black, injured a knee on this drive and was lost for the remainder of the season.

The Vols were all but stopped on their next drive but an Irish offsides penalty kept the drive alive so that Martin could roll out and fire a two-yard TD pass to Eric Parker for a 17-7 halftime lead. They stretched the lead to 24-7 in the third quarter when two Irish DBs bumped each other out of a long pass play, a 43-yard TD pass from Martin to Leonard Scott. At the end of the quarter, Travis Henry turned on the jets for a 40-yard TD run that went through two missed tackles. The Irish answered quickly: a 36-yard KOR by Jones, an 11-yard pass to the FL, then his reverse on the seventh play for an 11-yard TD run. Sanson executed a perfect on-side kick, but the Irish ran out of gas on a fourth-down play eight plays later. Tee Martin completed the scoring at 38-14 with a 14-yard TD run with two minutes left. All the pundits agreed that the Vols simply had better players (although coach Phillip Fulmer's .857 winning percentage for the decade indicates that he's no slouch). Indeed, Tee Martin had been recruited by the Irish. If Tennessee simply had the better players, the next question is whether there are enough student-athletes of that caliber who have the academic credentials to be recruited by places like ND, Michigan, Stanford, Virginia, and so forth, with enough of them attracted to the Dome.

The Irish would need seven wins to be eligible for a Bowl. They had played fairly well in some games, but the loss to Tennessee may have taken some starch out of them. Pitt was next, having lost the last eight contests by an average of more than four TDs each try. Perhaps the Irish took the Panthers lightly, but whatever the case, they played a terrible game overall, beaten by Pitt 37-27. John Turman, subbing at QB for Pitt, found Antonio Bryant with a nine-yard TD pass to open the scoring. Jim Sanson answered with a 36-yard FG. In the second quarter, Nick Lotz tacked on a 24-yard FG, but ND tied it up with a five-yard TD pass from Jackson to Getherall. The Irish intercepted Turman's next pass, but Sanson's 45-yard FG try was blocked, one of several chances that the Irish bungled this terrible day. In the third quarter, Pitt showed it could be opportunistic, if ND didn't want to be: they recovered a fumble, then jumped on the Irish DBs for a 44-yard pass completion, then used an unbalanced line for two Kevan Barlow runs, the second a three-yard TD. The Irish tied it up at 17-17 after Pitt botched a punt return, with a pass from Givens to the Bobby Brown, a 21-yard scoring affair. Pitt was just starting to roll, however, and came right back with a 33-yard FG, ripped the ball from an Irish TB three plays later, then used that for a 28-yard TD pass on the third play after that. The final Irish score came on a 27-yard TD pass by Jackson to the multi-talented Givens, but Pitt added another FG and a TD run while the Irish managed another fumble and a missed FG. Irish running backs managed only 72 yards on the ground all day, while an amazing performance by Bobby Brown with 12 receptions for 208 yards (the best day in three decades for an Irish receiver) could not offset other mangled opportunities.

The optimism generated by the comeback wins earlier in the season was turning to ashes for the 5-5 Irish. To make matters as bad as they could be, ND lost any hope for postseason play with a 31-29 home field loss to Boston College. This time, they squandered a 14-0 lead gained by TD runs from Fisher and Jones, five yards and 11 yards respectively. A deflected pass turned into an INT and BC moved for the score eight plays later, a 27-yard pass from Tim Hasselbeck to Bryan Arndt. In the second quarter, BC got another TD pass from Hasselbeck and a FG before Sanson tied it up 17-17 at the half with a 44-yard FG. In the third quarter, only BC scored, ending a 93-yard march with a QB sneak of one yard. Hasselbeck kept up the pressure with a 34-yard TD pass in the fourth quarter, giving BC a 31-17 lead. This score followed a drop of a seemingly sure INT by an Irish DB. Jackson led a furious passing attack, capped by a nine-yard TD lob to Fisher—but BC tipped the PAT try for a 31-23 lead, the sixth missed PAT of the season. Notre Dame's defense turned it up a notch on the next possession, forcing a BC punt that Jones hauled back for a 67-yard TD. With 3:27 left, the defense did its job again, and ND got the ball back with 2:18 left, plenty of time to move in for a FG. On the second play, however, Jackson looked too long at his intended receiver, and Pedro Cirino ended Irish hopes with an INT. For the second game in a row, ND did not gain 100 yards on the ground, but allowed BC 442 yards of total offense.

In a span of little more than two weeks, the Irish had gone from hoping to garner a bowl bid—perhaps any bowl bid—to hoping to save a .500 season. Stanford would see that the latter hope did not come true, pushing ND over the edge into the worst season, in terms of losses, since 1963. Ty Willingham's Stanford team wasted no time in getting on the scoreboard, scoring on a 62-yard pass from Todd Husak to Troy Walters with their second play from scrimmage. On ND's second play from scrimmage, Tim Smith caused a fumble and Aaron Focht returned it 37 yards for their second TD within 88 seconds. They waited until the end of the first quarter to register a 31-yard FG for a 17-0 lead. Davie inserted Battle at QB on the next possession, who led the first scoring drive, sparked by his 31-yard pass to Jay Johnson on a curl route. Notre Dame got its first TD of the game from the wishbone, Fisher slanting left for the one-yard TD. Not to be outdone, Jackson fired a 42-yard scoring pass to Fisher on the next drive. Stanford kept throwing passes with relative impunity, leading to another FG and a 20-14 lead. The Irish briefly took the lead with Fisher's third TD, a nine-yard run, but Stanford had enough time for yet another FG and the 23-21 halftime lead. To start the second half, ND unleashed Jones for a 24-yard TD on a sprint draw. The defense stopped the Cardinal, and ND drove well enough to try a 42-yard FG, but Tim Smith blocked the kick. Four plays later, Husak launched a 38-yard TD pass to Walters again. In the fourth quarter, Joe Borchard ran a bootleg play for a two-yard TD and a 37-29 lead. But ND recovered a fumble on the Stanford 32 and Jackson hit Holloway with a five-yard TD pass, then Getherall ran a reverse for the two-point conversion to tie it at 37-37. But they left Stanford 1:32 and it proved to be too much time—on the game's last play, Mike Biselli executed a 22-yard FG kick for the win.

Davie thus joined Joe Kuharich as the only ND coaches with four-game losing streaks in two different seasons. Also, this was the first ND team to give up 30 points or more in four straight games (for comparative purposes, Parseghian's 1966 team gave up 38 points for the entire season, his 1973 team only 66 points).

The young Irish offensive line proved to be a factor in the more than 30 sacks the team suffered, compared to only 11 for the opponents (which is a comment on the ND defense as well). Total offense was up in '99 over '98—up to 5,036 yards from 4,207 yards. The opposition also went up, from 3,819 yards to 4,605 yards. With no Autry Denson, the rushing yardage slipped somewhat, from 2,338 yards to 2,178 yards, although Julius Jones showed good signs of being able to fill the void in future seasons. The Irish gave up 1,706 yards on the ground, up from 1,560 yards in '98. Jarious Jackson had a season for the ages as an Irish QB: 184 completions in 315 attempts for 17 TDs, 14 INTs, and 2,753 yards, the bulk of Notre Dame's 2,858 passing yards, a 35 percent increase over the '98 total. The opposition also racked up good yardage through the air, 2,899 for 21 TDs, a measure of the difficulty the defensive backfield had growing into its job, as well as the absence of a dominating pass rush. The Irish slipped in the turnover ratio, from a plus-five in '98 to a minus-six in '99. FG kicking also slipped, from 11 of 15 to eight of 18, and four PATs went south as well. Somewhere out there must be a kicker who could turn this around.

So, a young team made some mistakes, played tough most of the way, but couldn't buy a win at the end of the season when they most needed one.

Unfortunately, the University of Notre Dame and its football team learned shortly after the completion of the season that sanctions levied against ND by the NCAA included a five-year probationary period and loss of two scholarships. The NCAA Committee on Infractions, following a 21-month investigation begun by the University's report of rules violations to the NCAA Enforcement Staff, found Notre Dame guilty of a major infraction involving players and a former member of the Quarterback Club, among other things. Notre Dame's President, Edward A. Malloy, told the press that "It makes you wonder about our role as educators. . . . I feel disappointed with our perceived failures."

The University immediately took comprehensive corrective action. Nevertheless, the pristine reputation established through more than a century of intercollegiate football and more than 1,000 games, and sustained by nearly 3,000 players and coaches for their playing and professional careers, lay besmirched in the public eye. Irish fans everywhere sincerely believe the school and its football program would resolve the problems identified and work diligently to re-establish its honored reputation.

1999 record: 5-7 (.416)
Record to date: 767-238-42 (.752)

2000-2009

2000

The 1999 season had been traumatic for all concerned with Notre Dame football. There had been flashes of brilliance for sure, but when things had to happen, the Irish just couldn't get it done. They were streaky in '99: three losses, then four wins, and then four more losses after a first-game win. They could score points, but they gave up almost as much as they scored (scoring 348, giving up 331). Jarious Jackson had a season that no other Irish QB could claim, but to have his enormous production result in a mere five wins simply bolstered the old cliché about statistics and winning. You can win the statistics, or you can win. A superstar year won't guarantee a successful season (see Hornung's magnificent '56 campaign for evidence of this, as the Irish garnered only two wins in spite of the incredible performance of their Heisman winner).

Davie would have to fill some significant holes: QB for starters, along with his center, SE, and FB on the offensive side, but also the entire defensive secondary, to go with a three of his linemen and an ILB. He had been grooming the promising Arnaz Battle for QB to replace the dangerous Jackson. Not as big as Jackson, Battle was blessed with more speed and perhaps elusiveness. The best-laid plans can turn to dust, however, which is precisely what happened with Battle when he broke his left wrist during the Nebraska game. The Irish would have to make do after that with an untested QB, Matt LoVecchio, and the coaches would earn every penny of their salaries prepping him for the rigorous campaign.

Javin Hunter would have some pretty big shoes to fill in Bobby Brown's SE spot, the leading Irish receiver in '99. Tom Lopienski would work in the departed and reliable Joey Goodspeed's FB spot, while the TBs would work on a committee basis, with Jones and Fisher garnering most of the duty. Jeff Faine, an utterly dogged blocker, would move in to the C spot and begin a string of starts at that position that would take him through three seasons. The secondary would have all new faces as starters, but there was some experience

in the background. Shane Walton would move into the secondary and, like Faine, stay there for the next few seasons, bringing superb speed and aggressiveness to the CB spot. Tony Driver at FS contributed good size, speed, and knowledge of the game. Ron Israel at SS and Brock Williams at the other CB rounded out the secondary. Tyreo Harrison moved up to a starter's role at ILB, as did a very quick Ryan Roberts at RE, a persistent Lance Legree at RT, while B.J. Scott took over for the injured Grant Irons at LE. Rocky Boiman and Anthony Denman, returning starters in LB spots, gave the 2000 unit a decidedly rugged look and attitude.

Notre Dame's 2000 edition came out of the gates fast, whipping Texas A&M 24-10 at the Dome on a brutally hot day. After a scoreless first quarter, A&M broke the deadlock with an eight-yard TD run by TB Rich Whitaker, capping a 46-yard drive on the eighth play. The Irish were unable to respond until the half was almost over, but Battle used his FB, Tom Lopienski, well from the A&M 28 with a 16-yard pass to set up his nine-yard TD pass to Joey Getherall. With the score, Notre Dame showed that they could sustain a 70-yard drive and do it in 10 efficient plays, in spite of the sweltering temperature. A&M regained the lead in the third quarter, eating up half of the quarter with a patient 15-play drive

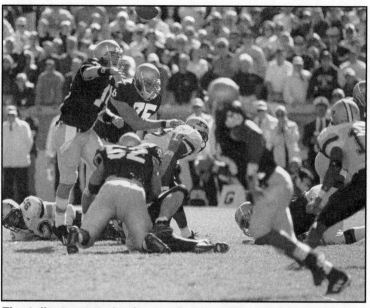

The tallest quarterback ever for the Irish, Gary Godsey saves the day against Purdue after Arnaz Battle is lost for the 2000 season (Photo provided by The Observer).

Nick Setta kicked the winning field goal as the clock ran out in the 23-21 thriller over Purdue in 2000 (Photo provided by **The Observer**).

that reached the Irish five, but then ND refused to budge and the Aggies could manage only a 23-yard FG. Taking a cue from their goal-line success, the Irish D pasted the Aggies on their next three possessions, allowing only nine yards on nine snaps. With this determined defensive mind set, it was all Notre Dame after that Aggie threat was blunted: Battle fired a 46-yard TD pass to Javin Hunter to finish a two-play drive, then he found Givens wide open for a 21-yard gain that set up Julius Jones's 17-yard TD run early in the fourth quarter. Nick Setta wrapped up the scoring with a 32-yard FG midway through the final frame. A&M's ground game was stymied, gaining only 90 yards on 37 rushes, to ND's 194 yards on 49 carries. Battle hit on 10 of 16 passes for two TDs and 133 yards. Tony Driver made his presence known with the season's first INT, followed by a 19-yard runback.

Nebraska had never won a game played at ND, but this time they had the number-one team in the country, along with the usual Brobdingnagian suspects in the line, and the proverbial bevy of good backs to go with a Heisman candidate in their scrappy QB, Eric Crouch. Furthermore, Husker fans must have used all of their guile and a good chunk of the state treasury to buy enough tickets from erstwhile ND

fans…enough to make large portions of the Notre Dame stadium take on a decidedly red color. Against all that corn-fed beef and firepower, and tens of thousands of Husker fans, the Irish nevertheless played Nebraska to an OT game, losing a thriller 27-24, while also losing the rising star of QB Arnaz Battle to a broken wrist. It certainly helped the cause that the ND student body literally rose to the occasion and out-yelled the more numerous, red-clad Husker fans—no mean feat in itself. Nebraska scored first after the teams had poked and prodded each other indecisively for most of the first quarter, with Crouch doing the honors on a splendid 62-yard TD run. Notre Dame didn't back down, however, and fought back to a 7-7 tie on their next possession, an 82-yard drive executed in 11 plays, the largest chunk going to Battle when he escaped the Husker defenders for a 14-yard gain before Tony Fisher banged it in from the two. Nebraska returned the favor on their next drive, although they first had to recover Crouch's fumble at the ND 15, before Crouch rehabilitated his reputation with a one-yard TD plunge, taking the lead into the halftime. The Huskers added to that lead in the third quarter, recovering yet another of their own fumbles before TB Dan Alexander broke loose for a 28-yard TD run. Seconds later, however, Julius Jones simply dusted the Huskers with a brilliant 100-yard KOR for a TD, putting himself in the Irish record books with players from the Rockne years who had also turned the trick, ahead even of the brilliant recent stars, Allen Rossum, Tim Brown, and Raghib Ismail. After that shock, the teams wrestled around some more before Getherall fielded a Husker punt on his 17 and turned on the jets for an 83-yard TD return. The excitement must have been too much again and the teams settled into another desultory deadlock for nearly the entire fourth quarter. The OT period saw the Irish with the ball first, not an advantage in such a situation, and they could only tally a 29-yard field goal by Nick Setta, kicked on the eighth play of their possession, shortly after Battle (with a broken wrist already) took a minus-seven yard sack. With that, Nebraska knew what they had to do and they did it…Crouch scored on a seven-yard option run after hitting Tracey Wistrom with a nine-yard pass on a third-and-nine play. It wasn't a crushing defeat for the Irish; they had played their hearts out and those in the stadium would never forget the game, it was that intensively played, with its staccato bursts of scoring interspersed with long periods of just plain, old-fashioned, tough football. The two offenses racked up a total of 601 yards of yardage against two rugged defensive units, 377 for Nebraska and 224 for ND, but when special teams yardage is put in the equation, the Huskers had a total all-purpose figure of 443 yards to ND's 544…987 yards racked up in one of the toughest ways that a football can be advanced against determined young men. What a game….

And what a disappointment to have lost Battle for the rest of the season, an injury that would remove him from the QB spot for his remaining years at ND.

Furthermore, DE Grant Irons was also lost for the season with a dislocated shoulder injured on one of his patented full-out pass rushes. Davie and his staff had one week to get a QB ready for Purdue…and they came up with a bit of a surprise, a very tall surprise, in fact, the tallest QB in ND annals—Gary Godsey, at 6'7", half a head taller than anyone else in this position since 1887. Godsey would save the day against the Boilermakers, and then eventually return to the anonymous trenches as a TE, thank you. (Kevin Rogers, ND's offensive coordinator and quarterbacks coach, had come to ND fresh from working with Syracuse's brilliant Donovan McNabb, not to mention how he contributed to Jackson's great '99 campaign. Looking at a 6'7" former QB-turned-TE-turned-QB must have been quite an experience for a coach who liked mobility in his QB).

Purdue was in a season that would take them to the Rose Bowl, so without ND's expected QB, this looked

Brock Williams gets ready to put a hit on the Air Force QB in ND's overtime win over the Falcons in 2000 (Photo provided by The Observer).

dire. Godsey enjoyed his day in the sun, however, and made it a memorable one with a nine-yard TD rumble after Glenn Earl had blocked a Boilermaker punt, putting the ball on the Boilermaker four. The teams jousted a bit until late in that first quarter when another DB, Shane Walton, snagged a Drew Brees throw and lit out for the territories, his TD jaunt ending 60 yards later. But this rivalry had been marked over the years by incredible comebacks, intense spirit, and individual heroics, and Purdue QB Brees was a throwback. He played pitch and catch with talented WR Vinny Sutherland, first a 54-yarder to set up Montrell Lowe's six-yard TD run—answered by a 47-yard Setta FG—and then a 19-yard TD pass to Sutherland. In the third quarter, Setta hit another FG, this one from 32 yards out. The teams then went into scoring hibernation until late in the fourth quarter when Purdue grabbed an INT from Godsey and the pesky and elusive Sutherland got back into the act with a 22-yard TD pass from Brees to cap the 77-yard drive, giving Purdue a 21-20 lead with 3:39 left in the game. And that's precisely the time needed for ND to receive the KO and move 59 yards in 13 careful, meticulous plays to get Setta close enough for a FG try—which he hit from 38 yards out as time expired, earning a fine 23-21 win for the beleaguered Irish. The call had gone out—and Gary Godsey answered, hitting 14 of 25 passes for 158 yards to go with seven carries and the TD. He directed a scaled-back version of the kind of offense that Battle would have commanded, but he did it well enough and with enough defensive help that Davie never had to ask him to do more than he could. Purdue won almost all of the statistical categories; the crushing blow was Walton's INT and TD return.

Luck for the Irish ran out in E. Lansing yet again when MSU pulled off a last-minute, fourth-down 68-yard TD pass for a 27-21 win. Jones got the Irish going late in the first quarter with a 56-yard scamper to the State one; after fiddling around a little, Godsey found FB Jason Murray outside the RE for a six-yard TD pass. For MSU, mammoth TB T.J. Duckett midway through the second quarter blasted in from the six to tie the game. The Spartans took the lead at the end of the half when David Schaefer banged in a 50-yard FG, following an INT. Things looked really grim for ND in the third quarter as Schaefer hit another FG and then freshman QB Jeff Smoker insisted on passes, first a 20-yarder to Chris Baker, then a 10-yard scoring strike to Travis Wilson. Notre Dame fought back in the fourth quarter as Matt LoVecchio replaced Godsey,

An acrobatic Joey Getherall gathers himself to make a long gain in 2000 home action (Photo provided by The Observer).

finding Javin Hunter wide open in the right flat for a 43-yard advance. Jones wrapped up that drive with a neat two-yard TD burst. Halfway through the final quarter, Anthony Weaver hauled in a Smoker pass on the MSU six, powering four yards before being stopped. Jones took the scoring honors again with a two-yard TD run on the next play. Neither team could move the ball on their next possessions, and ND seemed to have held MSU to a fourth-and-10 with less than two minutes in the game, when they decided to run a corner blitz on the freshman QB. It backfired as Smoker eluded the blitz and spotted a streaking Herb Haygood on a deep slant pattern, firing a strike that Haygood would take to the house for a 68-yard (crushing) score and their fourth consecutive victory over ND. No one would ever know what might have been had Battle been available, but without him, ND managed only eight first downs and 212 total yards, with a mere 63 yards coming on five completions—and 43 of those yards came on LoVecchio's only completion. ND managed only one third-down conversion in 11 attempts, a surefire way to guarantee a series of busted drives while surrendering time of possession to the opponent. Perhaps the coaches played it too conservatively.

Standing at .500 on the season, and not looking very settled in the QB situation, anyone could feel that the next game could be a turning point in the season. Following a bye week, Davie and his staff decided to go with LoVecchio against Stanford, after having worked with him for nearly a month following Battle's loss. The wide-eyed freshman handled the pressure just fine, thank you, firing two TD passes and completing 10 passes in 18 throws, to join three other Irish freshmen since 1950 to win their first start. The first Irish drive revealed that this

game was not going to be a conservative offensive effort: LoVecchio threw to his TE for a nice gain, operated the option to perfection, and helped block on a 23-yard gain by Javin Hunter on a reverse before espying David Givens open in a crease in the Stanford defense, hitting him with a 17-yard TD pass for the game's first score. Givens, the lanky FL for ND, put on quite a show late in the first half when he sped past the middle of Stanford's punting formation to block a punt, then caught his second TD pass of the day on an eight-yard toss from LoVecchio to cap his feat. Setta's PAT was blocked, so ND took an unexpected 13-0 lead to the locker room. Early in the third quarter, ND was victimized on yet another blitz when Brian Allen flared out of the backfield to snag a Chris Lewis pass and trundle 71 yards before the D forced him out of bounds. On the next play, Lewis fired a 13-yard TD pass to DeRonnie Pitts. Later in the third quarter, Tyreo Harrison blocked a Lewis pass attempt, leaving it to Brock Williams to record the INT at Stanford's 34. This time, LoVecchio favored Jones—a shovel pass for a 24-yard gain, followed shortly by Jones's seven-yard TD run. Stanford scored once more, late in the fourth quarter, and ND survived an onside kick try before LoVecchio could kneel with the ball to preserve a well-deserved win. Stanford was able to move the ball well between the red zones, but ND stiffened at the right times to deny them. In sum, Davie had his new QB open it up at just the right times, ND didn't give away any fumbles or INTs, and they were charged with only three harmless penalties. Meanwhile, Stanford went about accumulating quite a bit of real estate—384 total yards—that didn't produce enough points to win the game.

Well, if you have to play Navy, you might as well do it in a nice venue. A rejuvenated ND went to Orlando's Florida Citrus Bowl where they displayed near-total dominance and FS Tony Driver played an aggressive, alert game that garnered for himself two TDs on recovered Navy fumbles. Tyreo Harrison caused the first fumble, scooped up by Driver as he zipped 24 yards to pay dirt. LoVecchio kept up his good work on the next Irish drive, hitting Jabari Holloway with a 20-yard pass to set up a one-yard TD blast by Jones. Roughly a minute after that score, Driver plucked another Middie miscue and raced 22 largely unhindered yards for his second TD of the quarter and a 21-0 lead. Setta tacked on a 23-yard FG late in the half. Early in the third quarter, Dan O'Leary, a hulking TE, was the recipient of a LoVecchio TD strike of 11 yards, ending an 84-

yard Irish drive. In the fourth quarter, with ND leading 31-0, Tony Fisher tacked on another Irish score with a 32-yard pass from LoVecchio. Navy wrapped two TDs around yet another Irish score, a 46-yard TD pass from Godsey to Jay Johnson, a score that might not have been had not Tony Driver been there yet again to recover a Julius Jones fumble on a KOR. For the first time in quite a while, ND finished with good balance in its offensive production—218 yards on the ground and 229 via passing. Jones scampered around for 105 yards and LoVecchio pitched 13 completions in 20 tries. Even with that, it was Tony Driver's game.

Notre Dame stayed on the road for the next game, their first trip to West Virginia. The Mountaineers scored first, a 24-yard TD streak on a reverse by Antonio Brown. ND's two Tonys conspired to lead the first Irish scoring drive with five minutes left in the first quarter: a 33-yard KOR by Tony Driver before Tony Fisher took over on an 18-yard sideline dash, followed moments later by his one-yard TD caper. The Mountaineers showcased the talented Avon Cobourne on the next drive, finding him open for a 36-yard gain with a pass from the shotgun, followed shortly by his nine-yard TD sprint. In the second quarter, WV lost control of the game by allowing three unanswered Irish TDs: first, speedy Terrance Howard jetted up the middle for an 80-yard TD bolt, the longest run from scrimmage at WV's stadium; then Givens shook loose for a five-yard TD run; finally Fisher broke out of the pack with a 36-yard TD pass from LoVecchio. Fisher repeated in the third quarter with a seven-yard TD strike from LoVecchio, but Givens helped out big time with a 52-yard pass thrown to Getherall to set up Fisher's score. Properly warmed up with the long pass play from Givens, Getherall wrapped up ND's scoring with a 73-yard punt return for a TD. The Mountaineers tacked on two consolation TDs after that for the 42-28 final score. The two long-distance plays by Howard and Getherall proved to be the difference in a game that was in other respects quite close.

As their momentum was picking up, ND knew that Air Force would be more than a bump in the road. They didn't know, however, that the Falcons would come to the Dome and play well enough to take ND into an OT game, the first the Irish would ever win in their storied history. After a scoreless first quarter, ND tallied

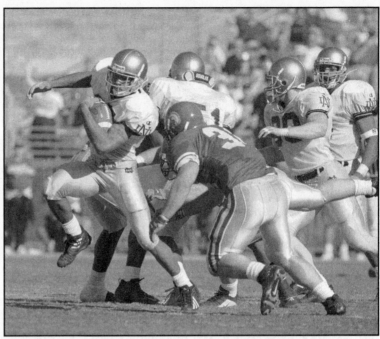

Tony Driver sidesteps a Trojan defender in 2000 Irish win over USC (Photo by Peter Richardson/The Observer).

first when LoVecchio fired a 10-yard TD pass to Javin Hunter, LoVecchio having helped his own cause with a 23-yard escape act to avoid a sack close to the Irish end zone. The Falcons zipped right along after that, scoring on a 23-yard pass and kicking a 27-yard FG. The Irish must have remembered how good it felt to score 21 in a quarter against another service academy, Navy, so they duplicated that feat against AFA: Jones rambled to midfield with a KOR, then Getherall scooted 28 yards to the promised land with a LoVecchio pass; Glenn Earl recovered a Falcon fumble on the ND 25, starting a drive that Givens would finish off with a 37-yard run; then Getherall again with a 68-yard cross-country pass from LoVecchio. Monkey see, monkey do—the Falcons promptly scored three times in the fourth quarter, with no response from the Irish: on a 30-yard pass, then a fumble recovery plus two-point conversion, then a 34-yard FG to tie the game at 28-28. They tried for a fourth score, but Glenn Earl made a stunning special teams play to block the kick, sending the game into overtime. The Falcons won the toss and took the ball, but the Irish D refused to budge and AFA kicked the FG they had missed moments earlier. On ND's possession, they maneuvered for four plays, including a screen pass to Jones, before turning loose Getherall on a nine-yard reverse for the winning TD and the 34-31 final score. The game stats finally lined up with the final score: both teams racked up good yardage and averaged more than five yards per play, both lost a fumble, neither had an INT, possession time was within a minute of being equal, and both teams converted fourth down plays twice.

The Irish next faced BC and wore them down to the nub with a stultifying ground game, 380 total yards rushing, led by Fisher's great effort for 196 yards on 26 carries, with Howard and LoVecchio tacking on 84 and 73 respectively. Jones scored early on a one-yard blast, but left the game with a bruised thigh. BC kicked a FG, but Fisher put the Irish ahead for good in the second quarter when he sped unimpeded for a 37-yard TD. Fisher struck again, in the third quarter, with a one-yard dive for a TD, following a great LoVecchio pass play of 17 yards to Jabari Holloway. BC managed to come back for a TD on a four-yard pass but Setta helped offset that with a surprise five-yard TD run off a fake FG. BC garnered a late TD in the fourth quarter to make the final score 28-16, and with that ND was sitting pretty with a 7-2 season record, ranked 11th in the polls, and with considerable momentum building.

Rutgers did nothing to slow down ND's momentum, falling to the Irish 45-17, as Fisher cavorted for another 135 yards to lead a solid ground game that reached 295 yards to go with LoVecchio's solid passing. Rutgers scored first on a FG, but ND struck back with a 43-yard TD pass from LoVecchio to Getherall, and then Setta got into the act, perhaps spurred by his TD against BC, by throwing a 25-yard TD pass to FB Tom Lopienski. (You can bet the house that no one in the country had ND scouted well enough to plan on a play where the Irish kicker would throw to the FB...heck, the QB almost never throws to the FB in this system.) Rutgers pushed in a one-yard TD early in the second quarter, but ND answered with 10 points, on a for-real 33-yard FG by Setta, *sans* the fake stuff, and then a one-yard TD by Terrance Howard. Rutgers wrapped up their scoring with a nifty 65-yard run by Dennis Thomas in the third quarter, but then the Irish deluge hit the Scarlet Knights—Givens blocked a Rutgers punt, followed shortly by a 25-yard TD pass from LoVecchio to Hunter; Rutgers put the ball on the carpet on their own 18, ND recovered, and Howard blasted in from the two four plays later; and Tony Fisher capped an 80-yard drive with another two-yard TD to make it 45-17.

The Irish hoped to cap the regular season with a solid game against USC; the Trojans were playing to avoid their first losing season in a decade. ND got their wish with a 38-21 win over Troy. Terrance Howard started the fireworks with a one-yard scamper near the end of the first quarter, the Irish taking advantage of a 14-yard Trojan punt and good field position. Trojan QB Carson Palmer leveled the score at 7-7 with a three-yard run to end the next possession. ND began to take control of the game in the second quarter as LoVecchio took off for a 13-yard TD run, capitalizing on Chad DeBolt's great hustle in blocking a Trojan punt and recovering it himself. Less than five minutes later, Driver nabbed a Palmer pass and hightailed 43 yards with the INT, giving the offense a short field to work with. Six plays later, Fisher hauled in the mail from the one-yard line to make it 21-7. Palmer showed his mettle, however, barely a minute later when he zipped a 59-yard TD pass to Kareem Kelly for the 21-14 halftime tally. In the third quarter, though, Glenn Earl saw his chance to pick off a Trojan throw, did so on the ND 48, and LoVecchio went for the jugular with a 48-yard bomb to Hunter. Shortly thereafter, the Irish QB made it into the end zone from the one for a TD. Early in the fourth quarter, Palmer struck again, with a 10-yard TD pass, but a Setta FG of 39 yards and a clock-killing 80-yard drive that Jones ended with a two-yard TD run more than made up for Palmer's work. For the game, the Irish rushed for 246 yards while holding the Trojans to a mere 76 yards. Palmer passed for 251 yards and two TDs but also gave up two INTs. Trojan turnovers in '00 amounted to 36 for the season, whereas ND had only eight giveaways, tying an NCAA season record. LoVecchio had only one INT in 125 passes for the season, setting a new record for ND in lowest INT percentage at .0080.

Ranked 10th, ND met fifth-ranked Oregon State in the Fiesta Bowl, a team

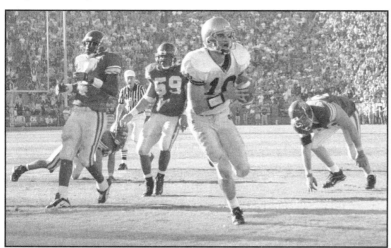

Freshman QB Matt Lovecchio scores on a 13-yard burst in 2000 Irish win over USC (Photo by Peter Richardson/The Observer).

on the rebound under Dennis Ericksen (of Miami fame) from decades of losing seasons. Ericksen's team was fast, mean, and capable of scoring from anywhere on the field. Even though it was a major bowl venue, the Irish just never seemed to have their hearts fully in the game. Perhaps that had something to do with the tremendous team speed they were up against; Irish plays designed to get outside OSU's flanks never worked. Irish runners were consistently forced to turn upfield before they should have, or were simply chased down by the speedy Beaver players, and they managed to gain only 17 ridiculous yards all night. Meanwhile, OSU tallied the first three scores—a first-quarter FG from 32 yards out, then a 74-yard TD bomb (in which the receiver, Charles Johnson, dropped the ball before reaching the end zone, the Irish DB failing to see this fumble, and the ref calling it a TD even though Johnson was yards away from the loose ball when he crossed into the end zone. . . oh well). Setta managed a FG with no time left on the clock to make it 12-3 at the intermission. A LoVecchio fumble on the first possession of the second half pretty much sealed ND's fate as OSU zipped in for a TD pass from the 23. The Beavers then piled on the points with a 45-yard TD punt return, a four-yard TD pass after an INT, and a four-yard TD run by their showcase back, Ken Simonton. Tony Fisher bulled his way into a score from the OSU one with less than half of the fourth quarter remaining in the game for the final score of 41-9, the worst loss for ND since the last game of the Faust years.

A review of the statistics revealed that the '00 Irish were quite a bit less productive in terms of sheer yardage: the '99 team, with only five wins, cranked out 5,036 total yards whereas the '00 team, with nine wins, managed only 3,803 yards, a dropoff of 25 percent. The bulk of the yardage that disappeared happened in the passing game, from the '99 total of 2,858 yards through the air to 1,454 yards in '00 (although there's no telling what might have happened had Battle stayed healthy). The turnover ratio of plus-six (13 INTs, nine fumble recoveries for ND) was much better than the minus-four of '99. The Irish pass D lopped off some 600 yards from the '99 figure, from 2,898 to the '00 figure of 2,268, so the reconstructed secondary held its own quite well. Scoring defense improved dramatically, with the '99 squad having allowed 331 points, for 27.6 points per game, to the 2000 squad's total of 226, or 20.5 points per game. LoVecchio's pass efficiency rating topped out at 151.7, better than Jackson's 140.3, but he was operating with a less risky system in order to protect

him from having to face extremely difficult reads.

LB Anthony Denman earned second-team All-America recognition; somehow, Tony Driver and Joey Getherall were overlooked.

2000 record: 9-3 (.750)
Record to date: 776-241-42 (.752)

2001

There was a certain pattern to Irish football fortunes in the last four seasons of the Bob Davie era—alternating winning and losing seasons. Although his teams twice won nine games, these seasons were punctuated by seasons during which the Irish could only win five games. No fan could have possibly hoped for a five-win season in 2001, following the nine wins of 2000, but that is what transpired. There was the constant sense that the Irish could be beaten on any given day. They seemed to have lost entirely the consistency of the Holtz years, when ND's teams racked up a decade of consecutive winning seasons. Along with the lost consistency, the Irish also seemed to have misplaced their confidence on the field, both confidence in themselves as well as in the program, and in the coaching. Davie, going into the 2001 campaign, had won only one of 10 games against ranked opponents. A certain defensiveness—almost a bunker mentality—set in; it seemed that Davie was offering excuses and not explanations. There were increasing calls for a change at the top, but Notre Dame extended Davie's contract. Fans prepared for the long haul.

Looking at the 2001 personnel, nine starters were gone from the 2000 season, four on the offense and five on the defense. It would not be an easy task replacing

Notre Dame President, the Rev. Edward Malloy, offers his thoughts to the nation before the Michigan State game, Notre Dame's first following the 9/11 attacks (Photo provided by The Observer).

Notre Dame Band Director Ken Dye leads part of the tribute to the victims of the 9/11 tragedy before the Michigan State game in 2001 (Photo provided by **The Observer***).*

WR Joey Getherall or the TE tandem of Jabari Holloway and Dan O'Leary. Lance Legree at NT and FS Tony Driver would leave pretty big gaps to fill. Davie could survey a veteran offensive line, and his running backs were solid, but Matt LoVecchio, a sophomore with most of the starting time in 2000, would be in a competitive situation with newcomer Carlyle Holiday, one of the most sought-after option QB recruits two seasons earlier. Only the left guard had to be replaced, but Sean Mahan would fill the bill. David Givens would provide steady playmaking at the FL spot. Julius Jones and Tony Fisher offered depth and speed at TB, and Jones looked like a potential 1,000-yard producer. Arnaz Battle returned to the offense, but in the guise of a WR after two years behind center; his skills offered the coaches some interesting possibilities. On defense, the Irish needed to replace their interior down linemen; Andy Wisne brought some experience to the task while newcomer

Cedric Hilliard would need to pass the test, although he brought good range and hustle to the job. The DEs, Anthony Weaver and Ryan Roberts, provided experience and steadiness for the newcomers inside. Courtney Watson, a former running back, would bring his speed to MLB, joining OLBs Rocky Boiman and Tyreo Harrison. Donald Dykes at FS and Jason Beckstrom at LCB would join veterans Ron Israel and Shane Walton. In sum, the 2001 season looked a bit tentative on the offensive side of the ball due to the unsettled QB situation and whether they could develop a sound passing game, especially in Getherall's absence (a loss that also impacted special teams). The defense, on paper, looked solid, with plenty of team speed. The nagging questions revolved around the core issue of team spirit, confidence, and the will to win for a program that did not seem to enjoy widespread fan support.

The 2001 season opener offered the Irish faithful a shock in that the team did not seem to be completely ready to play. Nebraska, to the contrary, rewarded their fans with 17 unanswered points in the first quarter, basically putting the game out of reach. Dahrann Diedrick slammed in from the two for the first score, even though ND had too many men on the field; then Heisman-winner-to-be Eric Crouch threw a 22-yard TD pass to John Gibson one play after an Irish fumble, and a 19-yard FG capped the first quarter explosion following yet another Irish fumble (one-fourth of the entire total of eight lost fumbles in the 2000 campaign). The first Irish points of the campaign came via Nick Setta's foot, a 29-yard FG more than halfway through

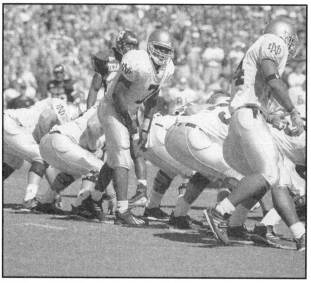

*Irish quarterback Carlyle Holiday surveys his new domain in his first career start, versus Texas A&M in 2001 (Photo by Ernesto Lacayo/*The Observer*).*

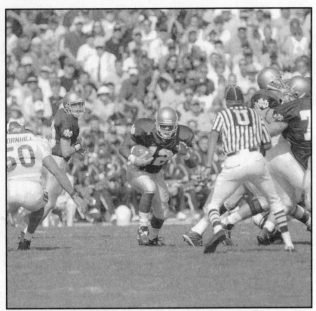

*Tony Fisher busts through a gaping hole in the Michigan State defense in tough 2001 Irish loss (Photo provided by **The Observer**).*

the second quarter, but Diedrick blasted in again from the three on their next drive after Crouch converted a third-and-14 situation with a pass to Tracy Wistrom. The Huskers closed out the first half scoring with a 21-yard FG with one second left on the clock. The dominance was almost total. The Irish looked unprepared; at one point, within a five-play sequence, they forgot to snap the ball, botched a punt snap, and had too many men on the field yet again. Nebraska had no problems exploiting these lapses. In the fourth quarter, Shane Walton blocked a Husker punt, leading to ND's only TD of the day, with Fisher slanting in from less than a yard away from a wishbone formation. For the game, Nebraska pretty much shut down the Irish offense, giving up only 162 total yards (allowing only 2.6 yards per play for ND). Nebraska picked off passes from both Matt LoVecchio and Holiday, and snagged two of three Irish fumbles. With these turnovers, several basic mistakes, and some signs of confusion, it was an inauspicious debut for the season opener, to say the least.

Three days after ND's loss in Lincoln, commercial airliners were hijacked and flown into three sites in NYC and DC, with tragic losses for the Notre Dame community, as for many groups throughout the country. In light of the overarching security concerns that swept the country, the Purdue game was postponed until the end of the season (a precedent was to be found in the 1963 Iowa game, following the JFK assassination,

that had been cancelled). Americans everywhere gave much thought to their priorities, including sports, as the country grieved, re-assessed, and renewed its commitments. Life would never truly be the same again after these events, but eventually Americans returned to the pastimes that perhaps promised to help them cope. For the Irish, the next opponent would be the Spartans of MSU rather than the Boilermakers. Somehow ranked 23rd, ND hoped to put an end to MSU's four-game winning streak against them. The Spartans, however, seemed keyed up, including a tussle in the tunnel before the opening KO, resulting in an unsportsmanlike conduct penalty being assessed against them for pushing Irish QB Matt LoVecchio. Even though MSU had lost 10 starters from their 2000 outfit, they still had TJ Duckett at TB, who helped them considerably on their first drive. The Spartans reached the ND six, but a penalty and sack by Weaver reduced them to a FG try. The Spartan kicker made it good from 29 yards out, but it was an ugly kick, floating through the goalposts sideways. The Irish were moving along on their next possession, although LoVecchio had to fall on a fumbled snap, until Jones later lost the handle for good and MSU recovered his fumble. They could not capitalize on the error, and ND kept moving on its next possession to tie the game 3-3 with 43-yard FG by Setta. The Irish D held MSU in check, but the O stumbled and bumbled. Holiday and LoVecchio were alternating at QB and the team seemed to have a problem establishing a functional rhythm. Holiday proved to be more mobile than LoVecchio, but his linemen didn't seem to notice, as Holiday ran into two ND linemen on one of his scrambles, before taking a sack. On MSU's ensuing possession, Jeff Smoker hit Herb Haygood for a 27-yard gain as Duckett distracted the Irish. They scored after another fake to Duckett, a six-yard rollout pass to their TE, taking a 10-3 lead. With less than a minute in the half, Jones returned a punt 54 yards and LoVecchio lobbed a pass to Javin Hunter, who made a stunning one-handed catch to tie the game at the half. Meanwhile, the Irish learned that the star-crossed Battle had fractured his right fibula fielding a punt.

At the halftime, the schools' combined bands played "Amazing Grace," then shared warm hugs.

The Irish did not seem to get their signals straight at the half; their third quarter possessions saw them miss more assignments and fumble the center snap again, basic errors that might be seen in spring football but should not be a regular part of the third week in the season. They also looked predictable, with 19 of 20

Irish linebacker Tyreo Harrison puts the stop to the Stanford quarterback in a 2001 loss the Irish could have won if the offense had been up to par (Photo by Peter Richardson/The Observer).

first-down plays being runs. The Spartans salted the win midway through the fourth quarter with a 46-yard TD pass to Charles Rogers, the score cinched when the Irish blitzed on the play, the pass went to the middle of the field, and the lone remaining DB, Vontez Duff, slipped on the ND stadium turf. MSU had seen this before late in the game with ND—a passing down, a blitz, a lone defender beaten on a long-scoring play. This time, it cost the Irish a 17-10 defeat.

Texas A&M was next up and the Irish had to get this thing turned around. As it turned out, they didn't, falling to the Aggies 24-3 at Kyle Field, setting an all-time ND record for futility to start a season, hitting rock bottom at 0-3 for the first time ever. Davie started Holiday at QB, but he held up for only a half or so before going out of the game with a sprained neck and two INTs for his trouble. The Aggies announced their intentions with an opening scoring drive, Derek Farmer earning the scoring honors with a fine 31-yard TD run. Shortly after the first Holiday INT, A&M scored again, making the 80-yard march look easy—a 45-yard pass

from Mark Farris to Terry Murphy, then a 22-yard TD pass off a fake reverse to QB Farris, hopelessly lost to the Irish D. They upped the score in the second quarter with a 29-yard FG, but ND answered that one, at last, with a 47-yard Setta FG. The Irish did reach the Aggie 23 with a Holiday pass to David Givens, but didn't reach any closer than that before settling for Setta's try. The scoreless third quarter, with LoVecchio giving it a try at QB, showed that halftime adjustments were not going to get ND on the scoreboard any time soon. The final score was reached in the fourth quarter when further ignominy was inflicted with a blocked Joey Hildbold punt, Jay Brooks doing the honors, Randall Webb garnering the TD from 13 yards out. The Aggies held ND to 191 total yards, 3.2 yards per play, as three INTs and six sacks basically demolished ND's possessions.

With three straight losses, would it be too early to say that the season was also demolished? For some schools, no. For ND, this was unknown territory… not even the dismal Joe Kuharich years had seen such a fiasco to start a campaign. The Irish offense was nearly non-existent: two TDs in 40 possessions to start the season. Somehow, the Irish rebounded to leave the slough of despond and beat Pitt handily 24-7. Although it would prove to be Holiday's best outing so far, it was Julius Jones who sparked the first score, late in the first quarter, with timely, productive short runs capped by a five-yard TD burst. Pitt's next possession, in the second quarter, tied it at 7-7, with a nifty 32-yard scoring pass from David Priestley to Antonio Bryant, but the Irish D finally asserted itself at that point to keep the Panthers pretty much caged for the rest of the game. In the third quarter, ND added a 40-yard FG by Setta, then dodged a bullet when Abram Elam landed on a Pitt fumble at the Irish one. The team showed some pluck and maturity by patching together a four-play, 99-yard drive, keyed by Fisher's 28-yard run and Holiday's 67-yard TD run moments later, a nice turnaround for once. Holiday's scoring run showed him breaking two tackles and jumping over a pile, the kind of gritty determination that had not been seen in some time. In the fourth quarter, Anthony Weaver and Shane Walton speared INTs and Jones copped his second TD of the day with a one-yard pop for the 24-7 final tally. Holiday's 122 yards on the ground proved to be the third most by any Irish QB, and the most since Tony Rice in 1989, perhaps a sign of good things to come?

If the Irish had not been clicking during the first month of the season, they put it all together to beat West Virginia 34-24. Irish runners almost came away with three men with 100 yards or more gained on the ground: Holiday gained 130 yards, Tony Fisher 119, and Julius Jones just missed with 92. Ball control and time of possession were the themes for this game, as ND's runners lugged the pigskin 69 times while throwing only 14 passes, hanging on to the ball for a stifling 37:54 minutes. The Irish struck swiftly, using only two plays in their first drive to score—a 27-yard Holiday run and a 19-yard Jones rumble to the end zone. Well, West Virginia returned the favor on their next possession—85 yards in three lightning-quick plays, with Avon Cobourne dashing 60 yards for the TD. The Mountaineers kicked off and Jones promptly zipped 58 yards to give ND great field position, but all they could manage was Setta's 21-yard FG. West Virginia matched that for a 10-10 tie at the end of the first quarter, one that had plenty of offensive fireworks. Perhaps the excitement

was too much, but things slowed down in the second frame, with only ND scoring, Jones again, capping a patient 55-yard drive done in 15 plays with his one-yard burst into the endzone. West Virginia had plenty of fight left, scoring twice to take the lead in the third quarter, QB Brad Lewis firing TD passes for the scores. Late in that quarter, however, Holiday got loose again for a 36-yard gain and Fisher took the cue to score the tying TD with a fine 25-yard run. Setta put ND ahead in the fourth quarter with a 42-yard FG on the stadium's wet turf, set up earlier by a successful fourth down gamble on the ND 33, Holiday getting the necessary distance on a keeper. Against a Mountaineer formation with five WRs, CB Justin Smith started to put the final nail in their coffin on their next drive when he intercepted a pass on the ND 12. Moments later, Fisher completed the job with a scintillating 55-yard TD run. The Irish kept their composure against a determined opponent, held their unforced errors to a bare minimum, and seemed to have taught themselves something about how to win a tough football game. Holiday became the first Irish QB to rush for 100-plus yards twice in a season, and averaged nearly seven yards per carry in the win over West Virginia.

Notre Dame brought its season to the .500 mark a week later with a 27-16 home field victory over archrival USC, their third straight win of the season, their third consecutive triumph over Troy. After six games, the Irish had an obvious first-down preference: they had run on 55 of 56 first downs. So this time they threw, Holiday hitting Givens for 17 yards to get USC's attention. Later, Setta got the scoring going with a 38-yard field goal, one set up when Holiday broke loose for a 43-yard gain on a

Defensive standout Grant Irons ending a Stanford back's run in 2001 action (Photo by Peter Richardson/The Observer).

QB draw. USC took the lead with a Carson Palmer 54-yard TD pass when Tyreo Harrison missed a sack and Duff missed an INT on the same play. In the second quarter, Holiday fumbled at the ND 20 on an option pitch, USC recovered, and, unbelievably, scored with a 20-yard TD pass while ND was still in its defensive huddle, waiting for the perfect play call, Davie said later. The PAT was missed, so there. The Irish fought back late in the second quarter when USC inexplicably tried a fake punt on their own 28; it failed when Shane Walton tackled the erstwhile runner, and the Irish were sitting pretty. Four plays later, Terrance

Anthony Weaver puts a stop to a Stanford runner in tough 2001 loss (Photo by Peter Richardson/The Observer).

Howard scored untouched with an option pitch from the four. In the third quarter, USC tacked on an 18-yard FG, but Holiday (who had bruised a leg in the second quarter) continued his heroics with a 35-yard TD run, set up by his 16-yard pass to Givens earlier. The teams tussled through most of the fourth quarter with ND hanging on to a slim 17-16 lead, but Setta opened up some distance with 29-yard field goal. On USC's next possession, Palmer fumbled when he was sacked, Donald Dykes recovered, and Jones rammed in a five-yard TD run moments later to wrap up the victory. Opportunistic defense resulted in this crucial fumble recovery, two INTs, and five sacks to make it a hard day at the office for one Carson Palmer and his USC teammates.

In a sign of the times, Boston College came into the next game favored over the Irish for the first time in their 14-game series going back to 1975. The three-game winning streak bubble burst for ND when the Eagles nipped the Irish 21-17. BC won the game in spite of a 2:1 edge in time of possession for ND, 82 offensive plays versus 47, two INTs and a fumble recovered by ND. What did happen for the Eagles is that they were extremely productive with their 47 snaps, gaining 354 yards, averaging 7.5 yards per play. Nevertheless, Holiday played well again, leading ND with 22 carries for 109 yards and firing two TD passes, but all for naught. His first TD pass went to Jones, a 21-yarder, following an INT by Grant Irons. But three plays later, William Green jetted 71 yards to pay dirt to knot the score. The teams played evenly until late in the third quarter, when Duff grabbed the other INT and Holiday found TE John

Owens for a five-yard score. Green struck again in the third frame when the Irish D failed to cover him on a wheel route, good for a 70-yard TD pass and run. The Irish were in the business of responding to that when a sack ended a drive, Setta kicking a 42-yard FG as the consolation prize. Seven plays later, BC scored again with a TD pass, then held on as ND used three long drives in the fourth quarter that all reached scoring territory and ate up the clock, but failed to score.

Seventh-ranked Tennessee next visited the Dome. The Irish had to be pretty low after the loss to BC, but they stuffed the Vols in the first half, allowing only two plays the entire half to be started from ND territory. While the D held the Vols in check, the offense strung together three drives that chewed up most of the clock, with one drive reaching the Tennessee one before Arnaz Battle put the ball on the ground as he ran a reverse, carrying the ball on his inside hip, an error that namesake Julian Battle did not fail to notice, his hit jarring the ball loose. After the Vols recovered from that threat, they saw Ryan Grant lose the handle, with the alert Julian Battle stripping the ball and hauling it in on the bounce, then zipping 81 yards for the only TD of the half. Setta managed to punch in a 41-yard FG with seconds remaining. The Irish D kept up its good work when Courtney Watson locked on to a Casey Clausen pass and took off for the promised land, dodging would-be tacklers and running over others, scoring after a 31-yard jaunt, giving ND a 10-7 lead. Tennessee used its next possession to garner its first offensive score of the day, capping an 80-yard march with a Travis Stephens TD burst of three yards. The Irish stalled, and the Vols kept up the pressure, going 81 yards in 12 patient plays, Clausen spying Donte Stallworth for a 17-yard TD strike. The Irish struck back with their own long drive, 75 yards, with Tony Fisher scoring from the wishbone from the one-yard line. ND wanted to go for a two-point conversion but seemed confused and had to call a time out, but it must have worked because Holiday found Fisher with a shovel pass for the two extra points, closing the score to 18-21. Tennessee was battle tested, however, and took command of the game when a Holiday aerial went astray for an INT on the ND 25, a pure gift, with less than three minutes left in the game. Seven plays later, the Vols scored when Clausen faked into the middle, rolled to his right, and dove for the one-yard score and the win. If there was a bright spot, it was that Holiday threw for 146 yards on 13 of 24 throws, his best day yet as a passer. Overall though, it was a frustrating game for the Irish…*that* close to a win over the number seven team in the country, but also *that* far away.

Having just missed with Tennessee, ND next faced its annual ho-hummer with Navy, having sunk the Middies for 37 consecutive games. The 2001 edition was no different, with ND prevailing over winless Navy 34-16, adding to the school's NCAA record for dominance over an opponent. Setta started the scoring with a 41-yard FG, his 11th consecutive game with a FG, tying John Carney's school record. Gerome Sapp made it 10-0 when Cedric Hilliard discombobulated an option play, caused a Navy fumble, and Sapp went the distance with the recovery for a 39-yard TD play. Navy fought back to 10-7 when QB Brian Madden shook loose on an option play to the left for a 38-yard TD run, then earned a tying FG at the end of the first quarter. The Irish offset that with a four-yard TD run in the second quarter by Terrance Howard, the score set up by a nifty 32-yard pass from Holiday to WR Carlos Campbell. Navy kept plugging away, hitting a FG just before the half. The Irish put the game away in the second half with an eight-yard TD run by Howard, who scored following a great Omar Jenkins block, a 44-yard TD burst up the middle by Jones, and a Setta FG of 32 yards, while Navy managed only one second-half FG for the 34-16 final tally. Jones led all rushers with 24 carries for 117 yards, and ND needed only 12 passes total as it played a ball control game, Holiday hitting six of those for 94 yards.

Those six completions would prove to be six times more than he would hit for the entire game against Stanford, a terrible 17-14 loss that all but sealed Coach Davie's fate. Actually, Holiday would catch as many passes in this game as he completed, as Battle would throw one to him on a flea flicker. The one pass that Holiday completed was for a 47-yard TD to Omar Jenkins to give ND a 7-3 lead, augmented later by two Setta FGs (setting a school record). As in the Tennessee game, this was another close one, but also another study in wasted opportunities, such as Julius Jones's 59-yard romp, the longest of his career, that put the ball on the Stanford seven … only to garner a FG. Stanford won the game in the final seven minutes with two TD runs, one from the nine and the other from the one. Davie inserted Matt LoVecchio to try to spark ND, but he threw an INT instead, and Stanford ran out the clock for the win. The Irish played well enough to win, especially with a good ground game and four sacks on Randy Fasani, but a 46-yard Fasani pass and a pass-interference call sparked the winning TDs, even though Fasani only completed eight passes. One has to wonder what Stanford Coach Tyrone Willingham thought of an opponent that could only complete two passes total in an entire game.

ND's offensive woes continued in the tragedy-delayed Purdue game. After the dismal passing game in the loss to Stanford, against Purdue the Irish could manage only 10 first downs and 162 total yards, with only 31 yards coming via seven Holiday completions. In spite of these stats, somehow, some way, this troubled Irish football team managed to pull out a win, 24-18 over their old nemesis, the Boilermakers. Purdue put up the first score, a first-quarter FG, but Ryan Grant put the Irish ahead with a 14-yard TD run in the second quarter. Purdue came back with another FG for a 7-6 halftime score. The teams traded FGs in the third quarter, but Vontez Duff followed up the Purdue score with a brilliant 96-yard KOR for a TD. In the fourth quarter, another Irish defender, Jason Beckstrom, espied a Boilermaker pass, intercepted it, and took it to the house, a 29-yard TD return. Purdue came right back for a TD on a 12-yard Kyle Orton pass, but the defense sealed the win when Clifford Jefferson capped his career with the final INT of the season as the last seconds ticked off the clock, also marking the final moments of the Bob Davie era at Notre Dame.

Five wins won't cut it under the Dome. Do it twice in five years and you have a problem. Early in his career as the head coach, Davie had said, "We aren't talking a national championship here." Indeed. To do that, a team has to play consistently across the board, on both sides of

Stanford's Ty Willingham gets the Gatorade as his team beats an inept Irish performance near the end of the 2001 season (Photo by David Gonzales/Gonzalesphoto.com).

the ball, has to play with composure, has to play above the tumult and the distractions, with a single-minded purpose, with intense discipline, and with imagination... but champions also execute the fundamentals with near-total regularity, avoid unforced errors, and do all the little things that go unnoticed by the pundits and many of the fans. If they lose a game, they come back even harder the next week. Champions find a way rather than find an excuse. They fix problems rather than fix blame.

The 2001 offense finished the season ranked 110th in the country for average total yardage per game (289.7 ypg). Opponents kept the Irish offense out of the end zone in four games. Holiday ended the season with a QB rating of 93.58, not exactly top of the line. He completed 73 of 144 passes for three TDs but also pitched seven INTs, all for a meager 784 total yards, 70 percent of the team's passing yards. Without a credible passing threat, opposing defenses could stack up against the run; it's nearly amazing that the Irish running game produced 2,070 yards. Still, Holiday showed some flashes of brilliance, including several long runs from scrimmage,

with a 67-yarder being the longest from scrimmage for all Irish runners. In high-stakes, big-time college football, you better have a durable quarterback if you're going to have him be the number two runner, or you don't hang him out there for some free shots by strong safeties and salivating linebackers. The Irish defense, to the contrary, showed its mettle time and time again, ending up ranked 14th in total defense, 10th in pass defense, and 22nd in scoring defense, garnering 12 fumbles, 14 INTs, and 25 sacks, for a plus-five in the turnover department.

Shortly after the win over Purdue, AD Kevin White announced the end of the Davie era. He would start the search for a replacement immediately and hoped to complete it quickly.

2001 record: 5-6 (.455)
Record to date: 781-247-42 (.749)

2002

Notre Dame players, fans, and school authorities had never experienced a transition from one season to the next like the one that heralded the 2002 season. The 2001 campaign had been an obviously frustrating season, with a young, talented team, featuring a stout defensive unit, a team however that never seemed to achieve its full potential, with a coach beset by the nagging doubts of others about his leadership, and a rising hue and cry for change from all quarters. Bob Davie's contract had been generously extended only recently, so change did not seem imminent. But Irish AD Kevin White had seen enough when the Irish looked totally inept, particularly Davie's offense, against Stanford. After announcing that Davie would not return as the head coach, White began an intensive search designed to find a suitable head coach as quickly as possible. Within a week, he had announced that Georgia Tech's George O'Leary would replace Davie. Irish fans began to rhapsodize about the various Irish possibilities under an O'Leary, a coach who had a good track record of taking undertalented teams

to unexpected heights, with exciting offensive schemes. Riding the high of the Christmas season's good cheer, O'Leary presented an enthusiastic vision at his coming-out press conference, with a firm promise of returning to ND's expected winning ways.

Instead of the Christmas football present that the Irish faithful anticipated, it all turned out to be a lump of coal within a week after White's announcement. Not long after O'Leary's introduction to the press, reports began to filter in to the highest ND authorities that there were irregularities in O'Leary's publicly stated football background credentials. A flurry of meetings and phone calls over two excruciating days ended up confirming the startling revelations that O'Leary had overstated his involvement as a varsity player in his playing days three decades earlier, and also lacked the needed credits for an advanced degree he claimed. O'Leary resigned his position, offering more apologies than explanations, having never coached an Irish player or finalized a recruiting offer. In disbelief and a strong measure of shame, Irish fans watched as an aggrieved White had to start the search all over.

Unfortunately, Notre Dame authorities had not

Intense, committed, disciplined, demanding—Ty Willingham introduces himself to the Notre Dame family on New Year's Day 2002 (Photo by Noah Amstadter/The Observer).

*Shane Walton creates mayhem against the Maryland Terrapins in the 2002 season opener (Photo by Brian Pucevich/*The Observer*).*

done the kind of background checks in the search process that would have uncovered the correct information that would have avoided the school and its reputation being embroiled in this lamentable episode. The football program was also beset with other embarrassing legal distractions involving former players, and key players were facing academic difficulties. For an institution that had taken justifiable pride for its academic and ethical stances, this constellation of malfeasances was almost too much to bear. Those who were not Irish fans took visible delight in the school's discomfort. Meanwhile, Kevin White—an honorable man—agonized on behalf of the programs, coaches, and athletes he headed.

Just as the longest night of the year is followed by a gradual increase in daylight, Irish fortunes were not destined to remain under this terrible cloud indefinitely. White's earlier search had put him in touch with a man well known to him from his AD days at Arizona State, the head coach at Stanford, Tyrone Willingham, a man who was not unfamiliar with Notre Dame, having played at Michigan State in the mid-'70s. Willingham pushed his case with White, calling him at ND repeatedly to reaffirm his desire for the job, indeed, that he was

the right man for the job. His quiet, firm insistence and well-known strength of character took him to the top of White's list. After leaving no stone unturned this time, and in the hopeful aura of the New Year, White introduced Willingham to the press and the Irish true believers as the school's 27th head coach. The nightmare was over.

Willingham took charge instantly, providing direction, firmness, goals, authority, realistic hopes, and high ideals for a program that felt itself much in need of those very qualities. At Stanford, Willingham had recruited and coached the kind of student-athlete that ND similarly appreciated and sought. His teams had been competitive in a tough conference, and his background included stints with some of the premier football minds on the national scene, notably Bill Walsh and Denny Green. Mike Holmgren, no stranger to excellence, having coached with Willingham a decade earlier, knew even then that he had brilliant potential.

Ever since 1986, Holtz's first year under the Dome, Notre Dame's offense, for better or worse, had been based on option football. Willingham made that one of the first things he changed. Under his leadership, the Irish would not be primarily focusing on attacking the flanks of a defense with option plays, but would stretch the field, going downtown often with its ambitious, sophisticated pass routes, using the West Coast offense that ND's Joe Montana had mastered under Walsh for four Super Bowl wins. He retained the defense's Greg Mattison but also brought in Kent Baer to provide the Irish D the kind of tactical thinker he appreciated on that side of the ball. But the big thing Willingham did as he prepared for the 2002 season was to provide a certain kind of structure and inner discipline for his players and staff. He could often be seen deeply involved physically in drills, constantly setting an example for the team. If the team did it, he did it. With his intensity, drive, focus, determination, and boundless energy, in his own inimitable way, Willingham was bringing this team together in ways not seen in many years, while also putting some much-needed distance between the Irish and the dark night of despair they had suffered with the 2001 season and the disastrous search.

When the new coach surveyed his domain, he could feel some relief in knowing that most of his offensive line returned, that the kicking game was in capable hands, that his interior linemen on defense returned, as well as most of the defensive secondary. Any coach, however, would have to be concerned about a returning starting quarterback, Carlyle Holiday, not yet proven, who had shown some flashes of brilliance, but also some glaring weaknesses in his overall game. In addition, Holiday had been recruited as an option threat, with his quickness and excellent outside speed. Willingham would have to convert his starter from that brand of offense into more of a dropback quarterback who would need the patience and skills to read keys and let receivers go deep into their patterns before throwing the ball. Stepping up at RT would be Brennan Curtin, Omar Jenkins at WR, sophomore Ryan Grant at RB, and Gary Godsey at TE. On the other side of the line, Kyle Budinscak would have to step up at LE, Ryan Roberts at RE, Mike Goolsby and Derek Curry would join the linebacking corps, and Glenn Earl would bring his hard-hitting style to FS. Looking at his team's 2001 offensive stats, Willingham knew that the Irish would have to improve the anemic output of 1,117 passing yards for a mere four TDs (only 101.5 yards per game, second worst in the country), but also that the offense would be hard-pressed to rush for more than 2,400 yards, as they had in 2001, due to the loss of starting TB Julius Jones for academic reasons. Holiday would present a real project for Willingham; he would need all the tutoring the coach could muster to improve his 2001 QB rating of 93.58, one of the lower ratings for the Irish in recent years. The leading Irish receiver in 2001 had gained only 387 yards through the air; the Irish air game would have to do better than that, and Willingham placed his hopes in Arnaz Battle, the fifth-year senior who had converted from QB two years earlier. For the D, the coaches could take heart in a set of speedy, aggressive, very athletic DBs who threatened to pick off any pass not perfectly thrown. Other starters who could be looked to for significant contributions included Nick Setta and Joey Hildbold in the kicking game, defensive linemen Cedric Hilliard and Darrell Campbell, and the exciting Shane Walton and Vontez Duff in the secondary.

Willingham took his unproven, unranked Irish up against Maryland in the 2002 Kickoff Classic at the Meadowlands, the first football meeting of the two schools. Coach Ralph Friedgen had taken the Terps to a stellar 10-2 record in '01, good for a 10th-place national ranking, while winning National Coach of the Year honors for his effort. The Irish D set the tone for the 2002 campaign when Shane Walton clutched an INT to stop Maryland's first drive. The Irish O looked a bit unsure of itself, and Setta was sent in to try a 56-yard field goal. He missed, but it was a good indicator of the confidence Willingham had in his kicker, and a good measure of the scoring pressure the Irish would consistently bring to opponents. Walton grabbed two more INTs and Setta banged five field goals as the Irish earned their first season-opening shutout since 1973. Holiday set a PR with 226 yards passing on 17 of 27 aerials, 63 percent of his attempts. Vontez Duff scored the game's only TD when he zipped 76 yards with a Terp punt in the third quarter. Overall, Willingham had to feel pretty good about this first game, especially the defensive unit that held Maryland to 133 total yards. The offense was unable to punch the ball in for any TDs, but they played within themselves and did not give anything away. The entire team played with improved discipline and confidence, while the offense worked with a much wider play selection.

With vastly improved morale, the Irish welcomed Joe Tiller's aerial circus, also known as Purdue, to South Bend for their 74th contest. Purdue QB Kyle Orton had bombed away with 52 passes in '01, but the Irish secondary might have been eager for that in '02. The first quarter ended in a scoreless tie, but the Irish D exploded for two TDs in the span of 11 seconds when Gerome Sapp snapped up a fumble and scooted 54 yards to the end zone, then Lionel Bolen reacted brilliantly

Gerome Sapp hauls the mail for a 54-yard TD fumble recovery and return in 2002 Irish win over Purdue (Photo by Tim Kacmar/The Observer).

Freshman wide receiver Maurice Stovall befuddles a Spartan defender for a nice gain in Irish comeback win in 2002 (Photo by Lisa Velte/The Observer).

to the fumbled kickoff, caused by fellow sophomore Quentin Burrell, snatching it in midair and zipping into the end zone just four yards away. Setta tacked on a field goal, but Purdue scored on a 76-yard punt return for the 17-7 halftime score. Purdue knotted the score with a field goal and a three-yard TD run before Duff iced the game for ND with a 33-yard INT return for a TD with little more than five minutes left in the game, in the process setting an Irish record by being the first ND defender to score in three consecutive games (on a 96-yard KO return in the rescheduled '01 Purdue finale, then the punt return the week before). Once again, the Irish D prevailed, holding the dangerous Boilermaker passing game to only 14 completions for 171 yards and hauling in three recovered fumbles. Joy prevailed under the Dome, but knowledgeable fans fretted that the Irish offense had yet to reach the end zone in '02; they also noted that Holiday's stats went retrograde with only seven completions in 22 attempts for 50 yards.

This would have to change if Willingham's team expected to do much with a powerful Michigan squad. Ranked 20th, ND welcomed the seventh-ranked Wolverines to the Dome for their 30th contest, the series having started in 1887. Without any offensive scores yet, some observers wondered if Willingham was getting it done with smoke and mirrors. If so, Michigan would be glad to end the illusion. Perhaps the Irish offensive

squad had taken note of these concerns; TB Ryan Grant had his best game of the young campaign, rushing for 132 yards on 28 carries, helping ND prevail in a great game, 25-23. Grant got it started with one-yard TD run, capping a 10-play drive. Michigan tied the game when DB Marlin Jackson made a perfect read and hauled in a Holiday pass to run untouched 19 yards for the score. In the second quarter, the persistent Irish D earned a safety by forcing a holding call in the end zone. On its next possession, Michigan fumbled and Holiday punched in a three-yard TD run to exploit the opportunity. In the third quarter, UM garnered a field goal before a Battle fumble gave them a short field and a two-yard TD run for a 17-16 lead. The Irish responded, Holiday finding Omar Jenkins with passes of 29 and 47 yards before Grant slammed in for a three-yard TD. Setta finished ND's scoring with a 46-yard FG, then the Irish had to hold on tight to their shillelaghs as Michigan scored inside the final three minutes with an eight-yard pass. Coach Lloyd Carr went for two points, only to see Shane Walton tip away the ball. Moments later, Walton stepped up again and hauled in another INT to close out the victory. In spite of giving up six sacks, the Irish offense rose to the occasion, gaining 311 total yards. Holiday passed sparingly, but gained 154 yards on eight completions. Overall team speed kept Michigan bottled up and frustrated; Setta's scoring threat actually forced Michigan into conservative play calling decisions that reduced their scoring punch.

For the previous five seasons, Michigan State had the Irish number, winning on lucky plays, blowouts, close games—whatever. With the Irish ranked 12th, riding a season-opening three-game win streak (the first since the Holtz years), fans had to worry that the Spartans would burst the bubble ... and they almost did it, with sophomore WR Charles Rogers snagging seven passes for 175 yards, including a 38-yard TD catch to go with an amazing 21-yarder in the last inches of the end zone. Before those Spartan heroics, Grant put up the first score, ending Notre Dame's opening drive with a six-yard TD run, a score set up when Battle threw a 30-yard pass to Holiday. MSU responded with a FG, then thwarted the next Irish possession, but Walton snapped their momentum with a tipped pass that Sapp hauled in and returned to the MSU 28. Holiday used the opportunity to locate freshman WR Maurice Stovall for a 15-yard TD strike with mere seconds left in the half. The third quarter was a scoreless affair, but the Irish saw their undefeated season seem to go down the drain when Holiday injured his left shoulder on a run out of bounds. Pat Dillingham, a walk-on who had earned a scholarship, found himself running the team in a tight 14-3 game. That lead disappeared in the fourth quarter when Rogers pulled off his TD heroics, setting up one of those sweet revenge scenarios that have a timeless quality about them. With less than 90 seconds in the game, Dillingham dropped back and sent a pass to Battle over the Spartan middle. The former QB snagged the ball just as two Spartan defenders eliminated each other on ill-timed hits and the remaining DB fell down as Battle broke loose for the stunning 60-yard TD catch and run—and win. With this fourth win, the Irish had their best start since 1994, and began to heal some of the lingering wounds from the five-game losing streak to the Spartans.

Sometimes ironies abound beyond imagination. For his fifth game as the Irish head coach, Willingham would face his former team, Stanford, with a quarterback who had gone to school with his own daughter, and whose father was the team physician for the Cardinals. Now ranked ninth, the Irish would have to place their hopes in the hands of Dillingham, running a scaled-back offense, and their stout defense. The first quarter revealed that Stanford was reading ND's offense well, and that Dillingham posed little threat as a runner, unlike Holiday. The Irish blocked a Stanford FG try, but Stanford closed out the quarter with a 14-yard TD catch by WR Teyo Johnson. With that, Stanford's scoring was completed for the day, while ND reeled off 31 unanswered points, with two RBs going over the century mark in the process, Grant and Rashon Powers-Neal, yet another sophomore. Setta started the landslide with a second quarter FG from 30 yards out, before Powers-Neal slammed in from the three late in the third quarter. Walton continued his DB magic with an INT and an 18-yard TD return, and LB Courtney Watson, injured earlier in the year, picked off another Cardinal pass and stormed 34 yards for yet another defensive score mere seconds after Walton had made his visit to the end zone. Gerome Sapp, helping his mother celebrate her birthday, snagged a tipped pass early in the fourth quarter, and Grant wrapped up the drive Sapp started with an untouched one-yard TD burst. Close observers of the game noted that Willingham managed a small smile in the fourth quarter, perhaps feeling that some of the pressures that attend his position might have been lifted at least temporarily with the 31-7 win—a win that put him in same lustrous bracket as Ara Parseghian, whose first Irish team, in 1964, would go deep into that season undefeated.

The Irish poll ranking inched up to the eighth spot as they prepared for an improving, dangerous Pitt Panther squad. The game had a certain asymmetry in that Pitt ran about as well as ND had been passing (97th in the country so far); whose defense would be best able to take advantage of the situation? Holiday returned as the QB starter, helped magnificently by Battle who set a PR with 10 catches for 101 yards, more than half of the Irish total for the day. Pitt outgained ND by more than 200 yards, but never reached the end zone. Two FGs were all the Panthers could manage, a point total that Battle equaled with a splendid catch for an 11-yard TD in the second quarter; Setta's PAT put the Irish ahead for good. Glenn Earl made one of his patented big hits on the Pitt QB in the fourth quarter, causing a fumble on the Panther 12. Five plays later, Grant rumbled in from the one for the final score of 14-6. With the offense not exactly hitting its stride, other than Battle's heroics, the difference in the close game could be found in eight Irish sacks and pinpoint punting by Joey Hildbold that forced Pitt to start most of their second-half drives deep in their territory.

Notre Dame had to take its act to meet undefeated Air Force, a team that was the perennial rushing champs in the country with their vaunted triple-option wishbone, also a team that had proven they could play up to Irish standards throughout the years. Ranked seventh, facing number 15, the Irish did not let past difficulties get in the way, basically manhandling and frustrating the smaller Falcons, outgaining them with 447 total yards to 161, holding them to 104 yards

Vontez Duff secures an Irish win over Purdue with a 33-yard interception return for a TD in 2002 (Photo by Andy Kenna/The Observer).

rushing, about one-third of their usual output. The final score, 21-14, did not reflect the degree of dominance, as three Irish fumbles kept Irish scoring chances down, with two of them leading to AFA gift scores. The first fumble, a Holiday miscue, gave Falcon LB Marchello Grady a free pass to the end zone from the Irish 21 for the game's first score. Miffed, Holiday took charge on the next drive, hitting Battle with a 15-yard pass, then breaking loose for a 53-yard TD romp, tying the game. The Falcons hung in there throughout the second quarter, until the Irish pulled together a 12-play drive covering 79 yards. Ryan Grant, having his best day as a running back (30 carries for 190 yards), blasted for a TD from the AFA 18, with FB Tom Lopienski obliterating a cast of Falcons with a tremendous block to clear the way. Vontez Duff helped out the Falcons in the third quarter when he fumbled the kickoff, giving them the ball at the Irish 16. From there, it took the triple option six plays to score, with Falcon QB Chance Harridge scooting in from the one to tie the game. Duff did better with the next kickoff, rambling 31 yards to give ND a shorter field; Holiday crafted a 58-yard drive, scoring from the one with the game-winning TD. Neither team scored in the fourth quarter, although ND stymied AFA with superior defense and ball possession tactics that consumed 12 precious minutes in the final frame. The Falcon offense was frustrated at every turn, with Irish defenders seemingly waiting for Harridge and his runners at every possible gap. There was nothing to exploit, no bad match-ups, as the Irish D never lost its cohesion to dominate AFA almost totally.

Continuing to edge up in the polls, 7-0 and sixth-ranked (third in the BCS poll) ND next went to Tallahassee to meet the 11th-ranked Seminoles. If there was ever a team, a coach, and a game that could bring things to a screeching halt for ND—this would be that game. Willingham knew what he was getting into and had the team practice indoors during the week, with the Seminole fight song blasting at the captive players until they were sick of it. The young Irish team took the cue, then nutted up to put on a superior display of football, dismantling FSU 34-24, including a characteristic explosion of points in the third quarter when Seminole miscues, caused by Irish hustle and outstanding hitting, produced 17 points for ND in little more than two minutes. Notre Dame served notice quickly by stopping FSU's first possession cold,

Carlyle Holiday joins Irish immortals with four TD passes in 2002 Irish win over Rutgers (Photo by Chip Marks/The Observer).

then stunning the 'Noles and their fans when Holiday used the first Irish play from scrimmage to isolate Battle on a DB with a deep slant pattern good for a 65-yard TD, with Battle's speed leaving the helpless defender trailing the whole way. Superior scouting and coaching had spotted the potential for that match-up, and an opportunistic attitude led to the kind of call on the first play of a big game that had not been seen in many years by the Irish faithful. FSU fought back on its next possession to garner a 24-yard FG, matched at the end of the quarter by a 39-yard Setta FG, set up by a powerful 22-yard run by Ryan Grant, breaking two tackles along the way, and a nifty 26-yard rollout pass from Holiday to freshman WR Maurice Stovall. FSU strung together a long drive—one that should have never been due to a missed fumble call—for a one-yard TD run late in the second quarter. On the missed call, a Seminole WR caught a pass over the middle, had control of the ball, took two steps, dropped the ball—immediately recovered by Vontez Duff ... but no call came other than for an incomplete pass. If the Irish had no luck on that play, they must have saved it up for the third quarter: on the 'Noles' second possession, FSU's QB, Chris Rix, called an audible, then fired a pass to his right, but LB

Carlos Pierre-Antoine speared the ball and followed a convoy of blockers to the FSU 23. The Irish settled for a 35-yard Setta FG. On the third play from scrimmage after Setta's kick, Rix scrambled to his right only to be stood up by Glenn Earl's monumental hit, he fumbled, and the refs made the right call this time as Duff finally snagged the fumble at the FSU two. Willingham wasted no time, calling for an option pitch to Grant, who broke through some flailing arm tackles for a TD from the two and a 20-10 lead. By this time in the season, opposing coaches had to have a sinking feeling knowing that a kickoff was coming their way, and that their returners would have to face a devastatingly effective special team operation. Sure enough, the Irish KO found the speedy Pierre-Antoine causing a fumble by returner Leon Washington, with Brandon Hoyte recovering the loose ball for ND at the FSU 17. Be assured—this was no accident. Willingham went for the jugular, using a short run and two passes into the end zone, the second a 16-yard TD pass from Holiday to Omar Jenkins out of a trips right formation. In the fourth quarter, the Irish struck quickly after a punt, moving to the payoff in two quick plays—a 40-yard pass, then a penalty, followed by a Ryan Grant TD run of 31 yards off the left side, with Lopienski pancaking two defenders with a great block. Bowden threw in the towel, it seemed, when he pulled his starting QB, but the sub rallied his teammates for two TDs to make the final score 34-24, with Irish players perhaps celebrating a bit too soon. For the game, the Irish gained an average of 5.7 yards per play (53 plays for 301 total yards) while FSU racked up 418 yards, but had to use 75 plays for that total. Notre Dame's run defense in particular stood out, holding a normally productive FSU run game to 93 yards on 32 carries. Ryan Grant gained more than that with his 19 carries. What stood out once again was outstanding pressure on anyone carrying the football, stunning tackling, and the ability to score in clusters to turn a close game into a rout. For the first time in Notre Dame history, with this win over FSU the Irish had gone on the road to defeat ranked teams in consecutive games.

Things had gone well for eight games for Notre Dame. Willingham had used almost every motivational ploy he could think of, including "greening" the fans in the stand with tens of thousands of impressive "Return to Glory" t-shirts. Well, maybe green would be a slight advantage for the players as well, so he dressed them in green for the Boston College game. As the game turned out, it seems that he forgot one thing—the refs. The bubble burst with a bitter 14-7 loss to an unranked BC squad that played a gutsy, intense game, taking advantage of the breaks that came their way, much like the Irish had done for two months of the season. Notre Dame fumbled seven times, losing four, and with Holiday on the sidelines nursing an injury in the second quarter, Dillingham threw an ill-advised shovel pass under pressure that turned into a 71-yard TD return for LB Josh Ott. An imaginary call on a FG try more or less captured the picture of the day. The other BC score came on a three-yard run by Derrick Knight in the first quarter. The Irish flirted with the red zone no less than five times before they worked a consolation TD, a 20-yard TD pass from Holiday to Stovall in the game's waning moments. The Irish D held BC to 184 yards, with a mere 77 coming through the air, while the O ran and passed 84 times for 357 yards, with Grant gaining 107 yards on 27 carries. It was one of those games where winning most of the stats meant nothing as long as you were courteous enough to give the ball to the other team

Arnaz Battle negotiates through Scarlet Knights' defenders with a reception in 42-0 Irish rout of Rutgers in 2002 (Photo by Andy Kenna/The Observer).

Ryan Grant trying to get the Irish untracked in 2003 Gator Bowl loss to NC State (Photo by Tim Kacmar/The Observer).

at crucial moments. The team looked a bit flat, as if they had expended most of their mojo in the magnificent efforts of the prior weeks.

Wherever the mojo had gone, it didn't make an appearance in the next game either, yet another sleepwalking affair against what on paper seemed to be a badly overmatched Navy squad—a recipe for disaster. Navy actually led at the end of the first quarter and then again at the end of the third quarter. The Irish continued to be generous with their fumbles, offering up four with the Middies grabbing three of those. Furthermore, the Irish seemed reluctant to run and block with their usual *élan*, gaining only 68 yards on 41 carries, against a team that usually offered little resistance in this regard. For its part, Navy was unable to pass, completing only six passes for 52 yards, with two picked off by ND. The Irish scored first as WR Carlos Campbell nailed a desperate Middie punter for a safety after a bad center snap. Just prior to that, however, Omar Jenkins had punctured the Navy defense for a 61-yard gain with a Holiday pass, but promptly fumbled. Two possessions later, Navy capped a 95-yard drive with a 12-yard TD gallop by Aaron Polanco to take the lead as the first quarter ended. Notre Dame took back the lead with their own long drive, 81 yards, highlighted by a 26-yard Holiday pass to TE Gary Godsey and a 38-yard strike to Stovall, with Lopienski diving over the pile from the one for the culminating score. Polanco kept the pressure on ND with his second TD of the day in the third quarter, a one-yard run, but Duff responded brilliantly with a 92-yard KOR on the next play for a TD. The Irish lead didn't last too long, as Eric Roberts scored from the 10 after a 12-play, 80-yard

Navy drive. Gloom began to set in when Grant fumbled shortly thereafter, giving Navy a cheap FG and a 23-15 lead. The fourth quarter, however, was a different matter as ND worked a careful march to have Powers-Neal score from the one, followed by a two-point try made good when Battle snagged a Holiday throw. With the game tied at 23-23, Omar Jenkins stepped up to atone for his earlier fumble as he hauled in a Holiday pass for a 67-yard score keyed by a Stovall block that took out three Middies. Notre Dame's D held off a spirited rally by Navy after that score, with INTs by Glenn Earl and LB Courtney Watson blunting their threats. To help earn the win, Holiday had his best day as the Irish QB, completing 13 passes for 272 yards. Even though it was the 39th consecutive win for ND over Navy, no one could miss the fact that the Irish were not hitting on all cylinders, not where you want a team to be this late in the season.

The Irish apparently didn't need all cylinders as they dismantled Rutgers 42-0 for their 10th win of Willingham's first season. They did this without starting LT Jordan Black in the first half, suspended by Willingham for letting campus parking tickets pile up, a small but ominous sign of things to come. The initial scores came in the second quarter, the first on a pass to Battle from 38 yards out, the second when Walton picked off a tipped pass and darted 45 yards to pay dirt. The third quarter proved to be one of those all-time keepers as ND scored three times in five plays from scrimmage—Battle on a 63-yard catch and run, Jenkins with a 37-yard TD reception, and Ryan Grant on a 28-yard run. Holiday went on to tie other Irish QBs with four TDs in one game when he found Stovall roaming loose for a 26-yard TD, also in the third quarter, the 28 points being the most ever scored in one frame by a Notre Dame team. The Irish D faced little resistance, as Rutgers' runners managed only 14 yards on 28 carries.

Ranked seventh, Notre Dame met sixth-ranked USC and their Heisman-winner-to-be, QB Carson Palmer. Setta put up two FGs in the first quarter for an early lead, and Pierre-Antoine regained the lead when he blocked a punt and had the composure to recover the loose ball for a 27-yard TD play. But with only five seconds left in the half, Palmer found WR Mike Williams for a 19-yard TD and a 17-13 lead. The second half was all SC, 27 points' worth, as an aroused Trojan D held the hapless Irish to a mere four first downs for the game and an anemic 109 total yards while Palmer and mates racked up 610 total yards. Palmer was sacked only once and seemed unruffled by any semblance of a pass rush as he completed 32 of 46 passes for four scores and 425 yards, surely a Heisman performance if there ever was one. Courtney Watson showed his mettle for ND in the third quarter when he intercepted a Palmer throw and rumbled 60 yards before being stopped. The Trojans, however, wouldn't let ND take advantage of the play. Playing inspired football, the USC defenders held Holiday to 70 yards passing with 10 completions in 29 tries; Ryan Grant was the leading runner for ND with 16 yards gained on 10 carries. It had been that kind of day. If fans didn't know any better, this was the kind of inept performance that had led to disillusionment under other coaches. Along with the downturn in play, it seemed that there was a return to poor team discipline in certain areas. The team had been demonstrative throughout the season, but it had seemed to stay within the accepted bounds. The USC debacle revealed some poor decisions and questionable behavior. With Willingham, however, there is an adamant refusal to offer an excuse. Whatever had gone wrong, he would find it and fix it.

Notre Dame's 10 wins earned the team a national ranking of 10th and a Gator Bowl bid to play North Carolina State, a team enjoying its first 10-win season and a ranking of 17th. Willingham would have the usual month between the finale and the bowl game to work on whatever had plagued his team in the final five games, including 15 fumbles and some ill-considered personal fouls. By the time the team was in its final practices, however, it became evident that he'd have to do it without his starting tackles, both severed from the team by the university. Then, a special teams player was arrested in Jacksonville for trespassing a few days prior to the game. WLB Courtney Watson, the team's leading tackler, would miss the game with a leg injury.

Perhaps the game itself was a bit of an anti-climax, especially after the FSU high and the USC low, and all the distractions with discipline problems. Nevertheless, the Irish came out on their first two possessions and looked pretty sharp, with NC State making the basic mistakes, until a drive reached the Wolfpack 10 and Holiday ran a keeper to the right side, injuring his left shoulder on the hit. Dillingham came in, Grant was dropped for a loss, and Setta nailed a 23-yard FG for a 3-0 lead. It would be all downhill after that, with NC State pounding the Irish for three TDs in the second quarter—two short runs by T.A. McLendon and a nine-yard TD pass from Philip Rivers to Jerricho Cotchery as part of a stretch of 12 straight completions, the kind of surgical precision ND was unable to muster. Setta managed to add another FG in the third quarter, but that was more than offset in the final frame when Rivers kept his hot hand going with a seven-yard TD pass to Sean Berton. Irish luck never materialized; with Holiday out, Dillingham managed to complete 19 passes, but had three picked off. The running game never materialized, adding only 86 yards, with Grant earning most of that on 21 carries. NC State gained only 80 yards on the ground, but picked apart the defense for 255 yards passing, with Rivers looking like an east coast version of Carson Palmer as the Wolfpack prevailed handily 28-6.

Doubling the win total from '01 was no mean feat, to be sure. Shane Walton completed his Irish career as an All-American, with Jeff Faine gaining second team status, while Vontez Duff and Courtney Watson earned third team All-America status. Coach Willingham deservedly earned several Coach of the Year Awards. But no one could deny that the Irish had lost three of their last five games, with two of those losses looking like reruns of the bitter disappointments from previous seasons. No one could deny that discipline issues afflicted the operation, although it would be difficult to identify the precise cause. But with all the problems, Notre Dame football had definitely re-appeared on the national scene and the future looks promising.

Had Willingham done it with smoke and mirrors? Not really. He showed a strong ability to motivate his players, to get them to play to their full potential, and to execute an aggressive game plan. The defense in particular was supremely opportunistic, with great ball pursuit, and strong pass defense. If anything hampered the overall effort, it had to be his quarterback play: Holiday had not completely negotiated the transition from option football to the west coast offense, and when he was on the sidelines, the offense clearly lacked the extra dimension he could bring with his running ability. Two of the three final losses were at least partially related to his absence from the games.

2002 record: 10-3 (.769)
Record to date: 791-250-42 (.749)

2003

The Irish started the campaign, Willingham's second under the dome, ranked 19th nationally. Julius Jones returned to action following a year away from the team. QB Carlyle Holiday would be throwing to an average group of receivers, led by Rhema McKnight, Maurice Stovall, and Anthony Fasano. Justin Tuck, Glenn Earl, Corey Mays, and Victor Abiamiri would play key roles on defense.

The season started with an overtime win over Washington State, 29-26, but the bloom was lost a week later in a 38-0 debacle against Michigan in Ann Arbor, the most lopsided score in the series that started in 1887, and the first shutout. The Irish were inept in virtually every department, gaining only 49 yards rushing and 91 yards receiving. The disgruntlement with Willingham's coaching began to fester as memories of the flashy 8-0 start in 2002 wilted.

Michigan State added insult to injury with a 22-16 victory at Notre Dame. Needing to turn it around, Willingham started freshman QB Brady Quinn against Purdue. Quinn fired 59 passes for 297 yards, but the Irish folded 23-10 for their third straight loss.

The team seemed to find the way to win with a squeaker in Pittsburgh, 20-14, paced by an all-time ND rushing effort of 262 yards by Jones. Whatever momentum this win provided basically evaporated in a humiliating 45-14 home loss to USC, as future Heisman winners Matt Leinart and Reggie Bush showed flashes of their brilliance against a befuddled Irish defense. In two games against the Trojans, Willingham's defenses had given up 1,160 yards.

The slide continued with a tough 27-25 road loss to Boston College, then reached alarming proportions with a devastating 37-0 home field loss to Florida State. The QB fired 50 passes again, with only 20 completions. Irish fans are not used to such humiliating results on their home turf. The general ineptness of the offense, with its second shutout of the season, caused a crescendo of criticism against the coach.

Fortunately, Navy continued in its time-honored

Julius Jones escaping Syracuse's defenders. (Reproduced courtesy of the University of Notre Dame Athletic Media Relations Office.)

patsy role, falling 27-24 to an Irish rushing game that racked up 280 yards. BYU closed out the Irish home season by obliging the disgruntled fans with a 33-14 win for ND. Willingham took the team to his old stomping grounds and demolished Stanford 57-7 as Irish runners rambled for 320 yards and four TDs while the air game added another 192 yards and two more TDs. The offense was clicking like it should have, but it might have been too late. Nevertheless, one more win would make the team bowl eligible.

It was not to happen. Syracuse ended the dismal season with a 38-12 win on their home field, and the critics now had a long winter to fan their ire.

2003 record: 5-7 (.416)
Record to date: 796-257-42 (.746)

2004

Irish hopes were strong going into Willingham's third season. Although Julius Jones had graduated, the fourth-leading runner in Irish history, top recruit Darius Walker, might be able to fill the void. All eyes were on sophomore QB Brady Quinn, a big athlete with a strong arm capable of making the kinds of throws the West Coast offense demanded. All of the receivers were back; the defense promised to be a steady if not spectacular outfit.

Whatever optimistic bubble the fans lived in burst asunder with a 20-17 loss to BYU in Provo. Quinn played well enough with 26 completions for 265 yards, including a 54-yard screen pass for a TD to Rhema McKnight. The last possession, however, was a dud, and BYU held on for the win. The absence of Jones could be seen in the paltry ground offense for ND: 11 net yards. The undefeated 8th-ranked Wolverines pranced into the Notre Dame stadium but went home with a 28-20 defeat. Michigan racked up three field goals for the first-half lead, but Walker turned it around in the second half with two TDs and 115 yards rushing for the game. The Irish then took the short trip to East Lansing and managed a 31-24 win, highlighted by safety Tom Zbikowski's 75-yard spring for a TD with a recovered fumble. Walker and Ryan Grant slashed the Spartans for 175 yards on the ground; Quinn hit 11 passes for 215 yards.

Notre Dame's momentum picked up with a convincing 38-3 pasting of the Washington Huskies. Quinn passed for three TDs in the first half, then added one more in the fourth quarter, while Walker chipped

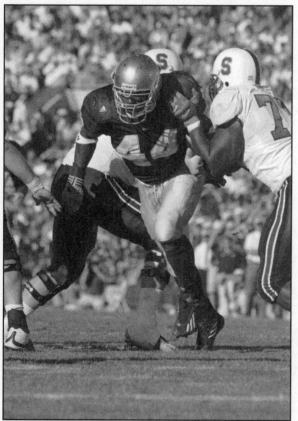

Justin Tuck defeating a Stanford double team. (Reproduced courtesy of the University of Notre Dame Athletic Media Relations Office.)

in with a ground score as the Irish racked up more than 400 total yards.

Ancient opponent Purdue brought the Irish family back to earth with a 41-16 rout in South Bend, their first win over ND at home in thirty years. Kyle Orton bombed the Irish with four TD passes and 385 yards, although Quinn bested him with an impressive 432 yards. Anthony Fasano snagged eight passes for 115 yards, a new record for an Irish tight end.

Notre Dame rebounded with a tough 23-15 win over visiting Stanford, its 800th career win. The Cardinal nursed a 9-3 lead in the third quarter, but Ryan Grant ended a long drive with a short TD run for a slim lead. He did it again after a bobbled Stanford punt attempt in the fourth quarter.

The traditional sinking of the Navy took place in Giants Stadium, with a 27-9 workmanlike win. Navy never found the key to stopping Ryan Grant, who ran for 114 yards and two scores.

Boston College continued its role as a chief nemesis with a 24-23 win under the Dome. The Irish had cracked the top 25, but it was short-lived. BC won in the final minute with a 54-yard TD pass. BC's 383 yards passing was more than the total yardage managed by Notre Dame.

Once more, Willingham's players rebounded from a terrible loss to cop a win against a tough opponent— Tennessee this time—17-13, to become bowl eligible. The Vols had a 10-7 lead when Irish linebacker Mike Goolsby snagged an errant pass and ploughed 26 yards for a TD in the third quarter. Tacking on a late field goal capped the win.

That was the high water mark of the season. Pittsburgh won a 41-38 slugfest at ND, with Pitt QB Tyler Palko racking up five TD passes for the first time ever in an Irish home game. USC continued its mastery with a 41-10 rout in LA. Willingham was summarily released three days after ND lost the third straight game to the Trojans by 31 points.

Interim head coach Kent Baer led the Irish in the 2004 Insight Bowl, but Oregon State looked like the team that beat ND in the Fiesta Bowl several years earlier, winning handily 38-21 as Derek Anderson threw the pill for 358 yards. It was the seventh consecutive bowl loss for ND.

Brady Quinn established a new season standard as the Irish QB: he completed 191 passes in 353 attempts, with 10 interceptions but 17 TDs.

2004 record: 6-6 (.500)
Record to date: 802-263-42 (.743)

2005

Very few Irish fans had been supportive of Willingham, who seemed rigid and aloof. Rumors had the school wooing Urban Meyer, a former assistant coach under the Dome, but he chose to leave Utah for Florida. Irish AD Kevin White turned to the NFL to nab the Patriots' offensive coordinator, Charlie Weis, luring him with a six-year contract. Weis brought pro style savvy and four Super Bowl rings, one with the Giants and three with the Pats. A '78 ND grad, Weis was a bit of a throwback—to the times when the Irish brought in a new head coach with no collegiate head coaching experience. There were two notables in this regard: Terry Brennan and Gerry Faust, both of whom had less than illustrious overall records. Nevertheless, the four gleaming rings made Irish eyes twinkle more than they worried about head coaching background.

Weis found an offense with ten returning players, including pro prospect Brady Quinn at QB. The defense, however, was stripped of seven starters, so this team would have to score in bunches and hang on for dear life.

That's what happened in the opener—a 42-21 win over Pitt on the road. Weis's offense had the Pitt DBs in deep trouble for the whole game, with an impressive 28 points scored in the second quarter. Quinn hit Jeff Samardzija with a 19-yard TD in that outburst, after hitting a first quarter 51-yard TD pass to Darius Walker. Notre Dame stayed on the road at the Big House in Michigan and showed some mettle with a nip and tuck 17-10 win over this major rival, ranked #3. The Irish defense stepped up, stopping Michigan on several crucial fourth-down plays, plus Tom Zbikowski's interception at the one-yard line to snuff a long Wolverine drive. With the win, ND reached #12 in the rankings. It was the first win for ND in Ann Arbor since Holtz had done it in '93, and Weis joined the immortal Rockne as the only head coach to start a career with two road wins.

Michigan State had pretty much been having its way with Notre Dame, with six wins in the last eight meetings, including four wins at Notre Dame. The trend continued with a shoot-out 44-41 overtime

MSU win. The Irish at one point were being drubbed 38-17, but they managed to tie it up at 38-38. In the overtime period, ND settled for a field goal, but the Spartans countered with a 19-yard TD pitch for the win. Quinn looked good with five TD passes, but the salt was in the wound.

Montana Mazurkiewicz was dying of an inoperable brain tumor. Weis heard of the ten-year-old child's plight and visited him at home before the Irish played Washington and Ty Willingham in Seattle. He promised the child that he could call the first play. "Pass right." So, Weis had a problem when the Irish recovered a Husky fumble on their own one-yard line in the first quarter. The next play would be their first play. What to do? Pass right…Quinn hit TE Fasano for a 13-yard gain, and the Irish had kept Weis's promise. Unfortunately, young Montana had died the day before. ND went on to prevail against their former coach with a 36-17 win.

Brady Quinn breaks out of the pocket in 2005 USC game. (Reproduced courtesy of the University of Notre Dame Athletic Media Relations Office.)

Weis led the team to their fourth road win, a 49-28 victory over Purdue. Quinn's maturing process as a QB showed with two telling facts: he tied ND's Heisman winner from '64, John Huarte, by throwing for TDs in ten straight games, and he went in the books as the first Irish QB to pass for 300+ yards in three consecutive games.

Weis was next faced with the problem that had haunted Irish coaches since 1926—how to beat USC. The Trojans had Matt Leinart, a Heisman winner, and Reggie Bush, to go with the usual NFL suspects. It was a see-saw affair, with ND holding slim leads twice. The Trojans broke Irish hearts with mere seconds left in the game when Reggie Bush pushed Leinart into the end zone for a TD and a 34-31 "win." Five years later, the Trojans had to vacate their '05 season wins due to a long-suspected scandal involving the same Reggie Bush.

ND rebounded convincingly with a 49-23 rampage against BYU, with Quinn firing six TD passes, three to Maurice Stovall. The win was capped by a Zbikowski interception and 88-yard TD scamper. Tennessee crumbled next, 41-21, with Quinn hitting two TD passes within a five-play sequence in the first quarter, then breaking a 21-21 tie in the fourth quarter with another TD pass, matched by yet another Zbikowski interception and TD return. Next, Navy fell for the

42nd consecutive time (an NCAA record), 42-21, with Quinn firing four TD passes and running his record to 14 straight games. Quinn kept up his assault on the record books with two more TD passes in a 34-10 win over Syracuse, and ND climbed to #6 in the country.

The Irish capped their regular season with a cliff-hanging 38-31 win over Stanford. It started out well enough, with an 80-yard TD pass from Quinn to Samardzija. Having served notice, the Irish seemed to rest on their laurels and needed a late six-yard TD run by Walker, capped by a two-point Walker run on a nifty direct snap play.

Notre Dame accepted a Fiesta Bowl invitation to play a loaded Ohio State team. Speed kills, and that's what Ted Ginn did to the Irish with a 56-yard TD reception and run to tie the game early on. The Irish played fairly well, but the Buckeyes prevailed 34-20, scoring a 60-yard TD on the last play of the game to wrap it up.

The 2005 season saw the Irish hit the record books with nearly four dozen new all-time records. Most notable: Quinn's 32 TD passes, Samardzija's 15 TD grabs, Walker's 43 receptions by a running back, and most points—440.

2005 record: 9-3 (.750)
Record to date: 811-266-42 (.743)

2006

The 2005 season would seem to be a hard act to follow. In his first season, Weis had made a major impact on the Notre Dame record book. Nevertheless, expectations were high—so high, indeed, that the Irish found themselves ranked #3. Maybe the thin air at that height reduced the team's effectiveness when they met unranked Georgia Tech. Notre Dame pulled it out with a field goal, a Brady Quinn run for a TD and a Darius Walker scamper for another TD to make the final score 17-10. Quinn's TD passing streak ended at 22 games.

Penn State looked to be better than Tech, but they suffered a 41-17 rout, with ND building a 20-0 halftime lead. Quinn fired three TD passes—to Samardzija, McKnight, and Walker. Zbikowski hauled in a fumble and rumbled for a TD, and

TE John Carlson running loose in the Spartan secondary. (Reproduced courtesy of the University of Notre Dame Athletic Media Relations Office.)

Jeff Samardzija escapes from a UCLA defender in Irish win. (Reproduced courtesy of the University of Notre Dame Athletic Media Relations Office.)

Travis Thomas legged in another one.

Michigan, however, was a different matter, as they dumped the #2 Irish 47-21, basically putting a severe chill on the rest of what had been a promising season. The Irish managed a 7-7 tie, but then the roof fell in as Michigan piled on 27 unanswered points until just before the half when Quinn hit a short pass for a TD. ND was blanked in the third quarter and Quinn tossed another TD, but the Wolverines kept the scoring juggernaut going for the final score.

A week later, the Irish met the Spartans in E. Lansing. They followed the Wolverine script by obligingly falling behind 31-14 at the half. It did not look good, but crazy things happen in football. The Irish could have folded, but they didn't. Quinn fired five TD passes in the game and DB Terrail Lambert picked off two Spartan passes, one for a TD, as ND nipped MSU 40-37.

Undefeated Purdue brought a gaudy offense to ND to meet the 12th-ranked Irish. The two teams would rack up 955 total yards, with 713 aerial yards. Boilermaker WR Selwyn Lymon snagged passes from Curtis Painter, good for a record 238 yards. Quinn fired two TD passes to McKnight, and Samardzija ran a fake for a field goal to go with rushing TDs by Walker and George West for the 35-21 win.

The Irish kept up their winning ways with a 31-10 workmanlike victory over Stanford. Quinn hit three TD passes—to Samardzija, McKnight and TE John Carlson.

UCLA was a different matter, leading for most of the game, keeping the Irish offense throttled. But they made the mistake of giving the ball to Quinn with :55 seconds left. He capped a great comeback with a TD pass to Samardzija, who hauled in the pass and juked around for the last 30 yards, absorbing a glancing hit by a safety before high-stepping into the end zone for the win.

Navy didn't have enough horses to stop Brady Quinn as the 11th-ranked Irish kept racking up TD passes, yardage, and points, crafting a 38-14 win. Quinn fired three more TD passes and racked up 296 yards through the air. He kept up the pace with four TD passes against North Carolina, while accumulating 346 yards through the air. Air Force was the next victim as Quinn hit yet another four TD passes in a 39-17 rout. The Irish made it a clean sweep of the service academies with a 41-9 clobbering of Army. Quinn had a TD pass to Samardzija and two to McKnight.

Arch-nemesis USC, sans two Heisman winners, put a convincing stop to ND's winning streak with a 44-24 win in LA. The Trojans had too many weapons on offense and nullified the hot hand Quinn had been showing, although he did pass for two TDs and scrambled for a 59-yard gain. In sum, the score showed which team had greater depth and talent. The Irish were not yet at the peak of the college game, as evidenced by their fifth straight loss to USC.

The disturbing trend continued with a 41-14 blow-out Sugar Bowl loss to LSU and their mammoth QB, Jamarcus Russell, who seemed to spend the evening toying with the Irish defenders. Played in Atlanta due to the hurricane damage to the Superdome, the Irish managed to make it a 14-14 tie in the second quarter, as Quinn hit two TD passes, but Russell ran for a TD, passed for two more, and LSU added two field goals for the final score. It was ND's ninth consecutive bowl loss. National respectability seemed a distant hope after giving up 82 points in important games on the national stage.

2006 record: 10-3 (.769)
Record to date: 821-269-42 (.743)

2007

Going into Weis's third season, there were plenty of question marks. He no longer had an experienced QB, and some excellent receivers were also gone. Nevertheless, it seemed that the Irish were gaining some momentum. No one expected that the 2007 season would turn into a nightmare.

The Irish never came out of the gates to start the season; indeed, they stumbled to five consecutive losses, an all-time record of ugliness that may never be surpassed. They would finish the dreary season with nine total losses—another all-time record.

Georgia Tech provided the first home licking with a convincing 33-3 pasting. The Irish looked unsure of some assignments and had to try to adjust to Tech's constant blitzes. ND's net rushing yards—eight—suggested the level of futility.. Of course, that will happen when the QBs are being sacked nine times.

Penn State continued the drought with a 31-10 character lesson. Weis started a freshman QB, Jimmy Clausen, who may not have completely recovered from elbow surgery—a measure of the desperation that was setting in. ND managed to snag an early lead with a 73-yard interception return by Darrin Walls. Then the defense gave up 31 points while the offense managed a field goal. Tech had surrendered eight yards rushing; Penn State held ND to zip on the ground; Clausen was sacked six times.

Michigan shut out the Irish 38-0. The ground game for the Irish exploded for six net yards; the porous line gave up eight more sacks.

Michigan State let the Irish have a 7-0 lead, then they scored 17 unanswered points on the way to a 31-14 win under the Dome. RB James Aldridge did manage to gain 104 yards on 18 carries, and the line gave up only four sacks. Overall—some improvement, but the long-term outlook was not looking very bright.

Purdue raced to a 23-0 lead before ND scored on a

Clausen pass to TE John Carlson. Clausen was beginning to show signs of wear and tear; Evan Sharpley subbed for him, and Golden Tate snagged a TD pass from him. The early Purdue lead held up for a 33-19 win.

Somebody had to do something; someone had to step up. It turned out to be linebacker Maurice Crum, who put in the game of his life: two interceptions, two recovered fumbles (one for a TD), one forced fumble, seven tackles, a sack, and general havoc as the Irish prevailed over UCLA 25-6 in the Rose Bowl. Crum had to do it because the Irish offense managed only 46 yards rushing and 96 yards passing.

Boston College brought the Irish back to losing reality with a 27-14 win at Notre Dame. Half of ND's scoring came from yet another linebacker, Brian Smith, who intercepted Matt Ryan and rumbled 25 yards for a TD. The other score came on a Sharpley pass to Robby Paris.

USC drilled the Irish 38-0, the kind of loss that turns Irish fans and alums into very harsh critics as it happened right under their home eyes. The Trojans held the Irish to 48 yards on the grounds while sacking the hapless Sharpley seven times.

ND reached the nadir was reached when Navy recorded a 44-41 victory in three overtimes. The last time Navy beat ND, Roger Staubach was their QB...43 years earlier. The Irish managed 235 yards rushing, far more than their season total at that point. But fans were approaching a catatonic state with ND's fifth loss at

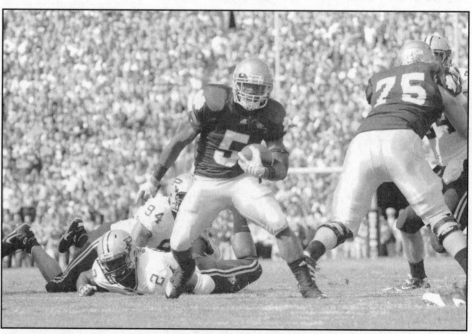

Armando Allen hits a big hole in action against Purdue. (Reproduced courtesy of the University of Notre Dame Athletic Media Relations Office.)

home—for the first time in their football history.

Air Force continued the humiliation (fans by this point were hearing echoes of Faust's four straight losses to AFA in the mid-80s). The final score was 41-24. The Falcons limited the Irish ground game to 58 yards, although Clausen hit three different receivers with TD passes. Unfortunately, he was also sacked six times.

The Irish ended the season with two wins, beating Duke 28-7 and Stanford 21-14. Clausen hit three more TD passes against Duke while generally staying upright. Irish runners added 220 yards, led by Robert Hughes. Stanford played the Irish pretty well, but came up short as the Irish running game jelled, Hughes hitting the century mark again.

So—a totally miserable season for the history books.

2007 record: 3-9 (.250)
Record to date: 824-278-42 (.738)

2008

Things could not become much worse for the Notre Dame football team. Charlie Weis seemed to have lost some of his swagger. No Irish coach had gone from a relatively successful season to a total disaster the following year. So many components that go into a successful team had gone awry…could they be corrected in time to avert yet another implosion? Weis did add defensive coach John Tenuta, previously at Georgia Tech, a team that had tormented ND with its blitz package.

San Diego State was the first test and the Irish managed a workmanlike 21-13 win, with a David Bruton goal line hit and fumble stopping an Aztec threat. Clausen used the break to throw a 38-yard TD pass to Golden Tate to secure the win and recover from a 13-7 deficit. In the second quarter, Clausen helped unveil a new Irish threat—Michael Floyd, who snagged a 22-yard TD pass. Floyd would prove to be a matchup nightmare for four seasons and eventually break almost all of the school's receiving records. David Grimes also caught a TD pass to put the game out of reach late in the fourth quarter.

Michigan made the short trip to ND but somehow managed to forget how to hang on to the ball, as they lost the ball six times to contribute to their own 35-17 undoing. The Irish put up 21 points in the first quarter,

with Clausen finding Duval Kamara and Golden Tate with TD passes to lead the way. Tate also snagged a Clausen pass good for 60 yards to lead to a rushing TD and a 28-10 lead. Linebacker Brian Smith rounded out the scoring with a fumble recovery and 35-yard TD burst.

The bubble burst with a 23-7 dud at MSU as Spartan RB Javon Ringer ran wild on 39 carries good for 201 yards. The Irish, to the contrary, managed only 16 yards on the ground. Clausen was sacked three times but did manage to locate Floyd for the only Irish score.

Purdue brought the Irish back to their winning ways thus far in 2008, falling 38-21. Armando Allen ran for 134 yards and a TD, DB Robert Blanton tacked on a 47-yard interception TD return. Clausen found WR David Grimes and TE Kyle Rudolph with TD passes.

Notre Dame kept up its momentum with a 28-21 win over Stanford. Clausen threw for 346 yards, with TD flings to Allen, Floyd and Rudolph, and Allen also scooting for a three-yard rushing TD.

At Chapel Hill, ND won the statistics but lost the game, 29-24. The Irish had a chance with seconds to go, but Floyd was ruled to have fumbled near the goal line and the opportunity evaporated. Clausen passed for 383 yards and threw TD passes to Tate and Floyd, to go with an Aldridge TD run as the Irish amassed 472 yards of total offense.

After a bye week, ND flew west to Seattle to meet the winless Huskies and the former Irish head coach, Ty Willingham, coming away with a 33-7 win that showcased some nifty play calling, highlighted by a 21-yard TD run on a reverse by Tate. Floyd opened the scoring with a 51-yard TD catch and run. Aldridge added two TD runs; a couple of field goals capped the scoring.

Pittsburgh put the Irish back in the losing column with a 36-33 win at ND. The Irish had a 17-3 halftime lead but gave up 33 points in the second half, including four field goals in overtime, to account for the loss. Clausen showed a growing command of Weis's complicated offense with three TD passes, two to the emerging Floyd and one to speedster Tate, but the inability to score a TD in overtime doomed the effort.

The promising season went retrograde with a home shutout loss to Boston College, 17-0. The Irish were not totally incompetent, but Clausen lost four passes to INTs, one for a 76-yard TD return. Killing one third of the drives that way pretty much insures the chances for a loss.

Fortunately, Navy was on the schedule to right the ship as the Irish won a close game in Baltimore, 27-21. A blocked punt led to an early TD by Toryan Smith, the running backs chipped in with two TDs on the ground, and special teams banged in two field goals. Clausen dinked and dunked on short passes, but it was consecutive onside kicks that Navy recovered in the closing moments that nearly led to an upset. The Irish defense stepped up after the second one, and Navy's rather basic pass offense couldn't pull it off.

Syracuse came to ND with eight losses...and left the stadium with eight losses. Notre Dame thus lost a home game for the first time to a team with that many losses, 24-23. The Irish looked flat and dispirited—or were looking beyond Syracuse to USC. To make it all the more galling, the Syracuse QB was the son of the great Irish hoopster, Adrian Dantley. Clausen tossed two TD passes to Golden Tate, to go with three Irish field goals, but Syracuse scored twice in the fourth quarter to give the Irish their fifth loss.

USC then made it a Notre Dame game with six losses, as they blasted ND 38-3—shades of the Willingham blowouts. The Irish looked like the 2007 edition, with a mere four first downs, and underwhelming figures for rushing and passing yardage—51 and 40 respectively. Twelve games after the most losses in a single season, the Irish looked even worse than they had a year

earlier. The Irish defense managed to get in the Trojans way just enough to allow 449 total USC yards.

Redemption? It's hard to tell if a blowout 49-21 win over Hawaii salved any wounds. The Irish frolicked for once, looking speedy and going deep at will. Golden Tate ran routes basically unhindered, hauling in TD passes covering 69, 18, and 40 yards, as he racked up 177 yards alone. Armando Allen finished it off with a scintillating 96-yard kickoff return to close the Hawaii Bowl's scoring. Weis called it a "great step forward" towards the team's 2009 season. He had to say something, as the 15 losses in the '07 and '08 seasons were the most ever for the sons of Ireland.

Time would tell if Weis was right.

2008 record: 7-6 (.538)
Record to date: 831-284-42 (.736)

2009

A 7-6 record in 2008, even though it was "better" than the 2007 disaster, was not the kind of season that Irish alumni, fans, players or coaches could deem as satisfactory. The Weis regime was under very close scrutiny. His NFL background was seen as both a

QB Jimmy Clausen has his receiver in his sights. (Reproduced courtesy of the University of Notre Dame Athletic Media Relations Office.)

strength in recruiting and play calling as well as a weakness in terms of conducting practices and helping players improve over their years of eligibility.

The season opener was against Nevada. Jimmy Clausen started off where he had finished in the Bowl game, firing five TD passes, with three bombs to Michael Floyd, including strikes covering 70 and 88 yards. Kyle Rudolph snagged another TD pass, and Armando Allen slammed in from the one-yard line for a rushing TD. The Irish defense kept the Nevada pistol formation in check, unloaded, throughout. It was the first shutout for Weis and seemed to validate the #23 national ranking.

Michigan was a different matter. In spite of more solid QB play by Clausen, who tossed three TD passes and accumulated 336 yards through the air, the Wolverines prevailed in a 38-34 shootout, the victory clinched when Weis called for passes on the final Irish possession, both incomplete, giving Michigan the ball with plenty of time for a winning drive. A Michigan TD pass with 11 seconds on the clock finished the job. With the loss, ND fell out of the national ranking scene.

Lou Holtz was the head coach for ND the last time ND defeated MSU at home—in 1993. It had been sheer torment since then. The Irish reversed the lamentable trend with a 33-30 win that took away some of the Michigan sting. ND jumped out to a 13-3 first quarter lead, then saw it melt as MSU scored twice for a 17-16 halftime lead. Michael Floyd went down with a broken clavicle after catching two passes; Clausen suffered a turf toe injury on a sack, but the Irish didn't throw in the towel. In the third quarter, DE Ethan Johnson blocked a PAT, a play that would be crucial in the waning moments. The Irish got back into the lead on a TD pass from the five-yard line by RB Armando Allen to Robby Paris. Clausen gimped around long enough to fire a 33-yard TD pass to Tate in the closing moments for the late lead, one that held up when Kyle McCarthy intercepted a Spartan pass with less than a minute to go.

Notre Dame maintained its momentum with a road win at Purdue, another last-second squeaker, 24-21. Clausen played with his injured toe and the offense lacked the injured Floyd, so the ground game picked up the slack. Robert Hughes and Golden Tate both had TD runs to go with a field goal and a TD pass to Rudolph in the closing seconds.

A team that had never experienced victory over the Irish in seven tries visited the Dome and lost again, but took it to overtime—the Washington Huskies finally bowing 37-30. It wasn't pretty, as a much tougher Washington defense stuffed Irish drives well enough that Irish kicker Nick Tausch booted five field goals. Clausen had his best day for passing yardage, firing away for 422 yards, with Golden Tate as a prime target with nine catches for a PR 244 yards, one a 67-yard TD and another a 77-yard gain that led to a field goal. Robert Hughes powered in from the one-yard line in OT for the winning margin.

Hopes had been high when Weis was hired that he would be able to outwit the USC coaches and juggernaut; he started well enough but had no wins while the losses were becoming more alarming, back to the big margins that had infuriated Irish fans in the Willingham years. The 6th-ranked Trojans did it again, tripping up the Irish lads 34-27, a respectable score, not a blowout by any means, but it was on home turf and might just have been the beginning of the end for Weis. Clausen played well, throwing two TD passes to Tate and running for one to go with a Hughes rushing TD. The Irish defense, however, leaked for 501 total USC yards.

Charlie Weis mulling over the next play call. (Reproduced courtesy of the University of Notre Dame Athletic Media Relations Office.)

The Irish overcame their disappointment to snag a 20-16 win over nemesis Boston College. Clausen and Tate hooked up for two TDs, and two field goals completed the scoring for ND. Kyle McCarthy snagged two of ND's interceptions to help keep BC's offense frustrated.

Bad memories of the USC loss seemed to be gone as the team blasted Washington State 40-14 in San Antonio, racking up nearly 600 yards of total offense while the Cougars' defenders seemed confused and inefficient. Clausen clicked for 22 completions in 27 throws; Tate scored twice, once with a 50-yard reception. Robert Hughes rumbled for 131 yards.

Then the bottom fell out of the season. Standing at 6-2, the Irish went into a tailspin with four consecutive losses. The month-long insult started with a 23-21 home loss to Navy, an unranked team prevailing over the #19-ranked Irish, a feat ND had not suffered since 1936. The Midshipmen did it their way, with 56 rushing plays and only three pass attempts. A safety with 1:00 left in the game put it out of touch, although Clausen found Tate with a 31-yard TD pass 24 seconds later.

Pitt put up a balanced attack for a 27-22 win on their home turf. They held ND to a field goal going into the fourth quarter, then Tate exploded for an 18-yard TD pass and an 87-yard TD punt return, but it wasn't enough.

Connecticut was the next victor, 33-30 in overtime. Clausen sneaked in for a short TD and clicked with Tate and Floyd for scoring passes, but the Huskies stayed close and jolted in a four-yard TD run in OT to earn the win.

Stanford snapped a seven-game losing streak to ND with a 45-38 victory in the Bay area. The Irish held a 24-20 halftime lead, but surrendered 18 points in a frenetic fourth quarter. Stanford controlled the game with 48 rushes, highlighting the strength and speed of massive Toby Gerhart, who thundered for three TD runs and 205 yards on 29 carries.

Charlie Weis was allegedly fired two days later, a Notre Dame grad who as a student complained to Pres. Hesburgh about Dan Devine's coaching, who had won 44 games in his first five years leading the team and who won at .764 clip. Weis managed 35 wins for a .565 winning percentage, far below the school's historical winning rate.

2009 record: 6-6 (.500)
Record to date: 837-290-42 (.733)

2010-2011

2010

For the third time in recent Notre Dame history, the football program under Weis had been led by a coach who entered the job with no college coaching experience. All ended unsatisfactorily (Brennan, Faust, Weis). Rather than repeat the mistake, AD Jack Swarbrick turned to the college ranks and plucked Cincinnati's Brian Kelly who had accumulated a sterling record in his prior assignments, winning three-fourths of his games, with 171 wins in college football against 56 losses. Kelly championed a version of the spread offense and had run up some gaudy figures at Cincinnati. Not surprisingly, Irish hopes rose, even though the program would have its fourth coach in little more than ten years.

The naysayers had plenty of ammunition: playing in the upper Midwest left much to be desired; recruiting the primary talent zones would be a difficult

Notre Dame's 25th head coach, Brian Kelly. (Reproduced courtesy of the University of Notre Dame Athletic Media Relations Office.)

proposition; more than twenty years since its last national championship, the luster normally associated with the ND program had dimmed somewhat.

Kelly attacked the recruiting with vigor, ingratiated himself across the campus, and went about installing a version of the spread offense. The main issue is that the cupboard was almost bare at the QB position. He had one upperclassman, Dayne Crist, who had seen some game action under Weis, but Jimmy Clausen had moved on to the NFL. Eventually, Kelly settled on freshman Tommy Rees, trusting to the youngster's ability to learn on the job. Full installation of the spread offense would take a while longer.

Purdue was Kelly's first opponent, and Crist led the team to a 23-12 win. T.J. Jones caught a short TD pass from Crist, Armando Allen ran one in from 22 yards out, and David Ruffer booted three field goals, while the Irish defense kept Purdue in check most of the game.

Michigan was next, and their QB Denard Robinson, who eschews tying his shoelaces, ran wild against a hapless Irish defense, passing for 244 yards but rushing for a staggering 258 yards, more than 100 yards beyond the Irish total. His last two yards, good for a TD, won the game with 27 seconds remaining. Crist played well enough, including overcoming an early injury to find TE Kyle Rudolph open for a 95-yard TD catch and run. Kelly also tried Tommy Rees and Nate Montana at QB, but decided to stick with Crist. Robinson's heroics insured the Wolverines' 28-24 win.

The Irish made the short trip to E. Lansing only to find themselves on the losing side of a 34-31 OT loss. So, after three games, things did not look much different compared to recent seasons, with the big Michigan schools having their way with Notre Dame. Still, the Irish had a chance, but the Spartans pulled off a great fake field goal play in OT to throw a 29-yard TD pass for the win. Crist had a good game, hitting 32 passes for 369 yards and four TDs, two to Floyd, one each to Rudolph and Theo Riddick.

Things got worse for the new coach when Stanford and Andrew Luck romped over ND 37-14 in yet another disappointing home loss. Luck didn't do it all be himself; Owen Marecic played both sides of the ball at fullback and linebacker and had the pleasure of scoring a TD each way within a 13- second span in the fourth quarter—

one on a one-yard burst, the next with a 20-yard TD interception. Marecic also helped stuff ND's running game, as the Irish managed only 44 yards on 23 carries, while giving up three sacks.

The Irish had to turn it around and started the road back with a 31-13 win at Boston College. Crist led the team to three first-quarter TDs with a seven-yard run and passes to Rudolph and Riddick. BC tacked on a TD and two field goals, but the Irish kicked their own three-pointer and Armando Allen powered in for a short TD.

Crist continued his good work and ND showed a flashy, speedy spread offense—for half of the 23-17 win over Pittsburgh. Once again, he ran for a TD and passed for another, while also completing 12 straight passes at one point. Kicker David Ruffer added three field goals and took his streak to 16 consecutive FGs.

Kelly got the team to be over the .500 mark with a convincing 44-20 beat down of W. Michigan. Floyd

Michael Floyd, the all-time Irish receiver, where opponents don't want to see him—wide open. (Reproduced courtesy of the University of Notre Dame Athletic Media Relations Office.)

and Crist hooked up for two TDs—80 yards and two yards; Floyd added another, 32 yards, on a pass from John Goodman. Crist added a TD run, another TD pass to TE Tyler Eifert, and freshman Cierre Wood scooted for a 39-yard score.

Unbelievably, Navy won another game against the Irish. It's as if ND forgot how it won more than 40 straight games against a team that seldom came close to its own talent level. This time, the sailors beat the Irish 35-17. They did it with 60 runs for 367 yards, a team record v. ND, to go with two interceptions of Crist. A frustrated Kelly put in freshman QB Tommy Rees. Back to the drawing board.

The tragic death of a student videographer in a windstorm at practice after the Navy loss certainly added to the team's general malaise; Tulsa then capped off the terrible week with an upset victory, 28-27. Crist was injured early and Kelly went with Rees, who had a chance to win the game but threw an interception, his third of the game, in the end zone to lose the opportunity. To his credit, Rees did fire four TD passes, two to Floyd and two to Wood. A blocked PAT was the point difference in the loss.

Utah, 15th ranked, came to ND and lost to the unranked Irish 28-3. Robert Blanton sped six yards with a blocked punt, and Rees threw three TD passes, one to Floyd and two to Duval Kamara, in his first career start.

ND crept back over the .500 level again with a 27-3 victory over Army at Yankee Stadium. Robert Hughes slammed for a one-yard TD, Eifert hauled in a 31-yard TD pass from Rees, Darrin Walls burned in from 42 yards out with an INT, and Ruffer booted two FGs. The Irish defense held Army to 39 yards in passing.

Willingham and Weis had not been able to beat USC during their abbreviated tenures, but Kelly got the job done in his first outing, as ND snagged a close one, 20-16. Rees almost handed the game to the Trojans with three INTs but managed to keep his team alive hitting 20 of 32 passes with twin 1-yard TD flicks to Floyd and Kamara in the second quarter. Hughes bulled in for the game's last score from the five, and Harrison Smith erased budding Trojan hopes with a timely goal line INT with :36 left in the game.

Notre Dame agreed to meet an old foe, Miami, in the Sun Bowl and dispatched the 'Canes 33-17. The Irish scored the game's first three TDs, two on Rees flings to Floyd, then a Cierre Wood TD run. Two kickers scored the remaining Irish points to offset Miami's late scoring, but their offense was stymied primarily by Harrison Smith's three INTs.

The inaugural season for Brian Kelly was not an unqualified success; he wasn't able to take down the Michigan teams. The team lost to two teams that had little right to expect wins, Navy and Tulsa. The win over USC was satisfying, but it came against a team in flux. The Kelly version of the spread offense may not have had a fair trial; the Irish turf is not designed for a track meet, and it was obvious that Kelly did not have the full complement of personnel who best operate a spread offense. Irish eyes may not have been totally smiling, but a little bit of a twinkle could be detected.

**2010 record: 8-5 (.615)
Record to date: 845-296-42 (.732)**

Kyle Rudolph steaming for a long gain against an absent Michigan defense. (Reproduced courtesy of the University of Notre Dame Athletic Media Relations Office.)

2011

That twinkle did not last long, however. The 2011 Irish, with Michael Floyd back to terrify opposing defenses on his way to all-time receiving records, with Tommy Rees emerging as a QB starter, and Manti Te'O and Harrison Smith hammering opposing offenses, looked to do better than Kelly's first team. Having said that, however, the 2011 Irish stumbled coming out of the gate, losing a shocker to Skip Holtz and South Florida in the home opener, and then yet another last-minute nail-biter to Michigan on the road.

USF opened up a 16-0 first-half lead, lowlighted by a 96-yard fumble recovery and TD return when Jonas Gray lost the ball to end an early Irish drive. Seemingly in shock, the Irish surrendered three field goals before Floyd snagged a 24-yard TD pass from Rees. USF's only TD scored by their offense came on two-yard run, then ND fought back valiantly with a Cierre Wood TD burst and another Floyd TD reception. Three Irish INTs doomed other drives in the 23-20 loss.

Michigan waited until the last two seconds of the next game to secure a 35-30 win in the Big House. Notre Dame came out hot, scoring twice in the first quarter for a 14-0 lead, but Michigan had Denard Robinson, still playing with untied cleats. He had romped over, around, and through the Irish for 502 total yards in 2010; this time, ND obliged him with another 446 total yards, for a two-game grand total of 948 total yards. Robinson fired back with a 43-yard TD pass. ND kept plugging away, with a Ruffer field goal and a 15-yard TD pass from Rees to T. J. Jones. Michigan bombed away in the fourth quarter with three TDs, one on the ground by Robinson and another with his passing. With :30 left in the game, Rees completed a nifty drive by finding Riddick with a 29-yard TD throw. The thirty seconds proved to be too long; Robinson put together three plays for the 80 necessary yards, hitting a receiver with a 16-yard TD pass at the two-second mark

to ruin ND's high hopes.

Part of the state of Michigan jinx was put to rest a week later when ND defeated MSU 31-13. ND jumped out to 14-3 first quarter lead, with a stunning 89-yard TD kickoff return by George Atkinson III. Cierre Wood had TD bursts of 22 yards and six yards, Rees flicked a 26-yard TD pass to T. J. Jones, and Ruffer chipped in with a FG.

The Irish next pulled out a squeaker over Pitt, 15-12. Jonas Gray redeemed his earlier fumble against USF with a 79-yard rumble for a TD, and Rees hooked up with Eifert with a six-yard TD toss followed by a two-point conversion pass also to Eifert.

Purdue offered little resistance on their home turf as ND prevailed 38-10 to raise the season record above .500. Cierre Wood seemed unstoppable, with 191 yards gained rushing to go with Gray's 94 yards. Wood busted loose for a 55-yard TD run after Floyd had opened the scoring with a 35-yard scoring pass. Gray scored on a short run, and Eifert and Jones also hauled in scoring passes from Rees.

Air Force offered even less resistance as ND romped at home 59-33, amassing 560 yards of total offense, averaging over eight yards per play. Rees found four different receivers with TD passes and four Irish runners rushed for scores. Sub QB Andrew Hendrix tallied a long run to show that he could be a serious threat in the spread offense.

Once again, USC burst the momentum bubble, beating ND at the Dome 31-17. They raced to a 17-0

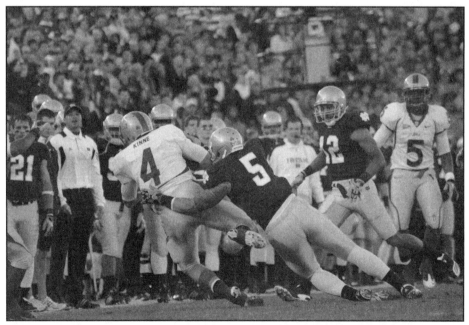

Leader of the Irish defense, Manti Te'O stops a scrambling QB. (Reproduced courtesy of the University of Notre Dame Athletic Media Relations Office.)

lead before Atkinson struck with a 96-yard kickoff return for a TD. The USC QB hit three TD passes and a Trojan ran back a recovered fumble 80 yards for a TD. Kelly was beginning to realize what it would take for his team to win the trifecta—victories over Michigan, Michigan State, and USC in the same season. That trick had not been done in many years, and the Irish will not be fully back in the national picture until they pull it off.

The loss to USC did not put the team into yet another tailspin. Instead, they upended Navy with an impressive 56-14 romp. Cierre Wood and Jonas Gray slammed in for rushing TDs, Floyd contributed one more on the ground and another with a 56-yard TD pass from Rees, and Atkinson finished off the scoring gala with a one-yard run. ND only had to punt one time.

Wake Forest put up a better fight, but eventually bowed in defeat, 24-17. The game was played close to the vest offensively, with the Irish getting just enough scoring to do the job: a 44-yard Ruffer FG, Rees passes to Eifert and Floyd for TDs, and a Jonas Gray TD burst.

Maryland toppled next, 45-21. Rees had a great day, hitting 30 of 38 passes for 296 yards, hitting his favorite targets, Floyd and Eifert, with TD passes. The Irish ground game clicked for 212 yards and 4 TDs. CB Lo Wood picked off a Maryland pass and jetted 57 yards to add to the rout.

Fourth-ranked Stanford loomed, but Boston College was next, and ND seemed to have overlooked the Eagles, stumbling around enough, however, to pull off a 16-14 win. Jonas Gray started the scoring with a 26-yard TD run, and Ruffer banged in three FGs. The Irish defense held the Eagles to 80 yards rushing and contained them when the game was on the line in the fourth quarter.

That was not the case with Andrew Luck, as the All-American fired four TD passes in a 28-14 win. Kelly benched Rees after an INT and a fumble halfway into the game and thrust Hendrix into the maelstrom. Hendrix put together one good drive, finding Floyd with a six-yard TD pass, and zipped in for the other Irish TD. Floyd and Eifert both put themselves in the Irish record books with their season receptions. But watching Luck in the same game as the Irish QBs was enough to make Notre Dame fans hope for major improvements in their team's QB play.

The Champs Sports Bowl game against Florida State bookended the season for Notre Dame with losses to teams from Florida, in this case an 18-14 loss suffered as ND lost a 14-0 second-half lead. The Irish passing game, even with a TD reception by Floyd, never hit its full stride, with only 19 completions in 35 throws by Rees and Hendrix. Floyd became a non-factor after an upper body injury in the third quarter. Zeke Motta dashed 29 yards with a recovered fumble for ND's first score. The defense worked hard for five sacks, but it wasn't enough to stop the Seminoles in the second half. Basically, the Irish offense went stagnant at the wrong time. Kelly's second Irish team thus brought in an identical 8-5 record as his first team—and left as many questions and concerns as had that first edition.

2011 record: 8-5 (.615)
Record to date: 853-301-42 (.730)

CHAPTER FIVE 5

FIGHTING IRISH PLAYER ROSTER

From 1887 to 2003, Notre Dame played 1,083 games of football, and some 2,500 players represented the university on the gridiron, although many more may have aspired to play. Memories of the vast majority of those who played for Notre Dame are somewhat vague, obscured—or enlarged in some cases—by time and distance. Perhaps the young man labored in the anonymity of the interior line, or played when records were kept haphazardly. As recently as 1950, at the height of the Leahy years, Ed Flynn made the team and appears to have played—but that's all that is known. At one point in the lifetime of this project, I had envisioned listing all Fighting Irish players, but that was not feasible. Instead, using no particular guidelines other than an abiding interest in Notre Dame football, a sense of its growth and development, and some notion of "what makes a story," roughly 300 players have been selected for inclusion in the roster that follows.

Most of them were heroes in their careers—but not all. There are some surprises. Most had some golden moments in that autumn light of a late afternoon playing football for Notre Dame. A select few knew only golden moments, even when tinged with the little failures that the game manages to propel into the stream of time at a crucial moment. Some men go beyond enjoying golden careers. These men are in the pantheon of American sports: Red Salmon, Knute Rockne, George Gipp, the Horsemen, Moose Krause, Angelo Bertelli, Johnny Lujack, Leon Hart, Johnny Lattner, Paul Hornung, Joe

Theismann, and perhaps Ross Browner, Joe Montana, Allen Pinkett, Tim Brown, Chris Zorich, and Raghib Ismail. All were stunning actors in the drama, both on the gridiron and in life. The brilliant play happens suddenly, unfolds in 10-12 seconds, and is gone. Film and video cannot revive the total moment—Gipp's frenetic playing against destiny, Shakespeare's winning pass to Millner to beat Ohio State in 1935, Lujack's open-field tackle of Blanchard in 1946, Penick's game-winning touchdown run to start the second half of the 1973 USC game, Montana's winning throw in the 1979 Cotton Bowl, or the team defense that beat Miami in 1988. Film, video, and books cannot fully catch the sounds, the sights, the collective emotion, the tension, the mounting hopes or fears, and the breathlessness. We try to stop the golden moment, suspend it, make it linger. But it leaves us ...

What follows involves players from all decades of Fighting Irish football and at all positions. Record-keeping today is an impressive effort, and players in the last few decades have had their careers recorded in exquisite detail. But when it started in 1887, and for many years after that, football was a fad. Who in 1887 could have foreseen what that mayhem would become? So many of the interesting facts and records of players are long gone. A few players still shine through—take a careful look at John Farley, for instance. Enough said. Here come the Irish ...

ALLAN, DENNY. 1968-1969-1970; HB; 5'11", 188; Ashtabula, OH. Two-year starter as RHB in 1969 and 1970. Teamed with Theismann for good outside quickness and excellent receiving skills. In 1968, made 33 runs for 105 yards and three TDs, caught seven passes for 93 yards and one TD, and returned seven kickoffs 183 yards. In 1969, had 148 carries for 612 yards and nine TDs, caught 11 passes for 199 yards, and returned 10 kickoffs for 185 yards. In 1970, had 111 carries for 401 yards and seven TDs, and caught 11 passes for 166 yards and one TD. For his career, had 292 runs for 1,118 yards and 19 TDs, caught 29 passes for 458 yards and two TDs, and returned 17 kickoffs 368 yards for a total of 1,944 yards.

ALLEN, ARMANDO. 2007-2008-2009-2010. RB, 5'10", 205. Opa Locka, FL. Speedy, multi-talented RB for Weis's last three teams and Kelly's inaugural Irish team. Could handle virtually any offensive assignment: KO returns, punts, rushing, receiving, passing. After four years, he stood 5th overall in Irish annals for all-purpose production, with 4,360 yards and 12 TDs. In 2007, started four games, rushing 86 times for 348 yards, catching 24 passes for 124 yards and one TD, returning 33 KOs 704 yards, for 1,176 yards on 143 attempts. As a sophomore in 2008, led the Irish ground game with 585 yards on 134 carries good for three TDs, contributing 50 pass receptions for 355 yards and two more TDs, with 21 KO returns for 543 yards, including a 96-yard TD return against Hawaii, and 66 yards on punt returns for a season total of 1,549 yards and six TDs. In 2009, saw action in only eight games but still led the team in rushing with 697 yards on 86 carries good for three TDs, snagged 28 passes for 217 yards, and completed one pass for a 5-yard TD. For the year, accumulated 919 yards and scored three TDs. In his senior campaign and in a new system under Kelly, played in eight games and rushed for 534 yards on 107 carries, scoring two TDs. He caught 17 passes for 138 yards, completed one pass for three yards, and returned two punts 47 yards.

ALM, JEFF. 1986-1987-1988-1989; DT; 6'7", 270; Orland Park, IL. Excellent DT for the first four Holtz teams, a key member of the stifling defense featured by the 1988 national champs. Great pass rusher, excellent pursuer, and tremendous obstacle for QBs. Teamed with Zorich. In 1986, backed up at DT; made four tackles. In 1987, backed up at DT; made five tackles. In 1988, started at DT for the national champs; made 50 tackles, eight for minus-25 yards, caused two fumbles, recovered one fumble, broke up three passes, and made three interceptions (to tie for the team lead) for eight return yards. In 1989, started at DT; made 74 tackles, one sack for minus-four yards and six others for minus-20 yards, caused one fumble, broke up six passes, and had one

Elmer Angsman, who started at fullback for the 1944 Fighting Irish, lost 11 teeth in a game against Navy, but continued to play.

interception for 16 return yards. Made All-American. In his career, made 133 tackles, with one sack for minus-four yards and 14 others for minus-45 yards, caused three fumbles, recovered one fumble, broke up nine passes, and made four interceptions for 24 return yards.

ANDERSON, EDDIE. 1918-1919-1920-1921; E; 5'10", 166; Mason City, IA. Four-year starter at right end; teamed with Gipp on undefeated squads of 1919 and 1920. Good receiver and excellent defensive player. In 1919, made an interception and TD runback in win over Purdue. In 1920, caught a 60-yard pass from Gipp in win over Valparaiso. Had a long reception from Gipp in shutout of Purdue. Scored twice with short passes in win over Northwestern. Scored last TD of season recovering a blocked MAC punt. In 1921, caught three passes from Mohardt in loss to Iowa. Helped beat Purdue by blocking a punt for an Irish TD. Caught four Mohardt passes in win over Indiana. Contributed to win over Nebraska by recovering two fumbles and blocking well for game's only TD. In win over Army, recovered a fumble on their 20 and blocked a field goal try. Scored against Rutgers with an 84-yard pass from Mohardt and recovered a fumble. Caught a 45-yard TD pass in win over Marquette to go with two sacks and two other catches. All-America pick.

ANGSMAN, ELMER. 1943-1944-1945; HB, FB; 6'0", 185; Chicago, IL. Tough, speedy runner during relatively lean years with Leahy gone to war; excellent defensive player. In 1944, started at FB and gained 233 yards on 58 carries. Lost 11 teeth in Navy game but continued to play. In 1945, started at RHB and led backs with 616 yards on 87 carries for seven TDs and seven yards per carry.

ARRINGTON, DICK. 1963-1964-1965; T, G; 5'11", 232; Erie, PA. Started at LT in 1963. Started at RG in 1964. Started at RG and DT in 1965. Tremendous upper-body strength and superb quickness; excellent blocker and also wrestled. In 1963, blocked a Syracuse PAT in close loss. Made 40 tackles for the year. In 1964, was an important member of the offensive line that helped Huarte win the Heisman and nearly went undefeated. In 1965, was a two-way starter even though two-platoon football was back. Made 36 tackles for the year. Consensus All-American.

ASHBAUGH, PETE. 1941-1942-1946-1947; QB, HB, K; 5'9", 175; Youngstown, OH. Known as a great defensive backfield specialist. Fine speed, great hitter. In 1941, had one interception and a 15-yard runback. In 1942, had a 40-yard punt return to the Illini one-yard line in 21-14 win. In 1946, in rout of Iowa made a fumble recovery on the ND eight, an interception plus a 38-yard runback to lead to a TD, and a 32-yard kickoff return. Caught one pass for 28 yards. In 1947, played exclusively as a defensive ace; saw 224 minutes of action.

AZZARO, JOE. 1964-1965-1966-1967; K; 5'11",190; Pittsburgh, PA. Starting kicker on early Parseghian teams. In 1964, booted two PATs and a 30-yard field goal in tough win over Pitt. For the year, made seven PATs and one field goal. In 1966, was an integral part of a great scoring machine. Hit eight straight PATs against Duke. Kicked the field goal that tied MSU 10-10, and missed one by a foot that would have won the game. Made a 38-yard field goal and six of seven PATs in rout of USC. For the year, hit 35 of 38 PATs and four of five field goals for 47 points. In 1967, kicked field goals of

Defensive back Reggie Barnett starred on Parseghian's last three teams, ending his career with an interception against Alabama to guarantee an Irish victory in the 1975 Orange Bowl.

23 and 24 yards in win over Cal. Beat Miami with a 22-yard field goal. For the year, hit 37 of 40 PATs and eight of 10 field goals for 61 points. In his career, kicked 74 PATs, 13 field goals, and scored 113 points.

BACHMAN, CHARLIE. 1914-1915-1916; G, FB; 5'11",187; Chisholm, MN. Rugged, spirited player for Jesse Harper's powerhouse teams in the early years of Notre Dame's emerging national fame. Started at RG in 1914. Started at fullback in 1915. Against Alma, scored on a short run and set up another with a 60-yard sprint. In win over Haskell, shed six tacklers and scored on a 40-yard punt return. In win over Creighton, ran for 89 yards, scored a TD, returned a kickoff 25 yards, and intercepted two passes. Scored a TD in big win over Texas. Led Irish runners with 120 yards in win over Rice. Started at LG in 1916. Named All-American.

BARNETT, REGGIE. 1972-1973-1974; DB; 5'11", 181; Flint, MI. Smart, fast defensive back for Parseghian's last three teams. Key player in 1973 national championship season. Started at RCB in 1972. For the year, made 24 tackles, broke up four passes, recovered one fumble, intercepted two passes for 16 return yards in 274 minutes. Started at LCB in 1973; made 29 tackles, one for minus-two yards, broke up six passes, had two fumble recoveries, and one interception. Started at LCB in 1974. Saved a narrow win over Alabama in Orange Bowl with an interception within game's last two minutes. For the year, made 37 tackles, three for minus-10 yards, led team with nine passes broken up, had one interception. For his career, made 90 tackles, four for minus-12 yards, broke up 19 passes, recovered three fumbles, and made four interceptions.

BARRY, NORM. 1917-1918-1919-1920; HB; 5'10", 170; Chicago, IL. Steady, heady player with the misfortune of playing behind Gipp for most of his career. Excellent blocker. Competed hard with John Mohardt for playing time, to the detriment of opponents. In 1917, ran more than 50 yards for a TD in win over MAC. In 1918, caught a 22-yard TD pass from Gipp in win over Purdue. In 1919, scored one TD in win over Northwestern. In 1920, started at RHB. Tallied two TDs in win over Kalamazoo. Ran for two TDs and caught a TD pass from Gipp in win over Northwestern—Gipp's last pass before his death three weeks later. Helped sustain a long TD drive with excellent end runs in win over MAC.

BARZ, BILL. 1968-1969-1970; HB, FB; 6'2", 216; Country Club Hills, IL. Theismann's fullback in 1969 and 1970. Excellent blocker, steady runner, and good receiver. In 1969, had 362 yards on 90 carries for five TDs, was second in receiving with 24 catches for 262 yards and two TDs (when it was rare to throw to fullbacks). In 1970, had 88 carries for 352 yards and four TDs and caught 13 passes for 127 yards and one TD. For his career, had 178 carries for 714 yards and nine TDs, and caught 37 passes for 389 yards and three TDs for 1,103 all-purpose yards.

BATTLE, ARNAZ. 1998-1999-2000-2001-2002; QB, FL; 6'1", 210; Shreveport, LA. Gifted athlete, oft-injured, made the switch to FL after two seasons as a QB. Rare player to earn five monograms for ND. As a freshman, played in four games; completed eight of 20 passes for 134 yards and two INTs; rushed 13 times for 53 yards. Played in seven games as a sophomore backup, completing seven of 15 passes for 84 yards and one INT, rushing 19 times for 100 yards and one TD. Started the season as the top QB in 2000; hit 13 of 31 passes for 173 yards, two TDs, and one INT; carried 26 times for 157 yards. Broke his wrist during the Nebraska game; at the time, was the leading rusher and passer for the Irish. As a senior, switched to FL and started; broke a fibula

in the second game and missed next four games; for the season, completed his only pass for 17 yards, rushed three times for eight yards, and caught five passes for 40 yards. In 2002, started at FL as a fifth-year senior; completed one pass in two tries for 30 yards, rushed once for minus-four yards, had 16 KOR for 335 yards, and caught 48 passes for 702 yards good for five TDs. Against NC State in 2003 Gator Bowl, rushed twice for six yards and caught 10 passes for 84 yards. For his career, gained 320 yards on 64 carries good for one TD; completed 30 passes in 69 attempts for 438 yards, four INTs and two TDs; caught 63 passes for 826 yards and five TDs; had 16 KOR for 335 yards, reaching a career total of 1,919 all-purpose yards, good for seven TDs, and an average of 11.09 yards per offensive play in 173 tries.

BAVARO, MARK. 1981-1982-1983-1984; TE; 6'4", 246; Danvers, MA. Tremendous talent; devastating blocker with good hands, size, and speed. In 1981, played briefly against Navy and Georgia. In 1982, was supposed to back up Tony Hunter. Played briefly in Michigan game and reinjured an old hand problem; lost for the season. In 1983, started at TE. Scored with a 17-yard TD pass from Kiel in win over Purdue. Caught a two-yard TD pass from Kiel in loss to MSU. Made 22-yard TD in win over Army, on a pass from Beuerlein. Caught a 59-yard option pass from Pinkett in win over USC. For the season, Bavaro caught 23 passes for 376 yards and three TDs. In 1984, saw more action than any other Fighting Irish receiver. Led in receptions with 32 for 395 yards. Caught four against MSU and Missouri and kept Notre Dame close with a five-yard TD catch in tough loss to South Carolina. Caught two passes in close loss to SMU in Aloha Bowl. For the season, Bavaro caught 32 passes for 395 yards and one TD. In his career caught 55 passes for 771 yards, good for four TDs. Made All-American.

BEACOM, PAT. 1903-1904-1905-1906; G, T; 6'2", 220; Sheldon, IA. One of the Fighting Irish mainstays at the turn of the century; not highly skilled at first, but developed into dominating player. In 1903, started at LG for an undefeated Irish team. In 1904, started at LG. Scored twice on "tackle back" plays against Ohio Medical. Rushed for more than 50 yards to help an ailing Notre Dame team beat DePauw. In loss to Purdue, was an effective runner in only TD drive. Started at LG in 1905. Scored three TDs and ran for more than 60 yards in win over North Division H.S. Wabash held him to 30 yards rushing in their surprising win. Tallied two TDs against American Medical. Ran for two more TDs in win over DePauw. Kicked PAT in win over Bennett Medical College. Started at LT in 1906. Scored two TDs and kicked one PAT in win over Franklin. Blocked a Hillsdale punt to set up TD on a linebuck; added insurance TD and PAT. Scored three TDs in shutout of Physicians and Surgeons. Lost a TD on a penalty, but Notre Dame won over Purdue 2-0.

BECKER, DOUG. 1974-1975-1976-1977; LB; 6'2", 224; Hamilton, OH. Key player in 1977 national championship season; quick, played with reckless abandon, good tackler. In 1974, made 12 tackles, one for minus-19 yards, recovered two fumbles, and played 36 minutes. In 1975, started as OLB. Made 72 tackles, four for minus-eight yards, broke up one pass, and recovered three fumbles in 184 minutes. Grabbed a Miami fumble on their 20 that led to a TD in win. In 1976, started as OLB. Made 89 tackles, four for minus-27 yards, broke up two passes, and had one interception in 233 minutes. His good hit created a Miami fumble to set up a TD in Irish win. In 1977, started as OLB; teamed with Golic and Heimkreiter. For the season, made 81 tackles, three for minus-16 yards, broke up one pass, recovered one fumble, and intercepted one pass for 29-yard runback. In Cotton Bowl win over Texas, intercepted a pass and returned it 23 yards to set up third Irish TD. For his career, made 254 tackles, 12 for minus-70 yards, broke up four passes, recovered six fumbles, and had three interceptions.

BECTON, LEE. 1991-1992-1993-1994; TB; 6'0", 191; Ernul, NC. Elusive, shifty TB for Holtz, a key component in the surprising '93 campaign as he joined backfield newcomers Ray Zellars at FB and QB Kevin McDougal to spark the Irish to a near national championship in what looked like a rebuilding year. In 1991, had 15 carries for 62 yards. In 1992, backed up Reggie Brooks at TB; gained 373 yards on 68 carries and scored three TDs; caught one pass for a nine-yard TD; returned four kickoffs 114 yards, including a 78-yard TD romp against MSU. Helped beat Texas A&M in the 1993 Cotton Bowl with five carries for 26 yards. In 1993, started at TB for an Irish squad that finished number two in the country. Became ND's fifth 1,000-yard rusher with 1,044 yards gained on 164 rushes for a glittering 6.4 yards per carry, racking up six TDs; caught 12 passes for 153 yards and one more TD. Led the Irish to another Cotton Bowl win over Texas A&M with 138 yards on 26 carries and three yards gained with one pass

Greg Bell, seen here carrying the ball against LSU in 1981, was speedy and powerful—yet injury-prone. In 1983 against Purdue, he scored four touchdowns in one game.

reception. Injuries limited his action in the disappointing 1994 campaign, but he gained 550 yards on 100 carries for three more TDs; caught six passes for 50 yards and one TD; and returned one kickoff 17 yards. In the 1995 Fiesta Bowl loss to Colorado, gained 81 yards on 17 carries and snagged three passes for 60 yards. In his career, he ranks ninth among ND's runners, with 2,029 yards gained on 347 rushing attempts in the regular season, good for 12 TDs and an impressive 5.8 yards per carry average; caught 19 passes for 212 yards and three TDs; and returned five kickoffs 131 yards, good for one TD. With Bowl games, Becton's total yardage comes to 2,274 yards on 395 carries, scoring 12 TDs; caught 23 passes for 275 yards and three TDs, and gained 131 yards for one TD on five KORs, bringing his total offensive output to 2,680 yards gained on 423 attempts, for a fine 6.33 yards per attempt.

BELL, GREG. 1980-1981-1982-1983; TB, WB; 6'0", 205; Columbus, OH. Speedy, powerful runner in Faust years. Effectiveness limited by injuries. In 1980, gained 66 yards on five carries, for 13.2 average, and scored one TD in 3:36 minutes. In 1981, backed up Hunter at WB, probably a misuse of his skills; gained 512 yards on 92 carries for four TDs, caught 11 passes for 135 yards, and led team with 13 kickoff returns for 371 yards, including 98-yard TD run against Miami. In limited action in

1982, carried 24 times for 123 yards, caught three passes for 20 yards, returned three kickoffs for 50 yards, and one punt for 12 yards. In 1983, another limited season, scored four TDs against Purdue in blowout win: on a two-yard run, a nine-yard pass from Kiel, another two-yard run, and a six-yard run. Ran 50 yards for TD in loss to MSU. Ran back punts in Liberty Bowl win over Boston College. In his career, Bell had 158 carries for 870 yards and nine TDs, caught 20 passes for 220 yards and one TD, returned 16 kickoffs for 421 yards and one TD, and one punt 12 yards. He reached 1523 yards for 11 TDs in 195 career attempts.

BERCICH, PETE. 1990-1991-1992-1993; LB, 6'2", 237; Mokena, IL. Sturdy, overachieving, intense, emotional defensive leader for Holtz; especially effective on run defense. Saw limited action for the Irish, all on special teams, in 1990. Made remarkable progress and started as ILB in 1991; was second leading tackler for ND with only seven starts, making 41 solo hits, 28 assists, with five for minus-11 yards, in 174:27 minutes of action, earning honorable mention All-America honors. In 1992, replaced the suspended Demetrius DuBose to start the first two games, then came in as a sub for 10 other games. For the season, had 16 solo hits, five assists, with two for minus-four yards, broke up one pass, caused one fumble, and had one interception in 71:15 minutes of game action. Made two tackles, one for minus-five yards, in Irish win over Texas A&M in the Cotton Bowl. In 1993, started again at LB, and was again the second leading tackler for ND in a campaign that almost won the national crown. Scored a TD on season's first play from scrimmage when he intercepted a Northwestern pass and tallied with the interception return run of 21 yards. For the season, made 39 solo hits, 32 assists, with four for minus-nine yards, had one sack for minus-six yards, broke up two passes, caused one fumble, and had the one interception for the TD in 203:05 minutes of starting time. Against Texas A&M in 24-21 Irish Cotton Bowl win in '94, made six tackles and snagged a fourth quarter Aggie pass to help seal the win. For his career, had 96 solo hits, 71 other tackles, for 167 total hits, with 11 for minus-24 yards, one sack for minus-six yards, four passes broken up, two fumbles caused, one interception, scoring one TD, in 453:55 minutes of game action.

BERGMAN, ALFRED (DUTCH). 1910-1911-1913-1914; HB, QB; 5'8",160; Peru, IN. Fast, shifty, smart runner and field general. Played with Dorais and

Angelo Bertelli, the "Springfield Rifle," earned the first Heisman Trophy by a Notre Dame player in 1943.

Rockne. In 1910, backed up at RHB. In 1911, started at RHB. Had 20-yard TD run, 40-yard kickoff return, and 40-yard punt return in win over Ohio Northern. Led Fighting Irish in rushing and scoring in win over St. Viator; scored on runs of 15, three, 40, and 40 yards and on pass from Dorais. Scored one TD on a 65-yard punt return in win over Butler. Entered record book with 105-yard kickoff return against Loyola—without scoring (the field was longer then), but scored three of 14 TDs for the day. In 1913, backed up at RHB. In 1914, started at QB. Scored two of 15 TDs against Rose Poly. Played well in shutout loss to Yale: had runs of 20 and 15 yards, a 35-yard punt return, and threw two passes for 48 yards. Rushed for 160 yards against South Dakota, scoring on end runs of 50 and 60 yards, passed for another 50 yards, and made one PAT. Against Haskell, scored on a 35-yard run with a lateral and on punt returns of 80 and 85 yards (and lost an 80-yard TD run for stepping out of bounds). Gained more than 245 yards of total offense in win over Carlisle with two kickoff returns of 50 yards each, 50-yard TD runback of a dropped punt, 60 yards on two punt returns, and two pass completions. Closed career with TD against Syracuse.

BERTELLI, ANGELO. 1941-1942-1943; HB, QB; 6'1", 173; West Springfield, MA. The "Springfield

Rifle;" first QB of early T-formation teams under Leahy. Great team leader, superb passer, somewhat slow for HB, so moved to QB. First Notre Dame player to win Heisman Trophy. In 1941, started at LHB and hit 70 of 123 passes for 1,027 yards and eight TDs; gained 56 yards with 40 carries; had one interception, a 17-yard kickoff return, and made three of three PATs. Completed six of seven passes in first game, one a 16-yard TD to Bob Dove, and kicked two PATs, in win over Arizona. Fired TD pass to George Murphy and hit four passes in a row on TD drive in shutout of Georgia Tech. In win over Illinois, fired 13-yard TD pass to Juzwik and 40-yard TD pass to Evans. In win over Navy, 42-yard pass to Earley set up first TD; fired 18-yard pass to Juzwik. Beat Northwestern with TD pass to Bolger. Teamed with Dove for brilliant passing in win over USC; made winning score with 18-yard pass to Evans. For the year, had 70 completions in 123 tries for 1,027 yards and eight TDs. In 1942, switched to QB. Got on wrong train as the team took the right train to Madison but made it to game; Irish tied Wisconsin 7-7; had only four completions; new backfield set dropped five fumbles. Had three passes intercepted in loss to Georgia Tech. Made nine straight completions in win over Stanford and hit four TD passes: 36 yards to Dove, 16 yards to Limont, 26 yards to Murphy, and 15 yards to Livingstone for 14 of 20 for 233 yards. Threw 47-yard TD to Livingstone in win over Iowa Pre-Flight. QB sneak for TD was the

difference in 21-14 win over Illinois. Scored on short TD run against Navy and had an endzone interception in 9-0 win. Threw 17-yard TD to Murphy in 13-0 win over Army. Had seven-yard TD pass to Dove in loss to Michigan. Helped beat Otto Graham and Northwestern with 31-yard TD pass to Creighton Miller. In win over USC, fired TDs of 48 yards to Miller and nine yards to Livingstone. For the season, completed 74 of 165 throws for 1,044 yards and 11 TDs. In 1943, won Heisman Trophy on six games played before his service call-up. Recovered Pitt fumble and dove two yards for TD in shutout win. To beat Michigan, completed five of eight passes for 172 yards, scored one TD, and threw two TDs, one a 70-yarder to Earley. Led starters to five TDs in 22 plays against Wisconsin in 50-0 blowout. In last home game, completed five of seven in shutout of Illinois, including 47-yard bomb to Julie Rykovich for the first score. Against Navy, threw three TD passes and ran for another. For the year, completed 25 of 36 for 511 yards and 10 TDs. He was in the Marines shortly thereafter. In his career, completed 169 of 324 passes for 2,582 yards and 29 TDs.

Fullback Jerome Bettis totaled 2,624 yards of total offense and scored 39 touchdowns in three seasons for Holtz's teams in the early 1990s.

Quarterback Steve Beuerlein held virtually all of Notre Dame's passing and total offense records when he graduated in 1986.

BETTIS, JEROME. 1990-1991-1992; FB; 6'0", 247; Detroit, MI. In 1992, carried 154 times for 825 yards and 10 TDs, caught 15 passes for 239 yards and two more TDs. Helped beat undefeated Texas A&M in the '93 Cotton Bowl with 20 carries for 75 yards and two TDs, and also caught one pass for a 26-yard TD. Played 195:27 minutes. Earned honorable mention All-America recognition. For his career, slammed into opposing lines 376 times for 2,164 yards, a 5.75 yards per carry average, good for 32 TDs; caught 34 passes for 460 yards and seven TDs. Played a total of 493:06 minutes. His total offense comes to 2,624 yards gained on 410 attempts for a 6.4 yards-per-attempt average, good for 39 TDs. Prorating his three-year stats to a fourth year, Bettis would have ended up as the third all-time rusher for ND, just ahead of Jerome Heavens, trailing Allen Pinkett and Vagas Ferguson. Instead, ended up as the 14th best rusher for the Irish, sixth in career rushing TDs, fifth in career TDs.

BEUERLEIN, STEVE. 1983-1984-1985-1986; QB; 6'3", 201; Fullerton, CA. One of the most impressive QBs for the Fighting Irish in recent years, perhaps the best pure passer since Montana. Excellent arm, good leadership skills, and pinpoint accuracy. Had some great offensive weapons to work with in Pinkett and Tim Brown. May not have been fully appreciated since his career spanned some rather dismal years. In 1983, started at QB for eight games. For the year, had 23 carries for minus-nine yards, and 75 completions in 145 throws for 1,061 yards, four TDs, and six interceptions. In 1984, started at QB. For the year, had 58 carries for minus-75 yards, completed 140 of 232 throws for 1,920 yards, seven TDs, and 18 interceptions, and caught one pass for six yards and a TD. In 1985, started at QB. In the Aloha Bowl, hit 11 of 23 passes for 144 yards and one TD as SMU won 27-20. For the season, had 43 carries for minus-19 yards and one TD, and completed 107 of 214 passes for three TDs and 13 interceptions. In 1986, had 53 carries for 35 yards and one TD, completed 151 of 259 passes for 2,211 yards, 13 TDs, and seven interceptions. For his career, had 177 carries for minus-68 yards and two TDs, completed 473 of 850 passes for 6,527 yards, 27 TDs, and 44 interceptions, and caught one pass for six yards and one TD. He was involved in 6,465 yards of offense for 30 TDs.

BLEIER, ROCKY. 1965-1966-1967; HB; 5'11", 195; Appleton, WI. Steady, dependable runner, blocker, and receiver for Parseghian on 1966 championship team with Hanratty and Seymour; captain in 1967. In 1965, as a reserve RB averaged 5.6 yards per carry on 26 runs for 145 yards and two TDs; caught three passes for 42 yards and made one tackle. In 1966, started at RHB with Hanratty, Eddy, and Conjar in the backfield. Gained 282 yards on 63 carries for four TDs; was second on team with 17 receptions for 209 yards; punted 16 times for a 39.6-yard average; and returned three kickoffs 67 yards. In 1967, started at LHB and gained 357 yards on 77 carries for five TDs; caught 16 passes for 171 yards and two TDs; punted 23 times for a 33.0-yard average; and returned nine kickoffs for 201 yards. For his career, made 166 runs for 784 yards and 11 TDs, caught 36 passes for 422 yards and two TDs, and returned 12 kickoffs 268 yards for a career total of 1,474 yards.

BOLAND, JOE. 1924-1925-1926; T; 6'0", 221; Philadelphia, PA. One of the all-time greats; assistant coach under Elmer Layden, 1936-40; well known speaker; and the radio "Voice of the Irish" for years. Very quick for a big man; was a good tactician as a key lineman in Rockne's shift offense in the final year of the Four Horsemen as a reserve and the first year with Christy Flanagan. Started at LT in 1925 and 1926, but an injury curtailed his senior year. In 1925, blocked two punts in a close win over Minnesota. In 1926, was headed for another blocked punt against Minnesota, but was kicked in the leg and was lost for the season.

BRACKEN, BOB. 1904-1905-1906; HB, QB; 5'11", 165; Polo, IL. Three-year starter in the backfield. Played good defense and was capable of breaking loose for long gains. In 1904, started at RHB. Playing under Red Salmon, scored three TDs in shutout of American Medical. In 1905, started at LHB. In 58-0 loss to Wisconsin, recovered a Badger fumble for a touchback, ran for short yardage gains, and stopped a probable Badger TD, after a 55-yard gain, with a flying tackle. Scored three TDs on long runs in 142-0 "game" against American Medical and started to give the linemen the ball for fun (they ended up with more TDs than the backs). In 1906, started at QB. In opening win over Franklin, scored on 35-yard run and 40-yard sprint. Scored one TD in 17-0 win over Hillsdale. Returned a punt 105 yards against Physicians and Surgeons, but it was called back for stepping out of bounds. Helped beat MAC 5-0 with runs of 20 and 15 yards on a muddy field. Rushed for important short yardage gains in 2-0 win over Purdue to go with a good punt return and a fumble recovery. Returned punts for 35 yards in loss to Indiana. Named to All-State team. Was an assistant coach in 1907.

BRADLEY, LUTHER. 1973-1975-1976-1977; SS, CB; 6'2", 202; Muncie, IN. Very quick defensive back for Parseghian and Devine; constant scoring threat. Played on two national championship teams (1973 and 1977). In 1973, started at SS and led Notre Dame with six interceptions for 37 return yards; made 27 tackles, one for minus-two yards; led the team with 11 passes broken up; and recovered one fumble. Missed 1974 over a parietals infraction. In 1975, started at RCB and made 56 tackles, two for minus-five yards; broke up two passes; blocked one punt; and made four interceptions for 135 return yards and one TD in 303 minutes of play. Entered the record book by intercepting a HB option pass intended for the Purdue QB and running 99 yards for a TD. Made All-American. In 1976, started at LCB and made 50 tackles, two for minus-23 yards; broke up seven passes; recovered one fumble; blocked one kick; and intercepted two passes in 272 minutes of action. Made All-American. In 1977, helped win the national championship with 45 tackles, seven passes broken up, and five interceptions for 46 return yards. Consensus All-American. For his career, made 153 tackles, five for minus-30 yards; broke up 27 passes; recovered two fumbles; blocked two kicks; and intercepted 17 passes for 218 return yards and one TD.

BRANDY, JOE. 1917-1919-1920; HB, QB; 5'8", 147; Ogdensburg, NY. Slick ball handler and excellent field general. Teamed with Gipp in two undefeated seasons, 1919 and 1920. In 1917, backed up at RHB. Led backs in rushing in tie with Wisconsin. Scored TD in win over South Dakota. Scored Notre Dame's only TD in 7-2 win over Army, a drive started by his interception; also recovered a fumble. In 1919, backed up at QB. Scored TD in rout of Western Normal. In 1920, started at QB. Kicked one PAT in win over Kalamazoo. Directed parade of TDs in rout of Western Normal. Scored winning TD against Indiana. Threw five-yard TD pass to Eddie Anderson in win over Northwestern. Recovered a fumble in win over MAC.

BRENNAN, TERRY. 1945-1946-1947-1948; HB; 6'0", 170; Milwaukee, WI. Started for three undefeated Leahy teams. Good, quick runner and receiver, and excellent defender. Became Notre Dame's head coach in 1954. In 1945, rushed 57 times for 252 yards and backed up at LHB. In 1946, started at LHB and led the nation's best rushing team with 329 yards on 74 carries, caught 10 passes for 154 yards, returned kickoffs for 111 yards, and scored six TDs. In 1947, gained 404 yards rushing, led team with 11 TDs, led in carries (87), led in receptions (16) and yardage (191), and led in punt returns with 11 for 115 yards—all despite a season-ending knee injury in the eighth game. In 1948, started at LHB and rushed 48 times for 284 yards, a 5.9-yard average, and caught five passes for 102 yards. For his career, made 266 runs for 1,269 yards; caught 31 passes for 447 yards; made 111 yards in kickoff returns and 115 yards in punt returns; and scored 17 TDs as he gained 1,942 all-purpose yards.

BRILL, MARTY. 1929-1930; HB; 5'11", 190; Philadelphia, PA. A transfer to Notre Dame from Penn, much to Rockne's delight. Teamed with Carideo, Savoldi, Elder, and Schwartz to give the Fighting Irish, undefeated in 1929 and 1930, tremendous depth and skill in the backfield. Very fast, powerful, a good blocker. Never played in a losing game for Notre Dame. In 1929, played great defense to help Notre Dame beat USC. Caught 25-yard pass to set up winning TD against Northwestern. In 1930, used lateral passes to Savoldi, who scored on two of them to beat Navy. Scored first Irish TDs in win over Pitt, from the 23 and two. Annihilated Penn with three TDs and 125-plus yards of rushing—including 65-yard TD run—in 60-20 win. Scored on three-yard run off a fake pass in win over Drake. In 7-6 win over Army, made a perfect open-field block in the secondary to spring Schwartz for 54-yard TD run. Scored six TDs for the year. Made All-American.

BROOKS, REGGIE. 1989-1990-1991-1992; TB; 5'8", 200; Tulsa, OK. Came into his own in the '92 season, when he compiled the third best single-season totals as an Irish runner, the first Holtz back to rush for 1,000 yards at ND. Shifty, strong, quick runner with excellent balance, an elusive target for defenders. In 1989, played in six games, carried 13 times for 43 yards, gaining 11:16 minutes of experience. In 1990, switched to CB. Made 22 solo tackles, had six assists, with one tackle for minus-one yard, one interception, returned nine yards, and broke up one pass in 86:13 minutes of action. In 1991, went back to offense but served as a sub at TB.

Had only 18 carries for 122 yards, but scored two TDs, including a 65-yard blast against Navy. Also had nine KORs for 198 yards, returned one punt 26 yards for a TD, but played only 16:22 minutes. In 1992, started at TB and had such a good season you have to wonder what he had been doing playing behind anyone in his other campaigns. For the year, rushed 167 times for 1,343 yards and a staggering 8.0 yards per carry average, scored 13 TDs, caught one pass for a 24-yard TD, and returned three kickoffs 39 yards. Played 182:37 minutes, earned second-team All-America honors, and was voted MVP by his teammates. Gained 115 yards on 22 carries in '93 Cotton Bowl win over Texas A&M. For his career as a TB, (in only nine starts), gained 1,623 yards on 189 rushes for 13 TDs, caught two passes for 28 yards and one TD; returned 12 kickoffs 237 yards, one punt 26 yards for one TD, and played 296:18 minutes. His 7.6 yards per carry for a career in regular season games stands as the best ever for an Irish back; his 8.0 average for '92 is the second best for any Irish runner in a season. His all-purpose totals come to 1,923 yards in 223 attempts, good for 15 TDs.

BROOKS, TONY. 1987-1988-1990-1991; TB; 6'2", 223; Tulsa, OK. Powerful, speedy TB for Holtz. Exploded to a quick start, broke tackles, and then accelerated in the open field. In 1987, backed up at TB. Carried three times for seven yards in 1988 Cotton Bowl against Texas A & M. For the year, carried 54 times for 262 yards and one TD, caught three passes for 38 yards, and returned one kickoff two yards. In 1988, backed up at TB for the national champions. Made 11 carries for 35 yards in Fiesta Bowl win over West Virginia. For the season, in spite of a painful foot injury, carried 117 times for 667 yards and two TDs, and caught seven passes for 121 yards and two TDs. Missed 1989 for academic reasons. In 1990, backed up at TB. For the year, made 105 carries for 451 yards and four TDs, caught three passes for 47 yards, and returned four kickoffs 67 yards. In 1991, started four games at TB. For the year, had 147 carries for 894 yards and five TDs, and caught 11 passes for 126 yards and one TD. Gained 68 yards on 13 carries in win over Florida in the 1992 Sugar Bowl. For his career, had 423 carries for 2,274 yards and 12 TDs, caught 24 passes for 332 yards and three TDs, and returned five kickoffs 69 yards. His career offense reached 2,675 yards in 452 attempts and 15 TDs.

BROWN, BOB. 1895-1896; HB; 5'10",162; Sheldon, IA. Came from same small Iowa town as Pat Beacom a few years later; part of the renewed interest in football at Notre Dame after three-year lapse (1889-1892). Tough, quick player, adept at long runs from scrimmage. In 1895, started at RHB and led Irish runners for yardage in the season even though he did not play all the way. Had 40-yard TD run in shutout of Northwestern Law. Helped beat Illinois Cycling Club with 130 yards rushing and two TDs; made seven runs of more than 13 yards. Rushed for 155 yards and one TD while recovering three fumbles in win over Physicians and Surgeons. In 1896, started at LHB and rushed for 120 yards against South Bend Commercial A.C., with TD runs of 50 and 65 yards to go with a TD plunge. Helped beat Albion with a TD and 50 yards of punt returns. Scored a TD in loss to Purdue. Helped demolish Highland Views 82-0 with three TD runs of 60 yards each.

BROWN, BOBBY. 1996-1997-1998-1999; SE-FL; 6'2", 193; Lauderhill, FL. Three-year starter for Irish as WR. Dependable, possession-type receiver, helped give ND its first pair of 40-reception receivers in '97, along with Malcolm Johnson, catching Ron Powlus aerials. In '96, caught two passes for 84 yards and an impressive 42-yard average in 47:08 playing time. Broke into the starting lineup in '97 as the FL and had a great campaign: 45 receptions for 543 yards and six TDs for 12.1 yards per catch. Snagged one pass for 10 yards in '97 Independence Bowl loss to LSU. Played 234:29 minutes. In '98, saw his production slip to 13 receptions for 286 yards, a 22-yard average, good for one TD in 152:59 minutes. Gained 42 yards on two catches in '99 Gator Bowl loss to Georgia Tech. Recovered well in '99 campaign to lead the Irish with 36 catches for 608 yards and a 16.9-yard average per catch, for five TDs and a two-point conversion. For his career, grabbed 97 passes for 1,547 yards, 12 TDs, and one two-point conversion.

BROWN, DEREK. 1988-1989-1990-1991; TE; 6'6", 252; Merritt Island, FL. Premier TE in college football, long-distance threat with superb size, good speed, and good hands. Integral part of offense since freshman year. In 1988, started at TE in fifth game for the national champions. For the year, caught 12 passes for 150 yards and three TDs. Caught two passes for 70 yards in Fiesta Bowl win over West Virginia. In 1989, started at TE. For the year, caught 13 passes for 204 yards. Had one reception for 12 yards against Colorado in the Orange Bowl. In 1990, started at TE. For the year, caught 15 passes for 220 yards and one TD. In Orange Bowl loss to Colorado, caught four passes for 56 yards. In 1991, caught 22 passes for 325 yards and four TDs. Caught one pass for 11-yard gain in Irish win over Florida in 1992 Sugar Bowl. For his career, caught 62 passes for 899 yards and eight TDs.

BROWN, TIM. 1984-1985-1986-1987; FL; 6'0", 195; Dallas, TX. Heisman Trophy winner in 1987, Notre Dame's seventh; tremendous deep threat for Faust and Holtz in passing game and on special teams. Had 4.38-speed in the 40-yard dash, superb instinctive moves, sixth sense for avoiding tackles, good hands, and a willingness to catch passes on crossing patterns over the middle. In 1984, backed up at SE. For the year, had one carry for 14 yards, caught 28 passes for 340 yards and one TD, and returned seven kickoffs 121 yards. In 1985, started at FL. For the season, carried four times for 30 yards and one TD, caught 25 passes for 397 yards and three TDs, returned 14 kickoffs 338 yards for one TD. In 1986, started at FL. For the year, had 59 carries for 254 yards and two TDs, caught 45 passes for 910 yards and five TDs, returned 25 kickoffs 698 yards for two TDs and two punts for 75 yards. Made All-American. In 1987, started at FL. For the season, had 34 carries for 144 yards and one TD, caught 39 passes for 846 yards and three TDs, returned 23 kickoffs 456 yards and 34 punts 401 yards for three TDs. Consensus All-American and Heisman Trophy winner. For his career, had 98 carries for 442 yards and four TDs, caught 137 passes for 2,493 yards and 12 TDs, returned 69 kickoffs 1,613 yards for three TDs and 36 punts 476 yards for three TDs. His career yardage was 5,024 yards on 340 attempts for 22 TDs, an average of 42.3 yards for each scoring play. He holds Notre Dame's records for most career receiving yards, most kickoff returns in a season (25 for 698 yards in 1986), most career kick returns, most career kick return yards, and is tied with Ismail for most career kick returns for a score (six).

BROWNER, JIM. 1975-1976-1977-1978; FB, SS; 6'3", 204; Warren, OH. Middle brother of three Browners to play at Notre Dame. Excellent defensive player, especially hard tackler. In 1975, backed up at FB, and was third in rushing with 394 yards on 104 carries for two TDs, caught two passes for 16 yards, and made two tackles in 137 minutes of play. In 1976, started at SS and led DBs with 80 tackles, four for minus-14 yards; broke up three passes; blocked one kick; and intercepted two passes in 242 minutes. In 1977, started at SS and led DBs again with 73 tackles, nine for minus-53 yards; broke up five passes; recovered five fumbles; made one

Ross Browner, winner of the Outland Trophy in 1976, closes in on Pitt's Tony Dorsett.

interception; and returned eight kickoffs 133 yards in 244 minutes for the national championship team. In 1978, started at SS and led DBs with 75 tackles, five for minus-38 yards; broke up four passes; recovered three fumbles; and made two interceptions for 64 return yards and one TD. For his career, made 230 tackles, 18 for minus-105 yards; broke up 12 passes; recovered eight fumbles; and made five interceptions.

BROWNER, ROSS. 1973-1975-1976-1977; DE; 6'3", 248; Warren OH. All-time great Notre Dame player—four-year starter, devastating pass rusher, extremely quick, extraordinary nose for the ball, and a threat to make a big play at any time. Played on two national championship teams (1973 and 1977). In 1973 as freshman, started at DE and was third on team with 68 tackles, led in tackles for losses with 15 for minus-104 yards, broke up one pass, recovered two fumbles, blocked one kick, and scored a safety. Did not play in 1974 after being suspended, with five others, over infractions of dorm regulations. In 1975, started at DE and made 71 tackles, 16 for minus-78 yards; broke up two passes; and scored one TD and a safety in 247 minutes. In 1976, started at DE and won the Outland Trophy for 97 tackles, 28 for minus-203 yards; broke up seven passes; recovered four fumbles; and blocked one kick in 273 minutes. In 1977, started at DE and made 104 tackles, 18 for minus-130 yards, and recovered two fumbles. In his career, made 340 tackles, 77 for minus-515 yards; broke up 10 passes; recovered eight fumbles; blocked two kicks; and scored two safeties and one TD. Consensus All-American in 1976 and 1977.

BUDKA, FRANK. 1961-1962-1963; QB; 6'0", 190; Pompano Beach, FL. Part of the QB shuffle in early 1960s; good runner, fair passer, and good defensive skills, who was probably played out of position for much of his career. In 1961, backed up at QB, but led Notre Dame in passing with 646 yards on 40 of 95 passes for three TDs; ran 31 times for 20 yards and one TD; returned one kickoff for 10 yards; made 21 tackles and two interceptions; broke up three passes; and led team with three fumble recoveries in 217 minutes. In 1962, backed up at QB. Hit only two of nine passes for 25 yards, gained 21 yards on 12 carries, returned one kickoff for 20 yards, caught one pass for 19 yards, made 51 tackles to lead DBs, broke up eight passes, and intercepted one pass for a 10-yard runback. Also played FL to help vitalize a moribund Irish offense. In 1963, back at QB and completed 22 of 41 passes for 251 yards

A guard and linebacker during a dismal period of Notre Dame football, Nick Buoniconti earned All-America accolades in 1961.

and four TDs; ran for 97 yards on 47 carries and scored four TDs; and made four tackles. For his career, hit 64 of 145 passes for 690 yards and seven TDs, rushed 78 times for 117 yards and five TDs, caught one pass for 19 yards, broke up 11 passes, made three interceptions,

recovered three fumbles, and made 71 tackles. His career all-purpose yardage was 826 yards in 143 attempts for 12 TDs.

BULLOCK, WAYNE. 1972-1973-1974; FB; 6'1",223; Newport News, VA. Powerful runner and excellent blocker under Parseghian; key backfield man in the 1973 championship season. Hard to stop in scoring range. In 1972, as a reserve, carried 27 times for 123 yards and caught two passes for 32 yards. In 1973, started at FB, teaming with Clements, Best, and Penick, and led the Fighting Irish with 752 yards on 162 carries for 10 TDs, caught eight passes for 83 yards and one TD, and returned two kickoffs 39 yards. In 1974, started at FB and led runners with 855 yards on 203 carries for 12 TDs, caught 11 passes for 103 yards, and returned one kickoff seven yards. For his career, ran 392 times for 1,730 yards and 22 TDs, caught 21 passes for 218 yards and one TD, and returned three kickoffs 46 yards for a career yardage total of 1,994 yards.

BUONICONTI, NICK. 1959-1960-1961; G, LB; 5'11", 210; Springfield, MA. Gritty, dependable, overachieving lineman and linebacker; excellent tackler; good blocker. Played in a dismal period of Notre Dame football. In 1959, started at LG and was third-leading tackler with 67; broke up one pass. In 1960, backed up at LG but led team with 74 tackles, blocked two kicks, and broke up one pass. In 1961, started at LG and was second on team with 71 tackles; broke up one pass, recovered one fumble, and blocked one kick. For his career, made 212 tackles, blocked three kicks, recovered one fumble, and broke up three passes. All-American in 1961.

BURGMEIER, TED. 1974-1975-1976-1977; SE, S, CB; 5'11", 187; East Dubuque, IL. Speedy, sure-handed DB on 1977 national championship team Three-year starter, with one spent at SE. In 1974, backed up at FS and made six tackles. In 1975, started at SE, had one carry for 50 yards, caught 10 passes for 185 yards and one TD, returned nine punts 52 yards, and made four tackles, one for minus-three yards. In 1976, switched to defense and started at RCB; made 54 tackles, one for minus-two yards; broke up three passes; recovered one fumble; intercepted two passes for 42 yards; and handled 20 punts for 138 yards in returns. In 1977, started at RCB; made 54 tackles, one for minus-nine yards; broke up six passes; ran once for 21 yards; threw one pass for a two-point conversion; made four interceptions and 100 yards in runbacks; and returned 18 punts 82 yards. For his career, carried twice for 71 yards, caught 10 passes for 185 yards, threw a two-point conversion pass, made 118 tackles, three for minus-14 yards, broke up nine passes, recovered one fumble, made six interceptions for 142 return yards, and handled 47 punts for 272 yards for a total of 670 yards.

BURRIS, JEFF. 1990-1991-1992-1993; FS, TB; 6'0", 204; Rock Hill, SC. Multi-threat, multi-talented player for Holtz. Great DB, kick returner, TB in full-house goal-line formations—blessed with great speed, good hands, and the ability to deliver a hard hit. In 1990, main contribution was in 119 special teams appearances, but also had six carries for 30 yards and one TD as a TB, and had three kickoff returns for 25 yards in 17:05 minutes of action. Saw special team duty in close loss to Colorado in Orange Bowl. In 1991, started at FS and CB. Made 48 solo hits, 15 assists, broke up four passes, and made two INTs to go with three KORs for 54 yards, and 18 punt returns for 227 yards in 280:04 minutes of play. Added three tackles and broke up one pass in '92 Sugar Bowl win over Florida. Earned honorable mention All-America status. In 1992, started at FS; led ND in INTs and was third in tackles. For the season, made 51 solo hits, 22 assists, broke up four passes, hauled in five INTs, returned them six yards, carried the ball as a TB seven times for 14 yards, scoring three TDs; scored one TD with a three-yard pass and had two KORs for 25 yards. Made five tackles, one for minus-four yards, broke up one pass, and carried twice for eight yards in Irish Cotton Bowl win over Texas A&M. Saw 289:40 minutes of action for the year. In 1993, started at FS, leading Irish defenders in playing time, all players in special teams plays with 204, and played as TB in goal-line situations, to rank as the team's second-best TD producer. On defense, had 36 solo hits, made 17 other tackles, broke up six passes, made three INTs, returning them 61 yards; on offense, carried 16 times for 92 yards, scoring TDs six times; had three KORs for 28 yards, and had one punt return of 60 yards for a TD. He played 208:07 minutes over the season and earned All-America recognition. In his busy career, Burris rushed 32 times for 148 yards, scoring 10 TDs, caught one pass for three yards and one TD, made 11 KORs for 132 yards, returned 19 punts 287 yards, scoring one TD; on defense, he had 135 solo hits, 71 other tackles, 15 passes broken up, caused one fumble, recovered a fumble, made 10 interceptions, and returned them 67 yards. His total all-purpose yardage came to 637 yards in 74 assorted attempts, good for 12 TDs in 868:56 busy career minutes of play.

CALHOUN, MIKE. 1976-1977-1978; DT; 6'5", 250; Austintown, OH. Three-year starter at DT; steady, dependable player, with good quickness; on national championship team in 1977. In 1976, started at DT and made 92 tackles, 12 for minus-41 yards; broke up eight passes; recovered two fumbles; and blocked one kick. In 1977, started at DT and made 76 tackles, 13 for

Jack "Boom Boom" Cannon, the last Notre Dame player with enough guts to play without a helmet, captained the 1929 national champions and was a consensus All-American.

minus-63 yards, and recovered three fumbles. In 1978, started at DT and led linemen with 99 tackles, eight for minus-39 yards, and broke up one pass. For his career, made 267 tackles, 33 for minus-143 yards; broke up four passes; recovered five fumbles; and blocked one kick.

CALLICRATE, DOM. 1905-1906-1907; E, HB; 5'11", 160; Granger, IN. All-purpose player and three-year starter, with good speed, toughness, and the ability to break a long gainer. Played with Red Miller and Bob Bracken, a good QB of the day. In 1905, started at RE. Scored one TD in 142-0 rout of American Medical. Ran for another TD in rout of DePauw. Used a "fake sideline play" for 12-yard gain in loss to Indiana. In 1906, started at RH. Scored one TD in shutout of Physicians and Surgeons. Lost 60-yard TD play on a penalty in 20-point win over Purdue. Was only effective Notre Dame runner in loss to Indiana. In 1907, started at RH and scored one TD in opening shutout of Physicians and Surgeons. Shocked Olivet with a 100-yard kickoff return, and scored on five-yard plunge. Made 75 yards in 0-0 tie with Indiana. Scored one TD in win over St. Vincent's.

CANNON, JACK. 1927-1928-1929; G; 5'11", 193; Columbus, OH. The last Fighting Irish player to play without benefit of a helmet. A very quick, rugged, reckless, determined ball player; good blocker; great tackler. In 1927, backed up at LG. In 1928, backed up at RG. In 1929, started at LG. In the 1929 game with Army, won by Elder's interception and TD return, was involved in half of Notre Dame's tackles. Consensus All-American in 1929.

CARBERRY, GLEN. 1920-1921-1922; E; 6'0", 180; Ames, IA. A tough, speedy player, especially good on defense; good football mind; later coached at Fordham. Played with both Gipp and the Four Horsemen. In 1920 and 1921, backed up at LE. In 1922, started at LE and captained the team.

CAREY, TONY. 1964-1965; DB; 6'0", 190; Chicago, IL. Excellent defensive back for early Parseghian teams—tough, rangy, fast; devastating tackler. Teamed with Longo and Rassas to make formidable secondary unit. In 1964, started at RCB and made 46 tackles, broke up 10 passes, recovered one fumble, and led team with eight interceptions for 121 return yards. Made second-team All-America. In 1965, started at RCB and made 34 tackles, broke up three passes, recovered one fumble, and made three interceptions for nine return yards. In relatively brief career, made 80 tackles, broke up 13 passes, recovered two fumbles, and made 11 interceptions for 130 return yards.

CARIDEO, FRANK. 1928-1929-1930; QB; 5'7",175; Mt. Vernon, NY. One of Rockne's best QBs: chesty, heady, excellent field general, good runner, blocker, good kicker, and excellent defender. Always found a way to win. Involved as a player in the 1928 win over Army ("Win One for the Gipper"). QB for the first recognized consecutive national championship teams in 1929 and 1930. Led famous backfield players: Marchy Schwartz, Marty Brill, Jack Elder, and Joe Savoldi. In 1928, subbed at QB. Scored TD against Drake on a sneak. Subbing for injured starter, scored only TD in shutout win over Penn State by crawling into the end zone. Returned a

punt 50 yards in loss to USC. In 1929, started at QB. In win over Navy, made two PATs, an interception plus runback to the Navy 32 to set up winning TD, and completed pass to Elder while on one knee. Helped beat Georgia Tech with a 75-yard punt return for TD, plus good passing and kicking. Against Northwestern made 85-yard interception return for TD. Made All-American. In 1930, started at QB. Against Northwestern, dropped five punts inside their five-yard line. With Brill, made block to spring Schwartz on 54-yard TD run in 7-6 win over Army; kicked PAT for the win. Kicked two PATs and caught 19-yard TD pass from Schwartz in win over USC—Rockne's last game. Repeat consensus All-American.

CARLSON, JOHN. 2003-2004-2005-2006. TE, 6'5", 255. Litchfield, MN. One of Brady Quinn's favorite targets in a good 2006 season; helped set numerous Irish passing records. Ideal TE size, good speed, very good hands, excellent blocker. Did not play his first year and saw limited action in the next two seasons. Caught six passes for 31 yards in 2004. Started 6 games in 2005, with 7 snags for 56 yards and a TD. Really came into his own in 2006, with 47 receptions, good for 634 yards and four TDs. Named a Mackey Award finalist and appeared on some All-American rosters. Chose not to take a fifth year. For his career, had 60 receptions for 721 yards and 5 TDs.

CARNEY, JOHN. 1983-1984-1985-1986; K; 5'10", 170; West Palm Beach, FL. Walk-on player who earned kickoff team start as freshman. Generated tremendous distance on kickoffs. All-time leader in field goals, attempts, and percentage when he finished. In 1983, handled kickoff duties. In 1984, handled place kicking duties. For the season, was perfect on 25 PATs and made 17 of 19 field goals for 76 points. In 1985, handled place kicking. For the year, made 21 of 24 PATs and 13 of 22 field goals for 60 points. In 1986, handled place kicking. For the year, made 24 of 26 PATs and 21 of 28 field goals for 87 points. For his career, made 70 of 75 PAT kicks and 51 of 69 field goals for 223 points.

CARROLL, JIM. 1962-1963-1964; G, LB; 6'1", 225; Atlanta, GA. Hard-nosed lineman and linebacker; spiritual leader of Parseghian's first team (1964). In 1962, started at LG; was third on team with 58 tackles, and recovered two fumbles. In 1963, started at RG; made 59 tackles, broke up one pass, and blocked one kick. In 1964, started at ILB, captained the team, and set new record for tackles with 140. Also intercepted one pass and broke up four others. Made second-team All-America. For his career, made 257 tackles, blocked one kick, recovered two fumbles, intercepted one pass, and broke up five passes.

CARTER, PHIL. 1979-1980-1981-1982; HB, TB; 5'10", 197; Tacoma, WA. Short, strong, quick runner; prototype of backs for the next several seasons. In 1979, played in nine games, rushed 27 times for 145 yards to lead team with 5.4-yard average; and caught one pass for four yards. In 1980, started at HB but missed four games. Set new record with 40 carries in one game, against MSU. Was second leading rusher with 186 runs for 822 yards and six TDs; also caught five passes for 27 yards. Averaged 117 yards per game, second best for all Irish runners to that point. In 1981, carried 165 times for 727 yards and six TDs, was third in receiving with 14 catches for 57 yards, and was second leading scorer with 36 points. In 1982, ran 179 times for 715 yards and two TDs, caught 12 passes for 85 yards, threw one pass for 54-yard TD, and returned one kickoff 18 yards. For his career, rushed 557 times for 2,409 yards and 14 TDs, caught 32 passes for 173 yards, threw one pass for 54-yard TD, and returned one kickoff 18 yards for 2,600 total yards.

CARTIER, GEORGE. 1887-1889; QB; Ludington, MI. Notre Dame's first QB, from the Iron Country of Northern Michigan, near the home of George Gipp. Cartier Field was named for him, and the Fighting Irish played there until 1930.

CASE, JAY. 1975-1977-1978-1979; DE, DT; 6'3", 239; Cincinnati, OH. Good defensive lineman for 1977 national champions. Part of a defensive line that made it hard for offenses to operate. Three-year starter but injuries ended his senior year early. In 1975, subbed at DT. In 1977, made 36 tackles, three for minus-16 yards; broke up one pass; recovered one fumble; and scored 30-yard TD on a blocked punt. In 1978, started at DE, replacing Browner; made 72 tackles, leading team in tackles for losses with 12 for minus-56 yards; broke up two passes; and recovered four fumbles. In 1979, made one tackle before season ended with an injury. For his career, made 109 tackles, 15 for minus-72 yards; broke up three passes; recovered five fumbles; and scored one TD.

CASEY, DAN. 1894-1895; G; 6'0", 173; Crawfordsville,

IN. Part of resurgent interest in football at Notre Dame after it was not played for several years. Good runner, kicker, and defender. In 1894, started at RG. Ran ball several times in Hillsdale game from "guards back" deployment. Rushed for more than 145 yards, scoring TDs from 50 and 25 yards, in shutout win over Wabash. Ran for 35-yard TD in close win over Rush Medical. In 1895, started at RG and captained team. Scored one TD, ran back one kickoff, and made two PATs in shutout of Northwestern Law. Sped for 15-yard TD against Illinois Cycling Club and made all three PATs in win. Scored one TD, made three PATs, and returned two kickoffs 25 yards in shutout of Physicians and Surgeons.

CASPER, DAVE. 1971-1972-1973; T, TE; 6'3", 252; Chilton, WI. A rare starter in the modern era at two line positions. Excellent technician in blocking, with superb lateral quickness for a tackle. As TE on 1973 national championship team, presented formidable problem for defenders. In 1971, backed up at LT and caught one pass for 12 yards. In 1972, played T for most of the year. Caught one pass for six yards and made two tackles for the year. In 1973, started at TE; made 19 receptions for 317 yards and four TDs to go with one tackle. Consensus All-American. For his career, caught 21 passes for 335 yards and four TDs; also made three tackles on special teams.

CASTNER, PAUL. 1920-1921-1922; HB, FB; 6'0", 190; St. Paul, MN. Never played high school football but was developed by Rockne into All-American. Fine athlete in football, hockey, and baseball. As pitcher with the Chicago White Sox, was victimized by Ty Cobb when Cobb stole home from third. Holds Notre Dame's record for career kickoff return average (21 for 767 yards and two TDs, a 36.5-yard average) and single season (11 in 1922 for 490 yards and two TDs, a 44.5-yard average). Played both with Gipp and the Four Horsemen. His broken hip in the 1922 Butler game gave Rockne the opportunity to make the moves that brought four gifted sophomores together as starters, and the rest is football history. A powerful, punishing runner, a fine passer, an excellent kicker, and a good defender. In 1920, backed up at FB. Ran for short yardage, kicked one PAT, and intercepted one pass for 35-yard runback in win over Kalamazoo. Made 25-yard TD run in win over Western Michigan. Fired 50-yard TD pass to Chet Grant in win over Purdue. In 1921, backed up at RHB. In close loss to Iowa, kicked 70-yard punt, just missed 50-yard drop-kick field goal, and caught 33-yard pass. Helped beat Purdue with punts of 50, 55, and 45 yards, field goals of 20 and 24 yards, and good short yardage runs. Manhandled Indiana with a fumble recovery, three interceptions, a pass reception for 11-yard TD, and 50-

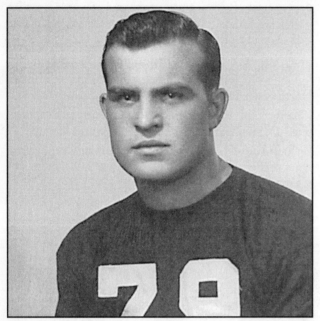

Corny Clatt started at fullback in 1942 and 1946, playing as a backfield starter with both Bertelli and Lujack.

yard TD sprint. In shutout win over Army, made one interception plus 27 yards, and punted 88 yards. Three days later, helped defeat Rutgers with 55-yard TD run, two-yard TD plunge, 55-yard punt, and field goals of 45 and 43 yards. Ran for three TDs against Haskell, one for 50 yards. Punted well against Marquette, ran for short yardage, and returned two kickoffs 28 yards. In win over MAC, made 65-yard kickoff return, one TD run, and a completed pass. Made second-team All-America as a sub. In 1922, returned a kickoff 95 yards in win over Kalamazoo. Caught TD pass from Stuhldreher in win over Georgia Tech. Personally beat Indiana with a 27-point performance in a 27-0 Irish win: booted two field goals of 43 and 35 yards, ran for TDs of 20 and 22 yards, intercepted a Hoosier pass and ran it back 35 yards for TD, and kicked three PATs. A hip injury against Butler ended it for him.

CHEVIGNY, JACK. 1926-1927-1928; HB; 5'9", 173; Hammond, IN. Good HB for Rockne; a teammate of Christy Flanagan; best known for scoring the first TD after Rockne's halftime pep talk in 1928 Army "Win One for the Gipper" game. When he crossed Army's goal, Chevigny cried out, "That's one for the Gipper!"

Later coached briefly at Notre Dame and was head coach at Texas. In 1926, back up at RHB. Scored TD in first varsity game in win over Beloit. Scored against Minnesota on 17-yard run. In 1927, backed up at RHB. His solid running against Georgia Tech helped secure an Irish win. In 1928, started at RHB. Scored Notre Dame's only TD on three-yard run in loss to Wisconsin. Scored on 10-yard sprint in win over Drake. Scored his TD for the Gipper with one-yard plunge on fourth down; had to be carried from the field later in the game after recovering a bad snap. Scored his final TD on 51-yard run off a fake reverse in loss to USC.

CLATT, CORNY. 1942-1946-1947; FB; 6-0, 200; East Peoria, IL. Solid performer for Leahy's first T-formation team and the immediate post-war, undefeated teams. In 1942, started at FB. Helped beat Iowa Pre-Flight with an interception and 37-yard TD return. Made 15-yard TD run in win over Illinois. Helped beat Otto Graham and Northwestern with five-yard TD buck, one-yard TD dive, 47 yards rushing on TD drive, and an interception to set up a Bertelli TD pass. In 13-13 tie with Great Lakes, scored on 82-yard TD burst. In 1946, backed up at FB and scored the last TD in win over Illinois. Slammed in from the Purdue two for TD in Irish rout. For the season, gained 105 yards on 28 carries. In 1947, backed up at FB and scored four-yard TD in win over Tulane after going 34 yards on three runs to get there. For the year, rushed 11 times for 49 yards and one TD.

CLAUSEN. JIMMY. 2007-2008-2009. QB, 6'2" 222. Thousand Oaks, CA. Much ballyhooed recruit out of a top California prep school. Played for Weis, but the Irish under him had already reached their peak. Thrown into the breach left by the graduated Brady Quinn. Accumulated some strong statistics as the starting QB, but left ND after three years, having accumulated the most losses of any Irish signal caller in their 120+ years of intercollegiate football. Blessed with a strong, accurate arm and good reading skills against defenses. Became Irish starter in his second collegiate game, in 2007. For the year, hit 138 passes in 245 throws for 1,254 yards, seven TDs and six INTs. Lost 187 yards in 62 rushing attempts, scoring two TDs, as ND fell to an abysmal 3-9 record. Started all 13 games as a sophomore in 2008. Weis opened up the play book and Clausen fired 268 completions in 440 throws, a good 60% completion figure, good for 3,172 yards to go with 17 INTs and 25 TDs. His linemen did a better job of protecting him, with 54 runs for -73 yards. His passing improved again in 2009, with 289 completions in 425 attempts, a 68% completion rate, racking up 3,722 yards. He fired 28 TDs against only four INTs. He also racked up three TDs on the ground, with 59 rushes for -95 yards. He did not play his senior year, although he was on track to threaten Quinn's records. In spite of all the losses, Clausen completed 695 passes in 1,110 attempts, a 62.6% completion rate, good for 8,148 yards, 60 TDs and 27 INTs. Trying to escape blitzers, he had 175 runs for -355 yards and five TDs.

CLEMENTS, TOM. 1972-1973-1974; QB; 6'0", 184; McKees Rock, PA. Three-year starter for Parseghian at QB; led offense in 1973 national championship season. Fine field general, excellent ball handler, good passer, and very quick. In 1972, started at QB. For the season, completed 83 of 162 passes for eight TDs and 1,163 yards, and rushed for 341 yards and four TDs on 86 carries. In 1973, led Notre Dame in total offense with 1,242 yards gained on 149 plays for 8.3-yard average. Completed 60 of 113 passes for 882 yards and eight TDs, picked up 360 yards and four TDs on 89 carries, and ran for a two-point conversion. Saved Sugar Bowl win with daring pass from his end zone to TE Robin Weber. In 1974, started at QB; threw 122 completions in 215 attempts for eight TDs and 1,549 yards, rushed 95 times for 369 yards and two TDs. Helped beat Alabama in 1975 Orange Bowl with 11 runs for 26 yards and four of seven passes for 19 yards. For his career, completed 265 of 490 passes for 3,594 yards and 24 TDs; rushed 270 times for 1,070 yards and 10 TDs and a two-point conversion for a career total of 4,664 yards and 34 TDs.

COADY, ED. 1888-1889; QB; Pana, IL. Starter at QB for fledgling Irish in four games over two seasons, part of the second wave of participants in the new sport. Was on the field for the first two Irish victories, after starting with three losses. In 9-0 win over Northwestern, faked to a lineman to score an easy TD.

COBBINS, LYRON. 1993-1994-1995-1996; ILB; 6'0", 245; Kansas City, KS. Tough, determined ILB for Holtz's last teams. Solid pass defender. In '93, made six tackles in 4:01 minutes of limited playing time. In '94, started two games, and made 34 stops in 104:54, adding two stops in '95 Fiesta Bowl loss to Colorado. Started all 11 games in '95, making an impressive 82 solo tackles to go with 23 assists for 105 total tackles, with three for minus-eight yards to go with one sack for minus-four yards, four PBU, one fumble caused, three fumbles

recovered, and a team-leading five INTs returned 86 yards in 283:32 minutes. Added eight tackles, two for losses, against FSU in '96 Orange Bowl loss. Started all 11 games in his senior year in '96; made 50 solo hits, adding 22 assists, for 72 tackles, three for minus-11 yards to go with four sacks for minus-32 yards, three PBU, one fumble recovery and one INT. For his career, had 227 tackles, six for minus-19 yards, five sacks for minus-36 yards, seven PBU, caused one fumble, recovered four fumbles, and made six INTs for 86 return yards.

COFALL, STAN. 1914-1915-1916; HB; 5'11", 190; Cleveland, OH. Three-year starter at LHB, the premier position in Harper/Rockne scheme. Fast, elusive; good passer and kicker. In 1914 started at LHB. Scored two TDs and kicked seven PATs in opening win over Alma. Scored four TDs playing only the first half against Rose Poly. In loss to Yale, had 30-yard run and 35-yard pass completion. Played both HB and QB in win over South Dakota and scored on 15-yard run, threw TD pass, returned two punts 65 yards, and booted one PAT. Played great defense and kicked three PATs in win over Haskell. Scored only Irish TD on one-yard plunge in loss to Army. Against Carlisle, kicked 50-yard field goal, three PATs, and 85-yard punt; completed 20-yard pass; and made TD plunge and assorted short runs. Scored one TD and one PAT in win over Syracuse. In 1915, started at LHB. Against Haskell scored TDs on runs of 20, 15, and 12 yards; added an interception and one PAT. In loss to Nebraska, ran for 50 yards, made two sacks, caught one pass, completed one pass, and scored on three-yard plunge. Threw 50-yard TD pass that beat Army 7-0. Against Creighton, rushed for 155 yards, scored two TDs and four PATs, completed two passes, and punted 65 yards. Led Notre Dame in 36-7 win over Texas with a TD on a short plunge, 75 yards rushing, one fumble recovery, one interception, 37-yard kickoff return, and three PATs. Two days later, battered Rice with three TDs, including 30-yard run and 90-yard kickoff return, five PATs, 70-yard punt, and 21-yard pass completion. In 1916, started at LHB and captained the team. Scored on 60-yard TD blast in rout of Wabash. Kicked one field goal and one PAT in loss to Army. Scored on two long runs in win over MAC. Made All-American.

COLLINS, GREG. 1972-1973-1974; LB; 6'3", 228; Troy, MI. Teamed with Mahalic and others to give Parseghian a solid linebacking corps in early 1970s. Fast, big, good tackler; good nose for the ball. In 1972, backed up at OLB; made 18 tackles during the season.

In 1973, led national champions with 133 tackles, 11 for minus-58 yards; broke up one pass; recovered two fumbles; and led linebackers with three interceptions and 25 return yards. In 1974, started at OLB and captained team. For the season, led Irish defense with 144 tackles, six for minus-22 yards, and recovered one fumble. For his career, made 295 tackles, 17 for minus-80 yards; broke up one pass; recovered three fumbles; and made three interceptions for 25 return yards.

CONJAR, LARRY. 1965-1966; FB; 6'0", 212; Harrisburg, PA. Powerful, quick, with good hands and excellent blocking skills. A rare example for his era of a player dedicated to weightlifting, now a routine aspect of a player's training. In 1965, started at FB. Was second leading rusher on ground-oriented team with 535 yards on 137 carries for seven TDs, caught four passes for 55 yards, had one kickoff return for 10 yards, and made one tackle. In 1966, carried 112 times for 521 yards and seven TDs, caught four passes for 62 yards, returned three kickoffs 39 yards, and ran for two-point conversion. Made All-American. Scored five career TDs against USC. For his career, carried 249 times for 1,056 yards and 14 TDs, caught eight passes for 117 yards, returned four kickoffs 49 yards, ran for two-point conversion, made one tackle, and accumulated 1,222 total yards.

CONLEY, TOM. 1928-1929-1930; E; 5'11", 175; Philadelphia, PA. Last team captain under Rockne. Always a deep threat and played solid defense. In 1928, backed up at RE. In 1929, started at RE. Caught Carideo pass for 26 yards to reach Georgia Tech's two and set up TD in Irish win. Scored first Irish TD in win over USC with 54-yard pass from Elder to go with several other receptions. In 1930, started at RE and captained the team. Caught 56 yard pass from Schwartz in win over Carnegie Tech. Played brilliant defensive game and blocked superbly in hometown showing against Penn in 60-20 rout. On Schwartz's "perfect play," helped cave in right side of Army's line with block on tackle to help release Schwartz. In big win over USC, Rockne's last before his death, made 37-yard reception from Schwartz. Made second-team All-America.

CONNOR, GEORGE. 1946-1947; T; 6'3", 225; East Chicago, IL. Tower of strength on one of Leahy's peerless lines; devastating blocker and fine tackler. In 1946, started at LT and won the Outland Trophy. In 1947, started at LT. Recovered USC fumble and later made

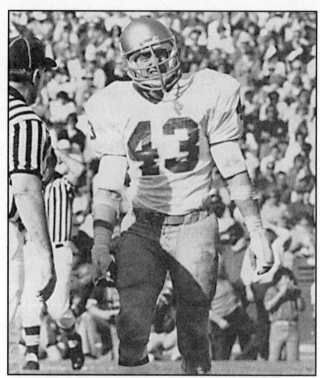

An all-time Irish player: Bob Crable, three-year starter at linebacker, consensus All-American in 1981.

the block to spring Sitko on 76-yard TD run.

COUTRE, LARRY. 1946-1947-1948-1949; HB; 5'9", 170; Chicago, IL. Speedy back; had poor eyesight but played great football for undefeated Leahy teams after war. Never played in a losing contest at Notre Dame. Good runner, receiver, and defender. In 1946, as a reserve, ran two times for 11 yards. In 1947, backed at LHB; gained 127 yards on 34 carries for two TDs, caught four passes for 87 yards, and returned three punts 37 yards. In 1948, backed up Sitko at RHB; gained 152 yards on 27 carries, caught two passes for minus-one yard, made one interception for 41-yard runback, and recovered one fumble. In 1949, started at RHB for the national champions; was second leading rusher, just behind Sitko, with 645 yards on 102 carries (6.2-yard average), caught 13 passes for 271 yards, and returned four kickoffs 48 yards; led team with all-purpose production of 964 yards. For his career, carried 163 times for 999 yards (6.12-yard average) for nine TDs; caught 19 passes for 357 yards; and returned three punts 37 yards, four kickoffs 48 yards, and one interception 41 yards, for a total of 1,482 yards (7.8 yards gained every time he got the ball), plus one fumble recovery.

COVINGTON, JOHN. 1990-1991-1992-1993; SS;

6'1", 211; Winter Haven, FL. Three-year starter for Holtz at SS, but also saw some time at LB and DE. One of 20 children, had a good combination of speed, strength, and quickness to handle a variety of defensive chores. In 1990, mostly with special teams, had five solo tackles and one assist in 4:02 minutes. In 1991, played SS and OLB. For the year, made 31 solo tackles, 27 assists, and broke up three passes in 208:49 minutes of play. Made five tackles in ND's defensive gem against Florida in '92 Sugar Bowl. In 1992, started the opener at DE then finished the year at SS. For the campaign, made 49 solo tackles, 14 others, broke up seven passes, and made three INTs, returning them six yards in 195:44 minutes of action. Against Texas A&M in the Cotton Bowl, tacked on four other hits. In 1993, started at SS, making 43 solo hits, 15 assists, broke up four passes, made two INTs and returned them seven yards, and recovered one fumble in 253:39 minutes of playing time. In '94 Cotton Bowl win over Texas A&M, made seven tackles and broke up one pass. For his career, made 128 solo tackles, 68 others, for a total of 195, with 15 passes broken up, five INTs, for 13 interception return yards, and recovered one fumble in 662:14 seconds of career game action.

CRABLE, BOB. 1978-1979-1980-1981; LB; 6'3",225; Cincinnati, OH. Fine linebacker for Devine and Faust. High on any list of modern-era Notre Dame stars. Had great range, mobility, reading skills, tackling skills, general toughness, and leadership qualities. In 1978, backed up at OLB; recovered Houston fumble on their 25 to lead to Irish TD in Cotton Bowl comeback win. For the season, made 13 tackles, broke up one pass, blocked one kick, and recovered one fumble. In 1979, started at MLB; won Michigan game with last-second block of a field goal. Made 26 tackles in loss to Clemson. For the season, made almost 20 percent of defense's tackles with 187 (a new record), with 10 for minus-29 yards; broke up three passes; recovered two fumbles; blocked three kicks; and made one interception—a performance in the range of Ross Browner's Outland Trophy year. Made All-American. In 1980, made 154 tackles, seven for minus-12 yards; broke up three passes; and recovered two fumbles. Named MVP by teammates; consensus All-American. In 1981, started at MLB. Set record for career tackles during Air Force game. For the year, made 167 tackles, 16 for minus-54 yards; broke up three passes; recovered two fumbles; and made two interceptions for 60 return yards. Repeat consensus All-American. For his career, made 521 tackles (a new

record), 33 for minus-95 yards; broke up 10 passes; recovered seven fumbles; blocked four kicks; and made three interceptions for 60 return yards.

CREANEY, MIKE. 1970-1971-1972; TE; 6'4", 232; Towson, MD. Big, fast TE for Theismann and Clements; capable of breaking a long one; good blocker; and three-year starter. In 1970, started at TE; caught 18 passes for 418 yards and two TDs (23.2-yard average). In 1971, started at TE; caught 11 passes for 151 yards and one TD (in a season when the passing game was in disarray). In 1972, started at TE; caught 17 passes for 321 yards and two TDs, and made two tackles. For his career, caught 46 passes for 890 yards and five TDs, and made two tackles.

CROTTY, JIM.1957-1958-1959; HB, FB; 5'10", 185; Seattle, WA. Good, general-purpose player for Brennan and Kuharich. In 1957, backed up at RHB and contributed to upset win of USC with 57 yards rushing and one TD. For the year, rushed for 69 yards on 14 carries and one TD, returned two kickoffs 91 yards, and broke up three passes. In 1958, started at RHB and was third in rushing with 315 yards on 67 carries; also caught 14 passes for 137 yards and a two-point conversion; was first on team in kickoff returns with nine for 228 yards; made one interception; returned five punts for 64 yards; recovered one fumble; made 38 tackles, and led team with four passes broken up. In 1959, backed up at FB. For the year, gained 184 yards on 62 carries for three TDs, caught eight passes for 104 yards, made one interception and six-yard return, and made 29 tackles. For his career, carried 143 times for 568 yards and four TDs, caught 22 passes for 241 yards and one TD conversion, returned five punts 64 yards, returned 11 kickoffs 319 yards, made two interceptions for six return yards, broke up seven passes, recovered one fumble, made 67 tackles, and accumulated 1,134 total yards.

CROTTY, MIKE. 1969-1970-1971; FB, S; 5'9", 180; Seattle, WA. Much like his brother, Jim, an all-purpose player under Parseghian. Originally on offense but switched to defense and stayed there for two years as starter. Had good speed and lateral quickness; good tackler. In 1969, backed up at LHB. For the year, gained 183 yards on 43 carries, caught two passes for eight yards, returned two punts six yards and four kickoffs 111 yards. In 1970, started at S. For the year, led DBs with 77 tackles, two for minus-eight yards; broke up four passes; recovered two fumbles; led the team with 19 punt returns for 100 yards; and returned three kickoffs

37 yards. In 1971, returned interception 65 yards for TD in win over Northwestern. For the year, led DBs with 65 tackles, made two interceptions for 66 return yards and one TD, and led team with nine passes broken up and 33 punt returns for 297 yards. For his career, gained 807 total yards, carried 43 times for 183 yards, caught two passes for eight yards, made 142 tackles with two for minus-eight yards, broke up 13 passes, recovered two fumbles, made two interceptions for 66 return yards and one TD, returned 54 punts 403 yards, and returned seven kickoffs 148 yards.

CROWLEY, JIM. 1922-1923-1924; HB; 5'11", 160; Green Bay, WI. Known as Sleepy Jim; the clown of the Four Horsemen. Very fast, but could lull a defense before bursting into action. Played for Curly Lambeau in Green Bay (who played for Rockne in 1918). Later coached at Fordham, where one of his Seven Blocks of Granite was Vincent Lombardi, who completed the cycle when he went to Green Bay and coached Paul Hornung. As one of the Horsemen, had the intangible talent of timing necessary for the dreaded Notre Dame Shift (ends and backfield flexed or shifted in unison just before the snap). The Horsemen operated in the shift before it was legislated into oblivion. In 1922, backed up Layden at LHB. Had 55-yard TD dash in win over DePauw. Led team with 566 yards rushing on 75 carries and in passing with 10 of 21 for 154 yards and one TD; also made two interceptions. In 1923, started at RHB. Ran 68 yards for TD in opening win over Kalamazoo. Intercepted Army pass and returned it 37 yards in 13-0 Irish win. For the season, gained 536 yards on 88 carries, led the team in passing with 13 of 36 for 154 yards and one TD, caught one pass for 44 yards, made four interceptions for 31 return yards, and returned four kickoffs for 89 yards. In 1924, started at RHB. Scored winning TD with 20-yard run in 13-7 Army game. Made 250 yards rushing and one TD in win over Princeton. Caught 65-yard TD strike from Layden to help end Nebraska's winning streak over Notre Dame. Scored on pass from Stuhldreher in win over Carnegie Tech. Made three PATs in win over Stanford in Rose Bowl. For the season, gained 731 yards on 131 carries for six TDs, completed 14 of 26 passes for 236 yards and two TDs, caught 12 passes for 265 yards and three TDs, and returned four kickoffs 52 yards. For his career, gained 1,841 yards on 294 carries for 15 TDs, completed 37 of 83 passes for 544 yards and four TDs, caught 13 passes for 309 yards and three TDs, made six interceptions for 40 return yards, returned four punts 36 yards and eight kickoffs 141 yards. His career totals

The irrepressible Ziggy Czarobski, starting right tackle for Notre Dame in 1946 and 1947, an All-America pick.

were 2,911 yards, 18 TDs, and 36 PATs. By any standard, stands as one of the all-time Fighting Irish heroes.

CULLINAN, JOE. 1900-1901-1902-1903; T; 5'10", 177; Notre Dame, IN. Known as Jepers. Teamed with Red Salmon to start to put the Fighting Irish on football map. Was small even then for T; quick, heady player. In 1900 backed up RT. In 1901, backed up LT. In 1902, started at LT. In 1903, started at LT and blocked punt in shutout of Lake Forest; later scored TD. Scored TD against American Medical in 52-0 blowout. Ran for short yardage and returned a kickoff 15 yards in win over Ohio Medical. Was integral part of powerhouse team that shut out nine opponents by combined score of 292 to 0, the only time in Fighting Irish annals for a team with a full slate of games to shut out all opponents.

CULVER, RODNEY. 1988-1989-1990-1991. FB, TB; 5'10", 226; Detroit, MI. Integral part of a bevy of talented backs playing for Holtz (Ricky Watters, Tony and Reggie Brooks, Dorsey Levens, Anthony Johnson, Lee Becton, Jerome Bettis). Brilliant speed (4.38 40-yard dash) in a sparkplug body made for a serious problem for defenders to solve—he could run them over or run by them. In 1988, played in all 12 games; started out on the D as a reserve SS, then switched to FB when injuries took out the top two players. Gained 195 yards and scored three TDs on 30 carries for team-leading 6.5 yards per carry average; caught one pass for 10 yards. Played 62:28 minutes. Scored one TD in four rushes for 20 yards as Irish whipped W. Virginia in the '89 Fiesta Bowl to take the national title. In 1989, played both TB and FB. Gained 242 yards on 59 carries, scoring five TDs; had three KORs for 28 yards. Played 104:20 minutes. Gained 29 yards on five carries in '90 Orange Bowl win over Colorado. In 1990, started at FB, leading the Irish in rushing and earning honorable mention All-American recognition. Rushed 150 times for 710 yards and five TDs; caught 13 passes for 145 yards and two TDs; returned five kickoffs 53 yards. Saw 231:22 minutes of action. In tough loss to Colorado in '91 Orange Bowl, gained nine yards on five carries. In 1991, switched to TB but injuries curtailed his productiveness. Started eight games, gained 550 yards on 101 carries; hauled in six passes for 76 yards; returned three kickoffs 56 yards, and played 123:26 minutes. Racked up 93 yards and one TD on 13 carries as ND beat Florida in the '92 Sugar Bowl. His 1,697 yards gained in regular-season rushing stood him at 19th on the all-time list of Irish backs. In his career, had 367 carries for 1,848 yards and 16 TDs, caught 20 passes for 231 yards and two TDs, had 11 KORs for 137 yards, and played 521:36

The speedy Frank Dancewicz started at quarterback for the 1944 and 1945 teams.

minutes. His all-purpose yardage total comes to 2,216 yards gained on 398 attempts, a 5.56 yards per attempt average for 18 TDs.

CZAROBSKI, ZYGMONT. 1942-1943-1946-1947; T; 6'0", 213; Chicago, IL. Leading orator, raconteur, and jokester of Leahy years, and a professional Irish personality after that. Leahy may have been impossible to take without Ziggy in the wings. Started for three national championship teams. In 1942, backed up at RT. In 1943, started at RT for the national champions. In 1946, started at RT for the national champions. Recovered fumble to lead to TD in win over Illinois. In 1947, started at RT for national champions. Recovered Tulane fumble at the Irish 40 to lead to TD. Made All-American.

DABIERO, ANGELO. 1959-1960-1961; HB; 5'8", 165; Donora, PA. Teamed with George Sefcik as one of "Gold Dust Twins." Fast, shifty runner and receiver; good defensive player. In 1959, backed up at RHB. For the season, made 36 carries for 118 yards, caught six passes for 64 yards, returned four kickoffs 70 yards and four punts 27 yards, and made 13 tackles. In 1960, started at RHB. Led team with 325 yards on 80 carries for two TDs, and in punt returns with eight for 102 yards; caught five passes for 112 yards and one TD; made one interception; returned five kickoffs 114 yards; led team with six passes broken up; and made 37 tackles. In 1961, helped defeat Oklahoma with 176 yards on 11 carries. For the year, led team with 637 yards on 92 carries (for 6.9-yard average) and four TDs; caught 10 passes for 201 yards and one TD; also led in punt returns with 11 for 97 yards; was second in kickoff returns with 203 yards on eight returns; third in tackles with 47; led with five interceptions for 78 return yards; and second with five passes broken up. For his career, rushed 208 times for 1,080 yards and six TDs, caught 21 passes for 377 yards and two TDs, returned 17 kickoffs 387 yards and 23 punts 226 yards, made six interceptions for 78 return yards, broke up 11 passes, and made 97 tackles. His career total was 2,048 yards, done mostly in two seasons.

DAHMAN, BUCKY. 1925-1926-1927; HB; 5'8", 156; Youngstown, OH. Teamed with Christy Flanagan in the years immediately following the Four Horsemen. Speedy, elusive runner; fine receiver; excellent defender; good kicker. Fit Rockne's shift tactics well. In 1925, backed up at RHB. Scored final TD in mismatch win over Baylor with interception and 50-yard runback. Scored in shutout of Lombard. In 1926, backed up at RHB. In opener with Beloit, scored one TD and three PATs in 77-0 win. Ran 65 yards for TD in tough win over Minnesota and Nagurski. Scored TD on 10-yard run in win over Penn State. Scored on five-yard plunge as Notre Dame beat Georgia Tech. Added two TD runs in shutout of Indiana. In 1927, started at RHB to team with Flanagan. Scored TD to cap five-play drive in 19-6 win over Indiana. Preserved 76 win over USC with 25-yard TD pass from Riley, one PAT kick, and interception on USC's last possession.

DANCEWICZ, FRANK. 1943-1944-1945; QB; 5'10", 180; Lynn, MA. One of fastest players on Leahy's teams, but played in shadows of Bertelli and Lujack. In 1944, started at QB. For the year, rushed 69 times for 230 yards and two TDs, and completed 72 of 153 passes for 999 yards and seven TDs. In 1945, started at QB. For the year, rushed 12 times for 12 yards, and completed 32 of 88 passes for 539 yards and four TDs. For his career, ran 81 times for 242 yards and two TDs, and completed 104 of 241 passes for 1,538 yards and 11 TDs.

DAWSON, LAKE. 1990-1991-1992-1993; FL; 6'1", 202; Federal Way, WA. With silky moves, deceptive speed, great hands, and precision routes, played WR for Holtz. In 1990, backed up at SE and played in all 11 games. For the season, caught 6 passes for 107 yards and had one KOR in 47:41 minutes of action. In 1991, started at FL and caught the second most passes for ND that year. In the campaign, snagged 24 passes for 433 yards and one TD, and ran once for 13 yards in 138:49 minutes of play. Hauled in a 40-yard TD pass from Rick Mirer to go with another for nine yards in the 792 Sugar Bowl win over Florida. In 1992, started at SE, becoming the top pass catcher for the Irish. For the season, caught 25 passes for 462 yards and one TD while also contributing 50 plays to the kicking game special teams in 140:37 minutes of action. Caught two passes for 46 yards in '93 win over Texas A&M in the Cotton Bowl. Earned honorable mention All-America recognition. In 1993, maintained his consistent performance with another 25 catches to lead ND's receivers for 395 yards and two TDs, while playing 174:38 minutes. Snagged two more passes for 41 yards in close win over Texas A&M in '94 Cotton Bowl. For his career, made 86 catches for 1,333 yards good for five TDs, returned one kickoff, and carried once for 13 yards in 501:45 minutes.

DEMMERLE, PETE. 1972-1973-1974; SE; 6'1", 196; New Canaan, CT. Fine receiver for Clements and 1973 national champions. Possession receiver rather than constant deep threat; had great hands and precise moves. In 1972, played only 5:22 minutes but scored Notre Dame's only TD in blowout loss to Nebraska in Orange Bowl. For the season, carried once for 23 yards and caught five-yard TD pass. In 1973, started at SE. For the year, led Fighting Irish receivers with 26 receptions for 404 yards and five TDs, including three against Miami, the game-winner against MSU, and a two-point conversion to help beat Alabama in Sugar Bowl. In 1974, started at SE; again led receivers with 43 receptions for 667 yards and six TDs. Consensus All-American and Rhodes Scholar finalist. For his career, caught 70 passes for 1,076 yards and 12 TDs and ran once for 23 yards.

DENSON, AUTRY. 1995-1996-1997-1998; TB; 5'10", 200; Lauderhill, FL. Notre Dame's all-time leading ground-gainer; with Pinkett, only the second runner for ND to compile three straight 1,000-yard seasons. Strong, quick, durable runner who specialized in brilliant cutback moves, with a great nose for the end zone. In '95, worked his way into the starting lineup for three games; had 137 carries for 695 yards, a 5.1 yards average, for eight TDs to go with six catches for 65 yards, four KOR

Notre Dame's all-time leading rusher, Autry Denson played both running back and receiver for Holtz's and Davie's teams in the late 1990s.

for 39 yards in 131:21 minutes. Added 11 carries for 67 yards in '96 Orange Bowl loss to FSU. Had a great sophomore campaign in '96: carried 202 times for 1,179 yards for a fine 5.8 average, good for eight TDs, adding 11 catches for 111 yards, two TDs, seven KOR for 141 yards, and 18 punt returns for 196 yards and one TD, in 193:36 busy minutes. Kept up the pace in his junior season in '97 with 264 carries for a career-best 1,268 yards and 12 TDs, accompanied by 30 receptions for 175 yards, one TD, to go with five KOR for 93 yards, and seven punt returns for 68 yards in 233:59 very productive minutes to go with a strong finish in the '98 Independence Bowl with 20 carries for 101 yards and three catches for 32 yards. In his senior campaign, served as a great team leader with 251 rushes for 1,176 yards, 15 TDs, six catches for 81 yards, five KOR for 93 yards, four punt returns for 40 another yards and a fine finish against Georgia Tech in the '99 Gator Bowl: 26 carries for 130 yards and three TDs to go with one catch for seven yards. For his sterling career, started 34 games, carried 911 times, good for 4,616 yards, a 5.06 yards per carry average and 46 TDs; caught 57 passes 471 yards and three TDs; returned 16 KO for 273 yards, returned 29 punts for 304 yards and one TD in 809:32 minutes. His total offensive yardage came to 5,664 total yards in 1,013 attempts, an average of 5.6 yards gained per attempt, good for 50 TDs.

DEVORE, HUGH. 1931-1932-1933; E; 6'0", 179; Newark, NJ. Rockne recruit who played with Moose Krause and for Hunk Anderson. Tough defensive player, tenacious blocker, and good hitter, with fair speed but very strong hands. In 1931, backed up at RE. In 1932, backed up at RE; as a sub in shutout of Army, played with broken hand and caught 45-yard TD pass, made numerous tackles, intercepted a pass, and recovered a fumble. In 1933, started at RE and captained team. Later served two stints as an assistant coach and as interim head coach in 1945 and 1963.

DIMINICK, GARY. 1971-1972-1973; HB; 5'9", 176; Mt. Carmel, PA. Speedy scatback, specialist in returning kicks. In 1971, backed up at LHB. For the season, rushed for 61 yards on 17 carries, caught two passes for 14 yards, and led the Fighting Irish with 199 yards on seven kickoff returns. In 1972, started at RHB. Ran 84 yards with kickoff return for TD in win over Navy. For the season, carried 71 times for 377 yards and two TDs, caught 14 passes for 143 yards and one TD, and

led team again with 15 kickoff returns for 331 yards and one TD. In 1973, backed up at LHB for the national champions. For the year, gained 121 yards on 19 carries (for 6.4-yard average) and one TD, caught two passes for 21 yards, and led for the third straight year with eight kickoff returns for 181 yards. For his career, rushed 107 times for 559 yards (5.22 yards per carry) and three TDs, caught 18 passes for 178 yards and one TD, and returned 30 kickoffs 711 yards (23.7 yards per return) for one TD.

DIMMICK, RALPH. 1908-1909-1910; T; 6'0", 225; Hubbard, OR. Bruising, dominant lineman prior to Rockne's arrival as player. Part of team that beat Michigan, and also part of the reason Yost cancelled series over eligibility. Played at Pacific University in Oregon, and apparently at Whitman College before going to Notre Dame. Yost objected to his playing in 1909, along with George Philbrook, also from the Northwest. In 1908, started at RT. Was deployed for short yardage in "tackle back" formation in win over Hillsdale. Ran well for short gains on cross bucks in loss to Michigan, to go with short kickoff return and sack for minus-five yards. Made run of 15 yards and recovered fumble in win over Wabash. Scored two TDs in beating Olivet, one on tackle around play. Ran for TD in win over Rose Poly and caught forward pass. In 1909, started at RT. Scored TD on 20-yard run and gained 80 plus yards in win over MAC. Played formidable defense in Irish 11-3 "upset" over Michigan. In 1910, started at RT and captained team. Cruised for three TDs in 51-0 win over Akron. Ran for three TDs in win over Rose Poly. Returned to Portland, OR, entered law school, and coached some football. In 1911, accepted invitation to play in Pacific's annual alumni game. During this contest, punctured a lung but kept playing and attended a party later. In tremendous pain and delirious, jumped through a window on upper floor of dormitory, and ran wildly around campus and the streets of Forest Grove with concerned police in hot pursuit. They subdued him and took him to a hospital, where he died 20 minutes later.

DINARDO, GERRY. 1972-1973-1974; G; 6'1", 242; Howard Beach, NY. Brother of Larry, Dominant interior lineman; integral member of the 1973 championship team. Excellent technique; good strength and quickness. In 1972, started at RG and played every minute offense was on the field. In 1973, key member of the line that set running backs free for rushing record of 3,502 yards on 673 carries (about 61 rushing plays per game, or 15 per quarter). In 1974, started at RG and made All-American.

Gerry DiNardo started at right guard from 1972 to 1974, a consensus All-America pick as a senior.

DINARDO, LARRY. 1968-1969-1970; G; 6'1", 243; Queens, NY. Must be counted among all-time greats. Greg Marx, himself an All-American, said that each practice session was a clinic in offensive blocking techniques. Instrumental player in success of Theismann-led offense under Parseghian. In 1968, started at LG. In 1969, started at LG and made All-American. In 1970, started at LG and was consensus All-American. Current head coach at Vanderbilt.

DOAR, JIM. 1901-1902; HB; 5'11",185; Cumberland, WI. Played with Red Salmon to give team tremendous striking potential with him on long excursions and Salmon bucking inside. Excellent runner and defender. In 1901, started at LHB. In 1902, started at LHB. Scored two TDs in 12-0 win over MAC, one on 65-yard sprint. Rushed for good short yardage gains and dropped several runners for losses in loss to Michigan. Helped beat Indiana with runs of 50 and 55 yards and kicked one conversion. Scored TD on 85-yard run in 92-0 rout of American Medical, and added 80-yard run later. Helped defeat DePauw with TD run. Shared rushing honors with Salmon in tie with Purdue.

DOLAN, ROSY. 1906-1907-1908-1909; T, G; 5'11", 210; Albany, OR. With Dimmick and Philbrook, part of Northwest connection. Combined with them to give

Notre Dame a line not to be lightly regarded. Despite portly appearance, could be counted on for gains of five and six yards when called on. In 1906, started at RT and ran effectively throughout season. Scored a TD the Physicians and Surgeons wipeout. In 1907, had surgery on knee early in season and hoped to play in big games at the end, but the knee did not respond well (one of the first such operations on record at Notre Dame). In 1908, started at RG. Played strong game against Michigan, including a sack. Ran back opening kickoff in win over Indiana. Played every minute of each game. In 1909, started at RG. Rushed for short yardage in win over MAC. Scored two TDs in win over Miami of Ohio. Played every minute for second consecutive year.

DORAIS, GUS.1910-1911-1912-1913; QB; 5'7",145; Chippewa Falls, WI. Only four-year starter at QB until Blair Kiel 70 years later. Excellent leader, superb field general, good throwing arm, fine speed, good defender, and very good kicker. Teamed with Rockne to make one of first great passing tandems in modern football. In 1910, started at QB. Made good impression against Akron with fine punt returning and cool demeanor. Kicked three PATs against Rose Poly. In 1911, started at QB. First recorded pass to Rockne was in blowout win over Ohio Northern; directed traffic for six players to score TDs; caught pass from FB Ray Eichenlaub. Helped demolish St. Viator in display of football skills: TD pass to Dutch Bergman, five conversion kicks, 25-yard dropkicked field goal, and short TD run. Booted five PATs in 80-0 win over Loyola. Narrowly missed field goal against Pitt that would have averted 0-0 tie. Made PAT kick against Wabash in 6-3 win. Missed two field goals in scoreless game with Marquette. In 1912, started at QB and captained team. Kicked three PATs and shared scoring among seven players as they obliterated St. Viator. Kicked eight conversions and had several long kickoff returns against Adrian. Scored one TD and kicked four PATs against Wabash. Kicked 25-yard field goal to beat Pitt 3-0. Led attack in win over Marquette with two TDs—one an 88-yard run during which he shed seven tacklers—to go with six conversion kicks and one field goal. In 1913, started at QB. Scored one TD and kicked seven PATs against Ohio Northern. In first "modern" football game against South Dakota, made two conversion kicks and mixed runs and passes to keep Coyotes befuddled in 20-7 Fighting Irish win. Returned punt 65 yards and kicked eight PATs in rout of Alma. In win over Army, completed 13 of 17 passes for TDs to Pliska and Rockne, returned punt 30 yards, intercepted a pass in the Notre Dame end zone, and was perfect with five PATs to go with nearly 300 yards of passing. Played brilliantly in win over Penn State: on one drive hit 40-yard pass to Pliska, ran 35 yards, and threw TD strike to Rockne; also made 15-yard kickoff return, two conversions, and 75-yard punt return lost to a sideline call. Beat Christian Brothers with 40-yard TD sprint, a long punt return for a TD, timely passing, and two conversion kicks. Against Texas five days later, scored on 15-yard run after a fake pass, drop-kicked three field goals, and tacked on two PATs. Led Notre Dame to three consecutive undefeated seasons and was instrumental in thrusting the team into the national spotlight.

DOWNS, BILL. 1905; FB; 5'11",195; Sayre, PA. Fine player for Notre Dame for one season; capable of breaking long gainers for TDs. In 1905, started at FB. Rushed for 75 plus yards in win over North Division, including 57-yard TD drive on five carries. Gained 50 plus yards on runs in loss to Wabash. Led all scorers in 142-0 rout of American Medical with four TDs on long runs and four conversion kicks; on one TD drive, went 70 yards on two runs. Scored six more TDs one week later against DePauw—10 TDs in a week must be an unofficial Irish record.

DOWNS, MORRIS. 1905; T; 5'10", 185; Sayre, PA. Brother of Bill Downs. In 1905, started at RT American Medical was just another game for this obscure lineman, except that the runners became fatigued from running for so many TDs and they turned it over to the linemen. Thus, this pudgy T scored two TDs and made four conversion kicks in 142-0 shutout. His scoring spree gave the family 43 points in one game—surely another unofficial record. Ran only for short yardage in losses to Indiana and Purdue.

DuBOSE, DEMETRIUS. 1989-1990-1991-1992 ILB, 6'2", 234; Seattle, WA. Intense, emotional, physical LB for Holtz. Had great quickness and lateral pursuit. In 1989, subbed as ILB; contributed mainly via 90 special teams appearances. Made three solo tackles and four assists in 20:28 minutes of play. Had two tackles in 1990 Orange Bowl win over Colorado, with one sack for minus-eight yards. In 1990, was a reserve ILB, but started four games, making 32 solo hits in the campaign, 16 assists, with two for minus-three yards, one sack for minus-eight yards, four passes broken up, done in 147:58

minutes of action. In 1991, started at ILB. Made an amazing 76 solo hits, 51 assists, with five for minus-six yards, broke up one pass, recovered two fumbles, and had one interception good for a 49-yard TD Had nine tackles in '92 Sugar Bowl, including one for negative yardage, and broke up two passes. Played 301:57 minutes and earned All-American accolades. In 1992, sat out first two games with an NCAA-imposed suspension, then stormed through another great season as starting ILB. Made 57 solo tackles, had 30 assists, 1.5 tackles for minus-three yards, one sack for minus-12 yards, broke up eight passes, and recovered one fumble. Against Texas A&M in Cotton Bowl win, had seven tackles, one sack for minus-seven yards, and recovered an Aggie fumble. Played 214:11 minutes and earned honorable mention All-America status. In his career, had 168 solo tackles, 111 assists, for a total of 279 tackles, with 8.5 for minus-12 yards, four sacks for minus-35 yards, 15 passes broken up, three fumble recoveries, one interception for a TD, and 684:34 minutes of playing time.

DUERSON, DAVE. 1979-1980-1981-1982; DB, SS; 6'3", 202; Muncie, IN. Fine defensive back for Devine and Faust; quick, extremely strong; heavy hitter. In 1979, backed up at LCB. For the season, led Fighting Irish with 12 punt returns for 209 yards; made 24 tackles, one for minus-one yard; broke up two passes, recovered one fumble; and made two interceptions for 43 return yards. In 1980, started at SS. For the year, made 34 tackles, three for minus-14 yards; broke up three passes; recovered two fumbles; intercepted one pass for 21-yard return; and returned 25 punts 194 yards. In 1981, started at SS. For the year, made 55 tackles, three for minus-eight yards; broke up five passes; had two interceptions for 88 return yards and one TD; and returned 32 punts 221 yards. In 1982, started at FS and was tricaptain. For the season, made 63 tackles, one for minus-two yards; broke up six passes, and made seven interceptions for 104 return yards; and returned 34 punts 245 yards. Made All-American. For his career, made 176 tackles, eight for -25 yards; broke up 16 passes; recovered three fumbles; had 12 interceptions for 256 return yards and one TD; and returned 103 punts for 869 yards. His total yardage was 1,125 yards.

DURANKO, PETE. 1963-1964-1965-1966; FB, LB, DT; 6'2", 235; Johnstown, PA. Recruited by Kuharich as FB; Parseghian saw lineman. Had tremendous strength and fine quickness as defensive lineman; played crucial role in defensive front for 1966 national champions. In 1963, backed up at FB. For the year, gained 93 yards on 26 carries and made one tackle. In 1964, started at LB; intercepted one pass against Wisconsin but was hurt and missed rest of the year. In 1965, started at LT. Against North Carolina, made 14 tackles. For the season, was second with 95 tackles. In 1966, started at LT. For the year, made 73 tackles, broke up one pass, and recovered one fumble. Made All-American. In his career, rushed 26 times for 93 yards, made 169 tackles, broke up one pass, recovered one fumble, and made one interception.

EDDY, NICK. 1964-1965-1966; HB; 6'0", 195; Lafayette, CA. Fast, elusive, excellent runner and receiver; tremendous ability to find seam and exploit it for long gain. Crucial component of championship efforts in 1964 and 1966. In 1964, started at RHB; gained 480 yards on 98 carries for seven TDs and a two-point conversion; caught 16 passes for 352 yards and two TDs; and returned seven kickoffs 148 yards. In 1965, started at RHB; led Irish with 582 yards on 115 runs for four TDs; also led in receiving with 13 catches for 233 yards and two TDs; returned three kickoffs 63 yards; and made two tackles. In the championship 1966 season, started at LHB. Consensus All-American. Gained 553 yards on 78 carries (7.1-yard average) for eight TDs; caught 16 passes for 123 yards; returned four kickoffs for 193 yards (48.3-yard average); and made two tackles. For his career, rushed 291 times for 1,615 yards, 17 TDs, and a two-point conversion; caught 45 passes for 708 yards and four TDs; returned 14 kickoffs 404 yards; and made four tackles. Scored 21 TDs and gained 2,727 total yards for an average gain of 7.8 yards every time he touched the ball.

EDWARDS, MARC. 1993-1994-1995-1996; FB; 6'0", 237; Norwood, OH. Powerful, determined runner and a good blocker, provided an excellent replacement for the Irish in short order for the departed Jerome Bettis. In his first season, 1993, carried 40 times for 186 yards, specializing in goalline situations in which he scored eight TDs, a record for Irish freshmen, playing 60:41 minutes. Scored a crucial TD and gained six yards on three carries in '94 Irish Cotton Bowl win over Texas A&M. Started four games for ND in 1994, carrying 48 times for 307 yards for two TDs, catching five passes for 58 yards, and seeing 131:35 minutes of play. Gained four yards on two carries in '95 Fiesta Bowl loss to Colorado. In 1995, teamed up with first-year player

Autry Denson and started all 11 games to give the Irish a great backfield tandem. On 140 rushes, he gained 717 yards and scored nine TDs while also showing good hands on 25 receptions for another 361 yards and three more TDs. Had a great game against FSU in '96 Orange Bowl against FSU—carrying 14 times for 67 yards and catching two passes for 25 yards. A knee injury suffered in the Boston College game curtailed his senior season, but still managed to gain 381 yards on 83 carries to score eight TDs to go with two more TDs on 16 catches for 169 yards. For his career, carried 330 times for 1,664 yards, scoring 28 TDs; caught 48 passes for 623 yards; and played 637:54 minutes for the Irish.

EGGEMAN, JOHN. 1897-1898-1899; C; 6'5", 256; Fort Wayne, IN. Brawny, tall, heavy, and immensely strong, which was required to do an effective job at center in the rough days of mass plays and wedges. Adept at fending off blockers with one arm and tackling with the other. Somewhat hampered in first two seasons by inexperienced guards, but he habitually pushed the middle of opponents' offensive lines back five or six yards at a time. In 1897, started at C. In 1898, started at C. Blocked an Illinois field goal to save game. Recovered MAC fumble and lurched four yards for TD in 53-0 blowout. Michigan triple-teamed him throughout their 23-0 win. In 1899, started at C.

A dynamic fullback on Holtz's last four teams, Marc Edwards scored 28 career touchdowns.

Clarence Ellis, a three-year starter in the defensive backfield for Parseghian, earned All-America honors in 1970 and 1971.

EICHENLAUB, RAY. 1911-1912-1913-1914; FB; 6'0", 210; Columbus, OH. Must be given serious consideration for any all-time Notre Dame team. Started four years at FB; crunching runner with good speed and tremendous strength; fine blocker; good receiver; and adequate passer. Against Army in 1913 his sledge-hammer blows into the line occupied the defense while Dorais and Rockne tuned up the passing game for win. In 1911, started at FB. Scored first TD with two-yard plunge in win over Ohio Northern, returned kickoff 30 yards, and completed pass to Dorais. Blocked St. Viator kick in easy Irish win. Scored two TDs in win over Butler. Bulled over for TD in win over Loyola. Grabbed Pitt fumble on their 35 in tie game. In 1912, started at FB; scored three TDs in 116-7 opener against St. Viator. Ran for 50-yard TD against Morris Harvey. Scored two TDs in win over Wabash that cinched state title. Had several long runs and one TD in win over St. Louis. Blasted Marquette's defense for four TDs, including 70-yarder in which he carried four defenders with him. In 1913,

started at FB; scored four TDs in wipeout of Ohio Northern. Scored two TDs against Alma. Against Army, ran for two TDs and kept the middle of the Cadet line busy with short yardage maneuvers. Finished off Penn State with TD burst. Ran at will and scored one TD against Christian Brothers. Against Texas, made two-yard TD plunge in Irish win. Made All-American. In 1914, started at FB. Played great game in a losing effort against Yale: a 45-yard kickoff return, then another for 15 yards, 35-yard pass completion, and two runs of 40 yards each to go with assorted shorter runs. Scored on 10-yard run against Carlisle.

ELDER, JACK. 1927-1928-1929; HB; 5'8", 165; Louisville, KY. Blazing fast speedster who defeated Olympic 100-yard sprinters; one of the fastest men ever to play for Rockne. In lack luster game, ran 18-yard TD to help defeat Drake. Threw 54-yard TD pass to Conley in win over USC. In one of the great moments in Irish football history, intercepted a Chris Cagle pass and ran 100 yards up the sidelines for game's only TD in win over Army, thus ensuring consecutive national championships.

ELLIS, CLARENCE. 1969-1970-1971; S, CB; 6'0", 178; Grand Rapids, MI. Fine leader in secondary under Parseghian; had great speed, superb lateral quickness, excellent leaping ability, excellent closing instincts, and good tackling skills. In 1969, started at S. For the year, made 31 tackles, led the Fighting Irish with 13 passes broken up, and made three interceptions for 98 return yards and one TD. In 1970, started at LCB. In Cotton Bowl win over Texas, caught 37-yard pass from the split-end position to lead to a field goal. For the season, made 27 tackles, broke up 11 passes, made seven interceptions for 25 return yards, and returned five punts 33 yards. In 1971, started at LCB. Caused Purdue fumble in their end zone that led to TD recovery and win. For the year, made 35 tackles, broke up eight passes, and made three interceptions for 34 return yards. Consensus All-American. For his career, made 93 tackles, broke up a 32 passes, made 13 interceptions for 157 return yards and one TD, returned five punts 33 yards, and caught one pass for 37 yards.

EURICK, TERRY. 1974-1975-1976-1977; HB; 5'11", 196; Saginaw, MI. Good all-purpose running back with Devine and Montana-led 1977 championship team. In 1974, backed up at RHB; gained 131 yards on 19 carries for one TD, caught one pass for six yards, and made one tackle. In 1975, backed up at LHB. For the year, led team in kickoff returns with 13 for 347 yards, gained 154 yards on 36 runs, and caught three passes for 30 yards. In 1976, backed up at LHB. For the year, gained 230 yards on 46 runs, caught five passes for 65 yards and one TD, and returned 10 kickoffs 181 yards. In 1977, backed up at LHB; scored twice in Cotton Bowl win over Texas. For the year, gained 291 yards on 68 carries for four TDs, caught 12 passes for 79 yards and three TDs, was second-highest scorer (behind kicker), returned nine kickoffs 211 yards, and made six tackles. For his career, carried 169 times for 806 yards and five TDs, caught 21 passes for 180 yards and four TDs, returned 32 kickoffs 739 yards, and made seven tackles. Accumulated 1,725 yards of all-purpose offense.

FAINE, JEFF. 2000-2001-2002; C; 6'3", 298; Sanford, FL. All-American C for ND in 2002, an iron man at the position with 35 consecutive starts and more than 900 minutes of action in his career. An absolutely dogged snap-to-whistle blocker, who often stayed in his man's chest until the poor guy had been totally run out of the picture. Part of a tradition of great Irish centers for Willingham, Davie and Holtz. Immensely strong, possessed a tortuous work ethic, Faine also executed the basics with proficient regularity, helping QB Carlyle Holiday become the first Irish signal caller to have three 100-yard games rushing in a season (and career).

FANNING, MIKE. 1972-1973-1974; DE, DT; 6'6", 255; Tulsa, OK. Big, quick, defensive lineman for Parseghian and a force in the 1973 championship year. Excellent pass rusher, part of defensive line that included Browner, Niehaus, and Stock. In 1972, backed up at DE. Made 13 tackles for the year, two for minus-10 yards. In 1973, started at DT. For the year, was Notre Dame's fourth leading tackler with 61, 12 for minus-76 yards; also recovered one fumble and led defensive linemen with 205 minutes of play. In 1974, started at DT. For the season, made 85 tackles, 12 for minus-52 yards; broke up one pass; and recovered one fumble. Made All-American. For his career, made 159 tackles, 26 for minus-138 yards; recovered two fumbles; and broke up one pass.

FARRAGHER, JIM. 1900-1901; T; 5'10",190; Youngstown, OH. Tough, gritty T who could score when needed and who played in spite of having only one eye. In 1900, started at LT and scored three TDs in 64-0 rout

of Howard Park. In 1901, started at LT. Blocked punt in 2-0 loss to Northwestern. Scored TD on fumble recovery in win over South Bend Commercial A.C.

FARLEY, JOHN. 1897-1898-1899-1900; E, FB; 5'9", 160; Paterson, NJ. Had extraordinary speed and elusiveness, capable of outflanking almost any defense; good defender; had absolute determination to score. In 1897, started at LE. Against Chicago Dental Surgeons, ran for 184 yards in first half, highlighted by 80-yard TD burst; in the second half, gained 280 more yards for one-game effort of 464 yards on the ground, surely an all-time Irish football feat. In the second half, scored on a short run and made 25-yard TD dash, 50-yard TD sprint, and 85-yard advance with a "backward pass." In 1898, started at LE. Crushed MAC with 220-plus yards running, including five runs of 20-plus yards, and two TDs on 38- and 45-yard runs. In 1899, started at LE. In 1900, scored on 75-yard run against Englewood High. In win over Howard Park, scored twice and made another 50-yarder. Against Rush Medical, had 35-yard run late in the game to save win; also blocked a field goal. Entered the priesthood and stayed at Notre Dame. Eventually lost his legs due to complications from diabetes.

FARRELL, JOE. 1962-1963-1964; HB, FB; 6'0", 205; Chicago, IL. Solid, dependable back who produced well under Parseghian. In 1962, backed up at FB. Carried 70 times for 278 yards and four TDs, caught one pass for 27 yards, returned one kickoff 19 yards, and made six tackles. In 1963, started at LHB. For the season, rushed 33 times for 79 yards, caught three passes for 33 yards, returned one punt 13 yards, made 30 tackles, broke up three passes, recovered one fumble, and intercepted one pass for 14-yard return. In 1964, started at FB for Parseghian. For the year, carried 93 times for 387 yards and four TDs, and caught six passes for 84 yards and one TD. For his career, rushed 196 times for 744 yards and eight TDs, caught 10 passes for 144 yards and one TD, returned one kickoff 19 yards and one punt 13 yards, made 36 tackles, broke up three passes, recovered one fumble, and had one interception plus 14-yard runback. His total career offense was 934 yards.

FASANO, ANTHONY. 2002-03-04-05. TE, 6'5", 255. Verona, NJ. Played during Willingham's tenure, but enjoyed a productive senior season under first Weis's aerial circus. Prototype TE for Brady Quinn: good size, fair speed, tough blocker, good hands, especially tough to bring down after catching a pass. Did not see game action in 2002 as a freshman. Started three games in 2003; caught 18 passes for 169 yards and two TDs. Became a full-time starter in 2004; snagged 27 passes for 367 yards and four TDs. Started all eleven games in 2005. Hauled in 45 passes for 564 yards and eight TDs. At the time, the 45 receptions was second-best for Irish TEs, as were his career totals. Nominated for the Mackey Award. For his career, he caught 90 passes good for 1,100 yards and eight TDs. Chose not to return for a fifth year.

FEENEY, AL. 1910-1911-1912-1913; C; 5'11", 190 Indianapolis, IN. Teammate of Rockne and Dorais; known for his sharp "passing"—snapping the ball—to *any* back, at various odd angles, and leading them with the ball if they were in motion. Always matched against behemoths that he dispatched. In 1910, backed up at C. In 1911, was tried at G but his talents could not be spared at C. Played good game in narrow win over Wabash. In 1912, started at C and made All-Western (a modified Big Ten). In 1913, started at C. Intercepted three passes against Alma, and two Army passes in classic win. Made interception against Penn State that saved win. Named All-Western again. In 1931 Indiana game, prevented Irish back from crashing into a barrier after a long run, and suffered a broken nose for his kindly gesture.

FERGUSON, VAGAS. 1976-1977-1978-1979; FB, HB; 6'1", 194; Richmond, IN. Among the very best who have ever played for Notre Dame. Fine blend of speed, power, finesse, balance, and good hands. Important factor in 1977 championship year as a backfield mate for Montana. In 1976, started at FB. In only eight games, was second leading rusher with 350 yards on 81 carries for two TDs; also caught three passes for 27 yards and one TD, and made two tackles. In 1977, started at LHB. For the year (although missing two games), was second on the team with 80 carries for 493 yards (a 6.2-yard average,) and six TDs, and caught six passes for 96 yards and one TD—in only 90:16 minutes of play. Ran three TDs against Texas in Cotton Bowl win; named outstanding offensive player of the game In 1978, started at RB and had the best year to date for an Irish running back: gained 1,192 yards on 211 carries for seven TDs, and caught 20 passes for 171 yards and one TD. Caught two-point conversion pass from Montana in 35-34 comeback win over Houston in Cotton Bowl. In 1979, started at RB and became first Irish runner to gain more than 1,000 yards twice. For his senior year, gained 1,437 yards on 301 carries for 17 TDs, caught

14 passes for 72 yards, and threw one incomplete pass. His rushing yardage was 71 percent of Notre Dame's ground game in 1979; his carries were 58 percent of all rushes; his 17 TDs were 58 percent of the team's TDs, both rushing and passing. Consensus All-American. For his career, rushed 673 times for 3,472 yards and 32 TDs, caught 43 passes for 366 yards and three TDs, made two tackles, and threw one incomplete pass. His totals were 35 TDs and 3,838 yards.

FIGARO, CEDRIC. 1984-1985-1986-1987; LB; 6'2", 246; Lafayette, LA. Three-year starter at LB for Faust and Holtz. Had good size, excellent strength, fine speed and quickness, and relentless pursuit. Always made things happen around the ball. In 1984, backed up at OLB. For the year, made 30 tackles, one for minus-seven yards, and broke up one pass. In 1985, started at OLB. For the year, made 62 tackles, two for minus-five yards; caused one fumble; and broke up two passes. In 1986, started at OLB. For the year, made 59 tackles, with 3.5 sacks for minus-31 yards and three others for minus-11 yards; caused two fumbles; recovered seven fumbles; and broke

Vagas Ferguson gets a quick start against Clemson in 1977. The halfback totaled 35 touchdowns and 3,838 yards for his career.

up four passes. Made All-American. In 1987, started at OLB. For the year, made 53 tackles, three sacks for minus-28 yards and five others for minus-15 yards, and broke up two passes. Made All-American. For his career, made 204 tackles, with 6.5 sacks for minus-59 yards and 11 others for minus-38 yards; caused three fumbles; recovered seven fumbles; and broke up nine passes.

FISCHER, BILL. 1945-1946-1947-1948; T, G; 6'2", 230; Chicago, IL. Powerful lineman for Leahy's great postwar years. Devastating blocker and tackler. In 1945, backed up at LT. In 1946, started at LG. In 1947, started at LG and led all linemen with 300 minutes of play. In 1948, started at LG. Blocked fourth-down pass to save win over Pitt. Recovered Husky fumble on their 24 to lead to TD in win. Consensus All-American in 1947 and 1948. Won Outland Trophy in 1948.

FISHER, TONY. 1998-1999-2000-2001; TB; 6'2", 226; Euclid, OH. Multitalented TB for the last four Davie teams, blessed with a good combination of speed and size, with good moves, and an excellent capacity for a burst of speed at the point of attack. Had his best year as a sophomore; shared time with a committee of TBs in other years, or suffered from nagging leg injuries that reduced his playing time. Ended up his career in 17th position for ND with yardage as a runner. As a freshman in 1998, played in eight games; carried eight times for 75 yards and saw action on 45 special teams plays. Started all 12 games as a soph in 1999; carried 156 times for 783 yards, good for five TDs, to go with 18 receptions for 297 yards and two more TDs. In his junior campaign on the '00 team, started five games, carried 132 times for 607 yards and six TDs, while snagging 12 passes for 106 yards and three TDs. Tallied ND's lone TD in Fiesta Bowl loss to Oregon State, with five carries for nine yards. In his senior campaign in '01, limited by a hamstring injury, started four games and played in five more, with 78 carries for 384 yards and four TDs, while catching three passes for minus-four yards. For his career, lugged the ball 379 times for 1,858 yards, good for 16 TDs, to go with 33 pass receptions for 399 yards and five TDs, with his total all-purpose yardage coming to 2,257 good for 21 TDs.

FLANAGAN, CHRISTIE. 1925-1926-1927; HB; 6'0", 170; Port Arthur, TX. Led Irish in ground yardage in each of his varsity seasons to join a select group, including Gipp and Sitko. Flashy, quick runner who fit well in Rockne's scheme whereby LHB did most of the

work, including passing. Followed Four Horsemen to give Notre Dame continued offensive threat. In 1925, started at LHB and ran 556 yards on 99 carries for seven TDs and kicked three PATs. In 1926, started at LHB and gained 535 yards on 68 runs (a 7.9-yard average), completed 12 of 29 passes for 207 yards, and returned six kickoffs 183 yards. Made All-American. In 1927, started at LHB. Ran 118 times for 731 yards, caught one pass for 30-yard TD. Made All-American. For his career, ran 285 times for 1,822 yards and 15 TDs.

FLANIGAN, JIM. 1990-1991-1992-1993; LB, DT; 6'2", 276; Sturgeon Bay, WI. Dependable, strong, quick, determined defender for Holtz; started out as a big linebacker and bulked up into a down lineman. In 1990, played in nine games, making three solo tackles and three assists along with 55 special teams appearances in 12:17 minutes. Had one tackle in bowl loss to Colorado. In 1991, started three games as ILB, but also played as a DT. For the campaign, made 19 solo tackles and 17 assists in 123:40 minutes of action. In 1992, spent time as a starter at RT and NT. For the season, made 36 solo hits and 15 assists, with 2.5 for minus-four yards, 3.4 sacks for minus-20 yards in 199:27 minutes in the trenches. Made four stops and recovered a fumble in the '93 bowl win three over Texas A&M. In 1993, split his starting

The great Christie Flanagan was a three-year starter at right halfback and another in a long line of excellent red-headed Irish players.

time between DE and DT. For the year, contributed 33 solo stops, 18 assists, with four for minus-17 yards and four sacks for minus-25 yards to go with two passes broken up and 75 special teams appearances in 240:39 minutes. Had a tremendous game against Texas A&M in '94 Cotton Bowl win with six tackles, including one sack for minus-11 yards in the game's final minute, to go with two other tackles for six more yards in losses. For his career, made 91 solo tackles, 64 other tackles, for a total of 155 tackles, with 8.5 for minus-27 yards, five sacks for minus-36 yards, and two passes broken up in 576:03 minutes of game action.

FLOYD, MICHAEL. 2008-09-10-11. WR, 6' 3", 224. St. Paul, MN. A match-up nightmare for the Irish under Weis and Kelly; towered over small DBs; could outrun the safeties. Re-set the Irish receiving records: In 2008, caught 48 passes for 719 yards and 7 TDs. In 2009, playing only seven games, caught 44 passes for 795 yards and nine TDs. In 2010, under Kelly, blossomed with 79 receptions for 1025 yards and 12 TDs. As a senior in 2011, hauled in an even 100 passes for 1147 yards, good for 10 TDs. His career receiving came to 271 receptions, good for a staggering 3686 Yds, with 13.6 yards per catch, and 38 TDs.

FOLEY, TIM. 1976-1977-1978-1979; T; 6'5", 265; Cincinnati, OH. Potent force on offensive line for Devine. Strong, with good speed; excellent technician in pass blocking. In 1976, backed up at LT. Played in all games at T and C, and with specialty teams. In 1977, was leader of national championship team. Had an excellent game against Texas in Cotton Bowl—even received MVP votes. In 1978, started at RT. In 1979, started at RT and made All-American.

FORTIN, AL. 1898-1899-1900-1901; T; 5'11", 180; Chicago, IL. Probably youngest man ever to play for the Fighting Irish—played against Illinois in October 1898, when he was 16 years old. In 1898, started at RT. In 1899, backed up at LT. In 1900, a veteran at age 18, was trusted to run with the ball. Scored two TDs against Highland Park. Earned praise for offensive line play in loss to Indiana. In 1901, scored TD in 6-0 win over Ohio Medical. Tallied one TD in win over Lake Forest. Ran for 40 plus yards in win over Purdue. Scored one TD in shutout of Chicago Physicians and Surgeons.

FROMHART, WALLY. 1933-1934-1935; QB; 5'11", 183; Moundsville, WV. Solid QB and team leader for Anderson and early Layden teams. Had good speed and was especially adept at broken field running. Also good blocker, fair passer, and good receiver. In 1933, was reserve QB. In 1934, started at QB. Led team with 33 punt returns for 288 yards. In 1934, started at QB. In what has been called the game of the century, caught two key passes on second scoring drive against Ohio State. For the year, led the team with 11 catches for 174 yards and one TD.

FRY, WILLIE. 1973-1975-1976-1977; DE; 6'3", 237; Memphis, TN. Perfect complement to Ross Browner on the opposite side of defensive line, giving Notre Dame two unstoppable ends. Probably best pair of DEs in Irish annals. Was very quick, had good strength, excellent backside pursuit, and a fine nose for the ball. In 1973, backed up Stock at DE. For the year, made 12 tackles, two for minus-16 yards, and broke up one pass. Missed 1974 due to suspension. In 1975, started at RE. For the season, made 78 tackles, with a team-leading 14 for minus-100 yards; recovered two fumbles; and blocked one kick. In 1976, started at RE. Made 77 tackles, nine for minus-65 yards, and broke up one pass. Made All-American. In the 1977 championship season, suffered variety of injuries that reduced his effectiveness but still made 47 tackles, four for minus-20 yards, and grabbed one fumble. Made All-American. For his career, made 214 tackles, 29 for minus-201 yards; broke up two passes; recovered three fumbles; and blocked one kick. With Browner, combined for 106 tackles for minus-716 yards—about the yardage for two complete games against the Irish.

FUNK, ART. 1902-1903-1904-1905; HB, FB, T; 5'8", 175; Lacrosse, WI. Light for a lineman, but was noted for offensive abilities with the ball. In 1902, backed up RHB. In 1903, backed up FB, behind Red Salmon. In 1904, started at LT. Came out late to the team and had to work his way into playing shape. Booted two PATs in tough win over Ohio Medical. Kicked conversion in 6-0 win over Toledo. Ran for important yardage in close win over DePauw. In 1905, started at T. Led Irish runners with 80-plus yards in loss to Wabash but could not score; contributed sack for minus-eight yards. Scored TD on four-yard plunge in shutout of Bennett Medical.

GANN, MIKE. 1981-1982-1983-1984; DE, DT; 6'5", 256; Lakewood, CO. Fine defensive player for Faust. Relentless pursuer with good quickness and tremendous upper body strength. In 1981, backed up at RE. Saw

Receiver Tom Gatewood, Theismann's favorite target in 1970, was an All-American in 1970 and 1971.

most playing time of any freshman. For the year, made 12 tackles. In 1982, started at DT. For the year, made 41 tackles, one for minus-one yard, and caused one safety. In 1983, started at DT and showed he could dominate in the line. For the year, led the Fighting Irish with six QB sacks for minus-54 yards, made 52 tackles, caused one fumble, broke up two passes, and had three other hits for minus-11 yards. In 1984, started at DT. For the year, made 60 tackles, 19 for minus-127 yards, and broke up two passes. Made All-American. For his career, made 165 tackles, 29 for minus-193 yards; caused one safety; caused one fumble; and broke up four passes.

GARVEY, ART. 1920-1921; T; 6'1", 215; Holyoke, MA. Played with Gipp and Hunk Anderson. Quick, excellent defender; always around the ball. In 1920, backed up LT. In 1921, started at LT. Had one sack in win over Kalamazoo. In win over Purdue, had a sack for minus-two yards and recovered a fumble on their 35-yard line. Returned a kickoff 12 yards in shutout of Indiana. Intercepted a Rutgers pass to set up TD in win. Recovered an Army fumble in 0-0 tie.

GATEWOOD, TOM. 1969-1970-1971; SE; 6'2", 208; Baltimore, MD. Teamed with Theismann to produce potent offensive duo. Had great speed, good size, silky moves, and great hands. In 1969, started at SE. In sophomore year, caught 47 passes from Theismann for

743 yards and eight TDs and ran once for no gain. In 1970, started at SE. Caught 79 passes for 1,166 yards and eight TDs; and gained four yards on one run. Made All-American. In 1971, started at SE but there was no Theismann to throw to him. For the season, caught 33 passes for 417 yards and four TDs, and carried twice for minus-seven yards. Repeat All-American. For his career, caught 159 passes for 2,326 yards and 20 TDs, and carried four times for minus-three yards.

GAY, BILL. 1947-1948-1949-1950; HB; 5'11", 175; Chicago, IL. Good all-purpose back for Leahy. Excellent pass defender; ran the open field with daring and was constant kicking game threat. In 1947, backed up at LHB; ran 12 times for 36 yards and caught two passes for 20 yards. In 1948, backed up at LHB; carried 64 times for 382 yards and four TDs, caught 10 passes for 131 yards and four TDs, and made 12 punt returns for 210 yards In the championship 1949 season, backed up at LHB but played plenty of defense. Carried 14 times for 47 yards, caught five passes for 60 yards and one TD, and led defenders with four interceptions for 80 return yards. In 1950, backed up at LHB and again played great defense. For the season, carried 21 times for 63 yards, caught seven passes for 57 yards, and returned two kickoffs 42 yards and 14 punts for 96 yards. For his career, carried 111 times for 528 yards, caught 24 passes for 268 yards and three TDs, returned 26 punts 306 yards and two kickoffs 42 yards, and made four interceptions for 80 return yards. Gained 1,224 yards of career offense.

GETHERALL, JOEY. 1997-1998-1999-2000; FL; 5'7", 175; Hacienda Heights, CA. Diminutive receiver and kick returner, used excellent speed and good hands to be an integral part of the Irish offense. As a freshman in '97, started two games and caught nine passes for 103 yards in 48:37 playing time. Played in all 11 games in '98, with 13 receptions for 197 yards and one TD, carried twice for six yards, returned 20 punts for 157 yards to go with four KOR for 43 yards, in 82:12 minutes of action. Had his best campaign as a junior in '99, hauling in 35 passes for 436 yards and three TDs, carried four times for 21 yards and two more TDs; returned five punts for 49 yards and four KO for 103 yards, all in 112:52 minutes. Started six games as a senior in '00, with 17 receptions for 323 yards and four TDs, eight carries for 78 yards and a TD, 24 punt returns for 392 yards and two TDs, and one KOR for 11 yards, in 147:30 minutes of action. In the '01 Fiesta Bow, caught one pass for 10 yards, carried once for minus–one yard, and returned two punts for two yards. For his career, caught 74 passes for 1,059 yards and eight TDs; carried 14 times for 105 yards and three TDs; returned 49 punts 598 yards for two TDs; and returned nine KO 157 yards for an all-purpose career total of 1,926 yards on 150 attempts for a per-play average of 12.18 yards, and 13 TDs in 401:11 minutes of playing time.

GIBSON, OLIVER. 1990-1991-1992-1993-1994; DT, NG; 6'3", 275; Romeoville, IL. Tenacious, strong, quick DL for Holtz, started on D line much of 1993 and 1994. Quick enough to be a walk-on basketball player for the '91 Irish hoopsters—even hit a three-pointer versus Missouri. Played in three games in 1990, but injuries ended his year and gained him a fifth season of eligibility. In 1991, backed up at LE; had seven solo tackles, eight assists, including two for minus-17 yards in losses, and one sack for minus-one yard, in 64:27 minutes, with a start against Penn State. In 1992, backed up Jim Flanigan at NG, garnering 13 solo tackles, six assists, credited with a half tackle for a nine-yard loss and two sacks good for minus-three yards, earning 103:14 minutes of play. In 1993, started at RDT for first five games of a sparkling Irish campaign; had 24 solo hits, 10 assists, 3.5 for minus-19 yards and shared a sack for minus-six yards in 145:12 minutes of action. In 1994, started at NG for the whole season, leading ND's down linemen in hits, garnering fourth on the team in tackles; in 211:28 minutes of action, made 37 solo hits, 22 assists, with seven for minus-23 yards and four sacks for minus-35 yards. In four Bowl games, made 11 solo hits, including seven in the 1995 Fiesta Bowl loss to Colorado. For his career, made 88 solo hits, 50 assists for 138 total tackles, with 13 for minus-68 yards and 7.5 sacks for minus-45 yards in 532:49 minutes of play.

GIPP, GEORGE. 1917-1918-1919-1920; HB; 6'0", 180; Laurium, MI. An immortal. There is perhaps no better player to be found among the 2,500 plus who have represented Notre Dame on the gridiron. Averaged 177 yards of offense every time he stepped on a field, and led Notre Dame to consecutive undefeated seasons in 1919 and 1920. Forever wedded in the collective memory to Knute Rockne, but was diametrical opposite. Rockne was not particularly gifted as an athlete but was a diligent worker. Gipp possessed a towering array of physical gifts but could have cared less. Painfully shy, yet witty; a gambler—morosely individualistic, diffident, extremely

intelligent, and perhaps very insecure; but competitive fires blazed with an intensity unmatched in American sports history.

On the football field, had more than enough speed, good size, enough strength, and an ability to improvise at precisely the right moment to avert a bad situation. This was the key to his prowess on the field, and had little to do with sheer physical gifts. Combination of raw athletic talent with uncanny capacity to do the most unexpected thing—a cutback against the grain, an invented option pass, a field goal try from an unbelievable distance, or some chicanery to upset the opposition. Finally, it is highly unlikely that he ever asked Rockne to "Win One for the Gipper." It's a nice story, and fit Rockne's romanticized notions of football, but Gipp was not a sentimentalist, nor did he talk like that.

In 1917, started at LHB on a team depleted by the demands of the war effort. Ran 40 yards (towards 110 for the day, his first game with more than 100 yards—nine others were to follow) against South Dakota as well as threw for a long gain in 40-0 win. Never

George Gipp—the best of the best.

scored in 7-2 win over Army, but his running, passing, and defensive play kept the Irish in the game. Suffered a broken leg in Morningside game to end his playing that year. For the year, carried 63 times for 244 yards, completed three of eight passes for 40 yards and one TD, returned eight punts 99 yards, and booted 13 punts 444 yards. In 1918, started at LHB in a non-season, due to the war. Scored twice against Case and made five of 12 passes for 101 yards. Scored two TDs in win over Wabash while rushing for 119 yards. In 7-7 tie with Great Lakes, punted eight times and narrowly missed 40-yard field goal that would have won the game. Hampered by mud against MAC, ran 52 yards, made three of six passes, and punted 10 times before being taken out with a ruptured blood vessel in his face in the third quarter. Dominant force in win over Purdue—two TDs plus 137 yards rushing, including 55-yard run; three of seven passes for 51 yards and one TD; four punts; 25-yard kickoff return; one PAT; and several broken-up passes. In scoreless tie with Nebraska, had two long runs toward 76 yards for the day; completed four of nine passes, two for long yardage; punted 12 times; returned kickoff 40 yards; and made one interception. For the season, led Irish with 98 carries for 541 yards and five TDs, led in passing with 19 completions in 45 tries for 293 yards and one TD, and led in scoring with six TDs and seven PATs. In 1919, started at LHB. Gained 148 yards rushing in win over Kalamazoo, but lost TD runs of 80 and 68 yards on penalties. Against Union, scored in three plays from 90 yards out, ending up with 123 yards on 10 runs, two pass completions for 49 yards, and two kickoff returns for 56 yards in 60-7 rout. In win over Nebraska, lateraled to Bergman for 90-yard TD, and hit five of eight passes for 124 yards. Scored twice, gained 85 yards on nine carries, hit two of three passes, and punted twice against Western Michigan in 53-0 win. Gained 82 yards on 18 runs, scored once (with a dislocated shoulder), threw for 57 yards, and drop-kicked 12-yard field goal in win over Indiana. Beat Army with 70 yards on the ground and 115 yards on seven passes. In win over Purdue, hit 11 of 15 passes for 217 yards and two TDs. Helped defeat MAC with 45 yards rushing and 73 yards on five of 10 passes for one TD and two interceptions. In wretched weather, beat Morningside with 94 yards rushing and 66 yards passing, including bomb to Kirk for last TD. For the season, led team with 106 carries for 729 yards and four TDs, completed 41 of 72 passes for 727 yards and three TDs, made 12 punts for 466 yards, led team in scoring, interceptions (three for 32 return yards), and

kickoff returns (eight for 7166 yards).

The last win closed Rockne's first undefeated season and gave Notre Dame the Western championship. In 1920, started at LHB. In win over Kalamazoo, made two runs of 30 yards, one for a TD, carried 16 times for 183 yards; and completed 28-yard pass to Kiley. In win over Western Normal, scored two TDs, rushed for 123 yards on 14 carries, and kicked two PATs. Beat Nebraska with two passes to Anderson for 60 yards, 25-yarder to Barry, seven-yard TD run towards 70 yards on the day, and one PAT. Against Valparaiso, completed 32- and 38-yard passes, made 10-yard TD run, returned kickoff 15 yards, ran 25 yards to keep a drive alive, scored three PATs, and gained 120 yards rushing and 102 passing. In win over Army, somewhat emaciated due to lingering illness, ran for 150 yards, passed for 123 yards and one TD, amassed 207 yards on kick returns, kicked three PATs, and averaged 43 yards on his punts.

Surveying the wreckage after his 480 yards of offense, the Army coach said, "He's not a football player...he's a runaway sonofabitch." In crunching Purdue, ran 80 yards from punt formation for TD, passed for 128 yards, and kicked three PATs. In narrow win over Indiana, scored TD on short plunge—with a dislocated shoulder. Closed out career with two TD passes, to Kiley and Barry, in fourth quarter in win over Northwestern. Stayed in Chicago for a few days after the game to help coach friend's football clinic. The bitter weather from the game and the clinic added to growing health problems. In midweek, attended team banquet at the Oliver Hotel in South Bend, but left early and checked into St. Joseph's Hospital. Gipp died three weeks later—and became an instant All-American legend. In his career, handled the ball 594 times and gained 4,781 yards. Many of his offensive records lasted 50-plus years.

GLADIEUX, BOB. 1966-1967-1968; HB; 5'11", 185; Louisville, OH. Fine, all-purpose running back for Parseghian. Had deceptive speed, good moves, good hands, and ability to run long distance. In 1966, backed up LHB. Playing for injured Nick Eddy; scored TD on 46-yard pass from O'Brien in 10-10 game with MSU. For the year, made 27 runs for 111 yards and three TDs, caught 12 passes for 208 yards and two TDs, punted 11 times for 35.1-yard average, returned two kickoffs 48 yards, and made one tackle. In 1967, backed up at LHB. For the year, made 84 carries for 384 yards and five TDs, caught 23 passes for 297 yards and two TDs, punted three times for 32.7-yard average, returned one kickoff 19 yards, and made three tackles.

In 1968, started at RHB and had one of the best years on record. Led Fighting Irish with 152 carries for 713 yards and 12 TDs, caught 37 passes for 442 yards and two TDs, returned six punts 91 yards and 11 kickoffs 262 yards to total 1,508 yards. Punted three times for 42.3-yard average; his best was a 61-yarder. In his career, carried 263 times for 1,208 yards and 20 TDs, caught 72 passes for 947 yards and six TDs, returned six punts 91 yards and 14 kickoffs 329 yards, made four tackles, and punted 17 times for a 35.94-yard average. His offensive career total was 2,575 yards and 26 TDs.

GMITTER, DON. 1964-1965-1966; DE, E; 6'2", 215; Mt. Lebanon, PA. Member of the 1964 class of sophomores who challenged for the national crown and won it as seniors (Lynch, Page, Hardy, Regner, Conjar, Goeddeke, and Swatland, among others). Multiskilled player, part of great defensive front four in 1964, then switched to TE. Excellent quickness and good strength; determined tackler; good blocker on offense. In 1964, started at DE; made 54 tackles for the year, recovered two fumbles, and broke up one pass. In 1965, moved to TE. Playing for a ground-oriented offense, caught six passes for 155 yards and two TDs, made six tackles, and recovered one fumble. In 1966, played much of the year with a bad knee (had surgery after the season) and saw most of passing game go to Seymour. For the year, made four catches for 72 yards and one tackle. In his career, made 61 tackles, recovered three fumbles, and caught 10 passes for 227 yards and two TDs.

GOEDDEKE, GEORGE. 1964-1965-1966; C; 6'3", 228; Detroit, MI. Starting center for Hanratty in 1966 championship year. Excellent blocker with good quickness; often dominating player. In 1964, backed up at C. In 1965, started at C. In 1966, started at C. Was hurt early in tie with MSU, but the injury allowed O'Brien to work with his regular C for the rest of the game. Made All-American.

GOHEEN, JUSTIN. 1991-1992-1993-1994; ILB; 6'2", 228; Wexford, PA. Steady, dependable ILB for Holtz, with a nose for the ball and good pass defender. In 1991, worked on special teams mostly but ended up with 10 solo hits, eight assists, and caused one fumble in the USC game while playing 70:33 minutes. In win over Florida in the '92 Sugar Bowl, had one tackle and broke up one pass. In 1992, served as a backup LB to Demetrius

DuBose and made 82 special teams appearances even though hampered by an ankle injury from fall drills. Had seven solo hits in the season in 26:35 minutes of play. In 1993, was scheduled as a backup to Anthony Peterson at ILB but started 10 games after injury ended Peterson's season. For the number-two ranked Irish, led with 92 hits—61 solo, 31 assists, with three for minus-five yards and five on a sack of minus-six yards; also broke up three passes. Played 252:11 minutes. Made three tackles in '94 Cotton Bowl win over Texas A&M. In 1994, started at ILB and was third on the Irish in tackles with 61, based on 42 solos, 19 assists, with two for minus-four yards, and four sacks for minus-31 yards to go with four passes broken up and two fumbles recovered in 192:40 minutes of action Made three tackles against Colorado in '95 Fiesta Bowl loss. His total stats for all games come to 120 solo hits, 65 assists, for 185 tackles, with five for minus-nine yards, 4.5 sacks for minus-37 yards, one fumble caused, eight passes broken up, and two fumbles recovered.

GOLIC, BOB. 1975-1976-1977-1978; LB; 6'3", 244; Cleveland, OH. Great linebacker for Devine. Had size, speed, quickness, tremendous strength, good reading skills, and excellent tackling. Dominating player on 1977 championship team. In 1975, started at MLB; made 82 tackles, fourth best on the squad as freshman, two for minus-13 yards. In 1976, started at MLB. Was second leading tackler for the season with 99, six for minus-25 yards; broke up one pass; and had one interception. In 1977, started at MLB. For the year, made 146 tackles, five for minus-33 yards; broke up five passes; recovered one fumble; blocked one kick; made three interceptions for 19 return yards; and returned one punt 16 yards. Made All-American. In 1978, started at MLB; set single-game record with 26 tackles in loss to Michigan. In his final season, made 152 tackles, five for minus-23 yards; broke up two passes; recovered one fumble; and had two interceptions for three return yards. Consensus All-American. For his career, made 479 tackles, 18 for minus-94 yards; broke up eight passes; made six interceptions for 22 return yards; recovered two fumbles; blocked one kick; and returned one punt 16 yards.

GRANT, RYAN. 2001-2002-2003-2004. RB, 6'1" 218. Nyack, NY. Seventh Irish runner to hit the 1,000-yard mark (2002). Good combination of speed, elusiveness, and power. Saw action in five games in 2001; scored one TD on 29 runs for 110 yards. Started all 13 games as a sophomore and made the most of it, gaining 1,085 on 261 carries, scoring nine TDs to go with nine pass receptions for 22 yards. In 2003, shared RB duties with Julius Jones; saw his production dwindle to 567 yards on 143 carries, good for three TDs; caught nine passes for 64 yards. Repeated split RB duties, this time with Darius Walker, in 2004. Ran for 536 yards on 127 carries, scoring five TDs; caught six passes for 51 yards. For his career, gained 2,298 yards on 561 carries, scoring 18 TDs, to go with 24 pass receptions that picked up 137 yards.

GREEN, MARK. 1985-1986-1987-1988; TB; 6'0", 184; Riverside, CA. Three-year starter at TB for Holtz; tri-captain of 1988 national championship team; leading rusher in 1986 and 1987. Superb runner, good receiver, and good blocker. Could play as WR as well as run inside. Had good speed, surprising power and toughness, and very good hands. In 1985, backed up at FL. For the year, carried five times for 64 yards, caught nine passes for 116 yards, and returned two kickoffs 29 yards. In 1986, started at TB for six games. For the year, made 96 carries for 406 yards and two TDs, and caught 25 passes for 242 yards. In 1987, started at TB. For the year, made 146 carries for 861 yards and six TDs, caught 13 passes for 98 yards, and returned one kickoff 17 yards. In 1988, started at TB. For the season, made 135 carries for 646 yards and seven TDs, caught 14 passes for 155 yards, and returned one kickoff 25 yards. For his career, carried 382 times for 1,977 yards and 15 TDs, caught 61 passes for 611 yards, and returned four kickoffs 71 yards. His career total was 2,659 yards and 15 TDs.

GRIFFITH, KEVIN. 1979-1981-1982; DT, DE; 6'3", 242; Kettering, OH. Solid, dependable defensive lineman for Devine and Faust. Very quick in spite of knee problems, good pursuit, and always in the vicinity of the ball. In 1979, started at DT. For the year, made 33 tackles, two for minus-seven yards; broke up one pass; and recovered three fumbles. Lost the 1980 season with knee problems. In 1981, started at DE. For the season, was third leading tackler with 63 hits, six for minus-23 yards; broke up five passes; and recovered three fumbles. In 1982, started at DE. For the season, made 65 tackles, six for minus-38 yards; broke up four passes; and recovered one fumble. For his career, made 161 tackles, 14 for minus-68 yards; broke up 10 passes; and recovered seven fumbles.

GROOM, JERRY. 1948-1949-1950; C, LB; 6'3", 215;

Des Moines, IA. Stellar defensive player for Leahy. Great tackler and inspirational leader. In 1948, backed up at C. Intercepted Nebraska pass deep in their territory to lead to TD in win. Recovered one of five Washington miscues to lead to TD in blowout win. In 1949, started at MLB for the national champions. Started rout of Indiana by grabbing Hoosier fumble on their 24. Played decisive part in defeating SMU 27-20 with blocked PAT and an interception to end their final drive. In 1950, started at MLB. Saved win over Tulane with fumble recovery on Notre Dame 10. Blocked Navy punt on their 17 that led to insurance TD in win. Played 465 minutes—86 percent of the total time the Fighting Irish played. Made All-American.

GRUNHARD, TIM. 1986-1987-1988-1989; G; 6'3", 292; Chicago, IL. Excellent offensive lineman for Holtz. Played three different positions (T, C, and G) and handled most of the special teams work as C. Had tremendous speed and quickness, especially seen on punting downs when he would snap to the punter and was often one of the first bearing down on the returner downfield. In 1986, worked mostly as snapper for the punt team. In 1987, backed up at RG. In 1988, started at G for the national champions. In 1989, started at G. Made All-American.

GUGLIEMI, RALPH. 1951-1952-1953-1954; QB; 6-0, 185; Columbus, OH. Leahy's last QB, inspirational leader, fine passer, pretty good runner, and slick pass

Ralph Gugliemi, a three-year starter at quarterback and consensus All-American in 1954.

defender; must be rated near the top of all Irish QBs. In 1951, backed up at QB. Led Irish in upset win over undefeated USC. For the year, completed 27 of 53 passes for 438 yards. In 1952, started at QB. Fired winning TD (16-yarder to Heap) in 27-21 game with Oklahoma. For the year, rushed 48 times for 31 yards and one TD, and completed 61 of 142 passes for 683 yards and four TDs. In 1953, started at QB and teamed with Heisman winner Johnny Lattner for potent backfield combination. Saved tie with Iowa with TD passes to Shannon with two seconds left in the first half and six seconds left in the game. For the year, completed 52 of 113 passes for 792 yards and eight TDs, made 60 carries for 74 yards and six TDs, kicked five PATs, made five interceptions for 47 return yards and one TD, and returned two kickoffs 15 yards in 410 minutes of play. In 1954, started at QB. For the season, completed 68 of 127 throws for 1,160 yards and six TDs, carried 79 times for 95 yards and five TDs, led team with five interceptions for 51 return yards, and made two fumble recoveries in 429 minutes. Consensus All-American. For his career, completed 208 of 435 passes for 3,073 yards and 18 TDs, carried 187 times for 200 yards and 12 TDs, kicked five PATs, made 10 interceptions for 98 yards and one TD, recovered two fumbles, and returned two kickoffs 15 yards. He accounted for 31 TDs and 3,386 total yards.

GULYAS, ED. 1969-1970-1971; DB, HB; 5'11", 190; San Carlos, CA. Dependable back for Parseghian's Theismann-led teams. Tough inside runner; good blocker and pass receiver. In 1969, was reserve DB; gained 20 yards on three carries, returned 14 punts 87 yards to lead team, and returned one kickoff 25 yards. In 1970, started at LHB. Led Irish backs with 558 yards on 127 carries for three TDs, caught nine passes for 189 yards and two TDs, and made one tackle. In 1971, started at LHB. Gained 220 yards on 56 carries for five TDs and caught three passes for 16 yards. For his career, carried 186 times for 798 yards and eight TDs, caught 12 passes for 205 yards and two TDs, returned 14 punts 87 yards and one kickoff 25 yards, and made one tackle. Accumulated 1,115 total yards and 10 TDs in his career.

HAINES, KRIS.1975-1976-1977-1978; SE; 6'0", 181; Sidney, OH. Speedy wideout for Devine; teamed well with Montana in 1977 national championship season and afterwards. Could go long as well as being possession receiver; had good moves, excellent hands, and good concentration. In 1975, backed up at SE; carried once

for 28 yards and returned one punt three yards. In 1976, backed up at SE; caught three passes for 64 yards. In 1977, started at SE. For the year, caught 28 passes for 587 yards and two TDs. In 1978, against Houston in "Frozen Bowl" caught four passes, including an eight-yard TD pass with no time showing to set up winning PAT, and a two-point conversion. For the year, led Irish receivers with 32 receptions for 699 yards and five TDs and made one tackle. For his career, ran once for 28 yards, caught 63 passes for 1,350 yards and two TDs, returned one punt three yards, and made one tackle.

HAMILTON, BRIAN. 1991-1992-1993-1994; DE, DT; 6'3", 276; Chicago, IL. Powerful, quick DL for Holtz, teamed with other stalwarts Bryant Young and Jim Flanigan to give Irish a great D line in '93. In 1991, in reserve DT role and limited special team work, made three solo hits in 4:03 minutes of play. In 1992, started four games at DT; had 22 solo hits, 12 assists, with 3.5 for minus-six yards and four sacks for minus–41 yards, caused one fumble, broke up one pass, and recovered two fumbles in 117:58 minutes of game time. In '93 Cotton Bowl win over Texas A&M, had five tackles, one sack for minus-five yards, and forced a fumble to lead to an Irish TD. In 1993, started at LDE. Had 23 solo hits, 19 assists, with four for minus-10 yards, four sacks for minus-22 yards, caused one fumble, and recovered three fumbles. Made three tackles in '94 Cotton Bowl win over Texas A&M. In 1994, started at LDE but also played inside when the D went to a four-man front. For the season, made 17 solo hits, 13 assists, with four for minus-14 yards, two sacks for minus-20 yards, caused one fumble, broke up one pass, and recovered three fumbles in 126:08 minutes of action. Made three tackles in '95 Fiesta Bowl loss to Colorado. In all games, had 65 solo hits, 55 assists, for 120 tackles, four for minus-14 yards, with three sacks for minus-25 yards, caused three fumbles, broke up two passes, and showed a good nose for the ball with eight fumbles recovered.

HAMILTON, DONALD. 1908-1909; QB; 5'10", 175; Columbus, OH. Excellent QB for era; fine punt returner; very adept on end runs for long gains. In 1908 started at QB. First man to throw TD pass for Notre Dame, a 40-yard pass and run bomb to Fay Wood in 64-0 rout of Franklin; also scored TD with 65-yard run, made 45-yard punt return, and returned a kickoff 25 yards in same game. Against Michigan ran for 15 yards, made one conversion kick, and picked up 70 yards on three punt returns to nullify Michigan's punting game (when punts were a first-down weapon to get out of a hole). Against Physicians and Surgeons, scored one TD and kicked three conversions and one field goal. Kicked two conversions against Ohio Northern. Scored all Notre Dame's points with two field goals and added two 50-yard punt returns in 8-4 win over Wabash. Hurt his hip in that game and missed a game, but then replaced another injured QB and led Notre Dame to a 6-0 victory over Marquette. In 1909, started at QB. Returned MAC punt 10 yards in Irish win. Did the same in close win over Pitt. Teamed with Red Miller to beat Michigan for the first time. Kicked three conversions in win over Miami of Ohio. Added five conversions and one 45-yard field goal in win over Wabash.

HANKERD, JOHN. 1977-1978-1979-1980; LB, DE; 6'4", 245; Jackson, MI. Good defensive lineman for Devine; quick, excellent pursuit; good tackler; good nose for the ball. In 1977, for the national champions, backed up MLB. Made 14 tackles and broke up one pass. In 1978, started at DE. For the year, made 55 tackles, nine for minus-50 yards (second best on the team); broke up one pass; and recovered one fumble. In 1979, started at DE; led linemen with 73 tackles, including a team-leading 14 for minus-90 yards; broke up one pass; and recovered three fumbles. In 1980, started at DE. Made 35 tackles, five for minus-11 yards; broke up two passes; recovered one fumble; and blocked one kick. For his career, made 177 tackles, 28 for minus-151 yards; broke up five passes; recovered five fumbles; and blocked one kick.

HANLEY, DAN.1930-1933-1934; FB, HB; 6'2",190; Butte, MT. Played for three head coaches—Rockne, Anderson, and Layden. Was part of elaborate ruse by Rockne to lull USC and the press into complacency prior to 1930 game. Had good speed, but various injuries kept him from going all out. Excellent defensive player. In 1930, backed up at FB for the national champions. In win over Drake, made 34-yard TD dash to go with 25-yard gain. Scored TD in win over Northwestern and made an interception and runback to their 15. Rockne, on train trip to LA, had the speedier Bucky O'Connor wear his uniform and limp in practice. Other fullbacks were gone or hurt, so it looked like the Fighting Irish would meet undefeated USC with a crippled backfield. It worked—O'Connor slashed USC for long TDs. Hanley intercepted a Trojan pass to set up Notre Dame's last TD

Dan Hanley played for three different Irish mentors—Rockne, Anderson and Layden.

of Rockne's last win. Injuries cost him both 1931 and 1932. In 1933, after much persistence, backed up HB. In 1934, backed up at RHB. Caught winning TD pass from Pilney to beat Army. Made five carries for 39 yards in win over Carnegie Tech.

HANLEY, FRANK. 1896-1899; T; 5'10", 186; South Bend, IN. Probably qualifies as a "tramp player"—moving from place to place to find a game of football. Was 23 years old when he began at Notre Dame, then played 1897 and 1898 seasons with South Bend Commercial A.C. (but not against Notre Dame). At age 26, finished up with Notre Dame. Was known for his ability to run low with the ball. In 1896, started at RT. Ran 15 yards and scored one TD in shutout of South Bend Commercial A.C. Tallied two TDs in win over Albion. Scored two TDs as the Fighting Irish beat Highland Views. Returned one kickoff, recovered one fumble, and scored one TD in win over Beloit. In 1899, started at RT. Played strong defensive game in win over Englewood H.S.

HANRATTY, TERRY. 1966-1967-1968; QB; 6'1", 200; Butler, PA. Great QB; best remembered for sophomore year (1966) under Parseghian when he teamed with sophomore Jim Seymour for potent passing offense that decimated virtually every team except MSU; he was hurt in that game. Had superb arm; excellent ball handler; great reader of defensive secondary coverages; good runner; and had intangible ability to take a team to new heights. In 1966 started at QB for the national champions. Took team to 8-0 start but a Bubba Smith tackle caused a shoulder injury against MSU. For the year, completed 78 of 147 passes for eight TDs and 1,247 yards; also carried 50 times for 124 yards and five TDs, his longest a 52-yard burst. In 1967, started at QB. For the season, completed 110 of 206 passes for 1,439 yards and nine TDs, carried 75 times for 183 yards and seven TDs, and caught one pass for minus-two yards. In 1968, surpassed Gipp's career yardage record against Illinois and hit 116 of 197 passes for 1,466 yards and 10 TDs while running 279 yards on 56 carries for four TDs. Consensus All-American. In his career, completed 304 of 550 passes for 4,152 yards and 27 TDs, carried 181 times for 586 yards and 16 TDs, and caught one pass for minus-two yards. His career total was 4,736 yards and 43 TDs.

HARDY, KEVIN. 1964-1965-1966-1967; DE, DT; 6'5", 270; Oakland, CA. Great three-sport athlete—as defensive lineman in football, center/forward in basketball, and right fielder in baseball. Must be considered for any all-time Notre Dame team. Stellar lineman for Parseghian; lined up next to Alan Page on right side in 1966 and to Mike McCoy a year later. Was hard to block, had great quickness, superior strength, and excellent pass rushing skills. O.J. Simpson credited him with the hardest tackle he ever experienced. In 1964, started at DT. For the year, made 38 tackles and blocked two kicks, one going to Page for a TD. In 1965, hurt his back in Purdue game and was lost for the year. In 1966, started at RT for the national champions; made 79 tackles, broke up four passes, recovered one fumble, and punted 10 times for 40.9-yard average. Made All-American. In 1967, was injured on a crackback block in Purdue game. Played with a hurt foot much of the year. For the season, made 33 tackles, broke up two passes, had one interception, and punted 20 times for 32-yard average. Consensus All-American. For his career, made 150 tackles, broke up six passes, recovered one fumble, blocked two kicks, had one interception, and punted 30 times for 35-yard average.

HARRISON, RANDY. 1974-1975-1976-1977-1978; FS; 6'1", 207; Hammond, IN. Had good speed and quickness, excellent coverage skills, was a good closer, and generally knew how to be around the ball. In 1974, as a freshman, led secondary with 57 tackles, one for

minus-three yards; broke up seven passes; recovered one fumble; and made two interceptions for two TDs (44 yards against Miami and 40 yards against Navy). In 1975, started at FS. For the season, made 54 tackles, one for minus-two yards; broke up two passes; had one interception and seven-yard runback; and returned two punts for 11 yards. In 1976, started at FS but broke his wrist against Purdue, the season's second game, and missed the rest of the year. Still managed to make 26 tackles and return two punts 17 yards. In 1977, backed up at FS for national champions. For the year, made 18 tackles, broke up one pass, had one interception and 13-yard runback, and returned six punts 36 yards and three kickoffs 46 yards. In 1978, backed up at FS. Started the great comeback of 1979 Cotton Bowl with 56-yard kickoff return. For the season, made 22 tackles, broke up one pass, returned seven punts four yards and five kickoffs 79 yards, and had one interception and 34-yard return. For his career, made 177 tackles, two for minus-five yards; recovered one fumble; made five interceptions for 138 return yards and two TDs; returned 17 punts 68 yards and eight kickoffs 125 yards for a total of 331 yards and two TDs.

Terry Hanratty, consensus All-American in 1968.

HART, LEON. 1946-1947-1948-1949; E; 6'4", 245; Turtle Creek, PA. One of only two linemen ever to win Heisman Trophy. Overpowering force on the lines of Leahy's glory years; instrumental in achieving 39-game winning streak. Never played in a losing contest in four years at Notre Dame. Devastating blocker and tackler; awesome, frightening sight when turned loose on his patented end run or from FB spot. Prototype of today's TE with size, speed, and good hands. In 1946, backed up at RE for the national champions. For the year, caught five passes for 107 yards and one TD. In 1947, started at RE for the national champions. Caught TD pass and recovered two fumbles against Navy and caught winning TD against Northwestern. For the year, caught nine passes for 156 yards and two TDs, recovered three fumbles, and led with 289 minutes of playing time. Named All-American. In 1948, started at RE. For the year, led Fighting Irish with 9.8-yard rushing average on four carries for 39 yards and one TD, caught 16 passes for 231 yards and four TDs, recovered one fumble, and led team with 389 minutes of playing time. Made All-American. In 1949, started at RE for national champions. For the season, rushed 18 times for 73 yards and one TD, caught 19 passes for 257 yards and five TDs, blocked one punt, and recovered three fumbles. Consensus All-American and won Maxwell and Heisman trophies. For his career, carried 22 times for 112 yards and two TDs, caught 49 passes for 751 yards and 12 TDs, blocked one kick, and recovered seven fumbles. His career total of 863 yards averaged 12.1 yards every time he handled the ball. He scored a TD one out of five times he got the ball. Ultimately, the stats are misleading because he changed the whole picture for opponents, both offense and defense; was a complete threat.

HEAP, JOE. 1951-1952-1953-1954; HB; 5'11", 180; Abita Springs, LA. Genuine triple-threat; part of extremely talented quartet of backfield stars under Leahy—teamed with Guglielmi, Lattner, and Worden. One of best small players ever to suit up for the Fighting Irish. Had fine speed and moves, good hands for passing game, and could throw option pass. In 1951, backed up at LHB. For the year, carried 38 times for 166 yards and two TDs, caught two passes for 25 yards, and returned two kickoffs 50 yards. In 1952, started at LHB. For the season, carried 89 times for 383 yards and two TDs, completed seven of 13 passes for 130 yards, caught 29 passes for 407 yards and two TDs, and returned 10 punts 126 yards for one TD and six kickoffs 145 yards

for a total of 1,191 yards. In 1953, started at LHB. For the year, rushed 62 times for 314 yards and two TDs, completed four of six passes for 48 yards, caught 22 passes for 336 yards and five TDs, returned seven punts 143 yards (including 99-yard TD return that clinched win over USC), returned four kickoffs 76 yards, made two interceptions, and recovered one fumble. In 1954, started at LHB and became career leader in pass receptions to that point in Irish football. For the season, led team in scoring, carried 110 times for 594 yards and eight TDs, completed all three passes for 32 yards and one TD, caught 18 passes for 369 yards to lead receivers, returned seven kickoffs 143 yards, and made two interceptions and two fumble recoveries. For his career, carried 299 times for 1,457 yards and 14 TDs, completed 14 of 22 passes for 210 yards and one TD, caught 71 passes for 1,137 yards and seven TDs, returned 17 punts for 269 yards and two TDs, returned 17 kickoffs 364 yards, made four interceptions, and recovered four fumbles. His career total was 3,437 yards and 24 TDs; amassed more than 1,000 career yards in both running and pass receiving (a rare feat to that point) and 843 yards on passing and kick returning. (Compare his career statistics with those of Paul Hornung.)

Jerome Heavens, Irish fullback in 1977 and 1978, teamed with Joe Montana and Vagas Ferguson to form a nightmare for opposing defenses.

HEAVENS, JEROME.1975-1976-1977-1978; FB; 6'0", 204; East St. Louis, IL. Solid, dependable player, with fine speed and moves for FB; excellent durability; and fine blocking skills. Teamed with Ferguson and Montana to give defenses serious headaches. In 1975, started at FB. As freshman, led Irish runners with 129 carries for 756 yards and five TDs, caught eight passes for 64 yards, and made one tackle. In 1976, hurt his knee in the third game and was lost for the year. In his shortened season, carried 54 times for 204 yards and caught two passes for 22 yards. In 1977, started at FB for the national champions and lost 1,000-yard season when tackled for a loss on the final play of blowout win over Miami. In win over Texas in Cotton Bowl, carried 32 times for 101 yards. For the season, carried 229 times for a team-leading 994 yards and six TDs and was third in receiving with 12 for 133 yards. In 1978, surpassed Gipp's career rushing record and helped beat Houston in Cotton Bowl comeback win with 16 carries for 71 yards and four receptions for 60 yards. For the year, carried 178 times for 728 yards and four TDs and caught 13 passes for 113 yards. For his career, carried 590 times for 2,682 yards and 15 TDs and caught 35 passes for 332 yards, a total of 3,014 yards of offense.

HEIMKREITER, STEVE. 1975-1976-1977-1978; LB; 6'2", 228; Cincinnati, OH. Three-year starter as LB alongside Golic and for two years with Becker to provide Notre Dame with a fearsome linebacking corps. Had good speed on pass coverage; excellent tackler. In 1975, injuries kept him sidelined most of the year, but still made 22 tackles and recovered one fumble. In 1976, started at OLB and led team with 118 tackles, one for minus-four yards, and recovered one fumble. In 1977, started at OLB for the national champions but missed three games with a sprained knee. For the year, made 98 tackles, two for minus-five yards; broke up two passes; and recovered one fumble. In 1978, started at OLB. For the year, set new tackling record with 160, three for minus-four yards; broke up two passes; and had one interception for a two-yard runback. For his career, made 398 tackles, six for minus-13 yards; broke up four passes; made one interception and two-yard return; and recovered three fumbles.

HEMPEL, SCOTT. 1968-1969-1970; K; 6'0", 235; Copley, OH. Handled most field goal and PAT work for Parseghian's teams led by Hanratty and Theismann. In 1968, kicked 45 of 50 PATs and five of nine field goals

for 60 points, made six tackles, and broke up one pass. In 1969, booted 41 of 44 PATs and five of seven field goals for 56 points; also made four tackles. In 1970, led team in scoring with 54 points on 39 of 41 PATs and five of six field goals; made five tackles. For his career, made 125 of 135 PATs, 15 of 19 field goals, scored 171 points, made 15 tackles, and broke up one pass.

HENTRICH, CRAIG. 1989-1990-1991-1992; K; 6'1", 196; Godfrey, IL. Excellent kicker for Holtz; handled both punting and place kicking. Has two best season averages for punting: 44.6 yards in 1989 and 44.88 in 1990. Set single-season mark for PATs in 1991 with 48. Career record holder for punting with 44.2-yard average on 83 punts. In 1989, made eight of 15 field goals and 44 of 45 PATs for 68 points; punted 26 times for 44.6-yard average. Had five punts for 40.1-yard average in win over Colorado in Orange Bowl. In 1990, hit 16 of 20 field goals, all 41 PATs, and averaged 44.9 yards on 34 punts. Made 73 consecutive PATs until one was blocked in loss to Colorado in Orange Bowl. In 1991, did most of the kicking until injured in Tennessee game. Made five of eight field goals, all 48 PATs, and punted 23 times for 42.9-yard average. Kicked one PAT in win over Florida in 1992 Sugar Bowl before re-injuring leg and leaving the game. In 1992, made 10 of 13 FG tries, hit 44 of 46 PATs, punted 35 times for 1,534 yards and a 43.8-yard average. Named All-American. For his career, scored 294 points on 34 FGs, and 177 PATs. His 294 points are the best by an Irish kicker, and second on the all-time scoring list, behind only Allen Pinkett. Punted 118 times for 5,205 yards for a Notre Dame record 44.1 yards per kick. Must be considered for the all-time Irish team.

HERING, FRANK. 1896; QB; 5'9",154; South Bend, IN. Invented Mother's Day; a number of awards in his name have been offered for excellence in Notre Dame's spring practices. Played E and QB for Chicago in 1893 and 1894; moved to Bucknell for 1895 season and to Notre Dame for final year. Infectious leadership; confident, poised, keen student of the game adept at exploiting an opponent's weaknesses. Both coach and captain in 1896. After 46-0 win over South Bend Commercial A.C., several of their players enrolled at Notre Dame and played in the following years. During 82-0 mangling of Highland Views, shared 15 TDs among nine players, with none for himself. First Notre Dame player to stay and coach full-time.

HOGAN, DON. 1962; HB; 5'11", 185; Chicago, IL. Great speed, moves, good hands during sophomore year. An automobile accident during Christmas vacation killed his sister and crushed his hip. Made valiant effort to recover, but had to leave the game. Wrote farewell letter to his teammates that stands as testament to his courage and determination in the face of terrible odds. In 1962, started at RHB. Led team with 454 yards and three TDs on 90 carries, was second in receiving with 12 catches for 146 yards, second in kickoff returns with nine for 206 yards, and made two-point conversion and 15 tackles. Of 1,000-yard rushers in the post-war era, his 1962 rookie yardage was second only to Worden's 686 yards.

HOLOHAN, PETE. 1978-1979-1980; FL; 6'5", 228; Liverpool, NY. Excellent wide receiver for Devine. His size made a great target; had good moves and great hands. In 1978, started at FL in Montana's final year. For the season, caught 20 passes for 301 yards and one TD. In 1979, started at FL; caught 22 passes for 386 yards, completed two of three passes for 81 yards, returned one kickoff for no gain, and tallied a two-point conversion to beat South Carolina. In 1980, started at FL. For the season, caught 21 passes for 296 yards and one TD, and lost 12 yards on his only carry. In his career, caught 63 passes for 983 yards and two TDs, carried once for minus-12 yards, completed two of three passes for 81 yards, returned one kickoff for no gain, and tallied a two-point conversion.

HORNUNG, PAUL. 1954-1955-1956; FB, QB; 6'2", 205; Louisville, KY. All-time Notre Dame star. Fine blend of size, speed, moves, passing and kicking skills, and leadership qualities. Unusually good on defense to go with obvious offensive talents. Won Heisman Trophy when Notre Dame won only two games for the year—the fourth Heisman winner in a decade. In 1954, backed up at FB but saw some action as QB. For the season, carried 23 times for 159 yards (6.9-yard average) and two TDs, hit five of 19 passes for 36 yards, averaged 39 yards on six punts, booted six PATs, returned one kickoff 58 yards, had three interceptions for 94 return yards, and recovered one fumble. In 1955, started at QB Carried 92 times for 472 yards and six TDs, completed 46 of 103 passes for 743 yards and nine TDs, kicked five PATs and two field goals, returned six kickoffs 109 yards, had five interceptions for 59 return yards, recovered two fumbles, and punted 30 times for 33.9-yard average. Made All-American.

In 1956, played with two dislocated thumbs near the end of the season. Carried 94 times for 420 yards and seven TDs and completed 59 of 111 passes for 917 yards and three TDs to be the first Irish player since 1938 to lead the team in both passing and running; returned 16 kickoffs 496 yards for one TD; returned four punts 63 yards; booted 14 PATs; had 55 tackles; and made two interceptions for 59 return yards. Consensus All-American and Heisman Trophy winner. For his career, carried 209 times for 1,051 yards and 15 TDs, completed 110 of 233 passes for 1,696 yards and 12 TDs, booted 25 PATs and two field goals, made 10 interceptions for 212 return yards, recovered three fumbles, returned 23 kickoffs 663 yards for one TD, returned four punts 63 yards, and punted 69 times for 36.1-yard average. His total was 3,622 yards and 28 TDs.

HOWARD, JOE. 1981-1982-1983-1984; SE, FL; 5'9", 170; Clinton, MD. Integral part of offense for Faust. Extremely fast, as shown in record-setting 96-yard TD pass and run against Georgia Tech in 1981 from Blair Kiel. In 1981, broke into starting lineup midway into

Paul Hornung, 1956 Heisman Trophy winner for a 2-8 team.

the season and had most playing time of freshman class, 114:29 minutes. For the year, caught 17 passes for 463 yards, a record 27.2-yard average, and three TDs. In 1982, started at SE; caught at least two passes each game except against Pitt (one, a 54-yard TD play). For the year, made 28 receptions for a team-leading 524 yards and two TDs, ran twice for 28 yards, returned one punt for minus-two yards and five kickoffs for 111 yards, and made five tackles. In 1983, started at SE. For the year, led team in yardage on receptions with 464 yards on 27 catches and two TDs, passed for 29-yard TD, carried four times for 61 yards. returned 28 punts 202 yards and one kickoff seven yards. Made one catch for 47 yards in Liberty Bowl win over Boston College. Played basketball as walk-on for Digger Phelps. In 1984, started at SE and became fifth leading receiver even though his stats fell off. Caught 13 passes for 212 yards for the season. In Aloha Bowl, caught two passes for 24 yards and returned four punts 42 yards as Notre Dame lost a close game to SMU. For his career, carried six times for 89 yards, caught 85 passes for 1,472 yards (17.3 yards per catch) and seven TDs, completed one pass for 29-yard TD, returned 29 punts 200 yards and six kickoffs 118 yards, and made five tackles. His total was 1,639 yards and eight TDs.

HUARTE, JOHN. 1962-1963-1964; QB; 6'0", 180; Anaheim, CA. Sixth Heisman Trophy winner for Notre Dame. Almost forgotten man on roster until Parseghian took a look around and told him, "You're my quarterback." The rest is history, but only a short, one-season history. Good ball-handler but had curious throwing delivery—almost sidearm—with great accuracy and soft touch; quiet, forceful leader. His 1964 stats with Jack Snow reveal how his talent had been wasted while the program floundered. His senior year also revealed the kind of passing tandems that Parseghian consistently produced: Hanratty to Seymour, Theismann to Gatewood, Clements to Demmerle. In 1962, backed up at QB. For the season, completed four of eight throws for 38 yards and lost 14 yards on three carries. In 1963 backed up at QB; showed flashes of his ability throughout pitiful season: completed 20 of 42 passes for 243 yards and one TD, also kicked one PAT. In 1964, started at QB. Led the Fighting Irish back to national prominence after five years of misery, making strong claim on the national championship (recognized as such by the MacArthur Bowl award). Completed 114 of 205 passes for 2,062 yards and 16 TDs, carried 37 times for seven yards and three TDs, and caught one

pass for 11 yards. For his career, carried 51 times for minus-60 yards and three TDs, completed 138 of 255 passes for 2,543 yards, 17 TDs, and 11 interceptions. His total was 2,483 yards and 20 TDs. Consensus All-American and Heisman Trophy winner.

HUFF, ANDY. 1969-1971-1972; HB, FB; 5'11", 212; Toledo, OH. Dependable, productive runner for Parseghian's teams led by Theismann and Clements. Especially valuable in short-yardage situations; good blocker; and good hands. In 1969, backed up at RHB. For the season, carried 69 times for 265 yards and five TDs, caught four passes for 28 yards and one TD, and returned one kickoff 12 yards. Lost 1970 due to severe shoulder injury during spring practice. In 1971, started at FB. For the year, carried 69 times for 295 yards and two TDs and caught four passes for 39 yards. In 1972, started at FB and had best day against Navy, gaining 121 yards on 16 carries. For the season, carried 115 times for 567 yards and a team-leading 10 TDs, caught nine passes for 102 yards, returned two kickoffs 40 yards, and made one tackle. For his career, carried 253 times for 1,127 yards and 17 TDs, caught 17 passes for 169 yards and one TD, returned three kickoffs 52 yards, and made one tackle. His career total came to 1,348 yards and 18 TDs.

HUFFMAN, DAVE. 1975-1976-1977-1978; T, C; 6'5", 245; Dallas, TX. Known for wearing red elbow pads so his mother could see him in the melee of the line. Dominant player for Devine, especially in 1977 championship season. Very dependable at C; excellent run and pass blocker. In 1975, backed up at T. Often used in double TE sets opposite MacAfee; caught one pass for 16 yards against Miami. In 1976, started at C. Made two tackles in 308 minutes. In 1977, starting C on great offensive line. Helped dominate line of scrimmage in Cotton Bowl win over Texas. Played 308 minutes and made two tackles. Made All-American. In 1978, started at C. Threw devastating block that helped spring Montana for a score on fourth-quarter rallying drive that beat Pitt. Consensus All-American.

HUGHES, ERNIE. 1974-1975-1976-1977; DE, G; 6'4", 253; Boise, ID. Fine offensive lineman for Parseghian and Devine; key member of offensive line on 1977 national championship team. Had good quickness, superior strength, and excellent technique. In 1974, backed up DE and made four tackles in 13 minutes of play. In 1975, started at G and played 322 minutes; made five tackles and recovered one fumble. In 1976, started at G; made two tackles, recovered two fumbles, and played 318 minutes. In 1977, part of a superb offensive line as starting G. For the season, made three tackles and ran one yard with kickoff return. Made All-American. Played super game in Cotton Bowl win over Texas to help Heavens and Ferguson both reach century mark in rushing; manhandled Outland Trophy winner, Brad Shearer, who made only one disappointed, frustrated tackle.

HUNTER, AL. 1973-1975-1976; HB; 6'0", 190; Greenville, NC. Fine back, though moody, who provided superior speed for 1973 national champions. Ran 9.3 in the 100; had good moves and strength. In 1973, backed up RHB. Shocked Alabama by running 93 yards with second-half kickoff for a TD in the Sugar Bowl. For the season, carried 32 times for 150 yards and three TDs, caught two passes for 12 yards, and returned three kickoffs 114 yards, including 74-yarder against Navy. In 1974, was suspended. In 1975, started at LHB. For the year, carried 117 times for 558 yards and eight TDs, caught 10 passes for 87 yards, returned five kickoffs 141 yards, and threw two-point conversion pass to Haines in loss to USC. In 1976, started at LHB to become Notre Dame's first 1,000-yard rusher in a season; against Miami became Notre Dame's all-time leading rusher at that point. For the year, carried 233 times for 1,058 yards and 12 TDs, caught 15 passes for 189 yards and one TD, completed one pass for 33-yard TD, returned 12 kickoffs 241 yards and four punts one yard, and made one tackle. Could have played in 1977 but turned pro under acrimonious circumstances. For his career, carried 382 times for 1,766 yards and 23 TDs, caught 27 passes for 288 yards and one TD, completed one pass for 33-yard TD, returned 20 kickoffs 496 yards and four punts one yard, threw a two-point conversion, and made one tackle. His offense totalled 2,584 yards and 25 TDs.

HUNTER, ART. 1951-1952-1953; C, E, T; 6'3", 226; Akron, OH. Multitalented lineman for Leahy. Had good size, speed, quickness, strength, and blocking and tackling skills. Leahy kept moving him around and he did well in all positions. Closest comparable player— Dave Casper. In 1951, started at C. In 1952, started at RE. Caught 16 passes for 246 yards and one TD. In 1953, started at RT; grabbed muffed snap in Georgia Tech's end zone for TD. Recovered three fumbles and led the team with 423 minutes of playing time. Consensus All-American.

HUNTER, TONY. 1979-1980-1981-1982; SE, WB, TE; 6'5", 226; Cincinnati, OH. Great size, speed, hands, moves, and strength. Multi-talented threat; played several positions and could create big gainer from each (but may have never found right position). In 1979, started at SE. Made 690 yards on 27 receptions (25.6-yard average) for two TDs to lead team. In 1980, started at SE. For the year, caught 23 passes for 303 yards and one TD and carried five times for 52 yards. In 1981, moved to WB; also played some TE, probably his natural position. For the year, caught 23 passes for 303 yards and two TDs and carried 27 times for 68 yards and one TD. In 1982, started at TE; caught 42 passes for 507 yards but did not score, and made five tackles. Made All-American. For his career, carried 32 times for 120 yards and one TD, caught 120 passes for 1,897 yards and five TDs, and made five tackles. His total was 2,017 yards and six TDs.

ISMAIL, RAGHIB. 1988-1989-1990; FL; 5'10", 175; Wilkes Barre, PA. Fastest player in Irish history. Timed at 4.12 in the 40 by NFL scouts. Not merely a speedster, could put moves on people and also go into the middle. Averaged 61 yards for TD plays for career. Tremendous ability to be near top speed in one or two strides. Could break tackles with leg drive, and was hard to hit. In

Raghib "Rocket" Ismail, the fastest player in Notre Dame history.

1988, started at SE for the national champions. For the year, made 12 catches for 331 yards and two TDs, and returned 12 kickoffs for 433 yards and two TDs and five punts for 72 yards. In 1989, started at FL. For the season, had 64 carries for 478 yards and two TDs, caught 27 passes for 535 yards, returned 20 kickoffs 502 yards for two TDs, and had seven punt returns for 113 yards and one TD. Consensus All-American. In 1990, started at FL and worked some at TB. For the year, carried 67 times for 537 yards and three TDs, caught 32 passes for 699 yards and two TDs, returned 14 kickoffs 336 yards for one TD, and returned 13 punts 151 yards. Consensus All-American; named Walter Camp Outstanding Player of the Year; was second in Heisman Trophy balloting. Bypassed final season to turn pro. For his career, made 131 carries for 1,015 yards (7.7 yards per carry) for five TDs, caught 71 passes for 1,565 yards (22 yards per catch) for four TDs, returned 46 kickoffs 1,271 yards (27.6 yards per return) for five TDs, and returned 25 punts 336 yards (13.4 yards per return) for one TD. His career totals were 273 attempts for 4,187 yards and 15 TDs—15.3 yards per attempt. In the 1,000-yard club in three different categories: runs, catches, and kickoff returns.

JACKSON, JARIOUS. 1996-1997-1998-1999; QB, 6'1", 228; Tupelo, MS. Waited in the wings while Powlus led the Irish for Holtz and Davie, then showed what he could do as the Irish QB in his final seasons. A powerful runner, he could improvise in a split second and turn a disaster into a long gain. Learned to be a good passer. Compiled the greatest single season for total offense for any Irish QB in his 1999 campaign. Played in six games for the high-scoring Irish in 1996; completed 10 of 15 passes for 181 yards and three TDs; carried 11 times for 16 yards; and played 54:06 minutes. In 1997, completed eight passes in 17 attempts for 146 yards and one TD and one INT; ran eight times for 36 yards and three TDs; hauled an onside KO attempt 40 yards for another TD, while playing 28:41 minutes. In '97 Independence Bowl loss to LSU, hit five of seven passes for 49 yards and carried the ball four times for minus-two yards. Started as the Irish QB in 1998 for all games except the USC game when an injury kept him out of action. Completed 104 passes in 188 attempts for 1,740 yards, good for 13 TDs and six INTs, while rushing for 441 yards on 113 carries for more more TDs. In tough '98 Gator Bowl loss to Georgia Tech, completed 13 of 24 passes for 150 yards while scoring one TD as he ran 12 times for 12 yards. For his senior campaign,

Jarious Jackson compiled the greatest single season for total offense by any Notre Dame quarterback in 1999.

1999, an outstanding personal effort in a difficult losing season turned out to be the best ever for an Irish QB: set the record for passing yards, 2,753 yards, surpassing Theismann's 1970 mark of 2,429 yards; set the record for passes attempted, 316, and completed, 184, in a season. Also set the record for total offense with 3,217 yards, zipping past Theismann's 2,820 yards from 1970. The only Irish QB to pass for more than 245 yards in four straight games (versus Michigan, Michigan State, Purdue, Oklahoma). Tallied 17 TDs against 14 INTs while also contributing seven TDs on the ground, with 140 carries for 464 yards. For his career, compiled the second best passing efficiency figure, mere fractions off Kevin McDougal's record. In little more than two full seasons, completed 324 passes in 567 throws for 4,702 yards, scoring 34 TDs against 21 INTs, while rushing for 14 TDs on 267 carries and 877 yards to go with the KO return TD. His total output came to 5,619 yards and 49 TDs on 835 attempts (6.72 yards per attempt). In 24 career starts, he averaged nearly 228 yards of total offense per start.

JEWETT, HARRY. 1887-1888; FB, HB; Chicago, IL. At one time reportedly held world's record for 100-yard dash, but his recorded time in a race with Michigan's fastest runner, prior to first Notre Dame football game, ended with him in second in a losing time of 11 seconds. In 1888, scored Notre Dame's first TD in 26-6 loss to Michigan. Grantland Rice wrote, ". . . Jewett secured the ball, and by a magnificent run made touchdown in Ann Arbor ground . . .[his] play was an elegant one and it caught the fancy of the crowd who were evidently pleased to see the Michigan team's [shutout] record broken."

JOHNSON, ANTHONY. 1986-1987-1988-1989; TB, FB; 6'0", 220; South Bend, IN. Powerful, hard-hitting, tough runner; played integral part on 1988 championship squad. Hard to bring down, seemed impervious to pain, and was pulverizing blocker. Especially tough in scoring territory. In 1986, backed up at TB. For the year, had 80 carries for 349 yards and five TDs, and caught six passes for 53 yards. In 1987, started at FB. Led Irish runners with eight carries for 20 yards against Texas A & M in Cotton Bowl. For the season, had 78 carries for 366 yards and a team-leading 11 TDs, caught four passes for 110 yards, and returned two kickoffs 55 yards. In 1988, started at FB. For the year, carried 169 times for 282 yards and five TDs, caught seven passes for 128 yards, and returned two kickoffs 27 yards. In 1989, started at FB and was a tri-captain. For the year, carried 131 times for 515 yards and 11 TDs, caught eight passes for 85 yards and two TDs, and returned three kickoffs 42 yards. For his career, had 358 carries for 1,512 yards and 32 TDs, caught 25 passes for 376 yards and two TDs, and returned seven kickoffs 127 yards. His career total was 2,015 yards and 34 TDs.

JOHNSON, JOE. 1981-1982-1983-1984; FS, SS; 6'2", 185; Fostoria, OH. Real hitter; excellent on safety blitzes and run support. In 1981, backed up at FS and played the most of any freshman on defense. Made 22 tackles, broke up two passes, and had one interception for the year. In 1982, started at SS. For the season, made 55 tackles, six for 22 yards; broke up two passes; and had two interceptions for 56 return yards. In 1983, started at SS. For the year, made 50 hits; caused three fumbles; recovered two fumbles; broke up three passes; and had four QB sacks for minus-47 yards, three other tackles for minus-23 yards, and one interception for a six-yard return. In 1984, started at SS and was a tri-captain. For the year, made 60 tackles, broke up two passes, caused

two fumbles, and registered one safety. For his career, made 187 tackles, 13 for minus-92 yards; had four interceptions for 61 return yards; caused five fumbles; recovered two fumbles; and forced one safety.

JOHNSON, MALCOLM. 1995-1996-1997-1998; SE; 6'5", 215; Washington, D.C. Big, rangy WR with good hands; paired with Bobby Brown and big TEs to give Irish QBs outstanding targets. Scored TDs in six consecutive games in the '98 season, a mark no other ND WR has met. Seventh all-time for Irish WRs in career pass receptions In '95, played behind Derrick Mayes in all 11 games; saw 20:50 minutes of action. Began a three-year stint as a starter in '96. Caught 25 passes that year for 449 yards and two TDs in 160:02 minutes. In '97, snagged 42 passes for 596 yards and two more TDs in 202:57 minutes. In '98, had his best season with 43 receptions for 692 yards and six TDs in 196:24 minutes. For his career, caught 110 passes in 29 starts for 1,737 yards, a 15.7 average, for 10 TDs in 580:13 minutes.

JOHNSTON, MIKE. 1980-1981-1982-1983; K; 5-11, 184; Rochester, NY. Walked on and did not receive scholarship until 1982. In 1980, handled kickoff duties and had one PAT. In 1981, handled kickoffs again. In 1982, set single-season record with 19 field goals in 22 that were the difference in win over Michigan, and was 19 of 19 on PATs for 76 points. In 1983, made 12 of 21 field goals and 33 of 34 PATs for 69 points. In his career, made 31 of 43 field goals and 53 of 54 PATs.

JUZWIK, STEVE. 1939-1940-1941; HB; 5'9", 185; Chicago, IL. Sturdy, quick HB for Layden and Leahy. Also played strong defense and was good kicker. In 1939, backed up at RHB. Made 32-yard run to set up only Irish TD in win over Northwestern. In 1940, started at RHB. Led team with 71 carries for 407 yards, also had 89 yards on passes, scored seven TDs, made one PAT, led in scoring with 43 points, including 84-yard interception runback for a TD. In 1941, was Bertelli's favorite receiver. For the year, carried 101 times for 386 yards; caught 17 passes for 305 yards; scored eight TDs; kicked 13 of 19 PATs; and had 23 punt returns for 290 yards, one kickoff return for 20 yards, and three interceptions for 39 yards for a total of 1,040 yards.

KADISH, MIKE. 1969-1970-1971; DT; 6'5", 260; Grand Rapids, MI. Dominant defensive lineman for Parseghian. Big, quick, strong; excellent pass rusher and run stopper. Teamed with McCoy, Patulski, and Marx to give Notre Dame a nearly impenetrable defensive line. In 1969, started at DT and made 68 tackles, six for minus-27 yards; had one interception; and broke up one pass. In 1970, started at DT; made 47 tackles, four for minus-15 yards, and recovered one fumble. In 1971, started at DT. Led team with 97 tackles (one of the last interior linemen to do so), eight for minus-40 yards, and broke up six passes. Made All-American. For his career, made 212 tackles, 18 for minus-82 yards; had one interception; broke up seven passes; and recovered one fumble.

KANTOR, JOE. 1961-1963-1964; FB; 6'1", 212; Cleveland, OH. Solid performer in a period of turmoil in the program; probably underutilized, but helped give stability and maturity in first year of Parseghian era. Had good size, adequate speed, good blocking skills, and good strength. In 1961, backed up at FB; made five carries for 39 yards, made six tackles, and broke up one pass. Injuries kept him out of action in 1962. In 1963, started at FB. For the year, led team with 88 carries for 330 yards and two TDs, caught two passes for 24 yards, returned one kickoff 11 yards, broke up one pass, and made one tackle. In 1964, backed up at FB. Scored what would have been winning TD in USC game to ensure undefeated season, but lost it on a holding call. For the season, carried 47 times for 158 yards and one TD, caught two passes for 43 yards, and returned one kickoff eight yards. For his career, carried 140 times for 527 yards and three TDs, caught four passes for 67 yards, returned two kickoffs 19 yards, broke up two passes, and made seven tackles. For his career, gained 613 yards and scored three TDs.

KEGLER, BILL. 1896-1897; FB; 6'0", 173; Bellevue, IA. Solid, all-around player—good runner, defender, and kicker. In 1896, started at FB and did place-kicking and some punting. Part of the decision the only time Notre Dame players quit a game. Trailing Physicians and Surgeons 4-0 and after a squabble over a possession matter, the Irish players simply walked off the field with 10 minutes remaining in the game. Made four conversions in 46-0 rout of South Bend Commercial A.C. Punted for 53-yard average against Albion, one for 65 yards, and made two conversion kicks in an Irish shutout. Scored one TD, rushed for 40-plus yards, but missed two crucial conversions in 28-22 loss to Purdue. Scored TD in 82-0 win over Highland Views a week

Mike Kadish, an All-American as a senior in 1971, was a three-year starter on the offensive line.

later. Helped defeat Beloit with one TD, good short yardage running, and good punting. In 1897, started at FB. In a tie with a much bigger Rush Medical squad, stopped some end runs, made a sack, punted well, and in the fashion of the day, was "pushed (by 256-pound Eggeman) into the line like a battering ram" on several plays. Scored only TD of game in win over DePauw, on five-yard run. Scored two TDs on long runs in win over MAC.

KELLY, BOB. 1943-1944; HB; 5'10", 182; Chicago, IL. Fine running back for Leahy; had excellent speed for breaking long runs and catching the long pass. In 1943, backed up at RHB. In shutout win over Army, rushed 11 times for 27 yards and, intercepted two passes. Caught two Lujack passes for TDs in win over Northwestern. Scored TD in win over Iowa Pre-Flight on four-yard run. Started at RHB in 1944. For the year, carried 133 times for 676 yards and eight TDs, scored five TDs with pass receptions, and kicked six PATs to lead team with 84 points. Made All-American.

KELLY, JIM. 1961-1962-1963; E; 6'2", 215; Clairton, PA. Fine player who labored for Fighting Irish teams that did not score well nor move the ball well. Had good size, speed, moves, hands, and defensive skills. In 1961, backed up at RE. For the year, caught nine passes for 139 yards and two TDs, made 26 tackles, and recovered one fumble. In 1962, started at RE; had record-setting day against Pitt with 11 catches for 127 yards and three TDs. For the year, set new season totals for receptions and yardage; caught 41 passes for 523 yards and four TDs, made 21 tackles, broke up one pass, and recovered one fumble. Made All-American. In 1963, started at LE. Playing for an inept offense, caught 18 passes for 264 yards and two TDs, made 21 tackles, broke up two passes, intercepted one pass for 10-yard runback, and returned one kickoff nine yards. Repeat All-American. For his career, caught 68 passes for 926 yards and eight TDs, recovered two fumbles, broke up three passes, made one interception for 10-yard runback, returned one kickoff nine yards, and made 68 tackles. His offensive total was 935 yards.

KELLY, LUKE. 1908-1909-1910-1911; T, G; 5'9", 185; Boston, MA. Tough lineman who specialized in quick penetration on defense to mess up plays; also adept at blocking kicks and catching passes. Called best player on 1911 team (which included Rockne, Dorais, Philbrook, Eichenlaub, and Bergman). In 1908, started at LT. Scored TD in 88-0 rout of Physicians and Surgeons. Scored TD in 11-0 win over Indiana by falling on a loose kick in the end zone; also made 15-yard pass reception. Blocked Ohio Northern kick near their end zone and Art Smith recovered and scored. In 1909,

Jim Kelly, who started at right end in 1962 and left end a year later, was an All-American in 1963.

backed up at RG. In 1910, backed up at RG. Knifed through Marquette's line and nailed their runner for a fumble, recovered for a TD and a 5-5 tie. In 1911, started at RT; elected captain. Blocked kick to avert a loss in 0-0 tie with Pitt. Caught five-yard pass in another scoreless game with Marquette. Named to second-team All-Western.

KIEL, BLAIR. 1980-1981-1982-1983; QB; 6'1", 206; Columbus, IN. First four-year starter at QB since Dorais 70 years earlier. Very strong for QB, good speed, good throwing arm for both distance and accuracy, and good punter. In 1980, started at QB. Played superbly at QB and as punter in 7-0 win over Alabama; also played well in Sugar Bowl loss to Georgia. For the year, carried 71 times for 148 yards and three TDs, completed 48 of 124 passes for 531 yards and five interceptions, averaged 40.1 yards on 66 punts, and had most playing time of any QB since Dorais—250 minutes. In 1981, started at QB. Led Irish in passing with 67 completions in 151 tries for 936 yards, seven TDs, and 10 interceptions; carried 31 times for 53 yards and one TD; and booted 74 punts for 39.9-yard average. In '82, completed 118 of 219 passes for 1,273 yards, three TDs, 10 interceptions, and .539 completion rate (fourth best in Irish history to that point); carried 44 times for minus-29 yards; and punted 77 times for 42.4-yard average. In 1983, started at QB. For the year, hit 64 of 115 passes for 910 yards, seven TDs, seven interceptions, and .557 completion rate; crunched 43 punts for 39.6-yard average; and carried 19 times for minus-eight yards and one TD. For his career, carried 165 times for 164 yards and five TDs; completed 297 passes in 609 throws for 3,650 yards, 17 TDs, and 32 interceptions; and punted 260 times for 40.67-yard average, second-best behind Shakespeare's 40.71 average at that point. His punts traversed 10,534 yards, but the number also signifies plenty of stalled drives. His 609 passes set record for most attempts, and was second only to Hanratty in completions (297 to 304). His career offense was 3,814 yards and 22 TDs.

KILEY, ROGER. 1919-1920-1921; E; 6'0", 180; Chicago, IL. Multi-talented athlete, teamed with Gipp as aerial tandem for undefeated 1920 squad. Had excellent speed, ran precise routes but had to ad lib when Gipp did, and played good defense. In 1919, backed up at LE. In 1920, started at LE. Caught 38-yard pass from Gipp in win over Valparaiso. Caught two passes from Gipp in win over Army, one a 35-yard TD. Caught several passes from Gipp in shutout of Purdue, one for 30 yards. Caught TD pass in win over Northwestern—Gipp's last game. All-America selection. In 1921, started at LE. Scored one TD in win over DePauw. Scored Notre Dame's only TD on 50-yard strike in 10-7 loss to Iowa; also made five other receptions and blocked a punt and returned it to the Iowa 25. Recovered Purdue fumble in Irish win. Caught 11-yard pass in win over Indiana. Scored two TDs on passes of 55 and 18 yards from Mohardt in shutout of Army. Scored against Rutgers three days later with 25-yard pass. All-American; captained basketball team; played second base for baseball team his senior year.

KIZER, NOBLE. 1922-1923-1924; G; 5'8", 165; Plymouth, IN. Originally went to Notre Dame to play basketball, but Rockne snatched him for football. Was perfect example, with Bert Metzger a few years later, of Rockne's "watch charm guard"—small, extremely quick, intelligent, and very tough. Rockne taught how to use leverage, angles, and the opponent's momentum to neutralize his charge, much like modern brush blocking. Fixture at RG for 1923 and 1924 seasons, when Seven Mules led Four Horsemen to fame and the national crown in 1924.

KLEINE, WALLY. 1983-1984-1985-1986; DT; 6'9", 274; Midland, TX. Fine DL whose size and agility posed problems for QBs intent on passing or staying in the pocket. In 1983, backed up at DT. For the season, made five tackles, one sack for minus-10 yards and one for minus-three yards, and caused one fumble. In 1984, started at DT. For the year, made 48 tackles, two sacks for minus-16 yards and 11 for minus-25 yards; broke up one pass; caused three fumbles; and recovered three fumbles. In 1985, started at DT but missed four games with a knee injury. For the season, made 36 tackles, five sacks for minus-21 yards and six for minus-25 yards, and caused two fumbles. In 1986, started at DT. For the year, made 74 tackles, five sacks for minus-40 yards and eight for minus-27 yards, and broke up three passes. Made All-American. For his career, made 163 tackles, 13 sacks for minus-87 yards and 26 for minus-80 yards; caused six fumbles; recovered three fumbles; and broke up four passes.

KOKEN, MIKE. 1930-1931-1932; HB; 5'9", 168; Youngstown, OH. Classic triple-threat—excellent speed, good passing arm, and good leg for kicking. In 1930,

backed up at LHB for national champions. Scored TD against Pitt with five-yard run around right end; also made 19-yard run. In 1931, backed up LHB. Led team with three TDs and four PATs in win over Drake. Threw lateral pass to Host for 11-yard TD in win over Pitt. Threw lateral pass to Leahy for 13-yard TD in win over Carnegie Tech. In shutout of Penn, ran 22 yards for TD and passed 11 yards for another to go with one PAT. Threw TD pass to QB in win over Navy. In 1932, started at LHB. Fired 20-yard TD pass to Banas in win over Haskell. Against Carnegie Tech, made 58-yard TD run, gained 116 yards rushing, completed 31-yard pass, and kicked two PATs. Closed Irish scoring in win over Kansas with three-yard plunge. Against Northwestern, threw 21-yard TD pass and 18-yarder to set up another score. Passed five yards to Melinkovich for TD in win over Army. Gained 375 yards on 105 carries and made four interceptions for 32 return yards in the year.

KOVALESKI, MIKE. 1983-1984-1985-1986; LB; 6'1", 218; New Castle, IN. Speedy, tough four-year starter at LB. Had excellent range; good hitter; had knack for being around the ball. In 1983, started at WLB. For the year, made 62 tackles, one sack for minus-10 yards and two for minus-four yards; caused two fumbles, broke up four passes; and had one interception for five return yards. In 1984, started at WLB. For the year, led team, despite nagging injuries, with 108 tackles, two for minus-four yards, and broke up two passes. In 1985, started at WLB. For the year, was second on team with 95 tackles, two for minus-20 yards; caused two fumbles; and broke up two passes. In 1986, started at ILB and captained team—first solo captain since Bleier in 1967. For the year, made 88 tackles, three for minus-eight yards, and broke up one pass. For his career, made 353 tackles, one sack for minus-10 yards and nine for minus-36 yards; caused four fumbles; broke up nine passes; and had one interception for five return yards.

KRAUSE, ED (MOOSE). 1931-1932-1933; T; 6'3", 220; Chicago, IL. One of greatest both in terms of athletic achievements and service to Notre Dame as coach, athletic director, and general figurehead of Fighting Irish excellence. Recruited by Rockne in response to rule changes that had all but gutted the shift, changes that placed a premium on size rather than sheer speed and quickness. Never played for Rockne, but was involved in fall and some spring practices, as well as Rockne's lectures on the game. Thus, important bridge to the past, having served as AD until the early 1980s.

Moose Krause, recruited by Rockne in 1930, remained at Notre Dame for more than 60 years as a player, coach, and administrator before his death.

First All-American for Notre Dame in both football and basketball. In football, was dominating lineman. In his words, "I was double- and triple-teamed for my entire career." In 1931, backed up at LT. In a scoreless tie with Northwestern, provided scoring opportunity with recovery of blocked punt, but offense couldn't capitalize. The Irish defense recorded six shutouts in nine games. In 1932, started at LT. Blocked two Drake punts in shutout win, one for a safety and the other for a TD. Recovered Carnegie Tech fumble to set up TD in shutout win. Was the main man in a defense that registered six shutouts. In 1933, started at LT. Made All-American. Hampered by offense that scored only 32 points in nine games. Led team to two shutouts. Blocked punt for a TD in 7-0 win over Northwestern and set up blocked punt to defeat Army 13-12.

KUECHENBERG, BOB. 1966-1967-1968; T, DE; 6'2", 245; Hobart, IN. Excellent lineman during Parseghian's Hanratty years, showing versatility by starting on both sides of line. Had excellent quickness and strength, and very good technique. In 1966 started at RT for national champions; part of offensive line that reached new levels of effectiveness and protection for Hanratty. Made one tackle. In 1967, switched to starting DE. For the season, made 32 tackles, returned one kickoff for no gain, and broke up four passes. In

1968, started at DE. For the year, made 44 tackles, eight for losses; broke up two passes; and recovered two fumbles. Never made All-American. In his career, made 77 tackles, eight for minus yardage; broke up six passes; recovered two fumbles; and fielded a kickoff for no gain.

KUHARICH, JOE. 1935-1936-1937; G; 6'0", 193 South Bend, IN. Excellent lineman for Layden—tough, smart, indomitable. Later had illustrious coaching career, but it didn't work at Notre Dame—his career record from 1959 to 1962 is the only losing one in school's history. In 1935, backed up at RG. In 1936, started at RG. In 1937, started at RG.

KUNZ, GEORGE. 1966-1967-1968; T, TE; 6'5",240; Arcadia, CA. Must be considered among all-time great linemen for Notre Dame. Had excellent size, mobility, and superb technique. Close observers called him most dominant lineman of the last quarter century. In 1966, started at RT for national champions but was injured in Northwestern game and sidelined. In 1967, played both T and TE; caught seven passes for 101 yards. In 1968, started at RT and was co-captain. Consensus All-American.

KURTH, JOE. 1930-1931-1932; T; 6'2", 204; Madison, WI. Fine lineman for Rockne and Anderson Had

Joe Kuharich, Notre Dame's starting right guard in 1936 and 1937, later returned as the team's head coach in the 1960s.

excellent quickness, good strength, and good technique. Especially good on defense. In 1930, started at RT for national champions. Helped save opening win over SMU with open-field tackle of back loose on a long run. Key blocker in many long TD runs for the year. In 1931, started at RT. Played strong defensive game against Pitt but ignored a doctor's warning not to play; spent three days in the hospital. Made All-American. In 1932, started at RT. In win over Northwestern, tackled punter for big loss to set up Irish TD drive and later blocked a punt to create another scoring opportunity. Deflected USC quick kick in losing effort. Repeat All-American.

LAMBEAU, CURLY. 1918; FB; 5'10", 188; Green Bay, WI. Flamboyant one-year player for Rockne in shortened season; teammate of Gipp. Excellent blocker and good short-yardage runner. In 1918, started at FB. Scored first TD of season in win over Case. Scored two TDs in slaughter of Wabash. Rushed for effective short yardage in win over Purdue and in tie with Nebraska. Returned to Green Bay. Later coached Jimmy Crowley before he went to Notre Dame.

LAMONICA, DARYLE. 1960-1961-1962; QB; 6'2", 205; Fresno, CA. One of best pure passers for Notre Dame; also could run and kick well. Had excellent arm, showed good leadership, and played defense well in last one-platoon era. Closest recent player with similar skills was Blair Kiel. In 1960, started at QB and showed good maturity as sophomore. For the season, hit 15 of 31 passes for 242 yards, five interceptions, and no TDs; gained 73 yards on 26 carries; punted 23 times for 37.4-yard average; had one interception and 18-yard runback; returned one punt for 10 yards; made 33 tackles; and broke up two passes. In 1961, started at QB. For the year, hit 20 of 52 passes for 300 yards, two TDs, and four interceptions; carried 44 times for 135 yards and three TDs; punted 29 times for 38.4-yard average; made 29 tackles; and had two interceptions for 54 return yards. In 1962, started at QB; completed 64 of 128 throws for 821 yards, six TDs, and seven interceptions; carried 74 times for 145 yards and four TDs; made three tackles; had one interception; broke up one pass; and punted 49 times for 36.5-yard average. For his career, carried 144 times for 353 yards and seven TDs; completed 99 of 211 passes for 1,363 yards, eight TDs, and 16 interceptions; made 65 tackles; made three interceptions for 54 return yards; broke up three passes; and punted 101 times for 37.25-yard average. His career offense totaled 1,770 yards and 15 TDs.

LANDRY, JACK. 1948-1949-1950; HB, FB; 6'1", 180; Rochester, NY. Good, dependable runner under Leahy. Wasn't flashy or given to many long gainers, but could be counted on for consistent gains and was hard to bring down near goalline. In 1948, backed up at RHB. For the year, carried 80 times for 309 yards and six TDs, caught one pass for 10 yards, and returned two punts 35 yards. In 1949, backed up at FB for the national champions. For the year, carried 37 times for 147 yards and two TDs. In 1950, started at FB. In the year, carried 109 times for 491 yards and two TDs, led in kickoff returns with 11 for 195 yards, and caught seven passes for 57 yards. For his career, carried 226 times for 947 yards and 10 TDs, caught eight passes for 67 yards, and returned 11 kickoffs 195 yards and two punts 35 yards. His career total was 1,244 yards and 10 TDs.

LARKIN, MIKE. 1981-1982-1984-1985; LB; 6'1", 210; Cincinnati, OH. One of speediest linebackers ever to suit up for Notre Dame; made up in intensity and quickness what he lacked in size. Brother of Cincinnati Reds' Barry Larkin. In 1981 backed up at OLB; made 10 tackles, one sack, and one fumble recovery. In 1982, started at OLB. Made 112 tackles, second best that year; led with eight hits for minus-23 yards; and broke up three passes. Lost 1983 with a twice-broken arm. In 1984, slated to start at OLB but a knee injury curtailed his action until late in the season. For the year, made 39 tackles, two for three yards, and broke up one pass. In 1985, started at ROLB. For the year, made 40 tackles, 11 for minus-46 yards, including five QB sacks. In his career, made 201 tackles, 21 for minus-72 yards; made six QB sacks; recovered one fumble; and broke up four passes.

LARSON, FRED (OJAY). 1918-1920-1921; C; 6'1", 190; Calumet, MI. One of toughest men to play for Rockne. Key lineman in blocking scheme for Gipp. In 1918, started at C. In 1920, started at C for undefeated Irish. Played most of second quarter in win over Army with torn muscles and partially dislocated hip. In 1921, backed up at C. Lost his monogram for playing in a semi-pro game.

LATTNER, JOHNNY. 1951-1952-1953; HB; 6'1", 190; Chicago, IL. Needs to be rated near top of all Fighting Irish players even though not outstanding in any particular phase of game. Good at almost everything—a rare commodity even in one-platoon football days. Best

Lean and lanky Johnny Lattner, Notre Dame's versatile 1953 Heisman Trophy winner.

compared to George Gipp for dramatic flair to get job done in any of a dozen different ways. Had certain raw-boned appearance, but closer examination showed a whippet in cleats. In 1951, backed up at RHB. For the season, carried 68 times for 341 yards and six TDs, caught eight passes for 157 yards, completed one of two passes for 23 yards, returned 10 punts 91 yards, made five interceptions for 66 return yards and recovered four fumbles to lead team in turnover recoveries, and punted 26 times for 32.4-yard average—all in 401 minutes. In 1952, started at RHB. For the year, carried 148 times for 732 yards and five TDs, caught 17 passes for 252 yards and one TD, completed two of five passes for 33 yards, returned seven punts 113 yards and three kickoffs 45 yards, recovered three fumbles, had four interceptions for 58 return yards, and punted 64 times for 36.6-yard average. Consensus All-American. In 1953, started at RHB. Carried 134 times for 651 yards and six TDs, caught 14 passes for 204 yards and one TD, completed only pass for 55-yard gain, returned eight kickoffs 321 yards for two TDs, returned 10 punts 104 yards, had four interceptions for four return yards, recovered one fumble, and punted 29 times for 35-yard average in 421 minutes of action. Consensus All-American and won Heisman Trophy (Leahy's fourth winner). For his career, carried 350 times for 1,724 yards and 17 TDs, caught 39 passes for 613 yards and eight TDs, completed four of eight passes for 111 yards, returned 27 punts 308 yards,

returned eight kickoffs 366 yards for two TDs, made 13 interceptions for 128 return yards, recovered eight fumbles, and punted 121 times for 35.3-yard average. His total offense was 3,250 yards and 22 TDs.

LAW, JOHN. 1926-1927-1928-1929; G; 5'9", 163; Yonkers, NY. Quality in small package; model for Rockne's type of guard—very tough and very quick. In 1926, backed up at RG. In 1927, backed up at RG. In 1928, started at RG. In 1929, started at RG for national champions.

LAYDEN, ELMER. 1922-1923-1924; HB, FB; 6'0", 162; Davenport, IA. The quiet Horseman; went in at FB in 1922 Butler game following Castner's injury to complete quartet—most famous and arguably greatest backfield in Irish history. Had tremendous acceleration; at 162 pounds, was largest of quartet. Great punter, a key skill in those days. In 1922, started at LHB. Intercepted Army pass to preserve 0-0 tie. Caught TD pass from Stuhldreher in win over Carnegie Tech. Threw TD pass to Miller in 14-6 loss to Nebraska. In 1923, started at FB. Broke open tight game with Princeton with interception and 40-yard TD runback in 12-0 win. Kept Purdue bottled up with punts averaging 48 yards in 34-7 win. Scored TD dive in win over Carnegie Tech.

Elmer Layden, an All-America fullback in 1923 and 1924, made the switch in 1922 from left halfback to fullback after Castner was hurt—and Rockne had his Four Horsemen.

Made two- and three-yard TDs in win over St. Louis. Made All-American. In 1924, started at FB for national champions. Scored first TD of game against Army that led to Grantland Rice's creation of the Horsemen mystique; also stole pass at midfield to begin drive that would win the game. Scored insurance TD with 17-yard run in win over Princeton. Scored on plunge in win over Georgia Tech. Played great game to avenge two earlier defeats by Nebraska—threw 65-yard TD pass to Crowley and ran for 30-yard TD. Intercepted pass and ran 40 yards for TD in 13-6 win over Northwestern. Scored two TDs in win over Stanford in 1925 Rose Bowl—on three-yard plunge, 78-yard interception return, and 70-yard interception return with 30 seconds left in the game; also returned punt 90 yards that kept Stanford mired at its end of the field. Consensus All-American.

LEAHY, FRANK. 1928-1929; T; 5'11", 183; Winner, SD. Very hard, driven worker. Tried to catch on as C, but that didn't work out. In 1928, backed up at LT. In 1929, subbed at RT and saw action in most games for national champions, but an arm injury limited effectiveness. In 1930, was ready to start, but in last practice before opener with SMU, tore knee cartilage. Spent part of his recuperation period at Mayo Clinic with Knute Rockne as a roommate, who was there for treatment of phlebitis. Their time together allowed him to imbibe Rockne's wisdom, and a coach was born. A few months later, Rockne was killed. A decade later, Leahy became head coach.

LEHMANN, BOB. 1961-1962-1963; G; 6'0", 215; Louisville, KY. Fine leader for struggling Irish. Had great desire and intensity; overachiever physically and was often overmatched, but willed his way into playing success. Good blocker but excelled on defense. In 1961, backed up at LG. Made 41 tackles in 258 minutes. In 1962, started at RG. Led goal-line stand that resulted in two yards from Notre Dame three before an Oklahoma fumble was recovered and the Fighting Irish won 13-7. For the year, was second with 61 tackles, recovered one fumble, and blocked one kick in 367 minutes. In 1963, started at RG and was captain. Made 20 tackles against Staubach and Navy in losing effort. Made 18 tackles against Pitt in loss. Intercepted Syracuse pass in loss. For the season, was second with 95 tackles, blocked one kick, recovered one fumble, and intercepted one pass. Made All-American. For his career, made 197 tackles, recovered two fumbles, blocked one kick, and had one interception.

LEMEK, RAY. 1953-1954-1955; G, T; 6'1", 205; Sioux City, IA. Solid, consistent lineman for Leahy and Brennan. Excelled on defense with good quickness. In 1953, started at LG. In rout of USC, intercepted pass and returned it to their 43 to set up TD. Intercepted pass to provide opportunity for last Irish TD in win over SMU. Played 347 minutes. In 1954, started at LG. Recovered Texas fumble at the Notre Dame six to preserve shutout. Helped tackle for a safety in loss to Purdue and broke up pass in win over Pitt. Set up score with interception of pass on the 37 in lopsided win over Penn. In 1955, started at RT and was captain. Grabbed Miami fumble on their 33 to lead to TD in shutout.

LEWIS, AUBREY. 1955-1956-1957; HB; 6'0", 185; Montclair, NJ. World-class sprinter's speed to complement Hornung in 1955 and 1956. Fastest man to have played for the Irish to that point. Tremendous threat to break long run or pass; played sterling defense. In 1955, backed up at LHB. For the season, carried 56 times for 222 yards and two TDs, caught 32-yard TD pass, returned four kickoffs 91 yards, and intercepted four passes for 38 return yards. In 1956, started at LHB. For the year, carried 59 times for 292 yards, caught 11 passes for 170 yards and one TD, returned six kickoffs 167 yards and five punts 46 yards, had three interceptions for 39 return yards, and recovered one fumble in 286 minutes. In 1957, had some excellent games but the stats fell off sharply: carried 11 times for 20 yards, caught two passes for 96 yards and one TD, returned one kickoff 21 yards and two punts 27 yards, missed two pass attempts, and recovered one fumble. For his career, carried 126 times for 534 yards and two TDs, caught 14 passes for 220 yards and three TDs, returned 11 kickoffs 279 yards and seven punts 73 yards, went 0 for two in passing, made seven interceptions for 77 yards, and recovered two fumbles. His career figures totaled 1,183 yards and five TDs.

LIND, MIKE. 1960-1961-1962; FB; 6'1", 200; Chicago, IL. Good FB for Kuharich's teams led by Lamonica. Career was cut short by a plague of injuries. In 1960, started at FB. For the season, carried 53 times for 167 yards and one TD, caught two passes for 10 yards, made 17 tackles, broke up one pass, and recovered one fumble in 147 minutes. In 1961, started at FB. For the campaign, rushed 87 times for 450 yards and four TDs, caught four passes for four yards, made 31 tackles, and broke up four passes in 261 minutes. In 1962, injuries limited him to eight carries for 13 yards and one pass for four yards. For his career, rushed 148 times for 630 yards and five TDs, caught seven passes for 18 yards, made 48 tackles, broke up five passes, and recovered one fumble. His career total was 648 yards and five TDs.

LINS, GEORGE. 1896-1897-1898-1899-1900-1901; C, G, FB, HB, E; 6'0",185; Wilmington, IL. Set record for varsity career longevity. May have played in 48 games, but records are spotty. Played with John Farley and Red Salmon. All-around player or at least pliable regarding coaches' playing suggestions. Played as many as three different positions in one season; had enough speed to go long distances; and was a good blocker. In 1896, backed up at C. In 1897, started at LG but played C too. Was C in shutout win over Rush. Helped in strong defensive effort that shut out DePauw. Played at LG in 62-0 win over Chicago Dental—the game in which Farley ran for more than 400 yards rushing from scrimmage and most TDs came on runs of over 50 yards. Tallied two TDs as RHB in win over MAC, his third starting position. In 1898, started at RHB. Had good short yardage runs in win over Illinois. Scored TD and ran 80 plus yards in 52-0 blowout over MAC. In 1899, subbed at RHB. Scored TD with six-yard run in win over Englewood H.S. Played well in 12-0 win over Northwestern; made one run for four yards, then quit team for unknown reasons. In 1900, came back. Started at LE much of the season, but scored on 95-yard run and long end run from FB spot in win over Goshen. Scored on 10-yard burst in win over Howard Park. Strong running near the goal helped earn 5-0 win over Rush. In 1901, started at LE but also played LHB. Scored only TD in win over Beloit. Went back to E in wins over Purdue and Indiana.

LIVINGSTONE, BOB. 1942-1946-1947; HB; 6'0", 175; Hammond, IN. True speed merchant; always a threat to break long play either running or receiving. Good kick returner and played well as DB. In 1942, started at LHB in new T-formation. Caught 42-yard TD pass from Bertelli in shutout of Stanford. Helped beat Iowa Pre-Flight with 47-yard TD reception from Bertelli. Scored on 14-yard run in win over Northwestern. Missed three seasons while serving in Army. In 1946, backed up at LHB. For the season, rushed 40 times for 191 yards and two TDs, caught three passes for 38 yards, and gained 146 yards on kickoff returns. In 1947, backed up at LHB for the national champions. For the year, gained 242 yards on 45 runs and scored four TDs, caught four passes for 78 yards, returned four punts 88 yards and two kickoffs 42 yards, and had two interceptions for 45 return yards.

LONERGAN, FRANK. 1901-1902-1903; E, HB; 5'10", 168; Palo, IL. Appreciated for speed, punt coverage, and lead blocking, as E, in blocking for plays coming in his direction. In 1901, started at RE. Made 50-yard TD run, kickoff return of 15 yards, 30-yard run from scrimmage, and fumble recovery in win over Physicians and Surgeons. Helped save narrow victory over Beloit with fumble recovery. Averaged 21 yards for four kickoff returns in win over South Bend Commercial A.C., the longest for 40 yards. In 1902, started at RE. Sprinted for 17-yard gain at crucial moment before Notre Dame took control of MAC in 33-0 win. Helped shut out Lake Forest with long TD run around end. Ran for short yardage against Michigan in loss. Recovered fumbled punt in Ohio Medical game, and ran 45 yards to score. Raced for three TDs against American Medical, two on runs of 85 and 90 yards, in 920 rout. In 1903, started at RHB for undefeated and unscored-upon Irish. Returned punt for TD, ran 45 yards from scrimmage, and made three conversions against American Medical in 52-0 win. Scored one TD against Missouri Osteopaths. Made 45-yard TD run against Northwestern, but lost it on a penalty call; game ended 0-0, the only blemish that year. Scored final Irish TD on 15-yard run against Ohio Medical.

LONGO, TOM. 1963-1964-1965; DB; 6'1", 200; Lyndhurst, NJ. Fine DB for first two Parseghian teams. Had good coverage speed, and was a great hitter. In 1963, played in special defensive situations. Made two interceptions for eight return yards. In 1964, started at RCB. Led DBs with 72 tackles, recovered one fumble, broke up 10 passes, and intercepted four passes for 27 return yards. In 1965, led DBs with 73 tackles, broke up two passes, recovered one fumble, and made four interceptions. For his career, made 145 tackles, recovered two fumbles, broke up 12 passes, and made 10 interceptions for 44 return yards.

LUHN, HENRY. 1887; HB. It all started with this man. Coach, captain, and first HB for Notre Dame (the one holding the football in the team photo). Became a physician and lived in Spokane, WA.

LUJACK, JOHNNY. 1943-1946-1947; QB; 6'0",180; Connellsville, PA. Strong candidate for all-time QB for the Fighting Irish. Tremendous competitor; had charisma that infected teammates with greater drive to win. Poised, with great arm, good quickness, and good running and kicking skills. Equally skilled on defense.

An all-time Irish quarterback, Johnny Lujack started Bertelli's unfinished season at quarterback in 1943, repeated in 1946 and 1947, was the Heisman Trophy winner once, and a consensus All-American twice.

In 1943, backed up at QB for the national champions (Leahy thus had two eventual Heisman Trophy winners stacked at one position). Led team in passing with 34 completions in 71 throws for 525 yards and four TDs, and carried 46 times for 191 yards. Served in Navy in 1944 and 1945. In 1946, started at QB. For the season, gained 108 yards on 23 carries, and completed 49 of 100 passes for 778 yards, six TDs, and eight interceptions. Recovered three fumbles to tie for lead. Consensus All-American. In 1947, started at QB for national champions. For the year, carried only 12 times but gained 139 yards for 11.1-yard average; hit 61 of 109 passes for 777 yards, nine TDs, and eight interceptions; and led in takeaway interceptions with three for 44 return yards. Won Heisman Trophy and was consensus All-American. For his career, completed 144 of 280 passes for 2,080 yards, 19 TDs, and 16 interceptions; and made 81 carries for 438 yards and two TDs. His offensive production totaled 2,518 yards and 21 TDs.

LUKATS, NICK. 1930-1932-1933; HB; 6'0", 185; Perth Amboy, NJ. Good reserve HB for Rockne's last

year and two-year starter for Anderson. Good passer, consistent runner, and fine blocker; played featured LHB position in football scheme of the day. In 1930, backed up at LHB. Missed 1931 with a broken leg. In 1932, backed up at LHB. Helped beat Haskell with 23-yard TD sprint. Scored one TD and threw 44-yard TD pass in win over Drake. Had great game against Carnegie Tech: hit passes of 21, 25, and 21 yards on long TD drive, made block that took out eight players to spring Jaskwich on TD punt return, and added 15-yard run on another long drive. Losing to Kansas early in the game, dashed 45 yards to tie score and provide impetus to win. Threw crucial 25-yard pass in win over Navy to set up TD chance at Middie 11; also punted once to their three. For the season, led team in passing with 13 completions in 28 tries for 252 yards and two TDs. In 1933, started at LHB. In 12-2 win over Indiana, had 53-yard TD run, four rushes for 19-yard TD drive, and 70-yard punt. Scored winning TD in 13-12 game with Army. For the year, led team with 339 yards on 109 carries, in passing with 21 of 67 for 329 yards, and in scoring with two TDs; also intercepted two passes.

LYGHT, TODD. 1987-1988-1989-1990; CB; 6'1", 184; Flint, MI. Outstanding DB under Holtz. Came as WR but made switch to defense and had immediate impact— had more starting time in 1987 than any other freshman. Superb speed and excellent coverage skills; at his best with the ball in the air. In 1987, backed up at RCB. For the season, made 29 tackles, caused one fumble, broke up two passes, and had one interception. In 1988, started at CB for national champions. Led team with six tackles in Fiesta Bowl win over West Virginia. For the year, made 36 tackles, three for minus-eight yards, and broke up nine passes. In 1989, started at CB. Made four tackles, one for a loss, in Orange Bowl win over Colorado. For the year, made 47 tackles, one for minus-one yard; broke up 6.5 passes; and had eight interceptions for 42 return yards and one TD. Made All-American. In 1990, started at CB. For the year, made 49 tackles, broke up three passes, and had two interceptions for 13 return yards. Made three tackles and one sack in Orange Bowl loss to Colorado. Consensus All-American. For his career, had 161 tackles, four for minus-nine yards; caused one fumble; broke up 20.5 passes; and had 11 interceptions for 55 return yards and one TD.

LYNCH, DICK. 1955-1956-1957; HB; 6'0", 180; Bound Brook, NJ. As any trivia buff knows, scored to

Dick Lynch, starting right halfback in 1957, scored the winning touchdown in the great upset of Oklahoma that year.

LYNCH, JIM. 1964-1965-1966; LB; 6'1", 225; Lima, OH. Must be seriously considered for place on any all-time Irish team. Fine competitor; intense but always under control. Had good speed, strength, and mobility, as well as nose for the ball. One of best strategic thinkers fielded by Notre Dame on defense. Saw team go from 2-7 in his freshman year to win it all in 1966. In 1964, started at OLB. Played in six games until injured during Navy game. For the year, made 41 tackles, broke up one pass, and played 117 minutes. In 1965, started at OLB (sixth in total defense nationally). For the year, led team with 108 tackles, broke up three passes, and intercepted one. In 1966, started at ILB and captained national champions. Led defense that put together three straight shutouts, with six for season; held 10 opponents to 38 points. For the year, made 106 tackles, three interceptions for 12 return yards, broke up two passes, and recovered one fumble. Consensus All-American; won Maxwell Award as top college player; Academic All-American. In his career, made 255 tackles, broke up six passes, made four interceptions for 12 return yards, and recovered one fumble.

beat Oklahoma in 1957. Prior to that, had not been used on regular basis in two seasons, but had broad range of skills. In 1955, backed up at RHB. For the year, carried 24 times for 124 yards and one TD. In 1956, backed up at RHB. For the season, carried 14 times for 10 yards, caught five passes for 54 yards, and returned two kickoffs 53 yards. In 1957, started at RHB. Scored with 3:50 remaining to give Notre Dame 7-0 win over Oklahoma and end their 40-game winning streak. On that play, QB Williams faked to Pietrosante up the middle and pitched out to Lynch on the right for three-yard TD run. For the year, was second in rushing with 77 carries for 287 yards and a team-leading five TDs, completed two of five passes for 26 yards, led in receiving with 13 for 128 yards, led in kickoff returns with six for 163 yards and in punt returns with four for 43 yards. In his career, carried 115 times for 421 yards and six TDs, caught 18 passes for 182 yards, completed two of five passes for 26 yards, and returned eight kickoffs 216 yards and four punts 43 yards. His career offense was 888 yards and six TDs.

Ken MacAfee, a three-year starter at tight end and consensus All-American in 1977, cuts to the middle of the Georgia Tech defense in the 1977 blowout.

MacAFEE, KEN. 1974-1975-1976-1977; TE; 6'4", 251; Brockton, MA. One of the best TEs ever to play for Notre Dame. Had perfect dimensions for the modern TE, with enough speed to have played from SE position. Had fine hands and uncanny sense for finding seams in coverages to help Clements and Montana. In 1974, backed up at SE until an injury gave him chance to move to TE. In win over Miami, caught 14 passes for 146 yards and one TD. In 1975, started at TE. For the year, led receivers with 26 catches for 333 yards and five TDs and returned one kickoff for no gain. Made All-American. In 1976, started at TE. For the year, led team with 34 catches for 483 yards and three TDs, returned three kickoffs 34 yards, and made one tackle. Consensus All-American. In 1977, started at TE for national champions. For the year, caught nine; 54 passes for team-leading 797 yards and six TDs to go with two tackles. Consensus All-American and the Walter Camp Player of the Year. For his career, caught 128 passes for 1,759 yards and 15 TDs, returned four kickoffs 34 yards, and made three tackles.

MacDONALD, TOM. 1961-1962-1963; HB, DB; 5'11", 180; Downey, CA. Speedy, crafty defensive specialist, one of best pass defenders in Irish annals. In 1961, backed up at LHB. For the year, carried two times for three yards, returned two punts four yards, had one interception for 23 return yards, made eight tackles, and broke up two passes. In 1962, played as defensive specialist and set new record with nine interceptions in a season. For the year, carried 10 times for 14 yards, caught one pass for no gain, made 29 tackles, had nine interceptions for 81 return yards, returned two kickoffs 30 yards, and broke up five passes. In 1963, played as defensive specialist. For the season, had six carries for 20 yards, caught two passes for 34 yards, returned eight kickoffs 146 yards, made 47 tackles, broke up six passes, had one fumble recovery, and made five interceptions for 63 return yards and one TD. For his career, had 18 carries for 37 yards, caught three passes for 34 yards, broke up 13 passes, made 85 tackles, made 15 interceptions (then a record) for 167 return yards and one TD, recovered one fumble, returned two punts four yards and 10 kickoffs 176 yards. His career total was 418 yards for one TD.

MAHALIC, DREW. 1972-1973-1974; LB; 6'4", 222; Farmington, MI. Converted from QB; fixture as LB and helped win national crown in 1973. Had good range; excellent hitter and good defensive thinker, probably helped by his knowledge of offense as former QB.

In 1972, started at LB and made 77 tackles, four for minus-15 yards; had two interceptions for 59 return yards and one TD; and broke up one pass. In 1973, started at LB. In the Sugar Bowl, intercepted Alabama pass on their 21 and took it to the 12; Penick scored winning TD on next play. For the year, made 59 tackles, one for minus-one yard; broke up two passes; recovered one fumble; and made one interception. In 1974, started at LB. For the year, had 117 tackles (second best on team), six for minus-27 yards; broke up four passes; recovered one fumble; and made one interception. For his career, made 253 tackles, 11 for minus-43 yards; had four interceptions for 59 return yards and one TD; broke up seven passes; and recovered two fumbles. Played in the last College All-Star game under Parseghian.

MARTIN, JIM. 1946-1947-1948-1949; E, T; 6'2", 204; Cleveland, OH. One of premier linemen during undefeated streak for Leahy. Very strong, cat quick, and tough competitor; had served as marine in WWII. As war hero, kept football in perspective. In 1946, started seven games at LE as freshman. Recovered three fumbles for the year. In 1947, started at LE for national champions. For the year, rushed 10 times for 86 yards and one TD, and caught 13 passes for 170 yards. In 1948, started at LE. Blocked Purdue punt which Panelli carried 70 yards for TD in one-point win. Caught 13-yard TD pass from Tripucka in blowout of Nebraska. For the year, caught 14 passes for 98 yards and one TD. In 1949, switched to T for national champions. Made All-American. For his career, carried 10 times for 86 yards and one TD, caught 27 passes for 268 yards and one TD, blocked one kick, and recovered three fumbles.

MARX, GREG. 1970-1971-1972; DT; 6'5", 265; Redford, MI. Integral part of impressive front four groups. Had excellent size and strength and very good quickness. Broke an arm in 1969 and missed the year. In 1970, started at LT. For the year, made 82 tackles, six for minus-25 yards, and broke up two passes. In 1971, started at RT. For the year, was second on team with 85 tackles, with 12 for minus-44 yards, and broke up three passes. In 1972, started at RT. Was second in stops with 96; led team with six for minus-36 yards; and broke up one pass. Consensus All-American. For his career, made 263 tackles, 24 for minus-105 yards, and broke up six passes.

MASZTAK, DEAN. 1978-1979-1980-1981; TE; 6'4", 240; Toledo, OH. Fine TE for Devine and Faust. Had great size, mobility, hands, and blocking skills. In 1978, backed up at TE. For the year, caught 13 passes for 236 yards, carried twice for three yards, and returned one kickoff for no gain. In 1979, started at TE. For the season, led Irish receivers in playing time and caught 28 passes for 428 yards and two TDs. In 1980, lost about half of the season with a bad ankle. For the year, caught eight passes for 97 yards. In 1981, missed final five games with another injury, but caught 13 passes for 163 yards and one TD. For his career, carried two times for three yards, caught 62 passes for 836 yards and three TDs, and returned one kickoff for no gain.

MAYES, DERRICK. 1992-1993-1994-1995; SE; 6'1", 204; Indianapolis, IN. Notre Dame's all-time pass reception yardage and all-time WR TD leader, with more than 2,500 yards gained through the air. With silky-smooth moves and incredibly soft hands, he could make routine catches look hypnotizing and the difficult catches appear beyond belief. In '92, led all Irish freshmen with 53:30 minutes; caught 10 passes for 272 yards and three TDs. In '93, had a solid sophomore season with 24 receptions for 512 yards and 2 TDs in 115:43 minutes of action. Grabbed two passes for 27 yards in Irish win over Texas A&M in '94 Cotton Bowl. In '94, led all Irish receivers with 47 catches for 847 yards and 11 TDs to go with four punt returns for 85 yards. In '95 Fiesta Bowl game against Colorado, hauled in four passes for 93 yards and two TDs. Had an outstanding senior campaign in '95 with 48 receptions, 881 yards, and six TDs in 263:56 minutes. Against FSU in '96 Orange Bowl, added two TDs on six catches for 96 yards. In his superlative career, Mayes caught 141 passes for 2,728 yards, for a 19.3 yards average, good for 26 TDs, and returned four punts for 85 yards to reach a total of 2,813 yards of all-purpose yardage in 678:46 minutes.

MAZUR, JOHN. 1949-1950-1951; QB; 6'2", 198; Plymouth, PA. Good QB for Leahy. Had good arm and leadership skills. In 1949, backed up at QB for national champions. For the year, completed two of five passes for 36 yards, both passes for TDs and carried two times for no gain. In 1950, backed up at QB. For the season, carried two times for minus-seven yards, and completed 13 of 24 passes for 177 yards, two TDs, and one interception. In 1951, started at QB. For the year, completed 48 of 110 passes for 645 yards, five TDs, and 12 interceptions; and scored three TDs. For his career, carried four times for minus-seven yards; completed 63 of 139 passes for 858 yards, nine TDs, and 13 interceptions; and scored three TDs.

McAVOY, TOM. 1905; E; 5'10", 160; Corning, NY. One-year starter and then oblivion. Fine year marked by some long gains. In shutout of MAC, his 60-yard run was highlight of the day. Had a fumble recovery, a 20-yard kickoff return, and good short yardage rushing in loss to Wisconsin. In loss to Wabash, returned punt 10 yards and kickoff 10 yards, and made sack for minus-10 yards. Scored three TDs and two conversions in 142-0 rout of American Medical—his longest score was on 110-yard run. Had longest run from scrimmage, 25 yards, in loss to Indiana. Ran 60 yards with kickoff in shutout of Bennett Medical.

McCOY, MIKE. 1967-1968-1969; DT; 6'5", 274; Erie, PA. Dominating force on defensive line; almost staggering physical dimensions and strength. In 1967, started at DT and teamed with Hardy to present fearsome defensive line. For sophomore year, made 43 tackles, two for losses, and intercepted one pass. In 1968, started at DT. For the season, made 72 stops, eight for 34 yards, and broke up seven passes. In 1969, started at DT. Made 88 tackles, 10 for losses; made one interception; broke up seven passes; and returned one punt 25 yards. Consensus All-American. For his career, made 203 tackles, 20 for losses; intercepted two passes; and returned one punt 25 yards.

McDONALD, DEVON. 1989-1990-1991-1992; OLB, DE; 6'4", 241; Paterson, NJ. Big, quick, physical DE for Holtz, especially determined on his pass rush, a sack threat on any play. In 1989, started four games but otherwise subbed at DE. Had eight solo tackles, 26 assists, with four sacks for minus-15 yards and one other for minus-five yards; recovered one fumble and broke up one pass. Played 132:27 minutes. Had five tackles in win over Colorado in '90 Orange Bowl. In 1990, subbed at OLB; started two games. For the campaign, had 23 solo stops, 15 assists, one sack for minus-six yards, five others for minus-14 yards, and recovered two fumbles. Saw action for 176:31 minutes. Started against Colorado in '91 Orange Bowl; made five tackles. In 1991, started 13 games at OLB. For the season, made 29 solo hits, 31 assists, two sacks for minus-10 yards, 11 tackles for minus-nine yards, caused three fumbles and recovered one. Saw 297:22 minutes of game action. Had four tackles and one for lost yardage in '92 Sugar Bowl win over Florida. Earned honorable mention All-American. In 1992, started at DE. Contributed 30 tackles, 17 assists, with 8.3 sacks for minus-73 yards, 4.5 tackles for minus-11 yards, caused one fumble and broke up one pass. Played 247:57 minutes. Obliterated Texas A&M in the '93 Cotton Bowl with 10 tackles, four for minus-22 yards. Named outstanding defensive player in the game. Achieved honorable mention All-American again. For his career, made 90 tackles, 114 other hits, with 15.3 sacks for minus-104 yards, 25.5 tackles for minus-61 yards, caused four fumbles, recovered four fumbles, and broke up two passes, all in 854:17 minutes.

McDONALD, PAUL. 1907-1908; FB, HB; 6'0", 180; Columbus, OH. Well-rounded player just before Rockne and Dorais era. Had exceptional speed and could break long gainer either from inside or outside. Also kicked, passed, and played great defense. In 1907, started at FB. Scored two TDs in win over Franklin. Scored two TDs in win over Olivet by recovering a fumble and running 40 yards for one score and then executing cross-buck for 50 yards for the other. Had longest run from scrimmage, 25 yards, in 0-0 tie with Indiana. On an end run, scored on 75-yard run and added 60-yard dash against St. Vincent's to help secure 21-12 win. In 1908, backed up at LH. Made 65-yard TD run and kicked one conversion. Slashed through Franklin's defense for three TDs, one a 65-yard run, and kicked three conversions in a Fighting Irish victory. Scored two TDs and kicked one conversion in win over Physicians and Surgeons. Scored three TDs and one conversion in win over Ohio Northern. In win over Wabash, rushed for short yardage, threw one completed pass, and made the first recorded Irish interception.

McDOUGAL, KEVIN. 1990-1991-1992-1993. QB; 6'2", 194; Pompano Beach, FL. Only had one year to shine, but what a year: after languishing in the shadow of Rick Mirer, used his senior year in 1993 to take over the top spot in Irish records for passing accuracy while leading Notre Dame to being within one play of going undefeated for the campaign, earning the number-two rank with an 11-1-0 record. Had a nice blend of size, quickness, passing touch, good hands on fakes, and the ability to outrun a defense on the option, in some ways a model QB for Holtz. In 1990, saw 11 minutes of action in two games; completed one of two passes for 10 yards, and carried once for three yards. In 1991, played in six games for 13:34 minutes: hit five of eight passes for 177 yards; carried four times for 30 yards and one TD. In 1992, played in seven games for 24:31 minutes, completing eight of 11 passes, with one interception but three TDs; carried 11 times for 41 yards and one TD. In 1993, started at QB for a great Irish team, completing

98 of 159 passes for 1,541 yards and seven TDs, with five INTs; carried 55 times for 85 yards and four more TDs, including a 43-yard burst against Michigan, in 237:46 minutes as a starter. Against Texas A&M in the '94 Cotton Bowl, completed seven of 15 passes for 105 yards and ran the three option for a 19-yard TD score as ND beat the Aggies. For his career, completed .622 of his passes (not counting the Bowl game), 112 of 180, for 1,726 yards, good for 10 TDs and only six INTs; ran 71 times for 159 yards and six more TDs, in a total of 286:51 minutes of action. His total offense came to 119 of 195 passes for 1,831 yards, 10 TDs, six INTs, with 80 rushes for 172 yards and seven TDs, bringing his total output to 2,003 yards of all-purpose production good for 17 TDs. His final campaign leaves behind records that will be difficult to beat: the single-season completion percentage mark of .616 (98 of 159); ND's career leader in completion percentage, .622 (112 of 180); the best mark for career passing efficiency—154.41 (over Mirer's 138.9); and the best in ND's books for yardage-per-attempt for a career—9.58 yards, not to mention the second best yardage-per-attempt for a season, 9.69 yards per attempt, just behind John Huarte's mark of 10.1 yards per attempt (1964). Not far away from the best is his career interception avoidance standard of .0333, second to Mirer's .0329. McDougal's achievements should not be minimized . . . his records should be around for quite a while, and attest to both the overall strength of Holtz's program (this QB would have been starting anywhere else in the country) and McDougal's maturity and class as he waited for his moment in the golden reflection of the Dome.

McGEE, COY. 1945-1946-1947-1948; HB; 5'9", 155; Longview, TX. Speedy, elusive runner—very hard to contain. Part of talent for postwar Leahy teams. In 1945, backed up at HB. Had three carries for 29 yards. In 1946, backed up at LHB. For the year, averaged 11.9 yards per carry with 250 yards on 21 carries for three TDs. In 1947, backed up at LHB for national champions. For the year, carried 36 times for 158 yards, caught six passes for 92 yards, and returned six punts for a team-leading 162 yards. In 1948, carried only twice for five yards. For his career, carried 62 times for 442 yards and five TDs, caught six passes for 92 yards, and returned six punts 162 yards. His career offense totaled 696 yards and five TDs.

McGLEW, HENRY. 1900-1901-1902-1903; QB, E; 5'8", 170; Chelsea, MA. Teammate of Red Salmon.

Especially adept at breaking long gainers and played excellent defense. Was not prone to making mistakes. In 1900, backed up at QB, but also played elsewhere. Subbed for Salmon at LE in win over Goshen. In 5-0 win over Rush, fell on a loose kick on their 20 to help save win. In 1901, started at QB. In 2-0 loss to Northwestern, recovered blocked punt and prevented TD, stopping a runner on a long gain with a desperation tackle. The Indiana coach called him the best QB in the state after engineering 18-5 win. In 1902, started at QB. Against American Medical, made runs of 80, 65, and 40 yards and scored one TD. In 1903, started at LE for undefeated Irish as they racked up a season of shutouts. Scored one TD and ran all over American Medical in 52-0 rout. Scored one TD in win over Missouri Osteopaths and teamed well with Salmon and his booming punts to execute perfect downfield coverage, often stopping runners before they could take a step. Helped tame Ohio Northern 35-0. Never fumbled, a difficult feat given the conditions and kind of football played.

McKENNA, JIM. 1935; QB; 5'10",169; St. Paul, MN. The man in the street who found himself directly involved in "the game of the century," Notre Dame against Ohio State in 1935. A marginal player; was not even on the traveling squad. Layden told him that he could pay his own way to the game and lurk on the sidelines. Was last player available for duty as substitute when Layden needed a replacement for injured Andy Pilney. Went in with the play that won game. After football, earned a Ph.D. in chemical engineering.

MELINKOVICH, GEORGE. 1931-1932-1934; HB, FB; 6'0", 180; Tooele, UT. Recruited by Rockne as all-purpose back; three-year starter for Anderson and Layden. Had good speed, power, and hands. In 1931, switched to FB and started after Lukats broke his leg. Scored two TDs in 63-0 shutout of Drake. Plunged for one TD and caught 17-yard TD pass from Schwartz in win over Pitt. Scored from the Haskell five and six within moments of each other in win. In 1932, started at FB. Ran 31 yards for TD in shutout win of Drake. Scored one TD on short plunge, caught 25-yard pass, and ran 27 yards to keep another drive alive in win over Carnegie Tech. Made 20-yard TD run in win over Kansas. Against Northwestern, sped 98 yards with kickoff for a TD; also ran for 56 yards on three carries in the fourth quarter to preserve a shutout. Caught five-yard pass from Koken for first TD in win over Army. Led team for the year in rushing with 88 carries for 536 yards and four TDs

and in receiving with seven catches for 106 yards and one TD. Missed 1933 with kidney ailment. In 1934, switched to RHB due to death of Johnny Young and started. Made only Irish score in loss to Texas (coached by Jack Chevigny). Ran 60 yards for TD in win over Purdue and caught five-yard pass from Layden to set up TD plunge. Workhorse in win over Wisconsin with 25 carries for 86 yards. Led backs with 63 yards on 11 carries in win over Carnegie Tech. For the year, led team with 324 yards on 73 carries and in scoring with six TDs.

MELLO, JIM. 1942-1943-1946; FB; 5'11", 185; West Warwick, RI. Powerful, low-slung FB for Leahy. In 1942, backed up at FB. Scored three-yard TD in 7-7 tie with Wisconsin. In 1943, started at FB for national champions. For the season, was second among Irish runners with 137 carries for 714 yards and five TDs. Was in Navy in 1944 and 1945. In 1946, started at FB. For the year, carried 61 times for 307 yards and six TDs, and caught two passes for 40 yards. In his two seasons as a starter, carried 198 times for 1,021 yards and 11 TDs.

METZGER, BERT. 1928-1929-1930; G; 5'9", 149; Chicago, IL. Epitome of Rockne's "watch-charm guards." But even Rockne had his doubts and questioned him, to receive the polite reply: "Yes, sir, I'm small but I'm rough." Often outweighed by 80 or 90 pounds, used incredible speed to be halfway into his block before an opponent knew what was happening. Typified

Bert Metzger, perhaps the smallest All-American for the Irish at just 149 pounds, started at right guard for the 1930 national champions.

Rockne-style of line play. In 1928, backed up at RG. In 1929, backed up at RG for national champions. In 1930, started at RG for national champions. Wreaked havoc in Army secondary, especially on Schwartz's "perfect five play" for the 7-6 win. Unanimous All-America selection.

MILLER, CREIGHTON. 1941-1942-1943; FB, HB; 6'0", 185; Wilmington, DE. Son of Red Miller and nephew of Don Miller; last of Miller clan that played for Notre Dame over 35-year span. Could do almost anything on the field, and appears to have done quite a bit off the field, too. Never accepted a scholarship, so he had some leverage with Leahy. Very much in the Gipp mold. His senior year stands among the very best for any Fighting Irish player. In 1941, backed up at FB. Carried 23 times for 183 yards and one TD, caught 40-yard TD pass, and punted four times for 49-yard average. In 1942, started at RHB. In 32-20 loss to Michigan, scored on three-yard run and on 14-yard run off a Statue of Liberty play. Against a loaded and highly favored Great Lakes team, ran for 68-yard TD in 13-13 tie. In 1943, started at LHB for national champions. In win over Michigan, scored on 66-yard burst and gained 159 yards for the day. For the season, led team with 911 yards on 151 carries (only second time an Irish runner gained more than 900 yards to that point), led in scoring with 13 TDs (the most scored until Gladieux got 14 in 1968), led with seven punt returns for 151 yards, and led in kickoff returns with four for 53 yards.

MILLER, DON. 1922-1923-1924; HB; 5'11", 160; Defiance, OH. Rockne called him the best open field runner he ever had. Averaged 6.8 yards per carry for his career. Was especially good shaking loose on runs to the outside. In their three years together, led the Horsemen in rushing two of three years, in receiving all three years, and in scoring once. Almost did not go to Notre Dame; Rockne cajoled him into attending. In 1922, started at RHB. Opened with 95-yard kickoff return and TD runs of 30 and 14 yards. Scored 10-yard TD run in win over Carnegie Tech. Scored only Irish TD in loss to Nebraska on pass from Layden. For the year, gained 472 yards on 87 carries for three TDs, caught six passes for 144 yards and one TD, and returned five kickoffs 179 yards. In 1923, started at RHB. Ran for 59-yard TD in 74-0 shutout of Kalamazoo. Caught 35-yard pass from Stuhldreher and scored on 22-yard run in 13-0 win over Army. Made two-yard TD run in 25-2 win over Princeton. Crunched Georgia Tech with

Creighton Miller, who could do just about anything he wanted to on a football field, started at left halfback in 1942 and 1943.

scoring runs of 59 and 23 yards to go with 30-yard reception; also lost 88-yard TD run on penalty. Scored two TDs against Purdue. Made 38-yard TD run in win over Butler. For the year, gained 698 yards on 89 rushes for 7.7-yard average and nine TDs, caught nine passes for 149 yards and one TD, had one interception, and returned four punts 69 yards and one kickoff 15 yards. In 1924, started at RHB for national champions. Scored two TDs in shutout of Lombard. Had key runs of 11 and 35 yards and 35-yard reception to keep drives alive in win over Princeton. Ran 40 yards with Stuhldreher pass for TD in win over Carnegie Tech. For the year, carried 107 times for 763 yards and five TDs, caught 16 passes for 297 yards and two TDs, threw one incomplete pass, had two interceptions for 43 return yards, and returned one kickoff 20 yards. For his career, carried 283 times for 1,933 yards and 17 TDs, had one incomplete pass, caught 31 passes for 590, yards and four TDs, had three interceptions for 43 return yards, returned four punts 66 yards and seven kickoffs 214 yards, and scored 22 TDs. His career offense totaled 2,846 yards in 329 attempts for 22 TDs, an average of 8.65 yards per attempt.

MILLER, RED. 1906-1907-1908-1909; HB; 6'0",175; Defiance, OH. First of Miller clan to attend Notre Dame; father of Creighton. First truly great back to play for Notre Dame after Salmon; a four-year fixture at LHB. In 1906, started at LHB; returned kickoff the

Kory Minor, a four-year starter at outside linebacker under Holtz and Davie, finished his career with 261 tackles and 24.5 sacks.

length of the field against MAC in 5-0 win. In 1907, started at LHB. Scored one TD in win over Physicians and Surgeons. Called upon to play C for the rest of the season; scored two TDs against Franklin. In 1908, started at LHB. Scored three TDs and two conversions in win over Physicians and Surgeons. Dashed Indiana's hopes with 175 yards rushing, including runs of 20, 25, 40, 45, and 20 yards, to go with fumble recovery in 11-0 win. In 1909, started at LHB. Scored one TD against Olivet, and ran back a punt 90 yards. Against Rose Poly, scored four TD runs. In close win over Pitt, rushed for 53 plus yards and recovered onside kick. Scored two TDs in win over Wabash. Walter Camp saw him play against Michigan and called him one of the best in the land.

MILLNER, WAYNE. 1933-1934-1935; E; 6'0", 184; Salem, MA. Fine E and three-year starter for Anderson and Layden. Excellent blocker and defender, good pass catcher. In 1933, started at LE. Blocked Army punt late in the game, and recovered it for a TD to preserve comeback win. In 1934, started at LE. In 1935, helped beat Kansas with 50-yard TD pass from Shakespeare. In best game of the century, caught game-winning TD pass from Shakespeare to beat Ohio State. Consensus All-American.

MINOR, KORY. 1995-1996-1997-1998; OLB; 6'1", 245; LaVerne, CA. Four-year starter at OLB; great pass rusher, sure tackler, an emotional leader, someone offensive coordinators had to account for in all their schemes. A bit undersized but stepped right in to start as a freshman in '95. Showed his mettle that year in 239:38 minutes of play in 10 starts with 27 solo hits, 20 assists, with two for minus-six yards in losses, six sacks for minus-30 yards, a safety, and three fumbles caused. Made five tackles against FSU in '96 Orange Bowl. In '96, stepped it up a bit with 32 solo tackles, 21 assists, seven tackles for minus-20 yards, eight sacks for minus-56 yards, caused three more fumbles, snagged one INT and returned it 17 yards, and broke up five passes in 231:54 minutes of play. Had his best season in '97 with 322:06 minutes of play producing 59 solo tackles, 26 assists, with eight for minus-16 yards, 3.5 sacks for minus-32 yards, three INTs for 50 yards in return, and five PBU. Added eight tackles in Independence Bowl loss to LSU, including four for minus-13 yards and two sacks for minus-10 yards. In his senior year, made 33 solo stops, added 27 assists, with four for minus-six yards, five sacks for minus-29 yards, three fumbles caused, had one INT and returned it seven yards, and broke up two passes while earning 277:26 minutes of action. For his career, had 261 tackles, with 25 for losses of minus-61 yards, 24.5 sacks for minus-157 yards, nine fumbles caused, five INTs and 74 yards in return, and 12 PBU.

MIRER, RICK. 1989-1990-1991-1992; QB; 6'2", 215; Goshen, IN. Irish QB for beginning of new decade. Excellent dropback passer: strong arm, good delivery, good reader of coverages; ran well enough to operate out of option occasionally. Good leadership skills. In 1989, backed up at QB. Played in eight games; carried 12 times for 32 yards; and completed 15 of 30 passes for 180 yards, no TDs, and one interception. In 1990, started at QB. In loss to Colorado in Orange Bowl, completed 13 of 31 throws for 141 yards and three interceptions; and carried six times for minus-two yards. Made 98 carries for 198 yards and six TDs, to go with 110 of 200 passes for 1,824 yards, eight TDs, and six interceptions. In 1991, started at QB. For the year, carried 75 times for 306 yards and nine TDs; and completed 132 of 234 passes for 2,117 yards, 18 TDs, and 10 interceptions. In 39-28 win over Florida in Sugar Bowl, completed 15 of 19 passes for 154 yards, one interception, and two TDs (40 yards and 4 yards). In 1992, started at QB and led ND to a 10-1-1 record and top four rating. Completed

120 passes in 234 attempts for 1,876 yards and 15 TDs, with only six INTs. Rushed 68 times for 158 yards and two TDs. Played 271:13 minutes. Led Irish to impressive 28-3 win over undefeated Texas A&M in the Cotton Bowl. Won outstanding offensive player award for hitting eight of 16 passes for 19 yards and two TDs while rushing 13 times for 55 yards. For his career, including bowl games, completed 412 passes in 766 attempts for 6,400 yards, 45 TDs, and 27 INTs; carried 278 times for 717 yards and 17 TDs. When he finished he was in the ND record book for: most career TDs (regular scheduled games) 41 TDs; total offense yards—6,691 yards; most career points running and throwing—350; best interception avoidance for a career—.0329 (23 INTs in 698 attempts); and in 1991 set the single-season TD mark of 18 TDs (broken by Ron Powlus in 1994 with 19). His total career offensive production comes to 7,117 yards and 62 TDs. Must be considered among the top four or five all-time ND QBs.

MOHARDT, JOHNY.1918-1919-1920-1921; HB; 5'11", 170; Gary, IN. Man behind Gipp; would have started anywhere else. Had fine speed, good hands, and passing arm needed by LHB in Rockne's offense. In 1918, backed up at RHB. In 1919, backed up at LHB for undefeated Irish. Scored one TD in blowout of

A three-year starter at quarterback, Rick Mirer passed for 7,117 yards and 62 touchdowns in his career.

Mt. Union. In 1920 backed up at LHB for undefeated team. Scored on short run in win over Western Normal. Subbing at RHB in win over Nebraska, ran 25 yards at a crucial moment and made several short gains to help win 16-7. Scored on five-yard blast in win over Valparaiso. Scored two TDs, ran well for short yardage, and caught a pass from Gipp in defeat of Army. Threw TD pass to Eddie Anderson and had an interception in win over Northwestern. Started at LHB against MAC as Gipp was on his deathbed; his end sweeps were a key in winning. In 1921, started at LHB. Rushed for 100 plus yards, scored on runs of 30 and 40 yards, and completed 35-yard pass to Anderson in win over Kalamazoo. In loss to Iowa, rushed for 75 plus yards; passed for 215 yards, including 50-yard TD strike to Kiley; and tackled a Hawkeye after a long interception return. In win over Purdue, carried 18 times for 80 yards and TDs of five and seven yards. In win over Nebraska, ran wild with off-tackle plays and scored game's only TD on a short plunge. Against Indiana rushed for 43 yards on 13 carries, and completed six straight passes for 53 yards, one an 11-yard TD. Beat Army with three TD passes, 45-yard kickoff return, and 15-yard TD run as part of 73 yards rushing and 200 yards passing. Against Rutgers three days later, threw TD passes of 25 and eight yards to go with 51-yarder to Wynne and one pass broken up. Ran twice for 50 yards against Haskell. Against Marquette, gained 96 yards on six carries, including 48-yard TD jaunt to go with 45-yard TD pass to Anderson. Scored once against MAC in shutout. His senior year was one of the best on record: led in rushing with 781 yards on 136 carries, led in passing with 53 of 98 for nine TDs and 995 yards, led in scoring with 12 TDs for 72 points, and personally accounted for 126 of Notre Dame's 375 points to outscore the opponents 126 to 41. Registered nearly 2,000 yards of offense (1,821 yards on the record). Walter Camp put him on the second-team All-America squad.

MONAHAN, BILL. 1897-1898-1899; HB, FB; 5'8", 150; Chicago, IL. Probably smallest FB in midwest, variously listed in contemporary accounts at 140-145 pounds. Good runner and packed unapparent power on his frame. Also described as "scientific" player. In 1897, started at RHB. In game in which Farley rushed for 464 yards, gained 106 plus yards on 18 carries for one TD, including runs of 30 and 23 yards, had 20-yard kickoff return, and fumble recovery for seven yards. In 1898, started at FB. In 5-0 win over Illinois, gained 110 plus yards; carried 10 straight times up the middle for 60 yards. Scored three TDs against MAC, all on short plunges, in 53-0 win. In 1899, backed up at FB.

MONTANA, JOE. 1975-1977-1978; QB; 6'2", 191; Monongahela, PA. Probably best Irish QB since Lujack; certainly among top three or four for all-time consideration. Known as "The Comeback Kid" for orchestrating unbelievable wins over several seasons. Not QB for any lengthy period until late in career, even in 1977 championship season. Classic QB: good size, fair speed, very quick feet, sharp, snappy release on passes, and fine downfield and peripheral vision. Had many intangibles—charisma, confidence in the clutch, teammates' respect, and general knowledge of the game. In 1975, backed up at QB. Saw action in seven games. For the season, hit 28 of 66 passes for 507 yards, four TDs, and eight interceptions; and made 25 carries for minus-five yards but two TDs. Missed 1976 due to a shoulder separation. In 1977, started as third-string QB. For the year, completed 99 of 189 passes for 1,604 yards, 11 TDs, and eight interceptions; and ran 32 times for five yards, six TDs, and a two-point conversion. In 1978, started at QB. For the year, completed 141 of 260 passes for 2,010 yards, 10 TDs, and nine interceptions; and carried 72 times for 104 yards and six TDs. For his career, completed 268 of 515 passes for 4,121 yards, 25 TDs, and 27 interceptions; and carried 129 times for 104 yards and 14 TDs. His career offense totaled 4,225 yards on 397 attempts for 39 TDs.

MORIARTY, LARRY. 1980-1981-1982; FB; 6'2", 223; Santa Barbara, CA. Did not play football for three years after high school due to illness and injury. Rare transfer player at Notre Dame; started at Santa Barbara City College in 1979. Tremendously strong—could bench press 485 pounds. Had good quickness and good blocking skills. In 1980, backed up at FB. Carried three for 78 yards. In 1981, backed up at FB. For the season, carried 20 times for 94 yards and one TD, and caught three passes for 30 yards and two TDs. In 1982, started at FB. For the year, carried 88 times for 520 yards and five TDs, and caught 18 passes for 170 yards and two TDs. For his career, carried 111 times for 692 yards and six TDs, and caught 21 passes for 200 yards and four TDs. His career offense was 892 yards in 132 attempts for 10 TDs.

MORSE, JIM. 1954-1955-1956; HB; 5'11", 175; Muskegon, MI. Fine, all-purpose running back; three-year starter. Had good speed, some fine moves, excellent hands, and ability to make something out of nothing. In 1954, started at RHB. For sophomore season, had 68 carries for 345 yards and two TDs, caught 15 passes for 236 yards and three TDs, gained 166 yards on five kickoff returns, and picked up 31 yards on four punt returns. In 1955, moved to LHB and started. For the year, carried 92 times for 404 yards and three TDs, led team with 17 receptions for 424 yards and three TDs, returned five kickoffs 88 yards and six punts 26 yards, and had two interceptions for 26 return yards. In 1956, started at RHB. For the year, rushed 48 times for 148 yards, led team with 20 receptions for 442 yards and one TD, completed five of seven passes for 68 yards, and returned four kickoffs 72 yards and one punt 12 yards. For his career, gained 2,443 yards for 12 TD in 292 attempts.

MULLEN, JACK. 1894-1895-1896-1897-1898-1899; E; 5'8",155; Iona. MN. Only three-time captain and one of two to play six seasons for the Fighting Irish (Lins was the other). Absolutely fearless player; "courageous almost to a fault." In 1895, started at RE. In 1896, started at RE. One of those who left the field in protest to end game with Physicians and Surgeons. Rushed for short yardage in loss to Stagg's Chicago team. Made 90-yard TD run

Jim Morse started at right halfback and captained the 1956 Fighting Irish squad.

and short TD run in win over South Bend Commercial A.C. Scored one TD in 82-0 rout of Highland Views. In 1897, started at RE and captained team. Made fine run for 18 yards around left end in 0-0 game with Rush. His good running set up lone score in 4-0 win over DePauw. In 1898, started at RE and captained team. Played well on defense and made short gains in 5-0 win over Illinois. Scored one TD and rushed for 50-plus yards in rout of MAC. In 1899, started at RE and captained team. Ran for 70 yards on 10 carries in win over Englewood H.S. Played well in 23-6 loss to Chicago. Let several different players serve as game captains and took himself out to allow others to get some experience.

MULLINS, LARRY (MOON). 1927-1928-1929-1930; FB; 6'0", 175; Pasadena, CA. Good FB for Rockne. Had good strength; was excellent blocker, but bad knees kept him from being fast. Was scoring threat close to the goalline. In 1927, backed up at FB. In 1928, backed up at FB. Gained most of the yardage in 80-yard TD drive in win over Drake. Recovered two fumbles and scored only Irish TD in loss to Carnegie Tech. In 1929, started at FB for national champions. Scored winning TD against Navy on one-yard plunge. Blasted for two-yard TD in win over Georgia Tech. In win over Drake, ran for 25-yard TD and carried three consecutive times inside the Bulldog 35 to sustain another TD drive. In 1930, competed with Savoldi for starter's job. Had bothersome knee injuries all year. Lost 60-yard TD run in win over SMU due to a penalty. Rammed in from the one in win over Pitt. Scored TD plunge in win over Drake. In win over Army, his block caved in Army's right end to let Schwartz loose in the secondary for "the perfect play."

MURPHY, GEORGE. 1940-1941-1942; E; 6'0", 175; South Bend, IN. Dependable, solid E for Leahy's first two teams. In 1940, backed up at RE. In 1941, started at RE. Caught Bertelli pass for first score in win over Georgia Tech and blocked a Tech punt to lead to another score. For the year, caught 13 passes for 130 yards and one TD. In 1942, started at RE and captained team. In shutout of Stanford, scored on 47-yard pass from Bertelli. In 17-0 win over Army, caught 17-yard TD pass from Bertelli. Longtime assistant coach at Notre Dame.

MUTSCHELLER, JIM. 1949-1950-1951; E; 6'1", 198; Beaver Falls, PA. Part of 1949 national championship team and twilight years of Leahy's era. Picked up slack when Hart graduated by breaking his single-season receiving record and Wightkin's yardage figures for

ends. In 1949, backed up LE and played mostly defense. Intercepted SMU pass in all-time great game to ensure undefeated season. For the year, caught two passes for 27 yards, recovered one fumble, and made one interception. In 1950, started at RE. For the season, led Irish receivers with 35 catches (breaking Hart's figure of 19) for 426 yards (breaking Wightkin's record of 309), scored seven TDs, and returned one kickoff 12 yards. In 1951, started at RE and captained team. For the year, led team with 20 catches for 305 yards, scored two TDs, and returned one kickoff 13 yards. Made All-American. In his career, caught 57 passes for 458 yards and nine TDs, recovered one fumble, had one interception, and returned two kickoffs 25 yards.

NIEHAUS, STEVE. 1972-1973-1974-1975; DE, DT; 6'5", 270; Cincinnati, OH. Premier defensive lineman. Severe knee injuries during his first two seasons, limited playing time. Had it all—tremendous size, awesome strength, great speed, mobility, and relentless pursuit. Best DL under Parseghian, except possibly for Page. In 1972, started at DT for five games before an injury ended his season. For his partial year, made 47 tackles, two for minus-14 yards. In 1973 for national champions, played partial season. Had 35 tackles, three for minus-12 yards. In 1974, started at DT. Made 95 tackles, 13 for minus-82

After two injury-plagued years as an underclassmen, Steve Niehaus had two fantastic seasons in 1974 and 1975, earning consensus All-America honors in 1975.

yards; broke up two passes; and recovered one fumble. Made All-American. In 1975, started at DT. First modern lineman to lead Fighting Irish with 113 tackles, seven for minus-20 yards. Consensus All-American. For his career, made 290 tackles, 25 for minus-128 yards; broke up two passes; and recovered one fumble.

NIEMIEC, JOHN. 1926-1927-1928; HB; 5'8", 170; Bellaire, OH. Played in shadow of Christie Flanagan until 1928. In 1926, backed up at LHB. Scored one TD and kicked two PATs in win over Beloit. Booted two PATs in win over Minnesota. Kicked three PATs in drubbing of Penn State. Caught game-winning TD pass in win over Northwestern. Completed 18-yard pass in win over Georgia Tech. Caught game-winning TD pass against USC. In 1927, backed up at LHB. For the year, led Irish passers with 14 completions in 33 tries for 187 yards. In 1928, started at LHB. In loss to Wisconsin, completed passes of 20 and 16 yards to Colrick in Notre Dame's only scoring drive. Won Navy game with TD pass to Colrick on a slant pattern. In win over Drake, threw 13-yard TD pass to Colrick and kicked two PATs. Made PAT to ice win over Penn State. Before 78,188 people in Yankee Stadium, threw 45-yard desperation pass to Johnny "One-Play" O'Brien for the 12-6 winning margin in "Win One for the Gipper" game with Army.

NOSBUSCH, KEVIN. 1972-1973-1974; DT; 6'4", 265; Milwaukee, WI. Good defensive lineman for Parseghian. Had good size and quickness; impressive hitter. In 1972, started at DT. For the year, made 39 tackles, three for minus-9 yards. In 1973, backed up DT for national champions. For the season, made 21 tackles, four for minus-34 yards. In 1974, started at DT and had his best season: made 79 tackles, nine for minus-40 yards, and recovered one fumble. For his career, made 139 tackles, 16 for minus-83 yards, and recovered one fumble.

O'BRIEN, COLEY. 1966-1967-1968; QB, HB; 5'11", 180; McLean, VA. Remarkably talented player; "played bigger" than his true dimensions. Had good arm, good speed, fine football mind, and infectious intensity. Helped save 1966 national crown by going into MSU game when Hanratty was knocked out and a week later by leading 51-0 defeat of USC. In 1966, backed up at QB. For the season, rushed 40 times for 135 yards and two TDs, and completed 42 of 82 passes for 562 yards and four TDs. In 1967, carried 34 times for 123 yards and one TD, and completed 16 of 41 passes for 220 yards

and one TD. In 1968, started at LHB to provide "two-QB" look. Played in same backfield with both Hanratty and Theismann. For the year, made 64 carries for 314 yards and three TDs, caught 16 passes for 272 yards and four TDs, returned one punt 13 yards and four kickoffs 156 yards, and completed one pass for 13 yards. For his career, accounted for 1,808 yards of offense, ran for six TDs, caught three TD passes, and threw five TD passes.

OLSEN, BOB. 1967-1968-1969; LB; 6'0", 230; Superior, WI. Fierce competitor at ILB spot; three-year starter; rugged; physical; tremendous hitter. Led team all three years in tackles made. In 1967, started at ILB. For the year, made 98 tackles with six for losses, broke up five passes, and recovered one fumble. In 1968, started at ILB. Made 128 tackles (the most in five seasons) with eight for losses, and broke up three passes. In 1969, started at ILB. Set new record with 142 tackles with 10 for losses, had one interception for 15 return yards, broke up one pass, and recovered one fumble. Made All-American. For his career, made 368 tackles, 24 for losses, had one interception for 15 return yards, broke up nine passes, and recovered two fumbles.

O'MALLEY, JIM. 1970-1971-1972; LB; 6'2", 221; Youngstown, OH. Good ILB for Parseghian. Had good speed and could unload on ball carriers. In 1970, backed up at MLB. For the year, made 12 tackles. In 1971, started at RILB. For the season, made 72 tackles and broke up one pass. In 1972, started at ILB. Led team for the year with 122 tackles, three for minus-31 yards, broke up one pass, recovered one fumble, and had one interception. For his career, made 206 tackles, three for minus-31 yards, broke up two passes, recovered one fumble, and had one interception.

ORIARD, MIKE. 1968-1969; C; 6'3", 221; Spokane, WA. Walk-on who became team captain. Centered for both Hanratty and Theismann. Had good blocking technique and good quickness. In 1968, backed up at C. In 1969, started at C and was co-captain. Later, authored football book, *The End of Autumn*.

PAGE, ALAN. 1964-1965-1966; DE; 6'5", 238; Canton, OH. All-time great. Had almost unstoppable combination of size, speed, quickness, and strength. Part of extremely talented core of defenders for Parseghian. In 1964, started at DE. For the year, made 41 tackles, two fumble recoveries, and scored one TD on 57-yard runback of a blocked punt. In 1965, started at DE.

For the season, made 30 tackles, broke up one pass, and recovered two fumbles. In 1966, started at DE for national champions. For his final year, made 63 tackles and broke up one pass. Consensus All-American. For his career, made 134 tackles, recovered four fumbles, broke up two passes, and scored one TD.

PANELLI, JOHN. 1945-1946-1947-1948; FB; 5'11", 185; Morristown, NJ. Fine FB for Leahy's undefeated teams. Had good speed and could break a play wide open; excellent blocker; played good defense. His favorite play was to break a long run off a lateral pass, a play he worked to perfection with Lujack and Tripucka. In 1945, backed up at FB. For the season, carried 18 times for 115 yards and two TDs. In 1946, backed up at FB. For the year, carried 58 times for 265 yards and four TDs. In 1947, started at FB for national champions. For the year, carried 72 times for 254 yards and four TDs, and caught three passes for 38 yards. In 1948, started at FB. For the year, carried 92 times for 692 yards (7.5-yard average) for eight TDs, and returned one punt 70 yards. For his career, carried 240 times for 1,326 yards (5.5-yard average) and 18 TDs, caught three passes for 38 yards, and returned one punt 70 yards. Gained 1,434 yards of offense in his career.

PATULSKI, WALT. 1969-1970-1971; DE; 6'6", 260; Liverpool, NY. One of the very best; instant starter; three-year fixture on left side of some very impressive defensive fronts. Had excellent size, good speed, mobility, lateral quickness, and strength, a model of a DE. Should be ranked near top at this position for all-time consideration. In 1969, started at DE. For the season, made 54 tackles, six for losses; broke up three passes; and recovered two fumbles. In 1970, started at DE. For the year, made 58 tackles, 17 for a team-leading minus-112 yards; broke up one pass; and recovered two fumbles. In 1971, started at DE and led defense to number-three ranking against the run, and number four for total defense. For the season, made 74 tackles and led team with 17 for minus-129 yards; broke up six passes; recovered one fumble; and returned a blocked punt 12 yards. Consensus All-American. For his career, made 186 tackles, 40 for minus-241 yards; broke up 10 passes; recovered five fumbles; and returned one blocked punt 12 yards.

PENICK, ERIC. 1972-1973-1974; HB; 6'1", 209; Cleveland, OH. Fine running back for Parseghian. Had explosive speed, good strength, good moves, and good hands. Best remembered for 85-yard TD run against USC in 1973, a single play that did as much as any other to earn the national championship. In 1972, backed up at RHB; led team with 124 carries for 727 yards and five TDs, caught two passes for nine yards, and returned two kickoffs 20 yards. In 1973, started at RHB. Scored winning TD of Sugar Bowl against Alabama that cinched 11-0 season. For the year, carried 102 times for 586 yards and seven TDs, and caught two passes for 16 yards. In 1974, a knee injury suffered in spring practice ended his bright promise; played in four games. Gained 14 yards on 12 carries and caught one pass for two yards. For his career, carried 240 times for 1,327 yards and 12 TDs, caught five passes for 27 yards, and returned two kickoffs 20 yards for a total of 1,374 yards.

PERKOWSKI, JOE. 1959-1960-1961; FB, K; 6'0", 200; Wilkes-Barre, PA. Good all-purpose FB, defensive player, and K. Kicked game-winning field goal against Syracuse in 1961 after time had expired due to a penalty on the previous play when he faced making a 56-yarder. In 1959, backed up at FB. For the season, carried 53 times for 164 yards, caught two passes for 12 yards, made 12 tackles, had one interception, and broke up one pass. In 1960, backed up at FB and handled place kicking. For the year, carried 25 times for 131 yards, caught one pass for 10 yards, returned one kickoff 10 yards, made 10 tackles, and kicked nine PATs and one field goal. In 1961, did the place kicking and led team in scoring with 31 points. For the year, caught one pass for 25 yards, made three tackles, and kicked 16 PATs and five field goals. In his career, carried 78 times for 295 yards, caught four passes for 47 yards, made 25 tackles, had one interception, returned one kickoff 10 yards, broke up one pass, and made 25 PATs and six field goals. His career totals were 352 yards and 43 points.

PETITBON, JOHN. 1949-1950-1951; HB, S; 6'0", 185; New Orleans, LA. Excellent defensive player with exceptional speed. In 1949, played at S. For the year, carried three times for minus-nine yards, recovered one fumble, and made three interceptions for 62 return yards, including 43-yard TD against USC. In 1950, started at LHB. For the season, carried 65 times for 388 yards and three TDs, caught 18 passes for 269 yards and two TDs, had one interception, returned one punt 14 yards, and returned two kickoffs 69 yards. In 1951, had 48 carries for 227 yards and three TDs, caught eight passes for 105 yards, returned 14 punts 189 yards and three kickoffs 115 yards for one TD, and had two interceptions for three return yards. For his career, carried 116 times for 606 yards and six TDs, caught 26 passes for 373 yards and two TDs, recovered one fumble, had six interceptions for 65 return yards and one TD, and returned 15 punts 203 yards and five kickoffs 184 yards for one TD. Gained total of 1,432 yards of offense and scored 10 TDs.

PHELAN, JIM. 1915-1916-1917; QB; 5'11", 182; Portland, OR. Three-year starter at QB for Harper. Quadruple threat—kicker, passer, runner, and defender. In 1915, playing with reserves against Alma, scored fourth-quarter TD on straight buck over C, and passed to Yeager for TD. Started the next week against Haskell and threw several passes for short gains in shutout win. In loss to Nebraska, returned two punts for 25 yards, made short yardage rushes, returned a kickoff 10 yards, made one interception, and completed a pass to Cofall. Helped win close game with South Dakota on a daring punt return to the Coyotes 20; team scored on next play for game's only TD. Scored two TDs on plunges against Creighton, made an interception and 20-yard runback, completed one pass for 15 yards, kicked one conversion, rushed for 48 yards, and returned a punt 21 yards. Scored TD on plunge in win over Texas to go with an interception and a 12-yard kickoff return. Against Rice two days later, rushed for short yardage, made an interception, and returned a kickoff 12 yards. In 1916, started at QB. Scored one TD in blowout win over Wabash and led team to several annihilations in the season. In 1917, started at QB. Scored first TD of year with a plunge against Kalamazoo; added two more later in the win. Near end of Wisconsin game, tried to dropkick a 61-yard field goal, but the ball hit the cross bar and fell back on the field to keep it a scoreless tie. Played in only those two games before being sent to Camp Taylor in Louisville, Kentucky, for the war effort.

PHILBROOK, GEORGE. 1908-1909-1910-1911; G, T; 6'3", 225; Olympia, WA. Came with Dimmick from Northwest to become integral part of Notre Dame football. One of Irish greats for first third of this century, and perhaps any period. Excellent blocker; had good speed and great size for his era; could kick and receive passes. Best known for blocking—could make a hole just about where and when he wanted. In 1908, backed up LG; used mainly for punting. In 1909, started at LG. Rushed for one TD in 58-0 win over Olivet. Scored

50-yard TD pass in 60-11 rout of Rose Poly. Recovered MAC fumble and ran for short yardage in win. Scored two TDs in rout of Miami of Ohio. Scored TD against Jesse Harper's Wabash team in shutout. Named to All-Western team. In 1910, started at LT. Against Akron (nee Butchel), started around end on "tackle around" play but fumbled, recovered the ball, composed himself, dusted off three converging tacklers, and made a 75-yard run. In 1911, started at LT. The coach decided to use him only against major schools, but there were only two— Pitt and Marquette. Was used primarily as pass receiver because of his height. Caught 20-yard pass in 0-0 tie with Pitt.

PIEPUL, MILT. 1938-1939-1940; FB; 6'1", 206; Thompsonville, CT. Powerful FB for Layden. Could also kick and play solid defense. In 1938, backed up at FB. In 1939, started at FB. Scored two TDs in one-point win over SMU. Scored winning TD on one-yard plunge against Navy. In close loss to Iowa, slammed for four-yard TD. Smashed through Northwestern's defense for Notre Dame's only score in 7-0 win. Scored TD on a reverse in loss to USC. For the year, led in rushing with 414 yards on 82 carries and led in scoring with six TDs. Never fumbled in the season and was stopped for losses only three times. Made All-American. In 1940, started at FB. Tallied two TDs in rout of Carnegie Tech. Helped beat Stagg's Pacific team with 17-yard TD run and an interception a minute later to set up another TD. In 10-6 win over USC, booted 25-yard field goal

Nick Pietrosante, a two-year starter at fullback, earned All-America honors in 1958.

and scored on three-yard run. Led team with 122 yards on four kickoffs.

PIETROSANTE, NICK. 1956-1957-1958; FB; 6'2", 215; Ansonia, CT. Very powerful FB for Brennan. Punishing runner able to break tackles, could also punt well and play solid defense. In 1956, backed up at FB. For the season, made eight carries for 27 yards. In 1957, started at FB. In busy season, led team with 449 yards on 90 carries for two TDs, caught four passes for five yards, had one interception, made 37 tackles, recovered two fumbles, returned one kickoff 18 yards, broke up two passes, and punted 39 times for 39.6-yard average. In 1958, started at FB. For the year, led with 117 carries for 556 yards and four TDs, caught 10 passes for 78 yards, made 44 tackles, returned one kickoff 17 yards, broke up three passes, and punted 26 times for 33.7-yard average. Made All-American. For his career, carried 215 times for 1,032 yards and six TDs, caught 14 passes for 83 yards, had one interception, made 81 tackles, made two fumble recoveries, returned two kickoffs 35 yards, broke up five passes, and punted 65 times for 37.24-yard average. His career total offense was 1,150 yards and six TDs.

PILNEY, ANDY. 1933-1934-1935; HB; 5'11", 175; Chicago, IL. Good, all-purpose back for Anderson and Layden. Never started, but saw plenty of action and always made a contribution, often making the difference. Best remembered for heroics against Ohio State in 1935. In 1933, backed up at LHB. Scored winning TD against Northwestern on 13-yard run. His TD was one of only five scored all season by Notre Dame. Led team in punt returns with nine for 124 yards. In 1934, backed up at LHB. In win over Wisconsin, fired 30-yard completion to Davis to start first scoring drive, and made two runs near the goal to keep the drive moving. Pounded Carnegie Tech with 11 rushes for 46 yards in 13-0 win. In 10-6 loss to Navy, almost turned tide with 32-yard run, 62-yard kickoff return, and 27-yard TD throw to Peters. In 1935, backed up at LHB. Tossed TD pass in win over Wisconsin and ran 40 yards for another. Fired both TD passes to beat Navy 14-0. Against Ohio State, started at LHB in second half with the Irish trailing. Started first Irish TD drive with 47-yard punt return to their 13, then threw to Gaul reaching the Buckeye one, and Steve Miller scored; with less than three minutes to play, completed pass to Fromhart that reached the Ohio State 24, passed again to Fromhart for 10 yards, and ended with 15-yard TD pass to Layden; on winning TD

drive, took busted play from the Irish 45 to the Ohio State 19, but was hurt on the tackle and carried off on a stretcher. From there, saw Shakespeare's pass to Millner for winning TD. Made All-American.

PINKETT, ALLEN. 1982-1983-1984-1985; TB; 5'9", 184; Sterling, VA. Supremely gifted runner; among Notre Dame's best running backs. Had tremendous speed, leg drive, overall strength (bench pressed 385 pounds), lateral mobility, darting quickness, good hands, and ability to break any play wide open. In 1982, grew into playing time slowly, but carried 107 times for 532 yards and five TDs, caught nine passes for 94 yards, and returned 14 kickoffs 354 yards for one TD. In 1983, started at TB and had best sophomore year for any Irish running back. Carried 252 times for 1,394 yards and 16 TDs, caught 28 passes (to lead team) for 288 yards and two TDs, threw one pass for 59 yards, and scored a two-point conversion. Played well in Liberty Bowl win over Boston College with 28 carries for 111 yards and two TDs. Made All-American. In 1984, started at TB. For the year, carried 275 times for 1,105 yards and 17 TDs, and caught 19 passes for 257 yards and one TD. Made honorable mention All-America. In Aloha Bowl against SMU, carried 24 times for 136 yards and one TD; became all-time Irish rushing leader for bowl games. In 1985, started at TB and became first Irish running back to have three consecutive 1,000-yard seasons. For his final year, carried 255 times for 1,100 yards and 11 TDs, and caught 17 passes for 135 yards. Made All-American. For his career, had 889 rushing attempts for 4,131 yards and 48 TDs, caught 73 passes for 774 yards and three TDs, returned 14 kickoffs 354 yards for one TD, completed one pass for 59 yards, and scored a two-point conversion. Scored 320 points, had 21 games rushing for 100 plus yards, gained 5,259 yards, scored 53 TDs, was first Irish back to go over 4,000 yards rushing, and was fourth all-time NCAA TD producer (behind Tony Dorsett, Doc Blanchard, and Steve Owens).

PLISKA, JOE. 1911-1912-1913-1914; HB; 5'10", 170; Chicago, IL. Fine runner and pass receiver for team that launched Notre Dame into the national spotlight. Excellent speed and elusiveness made him a long-distance threat on any play. In 1911, backed up RHB. Scored one TD against Ohio Northern and added 30-yard run. Ran for one-yard TD in win over St. Viator. Scored TD in rout of Loyola. Against St. Bonaventure, scored three TDs, kicked three conversions, intercepted

Left guard Myron Pottios captained the 1960 Fighting Irish and earned All-America accolades.

a double pass, and returned kickoff 10 yards. In 1912, started at RHB. Scored career-high four TDs in win over Adrian. Led team with three TDs against St. Louis in 47-7 victory. Scored in first three minutes in shutout of Marquette. In 1913, started at RHB. Ran for three TDs in win over Ohio Northern. Scored three TDs in win over Alma. Against Army, caught two of Dorais's passes for 70 plus yards and scored two TDs. In 1914, started at RHB. Against Alma, had three TD runs up the middle and around the ends of 50 yards or better, a 65-yard punt return, and one conversion kick. Dashed for 35-yard TD in win over South Dakota. Had 110 plus yards rushing in win over Carlisle, scoring on runs of 60 and 35 yards. Ended career with TD in win over Syracuse.

POTTIOS, MYRON. 1958-1959-1960; C, G; 6'2", 220; Van Voorhis, PA. Strong lineman under Brennan and Kuharich; played for defense that was burdened by offensive ineptitude. Had excellent skills as LB and was good blocker. In 1958, backed up at C. For the year, made 32 tackles, had one interception, and recovered one fumble. In 1959, started at LG but was injured in fourth game to end his season. In his partial year, made 24 tackles. In 1960, started at LG and LB. Blocked Pitt PAT in close loss. Won game ball for defensive effort in

shutout win over USC when Trojans rushed for only 74 yards and lost 17-0. For the season, led Irish with 74 tackles and had one blocked kick. Made All-American. For his career, had 130 tackles, one blocked kick, one interception, and one fumble recovery.

POWLUS, RON. 1994-1995-1996-1997; QB; 6'3", 225; Berwick, PA. Irish pacesetter in numerous QB statistical categories. Played with great dignity and determination under tremendous pressure of expectations inherited from his Pennsylvania high school career. Blessed with a good arm and touch, labored a bit with the option scheme Holtz liked. Integral part of Irish teams that would produce both of the school's leading career passer and runner within two seasons. Missed the 1993 season with a broken collarbone. Started the next 44 games after that. In 1994, came out of the gates faster than any Irish QB, with four TD passes in his first game, tying an Irish record first set by Angelo Bertelli (he would do it twice more). For the season, completed 119 passes in 222 attempts, a .536 completion average, good for 1,729 yards, 19 TDs, nine INTs. On the ground, he gained 232 yards and scored one TD but sacks counted among his 78 carries led to minus-48

Ron Powlus, Notre Dame's last four-year starter at quarterback, set a standard in career numbers that will be difficult to surpass—7,602 passing yards, 52 touchdown passes, and 44 consecutive games completing a pass.

yards rushing as he played an even 277 minutes. In the '95 Fiesta Bowl loss to Colorado, hit 18 of 34 passes for three TDs, one INT, good for 259 yards, to go with 15 carries for 12 yards. In 1995, completed 124 passes in 217 attempts for 1,853 yards, 12 TDs, seven INTs, and a .571 completion percentage in 273:31 minutes of action. On the ground, in 58 carries, he lost minus-34 yards but scored one TD. A broken arm suffered in the Navy game kept him out of action against FSU in the '96 Orange Bowl. In the 1996 campaign, led the high-scoring Irish with 133 completions in 232 throws for a .573 completion figure, 1,942 yards, 12 TDs and only four INTs in playing time of 282:09. Playing for a new head coach in 1997, compiled an outstanding set of season stats: a career-high 182 completions in 298 tries, nine TDs, seven INTs, 2,078 yards and a sterling .611 completion percentage, done in 308:52 minutes of action. Carried 46 times for minus-49 yards. In the '97 Independence Bowl loss to LSU, completed eight of 18 passes for 66 yards and carried seven times for minus-13 yards. His career stats will keep him in the Irish record book for decades: 584 completions in 1,021 attempts, a .571 completion percentage, 55 TDs, 27 INTs, 7,927 yards gained passing; on the ground, sacks overcame ground gained on 242 carries for minus-124 yards and two TDs, all done in 1,142:32 minutes of playing time. His career records (not counting Bowl games) most likely to last for a while include: most career passes, 969; most career passes completed, 558; most consecutive games completing a pass, 44; most career passing yards, 7,602; most TD passes in a season, 19; most career TD passes, 52; lowest career INT percentage, .0278; most career offense attempts, 1,201; most career total offense, 7,479 yards. Anyone who breaks these records will have to start every game for four years, avoid serious injuries early in the season, and play in a pass-happy environment.

PRUDHOMME, EDWARD. 1887-1888-1889; FB, HB; Bermuda, LA. One of the founders. Hard to judge these players since their game is only vaguely related to what happens today. His play was characterized as "strong." In 1887, started at FB in second game. In 1888, started at FB; on April 20 kicked first-ever conversion for an Irish football team in 26-6 loss to Michigan. Kicked two conversions in Notre Dame's first win, 20-0 against Harvard in December. In 1889, switched to RHB and captained team. After graduation, returned to Louisiana and became state legislator.

PUPLIS, ANDY. 1935-1936-1937; QB; 5'8", 168 Chicago, IL. Typical multipurpose QB for Layden—good runner, receiver, and kicker. Had capacity to turn small gains into breakaway runs. In 1935, backed up at QB. Had 70-yard punt return against Wisconsin. In 1936, started at QB. For the year, led team in kickoff returns with five for 136 yards (27.2-yard average). In 1937, started at QB. Averaged almost 10 yards per run—18 carries for 177 yards; caught four passes, averaging 19.5 yards per catch. Completed two of four passes and made two interceptions for 31 return yards. Scored three TDs and made six of eight PATs to lead Irish in scoring with 24 points. His yardage for the season came to 569 yards on 46 plays, or 12.4 yards per play.

QUINN, BRADY. 2003-04-05-06. QB, 6'4" 227. Columbus, OH. Strapping QB for Willingham and Weis; set dozens of school records as a four-year starter. As a freshman, played in all twelve games, hitting 157 passes in 332 attempts with 15 INTs and nine TDs, good for 1831 yards; rushed 48 times for 25 yards. In his sophomore season, completed 191 passes in 353 attempts, with ten INTs and 17 TDs, good for 2586 yards; rushed 54 times for -4 yards. As a junior, hit 292 out of 450 passes for 3919 yards, with seven INTs and 32 TDs; rushed 70 times for 100 yards. As a senior, he put it all together with 289 completions in 467 attempts with seven INTs and a staggering 37 TDs and 3426 yards; rushed 82 times for 71 yards. Career passing: 929 completions in 1602 attempts, good for an all-time 11762 yards, 39 INTs and 95 TDs. Career rushing: 254 runs, 182 yards, 0.7 avg, six TDs. Career punting: two Punts, 85 yards, 42.5 average. Career Scoring: six TD, 36 points. Heisman Voting: 4th in 2005 and 3rd in 2006.

RASSAS, NICK. 1963-1964-1965; HB, DB; 6'0",185; Winnetka, IL. Walk-on who became consensus All-American. Had good speed and moves for offense but defending in secondary was natural gift. Covered ground well, had real nose for the ball, and was instant threat to return interceptions and kicks for TDs. In 1963, backed up at HB. Saw spot action; made eight carries for 33 yards, caught one pass for nine yards, and made two tackles. In 1964, started at S but also caught two-yard TD pass from Huarte in rout of Purdue. For the year, made 37 yards on three carries, caught two passes for four yards and one TD, returned four kickoffs 103 yards and 15 punts 153 yards, made 51 tackles, broke up four passes, and had one interception for 23 return yards. In 1965, started at S and had one of the best years for

DB on record. Made 53 tackles, broke up three passes, had six interceptions for 197 return yards and one TD, and returned four kickoffs 82 yards and 24 punts 459 yards for three TDs. Consensus All-American. For his career, carried eight times for 33 yards, caught three passes for 13 yards and one TD, made 106 tackles, returned eight kickoffs 185 yards and 39 punts 612 yards for three TDs, had seven passes broken up, and made seven interceptions for 220 yards and one TD. His total reached 1,063 yards, virtually all on runbacks and turnovers, for five TDs.

REEVE, DAVE. 1974-1975-1976-1977; K; 6'3", 216; Bloomington, IN. Strong-legged K for Parseghian and Devine; leading scorer for 1977 championship team. In 1974, handled place kicking; made 38 of 40 PATs and seven of ten field goals for 59 points, second on team. In 1975, did the place kicking and made 24 of 26 PATs and 11 of 16 field goals for team-leading 57 points. In 1976, was kicking specialist and set record with 53-yard field goal in losing effort to Pitt. Helped beat Penn State with two PATs and two field goals in Gator Bowl. For the year, made 29 of 33 PATs and nine of 18 field goals for 56 points. In 1977 championship season, helped beat Texas with a field goal and five PATs. For the season, made 39 of 44 PATs and 12 of 20 field goals for 75 points. In his career, kicked 130 of 143 PATs and 39 of 64 field goals for 247 points.

RESTIC, JOE. 1975-1976-1977-1978; P, S; 6'2", 190; Milford, MA. Good punter and DB for Devine. Had great leg for punting and was heady man on secondary coverage, with especially good anticipation. In 1975, handled punting in six games and tossed 10-yard TD to MacAfee in win over Miami. For the year, completed one pass for 10-yard TD and punted 40 times for 43.5-yard average (longest was 61 yards). In 1976, started at FS and punted. For the year, punted 63 times for 41.7-yard average (longest was 63 yards); completed one pass for four-yard gain; made 54 tackles, three for minus-10 yards; made four interceptions for 92 return yards; and recovered one fumble. In 1977, punted and started at FS for national champions. For the season, punted 45 times for 38.1-yard average; made 51 tackles, one for minus-five yards; led defense with six interceptions for 25 return yards; and carried once for minus-10 yards. In 1978, punted and started at FS. For the year, had 61 punts for 38.2-yard average (longest was 66 yards); made 51 tackles; broke up eight passes; recovered two fumbles; and had three interceptions for 59 yards. For his career,

punted 209 times for 40.24-yard average; carried once for minus-10 yards; completed two of two passes for 14 yards and one TD; made 156 tackles, four for minus-15 yards; made 13 interceptions for 176 return yards; broke up eight passes; and recovered three fumbles.

RICE, TONY. 1987-1988-1989; QB; 6'1", 200; Woodruff, SC. Great option QB for Holtz. Had tremendous judgment about run/pitch options, and could throw well enough that it was hard to defend the whole package. At his best when he could break outside around a seal block, with a trailing back, and have two isolated on one defender. Had good speed, tremendous leg drive, and deceptive power. Led team to 28-3 record as starter, including longest winning streak in Irish history—23 games; QB for 1988 national championship season. In 1987, started at QB in fifth game. For the year, made 89 carries for 337 yards and seven TDs; and threw 35 completions in 82 tries for 663 yards, one TD, and four interceptions. In 1988, started at QB. Was Fiesta Bowl MVP with seven of 11 passes for 213 yards and 75 yards rushing. For the year, had 121 carries for 700 yards and nine TDs; and threw 70 completions

A great option quarterback, Tony Rice led the 1988 Fighting Irish to the national championship.

in 138 attempts for 1,176 yards, eight TDs, and seven interceptions. In 1989, started at QB and was tri-captain. Helped beat Colorado in Orange Bowl with 14 carries for 50 yards and five completions in nine throws for 99 yards. For the season, made 174 carries for 884 yards and seven TDs, and completed 68 of 137 passes for 1,122 yards, two TDs, and nine interceptions. Made All-American. For his career, rushed 384 times for 1,921 yards and 23 TDs; and completed 173 of 357 passes for 2,961 yards, 11 TDs, and 20 interceptions. In his career, was involved in 741 offensive attempts and produced 4,882 yards and 34 TDs.

ROBINSON, JACK. 1932-1934; C; 6'3", 200; Huntington, NY. Gutty C for Anderson and Layden. Played great football in spite of serious eye problems that cost him 1933 season. In 1932, started at C. In 1934, went through five eye operations to be ready to start at C. Saw kickoff that caromed high off shoulder pads of one of the kicking team's linemen and recovered it on a dead run. Had sixth eye operation in mid-season and played the following week. Made All-American.

ROCKNE, KNUTE. 1910-1911-1912-1913; E; 5'8", 165; Chicago, IL. Important as a player, unsurpassed as a coach. Was not supremely gifted as an athlete or player—though did pole vault near world mark. Success came through diligence and sheer determination. Had fair blend of strength and speed, and keen intellectual and psychological approach. Consummate team man; proficient tackler and fierce runner. In 1910, backed up RE and worked some at FB (called himself "the drawback"). In 1911, started at LE. Scored what would have been winning TD against Pitt with 40-yard advance of a fumble, but an inadvertent whistle stopped the play in the 0-0 tie. In 1912, started at LE but suffered from a sprained knee all season. Caught 33-yard pass from Dorais in 3-0 win over Pitt. In 1913, started at LE and captained team. Added long, downfield pass catching to his bag of tricks, but tore rib cartilage in opener with Ohio Northern. Against Army, removed Merrillat, their star E, with a hard tackle and dropped a runner for a loss at Notre Dame's two for a safe margin of victory—but is better known for catching 110-plus yards of Dorais passes, including 25-yard TD. Caught long TD pass from Dorais in 14-0 win over Penn State. Selected to All-State team for third time, All-Western, and honorable mention All-America by Walter Camp.

An outstanding defensive back and special teams player, Allen Rossum's nine career special teams and defensive touchdowns set an NCAA record.

ROSSUM, ALLEN. 1994-1995-1996-1997; CB; 5'8", 179; Dallas, TX. Outstanding DB for the Irish, capable of scoring on any defensive or special teams play—and did so often enough, nine times, to set an NCAA record. Possessed sheer trackster's speed perhaps unsurpassed by most other ND players. Ran the fastest 100 meters, 10.02, in the country as a Texas high school senior in '93. Won NCAA All-America status for indoor track as a freshman with a 6.29 time in the 55-meter sprint. Played as a backup to Bobby Taylor in 1994; had four solo tackles, one assist, three PBU in 12:30 minutes. Tacked on a solo tackle in the '95 Fiesta Bowl game with Colorado. Began a three-year stint as a starter in 1995. Made 24 solo hits and 12 assists to go with four PBU, three KOR for 94 yards and three INTs returned 105 yards for two TDs in 235:23 minutes. Against FSU in the '96 Orange Bowl, made five tackles, had two PBU, a sack, and two KOR for 43 yards. As a junior in '96, made 30 solo stops, added 20 assists, with two for minus-four yards, three PBU, two INT for eight return yards, to go with six KOR for 227 yards, including a 99-yard TD return, 15 punt returns for 344 yards and three more TDs, all done in 247:02 busy minutes. In his senior campaign, had 34 solo tackles, 19 assists, one for minus-seven yards, two PBU, two INT for 38 return yards and a TD, 20 KOR for 570 yards and two

TDs, 12 punt returns for 83 yards, in 275:39 minutes of action. Added three tackles in Independence Bowl loss to LSU. Averaged 20 yards every time he carried the ball in '96. For his career, had 92 solo tackles, 52 assists, nine more in Bowl games, three tackles for minus-11 yards 13 PBU, three sacks, 29 KOR for 891 yards and three TDs, 27 punt returns for 427 yards and three TDs, and seven INTs for 151 yards and another three TDs, in 770:34 minutes of action. His all-purpose career yardage comes to 1,469 yards gained on 63 plays for nine TDs, an average of 23 yards per play.

RUDDY, TIM. 1990-1991-1992-1993; G, C; 6'3", 286; Dunmore, PA. A model of what Notre Dame produces as a two-time Academic All-American, with a 3.86 GPA in mechanical engineering that qualified him for two prestigious post-graduate scholarships, one from the National Football Foundation and one from the NCAA. Fundamentally sound as a lineman, with good strength and quickness, and the intellectual acuity needed to make good line calls, helped lead ND's offense to impressive national finishes. In 1990, earned second-string spot at C; played in four games for 15:22 minutes. In 1991, started two games and played in all 11 as a G and C, earning 77:27 minutes of game action. In 1992, started all games at C and worked the trenches for 271:13 minutes, earning his first of two Academic All-America awards. In 1993, started at C for the number-two team in the country, playing more minutes than any other Irish player, 298:57, repeating his Academic All-America status but also garnering numerous other honors. Notre Dame went 21-2-1 in his two seasons as the starting C.

RUETTIGER, DAN. 1975; DE; 5'7", 200; Joliet, IL. Fine study in persistence and determination; DE with impish dimensions; campus security guard; service veteran; and oldest man on 1975 team at 27. In 1975, backed up at DE (for Browner). In last 28 seconds of 24-3 win over Georgia Tech, sacked QB for five-yard loss.

RYAN, BILLY. 1907-1908-1909-1910; QB, HB; 5'9", 160; Cleveland, OH. Dependable player during growth spurt before the Irish became a national entity. Good runner and kicker; could be used in variety of ways; and often managed to score. In 1907, started at QB. Ran for one TD and kicked one conversion in shutout of Physicians and Surgeons. Kicked conversion in win over Franklin. Returned two punts for 35 yards in 0-0 tie with Indiana. Helped defeat St. Vincent's with 30-yard field goal. In 1908, backed up RHB. Scored two TDs (one

a 10-yard run), made three conversions, and ran for 25 yards in win over Hillsdale. Scored two TDs and booted six conversions in defeat of Franklin. In 1909, backed up at RHB. Kicked three conversions against Olivet. Scored one TD and added three conversions in 60-11 win over Rose Poly. Was leading rusher from scrimmage with 90 plus yards in 17-0 win over MAC; also returned punt 10 yards and kicked two conversions. Rushed for short yardage in win over Pitt. Scored clinching TD and kicked one conversion in 11-3 win over Yost's Michigan team—surely most significant win prior to 1913 Army game. Kicked one conversion in 46-0 win over Miami of Ohio. In 1910, backed up at RHB. A bad knee severely curtailed his action for the year.

SALMON, LOUIS (RED). 1900-1901-1902-1903; E, HB, FB; 5'10",175; Syracuse, NY. Notre Dame's first All-American. Greatest Irish player—at least until Gipp matriculated. In an age when record keeping was inaccurate, some feats are amazing: scored 104 points in 1903 when TDs were five points; led team to 8-0-1 record without a point being scored against it. Absolutely fierce player; unafraid to throw his 175 pounds into any melee; fierce determination to succeed. Excellent punter and defender; had good speed and moves, but was best at bucking into line. In 1900, first known to newspaper readers as "Sammon," started at LE in 55-0 win over Goshen; instrumental in springing several long TDs by Farley and Lins. Stayed at LE for 68-0 shutout of Englewood H.S. Played both LE and FB against Beloit, scoring two-yard TD and returning one kickoff. Dropped for safety in a 7-0 loss to Michigan. Scored only TD in 5-0 win over Rush Medical. In 1901, started at FB. In 0-0 tie with South Bend Commercial A.C., dashed for 40 and 32 yards and had one punt return. Was tackled for safety in 2-0 loss to Northwestern. Punted for 70 yards in win over Beloit. Scored one TD, made one conversion kick, and had 25-yard kickoff return that featured "clever dodging" in win over Lake Forest. Rushed for 50 plus yards, scored one TD, and kicked two conversions in 12-6 win over Purdue Played C briefly against Physicians and Surgeons to allow John Pick charity TD, but tallied one himself and kicked four conversions. To help the Fighting Irish claim state championship, scored two TDs, kicked three conversions, streaked for 55-yard kickoff return, had 40 plus yards from scrimmage, and 65-yard punt return in win over Indiana. In second game against South Bend A.C., an Irish win, blasted 70-yard punt, had 20-yard punt return, recovered a loose kick, and made one conversion kick. In 1902, started at FB. Made one conversion kick and had 15-yard kickoff return in shutout of MAC. In win over Lake Forest, had several punts of 50-60 yards, recovered kick for TD, and ran 15 yards for another TD. Rushed for 90 plus yards in 23-0 loss to Yost's Michigan team, including carrying the ball 15 consecutive times on 80-yard drive; also knocked out four times. In 11-5 victory over Indiana, scored two TDs, one a 40-yarder through the assembled Hoosiers; ran 60 plus yards from scrimmage; and returned two kickoffs 40 yards each. His punting in 6-5 win over Ohio Medical was the difference; several were bobbled to Notre Dame's advantage. In 12-5 loss to Knox, went ballistic with 85-yard punt, scored a TD, rushed for 40 plus yards, and returned one kickoff. In 92-0 defeat of American Medical, scored three of 17 TDs and hit six conversion kicks. Rushed for one TD, kicked two conversions, had 35-yard field goal, and punted for 75 yards on several occasions in 22-0 win over DePauw. His one-yard TD plunge, the conversion, and a fumble recovery helped tie Purdue 6-6. In 1903, started at FB. Scored three TDs and made three conversions in 28-0 win over Lake Forest. Scored one TD and kicked four conversions in 520 win for American Medical. Scored three TDs and three conversions against the Missouri Osteopaths. Rushed for short yardage in tie with Northwestern and made 50-yard punt and a fumble recovery. Coached 1904 team to a 5-3 record.

SAMARDZIJA, JEFF. 2003-2004-2005-2006. WR, 6'5", 218. Valparaiso, IN. Two-sport athlete for the Irish, baseball and football. Rangy and very fast for his size. All-American in 2005-06. As a freshman in 2003, caught seven passes for 53 yards and made 75 special teams appearances. In 2004, snagged 17 passes for 274 yards and got into 70 plays with special teams. Really came on strong in 2005, making 77 catches for 1240 yards and 15 TDs. As a senior, caught 78 passes for 1017 yards and 12 TDs. For his career receiving: 179 receptions, for 2593 Yds, a 14.5 average, 27 TDs. Career Passing: zero completions, two attempts, zero yards, zero TD. Career Punt Returns: two returns, four yards, 2.0 average, zero TD. Rushed for one TD. Career Scoring: 28 TDs, 168 Pts. Consensus All-America: 2005

SCHAEFER, DON. 1953-1954-1955; QB, FB; 5'11", 190; Pittsburgh, PA. Good, all-purpose player for Leahy and Brennan. Made unusual shift from QB to FB. Good runner and kicker; played fine defense. In 1953,

backed up at QB. For the season, carried 23 times for 100 yards and two TDs, caught one pass for 42 yards, completed three of eight passes for 39 yards, made one interception for 37 return yards, punted four times for 34.5-yard average, and kicked six PATs. In 1954, started at FB. For the year, led team in rushing with 766 yards on 141 carries and three TDs, caught three passes for 60 yards, returned five kickoffs 82 yards and three punts 60 yards, kicked 22 PATs, and made one interception and one fumble recovery. In 1955, started at FB. Led team with 145 carries and 639 yards and one TD, caught six passes for 36 yards and two TDs, returned two kickoffs 27 yards, completed one pass for 24 yards, made 16 PATs, and had one interception for 21 yards. Made All-American. For his career, carried 309 times for 1,505 yards and six TDs, caught 10 passes for 138 yards and two TDs, returned seven kickoffs 109 yards and three punts 60 yards, completed four of nine passes for 63 yards, made three interceptions for 64 return yards, had one fumble recovery, and kicked 44 PATs and four punts for 34.5-yard average. His career offense totaled 1,939 yards and eight TDs.

SCHILLO, FRED. 1892-1893-1894-1896-1897; T, HB; 5'11", 180; Chicago, IL. Teamed with Lins and Mullen for three seasons to give Notre Dame core of veterans since the three men played a total of 17 years—thanks to liberal eligibility "regulations." By 1896, the student newspaper was viewing him wistfully: "In days gone by, Schillo was looked upon as an extraordinary football player, and this year showed improvement." Had many football skills, but was not a gamebreaker. In 1892, started at LT. In 1893, started at LT. Rushed for 89 yards against Albion, including runs of 20 and 25 yards, in 8-6 win. Ran for 65 yards against DeLaSalle in shutout win, including short TD burst and 20-yarder. Ran for eight-yard gain in 22-10 win over Hillsdale. In 1894, backed up at RT. In 1896, started at LT. Rushed for short yardage and returned kick in 4-0 forfeit loss to Physicians and Surgeons. Picked up at least 12 yards in loss to Stagg's team. Tallied one TD in shutout of Albion. In 28-22 loss to Purdue, scored one TD, rushed for short yardage, returned one kickoff 12 yards, and missed his only conversion attempt. Was instrumental in beating Beloit 8-0 by recovering two fumbles and rushing for 25 plus yards. In 1897, started at RT.

SCHOEN, TOM. 1965-1966-1967; QB, S; 5'11",178; Euclid, OH. Fine secondary player for Parseghian's powerful 1966 team. Started as QB in lean offensive year; shifted to defense. Took his understanding of offense into the secondary. Had good speed and instincts; real ball hawk. In 1965, backed up at QB. For the year, completed 13 of 24 passes for 229 yards, one TD, and one interception; had 35 carries for 81 yards; caught one pass for one yard; and made one tackle. In 1966, started at S for national champions. Made 30 tackles, had seven interceptions for 118 yards and two TDs, and led team in punt returns with 29 for 252 yards and one TD. Made All-American. In 1967, started at S. Led DBs with 52 tackles and 11 passes broken up, had four interceptions for 108 return yards, recovered one fumble, and returned 42 punts for 447 yards and one TD. Consensus All-American. For his career, had 35 carries for 81 yards; caught one pass for one yard; completed 13 of 24 passes for 229 yards, one TD, and one interception; made 83 tackles; broke up 11 passes; had 11 interceptions for 226 return yards and two TDs; recovered one fumble; and returned 71 punts 699 yards for two TDs. His career total was 1,236 yards and five TDs.

SCHWARTZ, MARCHY. 1929-1930-1931; HB; 5'11", 167; Bay St. Louis, MS. Best back to play for Rockne other than Gipp. Could do it all—run, throw, catch, block, and tackle. Dominating player, especially in 1930 and 1931 when led in rushing, passing, and scoring. In his three years, team was 25-2-1, won two consecutive national crowns for first time in college football history, and was twice consensus All-America. Would have won Heisman Trophy—if there had been one when he played. In 1929, backed up at LHB for national champions. Ran eight-yard TD in win over Georgia Tech. Ran 40 yards to set up score in win over Northwestern, and passed 25 yards to Brill to set up his own 10-yard TD run. For the year, carried 65 times for 326 yards and three TDs. In 1930, started at LHB for national champions. Scored TD plunges of five and four yards and threw 21- and 25-yard passes to Conley and Kosky to ensure narrow victory over SMU. Threw 56- and 13-yard TD passes and dove two yards for another in victory over Carnegie Tech. In win over Pitt, gained 109 yards on eight carries, including 60-yard TD run. Scored TD on 26-yard run; picked off fumbled kickoff in midair and ran 79 yards before being tackled in win over Indiana. Against Drake, returned kickoff to their 13, completed two passes to set up TD run from their 13, and made 43-yard TD run. On patented "perfect play," a delayed half-spinner, scored 18-yard unmolested run down the sideline to help beat Northwestern. In win over

Army at Soldier Field in Chicago, executed classic "51" play (with LHB going off RT) for 54-yard TD run on a terrible field. Threw 19-yard TD to Carideo, lateral pass to O'Connor for seven-yard TD, and 37-yard strike to Conley to keep another drive going; rushed twice for 65 yards to keep USC in hole for Irish shutout—Rockne's last regular game before his death. For the year, led in rushing with 927 yards on 124 carries for 7.47-yard average, led in passing with 17 of 56 for 319 yards and three TDs, and led in scoring with nine TDs. Consensus All-American. In 1931, started at LHB. Ran 11 yards for TD in win over Indiana. Gained 60 yards on 12 carries on sloppy field in 0-0 tie with Northwestern; averaged 46 yards per punt with five booted from his own end zone. Ran 63 yards on 18 carries and fired two TD passes to help beat Pitt. Amassed 188 yards against Carnegie Tech a week later, with 59-yard TD on a spinner and 16 yards on another similar play. Ran 16 yards for TD and threw 50 yards to Chuck Jaskwhich for TD in shutout of Penn. Tallied TD on 16-yard end run in shutout of Navy. Consensus All-American. Led in rushing with 692 yards on 146 carries for 4.7-yard average, led in passing with nine completions in 51 tries for 174 yards and three TDs, and scored five TDs. For his career, rushed for 1,945 yards in 335 carries and 16 TDs.

SCULLY, JOHN. 1977-1978-1979-1980; T, C; 6'5", 255; Huntington, NY. Fine lineman for Devine. Had good size, excellent strength, and exceptional quickness. Overcame injuries early in his career, and a position move, to become one of best interior linemen in recent decades. Most error-free, consistent lineman of his years. In 1977, backed up at T for national champions. In 1978, backed up at LT; played in six games. In 1979, started at C. In 1980, started at C and was tri-captain. Consensus All-American.

SEFCIK, GEORGE. 1959-1960-1961; HB; 5'8", 170; Cleveland, OH. With Dabiero, comprised "Gold Dust Twins." Like Dabiero, was small back who played much larger. Could do many things well—run, catch, block, tackle, play defense, kick, and return kicks. In 1959, started at LHB. Carried 43 times for 206 yards and one TD, caught 11 passes for 203 yards and two TDs, returned seven kickoffs 140 yards, led in punt returns with 10 for 138 return yards, made 22 tackles, broke up four passes, recovered two fumbles, had three interceptions for 35 return yards, and led in punting with 25 for 37.4-yard average. In 1960, started at LHB. For the season, made 50 carries for 248 yards, caught five

George Sefcik started at left halfback from 1959 through 1961, comprising the "Gold Dust Twins" backfield with Angelo Dabiero.

passes for 106 yards, returned 12 punts 71 yards and seven kickoffs 170 yards, made 35 tackles, broke up three passes, had two interceptions for 17 return yards, and recovered one fumble. In 1961, started at LHB. Made 72 carries for 335 yards and two TDs, caught five passes for 58 yards, returned five punts 40 yards and three kickoffs 57 yards, made 41 tackles, had three interceptions for 56 return yards, led team with nine passes broken up, and led in punting with eight for 39.4-yard average. For his career, made 165 carries for 789 yards and three TDs, caught 21 passes for 367 yards and two TDs, returned 17 kickoffs 367 yards and 27 punts 249 yards, made 98 tackles, broke up 16 passes, recovered three fumbles, had eight interceptions for 108 return yards, and punted 33 times for 37.88-yard average. His career offense was 1,880 yards and five TDs.

SEYMOUR, JIM. 1966-1967-1968; E, SE; 6'4", 205; Berkley, MI. Three-year starter and three-year All-American. Had fine speed, size, great hands, concentration, and silky moves. Provided deep threat. Appeared suddenly with Hanratty on national scene in 1966 and became media darling. His statistics for individual games were often greater than season or career totals for other players. In 1966, started at LE for national champions. Caught 48 passes for 862 yards and eight TDs. Made All-American. In 1967, started at SE.

For the year, made 37 receptions for 515 yards and four TDs. Made All-American. In 1968, made 53 catches for 736 yards and four TDs and recovered fumble for TD. Made All-American. For his career, had 138 receptions for 2,113 yards and 16 TDs as well as TD via recovered fumble.

SHAKESPEARE, BILL. 1933-1934-1935; HB; 5'11", 179; Staten Island, NY. Fine player for Anderson and Layden; significant feature of struggle between Ohio State and Notre Dame in 1935. Could do it all—run, pass, kick, catch, block, and tackle. Had excellent leadership qualities. In 1933 backed up at LHB. Caused safety in 12-2 win over Indiana In 1934, started at LHB. Helped win shutout with Carnegie Tech with 56-yard TD sweep. Fired 70-yard TD pass to Vairo in win over Army; his punting kept Army bottled up all day. Scored TD on a plunge in 20-7 win over Northwestern. Fired 51-yard TD pass in 14-0 triumph over USC. For the year, led in passing with nine of 29 for 230 yards and two TDs, and in kickoff returns with four for 60 yards. All-American. In 1935, started at LHB. Threw 41-yard TD pass to Millner in win over Kansas. Made 24-yard TD run in win over Carnegie Tech. Caught TD pass in win over Wisconsin to go with 50 yards on 12 rushes. Blasted 90-yard punt in win over Pitt and scored only Irish TD with five-yard run. In comeback win over Ohio State, replaced injured Pilney with seconds to go and threw game-winning TD to Millner. Against Army, made runs of 16, 15, and 11 yards to keep drives moving; completed 44-yard pass to Millner to set up Notre Dame's only score in 6-6 tie. Completed two long passes in a row for score—a 45-yarder to Fromhart—and swept eight yards for the final score in win over USC For the year, led in rushing with 104 carries for 374 yards, in passing with 19 of 66 for 267 yards and two TDs, in scoring with four TDs, and in kickoff returns with five for 123 yards. Consensus All-American.

SHANNON, DAN. 1951-1952-1953-1954; LB, E; 6'0", 190; Chicago, IL. Four-year starter; known best as devastating tackler. In 1951, started at LB. Helped stop Purdue with interception on the Irish 26. Recovered Navy fumble on Middie 22 and blocked for Barrett on 74-yard TD punt return. For the season, had two interceptions and four recovered fumbles. In 1952, started at LB. Slammed into Texas punt returner causing a fumble; recovered it on their two, setting up insurance TD in 14-0 win. Against Oklahoma, hit kickoff returner

Grigg; flipped him in midair and caused a fumble, which led to winning Irish TD. Intercepted pass to stymie drive in shutout of undefeated USC. Ended year with two interceptions for 19 return yards. In 1953, started at LE with return of one-platoon football. Scored both Irish TDs in 14-14 tie with Iowa, with two seconds left in the first half and six seconds left in the game. Caught Lattner pass for 55-yard advance to the SMU four and 31-yard strike from Guglielmi to keep the rout going. For the year, caught seven passes for 138 yards and two TDs. In 1954, started at LE and was co-captain. In shutout of Texas, caught 19-yard TD strike from Guglielmi. Caught 41-yard pass from Guglielmi to set up TD in loss to Purdue. Caused Pitt fumble in shutout win. Caught 16-yard pass from Guglielmi in late drive in win over Navy. Caught two Guglielmi passes for TDs, 22 and 18 yards, in win over Penn. Made All-American. For the year, caught 11 passes for 215 yards and three TDs. For his career, caught 18 passes for 353 yards and five TDs, recovered two; four fumbles, and made four interceptions for 19 return yards.

SHAUGHNESSY, FRANK. 1901-1902-1903-1904; E; 6'0", 178; Amboy, IL. Fast, shifty, excellent runner, prone to long-distance gains. In 1901, backed up at LE and also reserve QB. Improved on defense as season progressed. In 1902, started at LE. Made 40-yard run in loss to Michigan. Returned punts 20, 35, and 25 yards in 11-5 victory over Indiana. In 1903, started at RE. Made 40-yard TD run in shutout of MAC. Made two long TDs in 52-0 rout of American Medical. Recovered a fumble in tie with Northwestern. Rushed for 140 plus yards against Ohio Medical, recovered a fumble, and scored 90-yard TD. In 1904, started at RE. Recovered Wabash fumble and sprinted 80 yards for a TD, made 30-yard run from scrimmage, and returned punt 10 yards in 12-4 win. Gained 200-plus yards rushing and scored TDs on runs of 45 and 101 yards in 44-0 rout of American Medical. Against Kansas, made 100-yard TD run from scrimmage for the only Irish score in 24-5 loss. Led Irish runners with 70-plus yards in loss to Purdue, including runs of 30 and 25 yards.

SHAW, LAWRENCE (BUCK). 1919-1920-1921; T; 6'0", 185; Stuart, IA. Quiet, efficient lineman who had good kicking leg and uncanny ability to be around loose balls and kicks ready to be blocked. It was said that the end next to him would only be a spectator. Part of great lines that paved way for Gipp. In 1919, backed up at LT. In 1920, blocked punt for safety in win over Nebraska.

In shutout of Purdue, recovered Irish fumble for TD. Made two PATs in win over Northwestern. Blocked five punts during the season, the last against MAC, to help clinch an undefeated season and Notre Dame's first national championship. In 1921, started at LT. In win over Kalamazoo, deflected punt out of bounds and kicked seven PATs. Recovered DePauw fumble at midfield in win. Had one PAT in loss to Iowa (only loss of varsity career). Booted two PATs in defeating Purdue. Kicked four PATs and deflected punt in win over Indiana. Kicked four PATs in win over Army. Against Rutgers three days later, booted six PATs in rout. Against Marquette, made three tackles and kicked three PATs. Ended season with 38 PATs in 40 tries. Named All-American.

SHEEHAN, CLARENCE. 1903-1904-1905-1906; C; 6'0", 190; Grand Ridge, IL. Tough, active C who had a knack for blocking kicks, finding loose balls, and scoring. Noted for accurate "passing" (snaps to backfield). In 1903, started at C for undefeated, unscored-upon team led by Red Salmon. In 1904, injuries hampered play; backed up at C. Blocked Toledo kick and recovered fumble to preserve narrow victory. Recovered Purdue fumble on Notre Dame's 20 to stop a drive in Irish loss. In 1905, started at C. Led TD parade against American Medical, scoring on 25-yard run, 50-yard run, and recovered kickoff in the end zone; added 35-yard kickoff return. Blocked Indiana field goal attempt in 22-5 loss and showed excellent downfield coverage. In 1906, started at C. Recovered loose kickoff for TD in shutout of Franklin. Grabbed blocked punt on Hillsdale's 20 in win. Blocked MAC punt attempt from their end zone, leading to TD in 5-0 win. Scored TD but lost it on a penalty in 2-0 win over Purdue.

SILVER, NATE. 1902-1903-1904-1905; QB; 5'8", 150; Chicago, IL. Nifty, slippery, quick QB; important in 1903 undefeated season and its consecutive shutouts. Had very quick feet. In 1902, backed up at QB. Scored one TD against American Medical to accompany runs of 65 and 50 yards. Played strong defensive game in 6-6 tie with Purdue; recorded several sacks. In 1903, started at QB and orchestrated undefeated season. In 1904, started at QB. Ran 35 and 25 yards from scrimmage in 12-4 win over Wabash. Played E against Toledo A.A. due to mounting injuries; helped crippled Irish team win 6-0. In 1905, started at QB. Against North Division H.S., returned kicks of 30 and 20 yards as part of a 44-0 rout. In shutout loss to Wisconsin, returned two punts 60 and

45 yards. Tallied three TDs in 142-0 rout of American Medical: 40-yard run, 80-yard kickoff return, and a more modest run; gained 130 plus yards on other kick returns.

SITKO, EMIL. 1946-1947-1948-1949; HB, FB; 5'8", 180; Fort Wayne, IN. Key figure in success of Leahy's postwar teams. Bundle of high-strung muscle; averaged six yards from a set position. Hit high gear almost instantly and was good for certain gain; his only problem was in the open with a long run ahead—his muscled legs would tighten up and he was fairly easy to catch, if not tackle. Among very best players. Like Hart, never played in losing game. In 1946, started at RHB; led team with 346 yards on 54 carries for 6.4-yard average, scored three TDs, caught three passes for 55 yards, and made two interceptions for three return yards. In 1947, started at RHB for national champions. Carried 60 times for 426 yards and five TDs (7.1-yard average), caught four passes for 48 yards, and returned two kickoffs 52 yards. In 1948, started at RHB. Led team with 742 yards on 129 carries and nine TDs, caught seven passes for 70 yards, and returned one kickoff 76 yards. Made All-American. In 1949, started at FB for national champions. Led team with 120 carries for 712 yards and nine TDs, caught two passes for 15 yards, and returned four kickoffs 89 yards and one punt 23 yards. Consensus All-American; won Walter Camp Trophy as outstanding college player. For his career, carried 363 times for 2,226 yards and 26

TDs, caught 16 passes for 188 yards, and returned seven kickoffs 217 yards and one punt 23 yards. His career total was 2,654 yards and 26 TDs.

SLAGER, RICK. 1974-1975-1976; QB; 5'11", 190; Columbus, OH. Good QB for Devine. Had fair arm and was good runner. Played hard-nosed brand of football. In 1974, backed up at QB. Carried 12 times for 82 yards and completed three of eight passes for 39 yards. In 1975, started at QB though Montana was in the wings. Made 27 carries for 51 yards and one TD, and completed 66 of 139 passes for 686 yards, two TDs, and three interceptions. In 1976, started at QB. In Gator Bowl win over Penn State, hit 10 of 19 passes for 141 yards. For his senior year, carried 49 times for minus-78 yards and two TDs; completed 86 of 172 passes for 1,281 yards, 11 TDs, and 12 interceptions; made one tackle; and recovered one fumble. For his career, made 88 carries for 55 yards and three TDs; completed 155 of 319 passes for 2,006 yards, 13 TDs, and 15 interceptions; made one tackle; and recovered one fumble. His career offense was 2,061 yards and 16 TDs.

Jack Snow, who languished in the shadow of mediocrity until Ara Parseghian took over the Irish, earned All-America honors at left end as a senior in 1964.

Emil "Six-yard" Sitko started at right halfback from 1946 through 1948, earning All-America honors as a senior.

SNOW, JACK. 1962-1963-1964; HB, E; 6'2", 215; Long Beach, CA. Languished in shadow of mediocrity until Parseghian came. Combined with Huarte to provide preview of other game-breaking tandems. Had excellent speed, smooth moves, good power, and great hands. Also punted well. In 1962, backed up at E. For the year, caught four passes for 46 yards, had one interception for 23 return yards, and caught two-point conversion pass. In 1963, started at RHB; carried three times for 26 yards, caught six passes for 82 yards, and intercepted one pass for three return yards. In 1964, started at LE. Had spectacular season, setting reception records. For the year, caught 60 passes for 1,114 yards and nine TDs, made one tackle, and punted 29 times for 36.4-yard average. Consensus All-American. For his career, carried three times for 26 yards, caught 70 passes for 1,222 yards and nine TDs, had two interceptions for 26 return yards, made one tackle, caught one two-point conversion pass, and punted 29 times for 36.4-yard average. His career offense totaled 1,294 yards and nine TDs.

SPANIEL, FRANK. 1947-1948-1949; FB, HB; 5'10", 184; Vandergrift, PA. Fine all-purpose back for Leahy; played on two national championship teams. Could run inside and outside, catch passes for long gains, and return kicks for good yardage. Serious TD threat. In 1947, backed up at RHB for national champions. Carried four times for 13 yards. In 1948, backed up at FB. For the season, made 24 carries for 174 yards and one TD, caught one pass for three yards and one TD, and had two interceptions for 33 return yards. In 1949, started at LHB for national champions. Made 80 carries for 496 yards and four TDs, caught 16 passes for 212 yards and three TDs, returned five kickoffs 70 yards and three punts 32 yards. For his career, carried 108 times for 683 yards and five TDs, caught 17 passes for 215 yards and four TDs, had two interceptions for 33 return yards, and returned five kickoff for 70 yards and three punts for 32 yards. His career offense was 963 yards and nine TDs.

STEVENSON, HARRY. 1937-1938-1939; HB; 6'1", 189; Bloomfield, NJ. One of last good players to fill LHB spot in old Notre Dame box backfield. Had good speed, could throw well, and was proficient punter and place kicker. In 1937, backed up at LHB. In 1938, started at LHB. Fired 30-yard TD pass in 52-0 win over Kansas. His 47-yard TD pass was the difference in 14-7 win over Illinois. In 1939, started at LHB and handled most punting chores. Kicked winning field goal in 17-

14 victory over Georgia Tech. Fired 50-yard TD pass to Zontini in win over SMU. Scored on seven-yard sweep against Army—his passing got them there; also kicked two PATs in 14-0 win. For the year, led in kickoff returns with five for 85 yards and in passing with 14 of 50 for 236 yards and one TD.

STICKLES, MONTY. 1957-1958-1959; E; 6'4", 225; Poughkeepsie, NY. Fine E for some weak Irish teams. Had excellent size and strength, good speed, good hands, and very good kicking skills. In 1957, started at RE. For the year, made 11 catches for 183 yards and three TDs; led team in scoring with 11 PATs, one field goal, and three TDs for 32 points; made 27 tackles; and broke up two passes. In 1958, started at LE. For the season, led team with 20 receptions for 328 yards and seven TDs; led scoring with 15 PATs, one field goal, and six TDs for 60 points; made 31 tackles; recovered two fumbles; and broke up two passes. Made All-American. In 1959, started at LE. For the season, caught 11 passes for 235 yards and two TDs, had 16 PATs and three field goals for 37 points, made 52 tackles, recovered one fumble, broke up two passes, and blocked one kick. Consensus All-American. For his career, made 42 receptions for 746 yards and 12 TDs, kicked 42 PATs and five field goals, made 110 tackles, broke up six passes, recovered three fumbles, and blocked one kick.

STOCK, JIM. 1972-1973-1974-1975; DE, LB; 6'3", 217; Barberton, OH. Excellent DE and LB for Parseghian and Devine. Exceptional speed and mobility, especially for pass rushing and coverage duties. Good hitter and had knack for getting to loose balls. In 1972, backed up at LE. Made three tackles and one fumble recovery. In 1973, started at RE for national champions. For the season, made 41 tackles, 11 for minus-66 yards; led the team with four fumble recoveries; and caused one safety. In 1974, started at RE. For the season, made 76 tackles, led defense with 19 hits for minus-120 yards, led with three fumble recoveries, and broke up two passes. In 1975, started at OLB and was co-captain. For the season, made 84 tackles, two for minus-12 yards, and broke up one pass. For his career, made 204 tackles, 32 for minus-198 yards; broke up three passes, had eight fumble recoveries; and caused one safety.

STONE, JIM. 1977-1978-1979-1980; HB; 6'1", 198; Seattle, WA. Backup HB all four seasons but made contribution as kick returner; replacing injured Phil Carter in his senior year. Had a good blend of size and speed; was at his best in the open field. In 1977, backed up at HB for national champions. For the season, carried 29 times for 193 yards and two TDs, and caught three passes for 30 yards and one TD. In 1978, backed up at RB. For the season, had 28 carries for 109 yards and one TD, caught eight passes for 69 yards, and returned 13 kickoffs 242 yards. In 1979, backed up at RB. For the year, carried 37 times for 156 yards and one TD, caught one pass for three yards, and led team with 19 kickoffs for 493 yards (25.9-yard average). In 1980, backed up at RB but saw plenty of playing time, including four games with 100-plus yards rushing in each. For the season, led team with 192 carries for 908 yards and seven TDs, caught three passes for 29 yards, and led in kickoff returns with 17 for 344 yards. Joined select group of runners in two different 1,000-yard clubs—from scrimmage and on kick returns; had 286 carries for 1,366 yards and 11 TDs, caught 15 passes for 131 yards, and returned 49 kickoffs 1,079 yards. Involved in 350 offensive plays for 7.3-yard average. His career offense totaled 2,576 yards for 11 TDs.

STOVALL, MAURICE. 2002-2003-2004-2005. WR, 6'5", 222. Philadelphia, PA. Played three seasons for Willingham, then hooked up under Weis with Brady Quinn to present a pro-style passing attack. Very big for a WR, with TE height, good leaping ability, strong hands. Could manhandle smaller DBs. Snagged 18 passes as a freshman in 2002, scoring three TDs while picking up 312 yards. In 2003, started three games and used his big body and speed to catch 22 passes for 421 yards and three TDs. Started eight games in 2004, but production slipped as Irish fortunes went into reverse: he scored one TD on 21 receptions that garnered 313 yards. Really thrived in Weis's first year: caught nearly as many passes in his senior year as he had in the three prior campaigns…mauling defenders for 60 receptions, 1,023 yards, and 11 TDs. In his career, hauled in 121 passes, covering 2,069 yards, and scored 18 TDs.

STUHLDREHER, HARRY. 1922-1923-1924; QB; 5'7", 151; Massillon, OH. One of the great ones. Had everything that Rockne demanded of a QB—fine, analytical football mind, certain chestiness, commanding voice, fine arm, excellent punt returning skills (though not particularly fast), and superb blocking abilities (crucial for Rockne's offense). Probably most feared of the Horsemen. Caught Rockne's eye immediately in his freshman year. In 1922, backed up at QB. Scored TD in 46-0 rout of Kalamazoo. Scored TD in 34-7 win

over DePauw. Scored TD in 13-3 win over Georgia Tech and fired TD pass to Castner for the other. Saw Four Horsemen come together as a unit in win over Butler when Castner went down with a hip injury and Layden went in at FB. After that, won 22 games and lost only to Nebraska. For the year, carried 26 times for 49 yards and five TDs, completed eight of 15 passes for 68 yards and three TDs, caught six passes for 95 yards and one TD, and returned 28 punts 199 yards and one kickoff 10 yards. In 1923, started at QB. Returned punt 46 yards in win over Georgia Tech. Threw 20-yard TD pass to Cerney in 14-7 loss to Nebraska. Broke open Butler game with 65-yard TD punt return. Led team for the season with 32 punt returns for 308 yards. For the year, carried 26 times for 50 yards and two TDs, completed 10 of 19 passes for 205 yards and three TDs, caught seven passes for 63 yards, made three interceptions, returned 38 punts 308 yards for three TDs, and tallied one PAT. In 1924, started at QB for national champions. Returned punt 35 yards against Princeton, and threw 20-yard pass to Miller to keep another drive going in 12-0 win. Facing 6-0 deficit in game with Northwestern, fired 80-yard TD pass to Crowley and scored on two-yard sneak. Passed for three TDs in Carnegie Tech game; completed 12 passes in a row for 15 of 19 and scored on one-yard sneak. In 1925 Rose Bowl win over Stanford, played much of

Harry Stuhldreher, the slick quarterback of the Four Horsemen, had everything that Rockne demanded of a signal caller.

the game with a broken bone in his ankle. For the year, carried 17 times for 19 yards and three TDs, completed 25 of 33 passes for 471 yards and four TDs, caught five passes for 52 yards, returned 22 punts 194 yards for three TDs and two kickoffs 13 yards, and scored one PAT. For his career, carried 69 times for 118 yards and 10 TDs, completed 43 of 67 passes for 744 yards and 10 TDs, caught 18 passes for 210 yards and one TD, made three interceptions, returned 88 punts 701 yards for 12 TDs and three kickoffs 23 yards, and tallied two PATs. Gained 1,796 yards on 221 attempts (8.12-yard average) for 32 TDs and two PATs.

SZYMANSKI, DICK. 1951-1952-1953-1954; LB, C; 6'2", 215; Toledo, OH. Fine LB for Leahy and Brennan. Good hitter; good on pass coverage; always making things happen. In 1951, started at MLB. Recovered Indiana fumble on their 17 to set up Worden's third TD in wild second quarter that doomed Indiana. Intercepted Pitt pass to lead to final TD of shutout. For the season, made three interceptions for five return yards and two fumble recoveries. In 1952, started at RLB. Made interception in win over Navy. In 1953, one-platoon rules cut down his playing time. Backed up at C. For the year, made one interception for nine return yards. In 1954, started at C for six games but was lost in Penn game with ruptured spleen. For the year, had one interception for two return yards and one fumble recovery. For his career, made six interceptions for 16 return yards and three fumble recoveries.

TATE, GOLDEN. 2007-2008-2009. WR, 5'11", 195. Hendersonville, TN. Flashy, speedy, strong WR for Charlie Weis's Irish. Helped fill a void after graduation of Jeff Samardzija; teamed with Michael Floyd to give the Irish a great receiving tandem. In 2007, started two games; for the season, caught six passes for 131 yards and one TD; ran once for four yards; returned 15 KOs for 326 yards. In 2008, hauled in 58 passes for 1080 yards and ten TDs, averaging 18.6 ypc; rushed five times for 50 yards and one TD; returned 14 punts 162 yards; handled 26 KOs for 521 yards. In 2009, led the team with 93 catches for 1496 yards and 15 TDs; rushed 25 times for 186 yards and 2 TDs. For his career, snagged 157 passes for 2707 yards and 26 TDs; rushed 31 times for 240 yards and three TDs; handled 41 KO returns for 847 yards; and returned 14 punts for 162 yards. His all-purpose yardage came to 3956 yards in 243 attempts, a 16.27 ypa average, good for 29 TDs.

TAYLOR, AARON. 1990-1991-1992-1993; OG, OT; 6'4", 299; Concord, CA. A pillar of strength and consistency on the Irish offense for three seasons, one of the most highly acclaimed Notre Dame linemen in recent decades. A dominant force on the line, manhandled opponents with either speed, moves, or sheer strength. With him playing the left side, Irish QBs had little to worry about on their blind side in dropback situations. In 1990, saw 7:56 minutes in two games as a reserve guard. In 1991, blossomed into the starting LG for 10 of the season's 12 games, earning 239:13 minutes of action. In 1992, started all 11 games as LG, working the line for 269:07 minutes of playing time. Earned consensus All-America honors. In 1993, moved to and started at LT for all 11 games, dominating opponents for 298:57 minutes, repeating as a consensus All-American, winning the Lombardi Trophy as the country's outstanding lineman, and placing in the final three for the Outland Trophy.

TAYLOR, BOBBY. 1992-1993-1994; CB; 6'3", 201; Longview, TX. One of the best DBs ever to play for ND—son of former Olympic track star Robert Taylor; blessed with the speed, size, and agility to take away an opponent's best WR. In 1992, started six games at FS, was involved in 54 special teams appearances, made 28 solo tackles, nine assists, broke up nine passes, blocked one kick, and added two more tackles in the Cotton Bowl win over Texas A&M. Had the most playing time of the freshmen in '92 with 175:13 minutes. In 1993, started at CB. Led the Irish with four INTs, returned for 100 yards, made 151 special teams appearances, 45 solo tackles, nine assists, with two hits for minus-two yards, one sack for minus-six yards, recovered one fumble, scored one TD, broke up nine passes, and blocked two kicks in 265:09 minutes of action. Was a one-man wrecking crew in Cotton Bowl game with Texas A&M, with seven tackles, a blocked FG attempt, and a recovered fumble, as Irish eked out a narrow win over the Aggies. Was one of three finalists for Jim Thorpe award for DBs and made several All-America lists. In 1994, started at CB. For the year, made 29 solo tackles, 17 assists, with one sack for minus-15 yards, one fumble recovery good for a 57-yard TD return, one interception returned 38 yards, broke up five passes, and played final three games with a cast on his right hand after breaking a bone against Stanford. Played 281:57 minutes. Honored as a consensus All-American. Bypassed his senior year to play in the NFL. For his career, made 102 solo hits, had 41 assists, broke up 23 passes, had two tackles for minus-two yards, two sacks for minus-21 yards, recovered three fumbles, had five INTs for 138 return yards, scored two TDs, blocked four kicks, and played 722:19 minutes.

TE'O, MANTI. 2009-2010-2011-2012. ILB, 6'2", 255. Laie, HI. Excellent ILB for Weis and Kelly; tough against the run and receivers tread cautiously in his area. Started 36 games his first three seasons. Made 63 stops his freshman year, with one sack and 5.5 for losses. As a sophomore, added 133 hits to lead the Irish, with 9.5 for losses and one sack. In 2011, he kept bringing it, with 128 stops, five sacks, and 13.5 stops for losses. His three-year totals show 324 total tackles, 28.5 for losses, and seven sacks.

THAYER, TOM. 1979-1980-1981-1982; DT, T, G; 6'5", 268; Joliet, IL. Versatile, immensely strong, highly polished lineman. Good pass blocker and also devastating as pulling lineman for downfield blocking. In 1979, backed up at DT; made three tackles for the year. In 1980, started at RG for six games and led all guards in playing time. In 1981, started at LT and logged most playing time of any offensive lineman. In 1982, had an interesting season due to injuries elsewhere: Started three games at strong G, then four at C, and finished up with four at quick G.

THEISMANN, JOE. 1968-1969-1970; QB; 6'0", 170; South River, NJ. One of top-ranked QBs of all time for Notre Dame. Senior year ranks among top individual performances of any era. Had a great arm, quick feet, superb mobility, fine grasp of reading downfield coverages, quick release, supreme confidence, and toughness that belied his slim build. In 1968, backed up at QB, but started last three games when Hanratty was hurt. For the season, made 59 carries for 259 yards and four TDs, hit 27 of 49 passes for 451 yards and two TDs, caught one pass for 13 yards, and returned 14 punts for 99 yards. In 1969, started at QB. In Cotton Bowl, set records with 231 yards passing and 279 yards of total offense, including TD passes of 54 yards and 24 yards. For the season, had 116 carries for 378 yards and six TDs; and completed 108 of 192 passes for 1,531 yards, 13 TDs, and 16 interceptions. In 1970, started at QB. In Cotton Bowl win over Texas, completed nine of 16 passes for 176 yards and ran for TDs of three and 15 yards. For his final season, carried 141 times for 406 yards and six TDs, completed 155 of 268 passes for 2,529 yards and 16 TDs, caught one pass for seven yards, and made a two-point conversion. For his career, made 316 carries

for 1,043 yards and 16 TDs; completed 290 of 509 passes for 4,411 yards, 31 TDs, and 35 interceptions; caught two passes for 20 yards; and returned 14 punts 99 yards. His total offense was 5,749 yards and 47 TDs. For many years, he was in the record book for most passes in a season (268 in 1970), most completions in a game (33 against USC in 1970), most completions in a season (155 in 1970), highest career completion percentage (.570), highest passing efficiency rating for more than 100 career passes (136.1), most passing yards in a game (526 against USC in 1970), most passing yards in a season (2,429 in 1970), most passing yards per game (242.9 in 1970), most TD passes in a career (31), most total offense attempts (391 in 1970), most total offense yards in a game (512 against USC in 1970), most total offense yards for a season (2,813 in 1970), most total offense yards per game (281.3 in 1970), most total offense yards per game in a career (187.3 for 29 games), most games with 200 yards or more total offense (eight in 1970), and most points per game (12.4 in 1970).

THOMAS, BOB. 1971-1972-1973; K; 5'10", 178; Rochester, NY. Fine place kicker for Parseghian. Key figure in 1973 championship season. In 1971, led team in scoring with 21 of 22 PATs and five of nine field goals. In 1972, hit all 34 PATs and seven of 11 field goals for 55 points. In 1973, helped win national crown by scoring 70 points 43 of 45 PATs and nine of 18 field goals, including a carryover streak from 1972 of 62 straight PATs, the second highest for the NCAA at the time.

TONEFF, BOB. 1949-1950-1951; DT, T; 6'2", 230; Barberton, OH. Powerful, dominating lineman on both defense and offense. Good size and strength made him a constant threat to both runners and passers. In 1949, started at RT on defense for the national champions. Slammed into Hoosier punter for a safety in his first game. Also blasted through Washington line to block punt in win. In 1950, started at RT on defense. Recovered fumbled snap on North Carolina 10 to lead to first score of Irish win. In 1951, started at RT on offense. Blocked Iowa PAT to earn a 20-20 tie. Made one pass reception for 21-yard gain on tackle eligible play. Made All-American.

TORAN, STACEY. 1980-1981-1982-1983; DB; 6'4", 206; Indianapolis, IN. One of best DBs in Fighting Irish history. Had great size for covering his territory, fine speed, and tenacity and power to make pass-catching in his zone worrisome for a receiver. In 1980, started at LCB after the first two games. For the season, made 30 tackles, two for minus-10 yards; broke up six passes, had one interception for 10 return yards; and returned two punts 19 yards. In 1981, started at WCB; made 54 tackles, two for minus-nine yards; broke up four passes; and had two interceptions for three return yards. In 1982, started at SCB; led DBs with 77 tackles, seven for minus-20 yards; broke up six passes; and had two interceptions. In 1983, started at SCB but arm injuries limited effectiveness. For the year, made 23 tackles and broke up one pass. For his career, made 184 tackles, 11 for minus-39 yards; broke up 17 passes; had five interceptions for 13 return yards; and returned two punts 19 yards.

TOWNSEND, MIKE. 1971-1972-1973; DB, S; 6'3", 183; Hamilton, OH. Fine DB for Parseghian. Had good size, excellent speed, great vertical leap, and uncanny ability to intercept passes. In 1971, backed up at S. For the season, made five tackles. In 1972, started at LCB. Set new Irish record with 10 interceptions for the year for 39 return yards, made 34 tackles, and broke up four passes. In 1973, started at FS for the national champions. For the season, had 26 tackles, made three interceptions for 47 return yards, and recovered three fumbles. Consensus All-American.

TRIPUCKA, FRANK. 1945-1946-1947-1948; QB; 6-2, 172; Bloomfield, NJ. Very talented QB for the postwar Leahy teams, but played behind Lujack until senior season. Fine arm, sheer daring, and excellent ball-handling skills. In 1945, backed up at QB. For the season, carried twice for eight yards and completed his only pass for 21 yards. In 1946, backed up at QB. For the season, carried once for minus-six yards, and completed one of five passes for 19 yards. In 1947, backed up at QB for the national champions. For the season, carried five times for minus-36 yards and completed 25 of 44 passes for 422 yards, three TDs, and one interception. In 1948, started at QB and carried 16 times for minus-28 yards, and completed 53 of 91 passes for 660 yards and 11 TDs. In his career, carried 24 times for minus-62 yards, completed 80 of 141 passes for 1,122 yards, 14 TDs, and one interception. His offense total was 1,060 yards and 14 TDs.

TUCK, JUSTIN. 2001-2002-2003-2004. DE, 6'5", 261. Kellyton, AL. One of the best pass rushers in Irish history, a splendid blend of size, strength, quickness, and explosiveness. Entered ND as a linebacker; switched to DE. Did not play as a freshman. Chipped in with 33 solo tackles as a sophomore, adding 11 assists, 10 tackles for

Defensive back Stacey Toran was a key player on Gerry Faust's teams in the early 1980s.

Frank Tripucka started at quarterback for Leahy in 1948, passing for 660 yards and 11 touchdowns.

lost yardage, five sacks, five passes broken up, and one forced fumble. In 2003, came into his own with one of the best years ever for an Irish defensive lineman: 13.5 sacks for 106 lost yards, 43 solo tackles, 30 assists, 19 tackles for lost yardage, two passes broken up, and three forced fumbles. Opposing offenses wised up a bit by his senior year, but he still managed an impressive campaign: 27 solo hits, 20 assists, 14 tackles for lost yardage, and six more sacks for -38 yards. His career totals put him among the best (Ross Browner, Kory Minor): 103 solo hits, 61 assists, 43 tackles for -210 yards, 24.5 sacks for -170 yards, seven passes broken up, and four forced fumbles. He chose not to play a fifth year.

VARRICHIONE, FRANK. 1951-1952-1953-1954; G, T; 6'0", 210; Natick, MA. Good lineman for Leahy's last three teams and Brennan's first. Most famous for fainting tactic at end of first half in 14-14 tie with Iowa. In 1951, backed up at RG. In 1952, started at LT. In 1953, started at LT. In opening win over Oklahoma, blocked quick kick to lead to TD. In close win over Pitt, scored a safety. Achieved immortality against Iowa—Guglielmi threw TD pass to Shannon on the next play to end half (Leahy's tactic was legal in 1953; Iowa's Evashevski had used it earlier in the season). Scored TD on a fumble recovery in 40-14 win over SMU. In 1954, started at RT. Recovered Texas fumble on their 48 to lead to final TD of shutout. For the season, led the Fighting Irish with four fumble recoveries. Made All-American.

VAUGHAN, PETE. 1908-1909; FB; 6'0", 195; Crawfordsville, IN. Some credit him with coining the term "Fighting Irish" when he chastised teammates in 1909 game with Michigan by accusing them of not "fighting like Irishmen." At least 11 of 21 names on the 1909 roster were of Irish ancestry, including Maloney, Lynch, Brennan, Kelly, Collins, Duffy, Ryan, and Moriarty. Also credited with being the first man to break a goalpost for Notre Dame, in the same game, when he hit it with (a) his head, (b) his shoulder, (c) both, or (d) none of the above, since he could not remember. In 1908, started at FB. Rammed for two TDs in Hillsdale game, one a 35-yard center buck play. Scored only Irish TD in 12-6 loss to Michigan with 50-yard run on which he broke eight tackles. Scored one TD in win over Physicians and Surgeons. Ran for TD against Ohio Northern. Rushed for 50-plus yards and intercepted a pass in 8-4 win over Wabash. In 1909, started at FB. Ran for three TDs in opener with Olivet. Repeated with

three TDs against Rose Poly a week later. Against MAC (eventually MSU), scored two TDs, rushed for 80-plus yards, returned a kickoff 15 yards, and intercepted one pass. Rushed for 50-plus yards in game with Pitt to go with two punt returns of 15 yards each and a fumble recovery. Scored one TD and took out goalpost as the Irish beat Michigan in Ann Arbor—the most important game for Notre Dame to that point. Scored one TD in 46-0 rout of Miami of Ohio.

WALSH, ADAM. 1922-1923-1924; C; 6'0", 187; Hollywood, CA. One of the best in the first 60 years of Notre Dame football; candidate for all-time status. Coined the phrase "The Seven Mules" to gain measure of respect and recognition for players who toiled in the obscurity of the trenches while the Four Horsemen cavorted to fame. Superb blocker and particularly adept at snapping the ball to the backs who each had specific needs and likes in receiving the ball. In 1922, backed up at C. In 1923, started at C. In 1924, started at C for the national champions and captained one of the most famous football teams in collegiate history. Played against Army with two broken hands and intercepted a Cadet pass and returned it 20 yards to help save a 13-7 win. Tied Salmon's record of being knocked out four times in one game. Made All-American.

WALTON, SHANE. 1999-2000-2001-2002; CB; 5'11", 185; San Diego, CA. Outstanding soccer player who converted to football after his first year at ND. All-American in 2002, played for the Irish from 1999 to 2002. Tenacious, aggressive, self-confident, superquick defender who could pick your pocket faster than the eye could see. In 1999, played in nine games. In 2000, started 10 games as a junior, was in on 40 tackles, with two for minus–eight yards, three PBU, two INTs, with 60 return yards and one TD. Started all 11 games in 2001 as a senior, contributing 43 tackles, seven for 20 yards in losses, with one sack for minus–six yards, one forced fumble, eight PBU, and two INTs for 37 return yards. As a fifth-year starter, started all 13 games, contributing 65 tackles, five for minus–12 yards, a team-leading seven INTs for 84 return yards, good for two TDs, nine punt returns for 85 yards, with seven PBU, one forced fumble and one fumble recovered. Added three tackles in the '03 Gator Bowl. For his career, made 151 tackles, had one sack for minus-six yards, seven tackles for minus-20 yards in losses, broke up 18 passes, had 11 career INTs for 181 return yards and three TDS, returned nine punts 85 yards, forced one fumble and recovered one fumble, with 266 yards of all-purpose return yardage in 34 career starts.

WATTERS, RICKY. 1987-1988-1989-1990; FL, TB; 6'2", 205; Harrisburg, PA. Multitalented runner and receiver for Holtz. Had excellent speed, good moves, good power, and very good hands. Started as an elusive runner but added some punch in last seasons. In 1987, backed up at TB. Made one carry for minus-three yards in Cotton Bowl loss to Texas A & M. For the year, carried 69 times for 373 yards and three TDs, caught six passes for 70 yards, and returned two punts 23 yards. In 1988, started at FL for the national champions. In Fiesta Bowl win over West Virginia, carried three times for six yards and caught one pass for 57 yards to set up TD. In the season, had 30 carries for 71 yards, caught 15 passes for 286 yards and two TDs, and returned 19 punts 253 yards for two TDs and two kickoffs 42 yards. In 1989, started at TB. In Orange Bowl win over Colorado, carried two times for three yards. For the year, had 118 carries for 791 yards and 10 TDs, caught 13 for 196 yards, and returned 15 punts 201 yards for one TD. In 1990, started at TB. For the season, made 108 carries for 579 yards and eight TDs, caught seven passes for 58 yards, and returned three punts 25 yards. For his career, carried 325 times for 1,814 yards and 21 TDs, caught 41 passes for 610 yards and two TDs, and returned 39 punts 502 yards for three TDs and two kickoffs 42 yards. His career total was 2,968 yards for 26 TDs.

WENDELL, MARTY. 1944-1946-1947-1948; FB, C, G; 5'11", 198; Chicago, IL. Won three monograms at three different positions; versatility was obviously his strong suit. In 1944, backed up at FB. For the year, carried 31 times for 82 yards and one TD. In 1945, played for Great Lakes and had a good defensive game against Notre Dame. In 1946, backed up at C. In 1947, started at LG for the national champions.

WESTON, JEFF. 1974-1975-1976-1977-1978. DT; 6'4", 258; Rochester, NY. Quick, mobile, determined DT for Parseghian's last team and Devine's first four teams. Knee injury in opening game of '76 cost him that season. In 1974, subbed as a DT but made 31 stops, with two hits for minus-22 yards. Started at RT in '75. Had a career game against Navy—led ND to a win with five solo hits, an amazing 17 assists, caused one fumble, recovered another, and intercepted a Middie pass on a

fake punt, returning it 53 yards for a TD. For the season, was second in tackles, with 101 hits for minus-61 yards, one fumble recovery, and the one interception for a TD. In 1976, was injured after making three tackles in only 8:17 minutes of play in opening loss to Pittsburgh; had surgery and was lost to the team for the year. In 1977, split time with Mike Calhoun at DT for the national champs. For the year, made 57 tackles, four for minus-11 yards, and recovered one fumble. In 1978, started at RT, making 75 tackles in the campaign, five for minus-47 yards, broke up three passes, and recovered two fumbles. For his career, made 267 tackles, 20 for minus-141 yards, caused one fumble, recovered four fumbles, broke up three passes, had one interception, and scored one TD.

WILLIAMS, BOB. 1956-1957-1958; QB; 6'2", 190; Wilkes Barre, PA. Played for Brennan's last three teams. Had a good arm, ran well, and played good defense. In 1956, backed up at QB. For the year, carried 22 times for 46 yards and one TD; completed 16 of 31 passes for 197 yards, one TD, and four interceptions; and returned three kickoffs 45 yards. In 1957, started at QB. For the season, carried 62 times for 144 yards and four TDs; completed 53 of 106 passes for 559 yards, three TDs, and five interceptions; made three interceptions for 28 return yards; returned six kickoffs 102 yards; and made 19 tackles. In 1959, started at QB (but Izo played nearly as much). For the year, carried 44 times for 140 yards and four TDs; completed 26 of 65 passes for 344 yards, four TDs, and nine interceptions; made 23 tackles; and broke up three passes. For his career, carried 128 times for 330 yards and nine TDs; completed 95 of 202 passes for 1,100 yards, eight TDs, and 18 interceptions; made 42 tackles and three interceptions for 28 return yards; broke up three passes; and returned nine kickoffs 147 yards. His career offense was 1,935 yards and 17 TDs.

WYNNE, CHET. 1918-1919-1920-1921; FB; 6'0", 168; Norron, KS. Like many others of this era, went to Notre Dame for another sport, in his case, track. Rockne (track coach, chemistry professor, and football coach) had misgivings about possible damage to his track career, but football beckoned. Had excellent speed and power, could catch passes, and play strong defense. In 1918, backed up at FB. In 1919, backed up at FB for the undefeated Irish. In 1920, started at FB in same backfield with Gipp for another undefeated campaign to give Notre Dame an almost unstoppable running game. Scored one TD in win over Kalamazoo.

Tommy Yarr, who started at center and captained the 1931 Fighting Irish.

Played fine game in win over Army, including 20-yard TD run down the sideline. In close win over Indiana, made crucial 32-yard kickoff return. Ran with power in victory over Northwestern with gains of 33 and 28 yards. In 1921, started at FB. Scored two TDs in shutout of Kalamazoo, an 80-yard kickoff return and a 10-yard run; also intercepted a pass and tackled a pass receiver for a loss. Scored two TDs in win over DePauw. Rushed for 40-plus yards and broke up one pass in close loss to Iowa. Ran 52 yards from scrimmage in 10 tries, including seven-yard TD run, in win over Indiana. Running from the E position, caught 45-yard TD pass against Army and returned two kickoffs 42 and 15 yards to help with win; his play caught the attention of the eastern press. Helped beat Rutgers three days later with 35-yard TD run, picked off a pass, and caught a 51-yard aerial, none of which hurt his image with the eastern press. Gained 55 yards on six carries against Marquette, including a five-yard TD burst, and threw the decisive block to spring Mohardt on a 48-yard run. Scored one TD in shutout of MAC.

YARR, TOMMY. 1929-1930-1931; C; 5'11", 197; Dabob, WA. Part of line that gave Notre Dame undisputed back-to-back championships in Rockne's last seasons. Like most of his linemen, was on the small side but compensated with incredible quickness, superb blocking technique, and tenacious defensive play. In 1929, backed up at C. In 1930, started at C for the undefeated national champs. Intercepted two SMU passes in closing moments of 20-14 Irish win. Wreaked havoc against Drake's aerial game with interceptions and deflected passes. In 1931, started at C and served as captain. Made All-American.

YOUNG, BRYANT. 1990-1991-1992-1993; DT; 6'3", 277; Chicago Heights, IL. Dominating DT for Holtz, blessed with speed, size, strength, determination, and overpowering moves that made him a nightmare for defensive coordinators and anyone assigned heads up on him. In 1990, appeared with special teams 92 times, playing in 10 games; made four solo stops, four assists, with one for minus-three yards in 31:48 minutes. In 1991, started at LT for one game, then moved to NT; lost playing time late in the season following a broken bone in his left ankle against Air Force. For the season, contributed 32 solo hits, 18 assists, with nine for minus-27 yards, a team-leading four sacks for minus-28 yards, recovered two fumbles, and broke up two passes, all done in 232:32 minutes of play. Had one stop in Sugar Bowl win against Florida—not bad, considering the fact that the Gators threw 58 passes that day. In 1992, started at DT and led the team in sacks and tackles for losses. Had 37 solo tackles, 14 assists, with 5.5 for minus-10 yards and an impressive 7.5 sacks for minus-64 yards, to go with one fumble recovery and one pass broken up, done in 259:08 minutes of action. Made two stops in Irish Cotton Bowl victory over Texas A&M. For his labors, earned honorable mention All-America accolades. In 1993, started at LT, repeating as ND's leader in sacks and hits for losses. For the campaign, made 44 solo hits, 23 assists, seven for minus-23 yards, 6.5 sacks for minus-49 yards, recovered one fumble, and broke up one pass in 266:16 minutes. Hammered Texas A&M with nine tackles and a sack in '94 Cotton Bowl win. Earned All-America recognition. For his career, made 117 solo tackles, 72 others, with 22.5 for minus-63 yards, 19 sacks for minus-141 yards, recovered four fumbles, and broke up four passes in 789:42 total minutes.

ZBIKOWSKI, TOM. 2003-2004-2005-2006. S, 6'0", 207. Arlington Heights, IL. Speedy high school option QB turned into a safety at ND. Fierce, fearless hitter who also relished in special team play. Did not see action as a freshman. Three years of starting began in 2004. That year, he made 37 solo tackles, assisted with another 33, had 2.5 tackles for losses, broke up a pass, forced two fumbles, and recovered one. In 2005, started returning punts—hauling the mail 27 times for 379 yards and two TDs. On defense, made 42 solo tackles, assisted with 29 others, broke up four passes, had one sack, one tackle for a loss, and forced one fumble. As a senior, while earning second team All-America honors, made 44 solo hits, assisted on another 35, made one tackle for a loss, broke up two passes, caused one fumble, recovered one fumble, and returned 16 punts 144 yards for one TD. For his career, was in on 220 tackles, had 4.5 tackles for losses, had one sack, broke up seven passes, caused four fumbles and recovered two, while adding 43 punt returns for 523 yards and three TDs. Chose not to return for a fifth year.

ZELLARS, RAY. 1991-1992-1993-1994; FB; 5'11", 221; Pittsburgh, PA. Replaced Jerome Bettis as FB for Holtz. Had surprising power in a small package, with an excellent burst of speed out of his stance, good balance, excellent blocking skills, and solid receiving skills out of the backfield. In 1991, was in the deep reserves as a FB. Played in seven games, carried six times for 51 yards, made 18 special teams appearances, and saw 3:42 minutes of action. In 1992, subbed at FB. Played in 10 games, starting in two others; carried 26 times for 124 yards, caught two passes for 14 yards, made 112 special teams appearances, and played 56:09 minutes. Carried once for three yards in Cotton Bowl win over Texas A&M. In 1993, started at FB, carrying 99 times for 494 yards good for five TDs, caught 14 passes for 109 yards and three more TDs, and played 215:58 minutes. Helped beat Texas A&M in '94 Cotton Bowl with nine carries for 25 yards and one TD. Made honorable mention All-America. In 1994, started at FB, missing several games with an ankle injury. For the season, carried 79 times for 466 yards and three TDs, caught 12 passes for 114 yards and two TDs, and played 171:52 minutes. Against Colorado in '95

Fiesta Bowl loss, ran five times for 21 yards and snagged two passes for 25 yards. For his career, carried 225 times for 1,184 yards, a 5.6 average yardage per carry, good for nine TDs, caught 30 passes for 262 yards and five more TDs, for a total offensive output of 1,446 yards gained in 255 attempts, for 5.7 yards per attempt, good for 14 TDs in 447:41 minutes played for the Irish.

ZORICH, CHRIS. 1988-1989-1990; NT; 6'1", 266; Chicago, IL. Dominating NT with combination of strength (455-pound bench press), speed (4.68-second 40-yard dash), and lateral quickness. In spite of constant double- and triple-teaming efforts against him, often tackled runners and receivers on sideline patterns—rare for interior linemen. Came as LB, but made the move to the line. In 1988, started at NT. For the year, made 70 tackles, four for minus-eight yards, 3.5 sacks for minus-17 yards, recovered three fumbles, and broke up three passes. In 1989, started at NT. For the season, made 92 tackles, five for minus-12 yards, three sacks for minus-27 yards, caused one fumble, recovered two fumbles, and broke up two passes. Consensus All-American. In 1990, started at NT and was a tri-captain. For year, marred by various injuries, made 57 tackles, 12 for minus-26 yards, had four sacks for minus-26 yards, caused two fumbles, recovered one fumble, and broke up one pass. Repeat consensus All-American and won Lombardi Trophy. For his career, had 219 tackles, 21 for minus-56 yards, 10.5 sacks for minus-70 yards, caused three fumbles, recovered six fumbles, and broke up six passes.

A unique combination of strength, speed and lateral quickness, Chris Zorich earned the Lombardi Award as nose tackle under Holtz.

CHAPTER SIX

FIGHTING IRISH STATISTICS

WON/LOST PERCENTAGE FOR NOTRE DAME'S COACHES

Coach	Record	W/L %	Years
1. John L. Marks	13-0-2	.933	1911-12
2. Thomas Barry	12-1-1	.893	1906-07
3. Victor M. Place	8-1-0	.889	1908
4. Knute Rockne	105-12-5	.881	1918-30
5. Jesse Harper	34-5-1	.863	1913-17
6. Frank C. Longman	11-1-2	.857	1909-10
7. Frank Leahy	87-11-9	.855	1941-43 1946-53
8. Ara Parseghian	95-17-4	.836	1964-74
9. James Faragher	14-2-2	.833	1902-03
10. Ed McKeever	8-2-0	.800	1944
11. Elmer Layden	47-13-3	.770	1934-40
12. Lou Holtz	100-30-2	.765	1986-96
13. Dan Devine	53-16-1	.764	1975-80
14. Patrick O'Dea	14-4-2	.750	1900-01
15. H.G. Hadden	3-1-0	.750	1895
16. J.L. Morison	3-1-1	.700	1894
17. Frank Hering	12-6-1	.658	1896-98
18. James McWeeney	6-3-1	.650	1899
19. Terry Brennan	32-18-0	.640	1954-58
20. Hunk Anderson	16-9-2	.630	1931-33
21. Louis Salmon	5-3-0	.625	1904
22. Bryan Kelly	16-10-0	.615	2010-2011
23. Bob Davie	35-25-0	.583	1997-2001
24. Charlie Weis	35-27-0	.568	2005-2009
25. Tyrone Willingham	21-16-0	.567	2002-2004
26. Henry J. McGlew	5-4-0	.556	1905
27. Gerry Faust	30-26-1	.535	1981-85
28 Hugh Devore	9-9-1	.500	1945-1963
29. Joe Kuharich	17-33-0	.425	1959-62
Total:	**853-300-42**		**.731**

Only the top 16 coaches listed above have career marks better than the Notre Dame historical average (which has steadily slipped in the years since Holtz's tenure). The records of such contemporary luminaries as Devine and Holtz are flirting with falling below the mark, but it will take years of winning at an .800 clip to raise the cumulative average.

NOTRE DAME'S UNDEFEATED SEASONS

Twenty Irish teams have completed undefeated seasons. In chronological order, they are:

Year	Record	ND-Opp Total score	Avg. Score
1903	8-0-1	292-0	29.2 to 0
1907	6-0-1	137-20	19.57 to 2.8
1909	7-0-1	236-14	29.5 to 1.75
1911	6-0-2	229-9	28.62 to 1.12
1912	7-0-0	389-27	55.57 to 3.85
1913	7-0-0	268-41	38.28 to 5.85
1919	9-0-0	229-47	25.44 to 5.22
1920	9-0-0	251-44	27.88 to 4.88
1924	10-0-0	285-54	28.5 to 5.4
1929	9-0-0	145-38	16.11 to 4.22
1930	10-0-0	265-74	26.5 to 7.4
1941	8-0-1	189-64	21 to 7.11
1946	8-0-1	271-24	30.11 to 2.66
1947	9-0-0	291-52	32.33 to 5.77
1948	9-0-1	320-93	32 to 9.3
1949	10-0-0	360-86	36 to 8.6
1953	9-0-1	317-139	31.7 to 13.9
1966	9-0-1	362-38	36.2 to 3.8
1973	11-0-0	382-89	34.72 to 8.09
1988	12-0-0	39-156	32.75 to 12.75
	173-0-10	**5611-1109**	**30.66 to 6.06**

In these 20 seasons, the Irish played at .978 clip. In 103 seasons, then, Notre Dame teams stood roughly a one in five chance of ringing up an undefeated campaign. In these 20 seasons, the Irish defeated the opposition by an average of 24.6 points.

Rockne's influence looms large here. He played in three undefeated seasons (1911-1913) and coached five others (1919-20, 1924, 1929-30). It is not stretching the point to note that his own protégé, Frank Leahy, coached another six undefeated seasons (giving his 1949 seniors the privilege of playing four seasons without suffering a loss—36-0-2—compared to Rockne's class of four playing years at 24-1-3). Rockne thus either directly played in or coached 40 percent of Notre Dame's undefeated seasons. His indirect influence, extended through Leahy, has amazingly touched a full 70 percent of Notre Dame's undefeated seasons.

Of these 20 seasons, two in particular stand out—1912 and 1929. The 1912 season, one of Rockne's as a player, saw the Irish manhandle their opponents by a whopping margin of 51 points per game. The 1929 season, a defensive masterpiece, was an incredible feat because the Irish won all nine games on the road—and often without Rockne on the sidelines, due to phlebitis of the leg caused by a sideline pile-up that smashed into the coach during the Indiana game. His doctors kept him off his feet as much as possible and curtailed his coaching activities to intolerable limits as far as Rock was concerned.

In the eight undefeated seasons in which Rockne either played or coached, the Irish played 69 games, won 67 of them, and tied two. In those games, they outscored the opposition by 2,061 points to 334, an average score per game of 29.85 to 4.84, a winning margin of slightly better than 25 points per game—better than three touchdowns and a field goal. In his five undefeated seasons as the head coach, Rockne won all 47 games, his Irish scoring 1,175 points to 257, for an average score of 25 to 5.46, a winning margin of 19.54 points per game. Leahy's Irish, in six undefeated campaigns, won 52 games and tied five. In those seasons, they scored 1748 points to the opposition's 458, for an average score of 30.66 to eight, a winning differential of 22.66 points. Leahy's juggernauts in those years beat the opposition by three more points than did Rockne's, but those three points, combined with Leahy's relentless approach to the game, did not endear him to American sports fans. Rockne whipped you, and you did not feel too bad about it; his guile and wit made it painless. Leahy crunched you, and it hurt. This is reflected in his national reputation. Ara Parseghian's great teams of 1966 and 1973 actually took it to the opponents worse than most of Leahy's crusades: beating the opposition by a hefty 32.4 points in 1966, and by 26.63 points in 1973.

But for sheer whippings, the 1903 season, with Red Salmon playing in his senior year for Coach James Faragher, wins the prize, since the opposition did not score for the whole year. Coach John Marks, a decade later, set the record for overmatching the opposition, especially in the 1912 season, when the Irish crunched seven teams 389 to 27, a scoring differential of 51.72 points! His two seasons as head coach, in which he won 13 games and tied two, saw the Irish outscore the opposition by the ridiculous figure of 618 points to 36, for an average score of 41.2 to 2.4, a 38.8 scoring differential—in today's scoring, a margin of five touchdowns and a field goal.

UNDEFEATED SEASONS IN RANK ORDER OF SCORING DIFFERENTIAL

	Year	Point diff.	Coach [Remarks]
1.	1912	+51.72	Marks [Rockne's junior year]
2.	1903	+32.44	Faragher [nine shutouts]
3.	1913	+32.43	Harper [Rockne's senior year]
4.	1966	+32.4	Parseghian [six shutouts]
5.	1909	+27.75	Longman [six shutouts, beat Michigan]
6.	1911	+27.5	Marks [Rockne's sophomore year]
7.	1946	+27.45	Leahy [first postwar machine]
8.	1949	+27.4	Leahy [Hart's Heisman year]
9.	1973	+26.63	Parseghian [ND's first 11-0 year]
10.	1947	+26.56	Leahy [Lujack's Heisman year]
11.	1924	+23.1	Rockne [Four Horsemen]
12.	1920	+23	Rockne [Gipp's senior year]
13.	1948	+22.7	Leahy [mid-39 game streak]
14.	1919	+20.22	Rockne [Gipp's junior year]
15.	1988	+20.36	Holtz [ND's first 12-0 year]
16.	1930	+19.1	Rockne [dedicated new stadium]
17.	1953	+17.8	Leahy [the Master's last year]
18.	1907	+16.77	Barry [four shutouts]
19.	1941	+13.89	Leahy [Leahy's first season]
20.	1929	+11.89	Rockne [all games played away]

NOTRE DAME'S WINNING STREAKS

Over the years, the Irish have been fortunate enough to put together some streaks of very impressive football. In chronological order, here are the seasons when opponents most regretted scheduling the Irish:

Seasons	Streak	(W-L-T)	Coaches
1902-04	14 games	(12-0-2)	Faragher
1908-10	16 games	(14-0-2)	Place/Longman
1911-14	24 games	(22-0-2)	Marks/Harper
1919-21	20 games	(20-0-0)	Rockne
1923-25	16 games	(16-0-0)	Rockne
1929-31	20 games	(20-0-0)	Rockne/Anderson
1946-50	39 games	(37-0-2)	Leahy
1969-70	18 games	(16-1-1)	Parseghian
1973-74	20 games	(19-1-0)	Parseghian
1988-93*	74 games	(64-9-1)	Holtz

* includes ND's longest pure winning streak of 23 straight wins.

NOTRE DAME'S LOSING STREAKS

Losing streaks are not characteristic of Irish football. The Irish did not lose more than two consecutive games until Hunk Anderson's punchless team of 1933. In nine games that year, the Irish had little fight in them, scoring only 32 points, suffering six shutouts, and losing four straight games in the middle of the campaign. Bob Davie's 2001 team started the season with three straight losses, the first time that ever happened at the Dome; his teams also had three other such streaks, including four-game losing streaks twice. Following are the few losing streaks that mar the Irish record.

Season	Streak	Total Score	Avg. Score	Coaches
1933	4 losses	0-47	0 to 11.75	Anderson
1956	5 losses	48-174	9.6 to 34.8	Brennan
1960	8 losses	93-181	11.6 to 22.6	Kuharich
1961	3 losses	27-42	9 to 14	Kuharich
1962	4 losses	27-107	6.75 to 26.75	Kuharich
1963	3 losses	15-46	5 to 15.33	Kuharich/Devore
1963	5 losses	49-112	9.8 to 22.4	Devore
1982	3 losses	44-71	14.6 to 23.6	Faust
1983	3 losses	68-78	22.6 to 26	Faust
1984	3 losses	52-88	17.3 to 29.3	Faust
1985-86	5 losses	58-148	11 to 29.6	Faust/Holtz
1997	4 losses	53-105	13.25 to 26.25	Davie
1999	3 losses	58-77	19.3 to 25.6	Davie
1999	4 losses	107-146	26.75 to 36.5	Davie
2000-01	4 losses	32-109	8 to 27.25	Davie
2003	3 losses	26-83	8.6 to 27.66	Willingham
2003	3 losses	39-109	13 to 36.33	Willingham
2004	3 losses	69-120	23 to 40	Willingham
2006-07	7 losses	84-251	12 to 35.85	Weis
2007	4 losses	82-152	20.5 to 38	Weis
2009	4 losses	111-128	27.75 to 32	Weis
2010	3 losses	69-99	23 to 33	Kelly

The only surprise here is Holtz, but his '86 team tacked on two losses to a string inherited from Faust's last three games. Otherwise, coaches who enjoy excellent reputations within Notre Dame history are not found on this list.

Looked at another way, certain coaches simply resisted consecutive losses in the regular season. Of those with more than five or more seasons leading the Irish, they are Harper and Parseghian (who lost a bowl game after a closing loss to USC in 1972—then came back to win the national crown in 1973). All other coaches have been the victims of consecutive losses. That Parseghian dodged this bullet for 11 seasons is a testament to his ability to field talented teams with great preparation, composure, and confidence.

Other coaches came close: in 12 seasons, Rockne had consecutive losses once (1928); in 11 seasons, Leahy lost twice in a row only once (1950); in seven seasons, Layden had consecutive losses twice (1934 and 1940); in five seasons, Brennan had two or more losses in a row twice (1956 and 1957); and in six seasons, Devine suffered consecutive losses twice (1978 and 1979).

In six seasons, Holtz has fallen into consecutive losses, surprisingly, five times (three times in 1986, 1987, and 1991). Bob Davie's several streaks reveal an inconsistency that seriously marred his teams' campaigns.

The coaches since Davie, especially Willingham and Weis, could not seem to avoid losing streaks, complete with some blowout losses. It's a bit early to tell with Kelly, after only two seasons at the helm. Nevertheless, the fourteen seasons since the departure of Holtz have witnessed several sustained dismal periods.

SCORING DIFFERENTIALS FOR NOTRE DAME COACHES

Notre Dame football teams have played 1,083 games since 1887. They have scored 27,145 points to the opposition's 12,283 points. In these 1,083 games, then, the average score has been 25.06 to 11.34; the scoring differential in Notre Dame's history has thus been 13.72 points, slightly less than two touchdowns per game. The following chart reveals the scoring differential over the careers of Notre Dame's coaches.

Years	Coach	Total Points	Avg. Score	Differential
1894	Morison	80-31	16 to 6.2	+9.8
1895	Hadden	70-20	17.5 to 5	+12.5
1896-98	Hering	502-124	26.42 to 6.52	+19.9
1899	McWeeney	169-55	16.9 to 5.5	+11.4
1900-01	O'Dea	406-92	20.3 to 4.6	+15.7
1902-03	Faragher	495-51	27.5 to 2.83	+24.67
1904	Salmon	94-127	11.75 to l5.87	4.12
1905	McGlew	312-80	34.66 to 8.88	+25.78
1906-07	Barry	244-32	17.42 to 2.28	+15.14
1908	Place	326-20	36.22 to 2.22	+34
1909-10	Longman	428-34	30.57 to 2.42	+28.15
1911-12	Marks	611-36	40.73 to 2.42	+38.31
1913-17	Harper	1219-170	30.47 to 4.25	+26.22
1918-30	Rockne	2847-828	23.33 to 6.78	+16.55
1931-33	Anderson	502-151	18.59 to 5.59	+13
1934-40	Layden	873415	13.85 to 6.58	+7.27
1941-43	Leahy	2835-996	26.49 to 9.3	+17.19
1946-53	Leahy			
1944	McKeever	272-118	27.2 to ll.8	+15.4
1954-58	Brennan	1007-825	20.14 to 16.5	+3.64
1959-62	Kuharich	724-901	18.1 to 22.52	4.42
1945&63	Devore	363-281	19.1 to l4.78	+4.32
1964-74	Parseghian	3193-1132	27.52 to 9.75	+17.82
1975-80	Devine	1742-963	24.88to 13.75	+11.13
1981-85	Faust	1283-984	22.5 to 17.26	+5.24
1986-96	Holtz	4287-2424	32.48 to 18.36	+14.12
1997-2001	Davie	1525-1326	25.42 to 22.1	+3.32
2002-2004	Willingham	822-822	22.21 to 22.21	+0.0
2005-2009	Weis	1722-1548	27.77 to 24.96	+2.81
2010-2011	Kelly	722-542	27.76 to 20.84	+6.92

COACHES SCORING DIFFERENTIALS IN RANK ORDER

1. Marks .... +38.31
2. Place .... +34
3. Longman ...... +28.15
4. Harper .... +26.22
5. McGlew .... +25.78
6. Faragher .... +24.67
7. Hering .... +19.9
8. Parseghian ..... +17.82
9. Leahy .... +17.19
10. Rockne .... +16.55
11. O'Dea........... +15.7
12. McKeever ...... +15.4
13. Barry .... +15.14
14. Holtz .... +14.12
15. Anderson ...... +13
16. Hadden......... +12.5
17. McWeeney.... +11.4
18. Devine .... +11.13
19. Morison........ +9.8
20. Layden.......... +7.27
21. Kelly .... +6.92
22. Faust............. +5.24
23. Devore.......... +4.32
24. Brennan .... +3.64
25. Davie .... +3.32
26. Weis.............. +2.81
27. Willingham... +0.0
28. Salmon .... -4.12 (had a winning season though)
29. Kuharich .... -4.45 (ND's only coach with a losing record)

POINTS SCORED PER COACH

1. Holtz 4287
2. Parseghian........3193
3. Rockne.............2847
4. Leahy 2835
5. Devine 1742
6. Weis.................1722
7. Davie 1525
8. Faust 1283
9. Harper 1219
10. Brennan 1007
11. Layden 873
12. Willingham......822
13. Kuharich..........724
14. Kelly 722
15. Marks..............611
16. Hering 502
17. Anderson 502
18. Faragher...........495
19. Longman 428
20. O'Dea..............406
21. Devore 363
22. Place 326
23. McGlew...........312
24. McKeever.........272
25. Barry................244
26. McWeeney.......169
27. Salmon.............94
28. Morison 80
29. Hadden............70

POINTS ALLOWED PER COACH

1. Holtz............... 2424
2. Weis 1548
3. Davie 1326
4. Parseghian 1132
5. Leahy 996
6. Faust 984
7. Devine 963
8. Kuharich 901
9. Rockne............ 828
10. Willingham......822
11. Brennan 825
12. Kelly 542
13. Layden 415
14. Devore 281
15. Harper 170

16. Anderson......... 151
17. Salmon............ 127
18. Hering............. 124
19. McKeever........ 118
20. O'Dea............. 92
21. McGlew.......... 80
22. McWeeney 55
23. Faragher 51
24. Marks.............. 36
25. Longman.......... 34
26. Barry.............. 32
27. Morison 31
28. Hadden........... 20
29. Place................ 20

HIGHEST COACHING CAREER AVERAGE SCORE PER GAME

1.	Marks 40.73	1911-12
2.	Place 36.22	1908
3.	McGlew.......... 34.66	1905
4.	Holtz.............. 32.48	1986-96
5.	Longman 30.57	1909-10
6.	Harper............ 30.475	1913-17
7.	Weis 27.77	2005-09
8.	Kelly 27.76	2010-11
9.	Parseghian 27.52	1964-74
10.	Faragher.......... 27.5	1902-03
11.	McKeever 27.2	1944
12.	Leahy.............. 26.49	1941-43; 46-53
13.	Hering............ 26.42	1896-98
14.	Davie.............. 25.42	1997-2001
15.	Devine............ 24.88	1976-80
16.	Rockne 23.33	1918-30
17.	Faust.............. 22.5	1981-85
18.	Willingham .. 22.21	2002-04
19.	O'Dea 20.3	1900-01
20.	Brennan 20.14	1954-58
21.	Devore........... 19.1	1945; 63
22.	Anderson 18.59	1931-33
23.	Kuharich......... 18.1	1959-62
24.	Hadden 17.5	1895
25.	Barry 17.42	1906-07
26.	McWeeney...... 16.9	1899
27.	Morison.......... 16	1894
28.	Layden............ 13.85	1934-40
29.	Salmon 11.75	1904

AVERAGE OPPONENT POINTS ALLOWED
PER GAME

1.	Place	2.22	1908
2.	Barry	2.28	1906-07
3.	Marks	2.42	1911-12
4.	Longman	2.42	1909-10
5.	Faragher	2.83	1902-03
6.	Harper	4.25	1913-17
7.	O'Dea	4.6	1900-01
8.	Hadden	5	1895
9.	McWeeney	5.5	1899
10.	Anderson	5.59	1931-33
11.	Morison	6.2	1894
12.	Hering	6.52	1896-98
13.	Layden	6.58	1934-40
14.	Rockne	6.78	1918-30
15.	McGlew	8.88	1905
16.	Leahy	9.3	1941-43; 46-53
17.	Parseghian	9.75	1964-74
18.	McKeever	11.8	1944
19.	Devine	13.75	1975-80
20.	Devore	14.78	1945; 63
21.	Salmon	15.87	1904
22.	Brennan	16.5	1954-58
23.	Willingham	16.69	2002
24.	Faust	17.26	1981-85
25.	Holtz	18.36	1986-96
26.	Kelly	20.84	2010-11
27.	Davie	22.1	1997-2001
28.	Willingham	22.21	2002-04
29.	Weis	24.96	2005-09

The foregoing charts reveal that the early coaches at Notre Dame were very stingy chaps, many of them allowing only a field goal or less. Harper, Rockne, and Layden stand out for miserliness over extended periods—for a quarter century of football games, these three gave up less than a touchdown per game. Parseghian, with 11 seasons, racked up both the most points and allowed the most at that point in N.D. history, but this was in an era when passing was wildly more successful than 50 years before. The high-scoring coaches from before Harper just played smashmouth against inferior opponents. Leahy's winning machines kept opponents under 10 points per game while pounding out big winning margins. Parseghian managed to hold opponents to less than 10 points, in an era when it was becoming more difficult to stop an offense. In the Holtz era, Irish fans had to hope for lots of scoring and held onto their seats in the face of plenty of points by opposing teams. Rockne, ever the student of theatrics, kept the games pretty close, even while strangling opponents' offenses. Davie's teams could score well enough, but were not consistent enough to be highly successful. It is no accident that the last four Irish coaches bring up the rear on this table. Modern defense is not predicated on shutting out the opponent. It's nice if it happens, but the idea is to manage four or five stopped drives with no scoring, and hang on from there, hoping that the Irish offense scores more often. Kelly's offense at Cincinnati in 2008 was the second highest scoring offense in the country, but was last in time of possession. Today, it's a track meet. One wonders what Rockne would have thought. Defensive purists, however, must not be happy.

NOTRE DAME SHUTOUTS OF OPPONENTS PER COACH

In 1,083 football games, the Irish have shut out their opponents 294 times (27.1 percent). The following chart shows the shutout percentages of all Irish coaches.

	Coach	Shutouts	Percentage	Years
1.	Barry	10 in 14 games	71%	1906-07
2.	Faragher	12 in 18 games	66%	1902-03
3.	Place	6 in 9 games	66%	1908
4.	Longman	9 in 14 games	64%	1909-10
5.	Hering	12 in 19 games	63%	1896-98
6.	Harper	25 in 40 games	62.5%	1913-17
7.	O'Dea	12 in 20 games	60%	1900-01
8.	Marks	9 in 15 games	60%	1911-12
9.	McGlew	5 in 9 games	55%	1904
10.	Anderson	14 in 27 games	51%	1931-33
11.	McWeeney	5 in 10 games	50%	1899
12.	McKeever	5 in 10 games	50%	1944
13.	Hadden	2 in 4 games	50%	1895
14.	Rockne	50 in 122 games	40.9%	1918-30
15.	Morison	2 in 5 games	40%	1894
16.	Salmon	3 in 8 games	37.5%	1904
17	Layden	20 in 63 games	31.74%	1934-40
18	Leahy	26 in 107 games	24.3%	1941-43; 46-53
19.	Parseghian	28 in 116 games	24.13%	1964-74
20.	Brennan	11 in 50 games	22%	1954-58
21.	Devore	3 in 19 games	15.78%	1945; 63
22.	Willingham	2 in 13 games	15.38%	2002
23.	Devine	10 in 70 games	14.28%	1975-80
24.	Holtz	8 in 135 games	5.93%	1986-96
25.	Kuharich	2 in 40 games	5%	1959-62
26.	Faust	2 in 57 games	3.5%	1981-85
27.	Davie	1 in 60 games	1.67%	1997-2001

MOST SHUTOUTS PER COACH

1. Rockne..............50 in 122 games
2. Parseghian ....28 in 116 games
3. Leahy ....26 in 107 games
4. Harper...............25 in 40 games
5. Layden ....20 in 63 games
6. Anderson............14 in 27 games
7. Hering................12 in 19 games
8. Faragher ....12 in 18 games
9. O'Dea ....12 in 20 games
10. Brennan..............11 in 50 games
11. Barry ....10 in 14 games
12. Devine...............10 in 70 games
13. Longman...........9 in 14 games
14. Marks................9 in 15 games
15. Holtz..................8 in 135 games
16. Place..................6 in 9 games
17. McGlew ....5 in 9 games
18. McWeeney ....5 in 10 games
19. McKeever...........5 in 10 games
20. Salmon ....3 in 8 games
21. Devore ....3 in 19 games
22. Hadden ....2 in 4 games
23. Morison..............2 in 5 games
24. Willingham ....2 in 13 games
25. Kuharich ....2 in 40 games
26. Faust...................2 in 57 games
27. Davie..............1 in 60 games

NOTRE DAME AS SHUTOUT VICTIMS

In 1,083 games through the '03 Gator Bowl, the Irish have failed to score 67 times—little more than 6 percent of the time, as opposed to their turning the trick 294 times, 27.15 percent of their games. Only five of Notre Dame's opponents through the years have an edge over the Irish in this category: Chicago with two in four games, Indianapolis Artillery with one in its only try, Michigan with five in 29 games, Missouri with one in four meetings, and Yale with one shutout in the only encounter of the two teams. Otherwise, the Irish have racked up more shutouts of all other opponents than they have suffered.

Here is the chronological record of Irish coaches as victims of the shutout:

Coach	Shutouts	Percentage of games	Coach	Shutouts	Percentage of games
Morison	0 in 5 games	0%	Anderson	10 in 27 games	37%
Hadden	1 in 4 games	25%	Layden	7 in 63 games	1.11%
Hering	3 in 19 games	15.79%	Leahy	3 in 107 games	2.8%
McWeeney	2 in 10 games	20%	McKeever	1 in 10 games	10%
O'Dea	5 in 20 games	25%	Brennan	1 in 50 games	2%
Faragher	2 in 18 games	11%	Kuharich	4 in 40 games	7.5%
Salmon	2 in 8 games	25%	Devore	1 in 19 games	5.26%
McGlew	3 in 9 games	33%	Parseghian	1 in 116 games	.008%
Barry	2 in 14 games	14.28%	Devine	1 in 70 games	1.42%
Place	0 in 9 games	0%	Faust	1 in 57 games	1.75%
Longman	2 in 14 games	14.28%	Holtz	1 in 132 games	0.0075%
Marks	2 in 15 games	13.33%	Davie	1 in 60 games	0.0166%
Harper	3 in 40 games	7.5%	Willingham	0 in 13 games	0%
Rockne	8 in 122 games	6.56%			

SHUTOUT LOSS RANKINGS FOR COACHES

	Shutout Losses	Worst Percentage	Best Percentage
1.	Anderson...... 10	Anderson........ 37%	Place 0%
2.	Rockne......... 8	McGlew 33%	Morison 0%
3.	Layden 6	Hadden 25%	Willingham... 0%
4.	O'Dea 5	Salmon 25%	Holtz .... .0082%
5.	McGlew 3	O'Dea 25%	Parseghian...... .008%
6.	Hering.......... 3	McWeeney 20%	Devine 1.42%
7.	Kuharich 3	Hering............ 15.78%	Davie 1.66%
8.	Harper 3	Barry 14.28%	Faust 1.75%
9.	Leahy 3	Longman........ 14.28%	Brennan 2%
10.	Salmon......... 2	Marks............. 13.33%	Leahy 2.8%
11.	McWeeney ... 2	Faragher 11%	Devore 5.26%
12.	Barry 2	McKeever 10%	Rockne.......... 6.56%
13.	Longman...... 2	Layden 9.52%	Harper 7.5%
14.	Marks........... 2	Kuharich 7.5%	Kuharich 7.5%
15.	Faragher 2	Harper............ 7.5%	Layden 9.52%
16.	Hadden........ 1	Rockne 6.56%	McKeever...... 10%
17.	McKeever..... 1	Devore 5.26%	Faragher........ 11%
18.	Devore 1	Leahy 2.8%	Marks........... 13.33%
19.	Brennan 1	Brennan.......... 2%	Longman 14.28%
20.	Faust 1	Faust............... 1.75%	Barry............ 14.28%

	Shutout Losses	Worst Percentage	Best Percentage
21.	Devine 1	Davie 1.6%	Hering 15.78%
22.	Holtz 1	Devine 1.42%	McWeeney 20%
23.	Parseghian 1	Parseghian .... .008%	O'Dea 25%
24.	Davie 1	Holtz .... .0082%	Salmon 25%
25.	Willingham ... 0	Willingham .... —	Hadden 25%
26.	Morison 0	Morison .... —	McGlew 33%
27.	Place 0	Place .... —	Anderson 37%

SHUTOUTS BY AND AGAINST NOTRE DAME

The Irish have played football against 133 different opponents. Of those, Notre Dame has recorded shutouts over 94 of them, while only 28 have returned the favor. The Irish hold shutouts over 71 opponents who have not, in turn, been able to keep them scoreless. Only five opponents have turned the tables entirely on Notre Dame, earning shutouts over the Irish, but never being on the receiving end (and two of those, Indianapolis Artillery and Chicago, are not in the football business anymore). The complete list of teams with shutouts of the Irish follows.

Team	Total games	Shutouts of ND	Shutouts by ND
Army	48	8	20
Carnegie Tech	19	2	10
Chicago	4	2	0
Chi. Phys. & Surgeons	9	2	7
Georgia Tech	32	1	4
Illinois	12	1	5
Indiana	29	3	11
Indiana Artillery	1	1	0
Iowa	24	2	4
Kansas	6	1	2
Marquette	6	2	4
Miami (Florida)	23	3	5
Michigan	29	5	0
MSU	65	4	14
Missouri	4	1	0
Navy	75	2	20
Nebraska	16	3	4
Northwestern	47	4	15
Oklahoma	9	1	2
Penn State	17	1	3
Pitt	60	5	12
Purdue	74	3	13
Rush Med.	4	1	3
USC	74	5	8
Wabash	11	1	5
Wisconsin	16	4	6
Yale	1	1	0

OTHER SIGNIFICANT OPPONENTS IN THE SHUTOUT DERBY ARE:

Team	Total games	Shutouts of ND	Shutouts by ND
Alabama	6	0	1
Duke	3	0	1
LSU	9	0	1
Minnesota	5	0	1
N. Carolina	16	0	3
Penn	6	0	1
Rutgers	4	0	3
S. Dakota	5	0	4
SMU	13	0	1
Stanford	16	0	1
Syracuse	3	0	1
Tulane	8	0	3

In sum, then, 70.7 percent of Notre Dame's opponents have been whitewashed by the Irish at least once, whereas only 21 percent of ND's foes have been able to do the same. A mere 3.8 percent have been able to do it to ND without the favor being returned, while 76 percent of Notre Dame's shutout victims have not been able to hold the Irish scoreless in a game.

WINNING STREAKS

The following list shows the longest winning streaks either by or against Notre Dame for those opponents who have won or lost more than three consecutive games.

Notre Dame streaks

Air Force	11	1964-81
Alabama	4	1973-80
Army	12	1965-98
Boston College	4	1975-1993 &
		1995-1998
Cal	4	1959-67
Colorado	3	1983-1989
GA Tech	6	1922-27 &
		1967-75
Illinois	10	1938-68
Indiana	14	1908-49
Iowa	5	1945-49
Miami (FL)	11	1967-80
Michigan	4	1987-90
MSU	8	1897-1909 &
		1987-1994
Navy	39	1964-02
Nebraska	3	1919-21
North Carolina	10	1949-59
Northwestern	14	1965-94
Oklahoma	6	1957-99
Penn St.	3	1926-76
Pitt	11	1964-74
Purdue	11	1986-96
Rice	4	1915-88
Rutgers	4	1921-2002
South Carolina	3	1976-83
SMU	3	1930-49
		1953-55
Stanford	3	1964-89
Texas	4	1970-1996
Tulane	8	1944-71
USC	11	1983-93
Washington	4	1948-1996
Wisconsin	4	1929-36

Opponents' streaks

Air Force	4	1982-85
Chicago	4	1893-1899
Iowa	3	1921-40 &
		1956-58
Miami	4	1983-87
Michigan	8	1887-1908
MSU	8	1955-63
MSU	5	1997-01

Northwestern	4	1959-62
Penn State	3	1981-83 &
		1985-87
Pitt	3	1932-34
		1958-60
		1983-87
Purdue	3	1958-60 &
		1967-69
Tennessee	3	1991-2001
USC	5	1978-82
USC	3	1996-98

ASSESSMENT OF THE TRENDS IN PLAYER SIZE

Generally speaking, the trend has been toward larger and, when possible, faster players. Early versions of football involved mass play, with team speed not a requirement, although some jackrabbits were necessary to break away from the melee. For the Irish, there were some remarkably large men in the early goings, such as John Eggeman at 256 pounds at the turn of the century, then Dimmick and Philbrook a decade later. Still, such specimens were surrounded by considerably smaller players, although the tendency from the middle of the 1890s until 1913 was to field increasingly larger players.

Harper began to shift away from that trend, and Rockne changed the pattern completely by fielding teams with much smaller players at four key positions: left guard, center, right guard, and right tackle. His backfields also reversed the trend toward larger players (although he did field large backs in 1929-30, in response to rule changes). The four interior line positions decreased about 10 pounds per man as Rock placed a premium on speed and mobility in the line to match that of his cat-quick backs. This was very subtle football, begun during the Harper years, in which it was not necessary to overpower an opponent, but just brush block, or interfere long enough for a defensive player to be neutralized rather than demolished. Perfection of execution was the desired end. Rockne's backs over 13 seasons averaged a mere 165 1/3 pounds, and three of the four backfield positions are the smallest on record.

The rules were changing, partially as a result of the way in which Rock's approach to the game demolished a good Stanford team in the 1925 Rose Bowl. Pop Warner was the chief antagonist in the debate that led eventually to the end of the Notre Dame shift shortly after Rock's death in 1931. It was felt that the shift, which allowed the backfield and the ends to flex or shift into a new position just prior to the snap, gave the offense an unfair advantage. Rock's theory was that it could get the maximum number of players to the point of attack as fast as possible. He was also enchanted with its aesthetic merits. Within a decade after his death, however, the Notre Dame box formation also went into oblivion, to be replaced by the T formation in Leahy's second year—a move against football tradition that required the approval of the Notre Dame administration. In essence, Anderson and Layden fielded teams that were using an obsolete formation, though it was still good enough to make a run at the national crown in 1938.

Leahy was both a pragmatist and an enormously intense competitor. Although Irish teams began to grow larger again after 1931, he accelerated the trend—increasing the size of his linemen by more than 10 pounds per man and his backs by nearly five pounds per man over Layden's teams. The T also shifted the glamour spot in the backfield from the Notre Dame box's left halfback (the position of Gipp, Christie Flanagan, and Marchy Schwartz), to the T's quarterback—(Bertelli, Lujack, and Tripucka, for instance).

Backfields continued to grow larger, although in incremental ways, except for Faust's huge fullbacks, at six foot three and 231 pounds, and Davie's fullbacks, shorter than Faust's, but nearly 20 pounds heavier, these backs easily the largest who ever started at Notre Dame. A major shift appears early in the Parseghian years with the split end. The first split end, as such, for Notre Dame was the silky Jim Seymour, a very large target at six foot four. After his playing years, pass catchers tended to become much smaller targets, about five inches shorter than Seymour. In general, there are outside limits to the relationship of a runner's size to his speed and quickness. The monstrous backs envisioned in the late Kuharich years—six foot four, 235 pounds—never found a starting niche. Within a few years, the size of the backs reached a plateau, except for Faust's fullbacks—and Holtz's Jerome Bettis who, at 252 pounds, is the largest runner for the Irish in any era (unless you count the few times when an Eggeman was turned loose). By the early '80s, the current pattern was set: offensive linemen averaging about six foot five, 265 pounds leading the way for rather small backs, Allen Pinkett being the perfect example at five foot nine, 183 pounds. Irish passers were throwing to receivers of about that same size, except for an excellent run of huge tight ends. In fact, this is a correlation to look for in a team's success—a good quarterback hooked up with an excellent tight end, as seen in the following pairs: Clements and Casper, Montana and MacAfee, Rice and Brown, and Mirer and Brown. Add to such pairs the devastating scoring possibilities of a Pinkett or an Ismail, and you can see how defensive coordinators can be driven to distraction. If you design a defense to limit the threatened damage of an Ismail, then you're probably vulnerable to either the shorter routes of a 6-6 tight end over the middle, or the inside blasts of a Bettis, as Florida found out in the 1992 Gator Bowl. All of this adds up to tremendous offensive firepower. In fact, Parseghian's great 1966 team, which allowed only 38 points in 10 games, may be the last time a Notre Dame team truly shuts down its opponents over a whole season. Modern college football rings up big scores; modern defenses are almost incapable of stopping offenses over the long haul of an 11-game season. So, you try to score as much as possible with your offense and special teams, construct long, time-consuming drives, and keep the other offense walking the sidelines. You give up three TDs and hope to score four. It's wide-open football and extremely fast.

Modern Irish defense began with two-platoon football in the late '40s. Leahy was able to use defensive specialists like Jerry Groom and John Petitbon. This faded in the '50s as the NCAA tinkered with the rules, but two-platoon football returned in 1964, just in time for Parseghian's first squad to enjoy the benefits. For a while, as seen in Parseghian's teams, a defensive line was likely to be bigger than an offensive line. Changes in pass-blocking rules altered that pattern forever in the late '70s, so that a defensive lineman's task was less of a rush through the chest of the offensive player than a battle of quickness and leverage. When pass blocking changed from an "in-your-face" struggle to leverage and finesse, the offensive linemen became taller and heavier, and the defensive linemen became, on average, smaller and quicker. This is a timeless conflict in football—the swing of the pendulum between offensive tactics and defensive reactions. In the modern era, though, both sides of the ball are designed around speed either getting it loose and in the open if you're on offense, or containing it or catching up to it if on defense.

As with backs, linebackers probably have an optimum size for the maximizing of speed and quickness. They seemed to have settled in under Davie and Willingham at about six foot three, 244, heralded by earlier players such as Bob Golic and Wes Pritchett. But linebackers have an unenviable task—they have to be physical enough, and big enough, to stop the run consistently (modern defenses are designed to "feed" plays into them for finishing off), but they also have to assume certain pass-coverage responsibilities, either in man-to-man or zone defenses. So, you have to find an athlete capable of taking on a Jerome Bettis at the point of attack on the line of scrimmage, but also fast enough to cover an Ismail or Tim Brown over portions of pass routes through a linebacker's territory. Of course, the nightmare is to be isolated on one of those receivers beyond one's range, either on a miscalled man-to-man, or a blown zone coverage.

Assuming that doesn't happen, a linebacker will pass off a receiver downfield after he's through his zone, and let a deep back take over. It's been said that pass defenders are fast men who can't catch the ball well; if you are both fast and can catch, then you're a receiver. In any case, the greatest consistency in physical dimensions has been in the secondary, again because there are optimum physical dimensions for the tasks required of players. You can't be six foot five, 235, and expect to cover Ismail on 50-yard, long-post patterns. The player needs to be about Ismail's size, perhaps a bit larger, and use angles, the sidelines, and speed to keep a receiver from breaking loose. This, of course, does not take into account the equally difficult aspect of pass defense involving the reading of fakes and run support—another unenviable job.

And so college football will continue to evolve in relationship to new rules, new or altered offensive and defensive formations and plays, and the physical attributes of the players. The Irish fielded their first 300-pound offensive line in 1999 and their first team in which all the starters could run 4.8 40s or less (the '88 national champs). It is hard to determine the point at which growth trends will level off. We might be in the position today of Rockne in 1925 when it was not conceivable that a 265-pound player could have the speed and lateral quickness of a Chris Zorich. Improved diets and better strength and conditioning programs are allowing players to reach their physical and performance potentials sooner than before. Where we go from here over the long haul is not easily detected. We may be sure, however, that it will always be interesting, challenging, and exciting— and that Notre Dame will be among the leaders.

SERIES SCORES

[Numbers following the season and before the result indicate AP rankings for both teams coming into the game. For example, 4-10 indicates Notre Dame stood fourth and the Irish opponent 10th in the AP poll that week].

* = home game

ADRIAN
(1-0-0)

*	1912	W	74	7
		Total	74	7
		Avg. Score	74	7
		Diff.	+67	

AIR FORCE
(24-7-0)

	1964	6-	W	34	7
*	1969	8-	W	13	6
	1972	12-	W	21	7
*	1973	5-	W	48	15
*	1974	5-	W	38	0
	1975	15-	W	31	30
*	1977	6-	W	49	0
	1978	20-	W	38	15
	1979	10-	W	38	13
*	1980	2-	W	24	10
	1981		W	35	7
	1982	18-	L	17	30
*	1983		L	22	23
*	1984		L	7	21
	1985	-17	L	15	21
*	1986		W	31	3
	1987	11-	W	35	14
*	1988	2-	W	41	13
	1989	1 -17	W	41	27
*	1990	1 -	W	57	27
	1991	5-	W	28	15
*	1994	19-	W	42	30
	1995	17-	W	44	14
*	1996	8-	L	17	20 (OT)
*	2000	19-	W	34	31 (OT)
	2002	6-	W	21	14
	2006	9-	W	39	17
*	2007		L	24	41
*	2011		W	59	33
		Total	943	504	
		Avg. score	30.41	16.25	
		Diff.	+ 14.16		

AKRON
(1-0-0)

	1910	W	51	0
		Total	51	0
		Avg. score	51	0
		Diff.	+51	

ALABAMA
(5-1-0)

SB	1973	3-1	W	24	23
OB	1974	9-2	W	13	11
*	1976	18-10	W	21	18
BM	1980	6-5	W	7	0
BM	1986	-2	L	10	28
*	1987	7-10	W	37	6
		Total	112	86	
		Avg. score	18.66	14.33	
		Diff.	+4.33		

ALBION
(3-1-1)

*	1893	W	8	6
*	1894	T	6	6
*	1894	L	12	19
*	1896	W	24	0
	1898	W	60	0
		Total	110	31
		Avg. score	22	6.2
		Diff.	+15.8	

ALMA
(4-0-0)

*	1913	W	62	0
*	1914	W	56	0
*	1915	W	32	0
*	1916	W	46	0
		Total	196	0
		Avg. Score	49	0
		Diff.	+49	

AMERICAN MED. COL.
(5-0-0)

*	1901		W	32	0
*	1902		W	92	0
*	1903		W	52	0
*	1904		W	44	0
*	1905		W	142	0
		Total		362	0
		Avg. score		72.4	0
		Diff.		+72.4	

ARIZONA
(12-1-0)

*	1941		W	38	7
	1980	4-	W	20	3
*	1982	9-	L	13	16
		Total		71	26
		Avg. score		23.66	8.66
		Diff.		+ 15	

ARMY
(40-8-4)

	1913		W	35	13
	1914		L	7	20
	1915		W	7	0
	1916		L	10	30
	1917		W	7	2
	1919		W	12	9
	1920		W	27	17
	1921		W	28	0
	1922		T	0	0
EF	1923		W	13	0
PG	1924		W	13	7
YS	1925		L	0	27
YS	1926		W	7	0
YS	1927		L	0	18
YS	1928		W	12	6
YS	1929		W	7	0
SF	1930		W	7	6
YS	1931		L	0	12
YS	1932		W	21	0
YS	1933		W	13	12
YS	1934		W	12	6
YS	1935		T	6	6
YS	1936		W	20	6
YS	1937	18-	W	7	0
YS	1938	7-	W	19	7

YS	1939	4-	W	14	0
YS	1940	2-	W	7	0
YS	1941	6-14	T	0	0
YS	1942	4-19	W	13	0
YS	1943	1-3	W	26	0
YS	1944	5- 1	L	0	59
YS	1945	2-1	L	0	48
YS	1946	2-1	T	0	0
*	1947	1 -9	W	27	7
P	1957	12-10	W	23	21
*	1958	4-3	L	2	14
SS	1965	7-	W	17	0
*	1966	3-	W	35	0
YS	1969	15-	W	45	0
*	1970	3-	W	51	10
	1973	8-	W	62	3
*	1974	7-	W	48	0
GS	1977	11-	W	24	0
*	1980	5-	W	30	3
GS	1983		W	42	0
*	1985	-19	W	24	10
GS	1995	17-	W	28	27
*	1998	18-	W	20	17
*	2006	6-	W	41	9
NYS	2010		W	27	3
		Total		896	435
		Avg. score		17.23	8.36
		Diff.		+8.87	

BAYLOR
(2-0-0)

*	1925		W	41	0
*	1998	16-	W	27	3
		Total		68	3
		Avg. score		34	1.5
		Diff.		+32.5	

BELOIT
(5-0-1)

*	1896		W	8	0
*	1900		T	6	6
	1901		W	5	0
*	1906		W	29	0
*	1925		W	19	3
*	1926		W	77	0
		Total		144	9
		Avg. score		24	1.5
		Diff.		+22.5	

BENNETT MED. COL.
(1-0-0)

*	1905		W	22	0
		Total		22	0
		Avg. score		22	0
		Diff.		+22	

BOSTON COLLEGE
(12-9-0)

FX	1975	9-	W	17	3
LB	1983	-13	W	19	18
*	1987	9-	W	32	25
*	1992	8-9	W	54	7
*	1993	1-16	L	39	41
	1994	8-	L	11	30
*	1995	12-	W	20	10
	1996	17-	W	48	21
*	1997		W	52	20
	1998	13-	W	31	26
*	1999	-25	L	29	31
*	2000	11-	W	28	16
	2001		L	17	21
*	2002	4-	L	7	14
	2003		L	25	27
*	2004	24-	L	23	24
*	2007	-4	L	14	27
	2008		L	0	17
*	2009		W	20	16
*	2010		W	31	13
*	2011	24-	W	16	14
		Total		533	421
		Avg. Score		25.38	20.04
		Diff.		+5.34	

BUTLER
(3-0-0)

*	1911		W	27	0
	1922		W	31	3
*	1923		W	34	7
		Total		92	10
		Avg. score		30.66	3.33
		Diff.		+27.33	

BRIGHAM YOUNG
(4-2-0)

*	1992	10-	W	42	16
	1993	3-	W	45	20
*	1994	17-	L	14	21
*	2003		W	33	14
	2004		L	17	20
*	2005	9-	W	49	23
		Total		200	114
		Avg. score		33.33	19
		Diff.		+ 14.33	

CALIFORNIA
(4-0-0)

	1959		W	28	6
*	1960		W	21	7
	1965	3-	W	48	6
*	1967	1-	W	41	8
		Total		138	27
		Avg. score		34.5	6.75
		Diff.		+27.75	

CARLISLE
(1-0-0)

C	1914		W	48	6
		Total		48	6
		Avg. score		48	6
		Diff.		+42	

CARNEGIE TECH
(15-4-0)

	1922		W	19	0
	1923		W	26	0
	1924		W	40	19
*	1925		W	26	0
	1926		L	0	19
*	1928		L	7	27
	1929		W	7	0
*	1930		W	21	6
	1931		W	19	0
*	1932		W	42	0

	1933		L	0	7
*	1934		W	13	0
	1935		W	14	3
*	1936		W	21	7
	1937		L	7	9
*	1938	5-13	W	7	0
	1939	2-	W	7	6
*	1940	6-	W	61	0
	1941	8-	W	16	0
		Total		353	103
		Avg. Score		18.57	5.42
		Diff.		+13.15	

CASE TECH
(2-0-0)

*	1916		W	48	0
	1918		W	26	6
		Total		74	6
		Avg. score		37	3
		Diff.		+34	

CHICAGO
(0-4-0)

	1893		L	0	8
*	1896		L	0	18
	1897		L	5	34
	1899		L	6	23
		Total		11	83
		Avg. score		2.75	20.75
		Diff.		- 18	

CHICAGO DENTAL
(1 -0-0)

*	1897		W	62	0
		Total		62	0
		Avg. score		62	0
		Diff.		+62	

CHICAGO PHYSICIANS & SURGEONS
(7-2-0)

*	1895		W	32	0
*	1896		L	0	4
*	1899		L	0	5
*	1900		W	5	0
*	1901		W	34	0
*	1903		W	46	0
*	1906		W	28	0
*	1907		W	32	0
*	1908		W	88	0
		Total		265	9
		Avg. score		29.44	1
		Diff.		+29.44	

CHRISTIAN BROTHERS (ST. LOUIS)
(1-0-0)

	1913		W	20	7
		Total		20	7
		Avg. score		20	7
		Diff.		+13	

CINCINNATI
(1-0-0)

*	1900		W	58	0
		Total		58	0
		Avg. Score		58	0
		Diff.		+58	

CLEMSON
(1-1-0)

	1977	5-15	W	21	17
*	1979	-14	L	10	16
		Total		31	33
		Avg.score 15.5		16.5	
		Diff.		-1	

COE
(1-0-0)

*	1927		W	28	7
		Total		28	7
		Avg. score		28	7
		Diff.		+21	

COLORADO
(3-2-0)

	1983		W	27	3
*	1984		W	55	14
OB	1989	4- 1	W	21	6
OB	1990	5- 1	L	9	10
FB	1995	-4	L	24	41
		Total		136	74
		Avg. score		27.2	14.8
		Diff.		+ 12.4	

CONNECTICUT
(0-1-0)

	2009	L (2 OT)	30	33
*		Total	30	33
		Avg. score	30	33
		Diff.	-3	

CREIGHTON
(1-0-0)

	1915	W	41	0
		Total	41	0
		Avg. score	41	0
		Diff.	+41	

DARTMOUTH
(2-0-0)

FP	1944	1-	W	64	0
*	1945	3-	W	34	0
		Total		98	0
		Avg. score		49	0
		Diff.		+49	

DE LASALLE
(1-0-0)

	1893	W	28	0
*		Total	28	0
		Avg. score	28	0
		Diff.	+28	

DE PAUW
(8-0-0)

*	1897	W	4	0
*	1898	W	32	0
*	1902	W	22	0
*	1903	W	56	0
*	1904	W	10	0
*	1905	W	71	0
*	1921	W	57	10
*	1922	W	34	7
		Total	286	17
		Avg. score	35.75	2.12
		Diff.	+33.63	

DETROIT
(2-0-0)

	1927		W	20	0
BS	1951	5-	W	40	6
		Total		60	6
		Avg. score		30	3
		Diff.		+27	

DRAKE
(8-0-0)

*	1926	W	21	0
	1927	W	32	0
*	1928	W	32	6
SF	1929	W	19	7
*	1930	W	28	7
*	1931	W	63	0
*	1932	W	62	0
*	1937	W	21	0
		Total	278	20
		Avg. score	34.75	2.5
		Diff.	+32.25	

DUKE
(2-1-0)

*	1958	12-	W	9	7
	1961		L	13	37
*	1966	1-	W	64	0
		Total		86	44
		Avg. score		28.66	14.66
		Diff.		+14	

ENGLEWOOD H.S. (CHICAGO)
(2-0-0)

*	1899		W	29	5
*	1900		W	68	0
		Total		97	5
		Avg. score		48.5	2.5
		Diff.		+46	

FLORIDA
(1-0-0)

SD	1992	18-3	W	39	28
		Total		39	28
		Avg. score		39	28
		Diff.		+ 11	

FLORIDA STATE
(2-5-0)

*	1981	-20	L	13	19
*	1993	2-1	W	31	24
O	1994	-8	L	16	23
OB	1995	6-4	L	26	31
	2002	6-16	W	34	24
*	2009	-5	L	0	37
	2011		L	14	18
		Total		134	176
		Avg. score		19.14	25.14
		Diff.		-6	

FRANKLIN
(3-0-0)

*	1906		W	26	0
*	1907		W	23	0
*	1908		W	64	0
		Total		113	0
		Avg. score		37.66	0
		Diff.		+37.66	

GEORGIA
(0-1-0)

SD	1980	7-1	L	10	17
		Total		10	17
		Avg. score		10	17
		Diff.		-7	

GEORGIA TECH
(27-6-1)

	1922		W	13	3
*	1923		W	35	7
*	1924		W	34	3
	1925		W	13	0
*	1926		W	12	0
*	1927		W	26	7
	1928		L	0	13
	1929		W	26	6
	1938		W	14	6
*	1939		W	17	14
*	1940		W	26	20
	1941		W	20	0
*	1942		L	6	13
*	1943		W	55	13
	1944	18-10	W	21	0
	1945		W	40	7
*	1953	1 -4	W	27	14
*	1959	-19	L	10	14
	1967	9-	W	36	3
*	1968	9-	W	34	6
	1969	9-	W	38	20
*	1970	1-	W	10	7
	1974	2-	W	31	7
*	1975	12-	W	24	3
	1976	11-	L	14	23
*	1977	5-	W	69	14
	1978	10-20	W	38	21
*	1979	10-	W	21	13
	1980	1-	T	3	3
*	1981		W	35	3
*	1997	11-	W	17	13
GB	1998	17-12	L	28	35
	2006	2-	W	14	10
*	2007		L	3	33
		Total		810	354
		Avg. score		23.82	10.41
		Diff.		+13.41	

GOSHEN
(1-0-0)

*	1900		W	55	0
		Total		55	0
		Avg. score		55	0
		Diff.		+55	

GREAT LAKES
(1-2-2)

*	1918		T	7	7
SF	1942	6-	T	13	13
	1943	1-	L	14	19
*	1944	9-12	W	28	7
	1945	5-	L	7	39
		Total		69	85
		Avg. score		13.8	17
		Diff.		-3.2	

HARVARD PREP (CHICAGO)
(1-0-0)

*	1888	W	20	0
		Total	20	0
		Avg. Score	20	0
		Diff.	+20	

HASKELL
(5-0-0)

*	1914	W	20	7
*	1915	W	34	0
*	1916	W	26	0
*	1921	W	42	7
*	1932	W	73	0
		Total	195	14
		Avg. Score	39	2.8
		Diff.	+36.2	

HAWAII
(3-0-0)

	1991	18-	W	48	42
	1997		W	23	22
HB	2008		W	49	21
		Total		120	85
		Avg. score		40	28.33
		Diff.		+11.67	

HIGHLAND VIEWS
(1-0-0)

*	1896	W	82	0
		Total	82	0
		Avg. score	82	0
		Diff.	+82	

HILLSDALE
(4-0-1)

*	1892	T	10	10
*	1893	W	22	10
*	1894	W	14	0
*	1906	W	17	0
*	1908	W	39	0
		Total	102	20
		Avg. score	20.4	4
		Diff.	+ 15.6	

HOUSTON
(1-0-0)

CB	1978	10-9	W	35	34
		Total		35	34
		Avg. score		35	34
		Diff.		+ 1	

ILLINOIS
(11-0-1)

	1898		W	5	0
	1937		T	0	0
*	1938		W	14	6
	1940	2-	W	26	0
*	1941	7-	W	49	14
	1942	8-5	W	21	14
*	1943	1-	W	47	0
	1944	1-14	W	13	7
*	1945		W	7	0
	1946		W	26	6
	1967		W	47	7
*	1968	6-	W	58	8
		Total		313	62
		Avg. score		26.08	5.16
		Diff.		+20.92	

ILLINOIS CYCLING CLUB
(1-0-0)

*	1895	W	18	2
		Total	18	2
		Avg. score	18	2
		Diff.	+ 16	

INDIANA
(23-5-1)

*	1898	L	5	11
*	1899	W	17	0
	1900	L	0	6
*	1901	W	18	5
	1902	W	11	5
	1905	L	5	22
I	1906	L	0	12
*	1907	T	0	0
I	1908	W	11	0
I	1919	W	16	3
I	1920	W	13	10
I	1921	W	28	7
*	1922	W	27	0
*	1926	W	26	0
	1927	W	19	6
	1929	W	14	0
*	1930	W	27	0
	1931	W	25	0
	1933	W	12	2
*	1941	W	19	6
	1948	1-	W	42	6
*	1949	W	49	6
	1950	11-	L	7	20
*	1951	14-	W	48	6
*	1955	4-	W	19	0
*	1956	17-	W	20	6
*	1957	16-	W	26	0
*	1958	5-	W	18	0
*	1991	7-	W	49	27

Total 571 166
Avg. score 19.68 5.72
Diff. + 13.96

INDIANAPOLIS ARTILLERY
(0-1-0)

*	1895	L	0	18

Total 0 18
Avg. score 0 18
Diff. - 18

IOWA
(13-8-3)

	1921		L	7	10
	1939	3-	L	6	7
*	1940	7-	L	0	7
*	1945	2-	W	56	0
	1946	2-17	W	41	6
*	1947	2-	W	21	0
	1948	2-	W	27	12
*	1949	1-	W	28	7
	1950		T	14	14
*	1951		T	20	20
	1952	9-	W	27	0
*	1953	1-20	T	14	14
	1954	4-19	W	34	18
*	1955	4-	W	17	14
	1956	-3	L	8	48
*	1957	9-8	L	13	21
	1958	15-6	L	21	31
	1959	-16	W	20	19
*	1960	-2	L	0	28
	1961		L	21	42
*	1962		W	35	12
*	1964	1-	W	28	0
*	1967	6-	W	56	6
	1968	5-	W	51	28

Total 565 364
Avg. score 23.54 15.16
Diff. +8.38

IOWA PRE-FLIGHT
(2-0-0)

*	1942		W	28	0
*	1943	1-2	W	14	13

Total 42 13
Avg. score 21 6.5
Diff. +14.5

KALAMAZOO
(7-0-0)

*	1893	W	34	0
*	1917	W	55	0
*	1919	W	14	0
*	1920	W	39	0
*	1921	W	56	0
*	1922	W	46	0
*	1923	W	74	0
	Total		318	0
	Avg. score		45.42	0
	Diff.		+45.42	

KANSAS
(4-1-1)

	1904	L	5	24
	1932	W	24	6
*	1933	T	0	0
*	1935	W	28	7
*	1938	W	52	0
ERC*	1999	W	48	13
	Total		157	50
	Avg. score		26.16	8.33
	Diff.		+17.83	

KNOX
(1-1-0)

	1902	L	5	12
*	1907	W	22	4
	Total		27	16
	Avg. score		13.5	8
	Diff.		+5.5	

LAKE FOREST
(4-0-0)

*	1899	W	38	0
*	1901	W	16	0
*	1902	W	28	0
*	1903	W	28	0
	Total		110	0
	Avg. score		27.5	0
	Diff.		+27.5	

LOMBARD
(3-0-0)

*	1923	W	14	0
*	1924	W	40	0
*	1925	W	69	0
	Total		123	0
	Avg. score		41	0
	Diff.		+41	

LOUISIANA STATE
(5-5-0)

*	1970	2-7	W	3	0
	1971	7-14	L	8	28
*	1981	4-	W	27	9
	1984	-6	W	30	22
*	1985	-17	L	7	10
	1986	-8	L	19	21
	1997	-11	W	24	6
IS	1997	-15	L	9	27
*	1998	10-	W	39	36
SD	2006	11-4	L	14	41
	Total			180	200
	Avg. score			18	20
	Diff.			-2	

LOYOLA (CHICAGO)
(1-0-0)

*	1911	W	80	0
	Total		80	0
	Avg. score		80	0
	Diff.		+80	

LOYOLA (NEW ORLEANS)
(1-0-0)

	1928	W	12	6
	Total		12	6
	Avg. Score		12	6
	Diff.		+6	

MARYLAND
(2-0-0)

GS	2002		W	22	0
	2011		W	45	21
	Total			67	21
	Avg. Score			33.5	10.5
	Diff			+23	

MARQUETTE
(3-0-3)

	1908		W	6	0
	1909		T	0	0
	1910		T	5	5
	1911		T	0	0
C	1912		W	69	0
	1921		W	21	7
	Total			101	12
	Avg. score			21.83	2
	Diff.			+ 19.83	

MIAMI (FLORIDA)
(16-7-1)

	1955	5-15	W	14	0
	1960		L	21	28
	1965	6-	T	0	0
	1967	6-	W	24	22
	1971	7-	W	17	0
*	1972	10-	W	20	17
	1973	5-	W	44	0
*	1974	7-	W	38	7
	1975		W	32	9
*	1976	13-	W	40	27
	1977	5-	W	48	10
*	1978	19-	W	20	0
MB	1979		W	40	15
*	1980	7-13	W	32	14
	1981	-9	L	15	37
*	1982	10-17	W	16	14
	1983	13-	L	0	20
*	1984	17-14	L	13	31
	1985	-4	L	7	58
	1987	10-2	L	0	24
*	1988	4-1	W	31	30
	1989	1-7	L	10	27

*	1990	6-2	W	29	20
SBS	2010		W	33	17
	Total			544	427
	Avg. score			22.66	17.79
	Diff.			+4.87	

MIAMI (OHIO)
(1-0-0)

*	1909		W	46	0
	Total			46	0
	Avg. score			46	0
	Diff.			+46	

MICHIGAN
(15-23 -1)

*	1887		L	0	8
*	1888		L	6	26
*	1888		L	4	10
	1898		L	0	23
	1899		L	0	12
	1900		L	0	7
T	1902		L	0	23
	1908		L	6	12
	1909		W	11	3
*	1942	4-6	L	20	32
	1943	1-2	W	35	12
*	1978	14-5	L	14	28
	1979	9-6	W	12	10
*	1980	8- 14	W	29	27
	1981	1-11	L	7	25
*	1982	20- 10	W	23	17
	1985	13-	L	12	20
*	1986	-3	L	23	24
	1987	16-9	W	26	7
*	1988	13-9	W	19	17
	1989	1-2	W	24	19
*	1990	1-4	W	28	24
	1991	7-3	L	14	24
*	1992	3-6	T	17	17
	1993	11-3	W	27	23
*	1994	3-6	L	24	26
	1997	3-6	L	14	21
*	1998	22-5	W	36	20
	1999	16-7	L	22	26
*	2002	20-7	W	25	23

	2003	15-5	L	0	38		1966	1-2	T	10	10
*	2004	-8	W	28	20	*	1967		W	24	12
	2005	20-3	W	17	10		1968	5-	L	17	21
*	2006	2-11	L	21	47	*	1969	- 14	W	42	28
	2007		L	0	38		1970	4-	W	29	0
*	2008		W	35	17	*	1971	4-	W	14	2
	2009	-18	L	34	38		1972	7-	W	16	0
*	2010		L	24	28	*	1973	8-	W	14	10
	2011	-15	L	31	35		1974	7-	W	19	14
		Total		668	837	*	1975	8-	L	3	10
		Avg. score		17.12	21.46		1976	18-	W	24	6
		Diff.		-4.34		*	1977	14-	W	16	6

MICHIGAN STATE
(46-28-1)

							1978		W	29	25
*	1897		W	34	6	*	1979	15-7	W	27	3
*	1898		W	53	0		1980	7-	W	26	21
*	1899		W	40	0	*	1981		W	20	7
*	1902		W	33	0		1982	11-	W	11	3
*	1903		W	12	0	*	1983	4-	L	23	28
*	1905		W	28	0		1984		W	24	20
*	1906		W	5	0	*	1985		W	27	10
*	1909		W	17	0		1986	20-	L	15	20
	1910		L	0	17	*	1987	9-17	W	31	8
	1916		W	14	0		1988	8-	W	20	3
*	1917		W	23	0	*	1989	1-	W	21	13
	1918		L	7	13		1990	1 -24	W	20	19
*	1919		W	13	0	*	1991	11-	W	49	10
	1920		W	25	0		1992	7-	W	52	31
	1921		W	48	0	*	1993	4-	W	36	14
*	1948	1-	W	26	7		1994	8-	W	21	20
	1949	1-10	W	34	21	*	1997	-17	L	7	23
*	1950	-15	L	33	36		1998	10-	L	23	45
	1951	11-5	L	0	35	*	1999	24-	L	13	23
	1952	6-1	L	3	21		2000	16-23	L	21	27
*	1954	8-	W	20	19	*	2001	23-	L	10	17
	1955	4-13	L	7	21		2002	20-	W	21	17
*	1956	-2	L	14	47	*	2003		L	16	22
	1957	15-4	L	6	34		2004		W	31	24
	1959		L	0	19	*	2005	10-	L (OT)	41	44
*	1960	-14	L	0	21		2006	12-	W	40	37
	1961	6-1	L	7	17	*	2007		L	10	31
*	1962		L	7	31		2008		L	7	23
	1963	-4	L	7	12	*	2009	-18	W	34	38
*	1964	1 -	W	34	7		2010		L (OT)	31	34
*	1965	4-1	L	3	12			Total		1538	1175
								Avg. score		20.5	15.66
								Diff.		+4.84	

MINNESOTA
(4-0-1)

	1925		W	19	7
	1926		W	20	7
*	1927		T	7	7
	1937	-4	W	7	6
*	1938	2-12	W	19	0
		Total		72	27
		Avg. score		14.4	5.4
		Diff.		+9	

MISSISSIPPI
(1-1-0)

J	1977	3-	L	13	20
*	1985		W	37	14
		Total		50	34
		Avg. score		25	17
		Diff.		+8	

MISSOURI
(2-2-0)

	1970	3- 18	W	24	7
*	1972	8-	L	26	30
*	1978	5-	L	0	3
	1984	19-	W	16	14
		Total		66	54
		Avg. score		16.5	13.5
		Diff.		+3	

MISSOURI OSTEOPATHS
(1-0-0)

*	1903		W	28	0
		Total		28	0
		Avg. score		28	0
		Diff.		+28	

MORNINGSIDE
(2-0-0)

	1917		W	13	0
	1919		W	14	6
		Total		27	6
		Avg. score		13.5	3
		Diff.		+ 10.5	

MORRIS HARVEY
(1-0-0)

*	1912		W	39	0
		Total		39	0
		Avg. score		39	0
		Diff.		+39	

MOUNT UNION
(1-0-0)

*	1919		W	60	7
		Total		60	7
		Avg. score		60	7
		Diff.		+53	

NAVY
(72-12-1)

B	1927		W	19	6
SF	1928		W	7	0
B	1929		W	14	7
*	1930		W	26	2
B	1931		W	20	0
CL	1932		W	12	0
B	1933		L	0	7
CL	1934		L	6	10
B	1935		W	14	0
B	1936	13-	L	0	3
*	1937		W	9	7
B	1938	4-	W	15	0
CL	1939	2-	W	14	7
B	1940	7-	W	13	7
B	1941	7-6	W	20	13
CL	1942	4-	W	9	0
CL	1943	1 -3	W	33	6
B	1944	2-6	L	13	32
CL	1945	2-3	T	6	6
B	1946	2-	W	28	0
CL	1947	1 -	W	27	0
B	1948	2-	W	41	7
B	1949	1-	W	40	0
CL	1950		W	19	10
B	1951	13-	W	19	0
CL	1952	13-	W	17	6
*	1953	1 -20	W	38	7
B	1954	6-15	W	6	0

*	1955	9-4	W	21	7		GS	2004		W	27	9
B	1956		L	7	33		*	2005	7-	W	42	21
*	1957	5-16	L	6	20		RS	2006	11-	W	38	14
B	1958	-15	W	40	20		*	2007		L (3 OT)	44	46
*	1959		W	25	22		RS	2008		W	27	7
P	1960	-4	L	7	14		*	2009		L	21	23
*	1961		L	10	13		NM	2010		L	17	35
P	1962		W	20	12		*	2011		W	56	14
*	1963	-4	L	14	35			Total			2343	955
P	1964	2-	W	40	0			Avg. Score			27.56	11.23
*	1965	4-	W	29	3			Diff.			+16.33	
P	1966	1-	W	31	7							
*	1967	10-	W	43	14							
P	1968	12-	W	45	14				**NEBRASKA**			
*	1969	10-	W	47	0				**(7-8-1)**			
P	1970	3-	W	56	7							
*	1971	12-	W	21	0			1915		L	19	20
P	1972	12-	W	42	23			1916		W	20	0
*	1973	5-	W	44	7			1917		L	0	7
P	1974	7-	W	14	6			1918		T	0	0
*	1975	15-	W	31	10			1919		W	14	9
CL	1976	11-	W	27	21			1920		W	16	7
*	1977	5-	W	43	10		*	1921		W	7	0
CL	1978	15-11	W	27	7			1922		L	6	14
*	1979	13-	W	14	0			1923		L	7	14
GS	1980	3-	W	33	0		*	1924		W	34	6
*	1981		W	35	0			1925		L	0	17
GS	1982		W	27	10		*	1947	2-	W	31	0
*	1983	19-	W	28	12			1948	2-	W	44	13
GS	1984		W	18	17		OB	1972	12-9	L	6	40
*	1985		W	41	17		*	2000	23-1	L	24	27 (OT)
B	1986		W	33	14			2001	23-5	L	10	27
*	1987	9-	W	56	13			Total			238	201
B	1988	2-	W	22	7			Avg. score			14.88	12.56
*	1989	1-	W	41	0			Diff.			+2.32	
GS	1990	2-	W	52	31							
*	1991	5-	W	38	0							
GS	1992	10-	W	38	7				**NEVADA**			
VS	1993	2-	W	58	27				**(1-0-0)**			
*	1994		W	58	21							
*	1995	8-	W	35	17		*	2009		W	35	0
CP	1996	19-	W	54	27			Total			35	0
*	1997	W		21	17			Avg. Score			35	0
JC	1998	12-	W	30	0			Diff.			+35	
*	1999	W		28	24							
CIT	2000	20-	W	45	14				**NORTH CAROLINA**			
*	2001	W		34	16				**(16-2-0)**			
B	2002	9-	W	30	23		YS	1949	1-	W	42	6
*	2003		W	27	24		*	1950	1-20	W	14	7

	1951		W	12	7
*	1952	16-	W	34	14
	1953	1-	W	34	14
*	1954	5-	W	42	13
	1955	5-	W	27	7
*	1956		W	21	14
*	1958	-11	W	34	24
*	1959		W	28	8
	1960		L	7	12
*	1962		W	21	7
*	1965	4-	W	17	0
*	1966	2-	W	32	0
*	1971	7-	W	16	0
	1975	15-	W	21	14
*	2006	11-	W	45	26
	2008	-22	L	24	29
		Total		471	202
		Avg. score		26.16	11.22
		Diff.		+ 14.94	

NORTH CAROLINA STATE
(0-1-0)

GB	2003	11-17	L	6	28
		Total		6	28
		Avg. Score		6	28
		Diff.		-22	

NORTH DIVISION H.S.
(1-0-0)

*	1905		W	44	0
		Total		44	0
		Avg. score		44	0
		Diff.		+44	

NORTHWESTERN
(37-8-2)

	1899		W	9	0
*	1899		W	12	0
	1901		L	0	2
	1903		T	0	0
	1920		W	33	7
SF	1924		W	13	6
*	1925		W	13	10
	1926		W	6	0
	1929		W	26	6

	1930		W	14	0
SF	1931		T	0	0
*	1932		W	21	0
	1933		W	7	0
	1934		W	20	7
*	1935		L	7	14
*	1936	11-1	W	26	6
	1937	12-	W	7	0
	1938	1-16	W	9	7
*	1939	9-	W	7	0
	1940	14-10	L	0	20
	1941	5-8	W	7	6
*	1942	8-	W	27	20
	1943	1-8	W	25	6
*	1944	11-	W	21	0
	1945	7-	W	34	7
*	1946	2-	W	27	0
	1947	1-	W	26	19
*	1948	2-8	W	12	7
*	1959	-2	L	24	30
	1960		L	6	7
*	1961	8-	L	10	12
	1962	-3	L	6	35
*	1965	8-	W	38	7
	1966	4-	W	35	7
*	1968	5-	W	27	7
*	1969	11-	W	35	10
	1970	6-	W	35	14
*	1971	2-	W	50	7
	1972	13-	W	37	0
*	1973	8-	W	44	0
	1974	1-	W	49	3
*	1975	7-	W	31	7
	1976		W	48	0
SF	1992	3-	W	42	7
*	1993	7-	W	27	12
SF	1994	3-	W	42	15
*	1995	9-	L	15	17
		Total		1010	347
		Avg. score		21.48	7.38
		Diff.		+14.1	

NORTHWESTERN LAW SCHOOL
(1-0-0)

*	1895		W	20	0
		Total		20	0
		Avg. score		20	0
		Diff.		+20	

OHIO MEDICAL U.
(4-0-0)

1901	W	6	0
1902	W	6	5
1903	W	35	0
1904	W	17	5
Total		64	10
Avg. score		16	2.5
Diff.		+13.5	

OHIO NORTHERN
(4-0-0)

*	1908	W	58	4
*	1910	W	47	0
*	1911	W	32	6
*	1913	W	87	0
	Total		224	10
	Avg. score		56	2.5
	Diff.		+53 5	

OHIO STATE
(2-3-0)

	1935		W	18	13
*	1936		W	7	2
	1995	15-5	L	26	45
*	1996	5-4	L	16	29
FB	2005	5-4	L	20	34
	Total			87	123
	Avg. score			17.4	24.6
	Diff.			-7.2	

OKLAHOMA
(8-1-0)

*	1952	10-4	W	27	21
	1953	1-6	W	28	21
*	1956	-2	L	0	40
	1957	-2	W	7	0
*	1961		W	19	6
	1962		W	13	7
	1966	1-10	W	38	0
*	1968	3-5	W	45	21
*	1999	-23	W	34	30
	Total			211	146
	Avg. score			23.44	16.22
	Diff.			+7.22	

OLIVET
(3-0-0)

*	1907	W	22	4
	1909	W	58	0
*	1910	W	48	0
	Total		128	4
	Avg. score		42.66	1.33
	Diff.		+41.33	

OREGON
(1-0-1)

*	1976	14-	W	41	0
	1982	15-	T	13	13
	Total			54	13
	Avg. score			27	6.5
	Diff.			+20.5	

OREGON STATE
(0-2-0)

FB	2001	10-5	L	9	41
BB	2004		L	21	38
	Total			30	79
	Avg. Score			15	34.5
	Diff.			-19.5	

PACIFIC
(1-0-0)

*	1940	W	25	7
	Total		25	7
	Avg. score		25	7
	Diff.		+18	

PENN STATE
(9-9-1)

	1913		W	14	7
	1925		T	0	0
*	1926		W	28	0
P	1928		W	9	0
GB	1976	15-20	W	20	9
	1981	-13	L	21	24
*	1982	13-5	L	14	24
	1983		L	30	34
*	1984		W	44	7
	1985	- 1	L	6	36

*	1986	-3	L	19	24
	1987	7-	L	20	21
*	1988	1-	W	21	3
	1989	1-17	W	34	23
*	1990	1-18	L	21	24
	1991	12-8	L	13	35
*	1992	8-22	W	17	16
*	2006	4-19	W	41	17
	2007	-14	L	10	31
		Total		382	335
		Avg. score		20.1	17.63
		Diff.		+2.47	

PENNSYLVANIA
(5-0-1)

	1930		W	60	20
*	1931		W	49	0
	1952	10-12	T	7	7
	1953	1-15	W	28	20
	1954	5-	W	42	7
	1955	6-	W	46	14
		Total		232	68
		Avg. score		38.66	11.33
		Diff.		+27.33	

PITTSBURGH
(46-20-1)

	1909		W	6	0
	1911		T	0	0
	1912		W	3	0
	1930		W	35	19
*	1931		W	25	12
	1932		L	0	12
*	1933		L	0	14
	1934		L	0	19
*	1935		W	9	6
	1936	7-9	L	0	26
*	1937	12-3	L	6	21
	1943		W	41	0
	1944		W	58	0
	1945	3-	W	39	9
*	1946		W	33	0
	1947		W	40	6
	1948		W	40	0
*	1950		W	18	7
	1951		W	33	0
*	1952	8-	L	19	22
*	1953	1-15	W	23	14

	1954	8-	W	33	0
	1956	-20	L	13	26
*	1957	7-	W	13	7
	1958	14-	L	26	29
	1959		L	13	28
*	1960	-14	W	13	20
	1961		W	26	20
*	1962		W	43	22
*	1963	-8	L	7	27
	1964	1-	W	17	15
	1965	4-	W	69	13
*	1966	1 -	W	40	0
	1967	9-	W	38	0
*	1968	12-	W	56	7
	1969	8-	W	49	7
*	1970	2-	W	46	14
	1971	8-	W	56	7
*	1972	7-	W	42	16
	1973	5-20	W	31	10
*	1974	5-17	W	14	10
	1975	9-	L	20	34
*	1976	11-9	L	10	31
	1977	3-7	W	19	9
*	1978	-9	W	26	17
	1982	-1	W	31	16
*	1983	18-	L	16	21
*	1986		L	9	10
	1987	4-	L	22	30
	1988	5-	W	30	20
*	1989	1-7	W	45	7
	1990	3-	W	31	22
*	1991	7-12	W	42	7
	1992	14-	W	52	21
*	1993	4-	W	44	0
*	1996	14-	W	60	6
	1997		W	45	21
	1999	13-	L	27	37
*	2001		W	24	7
*	2002	8-	W	14	6
	2003	-15	W	20	14
*	2004	24-	L	38	41
	2005	-23	W	42	21
*	2008		L (4 OT)	33	36
	2009	-8	L	22	27
*	2010		W	20	16
	2011		W	15	12
		Total		1830	954
		Avg. score		21.03	10.96
		Diff.		+10.07	

PRINCETON
(2-0-0)

1923		W	25	2
1924		W	12	0
	Total		37	2
	Avg. score		18.5	1
	Diff.		+17.5	

PURDUE
(55-26-2)

*	1896		L	22	28
	1899		T	10	10
*	1901		W	12	6
	1902		T	6	6
	1904		L	0	36
	1905		L	0	32
	1906		W	2	0
*	1907		W	17	0
	1918		W	26	6
	1919		W	33	13
*	1920		W	28	0
	1921		W	33	0
	1922		W	20	0
*	1923		W	34	7
*	1933		L	0	19
*	1934		W	18	7
*	1939		W	3	0
*	1946	3-	W	49	6
	1947	1-	W	22	7
*	1948		W	28	27
	1949	2-	W	35	12
*	1950	1-	L	14	28
	1951	15-	W	30	9
	1952	-9	W	26	14
	1953	1-	W	37	7
*	1954	1-19	L	14	27
	1955	11-	W	22	7
*	1956	18-	L	14	28
	1957		W	12	0
*	1958	11-15	L	22	29
	1959	8-	L	7	28
*	1960	12-	L	19	51
	1961		W	22	20
*	1962		L	6	24
	1963		L	6	7
*	1964	9-	W	34	15
	1965	1-6	L	21	25
*	1966	6-8	W	26	14

	1967	1-10	L	21	28
*	1968	2-1	L	22	37
	1969	9-16	L	14	28
*	1970	6-	W	48	0
	1971	2-	W	8	7
*	1972	10-	W	35	14
	1973	7-	W	20	7
*	1974	2-	L	20	31
	1975	9-	W	17	0
*	1976		W	23	0
	1977	11-	W	31	24
*	1978		W	10	6
	1979	5- 17	L	22	28
*	1980	11-9	W	31	10
	1981	13-	L	14	15
*	1982	10-	W	28	14
	1983	5-	W	52	6
HD	1984	8-	L	21	23
	1985		L	17	35
*	1986		W	41	9
	1987	8-	W	44	20
*	1988	8-	W	52	7
	1989	1-	W	40	7
*	1990	1-	W	37	11
	1991	5-	W	45	20
*	1992	6-	W	48	0
	1993	4-	W	17	0
*	1994	8-	W	39	21
	1995	25-	W	35	28
*	1996	9-	W	35	0
	1997	12-	L	17	28
*	1998	23-	W	31	30
	1999	16-20	L	23	28
*	2000	21-13	W	23	21
	2001		W	24	18
*	2002	23-	W	24	17
	2003	-22	L	10	23
*	2004	-15	L	16	41
	2005	13-22	W	49	28
*	2006	12-	W	35	21
	2007		L	19	33
*	2008		W	38	21
	2009		W	24	21
*	2010		W	23	12
*	2011		W	38	10
	Total			2011	1343
	Avg. score			24.22	16.18
	Diff.			+8.04	

RICE
(4-0-0)

	1915		W	55	2
	1973	9-	W	28	0
*	1974	6-	W	10	3
*	1988	1-	W	54	11
		Total		147	16
		Avg. score		36.75	4
		Diff.		+32.75	

ROSE POLY
(3-0-0)

*	1909	W	60	11
	1910	W	41	3
*	1914	W	103	0
	Total		204	14
	Avg. score		68	4.66
	Diff.		+63.34	

RUSH MEDICAL
(3-0-1)

*	1894	W	18	6
*	1897	T	0	0
*	1899	W	17	0
	1900	W	5	0
	Total		40	6
	Avg. score		10	1.5
	Diff.		+8.5	

RUTGERS
(4-0-0)

PG	1921		W	48	0
*	1996	10-	W	62	0
	2000	11-	W	45	17
*	2002	8-	W	42	0
		Total		197	17
		Avg. Score		49.25	4.25
		Diff.		+45	

SAN DIEGO STATE
(1-0-0)

*	2008	W	21	13
	Total		21	13
	Avg. score		21	13
	Diff.		+8	

ST. BONAVENTURE
(1-0-0)

*	1911	W	34	0
	Total		34	0
	Avg. score		34	0
	Diff.		+34	

ST. LOUIS
(3-0-0)

	1912	W	47	7
*	1922	W	26	0
	1923	W	13	0
	Total		86	7
	Avg. score		28.66	2.33
	Diff.		+26.33	

ST. VIATOR
(4-0-0)

*	1897	W	60	0
*	1908	W	46	0
*	1911	W	43	0
*	1912	W	116	7
	Total		265	7
	Avg. score		66.25	1.75
	Diff.		+64.5	

ST. VINCENT'S (CHICAGO)
(1-0-0)

	1907	W	21	12
	Total		21	12
	Avg. score		21	12
	Diff.		+9	

SOUTH BEND A.C.
(1-0-1)

*	1901	T	0	0
*	1901	W	22	6
	Total		22	6
	Avg. score		13	3
	Diff.		+ 10	

SOUTH BEND COMMERCIAL A.C.
(1-0-0)

*	1896	W	46	0
		Total	46	0
		Avg. score	46	0
		Diff.	+46	

SOUTH BEND H.S.
(1-0-0)

*	1892	W	56	0
		Total	56	0
		Avg. score	56	0
		Diff.	+56	

SOUTH BEND HOWARD PARK
(1-0-0)

*	1900	W	64	0
		Total	64	0
		Avg. score	64	0
		Diff.	+64	

SOUTH CAROLINA
(3-1-0)

	1976	12-19	W	13	6
*	1979	14-	W	18	17
	1983		W	30	6
*	1984	-11	L	32	36
		Total		93	65
		Avg. score		23.25	16.25
		Diff.		+7	

SOUTH DAKOTA
(5-0-0)

*	1913		W	20	7
SFS	1914		W	33	0
*	1915		W	6	0
SFS	1916		W	21	0
*	1917		W	40	0
		Total		120	7
		Avg. score		24	1.75
		Diff.		+22.25	

SOUTH FLORIDA
(0-1-0)

*	2011	16-	L	20	23
		Total		20	23
		Avg. score		20	23
		Diff.		-3	

SOUTHERN METHODIST
(10-3-0)

*	1930		W	20	14
*	1939		W	20	19
	1949	1-	W	27	20
*	1951	5-	L	20	27
*	1953	2-	W	40	14
	1954	4-	W	26	14
*	1955	11-	W	17	0
	1956	3-	L	13	19
	1957	10-	W	54	21
	1958	7-17	W	14	6
AS	1984	17-10	L	20	27
*	1986		W	61	29
*	1989	1-	W	59	6
		Total		391	216
		Avg. score		30.07	16.61
		Diff.		+ 13.46	

STANFORD
(17-9-0)

RB	1924		W	27	10
*	1942		W	27	0
	1963		L	14	24
*	1964	2-	W	28	6
*	1988	5-	W	42	14
	1989	1-	W	27	17
*	1990	1-	L	31	36
	1991	8-	W	42	26
*	1992	7-19	L	16	33
	1993	4-	W	48	20
*	1994	8-	W	34	15
	1997	-19	L	15	33
*	1998	23-	W	35	17

1999		L	37	40
* 2000	25-	W	20	14
2001	-13	L	13	17
* 2002	9-	W	31	17
2003		W	57	7
* 2004		W	23	15
2005	6-	W	38	31
* 2006	12-	W	31	10
2007		W	21	14
* 2008		W	28	21
2009		L	38	45
* 2010	-16	L	14	37
2011	-4	L	14	28
Total			751	547
Avg. score			28.88	21.03
Diff.			+7.85	

SYRACUSE
(3-3-0)

1914		W	20	0
* 1961	-10	W	17	15
YS 1963		L	7	14
2003		L	12	38
* 2005	6-	W	34	10
* 2008		L	23	24
Total			113	101
Avg. score			18.83	16.83
Diff.			+2	

TENNESSEE
(4-4-0)

* 1978	14-	W	31	14
1979	13-	L	18	40
1990	1-9	W	34	29
* 1991	5-13	L	34	35
1999	24-4	L	14	38
* 2001	-7	L	18	28
2004	-9	W	17	13
* 2005	8-	W	41	21
Total			207	218
Avg. Score			25.87	27.25
Diff.			-1.38	

TEXAS
(8-2-0)

1913		W	30	7
1915		W	36	7

* 1934		L	6	7
1952	19-5	W	14	3
* 1954	2-4	W	21	0
CB 1969	9-1	L	17	21
CB 1970	6-1	W	24	11
CB 1977	5- 1	W	38	10
* 1995	21-10	W	55	27
1996	9-6	W	27	24
Total			268	117
Avg. Score			26.8	11.7
Diff.			+15.1	

TEXAS A&M
(3-2-0)

CB 1987	12-13	L	10	35
CB 1992	5-4	W	28	3
CB 1993	4-7	W	24	21
* 2000	-23	W	24	10
2001		L	3	24
Total			89	93
Avg. score			17.8	18.6
Diff.			-0.8	

TEXAS CHRISTIAN
(1-0-0)

* 1972	13-	W	21	0
Total			21	0
Avg. score			21	0
Diff.			+21	

TOLEDO A.A.
(1-0-0)

* 1904		W	6	0
Total			6	0
Avg. score			6	0
Diff.			+6	

TULANE
(8-0-0)

* 1944		W	26	0
1945	5-	W	32	6
1946	2-	W	41	0
* 1947	2-	W	59	6
* 1949	1-4	W	46	7
1950	10-	W	13	9

	1969	12-	W	37	0
*	1971	8-	W	21	7
		Total		275	35
		Avg. score		34.37	4.37
		Diff.		+30	

TULSA
(0-1-0)

*	2011		L	27	28
		Total		27	28
		Avg. score		27	28
		Diff.		-1	

UCLA
(2-0-0)

*	1963		W	27	12
*	1964	4-	W	24	0
		Total		51	12
		Avg. score		25.5	6
		Diff.		+19.5	

SOUTHERN CALIFORNIA
(43-35-5)

	1926		W	13	12
SF	1927		W	7	6
	1928		L	14	27
SF	1929		W	13	12
	1930		W	27	0
*	1931		L	14	16
	1932		L	0	13
*	1933		L	0	19
	1934		W	14	0
*	1935		W	20	13
	1936	9-	T	13	13
*	1937	9-	W	13	6
	1938	1-8	L	0	13
*	1939	7-4	L	12	20
	1940		W	10	6
*	1941	4-	W	20	18
	1942	8-14	W	13	0
*	1946	2-16	W	26	6
	1947	1-3	W	38	7
	1948	2-	T	14	14
*	1949	1-17	W	32	0
	1950		L	7	9
	1951	-20	W	19	12
*	1952	7-2	W	9	0

	1953	2-20	W	48	14
*	1954	4-17	W	23	17
	1955	5-	L	20	42
	1956	- 17	L	20	28
*	1957	12-	W	40	12
	1958	18-	W	20	13
*	1959	-7	W	16	6
	1960		W	17	0
*	1961	8-	W	30	0
	1962	-1	L	0	25
*	1963	-7	W	17	14
	1964	1-	L	17	20
*	1965	7-4	W	28	7
	1966	1-10	W	51	0
*	1967	5- 1	L	7	24
	1968	9-2	T	21	21
*	1969	11-3	T	14	14
	1970	4-	L	28	38
*	1971	6-	L	14	28
	1972	10- 1	L	23	45
*	1973	8-6	W	23	14
	1974	5-6	L	24	55
*	1975	14-3	L	17	24
	1976	13-3	L	13	17
*	1977	11-5	W	49	19
	1978	8-3	L	25	27
*	1979	9-4	L	23	42
	1980	2- 17	L	3	20
*	1981	-5	L	7	14
	1982	-17	L	13	17
*	1983		W	27	6
	1984	-14	W	19	7
*	1985		W	37	3
	1986	-17	W	38	37
*	1987	10-	W	26	15
	1988	1-2	W	27	10
*	1989	1-9	W	28	24
	1990	7-18	W	10	6
*	1991	5	W	24	20
	1992	5-19	W	31	23
*	1993	2-	W	31	13
	1994	-17	T	17	17
*	1995	17-5	W	38	10
	1996	10-	L	20	27 (OT)
*	1997		L	17	20
	1998	9-	L	0	10
*	1999		W	25	24
	2000	11-	W	38	21
*	2001		W	27	16

	2002	7-6	L	13	44
*	2003	-5	L	14	45
	2004	-1	L	10	41
*	2005	9-1	L	31	34
	2006	6-3	L	24	44
*	2007	-13	L	0	38
	2008	-5	L	3	38
*	2009	-6	L	27	34
	2010		W	20	16
*	2011		L	17	31
	Total			1638	1533
	Avg. score			19.73	18.46
	Diff.			+1.27	

UTAH
(1-0-0)

*	2010	-15	W	28	3
	Total			28	3
	Avg. score			28	3
	Diff.			+25	

VALPARAISO
(1-0-0)

*	1920		W	28	3
	Total			28	3
	Avg. score			28	3
	Diff.			+25	

VANDERBILT
(2-0-0)

*	1995	24-	W	41	0
	1996	6-	W	14	7
	Total			55	7
	Avg. score			27.5	3.5
	Diff.			+24	

VIRGINIA
(1-0-0)

GS	1989		W	36	13
	Total			36	13
	Avg. score			36	13
	Diff.			+23	

WABASH
(10-1-0)

*	1894		W	30	0
	1903		W	35	0
*	1904		W	12	4
*	1905		L	0	5
	1908		W	8	4
*	1909		W	38	0
	1911		W	6	3
*	1912		W	41	6
*	1916		W	60	0
	1918		W	67	7
*	1924		W	34	0
	Total			331	29
	Avg. score			30.09	2.63
	Diff.			+27.46	

WAKE FOREST
(1-0-0)

	2011	W	24	17
	Total		24	17
	Avg. score		24	17
	Diff.		+7	

WASHINGTON
(8-0-0)

*	1948	2-	W	46	0
	1949		W	27	7
	1995	23-15	W	29	21
*	1996	11-16	W	54	20
*	2004		W	38	3
	2005	16-	W	36	17
*	2008		W	33	7
	2009		W (OT)	37	30
	Total			300	105
	Avg. Score			37.5	13.12
	Diff.			+24.38	

WASHINGTON STATE
(2-0-0)

*	2003	19-	W (OT)	29	26
SA	2009		W	40	14
	Total			69	40
	Avg. score			34.5	20
	Diff.			+14.5	

WASHINGTON & JEFFERSON
(1-0-0)

1917		W	3	0
	Total		3	0
	Avg. score		3	0
	Diff.		+3	

WASHINGTON (ST. LOUIS)
(1-0-0)

*	1936	W	14	6
	Total		14	6
	Avg. score		14	6
	Diff.		+8	

WESTERN MICHIGAN
(3-0-0)

*	1919	W	53	0
*	1920	W	41	0
*	2010	W	44	20
	Total		138	20
	Avg. score		46	6.66
	Diff.		+39.34	

WESTERN RESERVE
(1-0-0)

1916		W	48	0
	Total		48	0
	Avg. score		48	0
	Diff.		+48	

WEST VIRGINIA
(4-0-0)

FB	1988	1-3	W	34	21
*	1997	-22	W	21	14
	2000	20-	W	42	28
*	2001		W	34	24
	Total			131	87
	Avg. Score			32.75	21.75
	Diff.			+11	

WISCONSIN
(8-6-2)

	1900		L	0	54
M	1904		L	0	58
M	1905		L	0	21
	1917		T	0	0
	1924		W	38	3
	1928		L	6	22
SF	1929		W	19	0
*	1934		W	19	0
	1935		W	27	0
*	1936		W	27	0
	1942		T	7	7
	1943	1-	W	50	0
*	1944	1 -	W	28	13
	1962		L	8	17
*	1963	-6	L	9	14
	1964		W	31	7
	Total			269	216
	Avg. score			16.81	13.5
	Diff.			+3.31	

YALE
(0-1-0)

1914		L	0	28
	Total		0	28
	Avg. score		0	28
	Diff.		-28	

Totals for 1190 games: 848–300–42 (.730)

Cum. Points: ND: 29,878   OPP: 14,652
Cum. avg. score: ND: 25.00   OPP: 12.26
Cum. diff. +12.74

KEY TO NEUTRAL SITES

AS Aloha Stadium (Honolulu)
B   Baltimore
BB Insight Bowl, Bank One Ballpark (Phoenix)
BM Birmingham
BS Briggs Stadium
C   Chicago
CB Cotton Bowl
CIT Citrus Bowl
CL Cleveland
CP Croke Park (Dublin, Ireland)
EB Ebbets Field
ERC Eddie Robinson Classic
FB Fiesta Bowl
FP Fenway Park (Boston)
FX Schaefer Stadium (Foxboro)
GB Gator Bowl
GS Giants Stadium (E. Rutherford, NJ.)
HB Hawaii Bowl (Honolulu)
HD Hoosier Dome (Indianapolis)
I   Indianapolis
IS Independence Bowl (Shreveport)
J   Jackson (Mississippi)
JC Jack Kent Cooke Stadium (Raljon, MD)
LB Liberty Bowl
M   Milwaukee
MB Mirage Bowl (Tokyo)
NM New Meadowlands Stadium (E. Rutherford, N.J.)
NYS New Yankee Stadium (New York)
OB Orange Bowl
P   Philadelphia
PG Polo Grounds
RB Rose Bowl
RS Raven Stadium (Baltimore)
SA Alamo Dome (San Antonio)
SB Sugar Bowl (Tulane)
SBS Sun Bowl (El Paso)
SD Sugar Bowl (Superdome, N. O.)
SF Soldier Field
SFS Sioux Falls
SS Shea Stadium
T   Toledo
YS Yankee Stadium

AWARDS RECEIVED BY NOTRE DAME COACHES AND PLAYERS

No school matches the Irish for Heisman winners, and few are peers regarding the other major awards for excellence. Here are the winners:

The Heisman (outstanding college football player):

1943: Angelo Bertelli
1947: John Lujack
1949: Leon Hart
1953: John Lattner*
1956: Paul Hornung
1964: John Huarte
1987: Tim Brown

* Lattner's award gave Leahy the unbeatable record of having produced no less than four Heisman winners, three of whom played together (Bertelli and Lujack in '43, Lujack and Hart in '47). Hart is one of only two linemen to win the Heisman. Leahy, furthermore, recruited Hornung, but did not coach him during his three varsity seasons.

The Lombardi Award (outstanding lineman):

1971: Walt Patulski
1977: Ross Browner
1990: Chris Zorich
1993: Aaron Taylor

The Outland Trophy (outstanding interior lineman):

1946: George Connor
1948: Bill Fischer
1976: Ross Browner

The Walter Camp Award (to the top individual in college football):

1977: Ken MacAfee
1987: Tim Brown
1990: Raghib Ismail

The Maxwell Award (to the top college player):

1949: Leon Hart
1952 and 1953: Johnny Lattner
1966: Jim Lynch
1977: Ross Browner
2006: Brady Quinn

Coach of the Year:

1941: Frank Leahy (Am. Football Coaches Assoc).
1966: Ara Parseghian (Am. Football Coaches Assoc.)
1988: Lou Holtz (Football Writers)

Hall of Fame Coaches:

1951: Knute Rockne
1970: Frank Leahy
1971: Jesse Harper
1980: Ara Parseghian
1985: Dan Devine
2008: Lou Holtz

Others:

• Forty-three Notre Dame players in the National Football Foundation Hall of Fame (the most of any school).

• Eight former Irish players are in the Hall as coaches.

• Twenty-nine Irish players have been honored, winning 35 times, as top scholar athletes in the country since 1952 (the most from any school).

• Seventeen Notre Dame players have earned NCAA post-grad scholarships since 1964.

• Fourteen Notre Dame players have earned National Football Foundation and Hall of Fame scholarships for postgraduate study (the most chosen from any school).

• Notre Dame has been honored five times for having the highest graduation rate in a year for CFA members: 1982, 1983, 1984, 1988, 1991(120 of 138, 86.9 percent). Notre Dame consistently ranks in the top three. For all sports, the NCAA reported that Notre Dame graduated 99% of its athletes in a 2010 report.

• As of 2012, 467 Irish players have been drafted by the NFL since 1936.

• The Irish have nine former players in the NFL Hall of Fame.

CHAPTER SEVEN

FIGHTING IRISH RECORDS

This chapter is reproduced from the *Notre Dame 2011 Media Guide*, courtesy of the University of Notre Dame Athletic Media Relations Office.

NOTRE DAME INDIVIDUAL RECORDS

* denotes a Notre Dame record

RUSHING

YEAR-BY-YEAR LEADERS

		Rushes	Yards
1918	George Gipp	98	541
1919	George Gipp	106	729
1920	George Gipp	102	827
1921	John Mohardt	136	781
1922	Jim Crowley	75	566
1923	Don Miller	89	698
1924	Don Miller	107	763
1925	Christie Flanagan	99	556
1926	Christie Flanagan	68	535
1927	Christie Flanagan	118	731
1928	Jack Chevigny	120	539
1929	Joe Savoldi	112	597
1930	Marchy Schwartz	124	927
1931	Marchy Schwartz	146	692
1932	George Melinkovich	88	503
1933	Nick Lukats	107	339
1934	George Melinkovich	73	324
1935	Bill Shakespeare	104	374
1936	Bob Wilke	132	434
1937	Bunny McCormick	91	347
1938	Bob Saggau	60	353
1939	Milt Piepul	82	414
1940	Steve Juzwik	71	407
1941	Fred Evans	141	490

		Rushes	Yards
1942	Corwin Clatt	138	698
1943	Creighton Miller	151	911
1944	Bob Kelly	136	681
1945	Elmer Angsman	87	616
1946	Emil Sitko	53	346
1947	Emil Sitko	60	426
1948	Emil Sitko	129	742
1949	Emil Sitko	120	712
1950	Jack Landry	109	491
1951	Neil Worden	181	676
1952	John Lattner	148	732
1953	Neil Worden	145	859
1954	Don Schaefer	141	766
1955	Don Schaefer	145	638
1956	Paul Hornung	94	420
1957	Nick Pietrosante	90	449
1958	Nick Pietrosante	117	549
1959	Gerry Gray	50	256
1960	Angelo Dabiero	80	325
1961	Angelo Dabiero	92	637
1962	Don Hogan	90	454
1963	Joe Kantor	88	330
1964	Bill Wolski	136	657
1965	Nick Eddy	115	582
1966	Nick Eddy	78	553
1967	Jeff Zimmerman	133	591
1968	Bob Gladieux	152	713
1969	Denny Allan	148	612
1970	Ed Gulyas	118	534

		Rushes	Yards			Rushes	Yards
1971	Bob Minnix	78	337	1992	Reggie Brooks	167	1,343
1972	Eric Penick	124	726	1993	Lee Becton	164	1,044
1973	Wayne Bullock	162	752	1994	Randy Kinder	119	702
1974	Wayne Bullock	203	855	1995	Randy Kinder	143	809
1975	Jerome Heavens	129	756	1996	Autry Denson	202	1,179
1976	Al Hunter	233	1,058	1997	Autry Denson	264	1,268
1977	Jerome Heavens	229	994	1998	Autry Denson	251	1,176
1978	Vagas Ferguson	211	1,192	1999	Tony Fisher	156	783
1979	Vagas Ferguson	*301	*1,437	2000	Julius Jones	162	657
1980	Jim Stone	192	908	2001	Julius Jones	168	718
1981	Phil Carter	165	727	2002	Ryan Grant	240	1,017
1982	Phil Carter	179	715	2003	Julius Jones	229	1,341
1983	Allen Pinkett	252	1,394	2004	Darius Walker	185	786
1984	Allen Pinkett	275	1,105	2005	Darius Walker	253	1,196
1985	Allen Pinkett	255	1,100	2006	Darius Walker	255	1,267
1986	Mark Green	96	406	2007	James Aldridge	121	463
1987	Mark Green	146	861	2008	Armando Allen	134	585
1988	Tony Rice	121	700	2009	Armando Allen	142	697
1989	Tony Rice	174	884	2010	Cierre Wood	119	603
1990	Rodney Culver	150	710	2011	Cierre Wood	217	1,102
1991	Jerome Bettis	168	972				

Rushing Attempts

Game: 40   Allen Pinkett (162 yards) vs. LSU, 1984; Phil Carter (254 yards) vs. Michigan State, 1980

Season: 301   Vagas Ferguson (1437 yards), 1979; also holds per-game record at 27.4 (301 in 11)

Career: 889   Allen Pinkett (4131 yards), 1982-85; also holds per-game record at 20.6 (889 in 43)

Consecutive Rushing Attempts by Same Player

Game: 8   Mark Green vs. Boston College, 1987; Phil Carter vs. Air Force, 1980; Larry Conjar vs. Army, 1965; Neil Worden vs. Oklahoma, 1952; James Aldridge vs. Navy, 2006

Rushing Yards

Game: 262   Julius Jones (24 attempts) at Pittsburgh, 2003

Season: 1437   Vagas Ferguson (301 attempts), 1979

Career: 4318   Autry Denson (854 attempts), 1995-98

Rushing Yards Per Game

Season: 130.6   Vagas Ferguson (1437 in 11), 1979

Career: 96.1   Allen Pinkett (4131 in 43), 1982-85

Games Rushing for 100 Yards or More

Season: 9   Allen Pinkett, 1983

Career: 22   Autry Denson, 1995-98

Consecutive Games Rushing for 100 Yards or More

Season: 6   Lee Becton, 1993 (Pittsburgh, BYU, USC, Navy, FSU, BC)

Games Rushing for 200 Yards or More
Season: 3   Julius Jones, 2003 (Pittsburgh, Navy, Stanford)

Rushing Yards by a Freshman
Game: 148   Jerome Heavens (18 attempts) vs. Georgia Tech, 1975
Season: 786   Darius Walker (185 attempts), 2004

Rushing Yards by a Quarterback
Game: 146   Bill Etter (11 attempts) vs. Navy 1969
Season: 884   Tony Rice (174 attempts), 1989
Career: 1921   Tony Rice (394 attempts), 1987-89; holds career per-game record at 58.2 (1921 in 33), 1987-89

Rushing Yards Per Attempt
Game: (min. 10 attempts)   17.1   John Petibon (10 for 171) vs. MSU, 1950
Game: (min. 5 attempts)   24.4   Coy McGee (6 for 146) vs. USC, 1946
Season: (min. 100 attempts)   8.10   George Gipp (102 for 827), 1920
Career: (min. 150 attempts)   7.6   Reggie Brooks (198 for 1,508), 1989-92

Rushing Touchdowns
Game: 7   Art Smith vs. Loyola (Chi.), 1911
Season: 17   Allen Pinkett, 1984; Vagas Ferguson, 1979
Career: 49   Allen Pinkett, 1982-85

PASSING

YEAR-BY-YEAR LEADERS

Year	Player	Att.	Comp.	Yards	TD
1918	George Gipp	45	19	293	1
1919	George Gipp	72	41	727	3
1920	George Gipp	62	30	709	3
1921	John Mohardt	98	53	995	9
1922	Jim Crowley	21	10	154	1
1923	Jim Crowley	36	13	154	1
1924	Harry Stuhldreher	33	25	471	4
1925	Harry O'Boyle	21	7	107	0
1926	Christie Flanagan	29	12	207	0
1927	John Niemiec	33	14	187	0
1928	John Niemiec	108	37	456	3
1929	Jack Elder	25	8	187	1
1930	Marchy Schwartz	56	17	319	3
1931	Marchy Schwartz	51	9	174	3
1932	Nick Lukats	28	13	252	2
1933	Nick Lukats	67	21	329	0
1934	Bill Shakespeare	29	9	230	2
1935	Bill Shakespeare	66	19	267	3
1936	Bob Wilke	52	19	365	2
1937	Jack McCarthy	53	16	225	3
1938	Bob Saggau	28	8	179	3
1939	Harry Stevenson	50	14	236	1
1940	Bob Saggau	60	21	483	4
1941	Angelo Bertelli	123	70	1027	8
1942	Angelo Bertelli	159	72	1039	10
1943	Johnny Lujack	71	34	525	4
1944	Frank Dancewicz	163	68	989	9
1945	Frank Dancewicz	90	30	489	5
1946	Johnny Lujack	100	49	778	6
1947	Johnny Lujack	109	61	777	9
1948	Frank Tripucka	91	53	660	11
1949	Bob Williams	147	83	1374	16
1950	Bob Williams	210	99	1035	10
1951	John Mazur	110	48	645	5
1952	Ralph Guglielmi	143	62	725	4
1953	Ralph Guglielmi	113	52	792	8
1954	Ralph Guglielmi	127	68	1162	6
1955	Paul Hornung	103	46	743	9
1956	Paul Hornung	111	59	917	3
1957	Bob Williams	106	53	565	3
1958	George Izo	118	68	1067	9
1959	George Izo	95	44	661	6
1960	George Haffner	108	30	548	3
1961	Frank Budka	95	40	636	3

		Att.	Comp.	Yards	TD			Att.	Comp.	Yards	TD
1962	Daryle Lamonica	128	64	821	6	1987	Tony Rice	82	35	663	1
1963	Frank Budka	40	21	239	4	1988	Tony Rice	138	70	1176	8
1964	John Huarte	205	114	2062	16	1989	Tony Rice	137	68	1122	2
1965	Bill Zloch	88	36	558	3	1990	Rick Mirer	200	110	1824	8
1966	Terry Hanratty	147	78	1247	8	1991	Rick Mirer	234	132	2117	18
1967	Terry Hanratty	206	110	1439	9	1992	Rick Mirer	234	120	1876	15
1968	Terry Hanratty	197	116	1466	10	1993	Kevin McDougal	159	98	1541	7
1969	Joe Theismann	192	108	1531	13	1994	Ron Powlus	222	119	1729	*19
1970	Joe Theismann	268	155	2429	16	1995	Ron Powlus	217	124	1853	12
1971	Cliff Brown	111	56	669	4	1996	Ron Powlus	232	133	1942	12
1972	Tom Clements	162	83	1163	8	1997	Ron Powlus	298	182	2078	9
1973	Tom Clements	113	60	882	8	1998	Jarious Jackson	188	104	1740	13
1974	Tom Clements	215	122	1549	8	1999	Jarious Jackson	316	184	2753	17
1975	Rick Slager	139	66	686	2	2000	Matt LoVecchio	125	73	980	11
1976	Rick Slager	172	86	1281	11	2001	Carlyle Holiday	144	73	784	3
1977	Joe Montana	189	99	1604	11	2002	Carlyle Holiday	251	126	1766	10
1978	Joe Montana	260	141	2010	10	2003	Brady Quinn	411	195	2,149	9
1979	Rusty Lisch	208	108	1781	4	2004	Brady Quinn	353	191	2,586	17
1980	Blair Kiel	124	48	531	0	2005	Brady Quinn	450	*292	*3,919	32
1981	Blair Kiel	151	67	936	7	2006	Brady Quinn	*467	289	3,426	*37
1982	Blair Kiel	219	118	1273	3	2007	Jimmy Clausen	245	138	1,254	7
1983	Steve Beuerlein	145	75	1061	4	2008	Jimmy Clausen	440	268	3,172	25
1984	Steve Beuerlein	232	140	1920	7	2009	Jimmy Clausen	425	289	3,722	28
1985	Steve Beuerlein	214	107	1335	3	2010	Dayne Crist	294	174	2,033	15
1986	Steve Beuerlein	259	151	2211	13	2011	Tommy Rees	411	269	2,871	20

Pass Attempts

Game:	63	Terry Hanratty (completed 29) vs. Purdue, 1967
Season:	467	Brady Quinn (completed 289), 2006
Career:	1602	Brady Quinn (completed 929), 2003-06

Pass Attempts Per Game

Season:	37.5	Brady Quinn (450 in 12), 2005
Career:	32.7	Brady Quinn (1602 in 49), 2003-06

Pass Completions

Game:	37	Jimmy Clausen (attempted 51) v. Navy, 2009
Season:	292	Brady Quinn (attempted 450), 2005
Career:	929	Brady Quinn (attempted 1602), 2003-06

Pass Completions Per Game

Season:	24.3	Brady Quinn (292 in 12), 2005
Career:	19.9	Jimmy Clausen (695 in 35), 2007-09

Consecutive Pass Completions

Game:	14	Ron Powlus v. MSU, 1997; Brady Quinn v. Ohio State, Fiesta Bowl, 2005
Season:	14	Ron Powlus v. MSU, 1997; Brady Quinn v. Ohio State, Fiesta Bowl, 2005

Consecutive Games Completing a Pass
Career: 49   Brady Quinn (12 games in 2003, 12 in 2004, 12 in 2005, 13 in 2006)

Completion Percentage
Game: (min. 10 completions)   .909   Steve Beuerlein (10 of 11) vs. Colorado, 1984
Season: (min. 100 attempts)   .680   Jimmy Clausen (289 of 425), 2009
Career: (min. 150 attempts)   .626   Jimmy Clausen (695 of 1110), 2007-09

Highest Passing Efficiency Rating
Season: (min. 50 completions)   161.42   Jimmy Clausen (429-289, 3,722 yards, 28 TD passes), 1949
    (min. 100 completions)   155.1   John Huarte (114-205, 11 INTs, 2,062 yards 16 TDs), 1964
Career: (min. 100 completions)   154.4   Kevin McDougal (112-180, 6 INTs, 1,726 yards, 10 TDs), 1990-93

Passes Had Intercepted
Game: 7   Frank Dancewicz vs. Army, 1944
Season: 18   Steve Beuerlein 1984; John Niemiec, 1928; also holds season per-game record at 1.8 (16 in nine)
Career: 44   Steve Beuerlein 1983-86; Terry Hanratty holds career per-game record at 1.3 (34 in 26), 1966-68

Lowest Interception Percentage
Season: (min. 100 attempts)   .0150   Brady Quinn (seven of 476), 2006
Career: (min. 200 attempts)   .02434   Brady Quinn (39 of 1602), 2003-06

Pass Attempts Without Interception
Game: 47   Brady Quinn v. BYU, 2004

Consecutive Pass Attempts Without Interception
Career: 226   Brady Quinn, Michigan State 2006 through Army 2006

Passing yards
Game: 536   Joe Theismann (33 of 58) vs. USC, 1970
Season: 3,919   Brady Quinn (292 of 450), 2005
Career: 11,762   Brady Quinn (929 of 1602), 2003-06

Passing Yards Per Game
Season: 326.6   Brady Quinn (3,919 in 12), 2005
Career: 340.0   Brady Quinn (11,762 in 49), 2003-06

Passing Yards Per Attempt
Game: (min. 20 attempts)   17.5   Jimmy Clausen (18 for 315) vs. Nevada, 2009
Season: (min. 100 attempts)   10.1   John Huarte (205 for 2062), 1964
Career: 9.58   Kevin McDougal (180 for 1726), 1990-93

Passing Yards Per Completion
Game: (min. 10 completions)   27.4   John Huarte (10 for 274) vs. Navy, 1964
Season: (min. 50 completions)   18.1   John Huarte (114 for 2,062), 1964
Career: (min. 75 completions)   17.3   George Izo (121 for 2,095), 1957-59

Touchdown Passes

Game: 6   Brady Quinn v. BYU, 2005
Season: 37   Brady Quinn, 2006 (13 games)
Career: 95   Brady Quinn, 2003-06 (49 games)

Touchdown Passes Per Game

Season: 2.85   Brady Quinn (37 in 13), 2006
Career: 1.94   Brady Quinn (95 in 49), 2003-06

RECEIVING

YEAR-BY-YEAR LEADERS

		Recps.	Yards	TD
1918	Bernie Kirk	7	102	1
1919	Bernie Kirk	21	372	2
1920	Eddie Anderson	17	293	3
1921	Eddie Anderson	26	394	2
1922	Don Miller	6	144	1
1923	Don Miller	9	149	1
1924	Don Miller	16	297	2
1925	Gene Edwards	4	28	0
1926	Ike Voedisch	6	95	0
1927	John Colrick	11	126	1
1928	John Colrick	18	199	2
1929	John Colrick	4	90	0
1930	Ed Kosky	4	76	1
1931	Paul Host	6	48	2
1932	George Melinkovich	7	106	1
1933	Steve Banas	6	59	0
1934	Dom Vairo	4	135	2
1935	Wally Fromhart	11	174	1
1936	Joe O'Neill	8	140	1
1937	Andy Puplis	5	86	1
1938	Earl Brown	6	192	4
1939	Bud Kerr	6	129	0
1940	Bob Hargrave	9	98	1
1941	Steve Juzwik	18	307	2
1942	Bob Livingstone	17	272	3
1943	John Yonakor	15	323	4
1944	Bob Kelly	18	283	5
1945	Bob Skoglund	9	100	1
1946	Terry Brennan	10	154	2
1947	Terry Brennan	16	181	4
1948	Leon Hart	16	231	4
1949	Leon Hart	19	257	5
1950	Jim Mutscheller	35	426	7
1951	Jim Mutscheller	20	305	2
1952	Joe Heap	29	437	2

		Recps.	Yards	TD
1953	Joe Heap	22	335	5
1954	Joe Heap	18	369	0
1955	Jim Morse	17	424	3
1956	Jim Morse	20	442	1
1957	Dick Lynch	13	128	0
1958	Monty Stickles	20	328	7
1959	Bob Scarpitto	15	297	4
1960	Les Traver	14	225	0
1961	Les Traver	17	349	2
1962	Jim Kelly	41	523	4
1963	Jim Kelly	18	264	2
1964	Jack Snow	60	1114	9
1965	Nick Eddy	13	233	2
1966	Jim Seymour	48	862	8
1967	Jim Seymour	37	515	4
1968	Jim Seymour	53	736	4
1969	Tom Gatewood	47	743	8
1970	Tom Gatewood	77	1123	7
1971	Tom Gatewood	33	417	4
1972	Willie Townsend	25	369	4
1973	Pete Demmerle	26	404	5
1974	Pete Demmerle	43	667	6
1975	Ken MacAfee	26	333	5
1976	Ken MacAfee	34	483	3
1977	Ken MacAfee	54	797	6
1978	Kris Haines	32	699	5
1979	Dean Masztak	28	428	2
1980	Tony Hunter	23	303	1
1981	Tony Hunter	28	387	2
1982	Tony Hunter	42	507	0
1983	Allen Pinkett	28	288	2
1984	Mark Bavaro	32	395	1
1985	Tim Brown	25	397	3
1986	Tim Brown	45	910	5
1987	Tim Brown	39	846	3
1988	Rickey Watters	15	286	2
1989	Raghib Ismail	27	535	0
1990	Raghib Ismail	32	699	2

		Recps.	Yards	TD			Recps.	Yards	TD
1991	Tony Smith	42	789	4	2002	Arnaz Battle	48	702	5
1992	Lake Dawson	25	462	1	2003	Rhema McKnight	47	600	3
1993	Lake Dawson	25	395	2	2004	Rhema McKnight	42	610	3
1994	Derrick Mayes	47	847	11	2005	Jeff Samardzija	77	1,249	*15
1995	Derrick Mayes	48	881	6	2006	Jeff Samardzija	78	1,017	12
1996	Pete Chryplewicz	27	331	4	2007	John Carlson	40	372	3
1997	Bobby Brown	45	543	6	2008	Golden Tate	58	1,080	10
1998	Malcolm Johnson	43	642	6	2009	Golden Tate	93	*1,496	*15
1999	Bobby Brown	36	608	5	2010	Michael Floyd	79	1,025	12
2000	David Givens	25	310	2	2011	Michael Floyd	*100	1,147	9
2001	Javin Hunter	37	387	1					

Pass Receptions

Game:	14	Maurice Stovall (207 yards) vs. BYU, 2005
Season:	100	Michael Floyd (1,147 yards), 2011
Career:	271	Michael Floyd (3,686), 2008-11

Pass Receptions Per Game

Season:	7.7	Tom Gatewood (77 in 10), 1970
Career:	271	Michael Floyd (3686), 2008-11

Pass Receptions by a Tight End

Season:	63	Tyler Eifert (803 yards), 2011
Career:	128	Ken MacAfee (1,759 yards), 1974-77

Pass Reception Yards

Game:	276	Jim Seymour (13 receptions) vs. Purdue, 1966
Season:	1,496	Golden Tate (93 receptions), 2009
Career:	3,686	Michael Floyd (271 receptions), 2008-11

Pass Reception Yards Per Game

Season:	124.7	Golden Tate (1,496 in 12), 2009
Career:	85.72	Michael Floyd (3,686 in 43), 2008-11

Pass Reception Yards Per Catch

Game: (min. 4)	47.3	Michael Floyd (four for 189) vs. Nevada, 2009
Season: (min. 20)	25.8	Matt Shelton (20 for 515 yards), 2004
Career: (min. 35)	22.0	Raghib Ismail (71 for 1,565), 1988-90

Touchdown Receptions

Game: 4 Maurice Stovall vs. BYU (2005)
Season: 15 Golden Tate, 2009; Jeff Samardzija, 2005; Rhema McKnight, 2005
Career: 36 Michael Floyd, 2008-11

Total Offense

Total Offensive Attempts

Game: 75   Terry Hanratty (420 yards) vs. Purdue, 1967
Season: 549   Brady Quinn(3,497 yards in 13 games), 2006
Career: 1,856   Brady Quinn (11,944 yards in 49 games), 2003-06

Total Offense Yards

Game: 512   Joe Theismann (71 attempts) vs. USC, 1970
Season: 4,009   Brady Quinn (520 attempts), 2005
Career: 11,944   Brady Quinn (1,856 attempts), 2003-06

Total Offense Yards Per Game

Season: 334.1   Brady Quinn (4,009 in 12), 2005
Career: 243.8   Brady Quinn (11,944 in 49)

Total Offense Yards Per Attempt

Game: (min. 20 attempts)   13.7   John Huarte (20 for 273) vs. Navy, 1964
Season: (min. 1000 yards)   9.37   George Gipp (164 for 1,536), 1920
Career: (min. 2000 yards)   7.46   John Huarte (306 for 2,283), 1962-64

Games Gaining 200 Yards Total Offense or More

Season: 12   Brady Quinn, 2006
Career: 33   Brady Quinn, 2003-06

Points Responsible For (scored and passed for)

Game: 37   Art Smith (seven TDs, five points each, two PATs) vs. Loyola (Chi.), 1911
Season: 234   Brady Quinn (13 games) (two rush TDs, 37 pass TDs), 2006
Career: 606   Brady Quinn (six rush TDs, 95 pass TDs), 2003-06

Points Responsible For Per Game

Season: 18.0   Brady Quinn (234 in 13), 2006
Career: 12.4   Brady Quinn (606 in 49), 2003-06

Points

Game: 37   Art Smith (seven TDs, five points each, and two PATs) vs. Loyola (Chi), 1911
Season: 120   Jerome Bettis (20 TDs), 1991
Career: 320   Allen Pinkett (53 TDs, one two-point PAT), 1982-85

Points Per Game

Season: 12.0   Alvin Berger (84 in seven), 1912
Career: 10.3   Stan Cofall (246 in 24), 1914-16

Touchdowns

Game: 7   Art Smith vs. Loyola (Chi.), 1911
Season: 20   Jerome Bettis, 1991
Career: 53   Allen Pinkett, 1982-85; Stan Cofall holds career per-game record at 1.25 (30 in 24), 1914-16

SCORING

YEAR-BY-YEAR LEADERS

		TD	XPts	FG	Pts
1918	George Gipp	6	7	0	43
1919	George Gipp	7	4	1	49
1920	George Gipp	8	16	0	64
1921	John Mohardt	12	0	0	72
1922	Paul Castner	8	10	2	64
1923	Don Miller	10	0	0	60
1924	Jim Crowley	9	17	0	71
1925	Christie Flanagan	7	3	0	45
1926	Bucky Dahman	6	5	0	41
1927	John Niemiec	4	7	0	31
1928	Jack Chevigny	3	0	0	18
1929	Jack Elder	7	0	0	42
1930	Marchy Schwartz	9	0	0	54
1931	Marchy Schwartz	5	0	0	30
1932	George Melinkovich	8	0	0	48
1933	Nick Lukats	2	0	0	12
1934	George Melinkovich	6	0	0	36
1935	Bill Shakespeare	4	0	0	24
1936	Bob Wilke	6	0	0	36
1937	Andy Puplis	3	6	0	24
1938	Benny Sheridan	4	0	0	24
1939	Milt Piepul	6	0	0	36
1940	Steve Juzwik	7	1	0	43
1941	Fred Evans	11	1	0	67
1942	Corwin Clatt	5	0	0	30
1943	Creighton Miller	13	0	0	78
1944	Bob Kelly	13	6	0	84
1945	Elmer Angsman	7	0	0	42
1946	Terry Brennan	6	0	0	36
1947	Terry Brennan	11	0	0	66
1948	Emil Sitko	9	0	0	54
1949	Emil Sitko	9	0	0	54
1950	Jim Mutscheller	7	0	0	42
1951	Neil Worden	8	0	0	48
1952	Neil Worden	10	0	0	60
1953	Neil Worden	11	0	0	66
1954	Joe Heap	8	0	0	48
1955	Paul Hornung	6	5	2	47
1956	Paul Hornung	7	14	0	56
1957	Monty Stickles	3	11	1	32
1958	Monty Stickles	7	15	1	60
1959	Bob Scarpitto	8	0	0	48
1960	Bob Scarpitto	5	0	0	30
1961	Joe Perkowski	0	16	5	31
1962	Joe Farrell	4	0	0	24
1963	Frank Budka	4	0	0	24
1964	Bill Wolski	11	0	0	66
1965	Bill Wolski	8	4	0	52
1966	Nick Eddy	10	0	0	60
1967	Joe Azzaro	0	37	8	61
1968	Bob Gladieux	14	0	0	84
1969	Scott Hempel	0	41	5	56
1970	Scott Hempel	0	36	4	48
1971	Bob Thomas	0	21	5	36
1972	Andy Huff	10	0	0	60
1973	Bob Thomas	0	43	9	70
1974	Wayne Bullock	12	0	0	72
1975	Dave Reeve	0	24	11	57
1976	Al Hunter	13	0	0	78
1977	Dave Reeve	0	39	12	75
1978	Vagas Ferguson	8	0	0	48
1979	Vagas Ferguson	17	0	0	102
1980	Harry Oliver	0	19	18	73
1981	Harry Oliver	0	28	6	46
1982	Mike Johnston	0	19	19	76
1983	Allen Pinkett	18	2 pt	0	110
1984	Allen Pinkett	18	0	0	108
1985	Allen Pinkett	11	0	0	66
1986	John Carney	0	24	*21	87
1987	Ted Gradel	0	33	14	75
1988	Reggie Ho	0	32	14	59
1989	Anthony Johnson	13	0	0	78
1990	Craig Hentrich	0	41	16	89
1991	Jerome Bettis	*20	0	0	*120
1992	Reggie Brooks	14	1 (2 pt)	0	86
1993	Kevin Pendergast	0	45	14	87
1994	Derrick Mayes	11	1(2 pt)	0	68
1995	Marc Edwards	12	2 (2pt.)	0	76
1996	Autry Denson	11	0	0	66
1997	Autry Denson	13	0	0	78
1998	Autry Denson	15	0	0	90
1999	Tony Fisher	7	1 (2pt.)	0	44
2000	Nicholas Setta	1	44	8	74
2001	Nicholas Setta	0	23	15	68
2002	Nicholas Setta	0	32	12	68
2003	Julius Jones	10	0	0	60
2004	D.J. Fitzpatrick	0	34	11	67
2005	Jeff Samardzija	15	0	0	90
2006	Rhema McKnight	15	0	0	90
2007	Brandon Walker	0	22	6	40
2008	Brandon Walker	0	39	14	81
2009	Golden Tate	18	0	0	108
2010	David Ruffer	0	37	18	91
2011	David Ruffer	0	47	10	77

Field Goals

Field Goals

Game: 5   Craig Hentrich (six attempts) vs. Miami, 1990; Nick Tausch (five attempts) vs. Washington, 2009; Nicholas Setta (six attempts) vs. Washington State, 2003 and vs. Maryland, 2002
Season: 21   John Carney (28 attempts), 1986
Career: 51   John Carney (69 attempts), 1984-86

Field Goal Attempts

Game: 7   Gus Dorais (made three) vs. Texas, 1913
Season: 28   John Carney (made 21), 1986
Career: 69   John Carney (made 51), 1984-86

Field Goal Percentage

Season: (min. 10 attempts)   .947   David Ruffer (18 of 19), 2010
Career: (min. 15 attempts)   .825   David Ruffer (33 of 40), 2008-11

Consecutive Field Goals

Season: 18   David Ruffer, 2010
Career: 23   David Ruffer, 2009-10

Consecutive Games with a Field Goal

Career: 16   Nicholas Setta   (last three games of 2000, all of 2001, first three games of 2002)

First Notre Dame Field Goal

Mike Daly vs. Chicago, 1897 (35 yards)

Extra Points

Extra Points (PATs)

Game: 9   by four players; last time Ken Ivan (10 attempts) vs. Pittsburgh, 1965
Season: 52   D.J. Fitzpatrick (54 attempts), 2005
Career: 177   Craig Hentrich (180 attempts), 1989-91

Extra Points Attempted

Game: 12   Frank Winters (made nine) vs. Englewood H.S., 1900
Season: 54   D.J. Fitzpatrick (made 52), 2005
Career: 180   Craig Hentrich (made 177), 1989-92

Extra Point Percentage

Season: (min. 20 made)   1.000   Brandon Walker (39 of 39), 2008; Nicholas Setta (38 of 38), 2002; Nicholas Setta (23 of 23), 2001; Craig Hentrich (48 of 48), 1991; Craig Hentrich (41 of 41), 1990; Bob Thomas (34 of 34), 1972; Ted Gradel (33 of 33), 1987; Steffan Schroffner (30 of 30), 1994; John Carney (25 of 25), 1984
Career: (min. 50 made)   .990   Nicholas Setta (99 of 100), 2000-02

Consecutive Extra Points

Career: 136   Craig Hentrich (from 9-30-89 vs. Purdue to 9-26-92 vs. Purdue, missed second attempt)

Points by Kicking (PATs and FGs)

Season: 89 Craig Hentrich (16 FGs, 25 PATs), 1990; also holds season per-game record at 8.1

Career: 294 Craig Hentrich (177 PATs, 39 FGs), 1989-92

Game: 91 David Ruffer (18 FGs, 32 PATs), 2010

Two-Point Conversions

Season: 2 Marc Edwards, 1995; Bob Minnix, 1971; Bill Wolski, 1965

Two-Point Conversion by Pass

Season: 2 Steve Beuerlein (attempted five), 1986; John Huarte (attempted nine), 1964

Two-Point Conversion Attempts

Game: 3 Joe Theismann vs. Pittsburgh, 1970; Terry Hanratty vs. Pittsburgh, 1966; John Huarte vs. Wisconsin and Michigan State, 1964

Season: 9 John Huarte, 1964

Career: 10 John Huarte, 1962-64

Tackles

YEAR-BY-YEAR LEADERS

1956	Ed Sullivan	79
1957	Jim Schaaf	88
1958	Al Ecuyer	78
1959	Bob Scholtz	84
1960	Myron Pottios	74
1961	Nick Buoniconti	74
1962	Ed Hoerster	73
1963	Bill Pfeiffer	101
1964	Jim Carroll	140
1965	Jim Lynch	108
1966	Jim Lynch	106
1967	Bob Olson	98
1968	Bob Olson	129
1969	Bob Olson	142
1970	Jim Wright	110
1971	Mike Kadish	97
1972	Jim O'Malley	122
1973	Greg Collins	133
1974	Greg Collins	144
1975	Steve Niehaus	113
1976	Steve Heimkreiter	118
1977	Bob Golic	146
1978	Steve Heimkreiter	160
1979	Bob Crable	*187
1980	Bob Crable	154
1981	Bob Crable	167
1982	Mark Zavagnin	113
1983	Tony Furjanic	142
1984	Mike Kovaleski	108
1985	Tony Furjanic	147
1986	Mike Kovaleski	88
1987	Ned Bolcar	106
1988	Wes Pritchett	112
1989	Ned Bolcar	109
1990	Mike Stonebreaker	95
1991	Demetrius DuBose	127
1992	Demetrius DuBose	87
1993	Justin Goheen	92
1994	Brian Magee	81
1995	Lyron Cobbins	105
1996	Kinnon Tatum	77
1997	Jimmy Friday	109
1998	Bobbie Howard	118
1999	A'Jani Sanders	91
2000	Anthony Denman	84
2001	Tyreo Harrison	97
2002	Courtney Watson	90
2003	Courtney Watson	117
2004	Mike Goolsby	97
2005	Brandon Hoyte	92
2006	Maurice Crum	100
2007	Trevor Laws	112
2008	Kyle McCarthy	110
2009	Kyle McCarthy	101
2010	Manti Te'O	133
2011	Manti Te'O	128

Interceptions

YEAR-BY-YEAR LEADERS
(Min. of three)

		No.	Yds.
1919	George Gipp	3	32
1920	(None)		
1921	Chet Wynne	4	43
	Harry Mehre	4	97
1922	(None)		
1923	Jim Crowley	4	31
1924	(None)		
1925	(None)		
1926	Vince McNally	3	0
1927	(None)		

1928	(None)				1971	Ken Schlezes	4	63
1929	Frank Carideo	5	151		1972	Mike Townsend	*10	39
1930	Carl Cronin	3	26		1973	Luther Bradley	6	37
	Marty Brill	3	8		1974	(None)		
	Tom Conley	3	4		1975	Luther Bradley	4	135
1931	Nordy Hoffmann	3	32			Tom Lopienski	4	79
1932	Mike Koken	4	18		1976	Joe Restic	4	92
1933	Nick Lukats	3	22		1977	Joe Restic	6	25
	Ray Brancheau	3	10		1978	Joe Restic	3	59
1934	(None)					Tom Gibbons	3	48
1935	(None)					Dave Waymer	3	10
1936	Bob Wilke	3	33		1979	Dave Waymer	4	77
1937	Ed Simonich	3	10		1980	(None)		
1938	(None)				1981	Mark Zavagnin	3	27
1939	(None)				1982	Dave Duerson	7	104
1940	Steve Bagarus	4	26		1983	Rick Naylor	3	24
1941	Bernie Crimmins	4	12		1984	Pat Ballage	3	41
1942	Angelo Bertelli	8	41		1985	Steve Lawrence	3	57
1943	Creighton Miller	6	78		1986	Steve Lawrence	3	28
1944	Joe Gasparella	4	28		1987	Corny Southall	3	80
1945	Frank Dancewicz	3	31			Marv Spence	3	18
1946	Terry Brennan	3	18		1988	George Streeter	3	39
1947	Johnny Lujack	3	44			Jeff Alm	3	8
1948	Bill Gay	6	83		1989	Todd Lyght	8	42
1949	Bill Gay	4	80		1990	(None)		
1950	Dave Flood	4	28		1991	Tom Carter	5	79
1951	John Lattner	5	66		1992	Tom Carter	5	0
1952	John Lattner	4	58			Jeff Burris	5	6
	Jack Whelan	4	35		1993	Bobby Taylor	4	100
1953	Ralph Guglielmi	5	50		1994	(none)		
1954	Ralph Guglielmi	5	50		1995	Lyron Cobbins	5	86
1955	Paul Hornung	5	59		1996	Benny Guilbeaux	4	42
1956	Aubrey Lewis	3	39		1997	Benny Guilbeaux	4	76
1957	Bob Williams	3	28		1998	A'Jani Sanders	3	29
1958	George Izo	4	11		1999	Deveron Harper	4	27
1959	George Sefcik	3	35		2000	Ron Israel	3	41
	Don White	3	39		2001	Vontez Duff	3	37
1960	(None)				2002	Shane Walton	7	84
1961	Angelo Dabiero	5	78		2003	Quentin Burrell	4	18
1962	Tom MacDonald	9	81		2004	(none)		
1963	Tom MacDonald	5	63		2005	Tom Zbikowski	5	136
1964	Tony Carey	8	121		2006	Mike Richardson	4	21
1965	Nick Rassas	6	*197		2007	David Bruton	3	20
1966	Tom Schoen	7	112		2008	David Bruton	4	57
1967	Tom Schoen	4	108		2009	Kyle McCarthy	5	30
	John Pergine	4	19		2010	Harrison Smith	7	54
1968	Chuck Zloch	5	31		2011	(none)		
1969	Ralph Stepaniak	4	84					
1970	Clarence Ellis	7	25					

Interceptions

Game: 3 by 14 players; last time by Harrison Smith vs. Miami (FL), Sun Bowl, 2010
Season: 10 Mike Townsend (39 yards), 1972
Career: 17 Luther Bradley (218 yards), 1973, 75-77

Interceptions by a Linebacker

Season: 5 Lyron Cobbins (86 yards), 1995; John Pergine (72 yards), 1966
Career: 9 John Pergine (91 yards), 1965-67

Interception Yards

Game: 103 Luther Bradley (two returns) vs. Purdue, 1975
Season: 197 Nick Rassas (six returns), 1965; also holds season per-game record at 19.7 (197 in 10)
Career: 256 Dave Duerson (12 returns), 1979-82

Interception Yards Per Return

Game: (min. two) 51.5 Luther Bradley (two for 103) vs. Purdue, 1975
Season: (min. four) 33.8 Luther Bradley (four for 135), 1975
Career: (min. six) 31.4 Nick Rassas (seven for 220), 1963-65

Interception Returns for Touchdowns

Game: 2 Dave Waymer vs. Miami, 1979
Season: 2 Allen Rossum, 1995; Dave Waymer, 1979; Bobby Leopold, 1977; Randy Harrison, 1974; Tom Schoen, 1966; Tom Zbikowski, 2005
Career: 3 Allen Rossum, 1994-97; Bobby Leopold, 1976-78; Tom Schoen, 1965-67; Shane Walton, 1999-02

Punt Returns

YEAR-BY-YEAR LEADERS

(min. one per game since 1970)

		No.	Yards	Avg.
1919	Joe Brandy	26	186	7.2
1920	Joe Brandy	27	249	9.2
1921	(None)			
1922	Frank Thomas	21	196	9.3
1923	Harry Stuhldreher	32	308	9.6
1924	Harry Stuhldreher	22	194	8.8
1925	Charlie Riley	7	38	5.4
1926	Vince McNally	8	153	19.1
1927	Charles McKinney	5	36	7.2
1928	Frank Carideo	22	239	10.9
1929	Frank Carideo	33	405	12.3
1930	Frank Carideo	37	303	8.2
1931	Emmett Murphy	10	105	10.5
1932	Chuck Jaskwhich	23	254	11.0
1933	Andy Pilney	9	124	13.8
1934	Wally Fromhart	33	288	8.7
1935	Andy Pilney	13	148	11.4
1936	Bob Wilke	5	73	14.6
1937	Andy Puplis	21	281	13.4
1938	Benny Sheridan	11	194	17.6
1939	Benny Sheridan	8	107	13.4
1940	Bob Hargrave	24	176	7.3
1941	Steve Juzwik	22	280	12.7
1942	Pete Ashbaugh	13	196	15.1
1943	Creighton Miller	7	151	21.6
1944	Bob Kelly	12	129	10.8
1945	Frank Dancewicz	18	240	13.3
1946	Bob Livingstone	7	103	14.7
1947	Coy McGee	6	162	27.0
1948	Lancaster Smith	5	157	31.4
1949	Bill Gay	19	254	13.4
1950	Bill Gay	14	96	6.9
1951	Billy Barrett	5	107	21.4
1952	John Lattner	7	113	16.1
1953	Joe Heap	8	143	17.9
1954	Dean Studer	5	62	12.4
1955	Dean Studer	6	92	15.3
1956	Aubrey Lewis	5	46	9.2
1957	(None)			
1958	Pat Doyle	7	64	9.1
1959	Bob Scarpitto	7	118	16.9
1960	Angelo Dabiero	8	102	12.8
1961	Angelo Dabiero	11	97	8.8
1962	Frank Minik	6	41	6.8
1963	Bill Wolski	6	31	5.2
1964	Nick Rassas	15	153	10.2
1965	Nick Rassas	24	*459	19.1
1966	Tom Schoen	29	253	8.7
1967	Tom Schoen	*42	447	10.6
1968	Bob Gladieux	6	91	15.2
1969	Brian Lewallen	7	75	10.7
1970	Mike Crotty	19	100	5.3
1971	Mike Crotty	33	297	9.0
1972	Ken Schlezes	10	138	13.8

		No.	Yards	Avg.			No.	Yards	Avg.
1973	Bob Zanot	19	141	7.4	1993	Michael Miller	26	213	8.2
1974	Ted Burgmeier	6	46	7.7	1994	(None)			
1975	Ted Burgmeier	9	52	5.8	1995	(None)			
1976	Steve Schmitz	18	168	9.3	1996	Allen Rossum	15	344	22.9
1977	Steve Schmitz	14	127	9.1	1997	Allen Rossum	12	83	6.9
1978	Dave Waymer	25	175	7.0	1998	Joey Getherall	20	157	7.8
1979	Dave Duerson	12	209	17.4	1999	Julius Jones	15	195	13.0
1980	Dave Duerson	25	194	7.8	2000	Joey Getherall	24	392	16.3
1981	Dave Duerson	32	221	6.9	2001	Julius Jones	18	192	10.7
1982	Dave Duerson	34	245	7.2	2002	Vontez Duff	40	385	9.6
1983	Joe Howard	28	202	7.2	2003	Vontez Duff	24	260	10.8
1984	Troy Wilson	11	84	7.6	2004	Carlyle Holiday	29	314	10.8
1985	Troy Wilson	17	144	8.5	2005	Tom Zbikowski	27	379	14.0
1986	Troy Wilson	26	222	8.5	2006	Tom Zbikowski	16	144	9.0
1987	Tim Brown	34	401	11.8	2007	Tom Zbikowski	23	234	10.2
1988	Ricky Watters	19	253	13.3	2008	Golden Tate	14	116	8.3
1989	Ricky Watters	15	201	13.4	2009	Golden Tate	12	171	14.3
1990	Raghib Ismail	13	151	11.6	2010	John Goodman	13	17	1.3
1991	Jeff Burris	18	227	12.6	2011	Michael Floyd	2	44	22.0
1992	Michael Miller	25	172	6.9					

Punt Returns

Game: 9   Tom Schoen (167 yards) vs. Pittsburgh, 1967
Season: 42   Tom Schoen (447 yards), 1967
Career: 103   Dave Duerson (869 yards), 1979-82

Punt Return Yards

Game: 167   Tom Schoen (nine returns) vs. Pittsburgh, 1967
Season: 459   Nick Rassas (24 returns), 1965
Career: 947   Frank Carideo (92 returns), 1928-30; also holds career per-game record at 33.8 (947 in 28)

Punt Return Yards Per Attempt

Game: (min. three)   52.3   Chet Grant (three for 157) vs. Case Tech, 1916
Game: (min five)   22.0   Frank Carideo (five for 110) vs. Georgia Tech, 1929
Game: (min. 1.5 per game)   20.2   Allen Rossum (344 for 15), 1996
Career: (min. 1.5 per game) 15.8   Allen Rossum (427 for 27), 1994-97

Punt Returns

Punt Returns

Game: 9   Tom Schoen (167 yards) vs. Pittsburgh, 1967
Season: 42   Tom Schoen (447 yards), 1967
Career: 103   Dave Duerson (869 yards), 1979-82

Punt Return Yards

Game: 167   Tom Schoen (nine returns) vs. Pittsburgh, 1967
Season: 459   Nick Rassas (24 returns), 1965
Career: 947   Frank Carideo (92 returns), 1928-30; also holds career per-game record at 33.8 (947 in 28)

Punt Return Yards Per Attempt

Game: (min. three)   52.3   Chet Grant
(three for 157) vs. Case Tech, 1916
Game: (min five)   22.0   Frank Carideo
(five for 110) vs. Georgia Tech, 1929
Game: (min. 1.5 per game)   20.2   Allen Rossum
(344 for 15), 1996
Career: (min. 1.5 per game)   15.8   Allen Rossum
(427 for 27), 1994-97

Kickoff Returns

YEAR-BY-YEAR LEADERS

		No.	Yards	Avg.
1919	George Gipp	8	166	20.8
1920	George Gipp	11	208	18.9
1921	Chet Wynne	9	258	28.7
1922	Paul Castner	11	490	*44.5
1923	Wille Maher	4	184	46.0
1924	Elmer Layden	5	111	22.2
1925	Rex Enright	4	86	21.5
1926	Christie Flanagan	6	183	30.5
1927	Jack Chevigny	4	91	22.8
1928	Jack Chevigny	5	115	23.0
1929	Joe Savoldi	4	81	20.3
1930	Joe Savoldi	4	186	46.5
1931	(None)			
1932	George Melinkovich	4	164	41.0
1933	Ray Brancheau	7	109	15.6
1934	Bill Shakespeare	4	60	15.0
1935	Bill Shakespeare	5	123	24.6
1936	Andy Puplis	5	136	27.2
1937	(None)			
1938	(None)			
1939	Harry Stevenson	5	85	17.0
1940	Milt Piepul	4	122	30.5
1941	Fred Evans	9	206	22.9
1942	Bob Livingstone	8	184	23.0
1943	Creighton Miller	4	53	13.3
1944	Bob Kelly	8	213	26.6
1945	Phil Colella	5	105	21.0
1946	(None)			
1947	(None)			
1948	Larry Coutre	4	70	17.5
1949	Emil Sitko	4	89	22.3
1950	Jack Landry	11	195	17.7
1951	Billy Barrett	4	86	21.5
1952	Joe Heap	6	145	24.2

		No.	Yards	Avg.
1953	John Lattner	8	331	41.4
1954	Jim Morse	5	166	33.2
1955	Dean Studer	5	115	23.0
1956	Paul Hornung	16	496	31.0
1957	Dick Lynch	5	159	31.8
1958	Jim Crotty	12	297	24.8
1959	Bob Scarpitto	12	247	20.6
1960	George Sefcik	7	167	23.9
1961	Angelo Dabiero	8	193	24.1
1962	Ron Bliey	13	309	23.8
1963	Ron Bliey	5	131	26.2
1964	Nick Rassas	4	103	25.8
1965	Bill Wolski	6	131	21.8
1966	Nick Eddy	4	193	48.3
1967	Dave Haley	5	119	23.8
1968	Coley O'Brien	4	156	39.0
1969	Mike Crotty	4	111	27.8
1970	Darryll Dewan	4	91	22.8
1971	Gary Diminick	7	199	28.4
1972	Gary Diminick	15	331	22.1
1973	Gary Diminick	8	181	22.6
1974	Al Samuel	8	150	18.8
1975	Dan Knott	10	284	28.4
1976	Al Hunter	12	241	20.1
1977	Terry Eurick	9	211	23.4
1978	Jim Stone	13	242	18.6
1979	Jim Stone	19	493	25.9
1980	Jim Stone	17	344	20.2
1981	Greg Bell	13	371	28.5
1982	Allen Pinkett	14	354	25.3
1983	Alonzo Jefferson	10	174	17.4
1984	Hiawatha Francisco	6	178	29.7
1985	Tim Brown	14	338	24.1
1986	Tim Brown	25	*698	27.9
1987	Tim Brown	23	456	19.8
1988	Raghib Ismail	12	433	36.1
1989	Raghib Ismail	20	502	25.1
1990	Raghib Ismail	14	336	24.0
1991	Clint Johnson	9	217	24.1
1992	Michael Miller	9	261	29.0
1993	Clint Johnson	10	409	40.9
1994	Emmett Mosely	13	320	24.6
1995	Emmett Mosely	15	419	27.9
1996	Allen Rossum	6	227	37.8
1997	Allen Rossum	20	570	28.5
1998	Darcey Levy	7	163	23.3
1999	Julius Jones	26	603	23.2
2000	Julius Jones	15	427	28.5

		No.	Yards	Avg.
2001	Julius Jones	18	405	22.5
2002	Vontez Duff	17	475	27.9
2003	Vontez Duff	16	346	21.6
2004	Chase Anastasio	19	353	18.6
2005	David Grimes	15	338	22.5
2006	David Grimes	21	514	24.5
2007	Armando Allen	33	704	21.3
2008	Armando Allen	21	543	25.9
2009	Theo Riddick	*37	849	22.9
2010	Bennett Jackson	29	645	22.2
2011	George Atkinson III	35	*915	26.1

Kickoff Returns

Game: 8   George Gipp (157 yards) vs. Army, 1920
Season: 37   Theo Riddick (849 yards), 2009
Career: 72   Julius Jones (1,678 yards), 1999-01, 2003

Kickoff Return Yards

Game: 253   Paul Castner (four returns) vs. Kalamazoo, 1922
Season: 849   Theo Riddick (37 returns), 2009
Career: 1,678 Julius Jones (72 returns), 1999-01, 2003

Kickoff Return Yards Per Attempt

Game: (min. two)   85.0   Raghib Ismail (two for 170) vs. Rice, 1988
Season: (min. 0.5 per game)   44.5   Paul Castner (11 for 490), 1922
Career: (min. 0.5 per game)   36.5   Paul Castner (21 for 767), 1920-22

Kickoff Returns for Touchdowns

Game: 2   Raghib Ismail vs. Michigan, 1989; vs. Rice, 1988; Paul Castner vs. Kalamazoo, 1922
Season: 2   Allen Rossum, 1997; Raghib Ismail, 1988,1989; Tim Brown, 1986; Nick Eddy, 1966; Johnny Lattner, 1953; Willie Maher, 1923; Paul Castner, 1922
Career: 5   Raghib Ismail, 1988-90

Total Kick Returns

Combined Punt and Kickoff Returns

Game: 10   George Gipp (two PR, eight KR, 207 yards) vs. Army, 1920
Season: 57   Tim Brown (34 PR, 23 KR, 857 yards)
Career: 105   Tim Brown (36 PR, 69 KR, 2089 yards), 1984-87

Kick Return Yards

Game: 254   Willie Maher (80 PR, 174 KR) vs. Kalamazoo, 1923
Season: 857   Tim Brown (401 PR, 456 KR), 1987;
Career: 2,104 Julius Jones (426 PR, 1,678 KR), 1999-01, 2003

Kick Return Yards Per Attempt

Game: (min. five)   35.0   Julius Jones (five for 175) v. Nebraska, 2000
Season: (min. 1.5 per game)   29.5   Raghib Ismail (17 for 505), 1988
Career: (min. 1.5 per game)   22.6   Raghib Ismail (71 for 1,607), 1988-90

Kick Returns for Touchdowns

Game:	2	Allen Rossum (PR), v. Pittsburgh, 1996; Raghib Ismail (KR) vs. Rice, 1988; vs. Michigan, 1989; Tim Brown (PR) vs. Michigan State, 1987; Vince McNally (PR) vs. Beloit, 1926; Paul Castner (KR) vs. Kalamazoo, 1922
Season:	4	Allen Rossum (three PR, one KOR), 1996
Career:	6	Allen Rossum (three PR, three KOR), 1993-97; Tim Brown (three PR, three KR), 1984-87; Raghib Ismail (five KR, one PR), 1988-90

All-Purpose Running
Yardage from Rushing, Receiving, and all Returns

All-Purpose Yards

Game:	361	Willie Maher (107 rushing, 80 PR, 174 KR) vs. Kalamazoo, 1923
Season:	1937	Tim Brown (254 rushing, 910 receiving, 75 PR, 698 KR), 1986; also holds season per game record at 176.1 (1,937 in 110)
Career:	5,462	Julius Jones (3,108 rushing, 250 receiving, 426 PR, 1,678), 1999-01, 2003

Total Yardage
Yardage from Rushing, Passing, Receiving, and all Returns

Total Yardage

Game:	519	Joe Theismann (526 passing, seven receiving, minus-14 rushing) vs. USC, 1970
Season:	4,009	Brady Quinn (3,919 passing, 90 rushing), 2005
Career:	11,944	Brady Quinn (11,762 passing, 182 rushing), 2003-06

Punting

Punts

Game:	15	Marchy Schwartz (509 yards) vs. Army, 1931
Season:	78	Joey Hildbold (3,088 yards), 2002
Career:	259	Blair Kiel (10,534 yards), 1980-83

Punts Per Game

Season:	7.4	Fred Evans (67 in nine), 1941
Career:	5.7	Joey Hildbold (256 in 46), 1999-02

Punting Average

Game: (min. five)	51.6	Joe Restic (five for 258) vs. Air Force, 1975
Game: (min. 10)	44.8	Paul Castner (12 for 537) vs. Purdue, 1921
Season: (min. 25)	44.9	Craig Hentrich (34 for 1,526), 1990
Career: (min. 50)	44.1	Craig Hentrich (118 for 5,204), 1989-92

Defense

Tackles by a Linebacker (since 1956)

Game:	26	Bob Crable vs. Clemson, Bob Golic vs. Michigan, 1978; 1979
Season:	187	Bob Crable, 1979
Career:	521	Bob Crable, 1978-81

Tackles by a Front Four Lineman (since 1956)

Season: 113   Steve Niehaus, 1975
Career: 340   Ross Browner, 1973, 75-77

Tackles for Minus Yardage (since 1967)

Season: 28   Ross Browner (203 yards), 1976
Career: 77   Ross Browner (515 yards), 1973,1975-77

Passes Broken Up (since 1956)

Season: 14   Shane Walton, 2002
Career: 32   Clarence Ellis, 1969-71

Fumbles Recovered (since 1952)

Season: 7   Cedric Figaro, 1986
Career: 12   Ross Browner, 1973,1975-77

NOTRE DAME TEAM RECORDS

Single Game Offense

Rushing

Rushing Attempts—91 vs. Navy, (597 yards), 1969
Fewest Rushing Attempts—17 vs. Michigan (four yards), 2006
                           17 vs. Michigan State (47 yards), 2006
Rushing Yards—629 vs. Drake, 1931; MR (Modern Record): 597 vs. Navy, 1969
Fewest Rushing Yards—Minus-12 vs. Michigan State (31 attempts), 1965
Rushing Touchdowns—27 vs. American Medical, 1905; MR: 10 vs. Dartmouth, 1944

Passing

Pass Attempts—63 vs. Purdue (completed 29), 1967
Fewest Pass Attempts—0, many times; MR: one vs. Iowa, 1945
Pass Completions—37 vs. Navy (attempted 51
Fewest Pass Completions—0, many times; MR: 0 vs. Iowa, 1945
Completion Percentage (min. 20 attempts)—.857 vs. Hawai'i (24 of 28), Hawai'i Bowl, 2008
Passing Yards—526 vs. USC (33 of 58), 1970
Fewest Passing Yards—minus-seven vs. Iowa, 1948
Passes Intercepted—eight vs. Army, 1944
Touchdown Passes—six vs. BYU, 2005

Total Offense

Total Offense

Attempts—104 vs. Iowa (587 yards), 1968
Fewest Total Offense Attempts—31 vs. Pittsburgh (87 yards), 1937
Total Offense Yards—720 vs. Navy, (99 attempts), 1969
Fewest Total Offense Yards—12 vs. Michigan State (42 attempts), 1965

Scoring

Points—142 vs. American Medical, 1905; MR: 69 vs. Georgia Tech, 1977; Pittsburgh, 1965

Touchdowns—27 vs. American Medical, 1905; MR: 10 vs. Georgia Tech, 1977; Pittsburgh, 1965; Dartmouth, 1944

Extra Points—12 vs. Rose Poly, 1914; MR: nine vs. Georgia Tech, 1977; Pittsburgh, 1965

Two-Point Conversions—two vs. USC, 1986; Michigan State, 1964

Two-Point Conversion Attempts—four vs. Pittsburgh, 1970; Michigan State, 1964

Field Goals—five vs. Miami (six attempts), 1990

            five vs. Washington (five attempts), 2009

            five vs. Washington State (six attempts), 2003

            five vs. Maryland (five attempts), 2002

Field Goal Attempts—seven vs. Texas, 1913; MR: six vs. Miami (made five), 1990

                       six vs. Washington State (six attempts), 2003

Interceptions

Interceptions—seven vs. Northwestern (185 yards), 1971; Wisconsin (75 yards), 1943

Interception Yards—185 vs. Northwestern (seven returns), 1971

Interception Returns for Touchdowns—two vs. Miami, 1979; Northwestern, 1971; USC, 1966

Punt Returns

Punt Returns—13 vs. Wabash, 1924; MR: 12 vs. Iowa, 1939

Punt Return Yards—231 vs. Pittsburgh (six returns), 1996

Punt Return Yards Per Attempt (min. three)—38.5 vs. Pittsburgh (six for 231), 1996

Kickoff Returns

Kickoff Returns—nine vs. Iowa (179 yards), 1956; Army (137 yards), 1945

Kickoff Return Yards—354 vs. Kalamazoo, 1922; MR: 192 vs. Michigan (three returns), 1989

Kickoff Return Yards Per Attempt (min. three)—64.0 vs. Michigan (three for 192), 1989

Punting

Punts—16 vs. Indiana, 1921; MR: 16 vs. Army, 1941

Fewest Punts—0, several times; last time vs. Navy 2009

Punting Average (min. five)—52.2 vs. Arizona State (five for 261), 1998

First Downs

First Downs—36 vs. Army, 1974

Fewest First Downs—two vs. Nebraska, 1917; MR: three vs. Pittsburgh, 1937

First Downs by Rushing—31 vs. Pittsburgh, 1993

Fewest First Downs by Rushing—one vs. Michigan State, 1965; Minnesota, 1938; Pittsburgh, 1937; Nebraska, 1917; Michigan, 2006

First Downs by Passing—19 vs. USC, 1970

Fewest First Downs by Passing—24 vs. Navy, 2009

First Downs by Penalty—six vs. N.C. State, 2003

Fumbles

Fumbles—10 vs. Northwestern, 1931; MR: 10 vs. Oklahoma, 1952; Purdue, 1952

Fumbles Lost—seven vs. Michigan State, 1952

SEASON OFFENSE

Rushing

Rushing Attempts—684 (3,119 yards), 1974
Rushing Attempts Per Game—67.3 (673 in 10), 1973
Rushing Yards—3502 (673 attempts), 1973
Rushing Yards Per Attempt—6.2 (556 for 3,430), 1921; MR: 5.4 (567 for 3,061), 1946
Rushing Yards Per Game—350.2 (3,502 in 10), 1973
Rushing Touchdowns—42, 1989

Passing

Pass Attempts—481 (285 in 13), 2010
Pass Attempts Per Game—37.8 (454 in 12), 2005
Pass Completions—301 (447 in 12), 2009
Completion Percentage—.673 (301 of 447), 2009
Passes Intercepted—22,1958
Lowest Pass Interception Percentage—.011 (5 of 447), 2009
Passing Yards—3,963 (294 of 454), 2005
Average Passing Yards Per Attempt (min. 125 attempts)—10.0 (185 for 1,857), 1993
Average Passing Yards Per Completion (min. 75 completions)—17.5 (120 for 2,105), 1964
Touchdown Passes—37, 2006

Total Offense

Total Offense Attempts—945 (5,728 yards), 2005
Total Offense Attempts Per Game—92.4 (924 in 10), 1970 (NCAA record)
Total Offense Yards—5,728 (945 attempts), 2005
Total Offense Yards Per Game—510.5 (5,105 in 10), 1970
Total Offense Yards Per Attempt—6.72 (671 for 4,512), 1921; MR: 6.59 (830 for 5,467), 1991

Scoring

Points—440, 2005
Points Per Game—55.6 (389 in 7), 1912; MR: 37.6 (376 in 10), 1968
Touchdowns—59,1991
Touchdowns Per Game—7.9 (55 in 7), 1912; MR: 5.3 (53 in 10), 1949
Extra Points—57, 1991
Extra Point Percentage—100.0 (41 of 41) 1990, (36 of 36) 1987, (34 of 34), 1972
Two-Point Conversion Attempts—12, 1964
Two-Point Conversions—three, 1999, 1971, 1970, 1965, 1958
Field Goals—21 (28 attempts), 1986
              21 (27 attempts), 2003
Safeties—2, 1989, 1987, 1983, 1979, 1973, 1959, 1958, 1954, 1949, 2002

Interceptions

Interceptions—29 (374 yards), 1977
Interception Yards—497 (26 returns) 1966
Interception Yards Per Return (min. 10 returns)—21.8 (12 for 261), 1998
Interception Returns for Touchdowns—five, 1996

Fumbles
Most Opponent Fumbles—51, 1952
Most Opponent Fumbles Lost—28, 1952

Punt Returns
Punt Returns—66, 1921; MR: 58 (617), 1939
Punt Return Yards—617 (58 returns), 1939
Punt Return Yards Per Game—68.6 (617 in nine), 1939
Punt Return Yards Per Attempt—18.7 (25 for 468), 1965
Punt Returns for Touchdowns—five, 1996

Kickoff Returns
Kickoff Returns—58 (1,142 yards), 2007
Kickoff Return Yards—1,223 (53 returns), 1999
Kickoff Return Yards Per Game—117.4 (1,174 in 10), 1956
Kickoff Return Yards Per Attempt—32.2 (36 for 1,160), 1922; MR: 27.6 (25 for 689), 1957
Kickoff Returns for Touchdowns—five, 1922

Punting
Punts—90, 1934; MR: 85, 1941, 1939
Fewest Punts—23, 1968
Punting Average—45.4 (50 for 2,272), 2006

First Downs
First Downs—314, 2005
First Downs Per Game—29.2 (292 in 10), 1968
First Downs By Rushing—193, 1989
First Downs By Passing—169, 2005
First Downs By Penalty—22, 1997

Penalties
Penalties—101, 1926; MR: 98 (933 yards), 1952
Fewest Penalties—29, 1939, 1937
Penalty Yards Per Game—93.3 (933 in 10), 1952
Fewest Penalty Yards—225, 1939
Fewest Penalty Yards Per Game—25.0 (225 in nine), 1937

Fumbles
Fumbles—57, 1952
Fewest Fumbles—12, 2000
Fumbles Lost—29, 1952
Fewest Fumbles Lost—four, 2000

SINGLE GAME DEFENSE

Rushing Defense
Fewest Rushing Attempts—eight by Kalamazoo, 1923; MR: 15 by Pitt (15 yards), 1968
Fewest Rushing Yards—minus-51 by Wisconsin (28 attempts), 1964
Most Rushing Yards Lost—141 by USC (43 attempts), 1961

Fewest Rushing Yards Per Attempt—Minus 1.8 by Wisconsin (28 for 51), 1964

Pass Defense

Fewest Pass Attempts—0 by Carnegie Tech, 1925; St. Louis, 1922; MR: one by Georgia Tech in 1976
Fewest Pass Completions—0, many times; last time by Georgia Tech in 1976
Fewest Passing Yards—0, many times; last time by Georgia Tech in 1976

Total Defense

Fewest Total Offense Yards—minus-17 by St. Louis, 1922; MR: two by Carnegie Tech, 1941

First Downs

Fewest First Downs—0 by Wabash, 1924; Kalamazoo, 1923; St. Louis, 1922; Michigan State, 1921; MR: one by USC, 1950; Carnegie Tech, 1941

Fumbles

Most Fumbles—11 by Purdue, 1952
Most Fumbles Lost—eight by Purdue, 1952

SEASON DEFENSE

Rushing Defense

Fewest Rushing Attempts Allowed Per Game—29.2 (263 in nine), 1920; MR: 35.7 (321 in nine), 1946
Fewest Rushing Yards Allowed—495,1921; MR: 611(340 attempts), 1941
Fewest Rushing Yards Allowed Per Game—45.0 (495 in 11), 1921; MR: 67.9 (611 in nine), 1941
Fewest Rushing Yards Per Attempt—1.4 (365 for 495), 1921; MR: 1.8(340 for 611), 1941
Rushing Yards Lost by Opponents—578, 1949

Pass Defense

Fewest Pass Attempts Allowed Per Game—6.9(69 in 10), 1925; MR: 9.7(87 in nine), 1937
Fewest Pass Completions Allowed Per Game—1.6 (14 in nine), 1924; MR: 3.0 (27 in nine), 1937
Lowest Completion Percentage— .215 (14 of 65), 1924; MR: .306 (41 of 134), 1938
Fewest Passing Yards Allowed Per Game—15.6 (140 in nine), 1924; MR: 49.4 (445 in 9), 1938
Fewest Touchdown Passes Allowed—0, 1931, 1924, 1922, 1921; MR: one, 1946, 1940

Total Defense

Fewest Total Offense Attempts Allowed Per Game—37.1, 1924; MR: 46.1, 1937
Fewest Total Offense Yards—651, 1924; MR, 1275, 1946
Fewest Total Offense Yards Allowed Per Game—72.3 (651 in nine), 1924; MR: 141.7 (1275 in nine), 1946
Fewest Total Offense Yards Per Attempt—1.8 (468 for 843), 1921; MR: 2.7 (481 for 1283), 1941

Scoring

Fewest Points Allowed—0, 1903 (nine games); MR: 24, 1946 (nine games)

Punt Returns

Fewest Punt Returns—five (52 yards), 1968
Fewest Punt Return Yards—47, 1954
Fewest Punt Return Yards Per Attempt—4.7 (33 for 156), 2000

Punting
Most Opponent Punts—119, 1921; MR: 98, 1939
Most Opponent Punts Blocked—seven, 1933, 1932; MR: 4, 2000, 1949, 1938

First Downs
Fewest First Downs Allowed—42, 1924; MR: 61, 1937
Fewest First Downs by Rushing Allowed—27, 1932, 1923; MR: 40, 1946
Fewest First Downs by Passing Allowed—eight, 1924; MR: 14, 1937

OPPONENT RECORDS

Individual Records

Rushing
Rushing Attempts—44, Charles White (261 yards), USC 1979
Rushing Yards—303, Tony Dorsett (23 attempts), Pitt, 1975
Longest Rush—88, Dick Panin, MSU, 1951

Passing
Pass Attempts—68, Steve Smith (completed 39), Stanford, 1989
Pass Completions—39, Steve Smith (attempted 68), Stanford, 1989
Passing Yards—424, Steve Walsh (31 of 50), Miami, 1988
Touchdown Passes—five, Matt Leinart, USC, 2004; Tyler Palko, Pittsburgh, 2004

Receiving
Pass Receptions—14, Robert Lavette (50 yards), Georgia Tech, 1981; John Jackson (200 yards), USC, 1989; Jim Price (98 yards), Stanford, 1989
Pass Reception Yards—238, Selwyn Lymon (8 receptions), Purdue, 2006
Touchdown Receptions—three, Dwayne Jarrett, USC, 2006; Mario Manningham, Michigan, 2006
Longest Pass—97 yards, Kyle Orton to Taylor Stubblefield, Purdue, 2004

Total Offense
Total Offense Attempts—69, Steve Smith (289 yards), Stanford, 1989
Total Offense Yards—420, Steve Walsh (52 attempts), Miami, 1988

Scoring
Points—36, Anthony Davis (6 TDs), USC, 1972
Touchdowns—six, Anthony Davis, USC, 1972
Extra Points—six, Paul Edinger, MSU, 1998; Eric Hipp, USC, 1979; Bernie Allen, Purdue, 1960; Bob Prescott, Iowa, 1956
Field Goals—five, Massimo Manca, Penn State, 1985; Arden Czyzewski, Florida, 1991 (Sugar Bowl); Nate Whitaker, Stanford, 2010; Conor Lee, Pittsburgh, 2008
Longest Field Goal—60, Don Shafer, USC, 1986

Returns
Interceptions—four, Adrian Young, USC, 1967
Longest Interception—100, Jeff Ford, Georgia Tech, 1969
Longest Punt Return—80, Jerry Mauren, Iowa, 1959

Longest Kickoff Return—100, Anthony Davis, USC, 1974; Frank Rieple, Penn, 1955; Joe Williams, Iowa, 1961; Jerome Brooks, Purdue, 2004
Longest Fumble Return—94, Leroy Keyes, Purdue, 1966

Punting

Punts—18, Joe Mihm, Carnegie Tech, 1934; Paul Dobson, Nebraska, 1918
Punting Average (min. five punts)—52.8, Bob Huston (5 for 264), Drake, 1937
Longest Punt—83 yards, Verl Lillywhite, USC, 1946

Career Records

Rushing

Rushing Attempts—120, Charles White, (648 yards), USC, 1976-79
Rushing Yards—754, Tony Dorsett (96 attempts), Pitt, 1973-76

Passing

Pass Attempts—163, Steve Stenstrom (completed 100), Stanford, 1991-94; Alex Van Pelt (completed 99), Pittsburgh, 1989-92
Pass Completions—100, Steve Stenstrom (attempted 163), Stanford, 1991-94
Passing Yards—1,020, Steve Stenstrom (100 completions), Stanford, 1991-94
Touchdown Passes—six, Alex Van Pelt, Pittsburgh, 1989-92
                              nine, Matt Leinart, USC, 2003-05

Receiving

Pass Receptions—23, R. Jay Soward (296 yards), USC, 1996-99
Pass Reception Yards—355, Dwayne Jarrett, (17 receptions), USC, 2004-06
Touchdown Receptions—three, Dwayne Jarrett, USC, 2004-05; Mario Manningham, Michigan, 2005-07

Total Offense

Total Offense Attempts—285, Carson Palmer (908 yards), USC, 1998-02
Total Offense Yards—947, Kyle Orton (172 attempts) Purdue, 2001-04

Scoring

Points—68, Anthony Davis, (11 TDs, one two-point conversion), USC 1972-74
Touchdowns—11, Anthony Davis, USC, 1972-74
Extra Points—16, Ryan Killeen, USC, 2002-04
Field Goals—six, Ryan Killeen, USC, 2002-04

TEAM RECORDS

First Downs—34, by Stanford, 1997
First Downs by Rushing—27, by Air Force, 1991
First Downs by Passing—23, by Miami, 1988
Rushing Attempts—76, by Nebraska, 1922
Rushing Yards—411, by Pitt (50 attempts), 1975; by MSU (60 attempts), 1962
Pass Attempts—68, by Stanford (completed 39), 1989
Pass Completions—39, by Stanford (attempted 68), 1989
Passing Yards—424, by Miami (31 of 50), 1988
Touchdown Passes—five, by USC, 2004; Purdue, 2004
Total Offense Attempts—95, by Stanford (421 yards), 1994

Total Offense Yards—617 by Oregon State (64 attempts), 2006
Points—59, by Army, 1944
Touchdowns—10, by Wisconsin, 1904

Longest Plays

Rushing
Bob Livingstone vs. USC, 1947 ... 92 yards

Pass Plays
Blair Kiel to Joe Howard vs. Georgia Tech, 1981.....96 yards

Interceptions
Jack Elder vs. Army, 1929.................... 100 yards

Kickoff Returns
Alfred Bergman vs. Loyola (Chi.), 1911*.. 105 yards
* did not score—field was 110 yards long

Field Goals
Dave Reeve vs. Pitt, 1976...........................53 yards

Punt Returns
Ricky Watters vs. SMU, 1989 ....97 yards

Fumble Return
Frank Shaughnessy vs. Kansas, 1904 ....107 yards

Punts
Bill Shakespeare vs. Pitt, 1935 ....86 yards

NOTRE DAME'S NCAA STATISTICAL LEADERS

The following Notre Dame players were either first or second in key NCAA football statistics for a given season:

Total Offense

	Year	Statistics
2. Paul Hornung	1956	1337
2. Joe Theismann	1970	281.3

Rushing

1. Creighton Miller	1943	911

Receiving

2. Jack Snow	1964	60
2. Tom Gatewood	1970	77

Interceptions
2. Tom MacDonald (tie)	1962	9
1. Tony Carey	1964	8
1. Mike Townsend	1970	10

Punt Returns
1. Nick Rassas	1965	459
1. Allen Rossum	1996	22.93

Kickoff Returns
2. Paul Hornung	1956	496
1. Raghib Ismail	1988	36.1

Scoring
2. Bob Kelly (tie)	1944	84
2. Allen Pinkett	1983	10.0
2. Allen Pinkett	1984	9.8

Individual NCAA Records

• Highest Percentage of Field Goals Made 40 Yards or More: John Carney, 1984, .909 (10 of 11)

• Highest Season Percentage of Field Goals Made 40-49 Yards: John Carney, 1984, 1.000 (10 of 10)

• Most Consecutive Career Field Goals Made 40-49 Yards: John Carney, 1984-85, 12

• Most Single-Game Touchdowns Scored on Punt Returns: Allen Rossum, 1996 vs. Pittsburgh, two; Tim Brown, 1987, vs. MSU, two (held by many others)

• Most Single-Game Touchdowns Scored on Kickoff Returns: Raghib Ismail, 1988 vs. Rice, 1989 vs. Michigan, two (held by five others)

• Tony Driver, two TDs, 2000 v. Navy (tied Minnesota's Tyrone Carter in 1996)

• Most Career Touchdowns on Interceptions, Punt Returns and Kickoff Returns (Must have at Least One Touchdown in Each Category): Allen Rossum, 1994-97, nine (three interceptions, three punt returns, three kickoff returns)

Team Records
Annual National Leaders

Total Offense:
1946   441.3 yards per game

Rushing Offense:
1946   340.1 yards per game

Scoring Offense:
1966   36.2 points per game

Punt Returns:
1958   17.6 yards per return

Kickoff Returns:
1966   29.6 yards per return

Total Defense:
1946   141.7 yards per game

Rushing Defense:
1974   102.8 yards per game

Scoring Defense:
1946   2.7 points per game

Miscellaneous Records

• Single-Game Touchdowns Scored on Kickoff Returns: two, vs. Rice in 1988 and vs. Michigan in 1989 (held by many teams)

• Single-Game Touchdowns Scored on Punt Returns: three, vs. Pittsburgh in 1996 (held by many teams)

• Season Total Offense—Most Plays Per Game: 92.4, 1970 (924 in 10)

• Season Pass Defense—Lowest Completion Percentage Allowed: (min. of 200 attempts) .333, 1967 (102 of 306)

• Season Punt Return Defense—Fewest Returns Allowed—five, 1968 (for 52 yards)

• Season Fewest Turnovers Lost: eight, 2000 (tied with Clemson 1940 and Miami of Ohio, 1966)

Miscellania

** A squad of up to 100 Irish student managers help prepare the team for home and away games. Freshmen apply the mix of lacquer, lacquer thinner, and gold dust on up to 120 Notre Dame helmets on Friday nights before home games and Thursday nights of away games. Sixty gallons of lacquer and five gallons of gold dust base are used in a typical season.

** The 14-floor tower of the magnificent Hesburgh Memorial Library at Notre Dame overlooks Notre Dame stadium. As the TV networks are fond of showing, the library's tower is covered by a mural of "Touchdown Jesus." This mural is 132 feet high, composed of 5,714 individual pieces deriving from 81 different types of stone from 16 countries. When the mural was being completed during the fall and winter of 1963-64, the tower was covered by a mammoth sheet of canvas that cracked like rifle fire in the frigid, snappy Indiana winds swirling around the building. Many Notre Dame students of that time speak of the difficulties of getting a good night's sleep with all the racket.

** Dutch Bergman was Notre Dame's first four-sport athlete. He competed for the Irish in football, basketball, baseball, and track from 1911 to 1915. With the addition of some 20,000 seats to the stadium—construction to continue through 1996 and 1997—the Irish will have a stadium that better meets the voracious demands of the alumni and the subway alumni, while also giving the Irish football team a venue where genuinely raucous noise can be generated. Some observers had claimed that the modest size of the current stadium did not provide enough volume of noise to distract opposing teams—a regular obstacle for the Irish when they play in places like Ann Arbor.

** "Win One for the Gipper"—a nice line in a 1940 Hollywood movie, a great motivational tool for Rockne in his 1928 win over Army. With a small pool of talent, barely scraping over .500 on the season, and faced with some rough customers in weeks ahead, Rockne knew he'd have to pull out all the stops to cop a win against a powerful Army team and avoid a losing season. He told Grantland Rice the night before the game that he might have to use—"Gipp's ghost." He had used Gipp on other occasions before over the years, but the results weren't as dramatic. The fact is, Gipp probably did not say this, in so many words, to Rock. Players who knew Gipp say that he never called himself "The Gipper." If, on his deathbed, he said anything at all, it is more likely that it was unprintable. It would have been more in character for Gipp to have remained cynical to the bitter end. It is also in character for Rockne to have embellished a story with sentimental, romantic overtones. In any case, it worked when he used it, and it has become one of the most famous lines in American sports history.

** The original Notre Dame Stadium, the house Rock built, contained more than two million bricks, 400 tons of steel, and 15,000 cubic yards of concrete. Rockne was the driving force behind its design, one loosely modeled on the cavernous Michigan stadium. He had the amazing foresight, in the late '20s, to know that modern technology would eventually bring the college game of football to the masses through some new medium, so he planned carefully for a stadium that would lend itself to television.

The growing ND alumni body and other demands on seating capacity expanded so much in recent decades that the original seating for 59,075 was simply not able to meet the increasing need. Restroom facilities, locker rooms, and concessions facilities, among other concerns, needed a boost, so the University's trustees voted in 1994 for a $50 million expansion project, one that took place over the 1996-97 football seasons.

The result is the nation's 14th largest stadium, now seating nearly 81,000 fans (opposing teams still get only 5,000 tickets), with improvements everywhere you turn, from the exterior gates, to the entrances, the ramps, the seats, the lights, the scoreboards, the press box, and the playing surface itself. The renovated stadium now better fits in architecturally and aesthetically with the nearby campus structures while providing a superior venue for Irish fans.

The improvements added 700,000 bricks, 240,000 concrete blocks, 500 cubic yards of mortar, 25,000 cubic yards of cast-in-place concrete, 8.5 miles of new redwood seating, permanent lighting, and beautiful exterior landscaping, complete with bronze statues of Frank Leahy and Moose Krause that bring the spirits from the past to the games played today.

But there's more to all this than the numbers for the materials, because for one thing, the extra 22,000 fans shake down the thunder more explosively than fans could before, while the great Irish Marching Band makes its own unique contribution to the powerful traditions and heart-thumping excitement of a Notre Dame football Saturday.